The University of Law

2 New York Street
Manchester
M1 4HJ

TERMINATION
FOR
BREACH OF CONTRACT

TERMINATION FOR BREACH OF CONTRACT

JOHN E STANNARD
Senior Lecturer in Law, Queen's University Belfast

DAVID CAPPER
Reader in Law, Queen's University Belfast

OXFORD
UNIVERSITY PRESS

OXFORD
UNIVERSITY PRESS

Great Clarendon Street, Oxford, OX2 6DP,
United Kingdom

Oxford University Press is a department of the University of Oxford.
It furthers the University's objective of excellence in research, scholarship,
and education by publishing worldwide. Oxford is a registered trade mark of
Oxford University Press in the UK and in certain other countries

Published in the United States of America by Oxford University Press
198 Madison Avenue, New York, NY 10016, United States of America

British Library Cataloguing in Publication Data
Data available

Library of Congress Control Number: 2013950401

ISBN 978–0–19–969597–3

Printed in Great Britain by
CPI Group (UK) Ltd, Croydon, CR0 4YY

PREFACE

The origins of this book lie in a PhD thesis submitted in 1989. One of the aims of that thesis was to try to bring some degree of clarity to a branch of Contract Law which is of immense importance, but which has always been bedevilled by unnecessary complexity and obscurity. Nearly twenty-five years have now elapsed since then, but as our first chapter shows all too clearly the problems of analysis associated with this area have not diminished to any great degree. What we are therefore trying to do, as in 1989, is to set out in detail the rules governing termination as a remedy for breach of contract in English law, to distil the very complex body of law on the subject to a clear set of principles, and to apply the law in a practical context. In doing so we have sought to draw on the work of the leading experts in the field, most particularly Professor John Carter, to whose profound and extensive scholarship and helpful advice we both owe a tremendous debt.

Termination for breach has always been a notoriously difficult subject to master, and our aim has been to try to explain it as clearly and simply as possible for academics and practitioners who may not be specialists in the area. Our exposition of the topic falls into four parts. In the first of these, which is by way of introduction, we explain the nature of termination by reference to some of the conceptual and analytical ambiguities to which the topic has traditionally given rise, and show how these can only be understood in the light of history. In the second part, we get to grips with the basic concepts outlined in the title, that is to say the twin processes of breach and termination, and explain how they work, with special reference to the so-called 'doctrine of election'. In the third part, we examine the situations in which a right to terminate for breach arises, including breach of condition, fundamental breach under the *Hongkong Fir* doctrine, repudiation and anticipatory breach. Finally, we set out the legal consequences that follow from an election whether to terminate or affirm, both in terms of the primary obligations to the parties to the contract and in terms of other remedies, including damages and restitutionary relief. Though our journey will take us through some difficult territory, we have tried to make the going as straightforward as possible. Our years of experience of teaching at a university have convinced us that a subject is not better understood for being inaccessible, and that even the most complex of topics can be explained in simple terms without necessarily compromising the accuracy of the explanation. Our own understanding of termination for breach has been greatly increased by the process of writing this book, and if others are helped in a similar way we will have succeeded in what we set out to do.

Thanks are due to the staff of Oxford University Press who have helped us with this project, most notably Rachel Alban, Joanna Dymond, Faye Judges, Jessica Huntley, Rachel Mullaly, Sally Pelling-Deeves, Eleanor Reedy, and Laura Williamson. We are also very grateful to those colleagues in the field of Contract who have taken the trouble to read over our drafts and to give their suggestions. Needless to say, we take full responsibility for any errors or omissions that may remain. We have endeavoured to state the law as it applies at the end of August 2013.

John E Stannard
David Capper

CONTENTS

III THE RIGHT TO TERMINATE

TABLE OF CASES

UNITED KINGDOM

AUSTRALIA

BARBADOS

TRINIDAD AND TOBAGO

UNITED STATES OF AMERICA

WEST INDIES

TABLE OF LEGISLATION

LIST OF ABBREVIATIONS

General

cif	cost, insurance, and freight included
fob	free on board

Journals

ALJ	Australian Law Journal
Can	BR Canadian Bar Review
CLJ	Cambridge Law Journal
Ind LJ	Indiana Law Journal
JBL	Journal of Business Law
JCL	Journal of Contract Law
LMCLQ	Lloyd's Maritime and Commercial Law Quarterly
LQR	Law Quarterly Review
MLR	Modern Law Review
NYU L Rev	New York University Law Review
NZULR	New Zealand Universities Law Review
OJLS	Oxford Journal of Legal Studies
SALJ	South African Law Journal
UCLA L Rev	University of California, Los Angeles Law Review
Univ BC L Rev	University of British Columbia Law Review
UNSW LJ	University of New South Wales Law Journal
Vand L Rev	Vanderbildt Law Review

Part I

INTRODUCTION

1

THE NATURE OF TERMINATION

Behind the concept of termination for breach[1] there lies a very simple notion which **1.01** can be summed up in three propositions: (1) I have made a deal with you; (2) you have failed to keep your side of the bargain; (3) I should therefore no longer be obliged to keep mine either. Whether or not this applies in any given case depends on the question identified by Tettenborn: to what extent are one person's obligations under a contract dependent on what the other party does—or indeed fails to do?[2]

---

[1] It has recently been argued that termination is best seen not as a response to breach as such but as an aspect of the law of unjust enrichment: C Langley and R Loveridge, 'Termination as a Response to Unjust Enrichment' [2012] LMCLQ 65. If this is right, this entire book is based on a misconception. The authors argue that their preferred analysis would better deal with a number of situations where the orthodox analysis causes difficulties, most notably termination for excused non-performance (para 1.28), concurrent rights of termination at common law and under the contract (Ch 8, paras 8.18–8.28), and the recovery of loss of bargain damages (Ch 10, paras 10.07–10.17). Whilst these issues certainly pose problems of analysis, abandoning the entire notion of termination for breach does seem a rather drastic solution to those problems; in any event, it is surely now too well engrained into the collective legal consciousness to be displaced by anything less than a complete statutory reformulation.

[2] AM Tettenborn, *An Introduction to the Law of Obligations* (Butterworths, 1984) p 141.

Simple though the basic notion may be, the law to which it gives rise has always been particularly difficult; as long ago as 1837 it was said that few questions were of so frequent occurrence or of so much practical importance, yet so difficult to solve, as those relating to discharge for breach.[3] As McKendrick points out, this is a topic that is complex in both a factual and a legal sense.[4] It is factually complex because it is often difficult to determine whether a breach of contract has occurred, and if so by whom.[5] It is legally complex because the rules are by no means clear, and the consequences of getting them wrong can be catastrophic.[6] In this opening chapter we shall clear the ground by defining the scope of our inquiry before going on to consider some of the problems of analysis to which it gives rise.

A. Defining the Question

1.02 The key question here is the one posed by Diplock LJ (as he then was) in *The Hongkong Fir*:[7] 'Every synallagmatic contract contains in it the seeds of the problem: in what event will a party be relieved of his undertaking to do that which he has agreed to do but has not done?' When the event relied on in this context is a breach by the other party, we have a case of termination for breach of contract, or as Carter says, 'exercise of a right to terminate the performance of the contract for breach or repudiation of obligation by the promisor'.[8] Though Diplock LJ refers to synallagmatic[9] or bilateral contracts in this connection, the same question can arise in relation to unilateral contracts where the promisor argues that the condition to which his or her promise is subject has not been fulfilled;[10] indeed, the rules governing these cases mirror very closely those governing termination for breach in bilateral contracts, and they derive from the same historical root.[11] While Diplock

---

[3] *Smith's Leading Cases* (A Maxwell, 1837) Vol 2, 1, quoted in F Dawson and DW McLauchlan, *The Contractual Remedies Act 1979* (Sweet & Maxwell, 1981) pp 2–3.

[4] E McKendrick, *Contract Law, Text, Cases and Materials* (5th edn, OUP, 2012) p 936.

[5] McKendrick, p 936 (n 4). Thus, for instance, a party who terminates performance in good faith after a breach by the other party may be found to have wrongfully repudiated the contract if the termination is found to have been unwarranted, as in *Federal Commerce and Navigation Co Ltd v Molena Alpha Ltd (The Nanfri)* [1979] AC 757 (HL): see Ch 7, para 7.35.

[6] McKendrick, p 936 (n 4).

[7] *Hongkong Fir Shipping Co Ltd v Kawasaki Kisen Kaisha Ltd (The Hongkong Fir)* [1962] 2 QB 26 (CA) 65.

[8] JW Carter, *Carter's Breach of Contract* (Hart, 2012) para 3-39.

[9] A synallagmatic contract has been defined as a 'reciprocal contract... characterised by mutual duties and rights': LB Curzon, *Dictionary of Law* (6th edn, Longman, 2002). In *United Dominions Trust (Commercial) Ltd v Eagle Aircraft Services Ltd* [1968] 1 WLR 74 (CA) 82 Diplock LJ admitted that the use of this term had left him open to the charge of 'gratuitous philological exhibitionism', but said that he preferred the term to 'bilateral' on the ground that there might be more than two parties to the contract.

[10] As in *United Dominions Trust v Eagle Aircraft Services* (n 9) itself: see para 1.29.

[11] See Ch 2, paras 2.06–2.12.

LJ is broadly correct in declaring that such a contract 'contains in it' the seeds of the problem we are considering, this does not mean that the problem is purely one of contractual construction;[12] on the contrary, as the *Hongkong Fir* case itself demonstrates, the answer to the question may very well depend on the effect of the breach in the given case.[13] While questions of termination for breach do indeed involve the question whether the promisor is relieved of his or her 'undertaking to do that which he [or she] has agreed to do but has not yet done', the two questions are not the same. For one thing, a party to a contract may claim to be relieved from such an undertaking by a wide range of factors, including not only breach but also frustration, failure of condition, misrepresentation, undue influence, and even mistake; while some of these are closely related to termination for breach, others raise very different issues.[14] As well as this, termination for breach may involve not only the discharge of contractual undertakings but a variety of other consequences too.[15]

The classic account of termination is that given in *Moschi v Lep Air Services* by Lord **1.03** Diplock.[16] Though he speaks in this context of 'rescission' rather than 'termination',[17] his words are still worth quoting at length in this context:

> It is no doubt convenient to speak of a contract as being terminated or coming to an end when a party who is not in default exercises his right to treat it as rescinded. But the law is concerned with the effect of that election upon those obligations of the parties of which the contract was the source, and this depends on the nature of the particular obligation and upon which party promised to perform it.
>
> Generally speaking, the rescission of the contract puts an end to the primary obligations of the party not in default to perform any of his contractual promises which he has not already performed by the time of the rescission. It deprives him of the right as against the other party to continue to perform them. It does not give rise to any secondary obligation in substitution for a primary obligation which has come to an end. The primary obligations of the party in default to perform any of the promises made by him and remaining unperformed likewise come to an end as does his right to continue to perform them. But for his primary obligations there is substituted by operation of law a secondary obligation to pay to the other party a sum of money to compensate him for the loss he has sustained as a result of the failure to perform the primary obligations.

---

[12] Such a view was broadly accepted in the first part of the 20th century, but was rejected by the Court of Appeal in the *Hongkong Fir* case: see Lord Devlin, 'The Treatment of Breach of Contract' [1966] CLJ 192. However, it has still been argued by Reynolds and others that the question ultimately depends on the intention of the parties: see for instance FMB Reynolds, 'Discharge of Contract by Breach' (1981) 97 LQR 541; SA Smith, *Contract Theory* (OUP, 2004) chs 8 and 9.

[13] See Ch 6, para 6.06.

[14] See Ch 4, paras 4.06–4.12.

[15] Thus, as Treitel says, the injured party may not only refuse to perform his or her own promise, but may also refuse to accept performance by the other party, and may even seek to 'undo' the transaction by returning the defective performance and claiming back the consideration provided for it: GH Treitel, 'Some Problems of Breach of Contract' (1967) 30 MLR 139, 140–1; E Peel, *Treitel: The Law of Contract* (13th edn, Sweet & Maxwell, 2011) para 18-001. The consequences of termination are discussed in Part IV of this work.

[16] [1973] AC 331 (HL) 350.

[17] See further Ch 4, para 4.07.

1.04 From this, we can see that the process of termination for breach generally involves certain elements. There is a breach by the party in default. There is an election by the other party to terminate in response to this. The consequences of this termination differ as between the injured party and the party in default. The consequence for the injured party is that he or she no longer has to perform any outstanding primary obligations under the contract; indeed, the innocent party loses the right to do so. The consequence for the party in default is the same, except that in this case there arises a secondary obligation to pay compensation to the injured party. All of these aspects of termination will be considered more fully in the course of the book.

B. Termination as a Process and a Remedy

1.05 Termination for breach can be seen both as a process and as a remedy. Traditionally the topic has been dealt with under the broader umbrella of 'discharge', alongside such topics as performance, frustration, and agreement.[18] This has the advantage of a certain conceptual symmetry, whereby the topics relating to the formation of a contract (offer and acceptance, consideration, intention to create legal relations, and so on) at the beginning of the book are mirrored by those relating to its discharge (agreement, performance, breach, and frustration) towards the end. Problems arise, however, when the notion of discharge is pressed too far; in particular, the idea of the contract 'coming to an end' can be a misleading one, and has given rise to various errors and misconceptions.[19] For this and other reasons more emphasis is now given to termination in the context of remedies.[20] Indeed, it has been stressed that termination (or in laymen's terms, 'cancelling the contract') can be one of the most useful weapons in the armoury for the victim of a breach of contract, not least because, unlike many other remedies, it does not require recourse to the courts.[21]

---

[18] This can be seen most clearly in the older editions of *Cheshire, Fifoot and Furmston's Law of Contract*, in which Part VII ('Discharge of Contract') had four chapters, one on each topic. The more recent editions are not split up into different parts, and performance and breach are now amalgamated into a single chapter. A similar scheme is followed in J Beatson, AS Burrows, and J Cartwright, *Anson's Law of Contract* (29th edn, OUP, 2010), where Part 4 ('Performance and Discharge') contains one chapter on performance and four on discharge (agreement, frustration, breach and operation of law). Older editions of Treitel, *The Law of Contract* (see n 15 for recent edition) deal with the matter under three headings, 'Performance', 'Breach' and 'Frustration'; in the most recent edition these have become 'Performance and Breach', 'Discharge by Breach' and 'Frustration'. All of these books deal with remedies at a later stage under one or more separate headings. In the same way, *Chitty* has a section devoted to discharge followed by a section devoted to remedies; see AS Burrows et al (eds), *Chitty on Contracts* (31st edn, Sweet & Maxwell, 2012).

[19] See para 1.36.

[20] The first person to do this seems to have been Hugh Beale in *Remedies for Breach of Contract* (Law Book Co, 1980), and this has been followed through in successive editions of Beale, Bishop, and Furmston (n 21) and also in McKendrick (n 4). See also FMB Reynolds, 'Discharge by Breach as a Remedy' in PD Finn (ed), *Essays on Contract* (Law Book Co, 1987) p 183.

[21] HG Beale, WD Bishop, and MP Furmston, *Contract: Cases and Materials* (5th edn OUP, 2007) p 549; JW Carter and MJ Tilbury, 'Remedial Choice and Contract Drafting' (1998) 13 JCL 5, 9.

However, this notion of termination as a remedy should not obscure the close relationship between termination and the other modes of discharge, most notably frustration. It is therefore essential to keep both aspects of the topic in view.

C. Problems of Terminology

One of the biggest problems in this area of the law is, as Lord Wilberforce has pointed out, the lack of any agreed or consistent terminology.[22] This relates not only to the process of termination itself, but also to some of the concepts surrounding it.

1.06

(1) The name of the process

The process which we are considering has been described in a wide variety of ways: for instance, the injured party may be said to repudiate the contract,[23] or treat the contract as repudiated[24] or discharged;[25] alternatively the contract may be discharged,[26] rescinded,[27] cancelled,[28] or terminated.[29] However, some of these

1.07

---

[22] See para 1.38 Treitel, 'Some Problems of Breach of Contract', p 139 (n 15). This problem goes back to the century before last: see WR Anson, 'Some Notes on Terminology in Contract' (1891) 7 LQR 337, who complains that 'a fig will as well produce thistles as a puzzled brain will produce a lucid explanation' (p 337); see also JL Montrose, 'Conditions, Warranties and other Contractual Terms' (1937) 15 Can BR 309.

[23] *Behn v Burness* (1863) 3 B & S 751 (Exchequer Chamber) 755, 122 ER 281, 283 (Williams J); *J & E Kish v Charles Taylor & Sons & Co* [1912] AC 604 (HL) 617 (Lord Atkinson); *Hongkong Fir Shipping Co Ltd v Kawasaki Kisen Kaisha Ltd (The Hongkong Fir)* [1962] 2 QB 26 (QBD: Commercial Ct) 38 (Salmon J).

[24] Sale of Goods Act 1979, s 11(2), (3), and (4); *Wallis, Son and Wells v Pratt and Haynes* [1910] 2 KB 1003 (CA) 1012 (Fletcher Moulton LJ (dissenting)). The appeal was allowed, and the sentiments of Fletcher Moulton LJ were approved, by the House of Lords at [1911] AC 394 (HL). For more recent examples of this terminology see *Hallam v Avery* [2000] 1 WLR 966 (CA) 969 (Judge LJ); *Meikle v Nottinghamshire County Council* [2004] EWCA Civ 859; [2005] ICR 1, para 34 (Keene LJ); *Azimut-Benetti SpA v Healey* [2010] EWHC 2234 (Comm); [2011] 1 Lloyd's Rep 473, para 32 (Blair J).

[25] *Kingscroft Insurance Co Ltd v Nissan Fire & Marine Insurance Co Ltd (No 2)* [1999] CLC 1875 (QBD: Commercial Ct) 1915 (Moore-Bick J); *TTM v Hackney LBC* [2011] EWCA Civ 4; [2011] HRLR 14 para 87 (Toulson LJ); *Masri v Consolidated Contractors International Co SAL* [2007] EWCA Civ 688; [2007] 2 CLC 49 (CA) para 33 (Lloyd LJ).

[26] *Humphreys v Chancellor, Master and Scholars of the University of Oxford and anor* [2000] ICR 405 (CA) 423 (Moore-Bick J); *ST Microelectronics NV v Condor Insurance Ltd* [2006] EWHC 977 (Comm); [2006] 2 Lloyd's Rep 525, para 61 (Christopher Clarke J); *ENE 1 Kos Ltd v Petroleo Brasileiro SA (The Kos)* [2010] EWCA Civ 772; [2010] 2 CLC 19, para 18 (Longmore LJ).

[27] *Stocznia Gdanska SA v Latvian Shipping Co* [1998] 1 WLR 574 (HL) 598 (Lord Lloyd of Berwick); *Hanson v South West Electricity Board* [2001] EWCA Civ 1377; [2002] 1 P & CR 35; *Eminence Property Developments Ltd v Heaney* [2010] EWCA Civ 1168; [2010] 3 EGLR 165, para 23 (Etherton LJ).

[28] This is the terminology used throughout the New Zealand Contractual Remedies Act 1979; Dawson and McLauchlan, *The Contractual Remedies Act*, chs 5 and 6 (n 3).

[29] *ERG Raffinerie Mediterranee SpA v Chevron USA Inc (t/a Chevron Texaco Global Trading)* [2007] EWCA Civ 494; [2007] 1 CLC 807, 810 (Longmore LJ); *Dadourian Group International v Simms* [2009] EWCA Civ 169; [2009] 1 Lloyd's Rep 601, para 9 (Arden LJ); *Parkwood Leisure Ltd v Alemo-Herron* [2011] UKSC 26; [2011] IRLR 696, para 12 (Lord Hope).

labels are more helpful than others. In particular, the notion of repudiation is also used in a more precise way to indicate a wrongful refusal to perform, or at the very least a total inability to perform,[30] and is now therefore best not used to describe a situation where the refusal to perform is justified, or where there is no question of refusal or inability at all. In the same way, rescission is now best used to describe the situation where a contract is avoided *ab initio*,[31] in contrast to that where the defaulting party still remains under what is termed a 'secondary obligation' to pay damages for the breach.[32] 'Discharge' is a useful term, but this is better used in a broader sense to cover cases of agreement and frustration as well as those of breach.[33] For this reason the present work will follow Cheshire, Fifoot, and Furmston and others in calling the process 'termination',[34] though of course it is not the contract itself that is terminated, but rather the obligation of the injured party to perform his or her obligations under that contract.[35]

(2) Performance and breach

1.08 One problem with the topic of termination for breach is that it is not necessarily discussed under a separate heading in the textbooks.[36] Rather, much of the material tends to be found under the broad headings of 'performance' and 'breach',[37] or alternatively 'discharge by performance' and 'discharge by breach'.[38] On the face of it this should cause no difficulty; a contract is performed when the promisor does what has been agreed, and breached when he or she fails to do so without lawful excuse. Unfortunately the classification adopted by the textbooks sometimes obscures this. In particular, much of the law relating to the topic presently under discussion has sometimes been set out not, as one would expect, under the heading of 'breach', but under the heading of 'performance'.[39] Of course, as Cheshire,

---

[30] *Universal Cargo Carriers Corp v Citati* [1957] 2 QB 401 (QBD: Commercial Ct) 426 (Devlin J); see Ch 7, para 7.32.

[31] *Johnson v Agnew* [1980] AC 367 (HL) 392–3 (Lord Wilberforce); *Photo Production Ltd v Securicor Transport Ltd* [1980] AC 827 (HL) 844 (Lord Wilberforce); see Ch 4, para 4.07.

[32] *Moschi v Lep Air Services* [1973] AC 332 (HL) 350 (Lord Diplock); see para 1.03.

[33] As in MP Furmston, CHS Fifoot, and AWB Simpson, *Cheshire, Fifoot, and Furmston's Law of Contract* (16th edn, OUP, 2012) chs 18–20; Beatson, Burrows, and Cartwright, *Anson's Law of Contract*, chs 13–16 (n 18).

[34] Furmston, Fifoot, and Simpson, *Cheshire, Fifoot, and Furmston's Law of Contract*, ch 18 (n 33); Carter, *Carter's Breach of Contract*, para 3-39 (n 8).

[35] *Heyman v Darwins* [1942] AC 356 (HL) 373 (Lord Macmillan); *Moschi v Lep Air Services*, 350 (n 32).

[36] FMB Reynolds, 'Warranty, Condition and Fundamental Term' (1963) 79 LQR 534, 550–1; Treitel, 'Some Problems of Breach of Contract', p 139 (n 15).

[37] As in Furmston, Fifoot, and Simpson, *Cheshire, Fifoot and Furmston's Law of Contract* (n 33) and the older editions of Treitel (*The Law of Contract* (n 15)).

[38] As in older editions of *Cheshire, Fifoot and Furmston's Law of Contract* (n 33). Beatson, Burrows, and Cartwright, *Anson's Law of Contract* (n 18) and the more recent editions of Treitel (*The Law of Contract* (n 15)) use a mixture of the two approaches.

[39] This was particularly marked in previous editions of Treitel (*The Law of Contract* (n 15)).

Fifoot, and Furmston point out, performance and breach are in many ways two sides of the same coin, and cannot easily be separated out.[40] Nevertheless, for the purposes of this book, the term 'performance' will be reserved for the situation where the party in question carries out the relevant obligation. 'Discharge by performance' will be used to denote the situation where a party is discharged from the relevant obligation by performing it, as opposed to that where the discharge comes about as a result of a failure in performance by the other party. In the same way, the term 'breach' will be used to denote a failure without lawful excuse to perform an obligation under the contract, and 'discharge by breach' will indicate the situation where the other party is discharged from one or more of his or her own obligations as a result of such failure.

(3) Conditions, warranties, and innominate terms

One key factor in determining whether a party has a right to terminate for breach is whether the term broken is a 'condition' or a 'warranty'.[41] This classification goes back to section 11(1)(b) of the Sale of Goods Act 1893, where a condition is described as a term 'the breach of which may give rise to a right to treat the contract as repudiated' and a warranty as a term 'the breach of which may give rise to a claim for damages but not to a right to reject the goods and treat the contract as repudiated'. Though this relates to the sale of goods, the same is true of contracts generally; breach of condition gives rise to the right to terminate, but not breach of warranty.[42] However, neither of these terms is free from ambiguity. The word 'condition' is used in many different ways in the law of contract,[43] and in the present context it can be used to mean not only an important term of the contract but also some agreed contingency that must occur before a particular obligation becomes due for performance.[44] In the same way, the word 'warranty' has been used to denote not only a minor term of the contract, but also: (1) a term of the contract

1.09

---

[40] Furmston, Fifoot, and Simpson, *Cheshire, Fifoot, and Furmston's Law of Contract*, p 665 (n 33).
[41] See Ch 2, paras 2.06–2.12.
[42] *Wallis, Son and Wells v Pratt and Haynes* [1910] 2 KB 1003 (CA) 1012 (Fletcher Moulton LJ (dissenting)). The appeal was allowed, and the sentiments of Fletcher Moulton LJ were approved, by the House of Lords at [1911] AC 394 (HL).
[43] A 'chameleon-like word that takes on its meaning from its surroundings': *Skips A/S Nordheim and ors v Syrian Petroleum Co Ltd and anor (The Varenna)* [1984] QB 599 (CA) 618 (Donaldson MR); SJ Stoljar, 'The Contractual Concept of Condition' (1953) 69 LQR 485.
[44] Or, in the words of Burchell, 'an external fact on which the existence of the obligation depends': EM Burchell, '"Condition" and "Warranty"' (1954) 71 SALJ 333. This confusion between a condition as a contingency and a condition as a promise is perhaps one of the least satisfactory aspects of the present law, and has been repeatedly discussed in the literature: see for instance Montrose, 'Conditions, Warranties and other Contractual Terms' (n 22); Stoljar, 'The Contractual Concept of Condition' (n 43); A Beck, 'The Doctrine of Substantial Performance: Conditions and Conditions Precedent' (1975) 38 MLR 413; GH Treitel, '"Conditions" and "Conditions Precedent"' (1990) 106 LQR 185; JW Carter, 'Conditions and Conditions Precedent' (1990–91) 4 JCL 90. The use of the word to denote a contingency is particularly associated with the old cases prior to the Sale of Goods Act 1893, and is still significant in relation to unilateral contracts and options: see paras 1.29–1.30.

as opposed to a 'mere representation';[45] (2) a guarantee of goods or services;[46] (3) a fundamental term in an insurance contract;[47] and even (4) a fundamental term generally.[48] In the present work, unless the contrary is stated, the words 'condition' and 'warranty' will be used as in the Sale of Goods Act, and the phrase 'condition precedent' used for an agreed contingency of the type described previously.[49]

1.10   The courts have also recognized a third class of term in this connection. In the *Hongkong Fir* case[50] it was said by Diplock LJ that not all contractual terms could be classified as 'conditions' or 'warranties', and that there were some terms of which the breach might or might not give rise to a right to terminate, depending on the gravity of the consequences.[51] This type of term has been classed as an 'innominate' or 'intermediate' term.[52] On this analysis there are three classes of term: (1) conditions (where a breach *always* gives rise to a right to terminate); (2) warranties (where a breach *never* (or at any rate, hardly ever)[53] gives rise to a right to terminate); and (3) innominate or intermediate terms (where a breach *sometimes* gives rise to a right to terminate). Given that the right to terminate for serious breaches can arise quite independently of the construction of the contract,[54] it can be argued that this three-fold analysis is over-subtle, and that it would be better simply to speak of: (1) conditions (where breach always gives rise to a right to terminate); and (2) warranties (where this can only be done if the consequences of the breach are sufficiently serious).[55] However, given the widespread acceptance by the courts of the concept of the innominate term,[56] it is probably too late to dispense with it now.[57]

---

[45] *Hopkins v Tanqueray* (1854) 15 CB 130 (Common Pleas) 142, 139 ER 369, 374 (Crowder J); *Oscar Chess Ltd v Williams* [1957] 1 WLR 370 (CA) 377 (Hodson LJ); *Dick Bentley Productions Ltd and anor v Harold Smith (Motors) Ltd* [1965] 1 WLR 623 (CA) 627 (Lord Denning MR).

[46] *Bernstein v Pamson's Motors (Golders Green) Ltd* [1987] RTR 384 (QBD) 393 (Rougier J); *Dandara Holdings Ltd v Co-operative Retail Services Ltd* [2004] EWHC 1476 (Ch); [2004] 2 EGLR 163, para 70 (Lloyd J); *National House Building Council v Revenue and Customs Commissioners* [2010] UKFTT 326 (FT); [2010] STI 2655, para 62 (Sir Stephen Oliver QC).

[47] Marine Insurance Act 1906, s 33(3); *De Maurier (Jewels) Ltd v Bastion Insurance Co* [1967] 2 Lloyd's Rep 550 (QBD: Commercial Ct) 560 (Donaldson J); *Bank of Nova Scotia v Hellenic Mutual War Risks Association (Bermuda) Ltd (The Good Luck)* [1992] 1 AC 233 (HL) 262 (Lord Goff); *Global Process Systems Inc v Syarikat Takaful Malaysia Bhd (The Cendor Mopu)* [2011] UKSC 5; [2011] 1 Lloyd's Rep 560, para 56 (Lord Mance).

[48] As in *Behn v Burness* (1863) 3 B & S 751 (Exchequer Chamber) 755 (Williams J).

[49] As in Peel, *Treitel*, para 17-015 (n 15); Carter, *Carter's Breach of Contract*, para 1-17 (n 8).

[50] *Hongkong Fir Shipping Co Ltd v Kawasaki Kisen Kaisha Ltd (The Hongkong Fir)* [1962] 2 QB 26 (CA).

[51] *The Hongkong Fir*, 70 (n 50).

[52] The two seem to be interchangeable: *Cehave NV v Bremer Handelsgesellschaft MBH (The Hansa Nord)* [1976] QB 44 (CA) 82 (Ormrod LJ); *Bunge Corp v Tradax Export SA* [1981] 1 WLR 711 (HL) 714 (Lord Wilberforce); *Dominion Corporate Trustees Ltd v Debenhams Properties Ltd* [2010] EWHC 1193 (Ch); [2010] 23 EG 106 (CS) para 22 (Kitchin J).

[53] See Ch 6, para 6.12.

[54] See Ch 6, para 6.06; see, however, Reynolds, 'Discharge of Contract by Breach' (n 12).

[55] See further Ch 6, para 6.13.

[56] JW Carter, 'Classification of Contractual Terms: the New Orthodoxy' [1981] CLJ 219; see further Ch 6, para 6.13, fn 42.

[57] Carter 'Classification of Contractual Terms' (n 56).

(4) Fundamental breach

According to *The Hongkong Fir*,[58] the right to terminate may be exercised not only **1.11** for breaches of condition but for other serious breaches too. Such breaches are described in various ways; for instance 'fundamental' breaches,[59] 'frustrating' breaches,[60] 'repudiatory' breaches,[61] or breaches that go to 'the root of the contract'.[62] Unfortunately none of these terms is without difficulty. The concept of 'fundamental breach' has been used in the past in a totally different connection, that is to say a breach of such gravity as to bar the party responsible from relying on an exemption clause in the contract,[63] and though that doctrine has long since been discredited,[64] there is still debate as to whether breaches of condition are also necessarily 'fundamental' in the present context.[65] To talk of a 'frustrating' breach creates the risk of confusion with the modern doctrine of frustration;[66] and it may not be appropriate to describe all breaches of this sort as 'repudiatory'.[67] The notion of a breach going to the 'root of the contract' has a long and respectable pedigree,[68] and for this and other reasons has been preferred by some judges,[69] but it has been

---

[58] *Hongkong Fir Shipping Co Ltd v Kawasaki Kisen Kaisha Ltd (The Hongkong Fir)* [1962] 2 QB 26 (CA).

[59] *Antaios Compania Naviera SA v Salen Rederiena AB (The Antaios)* [1983] 1 WLR 1362 (CA) 1375 (Fox LJ); *Hurst v Bryk and ors* [1999] Ch 1 (CA) 9 (Peter Gibson LJ); *Great Peace Shipping Ltd v Tsavliris Salvage International Ltd (The Great Peace)* [2002] EWCA Civ 1407; [2003] QB 679, para 82 (Lord Phillips).

[60] *The Hongkong Fir*, 35 (Salmon J) (n 58); *Suisse Atlantique Société d'Armement Maritime SA v NV Rotterdamsche Kolen Centrale* [1967] 1 AC 361 (HL) 436 (Lord Wilberforce); *Trade and Transport Inc v Iino Kaiun Kaisha (The Angelia)* [1973] 1 WLR 210 (QBD) 221 (Kerr J).

[61] *Miles v Wakefield Metropolitan District Council* [1987] AC 359 (HL) 562 (Lord Templeman); *Esanda Finance Corp Ltd v Plessnig* (1989) 63 ALJR 338 (HCA) 242 (Brennan J); *Esso Petroleum Co Ltd v Milton* [1997] CLC 634 (CA) 637 (Simon Brown LJ); *Associated British Ports v Ferryways NV* [2008] EWHC 1265 (Comm); [2008] 2 Lloyd's Rep 35, para 55 (Field J).

[62] *London Transport Executive v Clarke* [1981] ICR 355 (CA) 362 (Lord Denning MR); *Millers Wharf Partnership Ltd v Corinthian Column Ltd* (1991) 61 P & CR 461 (Ch D) 478 (Knox J); *ACG Acquisition XX LLC v Olympic Airlines SA* [2010] EWHC 923 (Comm); [2010] 1 CLC 581, para 35 (Hamblen J).

[63] *Karsales (Harrow) Ltd v Wallis* [1956] 1 WLR 936 (CA); *Charterhouse Credit Co v Tolly* [1963] 2 QB 683 (CA); *Harbutt's Plasticine Ltd v Wayne Tank & Pump Co Ltd* [1970] 1 QB 447 (CA).

[64] *Suisse Atlantique Société d'Armement Maritime SA v NV Rotterdamsche Kolen Centrale* [1967] 1 AC 361 (HL); *Photo Production Ltd v Securicor Transport Ltd* [1980] AC 827 (HL).

[65] Reynolds, 'Warranty, Condition and Fundamental Term', pp 540–50 (n 36); JL Montrose, 'Some Problems about Fundamental Terms' [1964] CLJ 60; see Ch 5, para 5.06.

[66] Though the two concepts derive from a common root, they have now diverged to a considerable extent: see Ch 2.

[67] Thus repudiation suggests an unwillingness or inability to perform in the future, whereas an injured party may terminate purely on the basis of the consequences of the breach that have already occurred. For this and other reasons it is argued by Carter (*Carter's Breach of Contract*, paras 6-43–6-45 (n 8)) that the doctrine in *The Hongkong Fir* operates independently from that of repudiation.

[68] Furmston, Fifoot, and Simpson, *Cheshire, Fifoot, and Furmston's Law of Contract*, p 679 (n 33) describes it as 'the favourite of the judges for at least 150 years'.

[69] *Decro-Wall International SA v Practitioners in Marketing Ltd* [1971] 1 WLR 361 (CA) 374 (Sachs LJ); Furmston, Fifoot, and Simpson, *Cheshire, Fifoot, and Furmston's Law of Contract*, p 679 (n 33).

described as a misleading metaphor,[70] besides which it is rather too unwieldy to be used as a technical term. Given that there is now no longer any risk of confusion with the law of exemption clauses, it is probably best to use the term 'fundamental breach' for a breach of this sort, whilst leaving open for the present the question whether it necessarily includes a breach of condition.[71]

(5) Repudiation and renunciation

1.12 The word 'repudiation' can be used in several different senses;[72] in particular, it can be used in a wide sense to describe any 'fundamental' breach of the sort mentioned earlier,[73] or in a narrower sense to mean a refusal by a party to perform his or her obligations under the contract.[74] In some cases the term is used to describe any such refusal, whether justified or unjustified,[75] but since the Sale of Goods Act 1893 it has generally carried the implication of a *wrongful* refusal to perform,[76] and this is the way in which it will be used in the present work. Though a repudiation in this sense will normally[77] amount to a fundamental breach, not every fundamental breach will be a repudiation, the distinction being that whereas the emphasis in fundamental breach is on what the defaulting party has done (or rather, not done) *in the past*, the emphasis in repudiation is on what he or she is likely to do (or rather, not do) *in the future*.[78] The essence of repudiation is that the party concerned demonstrates that he or she is not ready, willing, and able to perform.[79] Where the

---

[70] *Bank Line Ltd v Arthur Capel & Co* [1919] AC 435 (HL) 459 (Lord Sumner); Furmston, Fifoot, and Simpson, *Cheshire, Fifoot, and Furmston's Law of Contract*, p 679 (n 33).

[71] See further Ch 5, para 5.06.

[72] *Heyman v Darwins Ltd* [1942] AC 356 (HL) 378 (Lord Wright); Carter, *Carter's Breach of Contract*, paras 7-03–7-04 (n 8).

[73] See para 1.11; Carter, *Carter's Breach of Contract*, para 7-04 (n 8); *UCB Leasing Ltd v Holtom (t/a David Holtom & Co)* [1987] RTR 362 (CA) 369 (Lloyd LJ); *Glencore Grain Rotterdam BV v Lebanese Organisation for International Commerce* [1997] CLC 1274 (CA) 1281 (Evans LJ); *Gisda Cyf v Barratt* [2010] UKSC 41; [2010] ICR 1475, para 24 (Lord Kerr of Tonaghmore).

[74] Carter, *Carter's Breach of Contract*, para 7-03 (n 8); Furmston, Fifoot, and Simpson, *Cheshire, Fifoot, and Furmston's Law of Contract*, p 673 (n 33); *Shearson Lehman Bros Inc v Maclaine, Watson & Co Ltd (Damages: Interim Payments)* [1987] 1 WLR 480 (CA) 488 (Lloyd LJ); *Ali Shipping Corp v Shipyard Trogir* [1998] CLC 566 (CA) 581 (Potter LJ); *Pittack v Naviede* [2010] EWHC 1509 (Ch); [2011] 1 WLR 1666, para 24 (Mark Herbert QC).

[75] *Behn v Burness* (1863) 3 B & S 751 (Exchequer Chamber) 755, 122 ER 281, 283 (Williams J); *Goodman v Winchester & Alton Rly plc* [1985] 1 WLR 141 (CA) 144 (Lawton LJ); *Lancaster v Bird* (2000) 2 TCLR 136 (CA) 141 (Chadwick LJ).

[76] Sale of Goods Act 1893, s 11(1)(b); Sale of Goods Act 1979, s 11(3); *Chancery Lane Developments Ltd v Wades Departmental Stores Ltd* (1987) 53 P & CR 306 (CA) 310 (Slade LJ); *Credit Suisse Asset Management Ltd v Armstrong and ors* [1996] ICR 882 (CA) 891 (Neill LJ); *Golden Ocean Group Ltd v Salgaocar Mining Industries Pvt Ltd* [2011] EWHC 56 (Comm); [2011] 1 CLC 125, 128 (Christopher Clarke J).

[77] Though a refusal to perform a condition of the contract may perhaps also amount to repudiation: see further Ch 10, paras 10.15–10.16.

[78] The distinction is not an easy one to draw, as in many cases the injured party will be relying on a combination of *both* the past effects of the breach *and* the effects that it is likely to have in the future; see Ch 6, para 6.31.

[79] Carter, *Carter's Breach of Contract*, para 7-03 (n 8).

repudiation consists of an express or implied refusal to perform by the party concerned, it is generally termed a 'renunciation',[80] and most cases of repudiation fall into this category;[81] but repudiation can also be demonstrated by showing that the party concerned, though not unwilling to perform, was in fact unable to do so,[82] and this will be termed 'factual inability'.[83]

D. Common Law and Equity

One of the more tricky problems in this area of the law is the different way in which **1.13**
common law and equity have approached the question. At first sight this might
seem surprising; after all, the courts have had to administer both sets of principles
since the Judicature Act of 1873, and one might have expected the relationship
between the two to have been worked out by now. Nevertheless, the orthodox view
is that whilst there has been a fusion of jurisdictions,[84] equity and common law still
continue to exist as separate bodies of doctrine;[85] in the famous words of Walter
Ashburner,[86] whilst the two streams now run in a common channel, the waters
are not yet merged.[87] As far as termination for breach is concerned, there are three
main areas where the principles of the common law and equity appear to diverge,
and though efforts have been made to reconcile the two sets of rules, these have not
been met with universal approval by equity lawyers.

(1) Time stipulations in equity

The most obvious area of tension, at least from an historical perspective, has been **1.14**
the different approach of common law and equity to time stipulations. According
to the traditional approach, the courts of common law were more ready to allow
termination for breach of a time stipulation than those of equity, or as it was said,

---

[80] Beatson, Burrows, and Cartwright, *Anson's Law of Contract*, pp 512–16 (n 18); Peel, *Treitel*, para 17-074 (n 15); *Universal Cargo Carriers v Citati* [1957] 2 QB 401 (QBD: Commercial Ct) 436 (Devlin J); *Hurst v Bryk and ors* [1999] Ch 1 (CA) 18 (Hobhouse LJ); *Alan Auld Associates Ltd v Rick Pollard Associates and anor* [2008] EWCA Civ 655; [2008] BLR 419, para 13 (Tuckey LJ).

[81] See Ch 7, para 7.31.

[82] Carter, *Carter's Breach of Contract*, para 9-01 (n 8); see Ch 7, para 7.32.

[83] See *Carter*, para 9-13 (n 8).

[84] J McGhee (ed), *Snell's Equity* (32nd edn, Sweet & Maxwell, 2010) para 1.016; JE Martin, *Hanbury and Martin: Modern Equity* (19th edn, Sweet & Maxwell, 2012) paras 1-020–1-023.

[85] McGhee, *Snell's Equity*, para 1.019 (n 84).

[86] D Browne, *Ashburner's Principles of Equity* (2nd edn, Butterworth, 1933) p 18; Martin, *Hanbury and Martin: Modern Equity*, para 1-020 (n 84).

[87] In *United Scientific Holdings v Burnley Borough Council* [1978] AC 904 (HL) 925 Lord Diplock declared that this metaphor was no longer helpful, but the extent to which a fusion of principles has taken place continues to be a matter of hot dispute among equity lawyers: see PV Baker, 'The Future of Equity' (1977) 93 LQR 529; RP Meagher, JD Heydon, and MJ Leeming, *Meagher, Gummow and Lehane's Equity, Doctrines & Remedies* (4th edn, Butterworths LexisNexis, 2002) paras 2-100–2-320; A Burrows, 'We do this at Common Law but that in Equity' (2002) 22 OJLS 1.

time was generally of the essence at common law, but not in equity. This is well expressed by Maitland in his famous lecture on specific performance:[88]

> As a general rule a man cannot sue upon a contract at law if he himself has broken that contract, though of course as you know there are many exceptions to this statement. Now in contracts for the sale of land it very frequently happens that a breach of the terms of the contract has been committed by the person who wishes to enforce it. Such a contract will be full of stipulations that certain acts are to be done within certain times...Well you know that equity held as a general rule that these stipulations as to time were not of the essence of the contract—that for example a purchaser might sue for specific performance although he had not in all respects kept the days assigned to him by the contract of sale for his various acts. This was the general rule—these stipulations as to time were not essential unless the parties declared them to be so.[89]

This passage is noteworthy for three reasons. The first is that it shows the close connection between the equitable rules as to time and the doctrine of specific performance. The common law approach is to ask whether the innocent party can *terminate*, the general rule being that this can only be done if the breach *is* a sufficiently serious one. Equity, on the other hand, looks at the problem as it were from the other end, by asking whether the defaulting party can *enforce the contract*, the general rule being that this can be done provided that the breach is *not* too serious. Secondly, in declaring that someone 'cannot sue upon a contract at law if he himself has broken that contract', it assumes that the common law regarded termination as the norm in cases of breach rather than as the exception.[90] Thirdly, it shows that the whole point of the equitable rule in this regard was to enforce contracts which could be validly terminated at law; indeed, for this reason the equitable grant of specific performance in these cases was often accompanied by what was called a 'common injunction' to prevent the injured party taking proceedings at law on that basis.[91]

1.15 The status of these rules following the Judicature Act of 1873 has long been a matter of controversy. Section 25(7) of the Act provided that stipulations in contracts, as to time or otherwise, which would not prior to the passing of the Act have been deemed to be or to have become of the essence, should henceforth receive in all courts the same construction and effect that they would have had in equity. However, according to the House of Lords in *Stickney v Keeble*,[92] this did not

---

[88] FW Maitland, *Equity: a Course of Lectures* (2nd edn, revised by John Brunyate, CUP, 1947) ch 12.

[89] Maitland, *Equity*, p 307 (n 88).

[90] Whether this was so even in contracts for the sale of land is a moot point: see *Lang v Gale* (1813) 1 M & S 111 (KB) 105 ER 42, *Stowell v Robinson* (1837) 3 Bing NC 928 (Common Pleas), 132 ER 668 and *Sansom v Rhodes* (1840) 6 Bing NC 261 (Common Pleas), 133 ER 103.

[91] As in *Hearne v Tenant* (1807) 13 Ves J 287 (High Ct of Chancery), 33 ER 301 (action for ejection); *Levy v Lindo* (1817) 3 Mer 84 (High Ct of Chancery), 36 ER 32 (action for return of deposit).

[92] [1915] AC 386.

change the substantive law; in particular, the defaulting party would not be given relief in any case where formerly a decree of specific performance would not have been granted.[93] The effect of this was to preserve the equitable jurisdiction in a kind of bubble, insulated from the rest of the law. However, in 1978 an attempt was made by Lord Simon, in *United Scientific Holdings v Burnley Borough Council*,[94] to reformulate the equitable doctrine in common law terms. In the words of Lord Simon:[95]

> The law may well come to inquire whether a contractual stipulation as to time is (a) so fundamental to the efficacy of the contract that any breach discharges the other party from his contractual obligations ('essence'), or (b) such that a serious breach discharges the other party, a less serious breach giving rise to damages (if any) (or interest), or (c) such that no breach does more than give a right to damages (if any) (or interest) ('non-essential'). If this sort of analysis falls to be made, I see no reason why any type of contract should, because of its nature, be excluded.

> To put it another way, to say that time is of the essence would be another way of saying that timely performance is a 'condition'. To say that it is not of the essence would mean that it is a 'warranty'. There is also the possibility that it is an 'intermediate' or 'innominate' term, though this possibility is not reflected in the equitable classification.

Attractive though this analysis may be at first sight, there are a number of problems with it. In particular, while it works reasonably well for cases where time is of the essence, it falls down in cases where it is not. One can agree that where time is of the essence, untimely performance will be a breach of condition, and specific performance will not be available to the party in default. However, to equate a non-essential time stipulation with one 'such that no breach does more than give a right to damages' does violence to the historical roots of the doctrine, which was grounded on the assumption that that the breach *did* give a greater right at common law, namely the right to terminate.[96] Furthermore, the whole point of the doctrine was that where time was not of the essence, a decree of specific performance would be granted.[97] But even though it may now be true to say that a party whose untimely performance amounts to a breach of warranty may obtain specific performance in *some* cases, such a remedy is by no means available in *all*.[98] All in all, though Lord Simon may be right in saying that it may *eventually* be possible to express the law in these terms, that time has probably not yet come.

1.16

---

[93] *Stickney v Keeble*, 417 (Lord Parker) (n 92).
[94] [1978] AC 904 (HL).
[95] *United Scientific Holdings v Burnley BC*, 945 (n 94).
[96] See para 1.14.
[97] See para 1.14.
[98] On the contrary, specific performance will only be available in a minority of cases: McGhee, *Snell's Equity*, ch 17 (n 84); Martin, *Hanbury and Martin: Modern Equity*, ch 24 (n 84); see further Ch 12, paras 12.35–12.61.

(2) The notice procedure

1.17   Equity also allows for time to be made of the essence by notice.[99] This can happen in two cases, one being where the other party is in breach of a non-essential time stipulation,[100] and the other being when time was originally of the essence but the right to timely performance has been waived.[101] The issue of such a notice is subject to a number of conditions which need not be discussed at this point,[102] but its effect is to set a deadline for performance by the defaulting party; if this is not forthcoming, the right to specific performance is lost and the other party may terminate.

1.18   As in the case where time is originally of the essence, attempts have been made to reformulate the equitable doctrine in common law terms. However, it is not possible here to make use of the notion of a condition, as the law does not allow a term to be reclassified as a condition if it was not one to begin with.[103] However, in *United Scientific Holdings Ltd v Burnley Borough Council*[104] Lord Simon got round this problem by making use of the notion of repudiation, saying:[105]

> The notice operates as evidence that the promisee considers that a reasonable time for performance has elapsed by the date of the notice and as evidence of the date by which the promisee now considers it reasonable for the contractual obligation to be performed. The promisor is put on notice of these matters. It is only in this sense that time is made of the essence of a contract in which it was previously non-essential. The promisee is really saying, 'Unless you perform by such-and-such a date, I shall treat your failure as a repudiation of the contract.'

1.19   Once again, this is an attractive approach, and has the particular advantage of covering both types of case in which the procedure operates (that is to say cases where time was not of the essence to start with, and cases where an essential time stipulation has been waived).[106] This is of particular significance given that the use

---

[99]   McGhee, *Snell's Equity*, para 17-042 (n 84); JE Stannard, *Delay in the Performance of Contractual Obligations* (OUP, 2007) ch 8.

[100]   *Taylor v Brown* (1839) 2 Beav 180 (Rolls Court) 183, 48 ER 1149, 1150 (Lord Langdale MR); *Green v Sevin* (1879) 13 Ch D 589 (High Ct); *Compton v Bagley* [1892] 1 Ch 313 (High Ct); *Re Barr's Contract* [1956] Ch 551 (High Ct); *Behzadi v Shaftesbury Hotels* (CA) [1992] Ch 1.

[101]   As in *Charles Rickards Ltd v Oppenhaim* [1950] 1 KB 616 (CA).

[102]   See Ch 7, paras 7.35–7.40; Stannard, *Delay in the Performance of Contractual Obligations*, paras 8.07–8.32 (n 99).

[103]   *Green v Sevin* (1879) 13 Ch D 589, 599 (Fry J); *Raineri v Miles* [1981] AC 1050 (HL) 1085–6 (Lord Edmund-Davies); *Behzadi v Shaftesbury Hotels* [1992] Ch 1 (CA) 12 (Nourse LJ) and 24 (Purchas LJ); *Re Olympia & York Canary Wharf Ltd (No 2)* [1993] BCC 159 (Ch D: Companies Ct), 171–3 (Morritt J); *Morris v Robert Jones Investments Ltd* [1994] NZLR 275 (CA NZ) 280 (Hardie Boys J).

[104]   *United Scientific Holdings Ltd v Burnley BC* [1978] AC 904 (HL).

[105]   *United Scientific Holdings v Burnley BC*, 906 (n 104); see also *Taylor v Raglan Developments Pty Ltd* [1981] 2 NSWLR 117 (SC NSW Equity Division) 131 (Powell J); *Louinder v Leis* (1982) 149 CLR 509 (HCA) 526 (Mason J); *Laurinda Pty Ltd v Capalba Park Shopping Centre Pty Ltd* (1989) 166 CLR 623 (HCA) 644–5 (Brennan J); *Morris v Robert Jones Investments Ltd* [1994] 2 NZLR 275 (CA NZ) 281 (Hardie Boys J).

[106]   See para 1.17.

of the notice procedure in the latter situation is clearly not confined to cases where a decree of specific performance may be granted.[107] However, once again the fit between the notice procedure and the doctrine of repudiation is not an exact one; in particular, whereas failure by a party in default to comply with a properly served notice allows the other party to terminate more or less as a matter of course,[108] such failure, as Lord Simon concedes, can at best be *evidence* of repudiation.[109] Once again, therefore, it is probably still too early to dispense with the distinction between the doctrines of common law and equity in the present context.

(3) Relief against forfeiture

Another knotty problem in this context is the extent to which the right to termin- **1.20** ate for breach of contract can be restricted by the equitable jurisdiction for relief against forfeiture.[110] This jurisdiction has a long and venerable history,[111] the classic situation being where a lessor seeks to forfeit the lease for non-payment of rent and it can be shown either that the right of forfeiture was inserted purely by way of security, or that the lessee's breach was occasioned by fraud, accident, mistake, or surprise.[112] However, in 1973 the House of Lords put forward a wider principle, it being said that the courts had a general equitable jurisdiction to relieve against forfeiture for breach of covenant or condition where the primary object of the bargain was to secure a stated result which could effectively be attained when the matter came before the court, and when the forfeiture provision was added by way of security for the production of that result.[113]

The extent to which this affects the right to terminate for breach of contract in **1.21** English law is a moot point.[114] There is no doubt that this can be done as a matter of principle; the only debate is as to when, and under what conditions. The question is discussed more fully in Chapter 4,[115] but the equitable jurisdiction in this context seems to be subject to three clear limitations. The first and most important is that it

---

[107] *Hartley v Hymans* [1920] 3 KB 475 (KBD) (sale of goods); *Charles Rickards Ltd v Oppenhaim* [1950] 1 KB 616 (CA) (work and labour). Whether the procedure is confined to such cases in the former situation is not entirely clear, but the better view is that it is available as a general remedy: see Stannard, *Delay in the Performance of Contractual Obligations*, ch 8 (n 99).

[108] See Ch 7, para 7.40.

[109] See para 1.18; *Eshun v Moorgate Mercantile Credit Co* [1971] 1 WLR 722 (CA) 726 (Lord Denning MR); *Morris v Robert Jones Investments Ltd* [1994] NZLR 275 (CA NZ) 281 (Hardie Boys J).

[110] McGhee, *Snell's Equity*, paras 13-015–13-018 (n 84).

[111] M Pawlowski, *The Forfeiture of Leases* (Sweet & Maxwell, 1993) chs 9 and 10.

[112] *Hill v Barclay* (1811) 18 Ves J 56, 34 ER 238; *Re Lord de Clifford's Estate* [1900] 2 Ch 707 (Ch D).

[113] *Shiloh Spinners v Harding* [1973] AC 691, 723 (Lord Wilberforce) and 726 (Lord Simon); cf the general jurisdiction given in this context by the New Zealand Contractual Remedies Act 1979, s 9: Dawson and McLauchlan, *The Contractual Remedies Act 1979*, pp 140–66 (n 3).

[114] Stannard, *Delay in the Performance of Contractual Obligations*, paras 11.51–11.66 (n 99).

[115] See Ch 4, paras 4.77–4.81.

only applies to contracts involving the transfer of proprietary or possessory rights;[116] thus, for instance, it will not apply to a time charterparty, which gives the charterer no interest in the vessel itself but is in essence no more than a contract for services.[117] Secondly, the courts will be very slow to use the jurisdiction in the commercial context, where contracts are drafted for the purpose of trade between parties acting at arm's length.[118] Thirdly, the forfeiture against which relief is sought must be more than that of the defaulting party's expectation of performance;[119] rather there must be something in the case to make it unconscionable for the innocent party to rely on his or her legal rights, such as an element of unjust enrichment.[120]

E. Discharge and Damages

1.22 There are also problems concerning the relationship between discharge and damages. One is the extent to which the two overlap. Obviously the right to damages can exist without there being any question of discharge; this will be the case where there has been a breach of contract, but the term broken is not a condition and there is no evidence of repudiation or fundamental breach. A party to a contract may also be discharged from the obligation to perform without having any right to damages. This is well illustrated by *Jackson v Union Marine Insurance Co Ltd*,[121] where a charterparty provided that the ship was to proceed with all possible dispatch (dangers and accidents of navigation excepted) from Liverpool to Newport, and there load a cargo of iron rails for San Francisco. Soon after leaving Liverpool the ship went aground and was severely damaged, by which time the charterer had thrown up the charter and chartered another ship. A claim was subsequently brought by the shipowner on a policy of insurance on the chartered freight, and in this context the question arose whether the charterer had been bound to load the ship. It was found as a fact that the delay caused by the accident was sufficient to put an end, in a commercial sense, to the commercial speculation entered upon by the parties to the contract, but the insurers sought to argue that the owner was

---

[116] *BICC plc v Burndy Corp* [1985] Ch 232 (CA) 252 (Dillon LJ); *Celestial Aviation Trading 71 Ltd v Paramount Airways Pte Ltd* [2010] EWHC 185 (Comm); [2011] 1 Lloyd's Rep 9; McGhee, *Snell's Equity*, para 13-015 (n 84).

[117] *Scandinavian Trading Tanker Co AB v Flota Petrolera Ecuatoriana (The Scaptrade)* [1983] AC 694 (HL) 702 (Lord Diplock). However, the jurisdiction is not confined to the transfer of interests in land: *Barton Thompson & Co Ltd v Stapling Machines Co* [1966] Ch 499; *BICC plc v Burndy Corp* [1985] Ch 232 (CA); *More Og Romsdal Fylkesbatar AS v Demise Charterers of the Ship 'Jotunheim'* [2004] EWHC 671 (Comm); [2005] 1 Lloyd's Rep 181.

[118] *The Scaptrade* [1983] 1 Lloyd's Rep 146 (CA) 153 (Robert Goff LJ), affd [1983] AC 694 (HL); *Union Eagle Ltd v Golden Achievement Ltd* [1997] AC 514 (JCPC–Hong Kong) 519 (Lord Hoffmann).

[119] *Union Eagle v Golden Achievement*, 520 (Lord Hoffmann) (n 118).

[120] As in *Re Dagenham (Thames) Dock Co, ex p Hulse* (1872–73) LR 8 Ch App 1022 (land built on by purchaser); *Starside Properties Ltd v Mustapha* [1974] 1 WLR 816 (CA) (forfeiture of instalments of purchase price).

[121] (1874–75) LR 10 CP 125 (Exchequer Chamber).

protected by the exception relating to perils of the seas. However, this was held not to affect the matter. The clause had the effect of excusing the shipowner, but gave him no right.[122] In the words of Bramwell B:[123]

> The exception is an excuse for him who is to do the act, and operates to save him from an action and make his non-performance not a breach of contract, but does not operate to take away the right the other party would have had, if the non-performance had been a breach of contract, to retire from the engagement: and if one party may, so may the other.

To put it another way, the fact that the charterer had no right to damages did not deprive him of the right to throw up the charter.[124]

This brings out an important point; though termination is an important remedy **1.23** for breach of contract,[125] the discharge of contractual obligations is by no means confined to that situation.[126] On the contrary, there are at least three situations where discharge may take place in the absence of a breach. The first is where the contract is discharged by frustration, or by excused non-performance falling short of frustration.[127] Another is where the promisor in a unilateral contract argues that he or she is discharged from the obligation to perform by the failure of the event on which that obligation was conditioned.[128] A third case is where a party exercises a contractual right of termination predicated on events that may but need not necessarily include breaches by the other party.[129] All of this goes to show that the relationship between breach and discharge is much less close than that between breach and damages; while there can be no *damages* without breach in the contractual context, there can often be *discharge* without breach.

Another problem is that the quantum of damages recoverable may vary depend- **1.24** ing on the basis upon which termination took place. Where the termination has been occasioned by repudiation or fundamental breach, the law allows the injured party to recover damages not only for the particular breach but for loss of the expected benefit of the contract as a whole.[130] The same principle has been held to apply to breaches of condition, on the ground that these are deemed to amount

---

[122] *Jackson v Union Marine Insurance Co Ltd*, 144 (n 121).

[123] *Jackson v Union Marine Insurance Co Ltd*, 144 (n 121).

[124] The case is now generally treated as one of frustration, which means that the charterer had no choice; both parties were discharged automatically from their primary obligations; see further Ch 6, para 6.20.

[125] See para 1.03.

[126] This has led some to argue that termination is best not seen as a consequence of breach at all: see Langley and Loveridge, 'Termination as a Response to Unjust Enrichment' (n 1).

[127] See Ch 6, para 6.20.

[128] As in *United Dominions Trust (Commercial) Ltd v Eagle Aircraft Services Ltd* [1968] 1 WLR 74 (CA); see para 1.29.

[129] As in *Financings v Baldock* [1963] QB 104 (CA); *Shevill and anor v Builders' Licensing Board* (1982) 149 CLR 620 (HC Australia); see Ch 8.

[130] *Yeoman Credit Ltd v Waragowski* [1961] 1 WLR 1124 (CA); *Overstone Ltd v Shipway* [1962] 1 WLR 117 (CA).

to a repudiation of the contract.[131] But where the termination takes place under an express clause giving the right to do so, damages can only be recovered for the breach that has actually occurred.[132] The distinction between these different cases can be an exceedingly fine one, and can lead to seemingly arbitrary results.[133] For this reason it has been suggested that the law would be better if the two issues were separated; in particular, that the fact that termination is available should not necessarily carry with it a right to damages either at a particular level[134] or indeed at all.[135]

F. Withholding Performance and Termination

1.25 One of the most important aspects of the right to terminate is the right to refuse performance;[136] in the words of Lord Diplock, termination puts an end to the 'primary obligations' of the party not in default in so far as they have not already been performed at the time of the termination.[137] However, a party who is entitled to refuse performance is not necessarily entitled to terminate.[138] Thus an employer is normally entitled to withhold the payment of wages in certain circumstances,[139] but this does not mean that the contract is terminated; for this, the employee would have to be properly dismissed. Again, if a seller tenders goods that are not in conformity with the contract, the buyer may reject them, but this does not mean that the contract is terminated, as the seller may still have time to produce other goods that do meet that specification.[140] The buyer may only refuse a fresh tender of performance if it is made

---

[131] *Lombard North Central plc v Butterworth* [1987] QB 527 (CA); *Wallis, Son and Wells v Pratt and Haynes* [1910] 2 KB 1003 (CA) 1012 (Fletcher Moulton LJ).

[132] *Financings v Baldock* [1963] QB 104 (CA); *Shevill and anor v Builders' Licensing Board* (1982) 149 CLR 620 (HC Australia).

[133] See Ch 10, paras 10.07–10.17.

[134] JE Stannard, 'Delay, Damages and the Doctrine of Constructive Repudiation' (2013) 29 JCL 178.

[135] This is particularly a problem in the area of anticipatory breach: M Mustill, 'The Golden Victory–Some Reflections' (2008) 124 LQR 569, 572–3; see further Ch 7, para 7.33.

[136] Peel, *Treitel*, para 18-001 (n 15).

[137] *Moschi v Lep Air Services Ltd* [1973] AC 331 (HL) 350. In this context Lord Diplock speaks of 'rescission', but he is referring to the process which in the present work is called 'termination': see para 1.03.

[138] Beale, *Remedies for Breach of Contract*, p 91 (n 20).

[139] Thus an employee will normally have to work for a certain period before wages become due, and wages may also be withheld for non-performance in certain cases without the contract being terminated: see G Mead, 'Employer's Right to Withhold Wages' (1990) 106 LQR 192.

[140] *Borrowman, Phillips & Co v Free & Hollis* (1878) 4 QBD 500 (CA); *Agricultores Federados Argentinos Sociedad Co-operativa Lda v Ampro SA Commerciale, Industrielle et Financiere* [1965] 2 Lloyd's Rep 157 (QBD: Widgery J); *Motor Oil Hellas (Corinth) Refineries SA v Shipping Corp of India (The Kanchenjunga)* [1990] 1 Lloyd's Rep 391 (HL). This can cause problems where the seller seeks to repair and re-tender defective goods after they have been rejected by the buyer: see *J & H Ritchie v Lloyd Ltd* [2007] UKHL 9; KFK Low, 'Repair, Rejection and Rescission: an Uneasy Resolution' (2007) 123 LQR 536. See generally A Apps, 'The Right to Cure Defective Performance' [1994] LMCLQ 525; V Mak, 'The Seller's Right to Cure Defective Performance—a Reappraisal' [2007] LMCLQ 409.

too late,[141] or alternatively if the original tender was so bad as to amount to a repudiation of the contract.[142]

These principles are easy to state, but can be difficult to apply. The reason for this **1.26** is that the right to withhold performance may often crystallize into a right to terminate once the time for the other party's performance has passed, or in other cases where it is clear that he or she will not be able to perform.[143] This is well illustrated by the famous case of *Cutter v Powell*,[144] where a seaman agreed to serve on board ship for a voyage from Jamaica to Liverpool. The contract provided that his wages were to be paid ten days after arrival, provided that he had performed all his duties on the voyage. The seaman having died during the course of the voyage, it was held that his widow could recover nothing. In this case what was originally merely a right to withhold performance (until ten days after the arrival of the ship at Liverpool) was effectively converted by the seaman's death into a right to terminate. This case also illustrates another reason for the difficulty, which is historical. Prior to the beginning of the nineteenth century, questions of discharge were often couched in terms of whether a party to a contract had performed all the necessary 'conditions precedent' required to earn the right to demand performance from the other side.[145] Thus in *Cutter v Powell* the key finding of the court was that performance of the complete voyage was intended as a condition precedent to the right to recover wages.[146] Nevertheless, it is important that the two rights in question are not confused. The right to withhold performance is essentially a temporary one,[147] and depends basically on the agreed order of performance; if the contract provides that A should not have to perform until B has performed, then party A is entitled to withhold performance until this has happened.[148] The right to terminate, on the other hand, assuming that it is not waived by the injured party,[149] is fixed and final in nature, and depends not only on the intention of the parties but also on the nature and consequences of the other party's breach.[150]

---

[141] As in *Kwei Tek Chao v British Traders and Shippers Ltd* [1954] 2 QB 459 (QBD: Devlin J).

[142] As in *Texaco Ltd v Eurogulf Shipping Co Ltd (The Texaco)* [1987] 2 Lloyd's Rep 541 (QBD: Commercial Ct); Beale, *Remedies for Breach of Contract* (n 20); Peel, *Treitel*, para 17-004 (n 15).

[143] See further Ch 4, para 4.08.

[144] *Cutter v Powell* (1795) 6 TR 320, 101 ER 573 (KB).

[145] See Ch 2, para 2.04. The use of the term 'condition' in this context is also a further source of ambiguity: see para 1.09.

[146] (1795) 6 TR 320, 325, 101 ER 573, 576 (Ashhurst J).

[147] Apps, 'The Right to Cure Defective Performance', p 528 (n 140).

[148] Beale, *Remedies for Breach of Contract*, p 20 (n 20). The same rule applies to unilateral contracts and options: see para 1.29.

[149] See Ch 4, paras 4.54–4.68.

[150] See Ch 6, para 6.06, though see Reynolds, 'Discharge of Contract by Breach' (n 12).

G. Termination, Frustration, and Excused Non-performance

1.27 The cases demonstrate a close relationship between the doctrines of termination for breach and discharge by frustration. In particular, the concepts of fundamental breach, repudiation, and frustration all stem from the same historical root,[151] and cases which give rise to any one of these doctrines can, with a slight alteration of the facts, fall under the purview of another. In *Jackson v Union Marine Insurance Co Ltd* the charterparty was frustrated because of delay caused by the grounding of the ship;[152] the fact that this came within the scope of the excepted perils clause made it a case of frustration, but if the clause had not applied it would have been a case of discharge by breach. Both doctrines involve the extinction of the primary obligations of the parties concerned, and it has been said that the degree of failure in performance needed to trigger the doctrine of frustration is the same as that needed to trigger the right to terminate for fundamental breach.[153] Nevertheless, the doctrines in question differ in a number of key respects.[154] One is that whereas termination for breach by its very nature requires a breach of some sort,[155] frustration operates only where neither party is in default.[156] Another is that whereas termination for breach operates only by way of election on the part of the injured party,[157] frustration is automatic.[158] Moreover, whereas termination for breach gives rise to a secondary obligation to pay damages for the party in default,[159] frustration gives rise to no such obligation; both parties are discharged entirely from their obligations under the contract.[160]

---

[151] See Ch 2; *Hongkong Fir Shipping Co Ltd v Kawasaki Kisen Kaisha (The Hongkong Fir)* [1962] 2 QB 26 (CA) 66–9 (Diplock LJ).

[152] (1874–75) LR 10 CP 125 (Exchequer Chamber); see para 1.22.

[153] *The Hongkong Fir*, p 69 (Diplock LJ) (n 151); *Chilean Nitrate Sales Corp v Marine Transportation Co Ltd (The Hermosa)* [1980] 1 Lloyd's Rep 638 (QBD: Commercial Ct) 649 (Mustill J); *Great Peace Shipping Ltd v Tsavrilis Salvage (International) Ltd (The Great Peace)* [2002] EWCA Civ 1407; [2003] QB 697, para 82 (Lord Phillips MR); see, however, GH Treitel, *Frustration and Force Majeure* (2nd edn, Sweet & Maxwell, 2004) para 5-060.

[154] Peel, *Treitel*, para 15-005 (n 15).

[155] See Ch 3.

[156] *Bank Line Ltd v Arthur Capel and Co* [1919] AC 435 (HL) 452 (Lord Sumner); *Maritime National Fish Ltd v Ocean Trawlers Ltd* [1935] AC 524 (JCPC–Canada) 530 (Lord Wright); *Davis Contractors Ltd v Fareham UDC* [1956] AC 696 (HL) 729 (Lord Radcliffe); *Paal Wilson & Co A/S v Partenreederei Hannah Blumenthal (The Hannah Blumenthal)* [1983] AC 854 (HL) 909 (Lord Brandon); *J Lauritzen A/S v Wijsmuller BV (The Super Servant Two)* [1990] 1 Lloyd's Rep 1 (CA) 8 (Bingham LJ); Treitel, *Frustration and Force Majeure*, ch 14 (n 153).

[157] See Ch 4, para 4.13.

[158] *Hirji Mulji v Cheong Yue SS Co* [1926] AC 497 (JCPC–Hong Kong) 505 (Lord Sumner); *Denny, Mott & Dickson Ltd v James B Fraser & Co Ltd* [1944] AC 265 (HL(Sc)) 274 (Lord Wright); *The Super Servant Two*, 8 (Bingham LJ) (n 156); Treitel, *Frustration and Force Majeure*, para 15-002 (n 153).

[159] See para 1.03; see also Ch 10.

[160] *Taylor v Caldwell* (1863) 3 B & S 826, 840, 122 ER 309, 314 (Blackburn J); *Joseph Constantine SS Line v Imperial Smelting Corp* [1942] AC 154 (HL) 188 (Lord Wright); *The Super Servant Two*, 8 (Bingham LJ) (n 156); Treitel, *Frustration and Force Majeure*, para 15-010 (n 153).

Matters are further complicated by the existence of a third category of cases **1.28** involving excused non-performance falling short of frustration.[161] Thus an employee will not be liable for breach of contract by failing to turn up for work while he or she is ill,[162] or prevented by some other factor for which he or she is not to blame.[163] The point is that though performance is excused,[164] the contract will not be frustrated unless the employee's absence is of such nature or duration as to render performance of the contract radically different from that which was contemplated by the parties.[165] Such cases are relatively uncontroversial, but a fourth class of case has been mooted in which excused non-performance by one party allows the other to terminate even in the absence of either breach or frustration.[166] The case cited in this connection is *Poussard v Spiers & Pond*,[167] in which the plaintiff was engaged for a period of three months to sing in the defendants' opera. Shortly before the opening night the plaintiff fell ill, and the defendants engaged a substitute. The defendants then refused to take the plaintiff back when she recovered, and it was held that they were entitled to do so; the effect of the plaintiff's absence was serious enough to justify them dispensing with her services. This case has been cited as one of frustration,[168] but it has been argued that the illness of the plaintiff was not serious enough to bring this doctrine into operation, and that the defendants could have insisted on retaining her services had they wished to do so.[169] There is not the space in the present context to look at this argument in any detail;[170] suffice it to say at present that there is no bright line between termination for breach and frustration, and that some of the cases are not easy to classify.

---

[161] Peel, *Treitel*, para 17-059 (n 15); Treitel, *Frustration and Force Majeure*, paras 5-057–5-058 (n 153).

[162] *Jackson v Union Marine Insurance Co Ltd* (1874–75) LR 10 CP 125 (Exchequer Chamber) 145; *Poussard v Spiers & Pond* (1876) 1 QBD 410 (DC) 414; Treitel, *Frustration and Force Majeure*, para 5-058 (n 153).

[163] *Sim v Rotherham Metropolitan BC* [1987] Ch 216 (Ch D: Scott J) 254 (teacher locked in lavatory).

[164] ie the performance of the employee, in so far as he or she is prevented from carrying out the duties in question: *Marshall v Alexander Sloan & Co Ltd* [1981] IRLR 264 (EAT); J Stanner, *Tolley's Employment Law* (Tolley, 1994) para S5025.

[165] *Morgan v Manser* [1948] 1 KB 184 (KBD: Streatfeild J); *Condor v Barron Knights Ltd* [1966] 1 WLR 87 (Bedford Assizes: Thompson J); *Marshall v Harland and Wolff Ltd* [1972] ICR 101 (NIRC); *FC Shepherd & Co Ltd v Jerrom* [1986] ICR 802 (CA).

[166] Treitel, *Frustration and Force Majeure*, para 5-060 (n 153).

[167] (1876) 1 QBD 410 (DC).

[168] *Bank Line Ltd v Arthur Capel & Co* [1919] AC 435 (HL) 461 (Lord Sumner); *Robert H Dahl v Nelson Donkin* (1881) 6 App Cas 38 (HL) 52 (Lord Blackburn); *Tamplin SS Co Ltd v Anglo-Mexican Petroleum Co Ltd* [1916] 2 AC 397 (HL) 421 (Lord Atkinson); Treitel, *Frustration and Force Majeure*, para 5-060 (n 153).

[169] Treitel, *Frustration and Force Majeure*, para 5-060 (n 153).

[170] See further Ch 4, para 4.10.

H. The Problem of Options

1.29 By its very nature, the concept of termination for breach in the full sense can only apply to bilateral or 'synallagmatic' contracts, where the parties are subject to reciprocal obligations;[171] it cannot apply in relation to a unilateral contract or option where one party is not under any obligation at all. However, similar principles can apply, as is demonstrated by *Hare v Nicoll*,[172] where a contract for the sale of shares provided that the buyer could call on the seller to repurchase the shares provided that the price was paid before a particular day. The buyer sought to exercise the option, but failed to pay the price in time. It was held by the Court of Appeal that the option had not been validly exercised; options of this sort were in essence a privilege for the benefit of the party on whom they were conferred, and it was for that party to comply strictly with the conditions stipulated for the exercise of the option.[173] This is not a case of termination for breach, as the buyer had committed no breach; he was not obliged to call on the seller to repurchase at all, let alone within any particular time frame. The point was that if he wanted to do so, he had to do so on the terms agreed. In a bilateral contract, termination for breach can only occur if the breach is a sufficiently serious one, but in the case of a unilateral obligation or option there is no room for manoeuvre; either the conditions for the exercise of the option have been met, or they have not,[174] and if they have not, that is the end of the matter; a miss, as they say, is as good as a mile.

1.30 Efforts made by the courts to mitigate the harsh effects of this rule have led to some uncertainty in the law. Particular problems have been caused by rent review clauses; to what extent does the late service of 'trigger notices' deprive the landlord of the right to have the rent reviewed under a long lease?[175] The courts initially took the view that these notices were essentially options, and that they therefore could not be exercised at all unless the agreed time limits were strictly followed.[176] Needless to say, the effect of this at a time of rapid inflation was potentially catastrophic, and the courts had to modify their stance to some degree. In *United Scientific Holdings Ltd v Burnley Borough Council*[177] the House of Lords drew a distinction in this context between 'true options', which involved the creation of a new contract, and other

---

[171] See para 1.02.
[172] [1966] 2 QB 130 (CA).
[173] *Hare v Nicoll*, 141 (Willmer LJ) and 148 (Winn LJ) (n 172).
[174] *United Dominions Trust (Commercial) Ltd v Eagle Aircraft Services Ltd* [1968] 1 WLR 74 (CA) 84 (Diplock LJ); PS Atiyah (1968) 31 MLR 332.
[175] JE Stannard, *Delay in the Performance of Contractual Obligations*, paras 11.33–11.37 (n 99). Similar issues have been raised in relation to notification clauses in insurance contracts: see *Alfred McAlpine plc v BAI (Run-Off) Ltd* [2000] 1 Lloyd's Rep 437 (CA); *Friends Provident Life & Pensions Ltd v Sirius International Insurance* [2005] EWCA Civ 601, [2005] 2 Lloyd's Rep 517; J Lowry and P Rawlings, 'Innominate Terms in Insurance Contracts' [2006] LMCLQ 135.
[176] *Samuel Properties (Developments) Ltd v Hayek* [1972] 1 WLR 1064 (CA).
[177] [1978] AC 904 (HL).

provisions equivalent to options which merely led to the variation of obligations under an existing contract.[178] Provisions of the latter type, which may conveniently be termed 'quasi-options', are not subject to the strict rules for compliance governing true options, and in many ways are more akin to bilateral obligations of the usual sort; thus, for instance, both parties may take steps to have the provision invoked,[179] and a notice may even be served in some cases making time of the essence.[180] The relationship between quasi-options of this sort and true options is not at all clear, and as in the case of frustration and termination for breach no bright line can be drawn.

I. Liquidated Damages, Penalties, Options, and Deposits

One important consequence of termination is the right of the injured party to recover damages, not only for the actual breach in question, but for the loss of the entire bargain.[181] In many cases, however, the contract will contain an agreed damages clause, and the court may then be faced with the question whether the clause in question should be struck down as a 'penalty'.[182] The principles for deciding whether this is so are complex,[183] but generally speaking an agreed damages clause will be regarded as penal if it is designed not as a fair pre-estimate of the loss but as a measure to deter the other party for failing to perform the contract;[184] in particular, where the sum specified is out of all proportion to any possible loss sustained.[185]   **1.31**

The jurisdiction of the court to strike down penalties is relatively circumscribed; in particular, it only applies in relation to agreed *damages* clauses, that is to say sums payable in the event of a breach. A sum that is payable on the occurrence of some other event cannot be penal.[186] This leads to a strange paradox in relation to agreed sums payable on voluntary termination. Contracts of hire purchase and the like frequently contain provisions which allow the hirer to terminate on payment of an agreed sum. Even if this sum may be set at a level grossly in excess of any loss to the   **1.32**

---

[178] *United Scientific Holdings v Burnley BC*, 928–30 (Lord Diplock), 945–6 (Lord Simon), 951 (Lord Salmon), and 961–2 (Lord Fraser) (n 177).

[179] *Touche Ross & Co v Secretary of State for the Environment* (1983) 46 P & CR 187 (CA); *Metrolands Investments Ltd v JH Dewhurst Ltd* [1986] 3 All ER 659 (CA).

[180] *London and Manchester Assurance Co v Dunn* (1982) 265 EG 39 (CA); *Amherst v James Walker Goldsmith and Silversmith Ltd* [1983] Ch 305.

[181] See Ch 10, para 10.04.

[182] See Ch 10, para 10.18.

[183] *Dunlop Pneumatic Tyre Co Ltd v New Garage and Motor Co* [1915] AC 79 (HL).

[184] *Dunlop Pneumatic Tyre Co Ltd v New Garage and Motor Co*, 86 (Lord Dunedin) (n 183); *Lordsvale Finance plc v Bank of Zambia* [1996] QB 752 (QBD) 762 (Colman J); *Murray v Leisureplay plc* [2005] EWCA Civ 963; [2005] IRLR 946; McGhee, *Snell's Equity*, para 13-002 (n 84).

[185] *Dunlop Pneumatic Tyre Co Ltd v New Garage and Motor Co*, 87 (Lord Dunedin) (n 183); *Ringrow Pty Ltd v BP Australia Pty Ltd* (2005) 224 CLR 656 (HC Australia).

[186] *Associated Distributors v Hall* [1938] 2 KB 83 (CA); *Re Apex Supply Co Ltd* [1942] Ch 108 (Ch D); *Export Credit Guarantee Department v Universal Oil Products Co* [1983] 1 WLR 399 (HL).

other party, the doctrine of penalties cannot apply, as there is no breach involved;[187] the hirer is simply exercising an option of the sort considered previously.[188] This leads to the paradox that the law gives protection to one who breaks the contract, while denying it to one who keeps it.[189] This absurd state of affairs is now mitigated to some extent by statute,[190] but the limitation of the penalty doctrine to cases of breach still holds good.

1.33 Similar problems may arise when a party who terminates seeks to forfeit a deposit paid by the other, or to retain previous instalments of the purchase price.[191] In the past the equitable jurisdiction to relieve against forfeiture in such cases was thought to be confined to contracts for the sale of land,[192] but in *Workers Trust and Merchant Bank Ltd v Dojap Investments Ltd*[193] a broader principle was asserted by the Privy Council, Lord Wilberforce suggesting that any clause requiring one party either to pay or to forfeit a sum to the other in the event of breach could be treated as a penalty unless it could be justified as a genuine pre-estimate of the loss.[194] However, the jurisdiction of the court in relation to forfeiture is more restricted than its jurisdiction in relation to penalties; whereas the courts will refuse to enforce a penalty as a matter of principle, relief against forfeiture is not automatic, and will generally only be granted to a party who is ready and willing to perform his or her contractual obligations (for instance by paying any sums outstanding).[195] It has been said that there is no doctrinal or policy reason for this distinction,[196] which like so many in this area of the law can only be explained in the light of history.[197]

J. Damages and the Action for the Price

1.34 Where a breach of contract is serious enough to give rise to the right to terminate, the other party is left with a choice; he or she can either terminate or affirm.[198] A party who affirms may also sometimes have the option of completing performance and then bringing an action for the contract price. In *White and Carter (Councils) Ltd v*

---

[187] *Associated Distributors v Hall* (n 186).

[188] See para 1.29.

[189] *Bridge v Campbell Discount Co Ltd* [1962] AC 600 (HL) 629 (Lord Denning).

[190] Consumer Credit Act 1974, s 100.

[191] McGhee, *Snell's Equity*, para 13-015 (n 84).

[192] Law of Property Act 1925, s 49(2).

[193] [1993] AC 573 (JCPC–Jamaica); C Harpum, 'Deposits as Penalties' [1993] CLJ 389; H Beale, 'Unreasonable Deposits' (1993) 109 LQR 524; Carter (1993) 6 JCL 266.

[194] Beale, 'Unreasonable Deposits', p 578 (n 193); McGhee, *Snell's Equity*, para 13-014 (n 84).

[195] McGhee, *Snell's Equity*, para 13-001 (n 84).

[196] McGhee, *Snell's Equity*, para 13-001 (n 84).

[197] *Jobson v Johnson* [1989] 1 WLR 1026 (CA) 1042 (Nicholls LJ); C Harpum, 'Equitable Relief: Penalties and Forfeitures' [1989] CLJ 370; DR Harris, 'Penalties and Forfeiture: Contractual Remedies Specified by the Parties' [1990] LMCLQ 158.

[198] See Ch 4, para 4.13.

McGregor[199] a firm of advertisers contracted with the defendant to display advertisements for his business on litter bins in the Clydebank area. The defendant repudiated the contract very soon afterwards, but the claimants decided to ignore the repudiation and to carry on with performance regardless; having put the advertisements in place, they then brought a successful action for the contract price. At first sight this seems to go clean against the rule that the victim of a breach of contract is obliged to mitigate his or her loss, but this rule applies as such only to damages,[200] and there is a clear difference in law between such a claim and a claim for the contract price. Thus a claim for the price is a claim by the *promisor* for a *debt* owed on the basis of *performance* by the promisor; a claim for damages is a claim by the *promisee* for *compensation* on the basis of *non-performance* by the promisor.[201] This does not mean, of course, that the policy factors underlying the mitigation principle should not also restrict the availability of a claim for the contract price,[202] but the way in which these policy factors are addressed by the courts differs substantially as between the two kinds of claim,[203] and it is therefore important not to confuse the two.

K. Conditions and Contractual Rights of Termination

Commercial and consumer contracts often contain express rights of termination, **1.35** and the question then arises as to how these relate to the right to terminate for breach at common law.[204] Broadly speaking, termination for breach of contract at common law can take place in two cases, the first being where the other party has broken a condition of the contract, and the second where there has been some other breach with very serious consequences.[205] It is the first of these that gives rise to most of the problems in this connection. Since deciding whether a particular term is a condition is primarily a matter of construction,[206] the distinction between

---

[199] [1962] AC 413 (HL (Sc)); MP Furmston, 'The Case of the Insistent Performer' (1962) 25 MLR 364; PM Nienaber, 'The Effect of an Anticipatory Repudiation: Principle and Policy' [1962] CLJ 213; Mr Justice Priestley, 'Conduct after Breach: the Position of the Party Not in Breach (1990–91) 3 JCL 218; JW Carter, A Phang, and S-Y Phang, 'Performance Following Repudiation: Legal and Economic Interests' (1999) 15 JCL 97; see further Ch 12, paras 12.12–12.34.

[200] K Scott, 'Contract—Repudiation—Performance by Innocent Party' [1962] CLJ 12.

[201] *Re Park Air Services plc* [2000] 2 AC 172 (HL), 187; Peel, *Treitel*, para 21-001 (n 15).

[202] Beatson, Burrows, and Cartwright, *Anson's Law of Contract*, 575 (n 18); Furmston, Fifoot, and Simpson, *Cheshire, Fifoot, and Furmston's Law of Contract*, p 783 (n 33); Peel, *Treitel*, para 21-013 (n 15).

[203] See further Ch 10, para 10.31.

[204] JW Carter and Y Goh, 'Concurrent and Independent Rights to Terminate for Breach of Contract' (2009) 26 JCL 133; See Ch 8.

[205] See Part III.

[206] *Glaholm v Hays* (1841) 2 M & G 257 (Common Pleas), 133 ER 743; *Behn v Burness* (1863) 3 B & S 751 (Exchequer Chamber), 122 ER 281; *Schuler AG v Wickman Machine Tool Sales Ltd* [1974] AC 235 (HL); *Tradax Export SA v European Grain & Shipping Co* [1983] 2 Lloyd's Rep 100 (QBD: Commercial Ct); *George Hunt Cranes Ltd v Scottish Boiler and General Insurance Co Ltd* [2001] EWCA Civ 1964; [2003] 1 CLC 1.

termination for breach of condition and termination under a contractual right can be a very difficult one to draw.[207] Nevertheless, it is a distinction which can have serious implications when it comes to deciding what rights and remedies the injured party may have in addition to the basic right to terminate. In particular, a party who terminates for breach of condition may be in a much stronger position when it comes to damages than one who merely exercises a contractual right.[208] There are other problems associated with the distinction. For instance, to what extent can a party who wrongfully refuses to perform meet a claim for wrongful repudiation by arguing that he or she had made a bona fide mistake in interpreting the scope of a right to terminate that was expressly *given* by the contract, and that therefore his or her refusal to perform should not be construed as a refusal to be *bound* by that contract?[209] Again, to what extent can contractual rights of termination be taken to exclude a concurrent right of termination under the common law?[210] Given the importance of contractual rights of this sort in the commercial context, these questions are of crucial importance, but the law has still not fully worked out a satisfactory approach to the problem.[211]

L. Bringing the Contract to an End

1.36 References can frequently be found in reported cases to a contract being brought to an end by breach,[212] repudiation,[213] or even the election of the option to

---

[207] See Ch 8, paras 8.02–8.04.

[208] *Financings Ltd v Baldock* [1963] 2 QB 104 (CA); *Lombard North Central plc v Butterworth* [1987] 1 QB 527 (CA).

[209] *Sweet and Maxwell Ltd v Universal News Services Ltd* [1964] 2 QB 699 (CA); *Federal Commerce and Navigation Co Ltd v Molena Alpha Inc (The Nanfri)* [1979] AC 757 (HL); *Woodar Investment Development Ltd v Wimpey Construction (UK) Ltd* [1980] 1 WLR 277 (HL).

[210] *Stocznia Gdanska SA v Latvian Shipping Co (No 2)* [2002] EWCA Civ 889; [2002] 2 Lloyd's Rep 436; *Stocznia Gdynia SA v Gearbulk Holdings Ltd* [2009] EWCA Civ 75; [2010] QB 27; *Shell Egypt West Manzala GmbH v Dana Gas Egypt Ltd* [2010] EWHC 465 (Comm).

[211] See further Ch 8, paras 8.18–8.28.

[212] *H Dakin & Co v Lee* [1916] 1 KB 566 (CA) 578 (Cozens Hardy MR); *Emerald Construction Ltd v Lowthian and ors* (CA) [1966] 1 WLR 691, 704 (Diplock LJ); *Harbutt's 'Plasticine' Ltd v Wayne Tank and Pump Co* [1970] 1 QB 447, 464 (Denning MR); *Rasool and ors v Hepworth Pipe Co Ltd* [1980] ICR 494 (EAT) 504 (Waterhouse J); *Briggs v Oates* [1990] ICR 473 (Ch D) 483 (Scott J); *Delta Sound PA Ltd v Federal Signal Ltd* 2001 WL 1347085 (QBD: Manchester District Registry) para 127 (Nelson J); *Cooper & ors v Pure Fishing (UK) Ltd* [2004] EWCA Civ 375; [2004] 2 CLC 412, para 15 (Tuckey LJ); *Hayes (t/a Orchard Construction) v Gallant* [2008] EWHC 2726 (TCC) para 182 (Judge Toulmin QC).

[213] *Michael v Hart & Co* [1902] 1 KB 482 (CA) 490 (Collins MR); *Melachrino and anor v Nickoll and Knight* [1920] 1 KB 693 (KBD) 697 (Bailhache J); *Denmark Productions Ltd v Boscobel Productions Ltd* [1969] 1 QB 699 (CA) 721 (Salmon LJ); *Medway Packaging Ltd v Meurer Maschinen GmbH & Co KG* [1990] ILPr 234 (QBD) 238 (Hobhouse LJ); *SCI (Sales Curve Interactive) Ltd v Titus Sarl* [2001] EWCA Civ 591; [2001] 2 All ER (Comm) 416, para 36 (Rix LJ); *Prison Service v Beart (No 2)* [2005] EWCA Civ 467; [2005] ICR 1206, para 31 (Rix LJ); *Pioneer Freight Futures Co Ltd v TMT Asia Ltd* [2011] EWHC 1888 (Comm) para 25 (Gloster J).

terminate.[214] This is no doubt a useful metaphor as far as it goes, but problems have arisen when it is pushed too far. Thus, for instance, it has been suggested on this basis that arbitration clauses[215] and exemption clauses[216] no longer apply following termination; since the contract is totally at an end, none of its provisions can be relied on by either party. However, as has been affirmed on several occasions, this is a misunderstanding of how the process of termination works. What is terminated is not the contract as a whole, but merely the obligation of the parties to perform their primary obligations under it; other provisions, in so far as they are intended to regulate the obligations of the parties following termination, are unaffected.[217] The possibility of confusion would be less if the courts were to abandon the metaphor of the contract coming to an end, but given that it is to some extent implicit in the very notions of discharge and termination, such a hope must remain a vain one; indeed, despite being aware of the problems associated with its use, the courts seem to be as fond of the metaphor as ever they were.[218]

M. The Way Forward

When considering reform of the law relating to termination, one is reminded of **1.37** the old Irishman who, when asked the way to a certain destination, replied: 'If I wanted to go there, I wouldn't start from here!' Many of the anomalies and fine distinctions that pervade this area of the law can only be explained on historical grounds,[219] but have now become so ingrained into the jurisprudence of the courts that it would be impossible to get rid of them without abolishing the existing law in its entirety and starting again from scratch. Not that this is necessarily impossible; the Indian Contract Act of 1872 still forms the basis of Indian contract law to

---

[214] *Addis v Gramophone Co* [1909] AC 488 (HL) 501 (Lord Gorell); *Stickney v Keeble* [1915] AC 386 (HL) 415 (Lord Porter); *Martin v Stout* [1925] AC 359 (JCPC–Egypt) 364 (Lord Atkinson); *Littlejohn v LCC* [1938] 1 KB 78 (CA) 95 (Scott LJ); *Beard v Porter* [1948] 1 KB 321 (CA) 325 (Evershed LJ); *Jennings' Trustee v King* [1952] Ch 899 (Ch D) 904 (Harman J); *Maredelanto Compania Naviera SA v Bergbau-Handel GmbH (The Mihalis Angelos)* [1971] 1 QB 164 (CA) 198 (Edmund Davies LJ); *Millichamp v Jones* [1982] 1 WLR 1422 (Ch D) 1430 (Warner J); *Vitol SA v Norelf Ltd (The Santa Clara)* [1996] AC 800 (HL) 811 (Lord Steyn); *Berkeley Community Villages Ltd v Pullen* [2007] EWHC 1330 (Ch); [2007] 3 EGLR 101, para 80 (Morgan J); *Acre 1127 (in liq) v De Montfort Fine Art Ltd* [2011] EWCA Civ 87, para 15 (Tomlinson LJ).

[215] *Heyman v Darwins Ltd* [1942] AC 356 (HL) 359; *Johannesburg Municipal Council v D Stewart & Co Ltd* 1909 SC (HL) 53, 54 (Lord Loreburn) and 56 (Lord Shaw); *Jureidini v National British and Irish Millers Insurance Co Ltd* [1915] AC 499 (HL) 505 (Viscount Haldane LC); *Hirji Mulji v Cheong Yue SS Co* [1926] AC 497 (JCPC–Hong Kong).

[216] *Harbutt's Plasticine Ltd v Wayne Tank & Pump Co Ltd* [1970] 1 QB 447 (CA) 465–7 (Denning MR); see further Ch 9, paras 9.27–9.29.

[217] *Boston Deep Sea Fishing & Ice Co v Ansell* (1889) 39 Ch D 339 (CA) 361 (Bowen LJ); *Heyman v Darwins Ltd*, 373 (Lord Macmillan) and 399 (Lord Porter) (n 215); *Moschi v Lep Air Services* [1973] AC 331 (HL) 350 (Lord Diplock); *Photo Production Ltd v Securicor Transport Ltd* [1980] AC 827 (HL) 844–5 (Lord Wilberforce) and 848–50 (Lord Diplock); see further Ch 9, paras 9.19–9.34.

[218] See the cases cited at nn 212–214.

[219] See further Ch 2.

this very day,[220] similar codes can be found in New Zealand[221] and in Malaysia,[222] and there has even been discussion of a European Contract Code.[223] Indeed, it is easy to forget how much English contract law is now to be found in statutory form, especially in relation to specialized topics such as the sale of goods,[224] consumer credit,[225] and employment law.[226] Even where full scale recodification is not possible, a lot can be done by the agreement and formulation of sets of common principles, as seen in the work of the American Law Institute,[227] the International Institute for the Unification of Private Law (UNIDROIT),[228] and the Lando Commission.[229]

1.38   In the meantime, however, it is up to the courts to do their best to avoid creating unnecessary confusion. This is, of course, by no means an easy matter. Thirty years ago, commenting on the problems caused by the tortuous and now happily defunct doctrine of 'fundamental breach' as applied to exemption clauses, Lord Wilberforce claimed that a lot of the difficulties arose from the uncertain or inconsistent terminology as applied to the topic of this book; discharge, rescission, termination, the contract is at an end, or dead, or displaced; clauses cannot survive, or simply go.[230] He went on to concede that to plead for complete uniformity might be to cry for the moon, but added that the courts should not make use of these confusions to produce on purely analytical grounds doctrines that should be decided on the basis of policy.[231] Whilst it may be impossible at this stage to eliminate from the law the problems of analysis described in the present chapter, the courts can avoid some of their worst effects by ensuring that they do not distort the law by placing on matters of terminology a weight that they were not meant to bear.

---

[220] A Singh, *Contract and Specific Relief* (10th edn, Eastern Book Co, 2006).

[221] Contractual Remedies Act 1979; Dawson and McLauchlan, *The Contractual Remedies Act 1979* (n 3).

[222] Malaysian Contracts Act 1950; C Fong, 'The Malaysian Contracts Act 1950' (2009) 25 JCL 244.

[223] MP Furmston, 'Unification of the European Law of Obligations—an English View' in *Mélanges Offerts à Marcel Fontaine* (Larcier, 2003) p 371; Furmston, Fifoot, and Simpson, *Cheshire, Fifoot, and Furmston's Law of Contract*, pp 34–5 (n 33).

[224] Sale of Goods Act 1979; MG Bridge, *The Sale of Goods* (2nd edn, OUP, 2009).

[225] Consumer Credit Acts 1974 and 2006; F Philpott, *The Law of Consumer Credit and Hire* (OUP, 2009).

[226] Employment Rights Act 1996; I Smith and A Baker, *Smith and Wood's Employment Law* (11th edn, OUP, 2013).

[227] *Restatement of the Law Second, Contracts* (1981).

[228] *Unidroit Principles of International Commercial Contract: 2004* (2004); Furmston, Fifoot, and Simpson, *Cheshire, Fifoot, and Furmston's Law of Contract*, pp 34–5 (n 33).

[229] O Lando and H Beale, *Principles of European Contract Law* (Kluwer Law International, 2000).

[230] *Photo Productions Ltd v Securicor Transport Ltd* [1980] AC 827 (HL) 844.

[231] *Photo Productions v Securicor Transport*, 844 (n 230).

2

THE GENESIS OF TERMINATION

There is a right to terminate a contract for breach of condition or for a breach so ser- **2.01** ious in its consequences that the non-breaching party is deprived of substantially the entire benefit of the bargain. In Part III the full extent of these rights, when they arise, and what they really mean will be examined. For now the principal task is to explain how English law got to the point it is at now where it treats breach of condition and fundamental breach as the grounds on which a contract may be terminated. Today English law treats *condition* as a term of the contract so import- ant that a breach of it gives the other party the right to terminate the contract. But this is not by any means the most natural meaning of the word *condition* and it was not how that word was originally understood. Several commentators and judges have remarked that *condition* is used rather confusingly in this context but it is the way the word has been used in breach of contract situations for over a cen- tury now and change would be much too disruptive to contemplate.[1] This chapter attempts to explain how we got to the point where *condition* was used in this way and also explains how the parallel doctrine of fundamental breach (depriving the

---

[1] *Wallis, Son & Wells v Pratt & Haynes* [1910] 2 KB 1003 (CA) 1012 (Fletcher Moulton LJ); A Corbin, 'Conditions in the Law of Contract' (1918) 28 Yale LJ 739; MG Ferson, 'Conditions in the Law of Contracts' (1955) 8 Vand L Rev 537; FMB Reynolds, 'Warranty, Condition and Fundamental Term' (1963) 79 LQR 534; FMB Reynolds, 'Discharge of Contract by Breach' (1981) 97 LQR 541; MG Bridge, 'Discharge for Breach of the Contract of Sale of Goods' (1983) 28 McGill LJ 867.

non-breaching party of substantially the entire benefit of the bargain) developed alongside this.

A. Two Key Concepts

2.02 The story told in this chapter is one of how we got from using *condition* to mean something on which one party's contractual performance was dependent or conditional upon, to the concept of promissory condition. In the first sense, best illustrated by the condition precedent 'if X does not happen or you do not do X then I do not have to do Y', the non-occurrence of X merely releases the other contracting party from its obligation to do Y. It is not a breach of contract and does not give to the other contracting party any remedy for the first party's failure to perform. If something independent of the first party does not happen, no contractual obligation is owed by the second party. Similarly if the first party does not do something which is a condition of the other party's performance, the other party does not have to render this performance but has no right to treat the first party's omission to do the act in question as a breach. In the second sense the act or event upon which the second party's performance depends is a contractual obligation and its non-occurrence would be a breach of contract. In this sense the failure of condition is also a failure of *consideration*.[2] Failures of consideration come in two different forms in this context. First, there is what has come to be called *breach of condition*, where a contractual term of sufficient importance to justify the non-breaching party terminating the contract, is breached. Secondly, there is *breach of warranty*, where the non-breaching party is only permitted an action for damages.[3] A failure of consideration on a similar scale to breach of condition occurs when the term breached is an innominate term, as explained by Diplock LJ in *Hongkong Fir Shipping Co Ltd v Kawasaki Kisen Kaisha Ltd (The Hongkong Fir)*.[4] This is a term which the contract neither expressly nor by implication designates as condition or warranty. Whether the failure of consideration is sufficiently serious to give a right to terminate depends on whether the consequences of breach deprive the non-breaching party of substantially the entire benefit of the bargain. The failure of consideration concept used here should not be confused with its usage in the law of restitution to obtain the recovery of money paid for a consideration that totally failed.[5]

---

[2] Reynolds drew this distinction between the two different senses of contractual discharge in 'Warranty, Condition and Fundamental Term' (n 1) 534; 'Discharge of Contract by Breach' (n 1).

[3] See Ch 5.

[4] [1962] 2 QB 26 (CA) 65–73.

[5] See *Fibrosa Spolka Akynja v Fairbairn Lawson Combe Barbour* [1943] AC 32 (HL).

B. Conditions and Warranties

Although *condition* is used most frequently in the promissory sense, ie failure of con-   **2.03**
dition equates to breach of contract, it should not be thought that the more traditional
concept of *condition*, the dependent condition, is no longer of relevance. A contractual obligation may be dependent upon an external event, such as the obligation of an
insurer to pay up on the policy being dependent on the contingency insured against
actually occurring. A contractual promise could also be dependent upon the other
party first doing something. If the other party does not do the specified thing there is
no breach of contract but the counterparty's contractual obligation would not arise.

Two great cases of the eighteenth century illustrate how dependent conditions or   **2.04**
conditional promises work. First there is *Kingston v Preston*, decided in 1773.[6] The
defendant agreed to convey his business to the claimant, who in turn agreed to
provide good security for the purchase. The issue was whether the defendant was
obliged to convey the business if the claimant had not first provided good security. Lord Mansfield held that the answer depended on the nature of the mutual
relationship of the promises and these could be of three kinds.[7] First, they could
be 'mutual and independant' [*sic*], in which case either could be sued on without
proving the performance of the other. Secondly, they could be 'conditions and
dependant' [*sic*], meaning that the obligation to perform one depended on the prior
performance of the other. Thirdly, they could be 'concurrent', or 'mutual conditions to be performed at the same time', in which case one party could only sue if he
or she could demonstrate personal readiness and willingness to perform their own
side of the bargain. Lord Mansfield regarded it as inconceivable that the defendant would have agreed to convey his business without the claimant first providing
security so the promises were dependent and the claimant's action failed. The second great case was *Cutter v Powell*,[8] where a seaman agreed to serve as second mate
on the defendant's ship in consideration of a lump sum of 30 guineas 'provided he
proceeds, continues and does his duty as second mate in the said ship from hence to
the Port of Liverpool'. The seaman died before the ship reached Liverpool and his
widow was unable to recover anything for his labours as payment of the 30 guineas
was dependent on completion of the voyage.

---

[6] (1773) Lofft 194; S Stoljar, 'Dependent and Independent Promises' (1957) 2 Sydney L Rev 217.
[7] As was frequently the case before the Common Law Procedure Acts of the 1850s, the case
really turned on a pleading point, whether it was necessary to aver one's own proper performance of
legal obligations before suing for another's failure to perform theirs. See further on this, S Stoljar,
A History of Contract at Common Law (Australian National University Press, 1975) pp 147–63;
JW Carter and C Hodgekiss, 'Conditions and Warranties: Forebears and Descendants' (1976) 8
Sydney L Rev 31; GH Treitel, '"Conditions" and "Conditions Precedent"' (1990) 106 LQR 185;
O Black, 'Independent Promises and the Rescission of Contracts' [2003] Legal Studies 555.
[8] (1795) 6 TR 320, 101 ER 573; S Stoljar, 'The Great Case of *Cutter v Powell*' (1956) 34 Can BR
288; M Dockray, '*Cutter v Powell*: A Trip Outside the Text' (2001) 117 LQR 668.

2.05   As these 'all or nothing' conditions precedent of the kind seen in *Cutter v Powell* can produce very harsh consequences if they are not fully complied with, they are not often used today. In bilateral contracts courts are also reluctant to construe performance obligations as conditions precedent unless it is clear that they go to the whole consideration.[9] Instead the court is likely to favour a construction making terms 'mutual and independent' where a non-breaching party can sue for damages for any failure to perform a contractual obligation. Conditions precedent tend more often to be the stuff of unilateral contracts, where one party makes a promise in return for the other doing some requested act, for example: 'I will pay £1000 to anyone who returns my lost dog.' In this situation only the offeror is bound and only if another person does the act requested.

2.06   As the discussion of the great eighteenth-century cases suggests, it would be wrong to say that the dependent conditions of that time were never in any sense promissory, ie failure to perform a condition that another's contractual performance was dependent on was sometimes a breach of contract as well. The story that begins with *Boone v Eyre*[10] and effectively ends with the Sale of Goods Act 1893 is one where contractual conditions came to be seen almost entirely in a promissory sense. What began in the eighteenth century as a recognition that sometimes conditions meant the other party could sue for breach became an acceptance of the proposition that failure to comply with a condition usually did mean some sort of failure of consideration, either breach of condition giving the other party a right to terminate the contract or breach of warranty allowing a right to sue for damages.

2.07   In *Boone v Eyre*[11] the claimant covenanted to convey the equity of redemption in a West Indian plantation, together with the slaves on it, for a lump sum of £500 and an annuity of £160 for life. The claimant sued for failure to pay the annuity, the defendant pleading in his defence that the claimant was not lawfully possessed of all the slaves and so had not satisfied a condition precedent to the obligation to pay as he had no proper title to the property to be conveyed. In rejecting this plea Lord Mansfield had this to say:

> The distinction is very clear; where mutual covenants go to the whole of the consideration on both sides, they are mutual conditions, the one precedent to the other: but where they go only to a part, where a breach may be paid for in damages, there the defendant has a remedy on his covenant, and shall not plead it as a condition precedent. If this plea were to be allowed, any one negro not being the property of the plaintiff would bar the action.[12]

Despite the two allusions to *condition precedent* in this passage it is quite clear that Lord Mansfield was really talking about failure of consideration. The critical

---

[9] *Boone v Eyre* (1777) 1 Hy Bl 273n, 126 ER 160, 2 Bl W 1313n, 96 ER 267.
[10] *Boone v Eyre* (n 9).
[11] *Boone v Eyre* (n 9).
[12] *Boone v Eyre* (n 9).

distinction drawn was between contractual obligations which 'go to the whole of the consideration' and those which sound only in damages. The former corresponds to the modern promissory condition and allows a non-breaching party to terminate the contract and the latter corresponds to warranty and allows only a right to claim damages.

The next landmark case on this road was *Glaholm v Hays*.[13] A charterparty pro- **2.08** vided that a ship was to sail for a loading port on or before a certain date. Due to contrary winds it sailed late and when it finally turned up at the loading port the charterer refused to load. The court held that the charterer was not bound, Tindal CJ observing thus:

> Whether a particular clause in a charter-party shall be held to be a condition, upon the non-performance of which by the other party, the other is at liberty to abandon the contract, and consider it at an end; or whether it amounts to an agreement only, the breach whereof is to be recompensed by an action for damages, must depend on the intention of the parties to be collected, in each particular case, from the terms of the agreement itself, and from the subject matter to which it relates.[14]

This could hardly be clearer. There is no mention of the word *precedent* at all, and the only important interpretative exercise which the court has to carry out is distinguishing between breaches giving the right to terminate and those conferring only a right to damages.

The next landmark case, *Behn v Burness*,[15] was decided by the Court of Exchequer **2.09** Chamber in the decade after the Common Law Procedure Acts of the 1850s. The question was as to the status of a term in a charterparty which stated that the ship was currently in the port of Amsterdam. Williams J said this:

> But with respect to statements in a contract descriptive of the subject matter of it, or of some material incident thereof, the true doctrine, established by principle as well as authority, appears to be, generally speaking, that if such descriptive statement was intended to be a substantive part of the contract, it is to be regarded as a warranty, that is to say, a condition on the failure or non-performance of which the other party may, if he is so minded, repudiate the contract in toto, and so be relieved from performing his part of it, provided it has not been partially executed in his favour. If, indeed, he has received the whole or any substantial part of the consideration for the promise on his part, the warranty loses the character of a condition, or, to speak perhaps more properly, ceases to be available as a condition, and becomes a warranty in the narrower sense of the word—viz., a stipulation by way of agreement, for the breach of which a compensation must be sought in damages.[16]

---

[13] (1841) 2 M & G 257, 133 ER 743.
[14] *Glaholm v Hays*, 746 (n 13).
[15] (1863) 3 B & S 751, 122 ER 281.
[16] *Behn v Burness*, 755 and 283 (n 15).

Notwithstanding the somewhat confusing way in which the word 'warranty' is used here, the distinction is drawn between warranties as contractual promises that if breached give the non-breaching party the right to terminate and warranties of a lesser sort that offer a right to damages only. Significantly the former are referred to as conditions. Also importantly, it is said that breach of condition gives the non-breaching party a right to repudiate the contract in toto as well as to be relieved from performing his or her part of it. This makes clear that breach of a promissory condition goes beyond just preventing the other party's obligation from arising but actually gives that party the right to seek a remedy for breach. This distinction can also be seen in the case of a contract for the sale of goods by instalments where the seller delivers an instalment late. This will generally give the buyer the right to withhold the price for that instalment but not to terminate the contract as a whole unless the seller's conduct amounts to a total repudiation of the contract.[17]

2.10 On the eve of the Sale of Goods Act 1893 the Court of Appeal, in *Bentsen v Taylor, Sons & Co*,[18] essentially followed *Behn v Burness* in relation to the condition/warranty distinction, although this was again not without some confusing terminology being employed. The case concerned a charterparty which described the ship as 'now sailed or about to sail from a pitch pine port to the United Kingdom'. This was not so and the Court held that this term was a condition. Lord Esher actually called it a 'condition precedent' but later explained: 'The defendants had then a right to treat the contract as at an end, or they could, if they chose, treat it as still subsisting.'[19] Bowen LJ said that the court had to decide:

> ...whether [the term] amounts merely to a warranty, the breach of which would sound only in damages, or whether it is that kind of promise the performance of which is made a condition precedent to all further demands under the contract by the person who made the promise against the other party—a promise the failure to perform which gives to the opposite party the right to say that he will no longer be bound by the contract.[20]

Confusing though the references to 'condition precedent' are, it is still reasonably clear that this meant promissory condition in the sense of the non-breaching party being entitled to terminate the contract. In the end, however, the Court of Appeal held that the non-breaching party had waived the right to treat the relevant breach as one of condition and would have to settle for damages for breach of warranty.

2.11 The next development was by far the most significant of all, the enactment of the Sale of Goods Act 1893.[21] As the long title to the Act makes clear it was for the

---

17 JE Stannard, *Delay in the Performance of Contractual Obligations* (OUP, 2007) para 2.29.
18 [1893] 2 QB 274 (CA).
19 *Bentsen v Taylor, Sons & Co*, 279 (n 18).
20 *Bentsen v Taylor, Sons & Co*, 280–1 (n 18).
21 Stannard, *Delay in the Performance of Contractual Obligations*, paras 2.30–2.31 (n 17).

36

purpose of *codifying* the law relating to the sale of goods. Therefore the Act largely accepted the law as it stood before the Act and did not make significant change. As far as the move from dependent to promissory conditions was concerned, section 11(1)(b) clearly accepts the tolerably well settled differentiation between *conditions* and *warranties*:

> Whether a stipulation in a contract of sale is a condition, the breach of which may give rise to a right to treat the contract as repudiated, or a warranty, the breach of which may give rise to a claim for damages, but not to a right to reject the goods and treat the contract as repudiated, depends in each case on the construction of the contract.

This was the general contract law before the Act and it is not seriously in dispute that this provision and its modern equivalent in section 11(3) of the Sale of Goods Act 1979 is a statement of the general contract law and not limited to sale of goods contracts. Despite this, the drafter of the 1893 Act, Sir Mackenzie Chalmers, maintained that section 11(1)(b) reflected the old distinction between dependent and independent covenants.[22] As the distinction between conditions and warranties came about as a result of the courts' tendency to favour independent covenants categorized as those that gave a right to terminate and those allowing only for damages, it is very difficult to see how this could be the case. More plausible is the view of Carter and Hodgekiss that Chalmers simply misunderstood the previous law on this subject.[23] The 'condition' referred to in section 11(1)(b) is a term of the contract (a 'stipulation'), not an event, and gives to the other party a right to 'treat the contract as repudiated'.[24]

If there was any doubt about this matter it was surely settled by the decision of the **2.12** Court of Appeal in *Wallis, Son & Wells v Pratt & Haynes*.[25] Like *Bentsen v Taylor* the decision ultimately turned on issues other than the nature of contract terms, specifically whether the buyer of goods had accepted them and thus was no longer able to reject for breach of condition and whether the sellers had succeeded in excluding liability through another contractual term.[26] The decision is most useful in the present context for the magisterial statements of Fletcher Moulton LJ on the nature of contractual obligations generally and the effect of the Sale of Goods Act 1893. First, on the nature of contractual obligations the learned Lord Justice said:

> A party to a contract who has performed, or is ready and willing to perform, his obligations under that contract is entitled to the performance by the other contracting party of all the obligations which rest upon him. But from a very early

---

[22] Sir Mackenzie Chalmers, *The Sale of Goods Act 1893* (W Clowes & Sons, 1894) p 165.

[23] See JW Carter and C Hodgekiss, 'Conditions and warranties: forebears and descendants' (1976) 8 Sydney L Rev 31.

[24] See Stannard, *Delay in the Performance of Contractual Obligations* (n 17) para 2.31.

[25] [1910] 2 KB 1003 (CA).

[26] The decision of the Court of Appeal was reversed, and the dissenting judgment of Fletcher Moulton LJ affirmed, by the House of Lords at [1911] AC 394 (HL).

period of our law it has been recognised that such obligations are not all of equal importance. There are some which go so directly to the substance of the contract or, in other words, are so essential to its very nature that their non-performance may fairly be considered by the other party as a substantial failure to perform the contract at all. On the other hand there are other obligations which, though they must be performed, are not so vital that a failure to perform them goes to the substance of the contract. Both classes are equally obligations under the contract, and the breach of any one of them entitled the other party to damages. But in the case of the former class he has the alternative of treating the contract as being completely broken by the non-performance and (if he takes the proper steps) he can refuse to perform any of the obligations resting upon himself and sue the other party for a total failure to perform the contract.[27]

Then in relation to the Sale of Goods Act 1893 Fletcher Moulton LJ said that the usage of 'conditions' and 'warranties' 'has been followed in the codification of the law of contract of sale in the Sale of Goods Act'.[28] This very clearly parts company from Sir Mackenzie Chalmers' view of the effect of the Act.

2.13 The principal twentieth-century development was the recognition of the 'intermediate' or 'innominate' term in *Hongkong Fir Shipping Co v Kawasaki Kisen Kaisha Ltd*.[29] These are contractual terms which are neither conditions nor warranties. Whether the non-breaching party is entitled to terminate the contract depends on whether the consequences of breach are so serious as to deprive it of substantially the whole benefit of the bargain. If so the breach is treated as in effect a breach of condition, and if not as a breach of a warranty. But this should not be considered a third type of contractual term in addition to conditions and warranties. These are terms which the contract has neither expressly or by implication designated as condition or warranty, and in this sense the label 'innominate' is superior to 'intermediate'. A right to terminate arises, and always did arise, when the party in breach commits a repudiatory breach of the contract. This occurs when the scale of the breach and its consequences approximate to what Fletcher Moulton LJ described in *Wallis, Son and Wells v Pratt and Haynes* as a substantial failure to perform the contract at all.[30] It is still very much a failure of consideration analysis.

2.14 There was a tendency after *The Hongkong Fir* to think that all or most contract terms that had not been expressly designated as 'conditions' or 'warranties' must be innominate terms.[31] That this is not so and that courts may well decide that commercial certainty requires that certain undesignated terms should be treated as conditions appears from the decisions of the House of Lords in *Bunge Corporation v Tradax Export SA*[32] and *Compagnie Commerciale Sucres et Denrees v Czarnikow*

---

[27] [1910] 2 KB 1003, 1012.
[28] *Wallis, Son & Wells v Pratt & Haynes* (n 27).
[29] [1962] 2 QB 26 (CA).
[30] [1910] 2 KB 1003, 1012.
[31] See *Cehave NV v Bremer Handelsgellschaft (The Hansa Nord)* [1976] QB 44 (CA).
[32] [1981] 1 WLR 711.

Ltd (The Naxos).[33] More will be said about these cases in Chapter 4, but for now they should be taken as confirmation that the nineteenth-century migration of Contract Law away from dependent conditions to promissory conditions is well and truly established.

C. Frustration and Frustrating Breach

A contract is frustrated when some unforeseeable supervening event occurs that **2.15** without the fault of either party essentially destroys the bargain they have made. Where a contract is frustrated, both parties are released from their obligations of future performance.[34] A book on termination for breach of contract must address the question of frustration for two principal reasons. One is that whenever one party alleges that a failure to perform the contract amounts to the other party's breach, the latter may well allege that it was actually a frustrating event which releases both parties from their obligations to perform without any accompanying liability for breach. A book on discharge by breach must offer at least some outline distinction between these situations. The other is that certain discharge by breach situations, those not involving breach of an express promissory condition, require the occurrence of events as destructive of the bargain as frustrating events. What follows is a brief history of the development of the law on frustration focusing on the theoretical basis of the doctrine and the effect of the allegedly frustrating event on the contract.

(1) Destruction of the subject matter

The first case to recognize any doctrine of frustration in the English law of contract **2.16** was probably *Taylor v Caldwell*.[35] A music hall was hired for use as a concert venue but before the concert it was destroyed by fire and no longer available for use. When sued for damages for failing to perform their contract by making the hall available the defendants successfully invoked a plea summarized in the following dictum of Blackburn J:

> ...where, from the nature of the contract, it appears that the parties must from the beginning have known that it could not be fulfilled unless when the time for the fulfilment of the contract arrived some particular specified thing continued to exist, so that, when entering into the contract, they must have contemplated

---

[33] [1990] 1 WLR 1337.

[34] We are not much concerned with the remedial consequences of frustration but for completeness sake these are mainly laid down in the Law Reform (Frustrated Contracts) Act 1943. By section 2(5) the Act does not apply to contracts of insurance, certain charterparties, and sale of goods contracts to which section 7 of the Sale of Goods Act 1979 applies. In these situations the common law rules apply; see *Fibrosa Spolka Akcyjna v Fairbairn Lawson Combe Barbour Ltd* [1943] AC 32.

[35] (1863) 3 B & S 826, 122 ER 309.

such continuing existence as the foundation of what was to be done; there, in the absence of any express or implied warranty that the thing shall exist, the contract is not to be construed as a positive contract, but as subject to an implied condition that the parties shall be excused in case, before breach, performance becomes impossible from the perishing of the thing without default of the contractor.[36]

This doctrine, originating in Roman law it was subsequently said,[37] operates to excuse a contracting party where the subject matter of the contract is destroyed before contractual performance can be rendered. In *Taylor v Caldwell* there could clearly be no hire of a music hall for a concert when the hall had been destroyed, and as this was no party's fault the court felt justified in dismissing the breach of contract action.[38] The precise basis for this frustration defence, that a term (or condition) is implied into the contract that the parties are released from performance where essential subject matter is destroyed, is not entirely satisfactory, however. It is difficult to see how the parties could have impliedly agreed what was to happen in a situation which they could not reasonably have foreseen. But if Blackburn J's judgment is read, not as the implication of an additional term, but as a recognition that there was no contract covering the circumstances which transpired, it becomes easier to understand the basis for the frustration outcome.

(2) Impossibility of performance

2.17 The principle of *Taylor v Caldwell* was extended to situations of commercial impossibility in *Jackson v Union Marine Insurance Co Ltd*.[39] The claimant shipowner had chartered a ship to charterers for a voyage from Liverpool to Newport, there picking up a cargo of iron rails to take to San Francisco. The ship ran aground in Carnarvon Bay and it took over six months to complete the necessary repairs. In the meantime the charterers threw up the charter and chartered another ship to transport the rails. The claimant issued a claim on his freight insurance and it was held that this claim succeeded because the charter freight had been lost due to the frustration of the charterparty. The Exchequer Chamber held that the charterparty had been subject to an implied condition precedent that the ship should arrive in Newport within a reasonable time. The failure to do so meant that the completion of the commercial venture undertaken was a commercial impossibility. As the problem which occurred here was something quite readily foreseeable, this decision seems rather generous by today's standards. If this event was truly unforeseeable the implied term theory of frustration seems dubious for the same reasons as those stated for *Taylor v Caldwell* and the alternative basis of that decision, that the contract just did not provide for the events which occurred, may admit of doubt

---

[36] *Taylor v Caldwell*, 833–4 and 312 (n 35).

[37] *Krell v Henry* [1903] 2 KB 740 (CA) 748 (Vaughan Williams LJ).

[38] Today it is a distinct possibility that on facts similar to *Taylor v Caldwell* the contract might not be held to be frustrated. This is because where the event which prevents performance is foreseeable, the court may decide that the risk of this occurring was allocated to the defendant.

[39] (1874–75) LR 10 CP 125 (Exchequer Chamber).

too as the charterparty included an exception for dangers and accidents of naviga-tion. These points aside, the decision is important in showing that the impossibil-ity of performing a commercial venture is a ground on which a contract may be frustrated.

(3) Frustration of purpose

A further extension of the frustration principle occurred in the coronation cases of **2.18** *Herne Bay Steam Boat Co v Hutton*[40] and *Krell v Henry*.[41] In *Herne Bay Steam Boat* the claimants entered into an agreement in writing with the defendants to make their steamship *Cynthia* available to the defendants to take passengers from Herne Bay to see the naval review planned to mark the coronation of King Edward VII and for a cruise around the fleet. The coronation was postponed because the king was ill and the defendants argued that this totally undermined the purpose of the contract. The Court of Appeal rejected this argument because it would still have been possible to cruise around the fleet. For a contract to be frustrated any destruc-tion of the subject matter, commercial impossibility, or undermining of purpose had to be total.

A different result was reached in *Krell v Henry*. Here the defendant agreed to hire **2.19** a flat in Pall Mall for the purpose of viewing the coronation processions. The writ-ten contract made no express reference to the processions or any other purpose for which the flat was hired but the claimant had placed a notice on the premises stat-ing that the flat was available for hire to view the processions and the defendant had called on the claimant to negotiate the hire after seeing this notice. Hence the impli-cation of this purpose into the contract as a fundamental condition upon which the entire contract depended was easily understandable, although there seems con-siderable substance in Romer LJ's doubts as to whether the risk of cancellation/postponement had not been foreseen and allocated to the defendant. Both parties were fairly 'well heeled' private individuals and equally able to protect themselves by contractual provision. The frustration theory which underlay the judgment of Vaughan Williams LJ did not fall into the error of implying a term to govern a situ-ation (cancellation/postponement of the processions) not foreseen by the parties.[42]

(4) The Great War cases

The Great War (1914–18) served up several important frustration cases. One, *Ertel* **2.20** *Bieber & Co v Rio Tinto Co Ltd*,[43] was a case of frustration by illegality, specific-ally trading with the enemy in time of war, and nothing more needs be said of

---

[40] [1903] 2 KB 683 (CA).
[41] [1903] 2 KB 740 (CA).
[42] *Krell v Henry*, 747–55.
[43] [1918] AC 260 (HL).

it in the present context. Other cases were concerned with the effect of the war on contracts that did not involve trading with the enemy. In *Horlock v Beal*[44] the enemy's detention of a ship frustrated a seaman's contract of employment because it made performance of the contract impossible. In *FA Tamplin Steamship Co Ltd v Anglo-Mexican Petroleum Products Co Ltd*[45] a ship charterparty was held not to be frustrated by the Admiralty requisitioning it for the transport of troops. The charterers were content to continue paying the hire as they were reasonably well remunerated by the Admiralty for the use of the ship. In *Metropolitan Water Board v Dick, Kerr & Co Ltd*[46] the interruption of a six-year contract to build a reservoir by order of the Ministry of Munitions two years into the contract term frustrated that contract because it rendered it a radically different contract from the one originally conceived. Dicta in these cases as to the theoretical basis of frustration are not entirely consistent, but for the most part they proceed along lines essentially similar to the following passage from the speech of Earl Loreburn in *FA Tamplin Steamship Co*:

> ...a Court can and ought to examine the contract and the circumstances in which it was made, not of course to vary, but only to explain it, in order to see whether or not from the nature of it the parties must have made their bargain on the footing that a particular thing or state of things would continue to exist. And if they must have done so, then a term to that effect will be implied, though it be not expressed in the contract. In applying this rule it is manifest that such a term can rarely be implied except where the discontinuance is such as to upset altogether the purpose of the contract. Some delay or some change is very common in all human affairs, and it cannot be supposed that any bargain has been made on the tacit condition that such a thing will not happen in any degree.[47]

Two propositions are clear from this. First, the term implied is not directly addressed to something not foreseen but only as to the continued existence of some thing or state of affairs which construction of the contract as a whole indicates is essential to the contract's existence. If something happens which undermines this essential thing it is treated, as Viscount Haldane said in the same case, 'as being one about which no bargain at all was made'.[48] Secondly, the event which frustrates the contract must be very serious indeed. It may not have to be total destruction of the contract's assumptions but at the very least it has to be on a similar scale to the *Metropolitan Water Board* case, where it was argued unsuccessfully that the building of the reservoir could continue after the war was over. Finally, it should be stated that in all these cases the House of Lords pointed out that there could be no frustration if the risk of an event alleged to frustrate the contract had expressly or impliedly been allocated by the contract. It would have been a harsh application of

---

[44] [1916] AC 486 (HL).
[45] [1916] 2 AC 397 (HL).
[46] [1918] AC 119 (HL).
[47] [1918] AC 397, 403.
[48] *Tamplin Steamship v Anglo-Mexican Petroleum Products*, 406 (n 47).

the allocation of risk principle to hold that there had been any implied allocation in any of these cases.

(5) The Second World War cases

While the most significant frustration case in this era was clearly *Fibrosa Spolka* **2.21**
Akynja v Fairbairn Lawson Combe Barbour,[49] the latter's significance lay in the remedial consequences of frustration. More important in the present context was *Denny, Mott and Dickson Ltd v James B Fraser & Co Ltd*.[50] A contract between two timber merchants was frustrated when a wartime statutory order made further transactions between the parties impossible. Consequently one party's attempt to purchase the other's timber yard under a provision of the contract, allowing it to do so if the entire agreement were terminated by notice, failed because the contract had been terminated already by government action.[51] The speeches contain dicta emphasizing the need for any frustrating event to prevent substantial performance of the contract as a whole,[52] but the real significance of the case lies in Lord Wright's attack on the implied term theory of frustration:

> Though it has been constantly said by high authority...that the explanation of the rule is to be found in the theory that it depends on an implied condition of the contract, that is really no explanation. It only pushes back the problem a single stage. It leaves the question what is the reason for implying a term. Nor can I reconcile that theory with the view that the result does not depend on what the parties might, or would as hard bargainers, have agreed. The doctrine is invented by the court in order to supplement the defects of the actual contract. The parties did not anticipate fully and completely, if at all, or provide for what actually happened. It is not possible, to my mind, to say that, if they had thought of it, they would have said: 'Well, if that happens, all is over between us.' On the contrary, they would almost certainly on the one side or the other have sought to introduce reservations or qualifications or compensations. As to that the court cannot guess. What it can say is that the contract either binds or does not bind.[53]

While this dictum is an effective demolition of any implied term theory that requires the court to construct a term to govern the unforeseen circumstances that have arisen, it does not fully address the theory of frustration that most judges have based frustration principles on in previous cases. Courts have not attempted to determine what the parties have impliedly agreed or would have agreed had

---

[49] [1943] AC 32 (HL). This case was the inspiration behind the Law Reform (Frustrated Contracts) Act 1943.

[50] [1944] AC 265 (HL) (Sc).

[51] As Lord Macmillan crisply put it: 'The operation of the agreement having been compulsorily terminated, neither party can thereafter terminate it voluntarily. You cannot slay the slain.' *Denny, Mott and Dickson Ltd v James B Fraser & Co Ltd*, 273 (n 50).

[52] *Denny, Mott and Dickson Ltd v James B Fraser & Co Ltd*, 271 (Viscount Simon LC), 273 (Lord Thankerton) (n 50).

[53] *Denny, Mott and Dickson Ltd v James B Fraser & Co Ltd*, 275 (n 50). Lord Porter was the only other member of the House to mention this issue and this was only to say that it was unnecessary to decide the theoretical basis of frustration.

they thought of these circumstances. They have acknowledged the futility of this task and declared the contract frustrated because no provision was made for the circumstances which developed. That some judges have rationalized what they consider to be a fair outcome in terms of the meaning and extent of the contract the parties have made seems plausible, but there is no way of ascertaining whether this is what they actually did.

(6) *Davis Contractors Ltd v Fareham Urban District Council*[54]

2.22   This decision is probably the leading modern authority on frustration and contains some very extensive consideration of its theoretical basis. A firm of contractors entered into a contract with a local authority to build seventy-eight houses for a fixed sum within eight months. The contractors attached to their form of tender a letter stating that the tender was subject to adequate supplies of labour being available. Without the fault of either party adequate supplies of labour were not available and the work consequently took twenty-two months to complete. The contractors first contended that they were entitled to additional payment on the basis that the contract included the letter stating that the tender was subject to adequate supplies of labour being available. This argument was unanimously rejected by the House of Lords. Alternatively the contractors argued that the absence of adequate supplies of labour frustrated the contract and that they were entitled to payment on a *quantum meruit* basis. It was unanimously held that the absence of adequate labour supplies came nowhere near the sort of event that was capable of frustrating a contract. Viscount Simonds said that a frustrating event had to destroy the whole foundation of the contract and that whatever the theoretical basis for frustration the principle must be kept within very narrow limits.[55] Lord Reid said that frustration must result in a job of a different kind which the contract did not contemplate.[56] Lord Radcliffe said that hardship or inconvenience was insufficient and that there must be 'such a change in the significance of the obligation that the thing undertaken would, if performed, be a different thing from that contracted for'.[57]

2.23   None of the foregoing is contentious in any real way, so what is most significant about this decision is the extensive discussion of the theoretical basis of frustration engaged in by Lord Reid (with whose speech Lord Somervell agreed on this issue)[58] and Lord Radcliffe. Lord Reid said that whether frustration was an exercise in implying a term or construction of the contract on the one hand, or a rule of law on the other, may make a difference in two respects. First, implication or construction is a question of law, while applying the rule that the basis of the contract is

---

[54] [1956] AC 696 (HL).
[55] *Davis Contractors v Fareham UDC*, 714–15 (n 54).
[56] *Davis Contractors v Fareham UDC*, 723 (n 54).
[57] *Davis Contractors v Fareham UDC*, 729 (n 54).
[58] *Davis Contractors v Fareham UDC*, 733 (n 54).

overthrown requires the judgment of a skilled man comparing what was contemplated with what has happened. Secondly, if implication or construction has to be undertaken, extraneous evidence would be excluded[59] but could be admitted otherwise.[60] On the footing that frustration was not a rule of law Lord Reid went on to reject the implication of a term to specify what should happen in the frustrating circumstances. He did not believe, for example, that the seaman in *Horlock v Beal* would have agreed that his wages should cease on the capture of the ship and not go to his wife.[61] The true basis of frustration was that the court construed the contract as a whole in the light of its nature and the surrounding circumstances. A contract will cease to bind if on its true construction it does not apply in the circumstances that have developed.[62]

Lord Radcliffe's speech contained the most detailed judicial exposition of the doc- **2.24**
trine of frustration, certainly by that time. He began with the proposition that frustration was a rule of contract law 'which the courts will apply in certain limited circumstances for the purpose of deciding that contractual obligations, ex facie binding, are no longer enforceable against the parties'.[63] Then Lord Radcliffe went on to quote with approval the dictum from Earl Loreburn in *FA Tamplin Steamship Co Ltd v Anglo-Mexican Petroleum Products Co Ltd* (quoted at paragraph 2.20),[64] thus apparently indicating that the court is looking not for an implied term as to what would happen in the event of unforeseen circumstances, but for signs that the parties assumed something would continue to exist so that if it did not the contract was at an end.[65] At this point Lord Radcliffe rather bewilderingly changed tack and stated that Earl Loreburn based the contract's dissolution on an implied term of the contract. In response to this, Lord Radcliffe said 'there is something of a logical difficulty in seeing how the parties could even impliedly have provided for something which ex hypothesi they neither expected nor foresaw'.[66] This observation does not seem to indicate a full understanding of the basis on which Earl Loreburn and other judges have expressed the doctrine of frustration. Lord Radcliffe then continued his analysis by stating that as the parties could not have impliedly agreed on something they did not foresee, the implied term must be what they would have agreed had they considered the matter. Lord Radcliffe recognized that there is no reliable way of working this out in the following memorable passage:

> By this time it might seem that the parties themselves have become so far disembodied spirits that their actual persons should be allowed to rest in peace. In their

---

[59] As *Chartbrook Ltd v Persimmon Homes Ltd* [2009] UKHL 38 shows, some exclusions of extraneous evidence are still with us.
[60] *Davis Contractors v Fareham UDC*, 719 (n 54).
[61] *Davis Contractors v Fareham UDC*, 720 (n 54).
[62] *Davis Contractors v Fareham UDC*, 720–1 (n 54).
[63] *Davis Contractors v Fareham UDC*, 727 (n 54).
[64] See n 47.
[65] *Davis Contractors v Fareham UDC*, 727 (n 54).
[66] *Davis Contractors v Fareham UDC*, 728 (n 54).

place there rises the figure of the fair and reasonable man. And the spokesman of the fair and reasonable man, who represents after all no more than the anthropomorphic conception of justice, is and must be the court itself. So perhaps it would be simpler to say at the outset that frustration occurs whenever the law recognises that without default of either party a contractual obligation has become incapable of being performed because the circumstances in which performance is called for would render it a thing radically different from that which was undertaken by the contract. Non haec in foedera veni. It was not this that I promised to do.[67]

This most eloquent argument appears to go one way and then another. First it seems to suggest that a contract is frustrated when the court thinks it would be unreasonable to hold the parties to their bargain. Then it seems to ground frustration in the will of the parties, ie it was not this that they agreed to do. It is suggested that the proper sense in which to understand the passage is the way in which frustration has been presented in this chapter. Taking the passage as a whole and reading it in the light of Lord Radcliffe's speech as a whole it means that even though the literal meaning of the contract covers the events which have unfolded, the latter are completely different from what the parties envisaged when they made their contract. This conclusion is reached objectively, by asking whether the reasonable man would consider that the parties had contemplated these circumstances. If they have not, then the contract does not apply in these circumstances and is frustrated.

(7) *The Hongkong Fir*[68]

2.25 This seminal decision of the Court of Appeal is mainly concerned with 'innominate' or 'intermediate' terms. The Sale of Goods Act, in both its original 1893 and more modern 1979 forms, appears to recognize only two kinds of contractual terms relevant to the breach of contract scenario. Where a *condition* is breached the non-breaching party has the option of treating the contract as repudiated and terminating it. Where a *warranty* is breached the only remedy is damages. The 'innominate' or 'intermediate' term is one which is not described as a condition or a warranty and is 'in between' condition and warranty in the sense that it sometimes operates as a breach of condition and sometimes as a breach of warranty. But it was not recognized as a third category of term for the first time in *The Hongkong Fir*. All the judges in the Court of Appeal were very clear in stating that this kind of term had been around since well before the Sale of Goods Act 1893. That the Sale of Goods Act apparently recognized only conditions and warranties did not mean that in other contracts only the same division was available.[69]

---

[67] *Davis Contractors v Fareham UDC*, 728–9 (n 54).
[68] *Hongkong Fir Shipping Co Ltd v Kawasaki Kisen Kaisha Ltd (The Hongkong Fir)* [1962] 2 QB 26 (CA).
[69] *The Hongkong Fir*, 57–60 (Sellers LJ), 63 (Upjohn LJ), and 70 (Diplock LJ) (n 68).

The preceding discussion of frustration of contract becomes very important in   **2.26**
addressing the following crucial question relating to termination for breach. In
what circumstances will breach of an 'innominate' or 'intermediate' term be
treated as the equivalent of a breach of condition so that the non-breaching party
will be entitled to treat the contract as at an end? Upjohn LJ, after first recognizing
the case where the party in breach indicates by conduct that it will not perform the
contract,[70] then went on to pose the question with which we are truly concerned
as follows:

> …does the breach of the stipulation go so much to the root of the contract that
> it makes further commercial performance of the contract impossible, or in other
> words is the whole contract frustrated? If yea, the innocent party may treat the
> contract as at an end. If nay, his claim sounds in damages only.[71]

Diplock LJ posed the question in these words:

> The test whether an event has this effect or not has been stated in a number of
> metaphors all of which I think amount to the same thing: does the occurrence of
> the event deprive the party who has further undertakings still to perform of sub-
> stantially the whole benefit which it was the intention of the parties as expressed
> in the contract that he should obtain as the consideration for performing those
> undertakings.[72]

Where this sort of event occurs as a result of the default of one party to the contract,
the other may treat it as sufficient reason to treat the contract as ended. Where it
results from the default of neither party, the contract is frustrated and both are
relieved of their future obligations.[73]

What can be seen from the passages quoted in paragraph 2.26 is that the scale of the   **2.27**
breach of 'innominate' or 'intermediate' term necessary to discharge a contract on
this ground is the same as the scale of the calamity which befalls the contract where
it is discharged by frustration. In this sense we can speak of 'frustrating breach' and
of breach that arises from failure of consideration. Where the party in breach has
so undermined the contract that the other party has been deprived of substantially
the whole benefit of the bargain, the consideration for that party's performance has
totally failed and that party is afforded the right to terminate its own performance
immediately. The frustration cases are a very useful guide to when this will be the
case but it is clear that determining whether there has been a breach on this scale can
be a hazardous process. If the innocent party wrongly treats a breach of contract as
a frustrating breach when in the view of the court it falls short of this the court will
almost certainly treat it as guilty of a repudiatory breach, as described by Upjohn LJ
in paragraph 2.26. Hence the tendency for contracting parties to specify that certain

---

[70] *The Hongkong Fir*, 64 (n 68).
[71] *The Hongkong Fir*, 64 (n 68).
[72] *The Hongkong Fir*, 66 (n 68).
[73] *The Hongkong Fir*, 66 (n 68).

contractual obligations are express conditions giving express rights to terminate the contract is not difficult to understand.

(8) Later developments

2.28 Later developments in the related fields of frustration and frustrating breach have essentially confirmed the views expressed earlier as to the theoretical basis of the doctrine of frustration and also reaffirmed the message that this is a doctrine not lightly to be invoked.

2.29 As to theoretical basis, the first important statement after *Davis v Farnham* came from Lord Denning MR in *Ocean Tramp Tankers Corp v V/O Sovfracht (The Eugenia)*:

> It was originally said that the doctrine of frustration was based on an implied term. In short, that the parties, if they had foreseen the new situation, would have said to one another: 'If that happens, of course, it is all over between us.' But the theory of an implied term has now been discarded by everyone, or nearly everyone, for the simple reason that it does not represent the truth. The parties would not have said: 'It is all over between us.' They would have differed about what was to happen. Each would have sought to insert reservations or qualifications of one kind or another.[74]

The only thing wrong with this statement is that very few discarded the implied term theory because very few held to it in the first place.

2.30 Lord Radcliffe's view of frustration was strongly endorsed by the House of Lords in two decisions of the early 1980s, *National Carriers Ltd v Panalpina (Northern) Ltd*[75] and *Pioneer Shipping Ltd v BTP Tioxide Ltd*.[76] In *Panalpina* Lord Simon of Glaisdale said this:

> Frustration of a contract takes place when there supervenes an event (without default of either party and for which the contract makes no sufficient provision) which so significantly changes the nature (not merely the expense or onerousness) of the outstanding contractual rights and/or obligations from what the parties could reasonably have contemplated at the time of its execution that it would be unjust to hold them to the literal sense of its stipulations in the new circumstances; in such case the law declares both parties to be discharged from further performance.[77]

This dictum is instructive because it tells anyone required to make a judgment call about frustration to start with the literal terms of the contract. If these literally cover the case in point the question is whether both parties could reasonably have contemplated at the time they made the contract that it truly covered the situation which has developed. If there is such a gap between what the parties could

---

[74] [1964] 2 QB 226 (CA) 238.
[75] [1981] AC 675 (HL). The principal issue decided here was that frustration could in principle apply to leases of land, although the longer the lease the less likely it is to be frustrated.
[76] [1982] AC 724 (HL).
[77] [1981] AC 675, 700.

reasonably have contemplated and the situation which has developed that it would be unfair to hold the parties to the literal meaning of the contract then both parties are discharged from their duties of performance. Frustration is thus an exercise in contractual construction and if the events that have unfolded are not what both parties had agreed to do then the contract is frustrated.

The courts have not just *said* that frustration is not lightly to be invoked; they **2.31** have shown by their decisions that it is not lightly to be invoked. Courts have been particularly hard to convince that performance of a contract is impossible or that events have made it seem like something totally different from the bargain as originally conceived. They have also been slow to accept that the events that have unfolded are unforeseeable and hence that there has been no implied allocation of the risk of these events to one party or the other. Professor McKendrick has explained the courts' reluctance to recognize the frustration of contracts largely in terms of the availability of *force majeure* clauses and other clauses providing escape routes from unforeseen circumstances.[78] These clauses usually operate less drastically than frustration, which discharges the contract prospectively. In contrast a contractual provision can allow for temporary suspension of performance or for a neutral third party to intervene and settle disputes between the parties and perhaps assist them to find a way to adjust their contract to the new circumstances.

The brief survey of cases where the frustration doctrine was invoked begins with **2.32** one where the decision that the contract was frustrated was arguably a little generous. In *Pioneer Shipping Ltd v BTP Tioxide Ltd*[79] a one-year, seven-voyage charterparty that contained a clause providing that strikes at the loading port were not to be computed in the loading time was held to be frustrated by a strike that lasted for four months. The arbitrator made his decision just two days before the strike ended without any knowledge of the prospects for resolution in the immediate future. The case was the first commercial arbitration to reach the House of Lords after the Arbitration Act 1979 and its principal significance lay in the House's emphasis that arbitrators' decisions were not to be disturbed by the courts unless shown to be completely wrong. Whether a contract is frustrated is essentially a matter of judgment and in most cases the arbitrator is in the better position to decide.

In *J Lauritzen AS v Wijsmuller BV (The Super Servant Two)*[80] the defendants agreed **2.33** to transport the claimants' oil rig using, at their option, either of their self-propelling barges *Super Servant One* or *Super Servant Two*. Prior to performance of the contract the defendants allocated *Super Servant One* to other contracts and then suffered the misfortune of *Super Servant Two* sinking while transporting another rig.

---

[78] E McKendrick, *Contract Law* (10th edn, Palgrave Macmillan, 2013) pp 255–8. It may seem strange to say that one can draft a clause to deal with unforeseen circumstances, but these clauses are drafted in very wide terms and do not refer to specific events.

[79] [1982] AC 724 (HL).

[80] [1990] 1 Lloyd's Rep 1 (CA).

There was no negligence on the defendants' part in the sinking of *Super Servant Two* but the allocation of that vessel to the claimants' contract was not irrevocable. The contract could still be performed by allocating *Super Servant One* to the claimants' contract. This would probably have required the defendants to break another contract with a third party but the decision not to allocate *Super Servant Two* irrevocably to the claimants' contract was the defendants' alone. Accordingly the Court of Appeal decided that this was a self-induced frustration which the defendants could not rely on. There was no reason why the claimants should suffer when the defendants could have better protected themselves through different contractual provision. The defendants escaped liability under a *force majeure* clause but the decision clearly reveals how difficult it is to convince a court that performance of a contract is impossible or that better contractual provision could not have been made for the events that occurred.

2.34 In *CTI Group Inc v Transclear SA*[81] a seller of cement failed in an attempt to escape liability for non-delivery by arguing that its supplier had let it down by not delivering the cement to the loading port. The supplier had succumbed to pressure from Cemex, which took this action to protect a cartel situation in Mexico, the country to which the cement was to be shipped. Everyone knew about the cartel and the Court of Appeal took the view that the risk was allocated to the sellers. In *Edwinton Commercial Corporation v Tsavliris Russ (Worldwide Salvage & Towage) Ltd (The Sea Angel)*[82] the charterers of a small tanker used in a salvage operation off the coast of Pakistan failed in their attempt to persuade the courts that the charterparty was frustrated by a port authority's detention of the vessel as security for the costs of environmental damage. The port authority's detention was illegal and the vessel detained had very little to do with the environmental damage, most of which was caused by the shipwreck of an oil tanker the chartered vessel had been involved in salvaging. The charterparty was for twenty days' duration and the detention lasted for three and a half months, but the salvage work was all but done by the time of the detention and all that remained was redelivery of the ship and payment of any outstanding hire charges. Given also that it was open to the parties involved to find a resolution through a mixture of negotiation, diplomacy, and ultimately legal action in the Pakistani courts, the Court of Appeal was unconvinced that this was a frustration situation. In any event the problems which developed were a foreseeable risk in the salvage industry which the defendants had assumed.

2.35 Two recent first instance decisions illustrate the reluctance of the courts to conclude that a contract has been frustrated on frustration of purpose (*Krell v Henry*) grounds.[83] In *Gold Group Properties Ltd v BDW Trading Ltd (formerly Barratt*

---

[81] [2008] EWCA Civ 856, [2008] 2 CLC 112.
[82] [2007] EWCA Civ 547, [2007] 1 CLC 876.
[83] See paras 2.18–2.19.

Homes Ltd)[84] B were to build a large number of houses and flats that were to be sold by G, the freehold owner of the development site. Revenue generated was to be shared between the parties. G sued B for failing to do any construction work. B's defence was first, that there was a condition precedent in the agreement that the properties were to be sold for a minimum price and in the light of advice they had received, that the fall in the property market meant those prices would not be reached, they were not obliged to commence work. Although the agreement did contain a schedule of minimum prices giving some substance to B's argument, Coulson J held that this was not a condition precedent and did not justify B refusing to commence work. B's alternative defence was that both parties had a common expectation that the selling prices of the properties would be no less than the minimum prices in the schedule and that this justified the conclusion that the contract had been frustrated on *Krell v Henry* grounds. This argument was rejected on the basis that this problem did not render the entire contract pointless and that the risk of properties not reaching the minimum specified in the schedule had been allocated. In *North Shore Ventures Ltd v Anstead Holdings Inc*[85] guarantors of a loan to a company with which they were closely associated argued that the partial freezing of an account into which the loan money was paid because of the lender's links with someone suspected of money laundering, frustrated the loan and guarantee. Newey J rejected this argument because only $18m of the $50m loaned was frozen and use of the loan money was thus not entirely prohibited. In any event the frustration was self-induced because the guarantors had transferred the money into the account which was afterwards part frozen.

The principal significance of these decisions in the present context lies in their **2.36** message that frustration is not a defence which is likely often to avail a contracting party where the other decides to terminate the contract for breach of condition or any other ground that would entitle it to terminate. Also of importance is what these cases say about the scale of the breach that would entitle a contracting party to terminate in the absence of an express provision allowing it to do so. This scale is very large indeed and would admit of considerable uncertainty for contracting parties reviewing their options when performance from the other party seems difficult to obtain. It is easy to see why so many contracts are overloaded with promissory conditions giving a right to terminate.

D. The Current Analysis in English Law

The purpose of this last section of the chapter is to explain briefly the position **2.37** which English law has reached after the journey travelled in this chapter. There

---

[84] [2010] EWHC 323 (TCC), [2010] BLR 235.
[85] [2010] EWHC 1485 (Ch), [2011] 1 All ER (Comm) 81, [2010] 2 Lloyd's Rep 265.

will be much more detail on these matters later in the book but a short summary of the position is offered here to make the task of understanding those subsequent chapters a little easier.

(1) Failure of condition

2.38   We have seen how the English law concept of *condition* began as something upon which one party's duty to perform the contract depended. This condition could be an event external to the contract, such as weather conditions or the condition of land or sea that neither contracting party can readily control. Alternatively, one party's obligation to perform the contract may be dependent on the other party performing one or more of its obligations under the contract. These dependent conditions may be *conditions precedent*, something the other party must do first, or *conditions subsequent*, which effectively terminate the first party's obligation to perform, or they may be some variant of these conditions. This notion of condition still exists in English law but is not particularly common in synallagmatic (or bilateral) contracts today because the parties generally dislike the disruption and stop/go effect of these conditions. What has been seen is the emergence into prominence of the *promissory condition* under which a failure to perform an obligation classified as a condition gives to the non-breaching party a right to treat the other party's breach as going to the root of the contract and thus giving the non-breaching party the right to terminate it. A contractual term will be classified as a condition in this sense if the contract expressly makes it a condition, or if on construction of the contract as a whole the court is persuaded that it is a condition,[86] or if statute makes it a condition. The most significant example of the latter is the set of implied conditions in sale of goods contracts specified by sections 12 to 15 of the Sale of Goods Act 1979. The Sale of Goods Act essentially classifies contractual terms into *conditions* and *warranties*, the former having the effect already indicated and the latter allowing the non-breaching party only to sue for damages. The story told in this chapter of how English law came to think of *conditions* in the promissory sense is in many respects the story of how the Sale of Goods Act conception of *condition* came to be the general conception of condition throughout contract law. What this conception of the meaning of *condition* and *warranty* did not mean was that these were the only kind of contractual terms that English law recognized. There is also the *innominate* or *intermediate* term, about which more will be said when failure of consideration is revisited in paragraphs 2.40 and 2.41.

---

[86] See eg *Maredelanto Compania Naviera SA v Bergbau-Handel GmbH (The Mihalis Angelos)* [1971] 1 QB 164 (CA); *Bunge Corp, New York v Tradax Export SA, Panama* [1981] 1 WLR 711 (HL); *Compagnie Commerciale Sucres et Denrees v C Czarnikow Ltd* [1990] 1 WLR 1337 (HL).

Today the most frequent context in which the former conventional usage of *condi-* **2.39**
tion, usually as a condition precedent, is likely to be encountered is the unilateral
contract. In a unilateral contract the offeror is looking for acceptance of the offer by
the doing of the act requested. As the offeror makes no advance promise to anyone
who can make a reciprocal promise there is no contract until someone does the act
requested and at no time is anyone bound to do this act. If someone does it, the
offeror becomes bound to meet the promise he or she made to anyone who did the
act requested. Thus the person doing the act requested can be seen as satisfying a
condition precedent to the offeror's duty to honour the promise made.

(2) Failure of consideration

Failure of consideration may lead to the discharge of a contract where it takes **2.40**
the form either of a clear and unequivocal statement by words and/or conduct
by one contracting party that it is not going to perform the contract in future,
or where a breach occurs that goes to the very root of the contract. In the former
instance the breaching party's conduct may be styled a repudiation of the contract.
In the latter instance it may be possible to deduce from the scale of the breach
that the breaching party is making a repudiatory statement, but even if this is
not so the non-breaching party has a right to treat the contract as terminated
because the scale of the breach deprives the non-breaching party of essentially the
entire benefit of the bargain. The doctrine of frustration is relevant here especially
because the scale of a breach qualifying as *fundamental breach* is comparable to the
effect of an event sufficient to cause the contract to be discharged automatically by
frustration. Frustration is also relevant in this context, and in breach of condition
cases, because the party allegedly in breach may argue that the events that took
place were not the fault of either party, had not been foreseen by either party, and
could not reasonably have been foreseen by either. As a matter of construction of
the contract it does not provide for the events which have occurred and hence the
contract is frustrated due to the absence of any guide as to who is responsible or
what happens next.

Into this picture steps the *innominate* or *intermediate* term. This has been pre- **2.41**
sented in this chapter less as a third kind of contractual term in addition to conditions and warranties, and more as a term where the contract does not make clear,
either expressly or by reasonable implication, precisely what is to happen in the
event of a breach. The situation is that if the breach deprives the non-breaching
party of essentially the entire benefit of the bargain, that party may treat the contract as terminated; and if the consequences of breach are not so serious, an action
for damages is the only remedy. Where the consequences of breach deprive the
non-breaching party of the entire benefit of the bargain, the situation is analytic-
ally and practically indistinguishable from the fundamental breach discussed in
paragraph 2.40. It is not a third kind of failure of consideration to fundamental
breach and repudiation but a fuller description of what fundamental breach really

is. The parties have not made clear either expressly or by implication that any term in question is a condition. Those terms are necessarily either innominate/intermediate or warranties. In practice, contractual terms are rarely if ever expressly called warranties. They are either called conditions or they are not given a name. If they are not given a name they might be designated conditions by interpretation of the contract but they are more likely to be treated as innominate/intermediate and whether they operate as conditions or warranties depends on the consequences of breach. Predicting the outcome in such cases is a sufficiently hazardous process that many contracting parties who have sufficient bargaining power will try to specify as many obligations as conditions that they can to render the right to terminate for breach as crystal clear as they can make it.

Part II

BREACH AND TERMINATION

3

BREACH OF CONTRACT

A party seeking to exercise the right to terminate for breach of contract must prove **3.01** that the other party has broken the contract in the first place.[1] A useful starting point here is the definition given by Carter: a breach of contract occurs if a promisor either: (1) fails to perform a contractual obligation within the time stipulated for its performance, or (2) commits an anticipatory breach of contract.[2] The question of anticipatory breach is discussed later;[3] the present chapter will concentrate on the ingredients of what Lord Keith and others have termed 'actual' breach,[4] and on its consequences.

A. The Significance of Breach

Though one cannot have termination for breach of contract without a breach, the **3.02** proof of breach in the present context is not as important as it might at first sight appear. This is because different aspects of the right to terminate for breach are mirrored by various doctrines allowing termination, or consequences more or less equivalent to termination, without proof of breach.[5] Thus, for instance, the right to terminate

---

[1] This does not mean, of course, that there can be no termination on other grounds: see para 3.02.

[2] Carter, *Carter's Breach of Contract* (Hart, 2012) para 1-02.

[3] See Ch 7.

[4] *Woodar Investment Development Ltd v Wimpey Construction UK Ltd* [1980] 1 WLR 277 (HL) 297 (Lord Keith); *Afovos Shipping Co SA v R Pagnan and Fratelli (The Afovos)* [1983] 1 WLR 195 (HL) 201 (Lord Hailsham LC); *Fercometal Sarl v MSC Mediterranean Shipping Co SA (The Simona)* [1989] AC 788 (HL) 798 (Lord Ackner); *Torvald Klaveness A/S v Arni Maritime Corp (The Gregos)* [1994] CLC 1188 (HL) 1194 (Lord Mustill); *Kastor Navigation Co Ltd v AXA Global Risks (UK) Ltd (The Kastor Too)* [2004] EWCA Civ 277, [2004] 2 CLC 68, para 79 (Rix LJ); *Acre Ltd (in liq) v De Montfort Fine Art Ltd* [2011] EWCA Civ 87, 2011 WL para 50 (Tomlinson LJ).

[5] The reasons for this are largely historical; see Ch 2, paras 2.03–2.14.

for breach of condition is mirrored by the right to refuse performance of a unilateral obligation on the ground that an essential contingency has not been fulfilled, as in the case of an option to purchase which may not be exercised after a certain date;[6] though the party who tries to exercise the option late is not in breach, the effect of the delay, at least as far as the other party's obligations are concerned, is more or less the same as if there had been a breach of an essential time stipulation.[7] Again, the right to terminate for a repudiatory breach is mirrored by the doctrine of frustration[8] and by the right of the injured party to terminate in certain cases for excused non-performance falling short of frustration;[9] here the inability of the injured party to prove breach will exclude any claim for damages, but will not necessarily bar a claim to be excused from the obligation to perform.[10] All of this means that a party claiming wrongful repudiation will not necessarily succeed by showing that he or she was not in breach; this will certainly exclude the right of the other party to terminate *for breach*, but it may not exclude his or her right to refuse performance on some other ground.

B. The Elements of Breach

3.03 Bearing this in mind, we may now analyse the elements of a breach of contract. Proving that a breach of contract has occurred involves three basic elements: (1) the party in question must have been under a contractual obligation; (2) he or she must have failed to perform that obligation; and (3) there must be no lawful excuse for that failure. All of these elements involve complex issues of law.

(1) A contractual obligation

3.04 Before a party can be said to be in breach, it must be shown that he or she was under a contractual obligation with regard to the matter in question, or in other words that it was a term of the contract. There is not the space in the present context for a comprehensive discussion of the law relating to this topic, but broadly speaking such terms can be either express or implied.

(a) Express Terms

3.05 Deciding the express terms of a contract involves three questions; what did the parties say, what did they mean, and was it intended to have contractual force? The first of these questions is a fairly straightforward one, but the other two raise some difficult issues.

---

[6] As in *United Dominions Trust (Commercial) Ltd v Eagle Aircraft Services Ltd* [1968] 1 WLR 74 (CA); see para 1.29.

[7] JE Stannard, *Delay in the Performance of Contractual Obligations* (OUP, 2007) para 11.32.

[8] As in *Jackson v Union Marine Insurance Co Ltd* (1874–75) LR 10 CP 125 (Exchequer Chamber); see Ch 1, para 1.27.

[9] As in *Poussard v Spiers & Pond* (1876) 1 QBD 410 (DC); see Ch 1, para 1.28.

[10] See Ch 4, paras 4.09–4.10.

(i) What was said?   Deciding that what was said will not be a problem is basically   **3.06**
a question of fact, the burden of proof being on the claimant to show that his or her
version of what took place is correct. Where the contract is in writing, this will not
generally be a problem, but difficulties may arise where it is wholly or partly oral. In
Smith v Hughes[11] a contract was made for the purchase of oats according to sample.
The buyer later refused to accept and pay for the oats on the ground that they were
'new' oats, claiming that the seller had told him that they were 'old' oats.[12] The seller
denied having said any such thing.[13] In an action for the price by the sellers, the
first question left to the jury was whether the seller had actually used the word 'old';
if he had, the action failed.[14] On appeal by the seller this direction was affirmed as
correct by the Court of Queen's Bench.[15] Nowadays, of course, there would be no
jury involved, but the issue would still be one for the judge to decide as an issue of
fact; had the seller used the crucial words, or had he not? Even where it cannot be
shown that the disputed words were used, a party may still be bound if he or she
has acted in such a manner as to induce the other party to believe that the contract
was on certain terms, and the first party can be shown to have been aware of that
belief. As Blackburn J put it in *Smith v Hughes*, if, whatever a man's real intention
may be, he so conducts himself that a reasonable man would believe that he was
assenting to the terms proposed by the other party, and that other party upon that
belief enters into the contract with him, the man thus conducting himself would be
equally bound as if he had intended to agree to the other party's terms.[16]

(ii) What was meant?   In most cases there will be no problem in deciding what   **3.07**
the contract said, not least because that contract is likely to be in writing. However,
the courts may often be faced with a dispute between the parties as to the meaning of the words used, and it is then up to the court to provide its interpretation,
this being a question of law.[17] The construction of contracts is a vast topic in its
own right,[18] and it is not easy to formulate general principles, not least because

---

[11] (1870–71) LR 6 QB 597.
[12] *Smith v Hughes*, 598 (n 11).
[13] *Smith v Hughes*, 598 (n 11).
[14] *Smith v Hughes*, 599 (n 11).
[15] *Smith v Hughes*, 602 (Cockburn CJ) and 607–8 (Blackburn J) (n 11).
[16] *Smith v Hughes*, 607 (n 11); *Freeman v Cooke* (1848) 2 Ex 654, 154 ER 652; *HSBC Bank plc
v 5th Avenue Partners Ltd* [2007] EWHC 2819 (Comm), [2008] 2 CLC 770; *Statoil ASA v Louis
Dreyfus Energy Services LP (The Harriette N)* [2008] EWHC 2257 (Comm), [2008] 2 Lloyd's Rep
689. Apparently it would have been different if the seller had acquiesced in the buyer's belief that the
seller had *warranted* the oats to be old: *Smith v Hughes*, 607–8 (Blackburn CJ) and 610 (Hannen J)
(n 11); see *Hartog v Colin and Shields* [1939] 3 All ER 566 (KBD); *Chwee Kin Keong v Digilandmall
Com Pte Ltd* [2005] 1 SLR 502 (Singapore Court of Appeal).
[17] *Pioneer Shipping Ltd v BTP Tioxide Ltd (The Nema)* [1982] AC 724 (HL) 736 (Lord Diplock);
Carmichael v National Power plc [1999] 1 WLR 2042 (Lord Hoffmann); *Sirius Intl Insurance Co
(Publ) v FAI General Insurance Ltd* [2004] UKHL 54, [2004] 1 WLR 3251, para 3 (Lord Steyn);
Thorner v Major [2009] UKHL 18, [2009] 1 WLR 776, para 82 (Lord Neuberger).
[18] See G McMeel, *The Construction of Contracts* (2nd edn, OUP, 2011); K Lewison, *The
Interpretation of Contracts* (5th edn, Sweet & Maxwell, 2017); C Mitchell, *The Interpretation of
Contracts* (Routledge-Cavendish, 2007).

so much depends on the wording of the contract in the particular case before the court.[19] In the past much stress would have been placed on the so-called 'parol evidence rule', whereby extrinsic evidence was not allowed to add, vary, or contradict a written contract or other instrument.[20] However, this was always subject to numerous exceptions,[21] and the courts now take a rather broader approach to the question of interpretation; in particular, under the so-called principles of 'commercial construction'[22] they may now take into account not only the words used but the entire matrix of fact surrounding the making of the contract,[23] though evidence of pre-contract negotiations is still excluded.[24] The overall principle may be described as one of 'qualified objectivity';[25] the court will first ask itself how a reasonable person would construe the offer made, and then how the actual recipient of the offer construed the other's intentions.[26] If the answers to those

---

[19] E Peel, *Treitel: The Law of Contract* (13th edn, Sweet & Maxwell, 2011) para 6-006.

[20] *Shore v Wilson* (1842) 9 Cl & F 355, 565–6, 8 ER 450 (HL) 532 (Tindal LCJ); *Jacobs v Batavia & General Plantations Trust Ltd* [1924] 1 Ch 287, 295 (PO Lawrence J); *Rabin v Gerson Berger Association Ltd* [1986] 1 WLR 526 (CA) 537 (Balcombe LJ); KW Wedderburn, 'Collateral Contracts' [1959] CLJ 58; DW McLauchlan, *The Parol Evidence Rule* (Professional Publications, 1976); Law Commission, *Law of Contract—the Parol Evidence Rule* (Law Com No 154, 1986). For a discussion of the present status of the rule, see McMeel, *The Construction of Contracts*, paras 5.24–5.62 (n 18); Peel, *Treitel*, paras 6-013–6-030 (n 19).

[21] McMeel, *The Construction of Contracts*, paras 5.33–5.55 (n 18); AS Burrows et al (eds), *Chitty on Contracts* (31st edn, Sweet & Maxwell, 2012) paras 12-097–12-105.

[22] *Investors Compensation Ltd v West Bromwich Building Society* [1998] 1 WLR (HL) 912–13 (Lord Hoffmann). This is not the place to discuss the full implications of these principles, but it has been argued on the one hand that they state nothing new, and on the other that they lack clarity: see A Kramer, 'Common Sense Principles of Contractual Construction (and how we've been using them all along)' (2003) 23 OJLS 173; JW Carter, 'Commercial Construction and Contract Doctrine' (2009) 25 JCL 83. Certainly they have not been adopted with any great enthusiasm so far in the courts of Australia: see *Kooee Communications Pty Ltd v Primus Telecommunications Pty Ltd* [2008] NWSCA 5; D McLauchlan, 'Plain Meaning and Commercial Construction: has Australia adopted the ICS Principles?' (2009) 5 JCL 7.

[23] *Reardon Smith Ltd v Ynvar Hansen-Tangen (The Diana Prosperity)* [1976] 1 WLR 989, 957 (Lord Wilberforce); *Investors Compensation Ltd v West Bromwich Building Society* [1998] 1 WLR 896, 912–13 (Lord Hoffmann); *Bank of Credit and Commerce Intl SA v Ali* [2002] 1 AC 251 (HL); *R (Westminster City Council) v National Asylum Support Service* [2002] UKHL 38, [2002] 1 WLR 2956.

[24] *Prenn v Simmonds* [1971] 1 WLR 1381 (HL) 1384–5 (Lord Wilberforce); *Chartbrook Ltd v Persimmon Homes Ltd* [2009] UKHL 38, [2009] 1 AC 1101; Lord Nicholls of Birkenhead, 'My Kingdom for a Horse: the Meaning of Words' (2005) 121 LQR 577; PS Davies, 'Finding the Limits of Contractual Interpretation' [2009] LMCLQ 420; D McLauchlan, 'Contract Interpretation: What is it About?' (2009) 31 Sydney L Rev 5; R Buxton, '"Construction" and Rectification after Chartbrook' [2010] CLJ 253; C Mitchell 'Contract Interpretation: Pragmatism, Principle and the Prior Negotiations Rule' (2010) 26 JCL 134.

[25] McMeel, *The Construction of Contracts*, paras 3.16–3.31 (n 18).

[26] McMeel, *The Construction of Contracts*, paras 3.21 and 3.31 (n 18); *Paal Wilson & Co A/S v Partenreederei Hannah Blumenthal (The Hannah Blumenthal)* [1983] 1 AC 854 (HL) 915–16 (Lord Diplock); *OT Africa Lines Ltd v Vickers plc* [1996] I Lloyd's Rep 700 (QBD: Commercial Ct); *Hearn v Younger* [2002] EWHC 963 (Ch), [2002] WTLR 1317, para 81 (Etherton J).

questions are the same, that is the meaning that will be adopted; if they differ, there will be no contract at all.[27]

(iii) **Contractual force?**   Even where there is no doubt as to the words used and   **3.08** as to their meaning, there will be no breach of contract unless the words in question were intended to have contractual force. In this context two distinctions must be borne in mind, one being the distinction between terms and mere representations, and the other the distinction between promises and mere contingencies.

The courts are often faced with a situation where someone has been induced to   **3.09** enter into a contract by a statement that proves to be untrue. Where this is the case, the party responsible for the statement will generally be liable for *misrepresentation*,[28] but for him or her to be liable for *breach* the other party will have to show that the statement in question was intended to be a term of the contract.[29] Establishing such an intention is ultimately a question of construction,[30] and the principles are well established;[31] thus the statement is more likely to be a term if made by someone in a position to know the facts of the matter,[32] or where it is clear from the surrounding circumstances that particular importance was attached to its accuracy.[33] As well as this, there is section 13 of the Sale of Goods Act 1979, under which goods sold by description must correspond with the description.[34] However, this is one of the areas where establishing a breach is less important than might appear at first sight, given that even in the absence of breach the innocent party may still have the right to rescind the contract for misrepresentation.[35] However, such a right may not be as valuable as a right to terminate for breach. In particular: (1) the right to rescind for

---

[27] McMeel, *The Construction of Contracts*, para 3.21 (n 18).

[28] J Beatson, AS Burrows, and J Cartwright, *Anson's Law of Contract* (29th edn, OUP, 2010) ch 9; MP Furmston, CHS Fifoot, and AWB Simpson, *Cheshire, Fifoot and Furmston's Law of Contract* (16th edn, OUP, 2012) pp 338–88; Peel, *Treitel*, ch 9 (n 19).

[29] *Heilbut, Symons & Co v Buckleton* [1913] AC 30 (HL) 38 (Lord Haldane LC), 42 (Lord Atkinson) and 49–50 (Lord Moulton); Beatson, Burrows, and Cartwright, *Anson's Law of Contract*, p 134 (n 28).

[30] Peel, *Treitel*, para 9-050 (n 19); *Power v Barham* (1836) 4 A & E 473 (KB), 111 ER 865; *Miller v Cannon Hill Estates Ltd* [1931] 2 KB 113 (KBD); *Howard Marine & Dredging Co Ltd v A Ogden & Son (Excavations) Ltd* [1978] QB 574 (CA) 595 (Bridge LJ).

[31] Beatson, Burrows, and Cartwright, *Anson's Law of Contract*, pp 133–6 (n 28); Furmston, Fifoot, and Simpson, *Cheshire, Fifoot and Furmston's Law of Contract*, pp 170–7 (n 28); Peel, *Treitel*, paras 9-045–9-053 (n 19).

[32] *Oscar Chess Ltd v Williams* [1957] 1 WLR 370 (CA); *Dick Bentley Productions Ltd v Harold Smith (Motors) Ltd* [1965] 1 WLR 623 (CA).

[33] *Bannerman v White* (1861) 10 CBNS 844 (Exchequer Chamber), 142 ER 685; *Couchman v Hill* [1947] KB 554 (CA); *Harling v Eddy* [1957] 2 QB 739 (CA).

[34] *Beale v Taylor* [1967] 1 WLR 1193 (CA).

[35] Beatson, Burrows, and Cartwright, *Anson's Law of Contract*, pp 311–20 (n 28); Furmston, Fifoot, and Simpson, *Cheshire, Fifoot and Furmston's Law of Contract*, pp 359–68 (n 28); Peel, *Treitel*, paras 9-084–9-114 (n 19).

misrepresentation is subject to various restrictions;[36] (2) damages will not necessarily be available;[37] and (3) the court may award damages in lieu of rescission.[38]

3.10   Another possibility is that the provision in question is contingent rather than promissory, as in cases where a person offers a reward or a prize if certain conditions are met. This is the classic unilateral contract, where if the conditions are met, the reward or prize will have to be paid, but nobody is under any obligation to fulfil the conditions, and failure to do so cannot amount to a breach.[39] However, few cases are as clear cut as this.[40] One problem is that a particular provision in a contract may be both promissory and contingent. For instance, a lease may contain a provision allowing the tenant to renew provided that all the covenants in the lease have been duly observed, or a hire purchase contract may contain a provision allowing the hirer to purchase the goods provided that the instalments have been duly paid. In this situation the performance of the obligations in question is both a promise and a contingency; the tenant or hirer can be sued if the covenants are not kept or the instalments paid, and will not be able to renew the lease or purchase the property, as the case may be, if this has not been done. Another problem is that what may look like a unilateral option may be construed by the courts in a different way. This is illustrated by a long line of 'rent review' cases involving provisions in a lease allowing for the adjustment of the rent at certain intervals.[41] In many cases this would be done by the landlord serving a 'trigger notice' on the tenant specifying the new rent; the tenant would then be given the chance to challenge this by means of a counter-notice, after which there might be provisions for arbitration. The crucial question for the courts was whether time limits set in the contract for the service of such notices had to be strictly adhered to or not. Normally time is of the essence with regard to options,[42] but in some cases the courts refused to enforce the time limits strictly on the grounds that these provisions were not options in the strict sense, either because they did not involve the creation of any new contractual relationship between the parties,[43] or because the other

---

[36] Beatson, Burrows, and Cartwright, *Anson's Law of Contract*, pp 314–17 (n 28); Furmston, Fifoot, and Simpson, *Cheshire, Fifoot and Furmston's Law of Contract*, p 363–8 (n 28); Peel, *Treitel*, paras 9-094–9-114 (n 19).

[37] Damages for misrepresentation will only be available in four cases: (1) where the statement is a term of the contract; (2) under the Misrepresentation Act 1967, s 2(1); (3) in lieu of rescission under s 2(2) of the same Act; and (4) for negligent misstatement under the doctrine of *Hedley Byrne & Co Ltd v Heller & Partners Ltd* [1964] AC 465 (HL).

[38] Under the Misrepresentation Act 1967, s 2(2).

[39] Beatson, Burrows, and Cartwright, *Anson's Law of Contract*, pp 30–1 (n 28); Peel, *Treitel*, para 2-051 (n 19).

[40] K Llewellyn, 'On Our Case-Law of Offer and Acceptance' (1939) 48 Yale LJ 1, 799.

[41] Stannard, *Delay in the Performance of Contractual Obligations*, para 11.33 (n 7). Similar issues have been raised in relation to notification clauses in insurance contracts: see *Alfred McAlpine plc v BAI (Run-Off) Ltd* [2000] 1 Lloyd's Rep 437 (CA); *Friends Provident Life & Pensions Ltd v Sirius Intl Insurance* [2005] EWCA Civ 601, [2005] 2 Lloyd's Rep 517; J Lowry and P Rawlings, 'Innominate Terms in Insurance Contracts' [2006] LMCLQ 135.

[42] *Finch v Underwood* (1865) 1 LJ Ch 353; *Hare v Nicoll* [1966] 2 QB 130 (CA); *United Dominions Trust (Commercial) Ltd v Eagle Aircraft Services Ltd* [1968] 1 WLR 74 (CA).

[43] *United Scientific Holdings Ltd v Burnley BC* [1978] AC 904 (HL) 928–30 (Lord Diplock), 945–6 (Lord Simon), 951 (Lord Salmon), and 961–2 (Lord Fraser).

party could take steps to enforce them by issuing a notice making time of the essence.[44] All of this goes to show that though the difference between a promise and a contingency is an easy one to grasp, it can in many cases be hard to apply. However, it is submitted that the distinction ultimately depends on the same test as that for determining whether a statement amounts to a term of the contract, namely that of contractual intention.[45]

(b) Implied terms

There is also the possibility of breach of an implied term. A useful starting point here **3.11** is the judgment of Lord Denning MR in *Shell UK Ltd v Lostock Garage Ltd*,[46] where he drew a distinction between two categories of implied term. The first category comprehended 'relationships…of common occurrence', such as buyer and seller, landlord and tenant, owner and hirer, and so on, where the courts imposed obligations on one party or another on the basis of policy considerations.[47] The second category comprehended cases which were not of common occurrence where a term was implied into a particular contract on the basis of the particular circumstances of the case.[48] Terms of the first type are said to be 'implied in law', while the second are said to be 'implied in fact'.[49] In addition to this, terms may also be implied by custom.

(i) Term implied in law Terms implied in law are implied not into individual **3.12** contracts[50] but into contracts of a particular type.[51] Though it has been said several times that such terms should only be implied when it is necessary to do so,[52]

---

[44] *United Scientific Holdings Ltd v Burnley BC* (n 43) 933–4 (Lord Diplock); *London v Manchester Assurance Co v Dunn* (1982) 265 EG 39 (CA); *Amherst v James Walker Goldsmith and Silversmith Ltd* [1983] Ch 305.

[45] See para 3.09.

[46] [1976] 1 WLR 1187 (CA).

[47] *Shell UK Ltd v Lostock Garage*, 1196 (n 46).

[48] *Shell UK Ltd v Lostock Garage*, 1196–7 (n 46).

[49] Some cases, however, may be difficult to classify; for instance *The Moorcock* (1889) 14 PD 64 (CA). Another example is *Liverpool City Council v Irwin* [1977] AC 239 (HL); here Lord Cross (at 258) and Lord Edmund-Davies (at 266) were clearly of the view that no term could be implied on the basis of the common intention of the parties, but Lord Salmon (at 262) said that without the implication of some obligation on the landlord, the whole contract would be 'inefficacious, futile and absurd', and that such a result would not have been within the contemplation of either party to the contract (at 262). Perhaps Lord Wilberforce is right in saying that cases of this sort cannot be rigidly categorized, but are rather 'shade[s] on a continuous spectrum' (at 254). Attempts have been made to provide a synthesis of the two, most notably by the Privy Council in *BP Refinery (Westernport) Pty Ltd v Shire of Hastings* (1977) 180 CLR 266, and by Lord Hoffmann in *Attorney-General of Belize v Belize Telecom Ltd* [2009] UKPC 10, [2009] 1 WLR 1988 (Belize), but it has been argued that this does not succeed in eliminating the basic distinction: see GJ Tolhurst and JW Carter, 'The New Law on Implied Terms' (1996–97) 11 JCL 76; *Byrne v Australian Airlines Ltd* (1995) 131 ALR 422.

[50] *Clarion Ltd v National Provident Association* [2000] 1 WLR 1888 (Ch D) 1897 (Rimer J).

[51] Beatson, Burrows, and Cartwright, *Anson's Law of Contract*, pp 154–7 (n 28); Furmston, Fifoot, and Simpson, *Cheshire, Fifoot and Furmston's Law of Contract*, pp 185–95 (n 28); Peel, *Treitel*, paras 6-041–6-045 (n 19).

[52] *Mears v Safecar Securities Ltd* [1983] QB 54 (CA) 78 (Stephenson LJ); *Scally v Southern Health and Social Services Board* [1992] 1 AC 294 (HL) 307 (Lord Bridge); *Halliday v HBOS plc* [2007] EWHC 1780 (QB) para 8 (Underhill J).

deciding whether to do so inevitably involves consideration of the broader policy considerations,[53] and is therefore often said to be based ultimately on what is fair and reasonable.[54] In particular, the implication of terms of this kind may have little to do with the intention of the parties in the given case,[55] and for this reason the implication of a term in law is said to be no more than a way of specifying the legal duties which arise out of certain types of contract.[56] Indeed, such terms are often later codified into statutory form, as was the case with the implied terms relating to description, quality, and fitness for purpose in the Sale of Goods Act 1893.[57] Though these are still technically described as implied terms,[58] they are not 'terms' in any real sense of the word; rather, they are obligations laid down by the law, which may indeed sometimes apply irrespective of what the parties may intend in the given case.[59]

3.13   (ii) **Term implied in fact**   Terms implied in fact, however, are very closely linked to the intentions of the parties; here a term is implied on the ground that it is necessary so to do in order to give 'business efficacy' to the contract,[60] or on the ground that the parties would clearly have agreed to it had they thought about it.[61] Though the resulting term is said to be implied rather than express, it has

---

[53] *Crossley v Faithful & Gould Holdings Ltd* [2004] EWCA Civ 293, [2004] ICR 1615, para 36 (Dyson LJ).

[54] E Peden, 'Policy Concerns behind Implication of Terms in Law' (2001) 117 LQR 459.

[55] Peel, *Treitel*, para 6-042 (n 19).

[56] Peel, *Treitel*, para 6-044 (n 19); *Mears v Safecar Securities* [1983] QB 54 (CA) 78 (Stephenson LJ); *Tai Hing Cotton Mill v Liu Chong Hing Bank Ltd* [1986] AC 80 (JCPC–Hong Kong) 107 (Lord Scarman); *Jameson v Central Electricity Generating Board* [2000] 1 AC 455 (HL) 477–8 (Lord Hope); *Johnson v Unisys Ltd* [2001] UKHL 13, [2003] AC 518, para 24 (Lord Steyn); *Tullett Prebon plc v BGC Brokers LP* [2011] EWCA Civ 131, para 45 (Maurice Kay LJ).

[57] Sir Mackenzie Chalmers, *The Sale of Goods, including the Factors Act 1889* (William Clowes, 1890) p i.

[58] See the Sale of Goods Act 1979, ss 10–14, as amended by the Sale and Supply of Goods Act 1994, Sch 2, para 5.

[59] As with the Unfair Contract Terms Act 1977, s 6 (restrictions on excluding liability for breach of implied terms in the Sale of Goods Act). In other cases they are more akin to presumptions that apply unless the parties decide otherwise: JF Burrows, 'Implied Terms and Presumptions' (1968) 3 NZULR 121.

[60] *Luxor (Eastbourne) Ltd v Cooper* [1941] AC 108 (HL) 137 (Lord Wright); *Adler v Dickson (No 1)* [1955] 1 QB 158 (QBD) 174 (Pilcher J); *Lupton v Potts* [1969] 1 WLR 1749 (Ch D) 1753 (Plowman J); *C Czarnikow Ltd v Centrala Handlu Zagranicznego Rolimpex* [1979] AC 351 (HL) 372 (Lord Salmon); *Morris-Thomas v Petticoat Lane Rentals* (1987) 53 P & CR 238 (CA) 258 (May LJ); *Scally v Southern Health and Social Services Board* [1992] 1 AC 294 (HL) 307 (Lord Bridge); *Barclays Bank plc v Savile Estates Ltd* [2002] EWCA Civ 589, [2002] L & TR 28, para 14 (Aldous LJ); *AIC Ltd v ITS Testing Services Ltd (The Kriti Palm)* [2006] EWCA Civ 1601, [2007] 2 CLC 223, para 346 (Rix LJ); *Crosstown Music No 1 LLC v Rive Droite Music Ltd* [2010] EWCA Civ 1222, [2011] Bus LR 383, para 73 (Mummery LJ).

[61] This is the famous 'officious bystander' test: see *Shirlaw v Southern Foundries (1926) Ltd* [1939] KB 206 (CA) 227 (MacKinnon LJ); *EP Nelson & Co v Rolfe* [1950] 1 KB 139 (CA) 146–7 (Cohen LJ); *Weg Motors Ltd v Hales* [1961] Ch 176 (Ch D) 191–2 (Danckwerts J); *Ivory v Palmer* [1975] ICR 340 (CA) 351 (Roskill LJ); *Bourne v Colodense Ltd* [1985] ICR 291 (CA) 305 (Dillon LJ); *Wiggins v Arun DC* (1997) 74 P & CR 64 (CA) 71 (Evans LJ); *Owners of the Ship 'Borvigilant' v Owners of the Ship 'Romina G'* [2003] EWCA Civ 935, [2004] 1 CLC 41, para 47 (Clarke LJ); *Lowe v Powell* [2010] EWCA Civ 1419, para 2 (Moore-Bick LJ).

been said that the question in these cases is ultimately one of interpretation; what did the parties intend the contract to mean?[62] Since the question depends on the intention of the parties, a term cannot be implied on this basis unless it is clear that both parties would have agreed to it had they been asked;[63] still less where the proposed implied term contradicts the express terms of the contract.[64]

(iii) Term implied by custom A term may also be implied by custom or trade **3.14** usage.[65] For this to happen, two requirements must be met. First of all, the custom or usage in question must be shown to exist as a matter of fact,[66] the burden of proof here being on the party who wishes to rely on the custom. This means showing that it is well known in the relevant trade or locality[67] and followed as a matter of obligation by those concerned,[68] the rationale being that the parties must have been taken to have intended to bargain by reference to that practice.[69] Secondly, the practice in question must be 'fair and proper' and one which 'reasonable, honest and fair minded' people would adopt.[70] Once again, since the implication of this sort of term depends on the presumed intention of the parties,

---

[62] Beatson, Burrows, and Cartwright, *Anson's Law of Contract*, pp 153–4 (n 28); *A-G of Belize v Belize Telecom Ltd* [2009] UKPC 10, [2009] 1 WLR 1988 (Belize), para 21 (Lord Hoffmann); *Mediterranean Salvage & Towage v Seamar Trading & Commerce Inc (The Reborn)* [2009] EWCA Civ 531, [2009] 1 CLC 909, para 8 (Lord Clarke MR); *Talbot v General Federation of Trade Unions* [2011] EWHC 84 (QB) para 41 (Griffith Williams J). It has, however, been argued that when applying terms in this way the courts do more than just give expression to the actual but unexpressed intentions of the parties in question; rather, they may be attempting to approximate the terms the parties would have agreed if they had considered the matter: JM Paterson, 'Terms Implied in Fact: the Basis for Implication' (1998) 13 JCL 103; see also A Kramer, 'Implication in Fact as an Instance of Contractual Interpretation' [2004] CLJ 384; E Macdonald, 'Casting Aside "Officious Bystanders" and "Business Efficacy"'(2009–10) 26 JCL 97; PS Davies, 'Recent Developments in the Law of Implied Terms' [2010] LMCLQ 140.

[63] Peel, *Treitel*, para 6-034 (n 19); *Luxor (Eastbourne) Ltd v Cooper* [1941] AC 108 (HL); *Shell UK Ltd v Lostock Garage Ltd* [1976] 1 WLR 1187 (CA); *Nutting v Baldwin* [1995] 1 WLR 201 (Ch D).

[64] Peel, *Treitel*, para 6-033 (n 19); Beatson, Burrows, and Cartwright, *Anson's Law of Contract*, p 153 (n 28); *Duke of Westminster v Guild* [1985] QB 688 (CA) 700 (Slade LJ); *Johnstone v Bloomsbury HA* [1992] QB 333 (CA) 347 (Browne-Wilkinson VC) and 350 (Leggatt LJ); *Interactive Investor Trading Ltd v City Index Ltd* [2011] EWCA Civ 837, para 34 (Greer LJ).

[65] Beatson, Burrows, and Cartwright, *Anson's Law of Contract*, pp 157–9 (n 28); Furmston, Fifoot, and Simpson, *Cheshire, Fifoot and Furmston's Law of Contract*, pp 177–80 (n 28); Peel, *Treitel*, paras 6-046–6-048 (n 19).

[66] *The Lizzie* [1919] P 22 (CA) 34 (Swinfen Eady MR); *Cunliffe-Owen v Teather & Greenwood* [1967] 1 WLR 1421 (Ch D) 1438 (Ungoed-Thomas J).

[67] *Strathlorne SS Co Ltd v Hugh Baird & Sons Ltd* 1916 SC (HL) 134, 136 (Lord Buckmaster); *Three Rivers Trading Co v Gwinear and District Farmers* (1967) 111 SJ 831 (CA); *Grace v Leslie & Godwin Financial Services Ltd* [1995] CLC 801 (QBD: Commercial Ct) 808 (Clarke J); *Techarungreungkit v Alexander GTZ* [2003] EWHC 58 (QB) para 67 (Nelson J).

[68] Beatson, Burrows, and Cartwright, *Anson's Law of Contract*, p 158 (n 28); *Cunliffe-Owen v Teather & Greenwood* [1967] 1 WLR 1421 (Ch D); *Shearson Lehman Hutton Inc v Maclaine Watson & Co Ltd* [1989] 2 Lloyd's Rep 570 (QBD: Commercial Ct).

[69] *Hutton v Warren* (1836) 1 M & W 466, 150 ER 517; *Produce Brokers Co Ltd v Olympia Oil and Cake Co Ltd* [1916] 1 AC 314 (HL) 330–1 (Lord Sumner).

[70] *Produce Brokers Co Ltd v Olympia Oil and Cake Co Ltd* [1916] 2 KB 296 (KBD) 298 (Horridge J).

a term cannot be implied on this basis where it is contrary to the express terms of the contract.[71]

(2) Failure to perform

3.15 Given that contracts are made with a view to performance rather than breach, breach of contract is essentially negative in character; the party concerned has failed to perform the relevant obligation in one way or another. This in turn depends on a number of factors.

(a) Time of performance

3.16 The first of these is the time of performance.[72] Where a contract specifies a particular day for performance, failure to do so without lawful excuse is a breach for which damages can be obtained, irrespective of whether time is of the essence or not.[73] Where no time is specified, performance must take place within a reasonable time;[74] what amounts to a reasonable time is generally a question of fact,[75] depending on the nature of the contract, its terms, the relevant subject matter, the practice of the trade, and the general circumstances of the case.[76] It has been said that the consideration of whether there has been a breach of an obligation to perform within a reasonable time is not limited to what the parties contemplated or ought to have foreseen at the time of the contract;[77] rather, it involves a broad consideration—with the benefit of hindsight, and viewed from the time at which one party contends that a reasonable time for performance has been exceeded—of what would, in all the circumstances which are by then known to have happened, have been a reasonable time for performance.[78] In this respect, more latitude may

---

[71] *Les Affréteurs Réunis Société Anonyme v Walford* [1919] AC 801 (HL) 809 (Lord Birkenhead LC).

[72] Stannard, *Delay in the Performance of Contractual Obligations*, ch 1 (n 7).

[73] *Raineri v Miles* [1981] AC 1050 (HL); Stannard, *Delay in the Performance of Contractual Obligations*, paras 1.04–1.09 (n 7). Deciding whether the injured party can *terminate* for the breach is, of course, a different matter: see Ch 5, paras 5.38–5.52.

[74] Stannard, *Delay in the Performance of Contractual Obligations*, paras 1.11–1.34 (n 7); *Moel Tryvan Ship Co Ltd v Andrew Weir & Co* [1910] 1 KB 844 (CA) 857 (Kennedy LJ); *Jones v Gibbons* (1853) 8 Exch 920, 155 ER 1626; *Hick v Raymond and Reid* [1893] AC 22 (HL); *Re Lockie and Craggs & Son* (1902) 86 LT 388 (KBD); *Sims v Midland Rly* [1913] 1 KB 103 (KBD); *Johnson v Humphrey* [1946] 1 All ER 460 (Ch D); *Charnock v Liverpool Corp* [1968] 1 WLR 1498 (CA); *Astea (UK) Ltd v Time Group Ltd* [2003] EWHC 725 (TCC); *Fortis Bank SA/NV v Indian Overseas Bank* [2010] EWHC 84 (Comm), [2010] 1 CLC 16, para 75 (Hamblen J); Sale of Goods Act 1979, ss 29(3) and 37; Supply of Goods and Services Act 1982, s 14(1).

[75] *Nelson v Patrick* (1846) 2 Car & Kir 641, 175 ER 269; *Braithwaite v Crawshay* (1850) 16 LTOS 81; *Wigginton v Dodd* (1862) 2 F & F 844, 175 ER 1313; *Nosotti v Auerbach* (1899) 15 TLR 140 (CA); *Lafarge Redland Aggregates Ltd v Shepherd Hill Civil Engineering Ltd* (2000) 2 TCLR 642 (HL) 652 (Lord Hope).

[76] Adapted from *Pearl Mill Co Ltd v Ivy Tannery Ltd* [1919] 1 KB 78 (KBD) 83 (McCardie J); Stannard, *Delay in the Performance of Contractual Obligations*, para 1.15 (n 7).

[77] *Peregrine Systems Ltd v Steria Ltd* [2005] EWCA Civ 239 para 15 (Maurice Kay LJ).

[78] *Peregrine Systems v Steria*, para 15 (n 77); *Astea (UK) Ltd v Time Group Ltd* [2003] EWHC 725 (TCC) para 144 (Richard Seymour QC).

be allowed to a party who is obliged to perform within a reasonable time than to one who has to perform on a specified day;[79] in particular, delay may be excused in such cases where it is caused by events beyond the control of the promisor.[80]

(b) Place of performance

Determining the place of performance can be important not only for the purpose **3.17** of deciding whether a breach has taken place, but for other purposes too. Thus, for instance, where a contract is made involving different EU Member States the question may arise as to whether a particular court has jurisdiction to deal with the case; here the normal rule under the Brussels Convention is that a person domiciled in a Member State should be sued in the courts of that state,[81] but there is an exception allowing actions to be brought in the place where the relevant obligation is to be performed.[82] In the same way, a contract will only be frustrated by supervening illegality where performance of the relevant obligation is forbidden by the law of the place where the obligation is to be performed,[83] and the place of performance may be relevant also in the tax context[84] and in criminal cases involving cross-border fraud.[85] Normally the place of performance will be spelt out in the contract, but some cases can give rise to difficulties of interpretation. For instance, in *Scottish & Newcastle International Ltd v Othon Ghalanos Ltd*[86] a contract for the sale and carriage of goods from England to Cyprus provided that the seller should send the goods to the buyer and pay the freight, but the buyer had designated the carrier to be used.[87] The contract was expressed to be 'delivery CFR Limassol', and the relevant invoices also referred to Limassol as the place of delivery.[88] In a dispute about jurisdiction, the question arose as to where the contract was to be performed. Under section 32(1) of the Sale of Goods Act 1979 delivery to a carrier is *prima facie* presumed to be equivalent to delivery to the buyer, but the buyers

---

[79] *Hick v Raymond and Reid* [1893] AC 22 (HL); *SHV Gas Supply & Trading SAS v Naftomar Shipping & Trading Co Ltd Inc (The Azur Gaz)* [2005] EWHC 2528 (Comm), [2006] 1 Lloyd's Rep 163.

[80] *Hick v Raymond and Reid* (n 79).

[81] See Regulation 44/2001, art 2.1.

[82] Regulation 44/2001, art 5.1(a); *Color Drack GmbH v Lexx Intl Vertriebs GmbH* (C-386/05), [2010] 1 WLR 1909; *Claxton Engineering Services Ltd v TXM Olaj-es Gazkutato Kft* [2010] EWHC 2567 (Comm), [2011] 1 Lloyd's Rep 252. Which obligation is 'relevant' for this purpose will depend on the plaintiff's cause of action in the case; *Medway Packaging Ltd v Meurer Maschinen GmbH & Co KG* [1990] 2 Lloyd's Rep 112 (CA).

[83] *Toprak Mahsulleri Ofisi v Finagrain Compagnie Commerciale Agricole et Financière SA* [1979] 2 Lloyd's Rep 98 (CA); *Congimex Companhia Geral de Comercia Importadora e Exportadora Sarl v Tradax Export SA* [1981] 2 Lloyd's Rep 687 (QBD: Commercial Court).

[84] *Pintsch Bamag v Director of Income Tax (Intl Taxation)* (2009) ITL Rep 261 (authority for Advance Rulings) (India).

[85] *Treacy v DPP* [1971] AC 357 (HL); see now the Criminal Justice Act 1993, Pt 1.

[86] [2008] UKHL 11, [2008] 1 CLC 186.

[87] *Scottish & Newcastle Intl v Othon Ghalanos*, para 13 (n 86).

[88] *Scottish & Newcastle Intl v Othon Ghalanos*, para 27 (n 86).

argued that this was essentially a cif contract and that section 32(1) did not apply.[89] However, it was held by the House of Lords that this was to all intents and purposes indistinguishable from an fob contract, and that the use of the words 'delivery cost and freight Limassol' were not sufficient to turn it into an ex-ship contract.[90] Under section 32(1) the sellers were therefore deemed to have effected delivery by shipping the goods at Liverpool, and this was sufficient to give jurisdiction to the English courts. In the same way, the English courts were held to have jurisdiction over a consultancy contract between an Italian company and an Italian business-man domiciled in Italy, on the ground that a significant part of his work was to be done in London.[91] In the few cases where there is no express stipulation as to where the contract is to be performed, the matter will depend on the implied intention of the parties, to be judged from the nature of the contract and the surrounding circumstances.[92] Thus, for instance, in the absence of any agreement to the contrary a buyer of goods is bound to collect them from the seller;[93] the seller is not bound to send them to the buyer unless the contract provides otherwise.[94] Again, in a contract involving the payment of money it is the duty of the debtor to seek out the creditor rather than that of the creditor to seek out the debtor,[95] and similar rules may apply for other types of contract too.[96]

(c) Standard of performance

3.18 It has been said that performance must be 'precise and exact'.[97] This raises three questions, the first relating to the content of the obligation, the second relating to the standard of care required for its performance, and the third to the consequences that follow if it is not performed.

3.19 **(i) Content of obligation** A party to a contract must perform the relevant obligation exactly as it stands, no more and no less. Thus an obligation to ship goods 'from the East to New York direct' is not performed by sending them to Seattle and then on to New York by rail;[98] an obligation to deliver tins of fruit packed

---

[89] *Scottish & Newcastle Intl v Othon Ghalanos*, para 32 (n 86).

[90] *Scottish & Newcastle Intl v Othon Ghalanos*, para 7 (Lord Bingham), para 14 (Lord Rodger), and para 33 (Lord Mance) (n 86).

[91] *WPP Holdings Italy Srl v Benatti* [2007] EWCA Civ 263, [2007] 1 WLR 2316.

[92] Burrows et al, *Chitty on Contracts*, para 21-005 (n 21); *Reynolds v Coleman* (1887) 36 Ch D 453.

[93] Sale of Goods Act 1979, s 29(2).

[94] As in *Viskase Ltd v Paul Kiefel GmbH* [1999] 1 WLR 1305 (CA).

[95] Burrows et al, *Chitty on Contracts*, para 21-055 (n 21); Peel, *Treitel*, para 17-002 (n 19); *Walton v Mascall* (1844) 13 M & W 452 (Exch Ch), 153 ER 88; *Staton v National Coal Board* [1957] 1 WLR 893 (QBD) 895 (Finnemore J); *Carne v Debono* [1988] 1 WLR 1107 (CA); *Agrafax Public Relations Ltd v United Scottish Society Inc* [1995] CLC 862 (CA) 866; *Masri v Consolidated Contractors Intl (UK) Ltd* [2005] EWHC 944 (Comm), [2005] 1 CLC 1125, para 82 (Cresswell J).

[96] Thus, it has been said that where performance requires the concurrence of the promisee, it is the duty of the promisor to seek out the promisee and perform the promise wherever the promisee may happen to be; Burrows et al, *Chitty on Contracts*, para 21-005 (n 21); *Rippinghall v Lloyd* (1833) 5 B & Ad 742, 110 ER 534.

[97] Beatson, Burrows, and Cartwright, *Anson's Law of Contract*, p 441 (n 28).

[98] *Re Sutro & Co and Heilbut, Symons & Co* [1917] 2 KB 348 (CA).

in boxes of thirty is not performed by delivering the same quantity with some of it packed in smaller boxes;[99] an obligation to complete a sale of land by 5.00 pm on a certain day is not observed by tendering the necessary documents at 5.10 pm on that day.[100] It matters not whether the divergence is of any commercial significance to the promisee. Though the so-called 'doctrine of substantial performance' may affect the *remedies* of the injured party where the failure to perform is of minor significance, it does not alter the fact that such failure amounts to a breach.[101] Whilst the courts have occasionally applied a *de minimis* principle in this context by suggesting that the contract is *not broken at all* by trivial divergences from what was agreed,[102] these cases are better seen as depending on the original content of the obligation in question;[103] it is not so much a matter of saying that substantial performance of an obligation is sufficient as a general rule, as that in some cases substantial performance is all that the promisor agrees to do in the first place.[104] As Anson says, the question is to be approached in two stages; first the court must construe the contract to see what the parties meant by performance, and then they must apply the ascertained facts to that construction, to see whether that which has been done corresponds to that which was promised.[105]

(ii) Standard of care   In some cases contractual liability is strict, in the sense that a party is not excused by events beyond his or her control. Thus, unless the contract provides otherwise, it is no defence for a charterer who fails to load a proper cargo to claim that cuts in production made it impossible to obtain the contracted amount,[106] and where a seller contracts to deliver goods of a certain kind, inability to obtain the goods will not excuse failure to make delivery.[107] Again, an agent   **3.20**

---

[99]   *Re Moore & Co Ltd and Landauer & Co* [1921] 2 KB 519 (CA).

[100]   *Union Eagle Ltd v Golden Achievement Ltd* [1997] AC 514 (JCPC–Hong Kong).

[101]   See further Ch 6, para 6.21. Of course, where that doctrine applies, the remedies available for the breach may not be worth pursuing.

[102]   *Bowes v Chaleyer* (1923) 32 CLR 159 (High Court of Australia); *Luna Park (NSW) Ltd v Tramways Advertising Pty Ltd* (1938) 61 CLR 286 (High Court of Australia); Carter, *Carter's Breach of Contract*, para 2-04 (n 2).

[103]   Carter, *Carter's Breach of Contract*, para 2-04 (n 2).

[104]   cf *Reardon Smith Line Ltd v Yngvar Hansen-Tangen (The Diana Prosperity)* [1976] 1 WLR 989 (HL), where the words 'Osaka 434' in a charterparty were held to be no more than a means of identifying the ship; they were not part of the contractual description so as to enable the charterers to reject the ship when it transpired that the ship had been built in Oshima and not Osaka at all; see at 998–9 (Lord Wilberforce) and 1002 (Lord Russell).

[105]   Beatson, Burrows, and Cartwright, *Anson's Law of Contract*, p 441 (n 28).

[106]   Peel, *Treitel*, para 17-064 (n 19); *Postlethwaite v Freeland* (1880) 5 App Cas 599 (HL); *Ardan Steamship Co Ltd v Andrew Weir & Co* [1905] AC 501 (HL); *Steel Corp v Sardoil SpA (The Zuiho Maru)* [1977] 2 Lloyd's Rep 552 (QBD: Commercial Ct).

[107]   Peel, *Treitel*, para 17-064 (n 19); *Barnett v Javeri & Co* [1916] 2 KB 390 (QBD); *Intertradex SA v Lesieur Torteaux SARL* [1978] 2 Lloyd's Rep 509 (CA). It will be different if the contract is for specific goods: *Howell v Coupland* (1875–76) LR 1 QBD 258 (CA). In the same way, lack of fault is no excuse for breach of the implied terms as to quality in the Sale of Goods Act: *Frost v Aylesbury Dairy Co Ltd* [1905] 1 KB 608 (CA); *Grant v Australian Knitting Mills Ltd* [1936] AC 85 (JCPC–Australia); *Daniels and Daniels v White & Sons Ltd and Tarbard* [1938] 4 All ER 2598 (KBD).

may be liable for breach of warranty of authority even where he or she has acted in good faith and with all due care.[108] However, in other cases it is sufficient for the promisor to show reasonable care. Thus, where the contract is for the supply of a service, the promisor will generally only be liable on proof of negligence,[109] and the same applies in other contexts too.[110] In some cases it will not be possible to determine the appropriate standard of care either by the construction of the contract or by reference to previous authority; here the presumption appears to be that liability will be strict,[111] though the precise position is not entirely clear.[112]

3.21 **(iii) Remedies** The rule that performance must be precise and exact applies only to the question whether a breach has occurred in the first place; it says nothing about the remedies available for the breach, which may vary considerably depending on whether the breach was a major or a minor one. Thus the so-called doctrine of 'substantial performance' may prevent a party refusing to pay the contract price on the basis of minor defects in performance by the other side; though there is certainly a breach in such cases, the only remedy allowed is an appropriate deduction from the price.[113] Again, a party will not be allowed to terminate performance for a breach unless either the term in question is a condition of the contract or the breach is one with serious consequences;[114] in other cases the only remedy allowed will be damages. The practical effect of these rules is to deprive the requirement of 'precise and exact' performance of much of its force, for where the breach is a trivial one and the only remedy is damages, such damages will not generally be worth suing for.

(d) Order of performance

3.22 At the present day, problems with regard to the order of performance tend to arise in the following context: a party to a contract (A) refuses to perform; the other party (B) sues A for breach; A then claims that he or she was entitled to refuse performance because of failures in performance on the part of B. The question then comes down to

---

[108] *Knight Frank LLP v Aston du Haney* [2011] EWCA Civ 404, para 3 (Tomlinson LJ); PG Watts, *Bowstead and Reynolds on Agency* (19th edn, Sweet & Maxwell, 2010) Art 105.

[109] *Clark v Kirby-Smith* [1964] Ch 506 (Ch D); *Midland Bank Trust Co Ltd v Hett, Stubbs & Kemp* [1979] Ch 384 (Ch D); *Thake v Maurice* [1986] QB 644 (CA); *Henderson v Merrett Syndicates Ltd* [1995] 2 AC 145 (HL); *Killick v Pricewaterhouse Coopers (No 1)* [2001] PNLR 1 (Ch D); *Nicholson v Knox Ukiwa & Co (a firm)* [2008] EWHC 1222 (QB), [2008] PNLR 33; *Priory Caring Services Ltd v Capita Property Services Ltd* [2010] EWCA Civ 226, 129 Con LR 81; Supply of Goods and Services Act 1982, s 13.

[110] Carter, *Carter's Breach of Contract*, para 2-47 (n 2). Thus, under the Hague Rules in a contract for the carriage of goods by sea the obligation of the carrier to supply a seaworthy ship is not absolute but amounts only to the use of 'reasonable diligence': Carriage of Goods by Sea Act 1971, s 3; Hague Rules, Arts III and IV.

[111] *Raineri v Miles* [1981] AC 1050 (HL) 1086 (Lord Edmund-Davies).

[112] According to Carter, such a presumption would seem to conflict with other presumptions, in particular the rule that a party claiming a breach of contract must prove it: Carter, *Carter's Breach of Contract*, para 2-29 (n 2).

[113] *Dakin & Co v Lee* [1916] 1 KB 566 (CA); *Hoenig v Isaacs* [1952] 2 All ER 176 (CA); See Ch 6, para 6.21.

[114] See Part III.

this: is B entitled to claim performance from A without performing the relevant obligation on his or her own part, or to put it another way, does A have to extend credit to B with regard to the order of performance? Up to the reforms made in the middle of the nineteenth century by the Common Law Procedure Act of 1852, the question arose in the context of the pleadings in the action, the issue being whether one party could sue the other for breach without 'averring' his or her own performance in some relevant particular.[115] In *Kingston v Preston*[116] Lord Mansfield posited three possibilities in this context; promises or covenants might be dependent, independent, or concurrent. In the case of a dependent promise, performance of the relevant obligation is not due until after performance of a corresponding obligation on the part of the other party; thus, for instance, in a contract of employment wages are not generally due until after the employee has worked for a certain period,[117] and in a contract of carriage of goods by sea no freight is recoverable until the goods have been delivered to the agreed destination.[118] In the case of an independent promise, performance is due irrespective of whether the other party has performed the relevant obligation or not; thus, for instance, a landlord cannot refuse to repair the property on the ground that the tenant is in arrears with the rent,[119] and where a contract for the sale of goods provides for payment of the price on a certain day irrespective of delivery, the seller can demand the price even if the buyer makes it clear that he or she does not want the goods and will not accept them.[120] In the case of concurrent promises, neither party can claim performance from the other party without showing a readiness and willingness to perform on his or her own part, the classic example of this being a contract for the sale of goods where in the absence of any contrary stipulation delivery of the goods and payment of the price are concurrent conditions, so that the buyer cannot demand the goods without being ready and willing to pay the price, and the seller cannot demand the price without being ready and willing to deliver the goods.[121]

In some cases the order of performance is made clear by the contract.[122] In other cases it will be obvious from the circumstances that a particular obligation will **3.23**

---

[115] See Ch 2, para 2.04.

[116] (1773) Lofft 194, cited in *Jones v Barkley* (1781) 2 Dougl 684, 690, 99 ER 434, 437; *Tito v Waddell (No 2)* [1977] Ch 106 (Ch D) 290 (Megarry V-C).

[117] Beatson, Burrows, and Cartwright, *Anson's Law of Contract*, p 445 (n 28); *Morton v Lamb* (1797) 7 TR 125, 101 ER 890; *Cresswell v IRC* [1984] ICR 508 (Ch D); *Miles v Wakefield Metropolitan District Council* [1987] AC 539 (HL).

[118] *Vlierboom v Chapman* (1844) 13 M & W 230, 153 ER 96; *The Kathleen* (1874) LR 4 A & E 269 (High Court of Admiralty); *St Enoch Shipping Co Ltd v Phosphate Mining Co Ltd* [1916] 2 KB 624 (KBD).

[119] Peel, *Treitel*, para 17-019 (n 19); *Taylor v Webb* [1937] 2 KB 283 (KBD) 290 (du Parcq J) (revd on a different ground); *Lee-Parker v Izzet* [1971] 1 WLR 1688 (Ch D) 1693 (Goff J).

[120] Sale of Goods Act 1979, s 49(1); *Dunlop v Grote* (1845) 2 Car & K 153, 175 ER 64; *Ministry of Sound (Ireland) Ltd v World Online Ltd* [2003] EWHC 2178 (Ch) para 52 (N Strauss QC).

[121] Sale of Goods Act 1979, s 28; Peel, *Treitel*, para 17-018 (n 19).

[122] As in the case of conveyances and building contracts, which frequently provide detailed timetables for performance by either side: see Standard Conditions of Sale (4th edn) clause 4.3.1; JCT Agreement for Minor Building Works, clause 4:4.

have to be performed before another one becomes due; thus, for instance, a charterer is not obliged to load the ship until the owner has given notice of readiness to
load,[123] and a shipowner is not bound to sail to a nominated port until the nomination has been given.[124] Again, in some cases the order of performance is determined
by the class of contract, as in a contract of employment where the employee is not
generally entitled to wages until he or she has worked for a certain period.[125] In
cases where simultaneous performance is possible the presumption is in favour
of concurrence, so that neither party is entitled to demand performance without
being ready and willing to perform his or her own obligations.[126] This saves one
party from having to give credit to the other, whilst at the same time giving a degree
of security to both parties to prevent disappointment of their legitimate expectations under the contract.[127]

(e) Tender of performance

3.24 Where performance requires the cooperation of the other party, then a tender of
performance must be made to the other party.[128] Such tender must take place at
a reasonable hour of the day, when the other party can be expected to accept it.[129]
If the tender is in accordance with the contract, then the other party is obliged to
accept it; failure to do so will excuse performance of the obligation in question,[130]
and may amount to a repudiation of the contract as a whole.[131] The other party is
entitled to reject a tender which is not in accordance with the contract, but such
a tender will not necessarily amount to a breach, as there may still be time for a

---

[123] *Scandinavian Trading Co A/B v Zodiac Petroleum SA (The Al Hofuf)* [1981] 1 Lloyd's Rep 81;
Tradax Export SA v Italgrani di Francesco Ambrosio [1986] 1 Lloyd's Rep 112 (CA); *Warde v Feedex
Intl* [1985] 2 Lloyd's Rep 290.

[124] *Rae v Hackett* (1844) 12 M & W 724, 152 ER 1390.

[125] See Ch 4, para 4.08.

[126] *Morton v Lamb* (1797) 7 TR 125, 101 ER 890; *Stavers v Curling* (1838) 3 Bing NC 355;
Dimech v Corlett (1858) 12 Moo PC 199, 14 ER 887; *Seeger v Duthie* (1860) 8 CB(NS) 45, 141 ER
1081; *Simpson v Crippin* (1872) LR 8 QB 14; Peel, *Treitel*, para 17-021 (n 19).

[127] American Law Institute Restatement Second, Contracts, paras 231 and 234 and commentary.

[128] Furmston, Fifoot, and Simpson, *Cheshire, Fifoot and Furmston's Law of Contract*, pp 696–8
(n 28); *Startup v Macdonald* (1846) 6 M & G 593, 134 ER 1029.

[129] *Startup v Macdonald* (n 128); Stannard, *Delay in the Performance of Contractual Obligations*,
paras 4.08–4.10 (n 7).

[130] There is one exception to this rule. Where a creditor refuses to accept a tender of the debt due,
the debtor is not excused altogether from the obligation to pay the debt, but the debtor may pay the
sum into court if sued, and this will be a defence to the claim: Burrows et al, *Chitty on Contracts*,
para 21-084 (n 21); *Dixon v Clark* (1848) 5 CB 365, 377, 136 ER 919, 923 (Wilde CJ); *Graham v
Seal* (1918) 88 LJ Ch 31 (CA); *Canmer Intl Inc v UK Mutual SS Assurance Association (Bermuda) Ltd
(The Rays)* [2005] EWHC 1694 (Comm), [2005] 2 Lloyd's Rep 479, para 53 (Gloster J).

[131] Beatson, Burrows, and Cartwright, *Anson's Law of Contract*, p 450 (n 28). Thus, in a contract
for the sale of goods by instalments, the rejection of one instalment by the buyer will excuse the
seller from having to deliver *that instalment*, but whether it entitles the seller to *terminate the contract
altogether* depends on the terms of the contract and the circumstances of the case: Sale of Goods
Act 1979, s 31(2).

proper tender to be made.[132] However, even where this is the case a bad tender will amount to a breach if the circumstances indicate that the party making it is unable or unwilling to perform the contract according to its terms.[133]

(3) No lawful excuse

A failure to perform cannot amount to a breach if the party concerned has a lawful excuse for such failure. There is a wide range of excuses that may be relied on in this connection, and there is not the space to discuss them exhaustively in the present context,[134] but broadly speaking they can be broken down into four categories: (1) excuses and exemptions in the contract itself; (2) excuses based on the consent of the promisee; (3) excuses based on the conduct of the promisee; (4) and excuses based on supervening events. **3.25**

(a) Excuses and exemptions in the contract

In *Suisse Atlantique Société d'Armement Maritime SA v NV Rotterdamsche Kolen Centrale*[135] Lord Wilberforce pointed out that an act which, apart from an exceptions clause, might be a breach sufficiently serious as to justify refusal of further performance might be reduced in effect, or indeed not made a breach at all, by the terms of the clause in question.[136] A party who is sued for breach of contract will very often seek to rely on exemption clauses of one kind or another. The law relating to exemption clauses is a vast topic in itself,[137] but can be broadly summarized in three propositions; a person seeking to rely on such a clause must demonstrate that it has been incorporated into the contract, that as a matter of construction it covers the events or conduct concerned, and that it does not fall foul of statutory controls. **3.26**

(i) **Incorporation** There are four ways in which an exemption clause may be incorporated into a contract.[138] The first is by signature; if the contract has been signed by the relevant party[139] or by a person entitled to sign on his or her behalf,[140] **3.27**

---

[132] *Borrowman, Phillips & Co v Free and Hollis* (1878) 4 QBD 500 (CA); *Libau Wood Co v H Smith and Sons* (1930) 37 Ll LR 296 (KBD); A Apps, 'The right to cure defective performance' [1994] LMCLQ 525.

[133] *Decro-Wall Intl SA v Practitioners in Marketing Ltd* [1971] 1 WLR 361 (CA).

[134] For a fuller account, see Stannard, *Delay in the Performance of Contractual Obligations*, ch 5 (n 7).

[135] [1967] 1 AC 361 (HL).

[136] *Suisse Atlantique v NV Rotterdamsche Kolen Centrale*, 431 (n 135).

[137] See E Macdonald, *Exemption Clauses and Unfair Terms* (2nd edn, Tottel, 2006).

[138] Macdonald, *Exemption Clauses and Unfair Terms*, ch 1 (n 137); Burrows et al, *Chitty on Contracts*, paras 12.008–12.018 (n 21); Beatson, Burrows, and Cartwright, *Anson's Law of Contract*, pp 173–7 (n 28); Peel, *Treitel*, paras 7-004–7-013 (n 19).

[139] *Howatson v Webb* [1908] 1 Ch 1 (CA); *L'Estrange v Graucob* [1934] 1 KB 394 (CA); *Toll (FCGT) Pty Ltd v Alphapharm Pty Ltd* [2004] HCA 52; E Peden and JW Carter, 'Incorporation of Terms by Signature: L'Estrange Rules!' (2005) 21 JCL 96.

[140] *Bahamas Oil Refining Co v Kristiansands Tankrederie A/S (The Polyduke)* [1978] 1 Lloyd's Rep 211 (QBD) 215 (Kerr J).

then the party will be bound, unless there has been some misrepresentation as to the effect of the relevant clause,[141] or unless the document in question is not one which could reasonably be expected to have contractual effect.[142] The second is by notice; a party will be bound by an exclusion clause of which he or she has reasonable notice. What is reasonable is ultimately a question of fact,[143] but notice will not be reasonable if given after the contract was concluded,[144] or on a document which could not reasonably have been expected to have contractual effect,[145] or in an inadequate manner given the unusual or onerous nature of the clause.[146] The third is by course of dealing; here the party in question may not have been given proper notice of the clause at the time of the contract in question, but can reasonably have been expected to be aware of it on the basis of past dealings with the other party.[147] The fourth is where the clause is incorporated by reference to custom or trade usage,[148] or by statutory provision, as in the case of contracts for the carriage of goods by road or by sea.[149] The principles of incorporation are more fully discussed in specialist works on the subject.[150]

3.28 (ii) **Construction** The courts have a long history of strict construction of exemption clauses *contra proferentem*, that is to say against the party seeking to rely on them.[151] Thus it has been held that particularly clear words are required

---

[141] *Curtis v Chemical Cleaning and Dyeing Co Ltd* [1951] 1 KB 805 (CA); *Jaques v Lloyd D George and Partners Ltd* [1968] 1 WLR 625 (CA); *Horry v Tate and Lyle Refineries* [1982] 2 Lloyd's Rep 416 (QBD).

[142] *The Luna* [1920] P 20 (PDA), 28 (Hill J); *Bahamas Oil Refining Co v Kristiansands Tankrederie A/S (The Polyduke)* [1978] 1 Lloyd's Rep 211 (QBD) 215 (Kerr J).

[143] *Parker v South Eastern Rly* (1877) 2 CPD 416 (CA); *Richardson, Spence & Co v Rowntree* [1894] AC 217 (HL); *Hood v Anchor Line (Henderson Bros) Ltd* [1918] AC 837 (HL (Sc)).

[144] *Olley v Marlborough Court Ltd* [1949] 1 KB 532 (CA); *Hollingworth v Southern Ferries Ltd (The Eagle)* [1977] 2 Lloyd's Rep 70 (QBD); *Daly v General Steam Navigation Co Ltd (The Dragon)* [1979] 1 Lloyd's Rep 257 (QBD).

[145] *Chapelton v Barry UDC* [1940] 1 KB 532 (CA); *Taylor v Glasgow Corp* 1952 SC 440 (Court of Session); *Burnett v Westminster Bank* [1966] 1 QB 742 (QBD).

[146] *Thornton v Shoe Lane Parking Ltd* [1971] 2 QB 163 (CA); *Interfoto Picture Library v Stiletto Visual Programmes Ltd* [1989] 1 QB 433 (CA).

[147] *Hardwick Game Farm v Suffolk Agricultural and Poultry Producers Association* [1969] 2 AC 31 (HL); *Lamport & Holt Lines Ltd v Coubro & Scrutton (M & I) Ltd* [1981] 2 Lloyd's Rep 659 (CA); *Circle Freight Intl Ltd v Medeast Gulf Exports Ltd* [1988] 2 Lloyd's Rep 427 (CA); J Swanton, 'Incorporation of Contractual Terms by a Course of Dealing' (1988–89) 1 JCL 223.

[148] *British Crane Hire Corp Ltd v Ipswich Plant Hire Ltd* [1975] QB 303 (CA); *Smith v South Wales Switchgear Ltd* [1978] 1 WLR 165 (HL); *Victoria Fur Traders v Roadline UK Ltd* [1981] 1 Lloyd's Rep 571 (QBD: Commercial Ct); Peel, *Treitel*, para 7-013 (n 19).

[149] As with the Hague Rules, Art IV, incorporated into domestic law by the Carriage of Goods by Sea Act 1971, s 1. See also Carriage by Air Act 1961, s 4 (Warsaw Convention, Art 22); Carriage of Goods by Road Act 1965, s 1 (CMR Convention).

[150] See in particular Macdonald, *Exemption Clauses and Unfair Terms*, ch 1 (n 137); R Lawson, *Exclusion Clauses and Unfair Terms* (10th edn, Sweet & Maxwell, 2011) ch 1.

[151] Macdonald, *Exemption Clauses and Unfair Terms*, ch 2 (n 137); Lawson, *Exclusion Clauses and Unfair Terms*, ch 2 (n 150); Burrows et al, *Chitty on Contracts*, paras 14-005–14-019 (n 21). According to Peel, *Treitel*, para 7-015 (n 19) this principle covers not one but two rules of construction, the first applicable to exemption clauses in particular and the second applicable to contracts generally.

to exclude liability for negligence,[152] or to justify conduct that would seem to be contrary to the main purpose of the contract.[153] Given that much of the mischief caused by unfair exclusion clauses is now taken care of by statutory provisions,[154] it has been said that there is no longer any need for the courts to strain the rules of construction in ways thought appropriate in the past,[155] and it has also been asked whether the traditional approach is consistent with the broader canons of construction operated by the courts since *Investors Compensation Ltd v West Bromwich Building Society*.[156] However, it has been argued that the strict construction principle still has an important part to play in this area of the law;[157] though it has been said to be an aid to construction of last resort,[158] the principle continues to be cited and applied in the courts to the present day.[159]

(iii) Statutory controls Last but by no means least, exemption clauses **3.29** may be subject to statutory controls of one kind or another, most notably the Unfair Contract Terms Act 1977 and the Unfair Terms in Consumer Contracts Regulations 1999.[160] The effect of these provisions is to make certain types of

---

[152] *Canada Steamship Lines Ltd v R* [1952] AC 192 (JCPC–Canada); *Walters v Whessoe Ltd* (1968) 6 BLR 23 (CA); *Mediterranean Freight Services Ltd v BP Oil Intl Ltd (The Fiona)* [1994] 2 Lloyd's Rep 506 (CA); *HIH Casualty and General Insurance Ltd v Chase Manhattan Bank* [2003] UKHL 6, [2003] 2 Lloyd's Rep 61.

[153] *Glynn v Margetson & Co* [1893] AC 351 (HL); *Owners of the Cap Palos v Alder (The Cap Palos)* [1921] P 458 (CA); *Sze Hai Tong Bank v Rambler Cycle Co Ltd* [1959] AC 576 (JCPC–Singapore); *Suisse Atlantique Société d'Armement Maritime SA v NV Rotterdamsche Kolen Centrale* [1967] 1 AC 361 (HL); *MB Pyramid Sound NV v Briese Schiffahrt GmbH (The Ines)* [1995] 2 Lloyd's Rep 144 (QBD: Commercial Ct); *A Turtle Offshore SA v Superior Trading Inc (The A Turtle)* [2008] EWHC 3034 (Admiralty), [2009] 1 Lloyd's Rep 177.

[154] See para 3.35.

[155] *Ailsa Craig Fishing Co Ltd v Malvern Fishing Co Ltd* [1983] 1 WLR 964 (HL) 966 (Lord Wilberforce); *George Mitchell (Chesterhall) Ltd v Finney Lock Seeds Ltd* [1983] 2 AC 803 (HL) 810 (Lord Diplock).

[156] [1998] 1 WLR 896 (HL); see para 3.08; Peel, *Treitel*, para 7-015 (n 19); Macdonald, *Exemption Clauses and Unfair Terms*, pp 67–8 (n 137).

[157] Macdonald, *Exemption Clauses and Unfair Terms*, pp 68–9 (n 137).

[158] Peel, *Treitel*, para 7-015 (n 19); *Lakeport Navigation Co Panama SA v Anonima Petroli Italiana SpA (The Olympic Brilliance)* [1982] 2 Lloyd's Rep 205 (CA), 208 (Eveleigh LJ); *Macy v Qazi* [1987] CLY 425 (CA); *Thew v Cole* [2003] EWCA Civ 1828, [2004] RTR 25, para 17 (Tuckey LJ); *Lexi Holdings plc v Stainforth* [2006] EWCA Civ 988, (2006) 150 SJLB 984, para 20 (Carnwath LJ).

[159] See for instance *Frans Maas (UK) Ltd v Samsung Electronics (UK) Ltd* [2004] EWHC 1502 (Comm), [2005] 1 CLC 647, 694 (Gross J); *Whitecap Leisure Ltd v John H Rundle Ltd* [2008] EWCA Civ 429, [2008] CP Rep 31, para 22 (Moore-Bick LJ); *Kingsway Hall Hotel Ltd v Red Sky IT (Hounslow) Ltd* [2010] EWHC 265 (TCC), (2010) 26 Const LJ 542, para 252 (Judge Toulmin QC); *Dunavant Enterprises Inc v Olympia Spinning and Weaving Mills Ltd* [2011] EWHC 2028 (Comm) para 10 (Burton J).

[160] Burrows et al, *Chitty on Contracts*, paras 14-059–14-133 (n 21); Beatson, Burrows, and Cartwright, *Anson's Law of Contract*, pp 192–216 (n 28); Furmston, Fifoot, and Simpson, *Cheshire, Fifoot and Furmston's Law of Contract*, pp 231–57 (n 28); Peel, *Treitel*, paras 7-048–7.115 (n 19). Proposals have been made to rationalize the law in this area by replacing the 1977 Act and the 1999 Regulations with a single code: see the Draft Bill in the Law Commission and Scottish Law Commission Report, *Unfair Terms in Contracts. Report on a reference under section 3(1)(e) of the Law Commissions Act 1965* (Law Com No 292, 2005); P Nebbia, 'Reforming the UK Law on Unfair Terms: the Draft Unfair Contract Terms Bill' (2007) 3 JCL 228.

exemption clause ineffective, and to subject others to a test of reasonableness. No attempt will be made in the present context to analyse these and other legislative controls; details of these can be found in the specialist works on the subject.[161]

(b) Consent by promisee

3.30   In many cases the promisor may be excused from his or her obligation by the consent of the promisee. Such consent can take effect in four ways: (1) as a discharge of the contract by agreement; (2) as a variation; (3) as a waiver; and (4) under the doctrine of promissory estoppel.

3.31   (i) **Discharge by agreement**   The effect of a discharge by agreement, or 'rescission' as it is sometimes called, is that the contract is abandoned entirely.[162] Needless to say, this will not happen very often, as the effect is to prevent the contract being revived in the future;[163] all the parties can do is to make a new contract relating to the same subject matter.[164] Discharge by agreement can be express or implied. It is express where the parties agree in so many words to release each other from their outstanding obligations under the contract;[165] it is implied when it is reasonable to assume from the conduct of the parties that this was their intention,[166] or where one party has given the other party reasonable grounds to suppose that this was the case.[167] Mere inactivity will not normally be enough, as this may simply indicate that the parties have forgotten about the contract rather than that they intend to abandon it.[168] As well as this, the discharge of a contract by agreement requires proof of 'accord and satisfaction', that is to say some consideration on either side.[169] This will not be hard to demonstrate where each party has obligations outstanding under the contract—here the agreement to abandon is said to

---

[161] See Lawson, *Exclusion Clauses and Unfair Contract Terms* (n 150); Macdonald, *Exemption Clauses and Unfair Terms* (n 137).

[162] Burrows et al, *Chitty on Contracts*, paras 22-025–22-031 (n 21); Peel, *Treitel*, paras 3-057–3-061 (n 19); Beatson, Burrows, and Cartwright, *Anson's Law of Contract*, pp 462–4 (n 28).

[163] *R v Inhabitants of Gresham* (1786) 1 TR 101, 99 ER 996.

[164] As in *Morris v Baron & Co* [1918] AC 1 (HL).

[165] *Davis v Street* (1823) 1 C & P 18, 171 ER 1084; *Foster v Dawber* (1851) 6 Exch 839, 155 ER 785; *Morris v Baron & Co* [1918] AC 1 (HL); *Rose & Frank Co v JR Crompton & Bros Ltd* [1925] AC 445; Burrows et al, *Chitty on Contracts*, para 22.025 (n 21).

[166] *André et Compagnie SA v Marine Transocean Ltd (The Splendid Sun)* [1981] QB 694 (CA); *Paal Wilson & Co A/S v Partenreederei Hannah Blumenthal (The Hannah Blumenthal)* [1983] 1 AC 854 (HL); M Furmston, T Norisada, and J Poole, *Contact Formation and Letters of Intent* (John Wiley & Sons, 1998) pp 39–45.

[167] *Pearl Mill Co Ltd v Ivy Tannery Ltd* [1919] 1 KB 78 (KBD); *Fisher v Eastwoods Ltd* [1936] 1 All ER 421 (KBD).

[168] *Tracomin SA v Anton C Nielsen A/S* [1984] 2 Lloyd's Rep 195 (QBD); *Allied Marine Transport Ltd v Vale do Rio Doce Navegacio SA (The Leonidas D)* [1985] 2 Lloyd's Rep 18 (CA); *Compagnie Francaise D'Importation et de Distribution SA v Deutsche Continental Handelsgesellschaft* [1985] 2 Lloyd's Rep 592 (QBD); *Food Corp of India v Antclizo Shipping Corp (The Antclizo)* [1988] 1 WLR 603 (QBD).

[169] Burrows et al, *Chitty on Contracts*, para 22-012 (n 21); *British Russian Gazette and Trade Outlook Ltd v Associated Newspapers Ltd* [1933] 2 KB 616 (CA).

'generate its own consideration'[170] —but where it is fully executed on one side, some fresh consideration must be supplied by the other party.[171]

(ii) Variation Discharge by agreement involves the total abandonment of the   **3.32**
contract; variation involves a change in its terms. In some cases the contract itself
may provide for this possibility,[172] but it is equally possible for the parties to agree
to a variation after the contract has been made.[173] Once again, however, some
consideration must be shown for the variation to be enforceable; where the variation is capable of benefiting either party, the agreement generates its own consideration,[174] but otherwise some fresh consideration must be provided by the party
who benefits for the variation to be effective.[175]

(iii) Waiver The consent of the promisee in this context may also take effect as   **3.33**
a waiver. Waiver in the law of contract takes a number of forms,[176] but the most
relevant one in the present context is what is sometimes called 'waiver by forbearance'.[177] Waiver by forbearance takes place where the promisee agrees to accept a
substituted performance, such as a late delivery of goods or payment in a different
manner from that specified by the contract. Where this is done at the request of
the promisee, the law will clearly give binding effect to the agreement,[178] but the
position is less certain when it is done at the request of the promisor. As a general
rule, such promises are not binding without separate consideration,[179] but even in

---

[170] Peel, *Treitel*, para 3-057 (n 19).

[171] Burrows et al, *Chitty on Contracts*, para 3-079 (n 21).

[172] As where a building contract provides for variations to be made by the architect, or where
a creditor is allowed to vary the rate of interest payable by the debtor; Stannard, *Delay in the
Performance of Contractual Obligations*, paras 5.64–5.66 (n 7).

[173] Stannard, *Delay in the Performance of Contractual Obligations*, para 5.67 (n 7).

[174] *Alan (WJ) & Co v El Nasr Export and Import Co* [1972] 2 QB 189 (CA). The courts will generally be ready to find consideration if the variation is in practical terms beneficial to both parties and
not extracted by undue pressure: *Williams v Roffey Bros & Nicholls (Contractors) Ltd* [1991] 1 QB 1
(CA); *Adam Opel GmbH v Mitras Automotive (UK) Ltd* [2008] EWHC 3205 (QBD), [2008] CILL
2561. However, part payment of a debt can never constitute good consideration for a promise to
forgo the whole: *Foakes v Beer* (1883–84) LR 9 App Cas 605 (HL); *Re Selectmove Ltd* [1995] 1 WLR
474 (CA).

[175] *Pinnel's Case* (1602) 5 Co Rep 117a, 77 ER 237; *Stilk v Myrick* (1802) Camp 317, 170 ER
1168; *Foakes v Beer* (n 174); *Vanbergen v St Edmunds Properties Ltd* [1933] 2 KB 233 (CA); *Glencore
Grain Ltd v Flacker Shipping Ltd (The Happy Day)* [2002] EWCA Civ 1068, [2002] 2 Lloyd's Rep
487, para 61 (Potter LJ).

[176] *Ross T Smyth & Co Ltd v TD Bailey, Son & Co* (1940) 164 LT 102, 106 (Lord Wright);
The Happy Day, paras 64–68 (Potter LJ) (n 175); T Dugdale and D Yates, 'Variation, Waiver and
Estoppel: a Reappraisal' (1976) 39 MLR 680, 681–2; FMB Reynolds, 'The Notions of Waiver'
[1990] LMCLQ 453; JW Carter, 'Waiver (of Contractual Rights) Distributed' (1990–91) 4 JCL 59.
For waiver in the sense of election between inconsistent remedies, see Ch 4, paras 4.55–4.58.

[177] Peel, *Treitel*, para 3-069 (n 19); *Motor Oil Hellas (Corinth) Refineries SA v Shipping Corp of
India (The Kanchenjunga)* [1990] 1 Lloyd's Rep 391 (HL) 397 (Lord Goff). Another term is 'unilateral waiver': see *Banning v Wright* [1972] 1 WLR 972 (HL) 979 (Lord Hailsham LC); *Glencore
Grain Ltd v Flacker Shipping Ltd (The Happy Day)* [2002] EWCA Civ 1068, [2002] 2 Lloyd's Rep
487, para 64 (Potter LJ).

[178] *Levey & Co v Goldberg* [1922] 1 KB 688 (KBD).

[179] See para 3.32.

the absence of consideration the law will not allow the promisee to resile from the agreement without at least giving the promisor the chance to put matters right. This is well illustrated by *Panoutsos v Raymond Hadley Corporation of New York*,[180] where a contract for the sale of flour by instalments specified that payment should be made by confirmed banker's credit. The buyers opened an unconfirmed credit, on the basis of which a number of shipments were made by the sellers. It was held that the sellers could not summarily terminate the contract on the ground of the non-conforming credit without giving the buyers a reasonable opportunity of complying with the condition in question. Thus waiver by forbearance has the advantage over variation that it does not require proof of consideration, but the disadvantage is that it is generally only suspensory in its effect; the other party can always be required on reasonable notice to comply with the original mode of performance, unless the other party has put him or herself into a position where this is no longer possible.[181]

3.34 **(iv) Equitable estoppel** Consent can also be effective to excuse a failure to perform under the doctrine of equitable estoppel,[182] or 'promissory estoppel' as it is often called.[183] In the words of Lord Goff:[184]

> Equitable estoppel occurs where a person, having legal rights against another, unequivocally represents (by words or conduct) that he does not intend to enforce those legal rights; if in such circumstances the other party acts, or desists from acting, in reliance upon that representation, with the effect that it would be inequitable for the representor to enforce his legal rights inconsistently with his representation, he will to that extent be precluded from doing so.

There are four elements to this:[185] (1) a party who has legal rights against another;[186] (2) an unequivocal representation that he or she does not intend to enforce those

---

[180] [1917] 2 KB 473 (CA); *Hartley v Hymans* [1920] 3 KB 475 (KBD); *Besseler Waechter Glover & Co v South Derwent Coal Co* [1938] 1 KB 408 (KBD); *Tankexpress A/S v Compagnie Financière Belge des Petroles SA (The Petrofina)* [1949] AC 76 (HL); *Plastimoda Societa per Azioni v Davidson's (Manchester) Ltd* [1952] 1 Lloyd's Rep 527 (CA); *Enrico Furst & Co v WE Fischer* [1960] 2 Lloyd's Rep 340 (QBD); *MSAS Global Logistics Ltd v Power Packaging Ltd* [2003] EWHC 1393 (Ch), The Times, 25 June 2003.

[181] Peel, *Treitel*, para 3-074 (n 19); Burrows et al, *Chitty on Contracts*, para 22-042 (n 21); *Leather Cloth Co v Hieronimus* (1874–75) LR 10 QB 140; *Toepfer v Warinco AG* [1978] 2 Lloyd's Rep 569 (QBD: Commercial Ct); *Bottiglieri di Navigazione SpA v Cosco Qingdao Ocean Shipping Co (The Bunga Saga Lima)* [2005] EWHC 244, [2005] 2 Lloyd's Rep 1, para 31 (Gloster J).

[182] Beatson, Burrows, and Cartwright, *Anson's Law of Contract*, pp 468–70 (n 28); Furmston, Fifoot, and Simpson, *Cheshire, Fifoot and Furmston's Law of Contract*, pp 129–39 (n 28); Peel, *Treitel*, paras 3-076–3-099 (n 19); *Hughes v Metropolitan Rly* (1877) 2 App Cas 439 (HL); *Central London Property Trust v High Trees House Ltd* [1947] KB 130 (KBD) 134 (Denning J).

[183] See Furmston, Fifoot, and Simpson, *Cheshire, Fifoot and Furmston's Law of Contract*, p 132 (n 28) and the cases cited there.

[184] *Motor Oil Hellas (Corinth) Refineries SA v Shipping Corp of India (The Kanchenjunga)* [1990] 1 Lloyd's Rep 391 (HL) 399.

[185] Burrows et al, *Chitty on Contracts*, para 3-086 (n 21).

[186] Burrows et al, *Chitty on Contracts*, paras 3-087–3-088 (n 21). Though these will normally arise out of a pre-existing contractual relationship, the doctrine can apply to other kinds of legal relationship, as in *Durham Fancy Goods Ltd v Michael Jackson (Fancy Goods) Ltd* [1968] 2 QB 839 (QBD); *Maharaj v Jai Chand* [1986] AC 898 (JCPC–Fiji).

legal rights;[187] (3) the other party acts in reliance on that representation;[188] and (4) a situation where it would be inequitable for the first party to enforce his or her legal rights inconsistently with that representation.[189] Where this can be shown, the party making the representation will not be allowed to enforce those legal rights without at least giving the other party a chance to resume his or her position.[190] The effect of equitable estoppel in the present context is more or less the same as that of waiver by forbearance, and it has been argued that the latter doctrine is no more than an application of the former.[191] However, the two doctrines grew up independently, and also have different emphases; where the key element in waiver is *the conduct of the party making the representation*, the key element in equitable estoppel is *reliance by the party to whom that representation is made.*[192]

(c) Conduct of promisee

Another way in which performance may be excused is by the conduct of the prom- **3.35**
isee. This can take a number of forms.

---

[187] Such a representation may be implied from conduct, as in *Hughes v Metropolitan Rly* (1877) 2 App Cas 439 (HL), but the facts must point to a promise or representation of some kind: *Mardorf Peach & Co Ltd v Attica Sea Carriers Corp of Liberia (The Laconia)* [1977] AC 850 (HL); *Scandinavian Trading Tanker Co AB v Flota Petrolera Ecuatoriana (The Scaptrade)* [1981] 2 Lloyd's Rep 425 (QBD: Commercial Ct) 431 (Lloyd J). Any such representation must be clear and unequivocal in its effect: *Woodhouse AC Israel Cocoa Ltd SA v Nigerian Produce Marketing Co Ltd* [1972] AC 741 (HL); *Société Italo-Belge pour le Commerce et l'Industrie v Palm and Vegetable Oils (Malaysia) Sdn Bhd (The Post Chaser)* [1981] 2 Lloyd's Rep 695 (QBD: Commercial Ct); *HIH Casualty & General Insurance Ltd v Chase Manhattan Bank* [2001] 1 Lloyd's Rep 30 (QBD: Commercial Ct).

[188] *Hughes v Metropolitan Rly* (1877) 2 App Cas 439 (HL); *Hartley v Hymans* [1920] 3 KB 475 (KBD); *Avimex SA v Dewulf & Cie* [1979] 2 Lloyd's Rep 57 (QBD: Commercial Ct) 67–8 (Robert Goff J); *Cook Industries Inc Meunerie Liegieois SA* [1981] 1 Lloyd's Rep 359 (QBD: Commercial Ct) 368 (Mustill J); *Scandinavian Trading Tanker Co AB v Flota Petrolera Ecuatoriana (The Scaptrade)* [1981] 2 Lloyd's Rep 425 (QBD: Commercial Ct) 430–1 (Lloyd J); *Transcatalana de Commercio SA v Incobrasa Industrial e Commercial Braziliera SA* [1995] 1 Lloyd's Rep 215 (QBD: Commercial Ct) 219 (Mance J); *Collier v P & MJ Wright (Holdings) Ltd* [2007] EWCA Civ 1329, [2008] 1 WLR 643 (CA); *Carey Group plc v AIB Group (UK) plc* [2011] EWHC 594 (Ch) para 21 (Briggs J). It is sometimes said that such reliance has to be 'detrimental', but whether this is an additional requirement is a moot point: see Burrows et al, *Chitty on Contracts*, para 3-094 (n 21); *Collier v Wright (Holdings) Ltd* (earlier in this note) paras 32–40 (Arden LJ).

[189] *Williams v Stern* (1879) 5 QBD 409 (CA); *D & C Builders v Rees* [1966] 2 QB 167 (CA); *Société Italo-Belge pour le Commerce et l'Industrie v Palm and Vegetable Oils (Malaysia) Sdn Bhd (The Post Chaser)* [1981] 2 Lloyd's Rep 695 (QBD–Com Ct) 701–2 (Robert Goff J); *Southwark LBC v Logan* (1997) 29 HLR 40 (CA); *Emery v UCB Corporate Services Ltd* [2001] EWCA Civ 275 (CA) para 27 (Peter Gibson LJ); *Scinto v London Borough of Newham* [2009] EWCA Civ 837.

[190] *Central London Property Trust v High Trees House Ltd* [1947] KB 130 (KBD); *Tool Metal Manufacturing Co Ltd v Tungsten Electric Co Ltd* [1955] 1 WLR 561 (HL); *Ajayi v RT Briscoe (Nigeria) Ltd* [1964] 1 WLR 1326 (JCPC–Nigeria); *Collier v P & MJ Wright (Holdings) Ltd* [2007] EWCA Civ 1329, [2008] 1 WLR 643 (CA) para 37 (Arden LJ).

[191] Peel, *Treitel*, para 3-091 (n 19); *Prosper Homes v Hambro's Bank Executor & Trustee Co* (1979) 39 P & CR 395 (Ch D) 401 (Browne-Wilkinson J).

[192] *Glencore Grain Ltd v Flacker Shipping Ltd (The Happy Day)* [2002] EWCA Civ 1068, [2002] Lloyd's Rep 487, para 64 (Potter LJ).

3.36 **(i) Prevention by promisee** A promisor who is physically prevented by the promisee from performing will clearly not be liable for breach of contract.[193] Thus where a person covenants to build a house on another's land, and the other prevents him from coming on to the land to do the work, there is no duty to perform;[194] a builder does not have to pay liquidated damages for delay to the employer when the delays in question have themselves been caused by the employer;[195] and a shipowner is not liable for delay in loading where the ship has been prevented by the charterer's breach from getting to the point where notice of readiness to load could be given.[196] One obvious case of prevention is where a proper tender of performance is rejected by the other party.[197] Here the party whose tender has been refused will not be liable for breach; on the contrary, a promisee who prevents performance from taking place in this way will not only have broken the contract,[198] but may even be held to have wrongfully repudiated it.[199]

3.37 **(ii) Breach by promisee** In some cases a breach by the promisee may excuse the promisor from having to perform. For this to take place there must be either a breach of condition[200] or some other fundamental breach of the contract;[201] where this has taken place, the promisor may by 'accepting' the breach be discharged from his primary obligations under the contract.[202] Another possibility is that the breach may amount to a failure to perform a condition precedent, that is to say an obligation which has to be performed before the relevant obligation of the promisor itself becomes due for performance.[203] Here the effect of the breach is to excuse the promisor from performance unless or until the promisee has at least substantially performed the precedent obligation in question.[204]

3.38 **(iii) Other non-performance by promisee** A failure to perform by the promisee may provide an excuse for non-performance by the promisor even where the failure in question does not amount to a breach, as in *Cutter v Powell*,[205] where

---

[193] In the words of Tindal CJ, the promisor may say 'This is your own act, and therefore you are not damnified': *West v Blakeway* (1841) 2 M & G 729, 751, 133 ER 940, 949.

[194] 1 Roll Abr 453, Com Dig Condition N pl 6.

[195] *Holme v Guppy* (1838) 3 M & W 387, 150 ER 1195; *Thornhill v Neats* (1860) 8 CB (NS) 831, 141 ER 1392; *Courtnay v Waterford Rly* (1878) 4 LR Ir 11; *Peak Construction (Liverpool) Ltd v McKinney Foundations Ltd* (1970) 1 BLR 111 (CA); *Shawton Engineering Ltd v DGP Intl Ltd* [2005] EWCA Civ 1359, [2006] BLR 1.

[196] *Glencore Grain Ltd v Goldbeam Shipping Ltd (The Mass Glory)* [2002] EWHC 27 (Comm), [2002] 2 Lloyd's Rep 244; *Ocean Marine Navigation Ltd v Koch Carbon Inc (The Dynamic)* [2003] EWHC 1936 (Comm), [2003] 2 Lloyd's Rep 693.

[197] *Jones v Barkley* (1781) 2 Dougl 694, 99 ER 434.

[198] See para 3.30.

[199] See para 3.30.

[200] *Bunge Corp (New York) v Tradax Export SA* [1981] 1 WLR 711 (HL); see Ch 5, para 5.01.

[201] *Hongkong Fir Shipping Co v Kawasaki Kisen Kaisha Ltd (The Hongkong Fir)* [1962] 2 QB 26 (CA); see Ch 5, para 5.02.

[202] *Moschi v Lep Air Services Ltd* [1973] AC 331 (HL); see Ch 9, para 9.02.

[203] See para 3.28.

[204] *Sumpter v Hedges* [1898] 1 QB 673 (CA); *Hoenig v Isaacs* [1952] 1 TLR 1360 (CA); *Bolton v Mahadeva* [1972] 1 WLR 1009 (CA); see Ch 6, para 6.21.

[205] (1795) 6 TR 320, 101 ER 373.

the death of the plaintiff's husband prevented him from completing the work due under the contract and hence excused the defendant from the obligation to pay wages to his widow. The point here was that the completion of the work was a condition precedent to the right to claim wages, and this condition had not been fulfilled.[206] Indeed, such a condition need not be an obligation at all, as in the case of a unilateral contract or option that may only be exercised according to its terms; here the promisor need not perform unless the conditions for the exercise of the option have been duly fulfilled.[207]

(iv) Repudiation by promisee   Where the promisee repudiates the contract by **3.39** indicating that he or she does not intend to perform when the time comes, the promisor may 'accept' the repudiation and thereby be discharged from his or her own primary obligations under the contract.[208] Indeed, the promisee's repudiation may be a good excuse even before it is accepted.[209] Thus, for instance, a seller of goods cannot normally claim damages for non-acceptance without first tendering delivery of the goods, but where the buyer repudiates the contract by indicating that any such tender will be rejected, the seller may elect either to accept the repudiation and sue for damages at once, or to affirm and then sue for damages when the time for performance by the buyer has passed; in neither case is there any need for the seller to waste time and effort on making a pointless tender.[210] In the words of Dixon CJ, a claimant may be dispensed from performing a condition by the defendant expressly or impliedly intimating that it is useless for him to perform it and requesting him not to do it.[211] The extent to which one party may rely on a repudiation by the other in the absence of acceptance is considered further later.[212]

(d) Supervening events

Supervening events may also provide an excuse for non-performance. This can **3.40** work in at least two ways. The first is where the contract is frustrated; the test for this is whether the events in question render the performance 'radically different' from that which was undertaken by the contract,[213] so that it would be unjust to

---

[206] (1795) 6 TR 320, 325, 101 ER 573, 576 (Ashhurst J).

[207] *Hare v Nicoll* [1966] 2 QB 130 (CA); *United Dominions Trust (Commercial) Ltd v Eagle Aircraft Services Ltd* [1968] 1 WLR 74 (CA).

[208] *Golding v London and Edinburgh Insurance Co Ltd* (1932) 43 Ll L Rep 487 (CA) 488 (Scrutton LJ); *Heyman v Darwins Ltd* [1942] AC 356 (HL) 361 (Viscount Simon LC); see para 7.37.

[209] Carter, *Carter's Breach of Contract*, paras 7-58–7-66 (n 2).

[210] *Sinason-Teicher Inter-American Grain Corp v Oilcakes and Oilseeds Trading Co Ltd* [1954] 1 WLR 935 (QBD) 944 (Devlin J) see Ch 7, para 7.37; G Marston, 'Contractual Rights and Duties after an Unaccepted Repudiation' [1988] CLJ 340.

[211] *Peter Turnbull & Co Pty Ltd v Mundus Trading Co (Australasia) Pty Ltd* (1954) 90 CLR 235 (High Ct–Australia) 246–7; Carter, *Carter's Breach of Contract*, para 7-62 (n 2).

[212] See Ch 4, paras 4.32–4.36.

[213] Beatson, Burrows, and Cartwright, *Anson's Law of Contract*, pp 487–8 (n 28); *Davis Contractors Ltd v Fareham UDC* [1956] AC 656 (HL) 729 (Lord Radcliffe); *Tsakiroglou & Co Ltd v Noblee Thorl GmbH* [1962] AC 93 (HL) 131 (Lord Guest); *Paal Wilson & Co A/S v Partenreederei*

hold them to the literal sense of its stipulations.[214] The second is where an obligation becomes impossible to perform in circumstances falling short of frustration, as in the case of an employee who fails to turn up to work because he or she is sick.[215] There may also be a third class of case where the events in question, whilst not being grave enough to frustrate the contract as a whole, give the party affected the option of termination.[216] The details of these cases are discussed more fully later; suffice it to say at this stage that in none of them will the promisor's failure to perform the relevant obligation amount to a breach.

C. The Consequences of Breach

3.41   Where a breach of contract has occurred, there are various remedies that may be available to the injured party.[217] He or she will in all cases be entitled as of right[218] to an award of damages,[219] though if the breach has caused no loss these will only be nominal.[220] The injured party may sometimes also be entitled to specific relief, including a decree of specific performance and an action for the contract price.[221] There may also be restitutionary remedies of various sorts,[222] to say nothing of particular remedies stipulated by the contract in question. However, none of these need concern us here. Of more significance in the present context is the right of the injured party in such cases to refuse to perform his or her own contractual obligations, and this will now be dealt with in the chapters which follow.

Hannah Blumenthal (The Hannah Blumenthal) [1983] 1 AC 854 (HL) 909 (Lord Brandon) and 918 (Lord Diplock); *William Sindall plc v Cambridgeshire County Council* [1994] 1 WLR 1016 (CA) 1039 (Evans LJ); *Edwinton Commercial Corp v Tsavliris Russ (Worldwide Salvage & Towage) Ltd (The Sea Angel)* [2007] EWCA Civ 547, [2007] 1 CLC 876, para 84.

[214] Beatson, Burrows, and Cartwright, *Anson's Law of Contract*, pp 487–8 (n 28); *National Carriers Ltd v Panalpina (Northern) Ltd* [1981] AC 675 (HL) 700 (Lord Simon); *Great Peace Shipping Ltd v Tsavrilis Salvage Intl Ltd (The Great Peace)* [2002] EWCA Civ 1407, [2003] 2 CLC 16, para 70; *Edwinton Commercial Corp v Tsavliris Russ (Worldwide Salvage & Towage) Ltd (The Sea Angel)* [2007] EWCA Civ 547, [2007] 1 CLC 876, para 84.

[215] *Jackson v Union Marine Insurance Co Ltd* (1874–75) LR 10 CP 125 (Exchequer Chamber) 145 (Bramwell B); *Poussard v Spiers & Pond* (1876) 1 QBD 410 (DC) 414 (Blackburn J); GH Treitel, *Frustration and Force Majeure* (Sweet & Maxwell, 1994) para 5-058.

[216] Treitel, *Frustration and Force Majeure*, para 5-060 (n 215); *Poussard v Spiers & Pond* (n 215).

[217] DR Harris, DC Campbell, and R Halson, *Remedies in Contract and Tort* (2nd edn, Butterworths, 2002); AS Burrows, *Remedies for Torts and Breach of Contract*, (3rd edn, OUP, 2004).

[218] Beatson, Burrows, and Cartwright, *Anson's Law of Contract*, p 534 (n 28); Peel, *Treitel*, para 20-002 (n 19). But this does not apply to an unaccepted anticipatory breach: see Ch 7, para 7.37.

[219] Beatson, Burrows, and Cartwright, *Anson's Law of Contract*, ch 17 (n 28); Furmston, Fifoot, and Simpson, *Cheshire, Fifoot and Furmston's Law of Contract*, pp 746–96 (n 28); Peel, *Treitel*, ch 20 (n 19).

[220] Peel, *Treitel*, para 20-002 (n 19).

[221] Beatson, Burrows, and Cartwright, *Anson's Law of Contract*, ch 18 (n 28); Furmston, Fifoot, and Simpson, *Cheshire, Fifoot and Furmston's Law of Contract*, pp 796–805 (n 28); Peel, *Treitel*, ch 21 (n 19).

[222] Beatson, Burrows, and Cartwright, *Anson's Law of Contract*, ch 19 (n 28); Peel, *Treitel*, ch 22 (n 19).

4

THE PROCESS OF TERMINATION

Having looked at the notion of breach, we may now turn to the process of termin- **4.01**
ation. This chapter considers what termination is, how it should be described, and
what it involves; there is also consideration of how the right to terminate may be
limited, and how termination differs from other related concepts.

A. What is Termination?

From the discussion in the first chapter, it has been seen that the concept of ter- **4.02**
mination is not easy to define, not least because of the inconsistent terminology
used by the courts and by commentators, and also because of the overlap existing
between termination itself and other concepts that are akin to it.[1] We can begin by

---

[1] See further paras 4.06–4.12.

saying that termination is one way in which, in the words of Diplock LJ, a party to a contract is relieved of his undertaking to do that which he has agreed to do but has not yet done.[2] If we follow Anson and others by referring to this process as 'discharge',[3] it follows that termination is a sub-species of discharge, alongside discharge by agreement and discharge by frustration.[4] There are three key factors distinguishing termination from other types of discharge, the first being that it requires proof of a serious breach by the party in default,[5] the second being that it normally occurs only at the option of the innocent party,[6] and the third that it leaves the party in default liable in damages. To adopt the terminology used by Lord Diplock, both parties are freed from their *primary* obligations under the contract, but in the case of the party in default this is replaced by a *secondary* obligation to pay compensation to the innocent party.[7]

B. Terminology

4.03 The process under discussion has been labelled in various different ways, including 'repudiation',[8] 'treating the contract as repudiated',[9] 'rescission',[10] and 'termination'.[11] However, the word 'repudiation' nowadays suggests a *wrongful* refusal to perform,[12] and is therefore best not used where the innocent party is fully entitled to do so. 'Treating the contract as repudiated' has a respectable pedigree both in

---

[2] *Hongkong Fir Shipping Co Ltd v Kawasaki Kisen Kaisha Ltd (The Hongkong Fir)* [1962] 2 QB 26, 65 (CA).

[3] See J Beatson, AS Burrows, and J Cartwright, *Anson's Law of Contract* (29th edn, OUP, 2010), Part 4; AS Burrows et al (eds), *Chitty on Contracts* (31st edn, Sweet & Maxwell, 2012), Part 7.

[4] Older editions of *Cheshire, Fifoot and Furmston* (see n 15) also referred to 'discharge by performance' in this context, but most of the material discussed under that heading concerned the effects not of performance by the promisor but of *non*-performance by the promisee.

[5] For the forms which this can take, see Part III.

[6] See further para 4.13.

[7] *Moschi v Lep Air Services* [1973] AC 331, 350 (HL).

[8] *Behn v Burness* (1863) 3 B & S 751, 755, 122 ER 281, 283 (Williams J); *Andrew Millar & Co v Taylor & Co Ltd* [1916] 1 KB 402 (CA) 415 (Swinfen Eady LJ); *Behzadi v Shaftesbury Hotels Ltd* [1992] Ch 1 (CA) 32 (Purchas LJ).

[9] Sale of Goods Act 1979, s 11(3); *Wallis, Son and Wells v Pratt & Haynes* [1910] 2 KB 1003 (CA) 1012 (Fletcher Moulton LJ, dissenting). The decision of the Court of Appeal was reversed, and the judgment of Fletcher Moulton LJ affirmed, by the House of Lords at [1911] AC 394 (HL). See also *Suisse Atlantique Société d'Armement Maritime SA v NV Rotterdamsche Kolen Centrale* [1967] 1 AC 361 (HL) 394 (Viscount Dilhorne); *Lombard North Central plc v Butterworth* [1987] QB 527 (CA) 545 (Nicholls LJ).

[10] *Stickney v Keeble* [1915] AC 386 (HL) 401 (Lord Atkinson); *Heyman v Darwins* [1942] AC 356 (HL) 361 (Viscount Simon LC); *Moschi v Lep Air Services* [1973] AC 331 (HL) 349 (Lord Diplock). This terminology can be seen in older editions of Treitel and Peel, *The Law of Contract*, but has now been abandoned: E Peel, *Treitel: The Law of Contract* (13th edn, Sweet & Maxwell, 2011) para 18.001.

[11] *Schuler AG v Wickman Machine Tool Sales Ltd* [1974] AC 235 (HL) 251 (Lord Reid); *Federal Commerce & Navigation Co Ltd v Molena Alpha Inc* [1979] AC 757 (HL) 783 (Lord Fraser); *Union Eagle Ltd v Golden Achievement Ltd* [1997] AC 514 (JCPC–Hong Kong) 520 (Lord Hoffmann).

[12] See Ch 1, para 1.12.

statute and in case law, but the label presupposes that the consequences are the same whether the breach consists of a repudiation in the narrow sense or some other kind of serious breach that discharges the innocent party from the obligation to perform, which may not necessarily be the case.[13] The term 'rescission' has also been used in this context, but this is best reserved for the different process whereby the contract is annulled *ab initio* for misrepresentation, duress, or undue influence.[14] For these reasons the present work will follow other authors in using the word 'termination',[15] on the understanding that what is terminated is not the contract itself (whatever that may mean) but the primary obligations of the parties to that contract.[16]

C. Termination as a Process and a Remedy

The title of the present chapter reflects the traditional understanding of termin- **4.04** ation in English law as a process reflecting that of formation, the idea being that just as the latter *creates* obligations, the former *releases* one or both parties from those obligations.[17] This approach reflects the historical development of the subject, in which as we have seen it is not easy to disentangle termination for breach from other forms of contractual discharge.[18] However, while this is helpful in explaining the way termination has developed, it misses out on one important aspect of the subject, namely that termination is essentially something which the innocent party is entitled to *do*. Looked at in this way, termination can be seen as a remedy,[19] alongside other ways of proceeding more traditionally dealt with under that heading.[20] Indeed, it is one of the cheapest and most convenient remedies available;[21]

---

[13] See Ch 10, paras 10.07–10.17.

[14] *Johnson v Agnew* [1980] AC 367 (HL) 392–3 (Lord Wilberforce); N Andrews, M Clarke, A Tettenborn, and G Virgo, *Contractual Duties: Performance, Breach, Termination and Remedies* (Sweet & Maxwell, 2011), para 5-027; see para 4.07.

[15] Andrews et al, *Contractual Duties*, para 5-027 (n 14); Carter, *Carter's Breach of Contract* (Hart, 2012) para 3-24; MP Furmston, CHS Fifoot, and AWB Simpson, *Cheshire, Fifoot and Furmston's Law of Contract* (16th edn, OUP, 2012) pp 672–693; Peel, *Treitel*, ch 18 (n 10).

[16] *Photo Production Ltd v Securicor Transport Ltd* [1980] AC 827 (HL) 844 (Lord Wilberforce), and 850 (Lord Diplock).

[17] This is made explicit in *Cheshire, Fifoot and Furmston*, where the process of termination is construed in terms of an offer by the defaulting party to treat the contract as discharged followed by an acceptance of that offer; Furmston, Fifoot, and Simpson, *Cheshire, Fifoot and Furmston's Law of Contract*, p 680 (n 15). For further discussion of this analysis, see para 4.12.

[18] See Ch 2.

[19] HG Beale, *Remedies for Breach of Contract* (Sweet & Maxwell, 1980) chs 5 and 6; HG Beale, WD Bishop, and MP Furmston, *Contract: Cases and Materials* (5th edn, OUP, 2007) ch 21; E McKendrick, *Contract Law, Text, Cases and Materials* (5th edn, OUP, 2012) ch 22.

[20] Not all of the standard texts on remedies deal with termination: cf Beale, *Remedies for Breach of Contract* (n 19) and GH Treitel, *Remedies for Breach of Contract: a Comparative Account* (Clarendon Press, 1988) with A Burrows, *Remedies for Torts and Breach of Contract* (3rd edn, OUP, 2004), and DR Harris, DC Campbell, and R Halson, *Remedies in Contract and Tort* (2nd edn, CUP, 2002).

[21] Beale, *Remedies for Breach of Contract*, pp 66–7 (n 19); IR Macneil, *The Relational Theory of Contract* (Sweet & Maxwell, 2001) p 268.

instead of having to go to court, the innocent party can, broadly speaking, simply 'cancel the contract'.[22] Termination for breach of contract cannot be understood without keeping both of these aspects in mind.

D. Termination in Whole or in Part

4.05 Though termination is traditionally described as involving the termination of the contract as a whole,[23] it is perfectly possible for a contract to be terminated in part.[24] Obviously the contract may provide for this by an express term,[25] but partial termination may also be possible at common law.[26] Say, for instance, a seller of goods under an instalment contract fails to deliver one of the instalments. The buyer need no longer accept and pay for that instalment, but this does not necessarily mean that he or she can terminate the entire contract.[27] Again, it has been argued that in a building contract the architect can refuse to pay the builder for a particular piece of defective work without necessarily bringing the whole engagement to an end.[28] Indeed, even an ordinary case of termination is in a sense no more than partial;[29] as we shall see, the effect of termination is not to discharge the contract as a whole, but only such primary obligations of the parties as remain unperformed at the relevant time.[30]

E. Concepts Akin to Termination

4.06 Though termination is a mode of discharge, not all forms of contractual discharge involve termination. A party may rightfully be excused from performance in a number of other ways too, and it is important that these not be confused with termination.

(1) Termination and rescission *ab initio*

4.07 The process of termination is often referred to by judges and others as 'rescission'. There is no harm in this, provided that one keeps in mind that termination for breach of contract is very different in its effects from rescission for misrepresentation,

---

[22] So enabling him or her to get the relevant goods or services elsewhere; Beale, *Remedies for Breach of Contract*, pp 66–7 (n 19); H Collins, *The Law of Contract* (4th edn, CUP, 2008) pp 356–7.

[23] *Photo Production Ltd v Securicor Transport Ltd* [1980] AC 827 (HL) 849 (Lord Diplock).

[24] JW Carter, 'Partial Termination of Contracts' (2008) 24 JCL 1.

[25] Carter, 'Partial Termination of Contracts', pp 11–16 (n 24).

[26] Carter, 'Partial Termination of Contracts', pp 4–11 (n 24).

[27] Carter, 'Partial Termination of Contracts', p 6 (n 24); Sale of Goods Act 1979, s 31.

[28] Carter, 'Partial Termination of Contracts', pp 7–8 (n 24).

[29] Carter, 'Partial Termination of Contracts', pp 2–4 (n 24).

[30] See Ch 9, para 9.02.

duress, or undue influence. The distinction was aptly summarized in *Johnson v Agnew*,[31] a case involving the sale of land, by Lord Wilberforce in the following terms:[32]

> ... it is important to dissipate a fertile source of confusion and to make clear that though the vendor is sometimes referred to...as 'rescinding' the contract, this so-called 'rescission' is quite different from rescission ab initio, such as may arise for example in cases of mistake, fraud or lack of consent. In those cases, the contract is treated in law as never having come into existence...In the case of an accepted repudiatory breach the contract has come into existence but has been put an end to or discharged. Whatever contrary indications may be disinterred from old authorities, it is now quite clear, under the general law of contract, that acceptance of a repudiatory breach does not bring about 'rescission ab initio'.

Thus whereas rescission in its strict sense involves turning the clock back in the sense of *restitutio in integrum*, termination, as we shall see, operates to discharge the obligations of the parties in so far as they remain unperformed at the time of termination, but not otherwise.[33] Termination in this sense is an important remedy for breach of contract; rescission is not.[34]

(2) Termination and the withholding of performance

A party to a contract may be entitled to withhold his or her performance without **4.08** necessarily being entitled to terminate. Thus as a general rule an employer need not pay wages until the employee has worked for a certain period, but this does not mean that the employee has been dismissed. In the same way, if a seller tenders goods that are not in conformity with the contract, the buyer may reject them, but this does not necessarily mean that the buyer may terminate, as the seller may still be able to come up with a proper tender within the time stipulated by the contract.[35] However, if the seller is unable to do this, the buyer's right to withhold performance will become a right to terminate.[36] The same will be so if the defective

---

[31] [1980] AC 367 (HL).

[32] *Johnson v Agnew*, at 392–3 (n 31).

[33] See Ch 9, para 9.02.

[34] This has not always been appreciated, particularly in the conveyancing context: see M Albery, 'Mr Cyprian Williams' Great Heresy' (1975) 91 LQR 337; S Lurie, 'Towards a Unified Theory of Breach: Tracing the History of the Rule that Rescission ab Initio is not a Remedy for Breach of Contract' (2003) 19 JCL 250.

[35] *Borrowman, Phillips & Co v Free & Hollis* (1878) 4 QBD 500 (CA); *Motor Oil Hellas (Corinth) Refineries SA v Shipping Corp of India (The Kanchenjunga)* [1990] 1 Lloyd's Rep 391 (HL) 399 (Lord Goff); V Mak, 'The seller's right to cure defective performance—a reappraisal' [2007] LMCLQ 409; WCH Ervine, 'Cure and retender revisited' [2006] JBL 799.

[36] As Carter says, in a case of defective performance a breach occurs because the promisor has not provided the performance required at or within the time stipulated by the contract: Carter, *Carter's Breach of Contract*, para 2-12 (n 15); Lord Devlin, 'The Treatment of Breach of Contract' [1966] CLJ 192.

tender is such as to indicate that the seller has no intention of performing the contract according to its terms.[37]

(3) Termination and frustration

4.09   Frustration occurs, in the words of Lord Radcliffe, 'whenever the law recognises that without default of either party a contractual obligation has become incapable of being performed because the circumstances in which performance is called for would render it a thing radically different from that which was undertaken by the contract'.[38] The effect of frustration is to discharge both parties, the key difference being that unlike termination, frustration occurs automatically and does not depend on the choice of either party.[39] However, both doctrines to a certain extent share a common pedigree,[40] and in some cases the line between frustration and termination is a very fine one. For instance, in *Jackson v Union Marine Insurance Co Ltd*[41] a charterparty was held to be frustrated by a protracted period of delay resulting from the ship having gone aground. Since the grounding of the ship was an 'excepted peril' under the charterparty, neither party was to blame for the event, which made the case one of frustration. However, had it not been for the excepted perils clause the delay might very well have given the charterers the right to terminate on the grounds of fundamental breach.[42] Indeed, given that in cases of this sort the measure of delay needed to frustrate the contract is the same as that needed to amount to a fundamental breach giving rise to the right to terminate,[43] the same facts may often require consideration of both possibilities.

(4) Termination and excused non-performance

4.10   Even where the contract is not frustrated, a promisor may have a lawful excuse for failing or refusing to perform in circumstances not involving termination.[44] The classic illustration of this is the employee who fails to turn up to work because he or she is sick;[45] or is unable for some other reason to attend.[46] Again, such excuses may be provided in the contract itself, as in the case of a *force majeure* clause.[47] Where

---

[37] *PT Berlian Laju Tanker TBK v Nuse Shipping Ltd (The Aktor)* [2008] EWHC 1330 (Comm), [2008] 2 Lloyd's Rep 246, para 69 (Christopher Clarke J); Carter, *Carter's Breach of Contract*, para 2-12 (n 15).

[38] *Davis Contractors Ltd v Fareham UDC* [1956] AC 696 (HL) 729.

[39] *Hirji Mulji v Cheong Yue SS Co* [1926] AC 497 (JCPC–Hong Kong).

[40] See Ch 2.

[41] (1874–75) LR 10 CP 125 (Exchequer Chamber).

[42] As in *Hongkong Fir Shipping Co Ltd v Kawasaki Kisen Kaisha Ltd (The Hongkong Fir)* [1962] 2 QB 26 (CA); see Ch 6.

[43] *Universal Cargo Carriers Corp v Citati* [1957] 2 QB 401, 430–3 (Devlin J); *The Hongkong Fir* (n 42) 61 (Sellers LJ), 64 (Upjohn LJ), and 69 (Diplock LJ); see Ch 6, para 6.20.

[44] Peel, *Treitel*, paras 17-059–17-060 (n 10).

[45] *Poussard v Spiers & Pond* (1876) 1 QBD 410 (DC) 414 (Blackburn J); Peel, *Treitel*, para 17-059 (n 10).

[46] *Sim v Rotherham Metropolitan BC* [1987] Ch 216 (Ch D).

[47] Peel, *Treitel*, para 17-060 (n 10); D Robertson, 'Force Majeure Clauses' (2009) 25 JCL 62.

performance is excused in this way, the promisor is discharged from the duty to perform the obligation in question without any question either of breach by the other party or frustration of the contract as a whole.[48]

(5) Termination and discharge of unilateral obligation

A situation similar to termination is where a unilateral obligation is discharged for **4.11** failure of condition. If A agrees to do X *if* B does Y, A need *not* do X *unless* B does Y. Note that this does not involve any suggestion that B is bound or obliged to do Y—the doing of Y is no more and no less than a condition upon which the obligation of A to do X depends.[49] In *Hare v Nicoll*[50] an agreement under seal gave the plaintiff an option to repurchase shares at a set price, and provided that he should give notice of his intention to do so and pay the price on or before the dates set out in the agreement. The plaintiff later sought to exercise the option but was debarred from doing so on the grounds that he had not paid the price by the day stipulated. The effect of this was akin to termination in that the defendant was discharged from his obligation to sell the shares, but the obligation was a unilateral one; the plaintiff was not bound to pay for the shares, or even to purchase them at all. His obligation to pay for the shares by a certain date was no more than a condition upon which the defendant's obligation to sell the shares depended.

(6) Termination and discharge by agreement

Where a contract is fully or partly executory, that is to say when there are still obli- **4.12** gations outstanding on both sides, it may be discharged by mutual agreement.[51] Like termination, it has the effect of discharging the parties from their primary obligations, but it depends not on default by one party but on the agreement of both. However, the picture has been muddied to some extent by an analysis of the process of termination as involving an offer by the party in default to abandon the contract and an acceptance of that offer by the innocent party.[52] This analogy

---

[48] But if the excuse is sufficiently protracted, then the contract may be frustrated: *Jackson v Union Marine Insurance Co Ltd* (1874–75) LR 10 CP 125 (Exchequer Chamber); *Marshall v Harland and Wolff Ltd* [1972] ICR 101 (NIRC); *Hebden v Forsey & Son* [1973] ICR 607 (NIRC); *Egg Stores (Stamford Hill) Ltd v Leibovici* [1977] ICR 260 (EAT); *Hart v AR Marshall & Sons (Bulwell) Ltd* [1977] ICR 539 (EAT); *Williams v Watson's Luxury Coaches Ltd* [1990] 1 IRLR 164 (EAT); *Sharp & Co v McMillan* [1998] IRLR 632 (EAT); *Four Seasons Healthcare Ltd v Maughan* [2005] IRLR 324 (EAT); *Gryf-Lowczowski v Hinchingbrooke Healthcare NHS Trust* [2005] EWHC 2407, [2006] IRLR 100.

[49] This concept is, of course, a fundamental one in the whole law of contractual discharge; see Ch 2, para 2.02.

[50] [1966] 2 QB 130 (CA); *United Dominions Trust (Commercial) Ltd v Eagle Aircraft Services Ltd* [1968] 1 WLR 74 (CA); PS Atiyah, (1968) 31 MLR 332; see Ch 5, para 5.10.

[51] *Davis v Street* (1823) 1 C & P 18, 171 ER 1084; *Morris v Baron & Co* [1918] AC 1 (HL); *Rose & Frank Co v JR Crompton & Bros Ltd* [1925] AC 445 (HL); Burrows et al, *Chitty on Contracts*, para 22-025 (n 3).

[52] *Denmark Productions Ltd v Boscobel Productions Ltd* [1969] 1 QB 699 (CA) 731–2 (Winn LJ); Furmston, Fifoot, and Simpson, *Cheshire, Fifoot and Furmston's Law of Contract*, p 680 (n 15).

can be helpful for some purposes; in particular, it helps to stress that termination is not automatic, but only takes place if the innocent party chooses to respond to the breach in that way.[53] However, the analogy cannot be pressed too far, for three reasons. The first is that it does not normally reflect the intentions of the parties, even in an objective sense; in particular, whilst an outright repudiation by the party in default may in some ways be seen as an offer to abandon the contract, the same cannot be said of other serious breaches giving rise to termination, such as a breach of condition.[54] Secondly, the rules regarding termination differ in some respects from those of offer and acceptance; for instance, it may be that unlike the acceptance of an offer the acceptance of a breach does not always have to be communicated to the party in default;[55] similarly, it has never been suggested that some of the more technical rules relating to offer and acceptance, such as those regarding acceptances through the post, apply to termination.[56] Last but not least, the analogy confuses termination for breach with true cases of discharge by agreement, for which the rules are very different.[57] Ultimately, as the Chapter 3 shows, termination for breach is a doctrine with its own distinct pedigree,[58] and it does not do well to elide it with other doctrines, whatever the apparent similarities may be.[59]

F. The Requirement of Election

4.13 Though the phrase 'termination for breach' is a useful and well-recognized piece of legal shorthand for the process that we are describing,[60] it is nevertheless a misleading one in so far as it suggests that it is the breach that brings about the termination.[61] Though the ultimate effect of a serious breach of contract may be to absolve one or both parties from their obligations under the contract, this will only happen if the innocent party wants it to happen,[62] or to use technical language 'elects' to

---

[53] See para 4.13.

[54] Indeed, the very fact that the party in default is prepared to litigate the matter indicates that he or she did not have such an intention.

[55] See para 4.20.

[56] Though see Andrews et al, *Contractual Duties*, paras 14-046–14-051 (n 14).

[57] Beatson, Burrows, and Cartwright, *Anson's Law of Contract*, ch 13 (n 3); Furmston, Fifoot, and Simpson, *Cheshire, Fifoot and Furmston's Law of Contract*, ch 19 (n 15); Burrows et al, *Chitty on Contracts*, ch 22 (n 3).

[58] See Ch 2.

[59] Though the analogy is revived from time to time, it has been described in the House of Lords as 'discredited': *Hurst v Bryk* [2002] 1 AC 185 (HL) 195 (Lord Millett); J W Carter ' "Acceptance" of a Repudiation' (1994) 7 JCL 156; Carter, *Carter's Breach of Contract*, para 7-18 (n 15).

[60] Andrews et al, *Contractual Duties*, ch 10 (n 14); Peel, *Treitel*, ch 18 (n 10); M Bridge, *The Sale of Goods* (2nd edn, OUP, 2009) ch 5.

[61] Carter, *Carter's Breach of Contract*, para 10-01 (n 15).

[62] Carter, *Carter's Breach of Contract*, para 10-02 (n 15); Andrews et al, *Contractual Duties*, paras 14-001–14.003 (n 14); *Boston Deep Sea Fishing & Ice Co v Ansell* (1889) 39 Ch D 339 (CA) 344 (Bowen LJ); *Heyman v Darwins* [1942] AC 356 (HL) 373 (Lord Macmillan) and 399 (Lord Porter); *Moschi v Lep Air Services Ltd* [1973] AC 331 (HL) 349–50 (Lord Diplock); *Photo Production Ltd v Securicor Transport Ltd* [1980] AC 827 (HL) 844 (Lord Wilberforce) and 849 (Lord Diplock).

terminate rather than affirm.[63] In other words, the innocent party has a choice. The consequences of that choice will be discussed in more detail later;[64] at this stage it is necessary to consider whether there are any situations where there is no such choice—that is to say, whether there are exceptions to the requirement of election.

(1) Contracts of employment

The first possible exception relates to contracts of employment. Originally the **4.14** normal rule was said to apply to such cases,[65] but this was called into question on a number of grounds;[66] in particular, it was pointed out that where an employee was wrongfully dismissed, the contract was effectively at an end, since as a general rule the courts would not grant specific performance in such cases[67] and there could be no question of the employee insisting on remaining in post and then suing for his or her wages.[68] For these reasons it was suggested in a number of cases that a different rule applied to contracts of employment, at least where they involved wrongful dismissal.[69] However, in *Geys v Société Générale, London Branch*[70] the Supreme Court, by a majority of four to one, rejected this suggestion and held that contracts of employment were subject to the general rule requiring acceptance. In this case the defendant bank had summarily dismissed the claimant without good cause in November 2007 and had then made a payment into his bank in lieu of notice the following month. The claimant did not contest his dismissal as such,

---

[63] Andrews et al, *Contractual Duties*, paras 14-004–14-015 (n 14); Beatson, Burrows, and Cartwright, *Anson's Law of Contract*, pp 510–11 (n 3); Carter, *Carter's Breach of Contract*, para 10-02 (n 15); *Motor Oil Hellas (Corinth) Refineries SA v Shipping Corp of India (The Kanchenjunga)* [1990] 1 Lloyd's Rep 391 (HL) 397–9 (Lord Goff); *Tele2 International Card Co SA v Post Office Ltd* [2009] EWCA Civ 9, para 53 (Aikens LJ). It is occasionally argued that the elective theory is based on a misconception: see especially JM Thomson, 'The Effect of a Repudiatory Breach' (1974) 41 MLR 137 and JW Carter, 'Discharge as the Basis for Termination for Breach of Contract' (2012) 129 LQR 283, but the orthodox position has recently been reaffirmed by the Supreme Court in *Geys v Société Générale, London Branch* [2012] UKSC 63, [2013] 1 AC 523 (see para 4.14).

[64] See Chs 9–12.

[65] *Boston Deep Sea Fishing & Ice Co v Ansell* (1889) 39 Ch D 339 (CA) (Bowen LJ).

[66] See generally JM Thomson, Note (1980) 96 LQR 326; J McMullen, 'Synthesis of the Mode of Termination of Contracts of Employment' [1982] CLJ 110; KD Ewing, 'Remedies for Breach of the Contract of Employment' [1993] CLJ 405; BW Napier, 'Repudiation and the Contract of Employment' [1979] CLJ 56; B Hough and A Spowart-Taylor, 'Theories of Termination in Contracts of Employment: the Scylla and Charybdis' (2003) 19 JCL 134.

[67] *Firth v Ridley* (1864) 33 Beav 516, 55 ER 468; *Rigby v Connol* (1880) 14 Ch D 482 (Jessel MR); *de Francesco v Barnum* (1890) 45 Ch D 430 (Kay LJ). For a possible exception to this rule see *Hill v CA Parsons & Co Ltd* [1972] Ch 305 (CA).

[68] *Denmark Productions Ltd v Boscobel Productions Ltd* [1969] 1 QB 699 (CA) 737 (Harman LJ); *Gunton v Richmond-on-Thames LBC* [1981] 1 Ch 448 (CA) 474 (Brightman LJ); *Marsh v National Autistic Society* [1993] ICR 453 (EAT) (Ferris J).

[69] *Vine v National Dock Labour Board* [1956] 1 QB 658 (CA) 674 (Jenkins LJ), [1957] AC 488 (HL) 500 (Viscount Kilmuir LC); *Francis v Kuala Lumpur Councillors* [1962] 1 WLR 1411 (JCPC–Federated Malay States); *Sanders v Ernest A Neale* [1974] ICR 565 (NIRC); *Ivory v Palmer* [1975] ICR 340 (CA) 354 (Browne LJ).

[70] [2012] UKSC 63, [2013] 1 AC 523 (Lords Hope, Wilson, and Carnwath and Baroness Hale of Richmond, Lord Sumption dissenting).

but contended that it did not take effect until January 2008. The bank, however, argued that on the basis of the 'automatic' theory the dismissal was effective as from November 2007, or December at the latest. The court rejected the bank's contention, one reason being that to decide otherwise would allow the defaulting employer to take advantage of his or her own wrong. In the trenchant words of Lord Wilson:[71]

> In proposing that the court should endorse the automatic theory, the bank invites it to cause the law of England and Wales in relation to contracts of employment to set sail, unaccompanied, on a journey for which I can discern no just purpose and can identify no final destination. I consider, however, that we should keep the contract of employment firmly within the harbour which the common law has solidly constructed for the entire fleet of contracts in order to protect the innocent party, as far as practicable, from the consequences of the other's breach.

Be that as it may, it is still a moot point whether the requirement of election can operate in its full sense of allowing the employee to ignore the dismissal and affirm the contract. Indeed, it has been admitted that in cases of wrongful dismissal the right to affirm is effectively illusory, and that it would not be hard to conclude that the employee in such cases had elected to accept the repudiation and terminate the contract.[72] A wrongful dismissal does not legally terminate the contract in theory, but it may effectively do so in practice, and for this reason it must be conceded that the right of a wrongfully dismissed employee to affirm the contract is in most cases no more than an 'empty formality'.[73]

(2) Insurance contracts

4.15 A second exception relates to the so-called 'promissory warranty' in contracts of marine insurance. Section 33 of the Marine Insurance Act 1906 describes this as 'a warranty by which the assured undertakes that some particular thing shall or shall not be done, or that some condition shall be fulfilled, or whereby he affirms or negatives the existence of a particular state of facts',[74] and adds that if it is not exactly complied with the insurer is discharged from liability as from the date of the breach in question.[75] This provision, which codified the settled rule at common law,[76] was

---

[71] *Geys v Société Générale*, para 97 (n 70).
[72] *Gunton v Richmond-on-Thames LBC* [1981] 1 Ch 448 (CA) 469 (Buckley LJ).
[73] *Gunton v Richmond-on-Thames*, 459 (Shaw LJ) (n 72).
[74] Marine Insurance Act 1906, s 33(1).
[75] Marine Insurance Act 1906, s 33(3).
[76] *Newcastle Fire Insurance Co v McMorran and Co* (1815) 3 Dow 255, 3 ER 1057; *Anderson v Fitzgerald* (1853) 4 HL Cas 484, 10 ER 551; *Thomson v Weems* (1884) 9 App Cas 671, (1884) 11 R (HL) 48. This of course is the reverse of the normal meaning of the word 'warranty' in the contractual context, that is to say a term on the breach of which the innocent party can claim damages but is *not* discharged from further performance: see Ch 6, para 6.12.

applied by the House of Lords in *The Good Luck*[77] to a case where a ship had sailed into a prohibited zone contrary to the terms of such a warranty. It was held that the insurance policy had ceased to apply as soon as this had happened without any need for election by the insurer, the reasoning being that adherence to the warranty was a condition precedent to any claim being made on the policy.[78] This, of course, is similar to the analysis adopted in some of the older authorities,[79] and which still survives in relation to unilateral contracts and options.[80] Where bilateral or synallagmatic contracts are concerned, that analysis has been superseded in relation to contracts generally by the current requirement for election, but it still remains in use in the insurance context. As is often the case, we have here an exception that pre-dates the rule itself.

(3) Leases

It was said by the Court of Appeal in *Total Oil (Great Britain) Ltd v Thompson* **4.16**
Garages (Biggin Hill) Ltd[81] that the doctrine of termination for breach could not apply to leases, one reason being that a lease conveyed an interest in land, and therefore could not come to an end like an ordinary contract on the basis of repudiation and acceptance.[82] However, this approach was contrary to a number of older authorities,[83] and has not been followed in other jurisdictions.[84] The

---

[77] *Bank of Nova Scotia v Hellenic Mutual War Risk Association (Bermuda) Ltd (The Good Luck)* [1992] 1 AC 233 (HL); Peel, *Treitel*, para 18-007 (n 10); M Clarke, 'Breach of Warranty in the Law of Insurance' [1991] LMCLQ 437; M Leeming 'Discharge for Breach of Warranty in Contract for Marine Insurance' (1992) 5 JCL 163.

[78] *The Good Luck*, 262–3 (Lord Goff) (n 77); as Lord Goff puts it, the insurer only agrees to cover the assured so long as the warranty is kept. However, the rule can lead to injustice, and the Law Commission has issued a Discussion Paper including the question whether or not it should be modified or abolished: Law Commission and Scottish Law Commission, *Insurance Contract Law: Misrepresentation, Non-Disclosure and Breach of Warranty by the Insured* (LCCP No 182, SLCDP No 134, 2007); R Merkin and J Lowry, 'Reconstructing Insurance Law: the Law Commission's Consultation Paper' (2008) 71 MLR 95; B Soyer, 'Warranties in Commercial Insurance Contracts' (2009) 25 JCL 168.

[79] As in *Kingston v Preston* (1773) Lofft 194, cited in *Jones v Barkley* (1781) 2 Dougl 684, 690, 99 ER 434, 437; Samuel Stoljar, 'Dependent and Independent Promises' [1957] 2 Sydney L Rev 217; see further Ch 2, paras 2.03–2.05.

[80] *Hare v Nicoll* [1966] 2 QB 130 (CA); *United Dominions Trust (Commercial) Ltd v Eagle Aircraft Services Ltd* [1968] 1 WLR 74 (CA); see para 4.11.

[81] [1972] 1 QB 318 (CA).

[82] *Total Oil v Thompson Garages*, 324 (Lord Denning MR) (n 81).

[83] Such as *Edwards v Etherington* (1825) Ry & M 268; *Smith v Marrable* (1843) 11 M & W 5, 152 ER 693; *Wilson v Finch Hatton* (1877) 2 Ex D 336; HA Hill and JH Redman, *Hill and Redman's Guide to Landlord and Tenant Law* (Butterworths, 1999) paras 14-423–14-424.

[84] *Wood Factory Pty Ltd v Kiritos Pty Ltd* [1985] 2 NSWLR 105 (NSW CA); *Highway Properties Ltd v Kelly, Douglas & Co Ltd* [1971] 17 DLR (3d) 710 (Can SC); *Ripka Pty Ltd v Maggiore Bakers Pty Ltd* [1984] VR 629 (Victoria SC); *Progressive Mailing House Pty Ltd v Tabali Pty Ltd* (1985) 57 ALR 609 (HCA); JW Carter, 'Repudiation of Leases' [1985] Conveyancer 289; M Pawlowski, 'Acceptance of Repudiatory Breach in Leases' [1995] Conveyancer 379; JW Carter and J Hill, 'Repudiation of Leases: Further Developments' [1986] Conveyancer 262; M Pawlowski and J Brown, 'Repudiatory Breach in the Leasehold Context' [1999] Conveyancer 150.

reasoning used by the Court of Appeal in the *Total Oil* case was later rejected, albeit in the different context of frustration, by the House of Lords in *National Carriers v Panalpina (Northern) Ltd*,[85] and on that basis Stephen Sedley QC (as he then was) refused to follow the case in *Hussein v Mehlman*.[86] Others have since followed his lead,[87] and the better view is now said to be that a lease can be brought to an end by termination no less than any other type of contract;[88] at the very least, the rule in the *Total Oil* case is ripe for review by a higher court.

(4) Other cases

4.17   As far as other kinds of contract are concerned, the general rule applies in all cases, namely that the innocent party has a choice whether to terminate or affirm. However, the right to affirm is of more practical significance in some cases than in others. Affirmation is most valuable as an option in cases where a decree of specific performance is available,[89] or where the innocent party can complete performance without the cooperation of the party in default and has a legitimate interest in doing so;[90] here he or she can effectively force the other party to perform. In other cases, however, the right to affirm amounts to no more than a right to delay matters in the hope that the defaulting party will perform eventually.[91] In some cases, indeed, even this will not be a realistic option, as for instance where the effect of the breach is to destroy the subject matter of the contract or to render its performance impossible.[92]

G. What Amounts to Election?

4.18   Given that termination does not take place unless the innocent party chooses for it to take place, the next question is how such a choice is made. What does the innocent party have to do if he or she wishes to terminate? Though election has

---

[85] [1981] AC 675.

[86] [1992] 2 EGLR 87 (Wood Green County Court).

[87] *Chartered Trust plc v Davies* [1997] 2 EGLR 83 (CA); *Nynehead Developments v R H Fibreboard Containers Ltd* [1999] 1 EGLR 7 (High Ct).

[88] Pawlowski, 'Acceptance of Repudiatory Breach in Leases', p 379 (n 84); Hill and Redman, *Guide to Landlord and Tenant Law* (n 83); HA Hill, J Redman, and M Barnes, *Hill and Redman's Law of Landlord and Tenant* (looseleaf, LexisNexis) para A[5106].

[89] All the more so, given that such a decree can be issued even before the date for performance has arrived: *Hasham v Zenab* [1960] AC 316 (JCPC–Eastern Africa).

[90] *White and Carter (Councils) Ltd v McGregor* [1962] AC 413 (HL), discussed at Ch 12, paras 12.12–12.34.

[91] The danger in doing this is that when the date for performance arrives the party in default may have a good excuse for failing to perform, as in *Avery v Bowden* (1855) 5 E & B 714, 119 ER 647; see Ch 12, para 12.03. As well as this, the duty of the innocent party to mitigate his or her loss by obtaining performance from elsewhere may involve termination of the original contract: Peel, *Treitel*, para 18-008 (n 10).

[92] As in *Harbutt's 'Plasticine' Ltd v Wayne Tank & Pump Co Ltd* [1970] 1 QB 447 (CA); though the Court of Appeal was decidedly wrong in saying that the limitation clause in that case did not apply, it is difficult to envisage how the contract could have been effectively affirmed in that situation.

been described as a doctrine based on 'simple considerations of common sense and equity',[93] the law in this area is anything but simple; indeed, it is one of the most tricky areas of contract law.

(1) Termination by words or conduct

The most obvious way of electing to terminate is by an express statement to that **4.19** effect. Sometimes this can take the form of legal proceedings of some sort, such as an action for a declaration that the contract has been terminated,[94] or the issue of proceedings to forfeit a lease,[95] but such cases are exceptional; indeed, no set form of words is required at all,[96] so long as a reasonable person would conclude that the contract was terminated.[97] Election can also be by conduct, as where the innocent party puts himself or herself into a position where further performance is impossible,[98] or where new arrangements are made that are inconsistent with the previous contract.[99] Indeed, it has been said that any act by the promisee which is inconsistent with his or her intention to perform may count as an election to terminate for breach, whether or not that was the intention of the promisee.[100] As in the case of contract formation, what counts is not the subjective intention of the party in question, but what a reasonable person would conclude was his or her intention on the basis of the relevant words or conduct.[101]

(2) Election must be unambiguous

The election of the innocent party to terminate must be unambiguous, in the sense **4.20** that it must unequivocally and clearly indicate his or her intention to treat the

---

[93] *Johnson v Agnew* [1980] AC 367 (HL) 398 (Lord Wilberforce); JW Carter and MJ Tilbury, 'Remedial Choice and Contract Drafting' (1998) 13 JCL 5, 12–15; AM Sheppard, 'Demystifying the Right of Election in Contract Law' [2007] JBL 442.

[94] As in *Heyman v Darwins* [1942] AC 356 (HL); *Millers Wharf Partnership Ltd v Corinthian Column Ltd* (1991) 61 P & CR 461 (Ch D) (Knox J); *Samarenko v Dawn Hill House Ltd* [2011] EWCA Civ 1445, [2013] Ch 36, [2012] 1 P & CR 14.

[95] As in *Billson and ors v Residential Apartments Ltd* [1992] 1 AC 494 (HL); *Hynes v Twinsectra Ltd* (1996) 28 HLR 183 (CA); *Abidogun v Frolan Health Care Ltd* [2001] EWCA Civ 1821, [2002] L & TR 16; see S Bridge, 'Dusk Falls on Dawn Raids' [1992] CLJ 216.

[96] *Lakshmijit S/O Bhai Suchit v Sherani* [1974] AC 605 (JCPC–Fiji) 616; *Buckland v Farmar and Moody* [1979] 1 WLR 221 (CA) 225 ('rescind'); *Toepfer v Kruse* [1980] 2 Lloyd's Rep 397 (QBD: Commercial Ct) (Lloyd J) 400 ('cancelled'); *Roberts v West Coast Trains Ltd* [2004] EWCA Civ 900, [2005] ICR 254, para 12 ('you are dismissed'); *Dalkia Utilities Services plc v Celtech International Ltd* [2006] EWHC Civ 63, [2006] 2 P & CR 9, para 80 ('at an end').

[97] *Mannai Investment Co Ltd v Eagle Star Life Assurance Co Ltd* [1997] AC 749 (HL) 768 (Lord Steyn); PV Baker, 'Reconstructing the Rules of Construction' (1998) 114 LQR 55.

[98] As in *Gator Shipping Corp v Trans-Asiatic Oil Ltd SA (The Odenfeld)* [1978] 2 Lloyd's Rep 357 (Kerr J), where following the repudiation of a time charter by the charterers the owners put the ship into mothballs: Carter, *Carter's Breach of Contract*, para 10-18 (n 15).

[99] As where a wrongfully dismissed employee takes a new job, or where goods that have been wrongfully rejected by the buyer are sold elsewhere.

[100] *Carter*, para 10-18 (n 15).

[101] cf *Smith v Hughes* (1870–71) LR 6 QB 597, 607 (Blackburn J).

contract as discharged.[102] For this reason, a mere failure or even refusal to perform on the part of the innocent party in response to the breach will not normally be enough, as this may be equally consistent with the contract continuing in force.[103] In the same way, silence will not as a general rule amount to acceptance of a repudiation any more than it will amount to acceptance of an offer.[104] However, it has been said that the question whether the innocent party has elected to terminate is one of fact rather than one of law,[105] and for this reason even 'silence and inactivity' may be enough if the intentions of the innocent party are clear from the context. In *The Santa Clara*[106] the buyers of a cargo of propane gas sent a message to the sellers repudiating the contract, following which the sellers took no further steps to perform it. It was held by the House of Lords that the arbitrators were entitled to find that the repudiation had been accepted, as it must have been clear to the buyers that the sellers no longer regarded the contract as on foot.[107] As Lord Steyn said, if an employer tells a contractor in the evening that he need not come back next day because his services are no longer required, the fact that the contractor fails to put in an appearance the following morning will generally indicate that he considers the contract as at an end. Similarly, if a seller of goods is obliged to obtain an export licence, and the buyer repudiates the contract before he has done so, the failure of the seller to obtain the licence may be good evidence of termination.[108]

(3) The question of communication

4.21 Need the election to terminate be communicated to the party in default? The analogy of offer and acceptance would suggest that this is so, but the law is not entirely clear. In *The Santa Clara* Lord Steyn said that the fact of election had to come to the notice of the repudiating party,[109] and though this was not central

---

[102] *Norwest Holt Group Administration Ltd v Harrison* [1985] ICR 668 (CA); *Vitol SA v Norelf Ltd (The Santa Clara)* [1996] AC 800 (HL) 810–11 (Lord Steyn); *Rai v Somerfield Stores* [2004] ICR 656 (EAT) 662 (Judge Burke QC); *Sookraj v Samaroo* [2004] UKPC 50 (Trinidad and Tobago), para 17 (Lord Scott); *Stocznia Gdynia SA v Gearbulk Holdings Ltd* [2009] EWCA Civ 75, [2010] 1 QB 27, para 44 (Moore-Bick LJ); *Key Property Investments (Number Five) Ltd v Periasamy Mathialagan* [2005] EWCA Civ 220.

[103] Thus a buyer may reject goods that do not conform to the contract description without necessarily terminating the contract altogether, and an employer may withhold wages from an employee who is on strike without necessarily dismissing him or her: *Wiluszynski v Tower Hamlets LBC* [1989] ICR 493 (CA) 503 (Nicholls LJ).

[104] *State Trading Corp of India Ltd v M Golodetz & Co Inc Ltd* [1989] 2 Lloyd's Rep 277 (CA) 276 (Kerr LJ); *Glencore Grain Rotterdam BV v Lebanese Organisation for International Commerce (The Lorico)* [1997] 2 Lloyd's Rep 386 (CA) 394 (Evans LJ); cf *Felthouse v Bindley* (1862) 11 CB(NS) 869, 142 ER 1037.

[105] *J & E Kish v Charles Taylor & Sons & Co* [1912] AC 604 (HL) 617 (Lord Atkinson); *The Santa Clara*, 810 (Lord Steyn) (n 102); *Agrokor AG v Tradigrain SA* [2000] 1 Lloyd's Rep 497, 500 (Longmore J). But where the question involves the construction of a written document, it is one of law: *Norwest Holt Group Administration Ltd v Harrison* [1985] ICR 668 (CA) 679 (Cumming-Bruce LJ).

[106] *Vitol SA v Norelf Ltd (The Santa Clara)* [1996] AC 800 (HL).

[107] *The Santa Clara*, 811 (Lord Steyn) (n 106).

[108] *The Santa Clara*, 811 (Lord Steyn) (n 106).

[109] *The Santa Clara*, 811 (Lord Steyn) (n 106).

to the decision[110] it certainly appears to be the orthodox view.[111] However, it is argued by Carter that this is not an invariable rule,[112] and that it is enough if the decision to terminate is 'overtly evinced'.[113] The main situation in which this would be likely to be significant is where the party in default takes active steps to prevent communication taking place. As Carter points out, the law concerning rescission for misrepresentation clearly allows the requirement of communication to be dispensed with in cases of this sort,[114] and the same reasoning would seem to be relevant in cases of termination. The law would surely not allow the party in default to prevent this taking place simply by keeping out of the way.

H. The Time of Election

There are two issues regarding the time of termination. One is how long the inno- **4.22**
cent party has to decide whether to terminate or not; the other is when such a decision takes effect.

(1) A reasonable time for termination?

Under the Sale of Goods Act a buyer of goods who retains them for more than a **4.23**
reasonable time without rejecting them will lose that right,[115] and similar rules may

---

[110] In that case the buyers were clearly aware that the sellers were no longer performing the contract; the only issue was as to whether this was sufficiently unambiguous to indicate a decision to terminate: see para 4.06.

[111] Andrews et al, *Contractual Duties*, para 14-045 (n 14); *Lakshmijit S/O Bhai Suchit v Sherani* [1974] AC 605 (JCPC–Fiji) 616 (Lord Cross); *Wood Factory Pty Ltd v Kiritos Pty Ltd* (1985) 2 NSWLR 105 146 (McHugh JA); *Majik Markets Pty Ltd v S & M Motor Repairs Pty Ltd (No 1)* (1987) 10 NSWLR 49, 54 (Young J); *Stocznia Gdynia SA v Gearbulk Holdings Ltd* [2009] EWCA Civ 75, [2010] QB 27, para 44 (Moore-Bick LJ).

[112] 'Failure to Perform as "Acceptance" of a Repudiation' (1996–97) 11 JCL 255; Carter, *Carter's Breach of Contract*, para 10-18 (n 15). However, he concedes that communication may be essential in order to achieve some further consequence, such as the forfeiture of a lease.

[113] The point was left open by Phillips J at first instance in *The Santa Clara* [1994] 1 WLR 1390 (QBD: Commercial Ct), 1395; see also *Poort v Development Underwriting (Victoria) Pty Ltd (No 2)* [1977] VR 454, 459; *State Trading Corp of India Ltd v M Golodetz & Co Inc Ltd* [1989] 2 Lloyd's Rep 277 (CA) 286 (Kerr LJ); *Force India Formula One Team Ltd v 1 Malaysia Racing Team Sdn Bhd* [2012] EWHC 616 (Ch) para 207 (Arnold J). According to the unreported decision of the Employment Appeal Tribunal in *Atlantic Air Ltd v Hoff* (26 March 2008), communication is *not* required; cf *Gisda Cyf v Barrett* [2010] UKSC 41 (employment terminated when employee read letter or had reasonable opportunity to do so).

[114] Thus in *Car and Universal Finance Ltd v Caldwell* [1965] 1 QB 525 (CA) it was held that a man who had sold his car to a swindler who had then absconded could rescind the contract by informing the police and the AA without having to show that he had also located and notified the swindler!

[115] Sale of Goods Act 1979, s 35(4); Carter, *Carter's Breach of Contract*, para 11-37 (n 15); MG Bridge (ed), *Benjamin's Sale of Goods* (8th edn, Sweet & Maxwell, 2010) paras 12-040–12-068, discussed at paras 4.69–4.74. Note, however, that this rule differs from the normal rule of election in that knowledge of the breach is not required.

apply in the context of express rights of termination,[116] but the extent to which this represents the general law is open to question. It has been said that a right to terminate will not be lost by mere delay,[117] but on the other hand that the innocent party cannot be allowed an indefinite time to make his or her mind up.[118] Though the general law in this area is not entirely clear, three principles emerge from the cases.

4.24 The first is that mere delay on its own cannot be enough to bar the right to terminate.[119] Though it may seem plausible to say that the right to terminate must be exercised within a reasonable time, there is no authority for such a rule outside the particular areas mentioned previously.[120] In fact, such a rule would contradict the general requirement, stated earlier, that the decision to terminate must be clear and unambiguous;[121] after all, mere inactivity on the part of the innocent party may be as consistent with a decision to keep the contract on foot as with a decision to terminate it.

4.25 The second is that the innocent party is not obliged to make a decision the very instant he or she becomes aware of the breach. He or she must be given a reasonable opportunity to decide what to do,[122] all the more so given that a wrongful termination may itself amount to an unlawful repudiation of the contract.[123] How long that opportunity must be will obviously depend on the circumstances; some cases (for instance the withdrawal of a ship for late payment of hire) may call for a very quick decision,[124]

---

[116] *Mardorf Peach & Co Ltd v Attica Sea Carriers Corp of Liberia (The Laconia)* [1977] AC 850 (HL) 872 (Lord Wilberforce); *China National Foreign Trade Transport Corp v Evlogia Shipping Co SA of Panama (The Mihalos Xilas)* [1979] 1 WLR 1018 (HL) 1023 (Lord Diplock), 1030 (Lord Salmon), and 1037 (Lord Scarman); *Antaios Compania Naviera SA v Salen Rederiana AB (The Antaios)* [1983] 1 WLR 1362 (CA) 1370 (Sir John Donaldson MR), 1373 (Ackner LJ), and 1375–6 (Fox LJ); Carter, *Carter's Breach of Contract*, para 11-23 (n 15).

[117] Carter, *Carter's Breach of Contract*, para 11-22 (n 15).

[118] *Western Excavations (ECC) v Sharp* [1978] ICR 221 (CA) 226 (Denning MR); *Stocznia Gdanska SA v Latvian Shipping Co (No 2)* [2002] EWCA Civ 889, [2002] 2 Lloyd's Rep 436, para 87 (Rix LJ).

[119] *Cox Toner (Intl) Ltd v Crook* [1981] ICR 823 (EAT), 828 (Browne-Wilkinson J); *Bliss v South East Thames Regional Health Authority* [1987] ICR 700 (CA) 716 (Dillon LJ); *Nichimen Corp v Gatoil Overseas Inc* [1987] 2 Lloyd's Rep 46 (CA) 54 (Kerr LJ), 55–6 (Woolf LJ), and 58 (Sir John Megaw); Carter, *Carter's Breach of Contract*, para 11-22 (n 15).

[120] Carter, *Carter's Breach of Contract*, para 11-22 (n 15).

[121] See para 4.17.

[122] *Fisher, Reeves & Co Ltd v Armour & Co Ltd* [1920] 3 KB 614 (CA) 624 (Scrutton LJ); *Truk (UK) Ltd v Tokmakidis GmbH* [2000] 1 Lloyd's Rep 543 (QBD: Mercantile Ct) (Judge Jack QC); *Stocznia Gdanska SA v Latvian Shipping Co (No 2)* [2002] EWCA Civ 889, [2002] 2 Lloyd's Rep 436, para 87 (Rix LJ); *Ampurius Nu Homes Holdings Ltd v Telford Homes (Creekside) Ltd* [2013] EWCA Civ 577, [2013] BLR 400, para 63; Andrews et al, *Contractual Duties*, paras 14-026–14-031 (n 14).

[123] As in *Federal Commerce & Navigation Co Ltd v Molena Alpha Inc (The Nanfri)* [1979] AC 757 (HL); Carter, *Carter's Breach of Contract*, para 8-23 (n 15).

[124] *Mardorf Peach & Co Ltd v Attica Sea Carriers Corp of Liberia (The Laconia)* [1977] AC 850 (HL) 872 (Lord Wilberforce); *CMA CGM SA v Beteiligungs-Kommanditgesellschaft MS 'Northern Pioneer' Schiffahrgesellschaft mbH* [2003] EWCA Civ 1878, [2003] 1 WLR 1015, para 53 (Lord Phillips MR); Carter, *Carter's Breach of Contract*, para 11-24 (n 15); cf *The Nanfri* (n 123), Furmston, Fifoot, and Simpson, *Cheshire, Fifoot and Furmston's Law of Contract*, p 677 (n 15).

whereas in others (for instance cases involving the forfeiture of a lease for late payment of rent) more latitude can be allowed.[125]

The third is that if the conduct of the innocent party taken as a whole gives the party **4.26** in default good reason to believe that he or she has decided not to terminate but to keep the contract on foot, the right to terminate may be lost. In particular, a party with inconsistent rights and remedies cannot blow hot and cold, but must, in the end, choose whether to exercise one or the other.[126] In the same way, the conduct of the innocent party may sometimes be taken as equivalent to a representation that the right to terminate will not be exercised, and the party in default may have acted in reliance on that representation; here the innocent party will not be allowed to resile if it would be inequitable to do so.[127] These situations will be discussed in more detail later.[128]

(2) When does termination take effect?

Sometimes a court has to decide precisely when the decision to terminate takes **4.27** effect; for instance when time limits are specified either in the contract or by statute. This question arose in *The Brimnes*[129] in the context of a term in a charterparty allowing the owners to withdraw the ship for late payment of hire. Notice of withdrawal was sent to the charterers by telex fifteen minutes before their office was due to close, but the message was not read until the following morning, by which time the payment had been made. The question therefore arose whether the withdrawal had preceded the payment, or whether the opposite was the case.[130] Drawing an analogy with the cases on offer and acceptance,[131] the court held that the withdrawal had taken effect as soon as the message had been received on the charterers' machine.[132] In the words of Megaw LJ:[133]

> If a notice arrives at the address of the person to be notified, at such a time and
> by such a means of communication that it would in the normal course of business

---

[125] *Force India Formula One Team Ltd v Etihad Airways PJSC* [2010] EWCA Civ 1051, [2011] ETMR 10, para 122 (Rix LJ); cf *Woodar Investment Development Ltd v Wimpey Construction UK Ltd* [1980] 1 WLR 277 (HL); Furmston, Fifoot, and Simpson, *Cheshire, Fifoot and Furmston's Law of Contract*, p 677 (n 15).
[126] *Hartley v Hymans* [1920] 3 KB 475 (KBD), 495 (McCardie J); *Motor Oil Hellas (Corinth) Refineries SA v Shipping Corp of India (The Kanchenjunga)* [1990] 1 Lloyd's Rep 391 (HL) 398 (Lord Goff); see paras 4.55–4.58.
[127] *Hughes v Metropolitan Rly* (1877) 2 App Cas 439 (HL); *The Kanchenjunga*, 399 (Lord Goff) (n 126); see paras 4.59–4.67.
[128] See paras 4.54–4.68.
[129] *Tenax Steamship Co Ltd v The Brimnes (Owners) (The Brimnes)* [1975] QB 929 (CA), discussed in Andrews et al, *Contractual Duties*, para 14-050 (n 14).
[130] It was, however, also decided that since the payment in question was late the owners could have withdrawn the ship in any event: [1975] QB 929, 953 (Edmund Davies LJ), 957 (Megaw LJ), and 971 (Cairns LJ).
[131] Most notably the remarks of Denning LJ in *Entores Ltd v Miles Far East Corp* [1955] 2 QB 327 (CA) 333.
[132] [1975] QB 929, 945–6 (Edmund Davies LJ), 966–7 (Megaw LJ), and 969–70 (Cairns LJ).
[133] *Tenax Steamship Co Ltd v The Brimnes*, 966–7 (n 132) (passage quoted in Andrews et al, *Contractual Duties*, para 14-050 (n 14)).

come to the attention of that person on its arrival, that person cannot rely on some failure of himself or of his servants to act in a normal businesslike manner in respect of taking cognisance of the communication so as to postpone the effective time of the notice until some later time when it in fact came to his attention.

The basic rule therefore seems to be that termination takes effect when communicated to the party in default, or at any rate when the innocent party has done everything possible to bring it to his or her attention. However, this must be read subject to four qualifications.

4.28 The first is that *The Brimnes* is a case involving a contractual right of termination, to which special considerations may apply; in particular, the contract itself may regulate not only the circumstances in which such a right may arise, but also the manner in which it must be exercised.[134] Having said that, there may be cases in which the contract is silent as to the matter, and in which the ordinary rules of the common law will therefore apply.[135] Moreover, the rule set out in *The Brimnes* tallies nicely with the general rule stated previously, namely that a decision to terminate must either be communicated to the party in default or at least overtly evinced in some way.[136]

4.29 The second is to note that *The Brimnes* was decided in the context of a commercial transaction where it made sense to speak, as did Megaw LJ, of the 'normal course of business'. It has been argued that the result might have been different if the notice had been given to a private individual, who presumably cannot be expected to be on hand to deal with communications in the same way.[137]

4.30 The third is that while the rules concerning termination may reflect to some extent those regarding offer and acceptance, the analogy should not be pushed too far in this any more than in any other respect.[138] In particular, there is no authority for importing into the present context the anomalous rule whereby acceptance of an offer made in the course of the post takes effect when posted.[139]

4.31 The fourth is that in relation to particular types of contract the rules of the common law may be overridden either by the courts themselves or by statute. Thus, for instance, special rules apply to the termination of contracts of

---

[134] Carter, *Carter's Breach of Contract*, para 10-12 (n 15); JW Carter, 'Termination Clauses' (1990) 3 JCL 90.

[135] Carter, *Carter's Breach of Contract*, para 10-12 (n 15). Indeed, *The Brimnes* itself appears to have been such a case.

[136] See para 4.18.

[137] See the remarks of Bean J in *Gisda Cyf v Barratt*, quoted by Lord Kerr at [2010] UKSC 41, [2010] ICR 1475, para 16; see also Andrews et al, *Contractual Duties*, para 14-051 (n 14).

[138] See para 4.12.

[139] *Adams v Lindsell* (1818) 1 B & Ald 681, 106 ER 520; *Household Fire and Carriage Accident Insurance Co Ltd v Grant* (1879) 4 Ex D 216 (CA).

employment,[140] as they do in the consumer context[141] and in relation to the forfeiture of a lease.[142] Though these rules may differ in detail, the policy behind them is the same, namely to ensure that the party in default does not lose out without having a proper chance to know what the legal position is, and in some cases at least to remedy the default in question.[143]

I. A Third Option?

As it stands, the present law puts a great deal of pressure on the innocent party in deciding how to elect in cases of this sort. He or she must first decide whether the breach by the party in default is serious enough to give rise to the right to terminate in the first place, and then, assuming it is, whether to exercise that right. A wrong decision one way may amount to a repudiation, whereas a wrong decision the other way may amount to an affirmation of the contract. For this and other reasons it has been suggested that where the conduct of the party in default is such as to amount to an unlawful repudiation, the innocent party may, without actually terminating the contract, suspend performance until the party in default has indicated a readiness and willingness to perform his or her own obligations under the contract.[144] However, this so-called third option was firmly rejected by the House of Lords in *The Simona*.[145] This case involved a clause in a charterparty giving the charterers the right to cancel the charter if the ship was not ready to load by a certain day. The owners having indicated that the ship would not be ready on time, the charterers purported to invoke the clause and made arrangements for the cargo to be carried on another ship. The owners, however, indicated that the ship would still be available to carry the cargo. A few days later, the ship still not being ready, the charterers sent a second notice of cancellation. It was common ground that the first notice of cancellation was premature, and therefore amounted to an unlawful repudiation of the contract by the charterers. Did this prevent them relying on the second notice? The charterers argued that it did not; since the owners had not accepted the repudiation, they could not derive any rights from it.[146]

4.32

---

[140] *Brown v Southall & Knight* [1980] ICR 617 (EAT); *McMaster v Manchester Airport plc* [1998] IRLR 112 (EAT); *Gisda Cyf v Barratt* [2010] UKSC 41, [2010] ICR 1475; Andrews et al, *Contractual Duties*, paras 14-052–14-053 (n 14).

[141] Consumer Credit Act 1974, ss 87 and 88 ('default notice').

[142] Law of Property Act 1925, s 146(1); Carter, *Carter's Breach of Contract*, para 10-22 (n 15).

[143] The party in default may also seek to protect himself or herself by the provision of such a clause in the contract itself, for instance an 'anti-technicality' clause in a charterparty.

[144] Andrews et al, *Contractual Duties*, paras 14-017–14-025 (n 14).

[145] *Fercometal SARL v Mediterranean Shipping Co SA (The Simona)* [1989] AC 788 (HL).

[146] *The Simona*, 793–5 (n 145).

4.33 In response to this, the owners argued, on the basis of *Braithwaite v Foreign Hardwood Co*,[147] that their failure to accept the repudiation did not mean that it could be left out of the equation altogether.[148] The cancellation clause on which the charterers were relying could only be exercised on condition that the ship was not ready to load on the relevant date.[149] However, the owners argued that the charterers' repudiation, even if not accepted, absolved them from any obligation to have the ship ready on time,[150] the point being that in the circumstances they were entitled, even without going so far as to terminate, to hold back from performing until the intentions of the charterers with regard to the matter became clear.[151]

4.34 However, this argument was firmly rejected by the House of Lords. In the words of Lord Ackner:[152]

> When A wrongfully repudiates his contractual obligations in anticipation of the time for their performance, he presents the innocent party B with two choices. He may either affirm the contract by treating it as still in force or he may treat it as finally and conclusively discharged. There is no third choice, as a sort of via media, to affirm the contract and yet to be absolved from tendering further performance unless and until A gives reasonable notice that he is once again able and willing to perform. Such a choice would negate the contract being kept alive for the benefit of *both* parties and would deny the party who unsuccessfully sought to rescind, the right to take advantage of any supervening circumstance which would justify him in declining to complete.

4.35 So there is no third option; if the innocent party is not willing to risk termination, then he or she must affirm and take the consequences of doing so. However, this does not mean that the innocent party who affirms is necessarily bound to go to all the effort of rendering a performance that will be pointless, or which he or she knows will be rejected by the party in default. In particular, if the innocent party can show that his or her failure to perform was induced by the conduct of

---

[147] [1905] 2 KB 543 (CA), discussed further at para 4.39.
[148] [1989] AC 788 (HL) 790–3.
[149] *The Simona*, 790 (n 148); *Noemijulia SS Co v Minister of Food* [1951] 1 KB 223 (CA).
[150] *The Simona*, 791 (n 148). The argument was that repudiation by the party in default had the effect of absolving the innocent party from the duty to perform 'conditions precedent': *Jones v Barkley* (1781) 2 Dougl 684, 99 ER 434; *Cort and Gee v Ambergate, Nottingham and Boston and Eastern Junction Ry Co* (1851) 17 QB 127, 117 ER 1229. However, there seems to be some confusion here. First of all, the 'condition precedent' in the present case was not the readiness of the ship to load, but its unreadiness. Second, it was conceded by both parties that the clause in question placed no obligation on the owners to have the ship ready to load by the stated day; rather, the clause was in the nature of a unilateral option. Third, none of the cases relied on by the owners went so far as to say that the innocent party was absolved from performance even where the contract was affirmed, not even *Braithwaite v Foreign Hardwood Co* (n 147) itself, since, as Lord Ackner, demonstrated (at 801–4) that case was better viewed as one where the repudiation had been accepted.
[151] [1989] AC 788 (HL) 791.
[152] *The Simona*, 805 (n 151); G Marston, 'Contractual Rights and Duties after an Unaccepted Anticipatory Repudiation' [1988] CLJ 340.

the party in default, then that will be a good excuse even if the contract has been affirmed.[153] Say, for instance, the owners in *The Simona* would have been perfectly able and willing to have the ship ready to load in time, but had decided that it would be pointless to do so in the wake of the charterers' repudiation. In that case, the charterers would have effectively been estopped from using this as a ground for cancellation.[154]

As well as this, there may be other remedies available to an innocent party who **4.36** affirms. For instance, in some cases he or she may be able to obtain a decree of specific performance.[155] Even where this is not available, a fresh right of termination may arise if the party in default persists in failing to perform.[156] In particular, the innocent party may be able in these circumstances to issue a notice making time of the essence; the effect of this will be to set a deadline for the party in default, so that if performance is still not forthcoming, the innocent party may then go ahead and terminate.[157]

J. Termination for the Wrong Reason

A party to a contract who terminates without good reason will normally be held **4.37** to have repudiated the contract, so giving rise to a corresponding right of termination by the other party. But what if the party who terminates then becomes aware of some factor which would have justified the termination? Can he or she then rely on that factor as a defence? The general answer to this question is that this is allowed, so long as the relevant excuse existed at the time of the termination. A good example of this is *Boston Deep Sea Fishing & Ice Co v Ansell*,[158] where the defendant was dismissed for misconduct, following which the plaintiffs sued him for damages and an account of profits. The defendant then counterclaimed for wrongful dismissal. The plaintiffs were not able to substantiate the original allegations, but subsequently discovered that the defendant had been taking secret commissions contrary to the terms of his employment. It was held by the Court of

---

[153] *Peter Turnbull & Co Pty Ltd v Mundus Trading Co (Australasia) Pty Ltd* (1954) 90 CLR 235 (HCA); *Foran v Wight* (1989) 168 CLR 385 (HCA) 422 (Dawson J); Andrews et al, *Contractual Duties*, para 14-023 (n 14); RA Blackburn, 'Anticipatory Breach and Condition Precedent' (1955) 71 LQR 473; JW Carter, 'Foran v Wight' (1990–91) 3 JCL 70; A Beech, 'Terminating a Contract: Dispensing with the Requirement of Readiness and Willingness' (1992) 5 JCL 47.

[154] [1989] AC 788 (HL) 805–6 (Lord Ackner). Unfortunately for the owners in this case, they would not have been able to have the ship ready even if the charterers had not repudiated.

[155] In this sort of situation the remedy can be obtained even before the time for performance has arrived: *Hasham v Zenab* [1960] AC 316 (JCPC–Eastern Africa). For the general rules governing the availability of specific performance, see Burrows et al, *Chitty on Contracts*, ch 27 (n 3).

[156] Andrews et al, *Contractual Duties*, paras 14-032–14-036 (n 14).

[157] *Charles Rickards Ltd v Oppenhaim* [1950] 1 KB 616 (CA); see further Ch 7, paras 7.39–7.44.

[158] (1889) 39 Ch D 339 (CA); *Arcos Ltd v E A Ronaasen & Son* [1933] AC 470 (HL); *Force India Formula One Team Ltd v Etihad Airways PJSC* [2010] EWCA Civ 1051, [2011] ETLR 10.

Appeal that the plaintiffs could rely on this as a good reason for the dismissal. As Lord Sumner later said in *British and Beningtons Ltd v North Western Cachar Tea Co Ltd*,[159] a person who terminates without giving any reason at all can rely on any available defences that may exist; the court will not look into his or her reasons or motives for doing so. It therefore follows that even if the party terminating gives a bad reason, that will not prevent him or her later relying on a good reason if one can be found.[160] The only situation where this will not apply is where the problem is one that could have been put right if it had been brought to the notice of the party in default.[161] The general principle is well expressed by Lord Sumner:[162]

> What he says is of course very material upon the question whether he means to repudiate at all, and, if so, how far, and how much, and on the question in what respects he waives the performance of conditions still performable in futuro or dispenses the opposite party from performing his own obligations any further; but I do not see how the fact, that the buyers have wrongly said 'we treat this contract as being at an end, owing to your unreasonable delay in the performance of it' obliges them, when that reason fails, to pay in full, if, at the very time of this repudiation, the sellers had become wholly and finally disabled from performing essential terms of the contract altogether.

4.38 However, this only applies where the relevant excuse existed at the time of the termination. A party who accepts a repudiation does not have to show that he or she would, in fact, have been able to perform; after all, the main point of terminating is to release the innocent party from the duty to perform any future primary obligations under the contract. This is well illustrated by the facts of *British and Beningtons Ltd v North Western Cachar Tea Co Ltd* itself,[163] which involved a contract for the sale of tea for delivery in London. The tea having been diverted by the authorities to other ports, the buyers terminated the contract on the ground that

---

[159] [1923] AC 48 (HL) 71; see also *Taylor v Oakes Roncoroni & Co* (1922) 127 LT 267, 269 (Greer LJ); *Stocznia Gdanska SA v Latvian Shipping Co (No 2)* [2002] EWCA Civ 889, [2002] 2 Lloyd's Rep 436, para 32 (Rix LJ); *Stocznia Gdynia SA v Gearbulk Holdings Ltd* [2009] EWCA Civ 75, [2010] QB 37, para 153, (Moore-Bick LJ), *Tele2 International Card Company SA v Post Office Ltd* [2009] EWCA Civ 9, para 30 (Aikens LJ); Andrews et al, *Contractual Duties*, paras 8-048–8-053 (n 14).

[160] Perhaps this can best be explained on the ground that the innocent party's duty to perform was conditional on the other party performing his or her part; such performance not being forthcoming, the innocent party was never obliged to perform in the first place: F Dawson, 'Waiver of Conditions Precedent on a Repudiation' (1980) 96 LQR 239.

[161] *Heisler v Anglo-Dal Ltd* [1954] 1 WLR 1273 (CA) 1278 (Somervell LJ).

[162] [1923] AC 48 (HL), 71–2.

[163] [1923] AC 48 (HL). Thus a buyer under a cif contract cannot reject the documents merely because he or she suspects that the goods may not conform with the contract when tendered: *Gill & Duffus SA v Berger & Co Inc* [1984] AC 382 (HL); M Clarke, 'Papering over Cracked Goods—Contracts C.I.F.' [1984] CLJ 233. But it would be different if the seller could show that at the time the buyer was 'totally and finally disabled' from producing the goods in accordance with the contract under the principle in *Universal Cargo Carriers Corp v Citati* [1957] 2 QB 401; see *Sunbird Plaza Pty Ltd v Maloney* (1988) 62 ALR 195; J Harris, 'Anticipatory Breach—Innocent Party's Right to Terminate' (1988–89) 1 JCL 177, 180; see Ch 7, para 7.35.

a reasonable time for delivery had passed. The arbitrator having decided that the termination was premature, it was held by the House of Lords that the sellers could recover damages for repudiation without having to show that they were ready and willing to deliver the goods in London when the time came. Similarly, as Treitel says, a buyer of goods who indicates that he or she will not accept them cannot rely on the fact that the seller was about to tender goods that did not conform with the contract description; at that point, the seller was not in breach, and even if the wrong goods had been tendered, the sellers might have been able to make a proper tender at a later date.[164]

There are, however, three cases which cause difficulties in this connection. The **4.39** first is the notoriously difficult case of *Braithwaite v Foreign Hardwood Co.*[165] This involved a contract for the sale of rosewood for shipment in instalments to Hull, cash payable against bill of lading. While the first consignment was still en route, the buyers repudiated the entire contract on a ground that was later found to be baseless. The sellers then contacted the buyers and indicated that the bill of lading was ready to be handed over,[166] but the buyers said they would not accept it; the sellers then sold the goods elsewhere and claimed damages for non-acceptance. At this point it was discovered that the consignment in question did not fit the contract description, and the buyers argued that this provided them with a good defence. The Court of Appeal, however, found for the sellers, Collins MR saying that it was not open to the buyers, having wrongfully repudiated the contract, to 'hark back' and say that the sellers were not ready and willing to perform.[167] At first sight this seems to be contrary to the principle discussed earlier, whereby a party who repudiates can rely on any good excuse that existed at the time of the repudiation;[168] if the plaintiffs in *Boston Deep Sea Fishing & Ice Co v Ansell*[169] were allowed to 'hark back', why were the buyers in the *Braithwaite* case not equally entitled to 'hark back'? The facts of the case are not entirely clear, and it has been subject to adverse criticism,[170] but perhaps the best explanation is that the excuse relied on

---

[164] Peel, *Treitel*, para 17-061 (n 10).

[165] [1905] 2 KB 543 (CA); Carter, *Carter's Breach of Contract*, paras 9-29–9-31 (n 15).

[166] Whether this involved an actual tender of the bill of lading is not clear; if it did, it would have amounted to an affirmation of the contract by the sellers, which makes the decision even more inexplicable, as this should have kept the contract alive for the benefit of both parties and hence have allowed the buyers to rely on any supervening events, including further breaches by the sellers: see Ch 12, para 12.03. However, the orthodox interpretation of the case now seems to be that there was no actual tender and hence no affirmation: *Fercometal SARL v Mediterranean Shipping Co SA (The Simona)* [1989] AC 788, 801–4 (Lord Ackner); Carter, *Carter's Breach of Contract*, para 9-30 (n 15).

[167] [1905] 2 KB 543, 551.

[168] See para 4.37.

[169] (1889) 39 Ch D 339 (CA); discussed at para 4.37.

[170] MG Lloyd, 'Ready and Willing to Perform: the Problem of Prospective Inability in the Law of Contract' (1974) 37 MLR 121; JW Carter, 'The Higher Altitudes of Contract Law' [1989] LMCLQ 81; and see the cases cited by Carter, *Carter's Breach of Contract*, para 9-29, fn 164 (n 15). Carter himself says there that it should be 'confined to its own facts'.

by the buyers did not exist at the time of the repudiation; though non-conforming goods had been shipped, they had not yet been tendered, and there was nothing to stop the sellers coming up, when the time came for delivery, with goods that were in conformity with the contract.[171] On that basis the *Braithwaite* decision is more or less on all fours with *British and Beningtons Ltd v North Western Cachar Tea Co Ltd*,[172] and has therefore been described by Carter as, from that perspective at least, an orthodox decision on the effects of termination.[173] To adapt the words of Collins MR, the repudiating party is entitled to 'hark back' to an excuse that existed at the time of the repudiation, but cannot 'hark forward' to something that might have transpired later if the repudiation had not taken place or had not been accepted.

4.40 The second case is *Universal Cargo Carriers Corporation v Citati*,[174] which involved the termination of a charterparty by the shipowners on the basis that the charterers had failed to provide a cargo and were unlikely to do so within a reasonable interval. It was held there by Devlin J that the test to be applied was whether the charterers were in a position to furnish a cargo within such a time as would not frustrate the venture; if the owners could show that the charterers were 'wholly and finally disabled' from doing this at the relevant time, then they were entitled to cancel the charter. It has been argued[175] that this goes contrary to the principle in *British and Beningtons Ltd v North Western Cachar Tea Co Ltd*,[176] whereby a party who terminates can rely on an excuse existing at the time of the termination, but not on later events. However, the difference is more apparent than real. In so far as the *British and Beningtons* case suggests that a party who repudiates cannot justify his or her action by reference to future events, that case is certainly inconsistent with *Universal Cargo Carriers Corporation v Citati*, but it does not say this; what it says is that a party can accept a repudiation without having to show readiness and willingness to perform his or her own obligations under the contract.[177] It does not suggest that the repudiating party cannot excuse his or her actions by showing total disablement;[178] on the contrary, this would itself amount to an anticipatory breach by the other party,[179] so bringing the situation within the basic rule whereby the repudiating party can rely on any excuses existing at the time of the repudiation.

---

[171] See Peel, *Treitel*, para 17-026, (n 10).
[172] [1923] AC 48 (HL); see para 4.37.
[173] Carter, *Carter's Breach of Contract*, para 9-31 (n 15).
[174] [1957] 2 QB 401, discussed further in Ch 7, paras 7.32–7.36.
[175] Dawson, 'Waiver of Conditions Precedent' (n 160).
[176] [1923] AC 48 (HL); see paras 4.38–4.39.
[177] See para 4.39.
[178] Indeed, the very phrase used by Devlin J, 'wholly and finally disabled', is taken from the opinion of Lord Sumner in *British and Beningtons* quoted at para 4.37 (n 162), which was expressly approved by Devlin J: [1957] 2 QB 401, 445. Lord Sumner went on to say that the facts in *British and Beningtons* fell far short of showing such a state of affairs: [1923] AC 48 (HL) 72.
[179] See Ch 7, para 7.35.

The third of these tricky cases is *Panchaud Frères SA v Etablissement General Grain* **4.41**
Co,[180] decided by the Court of Appeal in 1970. This involved a contract for the
sale of maize at a price of '$65 per 1000 kilos gross for net delivered weight, c.i.f.
Antwerp'. The buyers duly made payment against the shipping documents without
complaint, but then rejected the goods on arrival on the grounds that they did not
comply with the description given in the bill of lading. The dispute having gone
to arbitration, an umpire upheld the buyers' claim to reject on this basis, but on
appeal the ground was abandoned on advice that it did not allow the goods to be
rejected vis-à-vis the sellers. However, it was then discovered that the date on the
bill of lading was false, and that the goods had not been shipped within the contract period. The buyer now sought to raise this as a ground for rejection, despite
the fact that it was now over three years since the goods had been shipped. The
sellers, however, claimed that by paying against the shipping documents without
complaint the buyers had waived the right to rely on the point, and an arbitration
appeal committee found for the sellers on this basis.[181] The decision was reversed
by Roskill J (as he then was), but an appeal by the sellers was allowed by the Court
of Appeal, albeit on uncertain grounds. According to Denning MR, this was not a
case of waiver strictly speaking, but rather of 'estoppel by conduct';[182] the principle
being that 'if a man, who is entitled to reject goods on a certain ground, so conducts
himself as to lead the other to believe that he is not relying on that ground, then
he cannot afterwards set it up as a ground of rejection, when it would be unfair
or unjust to allow him to do so'.[183] Winn LJ agreed that this was not waiver in the
legal sense, preferring to rely on what he called 'a criterion of what is fair conduct
between the parties... an inchoate doctrine stemming from the manifest convenience of consistency in pragmatic affairs, negativing any liberty to blow hot and cold
in commercial conduct'.[184] For his part, Cross LJ stressed the fact that though the
buyers were unaware of the discrepancy at the relevant time, it could have been discovered fairly easily.[185] But none of the four grounds given for the decision stands
up to scrutiny. It does not look like waiver, as the buyers had no actual knowledge
of the breach at the time of payment.[186] It does not look like estoppel, as it is hard
to see either an unequivocal representation by the buyers that they would not rely

---

[180] [1970] 1 Lloyd's Rep 53 (CA); T Dugdale and D Yates, 'Variation, Waiver and Estoppel: a
Reappraisal' (1976) 39 MLR 680; JW Carter, 'Panchaud Frères Explained' (1999) 14 JCL 239;
Carter, *Carter's Breach of Contract*, para 10-53 (n 15); Peel, *Treitel*, para 17-063 (n 10). It has been
pointed out that the problem is most likely to arise on a falling market: see LR Eno, 'Price Movement
and Unstated Objections to the Defective Performance of Sales Contracts' (1935) 44 Yale LJ 782,
and cf *Littlejohn v Shaw* 159 NY 188, 53 NE 810 (1899).
[181] *Panchaud Frères SA v Etablissement General Grain Co* [1970] 1 Lloyd's Rep 53 (CA) 56.
[182] *Panchaud Frères v Etablissement General*, 56 (n 181).
[183] *Panchaud Frères v Etablissement General*, 57 (n 181).
[184] *Panchaud Frères v Etablissement General*, 59 (n 181).
[185] *Panchaud Frères v Etablissement General*, 61 (n 181).
[186] *Motor Oil Hellas (Corinth) Refineries SA v Shipping Corp of India (The Kanchenjunga)* [1990]
1 Lloyd's Rep 391 (HL) 399 (Lord Goff); see further para 4.56.

on their rights or any conduct by the sellers undertaken in reliance on that representation.[187] The principle of 'fair conduct' set out by Winn LJ is too vague to be of any practical use,[188] and the approach of Cross LJ comes very near to a doctrine of constructive notice, something which is said to have no application in commercial affairs.[189] The case has subsequently been explained on a number of grounds,[190] but the orthodox view seems to be that it lays down no distinct principles of law,[191] and perhaps it is best regarded as a decision based very much on its own particular facts.

K. Restrictions on Termination

4.42 The common law right to terminate may be restricted in some cases; in particular, it may be subject to restrictions in the contract and to statutory restrictions.

(1) Contractual restrictions

4.43 Contractual restrictions on termination can be total or partial. In the first case, the right of the innocent party to terminate is excluded altogether, and he or she is restricted to other remedies, most notably damages.[192] In the second case the right is cut down in some way, for instance by making it subject to certain conditions, such as the duty to warn the party in default,[193] or setting a time limit for its exercise. In either case regard must be had to the general principles of the law regarding exemption clauses; such clauses must be properly incorporated into the contract, they must on their proper construction cover the events that have occurred, and they must not fall foul of statutory restrictions. The principles of incorporation have already been discussed,[194] and there is no need to refer to them in the present

---

[187] *The Kanchenjunga*, 399 (Lord Goff) (n 186); see further paras 4.60–4.61.

[188] Peel, *Treitel*, para 17-063 (n 10).

[189] *Manchester Trust v Furness* [1895] 2 QB 539 (CA) 545 (Lindley LJ); *Greer v Downs Supply Co* [1927] 2 KB 28 (CA) 36 (Scrutton LJ).

[190] According to Peel, *Treitel*, para 17-063 (n 10), the buyer's right to reject was lost by acceptance, and this explanation was also given by Robert Goff J in *BP Exploration Co (Libya) Ltd v Hunt (No 2)* [1979] 1 WLR 783, 811 and by the Court of Appeal in *Glencore Grain Rotterdam BV v Lebanese Organisation for International Commerce (The Lorico)* [1997] CLC 1274 (CA) 1288 (Evans LJ). However, as Carter points out (Carter, *Carter's Breach of Contract*, para 10-53 (n 15)) there is no reason to deny a cif buyer's right to reject non-contractual *goods* merely because he has accepted non-contractual *documents*.

[191] *V Berg & Son Ltd v Vanden Avenne-Izegem PVBA* [1977] 1 Lloyd's Rep 499 (CA), 504 (Roskill LJ); *Procter & Gamble Philippine Manufacturing Corp v Peter Cremer GmbH & Co (The Manila)* [1988] 3 All ER 843 (QBD), 852 (Hirst J); *The Lorico* [1997] CLC 1274 (CA) 1288 (Evans LJ) (n 190).

[192] Thus contracts for the sale of goods may contain clauses excluding the buyer's right to reject, as in *Robert A Munro & Co Ltd v Meyer* [1930] 2 KB 312 (Wright J).

[193] As in the case of 'anti-technicality' clauses in a charterparty: see *Afovos Shipping Co SA v Pagnan & Flli (The Afovos)* [1983] 1 WLR 195 (HL); *North Range Shipping Co Ltd v Seatrans Shipping Corp (The Western Triumph)* [2002] EWCA Civ 405, [2002] 1 WLR 2397; *Owneast Shipping Ltd v Qatar Navigation QSC (The Qatar Star)* [2010] EWHC 1663 (Comm), [2011] 1 Lloyd's Rep 350.

[194] See Ch 3, para 3.27.

context, but the other two requirements raise particular issues in relation to termination which need to be considered further.

(a) Rules of construction

As has been seen, an exemption clause must, as a matter of construction, have the **4.44** effect contended for by the party relying on it,[195] and some of the cases on this rule have particular relevance in the context of termination. Thus, for instance, a clause saying that no 'warranty' is given will not be effective to exclude the remedies for breach of condition;[196] a clause excluding the right to damages will not exclude the right to terminate,[197] or vice versa.[198] In the past the courts have sometimes applied this rule in an exceedingly pedantic manner, so as to avoid the application of terms that they considered unfair or harsh, but now that there is statutory protection in place, it has been said that the courts will be less inclined to place a strained construction on words which are clear and fairly susceptible of only one meaning.[199]

Some reference should perhaps also be made here to the so-called doctrine of **4.45** 'fundamental breach', not least because the present work makes use of that very useful concept.[200] The definition of 'fundamental breach' adopted by the present work is that given by Lord Upjohn in *Suisse Atlantique Société d'Armement Maritime v Rotterdamsche Kolen Centrale*,[201] namely a breach which goes to the root of the contract and entitles the other party to treat such breach or breaches as a repudiation of the whole contract.[202] However, the term was also used in the past in a different connection, namely as a principle derived from cases involving maritime deviation[203] that a party could not rely on an exemption clause in the contract when he or she had substantially failed to perform that contract.[204] At one level this was simply a rule of construction whereby it was presumed that the parties could not have intended an exemption clause to provide protection in

---

[195] E Macdonald, *Exemption Clauses and Unfair Terms* (2nd edn, Tottel, 2006) ch 2.

[196] *Wallis, Son & Wells v Pratt & Haynes* [1911] AC 394 (HL).

[197] *Suisse Atlantique Société d'Armement SA v Rotterdamsche Kolen Centrale* [1967] 1 AC 361 (HL); *SHV Gas Supply & Trading SAS v Naftomar Shipping & Trading Co Ltd Inc (The Azur Gaz)* [2005] EWHC 2528 (Comm), [2006] 1 Lloyd's Rep 163, para 28 (Christopher Clarke J); Carter, *Carter's Breach of Contract*, para 10-32 (n 15).

[198] *Ernest Beck & Co v K Szymanowski & Co* [1924] AC 43 (HL) 52 (Lord Shaw); *Toomey v Eagle Star Insurance Co (No 2)* [1995] 2 Lloyd's Rep 88 (QBD: Commercial Ct) (Colman J); Carter, *Carter's Breach of Contract*, para 10-32 (n 15).

[199] *Photo Production Ltd v Securicor Transport Ltd* [1980] AC 826 (HL) 851 (Lord Diplock); Beatson, Burrows, and Cartwright, *Anson's Law of Contract*, p 179 (n 3).

[200] See Ch 6.

[201] [1967] 1 AC 361 (HL).

[202] *Suisse Atlantique v Rotterdamsche Kolen Centrale*, 421–2 (n 201).

[203] *Davis v Garrett* (1830) 6 Bing 716, 130 ER 1456; *Hain Steamship Co v Tate & Lyle Ltd* (1936) 41 Com Cas 350 (HL).

[204] Carter, *Carter's Breach of Contract*, para 10-30 (n 15), Peel, *Treitel*, para 7-031 (n 10).

such circumstances,[205] and to that extent the principle is an uncontroversial one. However, there was also authority for regarding it as a rule of law,[206] the reasoning being that since a fundamental breach brought the contract to an end, exemption clauses in the contract could no longer apply.[207] There was always an element of circularity to this reasoning,[208] and it did not tally with the way termination works,[209] but for all its shortcomings the doctrine did admittedly serve to prevent parties exploiting a stronger bargaining position by the imposition of oppressive clauses of this nature.[210] However, following the advent of the Unfair Contract Terms Act 1977 the doctrine had served its purpose, and shortly afterwards it was given its *quietus* by the House of Lords.[211] Except perhaps in the very specialized context of deviation,[212] the doctrine (if indeed it still exists at all)[213] is one of construction only, and the term 'fundamental breach' is now free to be applied in a more suitable way.

(b) Statutory controls

4.46 As has been seen, the Unfair Contract Terms Act 1977 restricts the use of exemption clauses either by preventing a party from relying on them at all, or by allowing such reliance only in so far as the term in question satisfies the test of reasonableness.[214] Once again a number of provisions are of particular relevance to termination.

---

[205] *Leduc v Ward* (1888) 20 QBD 475 (CA); *Glynn v Margetson & Co* [1893] AC 351 (HL); *Connolly Shaw Ltd v A/S Det Nordenfjedlske D/S* (1934) 49 Ll LR 183 (KBD); *UGS Finance Ltd v National Mortgage Bank of Greece and National Bank of Greece SA* [1964] 1 Lloyd's Rep 446 (CA) 453 (Pearson LJ).

[206] *Karsales (Harrow) Ltd v Wallis* [1956] 1 WLR 969 (CA); *Charterhouse Credit Co Ltd v Tolly* [1963] 2 QB 683 (CA).

[207] *Harbutt's 'Plasticine' Ltd v Wayne Tank and Pump Co* [1970] 1 QB 447; JA Weir, 'Nec Tamen Consumebatur—Frustration and Limitation Clauses' [1970] CLJ 189; JH Baker, 'Suisse Atlantique Confounded' (1970) 33 MLR 441; PN Legh-Jones and MA Pickering, 'Harbutt's "Plasticine" Ltd v Wayne Tank and Pump Co Ltd: Fundamental Breach and Exemption Clauses, Damages and Interest (1970) 86 LQR 513; PN Legh-Jones and MA Pickering, 'Fundamental Breach: the Aftermath of Harbutt's "Plasticine"' (1971) 87 LQR 515.

[208] As Lord Wilberforce pointed out in the *Suisse Atlantique* case (see n 201), an act which, apart from the exceptions clause, might be a breach sufficiently serious to justify refusal of further performance, might be reduced in effect, or made not a breach at all, by the terms of the clause: [1967] 1 AC 361, 431.

[209] In particular: (1) it is not the breach that terminates the contract but the election of the innocent party consequent on the breach, and (2) termination does not bring the whole contract to an end, but only the primary obligations of the parties: *Photo Production Ltd v Securicor Transport Ltd* [1980] AC 826 (HL) 844 (Lord Wilberforce), and 847–51 (Lord Diplock).

[210] *Photo Production v Securicor Transport*, 843 (Lord Wilberforce) (n 209).

[211] *Photo Production v Securicor Transport* (n 209); AG Guest (1980) 96 LQR 324; A Nicol and N Rawlings, 'Substantive Fundamental Breach Burnt Out' (1980) 43 MLR 567; LS Sealy, 'Contract—Farewell to the Doctrine of Fundamental Breach' [1980] CLJ 252.

[212] J Livermore, 'Deviation, Deck Cargo and Fundamental Breach' (1989–90) 2 JCL 241; S Baughen, 'Does Deviation Still Matter?' [1991] LMCLQ 70; M Dockray, 'Deviation: a Doctrine All at Sea' [2000] LMCLQ 76; Peel, *Treitel*, para 7-032 (n 10).

[213] Carter, *Carter's Breach of Contract*, paras 10-30 and 12-32 (n 15).

[214] See Macdonald, *Exemption Clauses and Unfair Terms* (n 195).

The first is section 3 of the 1977 Act, which applies in cases where one party deals as **4.47** consumer or on the other's written standard terms of business.[215] In such cases the other party is prevented from doing three things by reference to any contract term except in so far as the term satisfies the test of reasonableness.[216] These are as follows: (1) exclude or restrict his or her liability for breach of contract,[217] or (2) claim to be entitled to render a contractual performance 'substantially different from that which was reasonably expected of him',[218] or (3) claim to be entitled in respect of the whole or part of his or her contractual obligation to render no performance at all.[219] The first of these is clearly relevant to termination; a clause which restricts the right of the innocent party to terminate where otherwise he or she would have been fully entitled to do so is clearly covered by the section,[220] as is one which makes the exercise of that right subject to restrictive or onerous conditions.[221] The third may also be relevant to termination, but in a different context, namely where the clause in question *grants* the innocent party an unreasonably wide right of termination; this will be discussed later.[222]

The next is section 6 of the Unfair Contract Terms Act 1977, which deals with **4.48** liability for breach of the implied terms as to title, description, quality, and fitness for purpose in sections 12 to 15 of the Sale of Goods Act 1979.[223] Section 6(1) says that the implied term as to title cannot be excluded or restricted by reference to any contract term. Section 6(2) goes on to say that the other implied terms cannot be excluded or restricted as against a person dealing as consumer; other cases are covered by section 6(3) which allows this to be done, but only in so far as the term satisfies the test of reasonableness. Since these implied terms are all conditions, giving the buyer the right to terminate for breach,[224] section 6 applies not only to attempts to exclude liability altogether, but also to situations where the seller seeks to restrict the buyer's rights in this regard.

---

[215] Unfair Contract Terms Act 1977 (UCTA 1977), s 3(1). For the definition of 'deals as consumer' see s 12; for 'other's written standard terms of business' see *Chester Grosvenor Hotel v Alfred McAlpine Management Ltd* (1991) 56 Build LR 115 (Judge Stannard, Official Referee); *Stewart Gill v Horatio Myer & Co Ltd* [1992] 2 QB 600 (CA); *St Albans City and District Council v International Computers Ltd* [1996] 4 All ER 481 (CA); *Paragon Finance plc v Nash* [2001] EWCA Civ 1466, [2002] 1 WLR 685; *Commerzbank AG v Keen* [2006] EWCA Civ 1536, [2006] 2 CLC 844; Macdonald, *Exemption Clauses and Unfair Terms*, pp 118–26 (n 195).

[216] As defined in UCTA 1977, s 11; see Macdonald, *Exemption Clauses and Unfair Terms*, pp 161–76 (n 195); J Adams, 'An Optimistic Look at the Contract Provisions of the Unfair Contract Terms Act 1977' (1978) 41 MLR 703.

[217] UCTA 1977, s 3(2)(a).

[218] UCTA 1977, s 3(2)(b)(i).

[219] UCTA 1977, s 3(2)(b)(ii).

[220] *Timeload Ltd v British Telecommunications plc* [1995] EMLR 459 (CA) 468 (Bingham MR).

[221] UCTA 1977, s 13(1)(a).

[222] See para 4.51.

[223] Macdonald, *Exemption Clauses and Unfair Terms*, pp 138–45 (n 195). UCTA 1977, s 7 makes similar provision for other contracts under which goods pass.

[224] See Ch 5. But where the buyer is not dealing as consumer, this may be subject to the restrictions in the Sale of Goods Act 1979, s 15A: see para 4.52.

4.49   Mention may also be made of the Unfair Terms in Consumer Contracts Regulations 1999,[225] which apply in relation to unfair terms in contracts concluded between a seller or supplier and a consumer.[226] A term which has not been individually negotiated will be regarded as unfair if, contrary to the requirement of good faith, it causes a significant imbalance in the parties' rights and obligations arising under the contract, to the detriment of the consumer.[227] Schedule 2 to the Regulations gives examples of terms which may be regarded as unfair;[228] in particular, a term 'inappropriately excluding or limiting the legal rights of the consumer vis-à-vis the seller or supplier or another party in the event of total or partial non-performance or inadequate performance by the seller or supplier of any of the contractual obligations'; this would clearly cover a provision excluding or restricting the consumer's right to terminate,[229] which would therefore not be binding on the consumer,[230] though the contract itself might continue to bind the parties if it was capable of continuing in existence without the unfair term.[231]

(2) Statutory restrictions

4.50   The right to terminate may also be restricted by statute. One common way in which this is done is to provide that the right cannot be exercised without giving the party in default due warning of the breach and allowing him or her a reasonable opportunity to put matters right; thus, for instance, section 146(1) of the Law of Property Act 1925 provides that a lease cannot be forfeited for a breach of covenant without first serving a notice on the tenant specifying the breach,[232] and requiring him or her to remedy it (if it is capable of remedy)[233] or pay compensation (if it is not);[234] only if such remedy or compensation is not forthcoming within a reasonable period may the lessor forfeit the lease. In the same way, section 87 of the Consumer Credit Act 1974 requires a creditor to serve a 'default notice' before terminating a regulated agreement as defined by the Act; such a notice must

---

[225] Macdonald, *Exemption Clauses and Unfair Terms*, ch 4 (n 195).

[226] Unfair Terms in Consumer Contracts Regulations 1999, SI 1999/2083, reg 3(1); Macdonald, *Exemption Clauses and Unfair Terms*, pp 198–206 (n 195).

[227] SI 1999/2083, reg 5(1) (n 226); Macdonald, *Exemption Clauses and Unfair Terms*, pp 227–49 (n 195).

[228] Macdonald, *Exemption Clauses and Unfair Terms*, pp 249–82 (n 195).

[229] SI 1999/2083, Sch 2, para 1(b) (n 226).

[230] SI 1999/2083, reg 8(1) (n 226).

[231] SI 1999/2083, reg 8(2) (n 226).

[232] Law of Property Act 1925, s 146(1)(a); *Akici v LR Butlin Ltd* [2005] EWCA Civ 1296, [2006] 1 WLR 201.

[233] Law of Property Act 1925, s 146(1)(b).

[234] Law of Property Act 1925, s 146(1)(c). A breach may be capable of remedy even though it is of a covenant the time of performance of which has passed: *Expert Clothing Service & Sales Ltd v Hillgate House Ltd* (1985) 50 P & CR 317 (CA) 336 (Slade LJ). But breaches of negative covenants are not capable of remedy within the subsection: *Rugby School (Governors) v Tannahill* [1934] 1 KB 695 (CA); *Scala House & District Property Co v Forbes* [1974] QB 575 (CA).

specify: (a) the nature of the alleged breach; (b) if the breach is capable of remedy, what action is required to remedy it, and the date before which that action is to be taken; and (c) if the breach is not capable of remedy, the sum (if any) required to be paid as compensation for the breach, and the date before which it is to be paid.[235] These and other provisions are designed to protect the party in default by ensuring that termination does not take place unless he or she is clearly unable or unwilling to perform the contract according to its terms.[236]

There are also provisions in place to prevent a party relying on unduly harsh termin-   **4.51** ation provisions in situations where the parties are not on equal terms. In the context of employment, the whole law of unfair dismissal may be seen as an example of this,[237] as may the law protecting residential tenants from summary eviction.[238] Again, one type of term which may fall foul of the Unfair Terms in Consumer Contracts Regulations 1999 is one 'enabling the seller or supplier to terminate a contract of indeterminate duration without reasonable notice except where there are serious grounds for doing so';[239] if found to be unfair within the meaning of the Regulations,[240] such terms will not be binding on the consumer.[241] Section 3(2)(b)(ii) of the Unfair Contract Terms Act 1977 may also be of relevance here; this provides that where a party deals as consumer or on the other's written standard terms of business, the other party cannot by reference to any term in the contract claim to be entitled to render no performance at all, except in so far as the term in question satisfies the test of reasonableness.[242] This could on the face of it apply to termination clauses, the whole point of which is to release the innocent party from the duty to perform his or her primary obligations under the contract.[243] It has, however, been argued that the provision in question was never intended to apply to clauses of this sort,[244] since in such cases the innocent party is claiming to be entitled to refuse performance not by reference to a contract term, but by reference to the other party's default.[245]

Section 15A of the Sale of Goods Act 1979 also merits mention in this regard.[246]   **4.52** This deals with the right to reject goods for breach of the implied conditions as to

---

[235] Consumer Credit Act 1974, s 88.

[236] The position is similar to that of a party who fails to comply with a notice making time of the essence: see Ch 7, paras 7.39–7.44.

[237] Employment Rights Act 1996, s 94. By section 95(1)(a) an employee is dismissed if the contract under which he or she is employed is terminated by the employer, whether with or without notice.

[238] Protection from Eviction Act 1977, s 2.

[239] SI 1999/2083, Sch 2, para 1(g) (n 226).

[240] SI 1999/2083, reg 5(1) (n 226); Macdonald, *Exemption Clauses and Unfair Terms*, pp 227–49 (n 195).

[241] SI 1999/2083, reg 8(1) (226).

[242] See para 4.47.

[243] Peel, *Treitel*, para 7-066 (n 10).

[244] *Paragon Finance Ltd v Nash* [2001] EWCA Civ 1466, [2002] 1 WLR 685, paras 76–77 (Dyson LJ).

[245] Peel, *Treitel*, para 7-066 (n 10).

[246] Andrews et al, *Contractual Duties*, paras 10-056–10-066 (n 14).

description, quality, and fitness for purpose under sections 13, 14, and 15 of the Act. The basic rule is that if one of these conditions is broken in any way, be it never so trivial, the buyer can reject,[247] but this rule was seen as unduly harsh by the Law Commission,[248] which recommended that it be modified except in the consumer context. This was duly implemented by the Sale and Supply of Goods Act 1994, which inserted the new section 15A into the main Act. The effect of this section is to prevent a buyer who is not dealing as consumer from rejecting goods for breach of one of the conditions mentioned in cases where the breach is 'so slight that it would be unreasonable of him to reject them';[249] instead, the buyer is restricted to his or her remedy in damages. Section 15A does not apply if a contrary intention appears in or can be implied from the contract,[250] but it nevertheless represents a significant departure from the traditional doctrine regarding conditions, the whole point of which is to give the innocent party the right to terminate irrespective of the seriousness of the breach in question.[251]

L. Loss of Right to Terminate

4.53 Even where a right of termination has arisen, it may subsequently be lost. In particular, the innocent party may lose the right as a result of waiver, or by virtue of the doctrine of 'acceptance' under the Sale of Goods Act 1979. In addition to this, the party in default may sometimes be able to avail themselves of equitable relief.

(1) Waiver

4.54 The word 'waiver' is used here not in its technical legal sense—if indeed such a technical sense exists[252]—but simply to denote the situation where the innocent party, despite having the right to terminate, relinquishes that right. That the innocent party may lose his or her right to terminate on this basis is not open to doubt, but the basis on which the right is lost is less certain. However, there seem to be two separate doctrines at work here, one being waiver by election and the other equitable or promissory estoppel.

---

[247] *Re Moore & Co Ltd and Landauer &Co* [1921] 2 KB 519 (CA); *Arcos Ltd v EA Ronaasen & Son* [1933] AC 470 (HL); R Brownsword, 'Retrieving Reasons, Retrieving Rationality: a New Look at the Right to Withdraw for Breach of Contract' (1992) 5 JCL 83; Andrews et al, *Contractual Duties,* paras 10-062–10-063 (n 14).

[248] Law Commission, *Sale and Supply of Goods* (Law Com No 196, 1987).

[249] Sale of Goods Act 1979, s 15A(1)(b); *Hi-Flyers Ltd v Linde Gas UK Ltd* [2004] EWHC 105 (Cox J).

[250] Sale of Goods Act 1979, s 15A(2).

[251] See Ch 5, para 5.06.

[252] According to Lord Wright in *Ross T Smyth & Co Ltd v TD Bailey, Son & Co* (1940) 164 LT 102 (HL) 106, the then current edition of *Stroud's Judicial Dictionary* listed at least thirteen different senses of the term. See also the analysis of Potter LJ in *The Happy Day* [2002] EWCA Civ 1068, [2002] 2 Lloyd's Rep 487, paras 64–68; T Solvang, 'Notice of Readiness under Voyage Charters' [2001] LMCLQ 465.

(a) Waiver by election

As Lord Goff pointed out in *The Kanchenjunga*,[253] the term 'waiver' can be used in **4.55** a number of different ways,[254] but the most significant one in the present context is what he describes as 'waiver in the sense of abandonment of a right which arises by virtue of a party making an election'.[255] What is at issue here is the election of the innocent party whether to terminate or affirm, and in this sense, Carter is right in saying that waiver does not exist as a separate doctrine in this context;[256] it is merely an application of the general rules regarding election. Termination for breach of contract does not occur automatically; the innocent party has a choice whether to terminate or to affirm, and in some cases the conduct of the innocent party will be consistent only with the latter option. In the passage which follows the requirements of waiver in this sense will be considered, before going on to look at its effect.

(i) Requirements According to Eder J in *The Mahakam*, waiver in the present **4.56** context involves 'the unequivocal affirmation of the continuation of a contract with knowledge of a breach justifying termination of the contract'.[257] This gives us two basic requirements: (1) knowledge by the innocent party; and (2) clear and unequivocal words or conduct on his or her part evincing an intention inconsistent with termination. According to Lord Goff in *The Kanchenjunga*, 'it is a prerequisite of election that the party making the election must be aware of the facts which have given rise to the existence of his new right'.[258] This means that the innocent party cannot be held to have affirmed without proof that he or she was at least aware of the relevant breach.[259] What about a party who knew of the relevant facts, but was unaware of their significance? According to the Court of Appeal in *Peyman v Lanjani*,[260] this is not enough; the innocent party must not only be aware of the facts, but of the legal right to which they give rise. This

---

[253] *Motor Oil Hellas (Corinth) Refineries SA v Shipping Corp of India (The Kanchenjunga)* [1990] 1 Lloyd's Rep 391 (HL).

[254] *The Kanchenjunga*, 397 (Lord Goff) (n 253). In particular, it can also denote: (1) 'rescission' in the sense of discharge by agreement (as in *Price v Dyer* (1810) 17 Ves 356, 364, 34 ER 137, 140 (Grant MR)); (2) variation (as in *Brikom Investments Ltd v Carr* [1979] QB 467 (CA) 488 (Roskill LJ)); (3) forbearance (as in *Hartley v Hymans* [1920] 3 KB 475 (KBD) (McCardie J)): Peel, *Treitel*, paras 3-066–3-075 (n 10).

[255] [1990] 1 Lloyd's Rep 391, 398.

[256] Carter, *Carter's Breach of Contract*, para 10-33 (n 15).

[257] *Parbulk II A/S v Heritage Maritime Ltd SA (The Mahakam)* [2011] EWHC 2917 (Comm), [2012] 1 Lloyd's Rep 87, para 94.

[258] [1990] 1 Lloyd's Rep 391, 398.

[259] *Hain Steamship Co v Tate & Lyle Ltd* (1936) 41 Com Cas 350 (HL) 372 (Lord Maugham); *UGS Finance Ltd v National Mortgage Bank of Greece and National Bank of Greece SA* [1964] 1 Lloyd's Rep 446 (CA) 450 (Lord Denning MR); *Panchaud Frères SA v Etablissements General Grain Co* [1970] 1 Lloyd's Rep 53 (CA) 57 (Lord Denning MR); *Kammins Ballrooms Co Ltd v Zenith Investments (Torquay) Ltd* [1971] AC 850 (HL) 877–8 (Lord Pearson); *Metropolitan Properties v Cordery* (1979) 251 EG 567 (CA).

[260] [1985] Ch 457 (CA); *Stevens & Cutting Ltd v Anderson* [1990] 11 EG 70 (CA); *Banner Industrial & Commercial Properties v Clark Paterson* [1990] 47 EG 64 (Hoffmann J); *Garside v Black Horse Ltd* [2010] EWHC 190 (QB).

was a case where an Iranian who spoke no English agreed to purchase leasehold premises for use as a restaurant. The vendor's title was defective, a previous assignment of the lease to the vendor having been obtained by fraud. The purchaser subsequently became aware of the fraud, but acting on the advice of his solicitor (who was also acting for the vendors in the transaction) he went ahead with the purchase and went into possession. However, having later changed his solicitor he subsequently purported to terminate the contract. The vendors argued that he had lost the right to do so by having gone into possession with knowledge of what had taken place, but the Court of Appeal held that this was not enough in the absence of proof that the purchaser was aware of his right to terminate at the relevant time. Whilst one can understand why the court were anxious to protect the purchaser in this situation, the case has been heavily criticized by Carter;[261] in particular, it creates an inconsistency between the requirements for termination and those for affirmation,[262] and between cases where the right to terminate was expressly conferred by the contract and those where it arose by operation of law.[263]

4.57   It is said that for the innocent party to lose the right of termination in this sort of case his or her decision to affirm must be 'clear and unequivocal'.[264] In some situations the innocent party may indicate in so many words that the contract is being affirmed; in others his or her conduct will be consistent only with affirmation, as where he or she requests a decree of specific performance,[265] or demands that the other party perform obligations arising after the right to terminate comes into existence.[266] In other cases, however, the conduct of the innocent party may be equally consistent with termination, as when, for instance, he or she demands that the party in default perform obligations that had already become due at the

---

[261]   Carter, *Carter's Breach of Contract*, para 11-14 (n 15).

[262]   A party can rely on a ground for termination even though it was unknown to him or her at the relevant time: see para 4.37.

[263]   Thus where a lease allowed a landlord to forfeit for breach of covenant and he demanded rent in knowledge of such breach, the right to forfeit was lost without the tenant having to show that the landlord was aware of his legal rights at the relevant time: *Blackstone Ltd v Burnetts (West End) Ltd* [1973] 1 WLR 1487, 1501 (Swanwick J).

[264]   *Scarf v Jardine* (1882) 7 App Cas 345 (HL) 361 (Lord Blackburn); *Matthews v Smallwood* [1910] 1 Ch 777 (Ch D), 786 (Parker J); *Hain Steamship Co v Tate & Lyle Ltd* (1930) 41 Com Cas 350 (HL) 355 (Lord Wright) and 601 (Lord Maugham); *China National Foreign Trade Transportation Corp v Evlogia Shipping Co SA of Panama (The Mihailios Xilas)* [1979] 1 WLR 1018 (HL) 1024 (Lord Diplock); *Motor Oil Hellas (Corinth) Refineries SA v Shipping Corp of India (The Kanchenjunga)* [1990] 1 Lloyd's Rep 391 (HL) 398 (Lord Goff); *Aktieselskabet Dampskibsselskabet Svendborg v Mobil North Sea* [2001] 2 Lloyd's Rep 127, 131 (Steel J); *MSAS Global Logistics Ltd v Power Packaging Ltd* [2003] EWHC 1393 (Davis J); *Peregrine Systems Ltd v Steria Ltd* [2005] EWCA Civ 239, para 18 (Maurice Kay LJ); Carter, *Carter's Breach of Contract*, para 11-15 (n 15).

[265]   *Johnson v Agnew* [1980] AC 367 (HL) 392 (Lord Wilberforce).

[266]   In particular, a landlord will lose the right to forfeit a lease for breach of covenant if he or she continues to demand rent falling due after the breach: *Segal Securities Ltd v Thoseby* [1963] 1 QB 887 (QBD); *Central Estates (Belgravia) Ltd v Woolgar (No 2)* [1972] 1 WLR 1048 (CA); *Blackstone Ltd v Burnetts (West End) Ltd* [1973] 1 WLR 1487 (Swanwick J); *Thomas v Ken Thomas Ltd* [2006] EWCA Civ 1504, [2007] L & TR 21.

relevant time, such as arrears of rent or other sums.[267] Does the innocent party lose the right to terminate by pressing for performance? Merely protesting about the breach, or even demanding that it be remedied, will not necessarily amount to an unequivocal election to affirm;[268] after all, the innocent party is not bound to terminate at once, and does at least have a reasonable interval in which to make his or her mind up about what to do.[269] On the other hand, it will be different if the demand for performance is in such terms as to make it clear that the innocent party has decided to go ahead with the contract; in particular, this will apply where time was of the essence of the contract but the innocent party continues to demand performance after the deadline has passed.[270] What if the innocent party does nothing to give any indication one way or the other? As a general rule, a right to terminate will not be lost by mere delay,[271] but in many cases the inactivity of the innocent party in the face of the breach will not be consistent with this option having been taken.[272] Since, ultimately, the question whether the innocent party has decided to terminate or affirm is said to be one of fact,[273] it is impossible to lay down any hard or fast rules that will apply to every possible situation.

(ii) **Effect**   The effect of waiver by election in this situation is that the right to   **4.58**
terminate is lost and cannot be revived without the party in default being given another chance to perform. In *Charles Rickards Ltd v Oppenhaim*,[274] the plaintiff car dealer agreed to deliver a Rolls-Royce chassis to the defendant customer by a certain date in March 1948. The car was not delivered on time, but the customer continued to press for delivery. At the end of June the defendant told the plaintiffs that if the car was not delivered in four weeks he would not accept it. In fact it

---

[267] *Re Debtor (13A-IO-1995)* [1995] 1 WLR 1127, 1131 (Rattee J); Carter, *Carter's Breach of Contract*, para 11-16 (n 15).

[268] *Yukong Line Ltd of Korea v Rendsburg Investments Corp of Liberia (The Rialto)* [1996] 2 Lloyd's Rep 604 (QBD: Commercial Ct) (Moore-Bick J) 608–9; *Parbulk II A/S v Heritage Maritime Ltd SA (The Mahakam)* [2011] EWHC 2917 (Comm), [2012] 1 Lloyd's Rep 87, para 94 (Eder J); Carter, *Carter's Breach of Contract*, para 11-16 (n 15).

[269] See paras 4.23–4.26.

[270] As in *Rickards v Oppenhaim* [1950] 1 KB 616 (CA).

[271] See para 4.24.

[272] *Holland v Wiltshire* (1954) 90 CLR 409 (HCA); *Heyman v Darwins* [1942] AC 356 (HL) 361 (Viscount Simon LC); *Maredelanto Compania Naviera SA v Bergbau-Handel GmbH (The Mihalis Angelos)* [1971] 1 QB 164 (CA) 204 (Megaw LJ); *The Leonidas D* [1985] 2 Lloyd's Rep 18 (CA) 24–6 (Robert Goff LJ); *State Trading Corp of India v M Golodetz & Co Inc Ltd* [1989] 2 Lloyd's Rep 277 (CA) 286 (Kerr LJ); *Glencore Grain Rotterdam BV v Lebanese Organisation for International Commerce (The Lorico)* [1997] 2 Lloyd's Rep 386 (CA) 394 (Evans LJ). cf the rules relating to 'acceptance' in the Sale of Goods Act 1979, s 35: *Clegg v Anderson (t/a Nordic Marine)* [2003] EWCA Civ 320, [2003] 2 Lloyd's Rep 32; *Jones v Gallagher (t/a Gallery Kitchens and Bathrooms)* [2004] EWCA Civ 10, [2005] 1 Lloyd's Rep 377.

[273] *J & E Kish v Charles Taylor, Sons & Co* [1912] AC 604 (HL) at 617 (Lord Atkinson); *Treitel*, para 18-009.

[274] [1950] 1 KB 616 (CA); *Panoutsos v Raymond Hadley Corp of New York* [1917] 1 KB 473 (CA) 477–8 (Viscount Reading CJ); *Hartley v Hymans* [1920] 3 KB 475 (KBD), 495 (McCardie J); *More OG Romsdal Fylkesbatar AS v The Demise Charterers of the Ship 'Jotunheim'* [2004] EWHC 671 (Comm), [2005] 1 Lloyd's Rep 181.

was not ready until October, by which time the defendant had had enough, and refused to take it. The Court of Appeal held that the defendant was entitled to reject the car. Time was originally of the essence, and the defendant could have terminated at once for failure to deliver on the agreed date. This right had been lost by waiver, and could not be revived without giving the plaintiffs another chance to perform. However, when they still failed to deliver, the defendant was entitled to serve a notice making time of the essence once more;[275] when this fresh deadline was still not met, the contract could then be terminated.

(b) Equitable estoppel

4.59 What if the innocent party goes ahead with the contract without being aware of the right to terminate? Here there can be no question of waiver by election or affirmation. However, the party in default may still be entitled to prevent termination on the grounds of equitable estoppel, or promissory estoppel as it is sometimes called.

4.60 **(i) Requirements** Equitable estoppel was defined by Lord Goff in *The Kanchenjunga* as follows:[276]

> Equitable estoppel occurs where a person, having legal rights against another, unequivocally represents (by words or conduct) that he does not intend to enforce those legal rights; if in such circumstances the other party acts, or desists from acting, in reliance upon that representation, with the effect that it would be inequitable for the representor to enforce his legal rights inconsistently with his representation, he will to that extent be precluded from doing so.

Applied to the present context, what this means is a situation where a party who has the legal right to terminate unequivocally represents that he or she does not intend to do so, and the other party acts or desists from acting in reliance on that representation. The three crucial requirements here are as follows: (1) there must be some kind of representation by the innocent party, (2) it must be unequivocal, and (3) the party in default must have acted (or refrained from acting) in reliance on that representation.[277]

4.61 The essence of equitable estoppel is a promise or representation that the contract will not be enforced according to its terms. In some cases the representation will be made expressly, but in others it will be implied from the conduct of the party in question. In *Hughes v Metropolitan Railway*[278] a lease contained a provision for forfeiture if repairs were not done. The landlords served a notice requiring such

---

[275] See Ch 8.

[276] *Motor Oil Hellas (Corinth) Refineries SA v Shipping Corp of India (The Kanchenjunga)* [1990] 1 Lloyd's Rep 391 (HL) 399; *Hughes v Metropolitan Rly* (1877) 2 App Cas 439 (HL) 448 (Lord Cairns); *Central London Property Trust v High Trees House Ltd* [1947] KB 130, 134 (Denning J); *BP Exploration Ltd v Hunt* [1979] 1 WLR 783, 810 (Robert Goff J); *Marseille Fret SA v D Oltmann Schiffahrts GmbH & Co KG (The Trado)* [1982] 2 Lloyd's Rep 157 (QBD: Commercial Ct), 160–1 (Parker J).

[277] Carter, *Carter's Breach of Contract*, para 10-48 (n 15).

[278] (1877) 2 App Cas 439.

repairs to be done within six months, but then entered into negotiations with the tenant for the purchase of the lease. When negotiations broke down, the landlords then sought to forfeit the lease on the ground that the six-month period had now elapsed without the repairs being done, but the claim was rejected by the House of Lords on the ground that the tenants had been led to suppose that the landlords did not intend to enforce their rights, and that it would now be inequitable for the landlords to do so having regard to the dealings that had taken place.[279] This was clearly not a case of waiver by election, as the relevant conduct on the part of the landlords took place before any right to terminate arose; even so, the fact that the tenants had been lulled into a false sense of security by the landlords' conduct was enough to debar the landlords from forfeiting the lease. However, the facts must point to a promise or representation of some sort. In *The Scaptrade*[280] the fact that shipowners had acquiesced in the late payment of hire on past occasions was held not to debar them from withdrawing the ship on that ground, since they had never expressly or impliedly represented that they would not insist on punctual payment. Again, this could never have been a case of waiver by election, as the conduct of the shipowners preceded the accrual of their right of termination, but if the necessary promise or representation could have been implied, then that right of termination would have been lost.

As in the case of waiver, the promise or representation has to be clear and unequivo- **4.62** cal.[281] One of the purposes of this requirement is said to be to prevent a party from losing his or her legal rights under a contract merely by failure to insist on strict performance of the contract at all times, or by granting some other indulgence. Thus in *The Scaptrade*[282] it was held by Lloyd J at first instance that the mere fact that the shipowners had accepted late payments of hire in the past did not imply any representation to the charterers that they did not intend to enforce the contract according to its terms. But in *The Petrofina*[283] it was held that shipowners who had allowed the charterers to pay the monthly instalments of hire by cheque rather than by cash in advance as stipulated by the contract could not withdraw the ship on this ground without giving the charterers proper notice that they intended to insist on their strict contractual rights from now on; in effect, the accepted method of payment under the charterparty had been modified.

---

279 *Hughes v Metropolitan Rly*, 448 (Lord Cairns) (n 278).
280 *Scandinavian Trading Tanker Co AB v Flota Petrolera Ecuatoriana (The Scaptrade)* [1981] 2 Lloyd's Rep 425 (Lloyd J), [1983] 1 Lloyd's Rep 146 (CA), [1983] 2 AC 694 (HL); *Mardorf Peach & Co Ltd v Attica Sea Carriers Corp of Liberia (The Laconia)* [1977] AC 850; *Balcombe Group plc v London Development Agency* [2007] EWHC 106 (QB) para 67 (Jack J).
281 *Motor Oil Hellas (Corinth) Refineries SA v Shipping Corp of India (The Kanchenjunga)* [1990] 1 Lloyd's Rep 391 (HL) 399 (Lord Goff); *Western Bulk Carriers K/S v Li Hai Maritime Inc (The Li Hai)* [2005] EWHC 735, [2005] 2 Lloyd's Rep 389; Carter, *Carter's Breach of Contract*, para 10-49 (n 15).
282 [1981] 2 Lloyd's Rep 425: see para 4.61; *Bird v Hildage* [1948] 1 KB 91 (CA).
283 *Tankexpress A/S v Compagnie Financière Belges des Petroles SA (The Petrofina)* [1949] AC 76 (HL).

4.63 The key element of equitable estoppel, and the one which distinguishes it from waiver by election, is the requirement of reliance; the representation or promise must, in the words of Denning J, have been 'acted on'.[284] In *Hughes v Metropolitan Railway*[285] this requirement was satisfied when the tenants allowed the deadline for the repairs to pass while they negotiated with the landlords for the sale of the lease, and in *The Petrofina*[286] the crucial point was that the charterers had paid by cheque rather than paying cash in advance. Where no such reliance can be shown, the doctrine of equitable estoppel will not operate. In *Avimex SA v Dewulf & Cie*[287] a buyer of goods was held not to have waived his rights by acceptance of a defective *force majeure* notice in the absence of any indication that the seller had acted on the faith of this acceptance, say by appropriating goods to the contract. In the same way, the charterers in *The Scaptrade*[288] were held not to have demonstrated any degree of reliance in failing to pay instalments of hire on time, despite the fact that this was done without any objection from the owner. No doubt they would have paid promptly if they had been warned that the owners were about to withdraw the vessel, but this was not enough.[289]

4.64 Some of the cases seem to suggest that mere reliance will not be enough unless it is accompanied by some degree of 'detriment'. In *The Post Chaser*[290] the sellers under a cif contract failed to declare a vessel on time as required by the contract. The buyers did not raise any objection, and later requested the sellers to present the shipping documents. It was held that though the buyers' request for the documents could be construed as an unequivocal declaration that they did not intend to rely on their rights,[291] the sellers had not shown the necessary reliance. They may have 'relied' on the buyers' request to the extent that they had conducted their affairs in accordance with it, but they had suffered no detriment by doing so and it was therefore not inequitable for the buyers to resile from their promise.[292] The requirement of detriment has been stated in other cases as well,[293] but it was denied by Lord Denning MR,[294] and is said to be based on a misleading analogy.[295] The point is not of great importance in the end. In cases where no detriment has been suffered

---

[284] *Central London Property Trust v High Trees House Ltd* [1947] KB 130, 134.

[285] (1877) 2 App Cas 439; see, para 5.79.

[286] See n 283.

[287] [1979] 2 Lloyd's Rep 57, 67–8 (Robert Goff J); *Cook Industries Inc v Meunerie Liegeois SA* [1981] 1 Lloyd's Rep 359, 368 (Mustill J).

[288] [1981] 2 Lloyd's Rep 425.

[289] *The Scaptrade*, 430–1 (Lloyd J) (n 288).

[290] [1981] 2 Lloyd's Rep 695.

[291] *The Post Chaser*, 700 (Robert Goff J) (n 290); *P v P* [1957] NZLR 854 (Supreme Ct of New Zealand).

[292] *The Post Chaser*, 701–2 (n 290).

[293] As in *Morrow v Carty* [1957] NI 174 (High Ct of N Ireland).

[294] *WJ Alan & Co Ltd v El Nasr Export and Import Co* [1972] 2 QB 189 (CA) 213.

[295] Peel, *Treitel*, para 3-084 (n 10). The analogy in question is that of estoppel by representation, which clearly *does* require proof of detriment; *Carr v London and North Western Rly* (1875) LR 10 CP 310, 317 (Brett J).

by the party concerned, it will generally not be inequitable for the other to go back on the promise or representation in question; and if it would be so inequitable, the courts are not likely to hold the doctrine inapplicable for lack of detriment.

(ii) Effect   The doctrine of equitable estoppel creates no new causes of action **4.65** where none existed before;[296] in that sense, it is said to be a shield and not a sword.[297] Rather, the effect is, in the words of Lord Cairns, that a person who otherwise might have enforced his or her rights will not be allowed to enforce them where it would be inequitable having regard to the dealings which have thus taken place between the parties.[298] This gives rise to two further issues: when is it inequitable to allow someone to enforce his or her rights in this situation, and to what extent can the party concerned resume these rights for the future?

Normally it would be inequitable to allow someone to go back on a promise or **4.66** representation he or she has made, especially where that promise or representation has been acted on by someone else.[299] However, there are cases where this will not apply. In *Williams v Stern*[300] the plaintiff gave the defendant a bill of sale as security for a loan, under which certain furniture could be seized if the loan was not paid on time. The plaintiff asked for extra time to pay, and the defendant agreed to this, but then, hearing that the plaintiff's landlord intended to distrain on the property, he went ahead and seized the furniture. It was held that in the circumstances it was not inequitable for the defendant to act as he did. In the present context it is also relevant to ask to what extent the party in default has changed position in reliance on the innocent party's undertaking not to enforce his or her contractual right to terminate. Where the party in default has incurred some degree of detriment it will generally not be equitable to allow the innocent party to resile from that undertaking, but this may not be so where the party in default has not been prejudiced in any way by relying on it. This is what happened in *The Post Chaser*,[301] where the buyers under a cif contract called on the sellers to present the shipping documents despite the fact that the vessel had not been nominated in time as required by the contract. Shortly afterwards the contract was terminated by the buyers on the ground of the delay, but it was held that though the buyers' request may have led the sellers to believe that the buyers had decided to overlook the late nomination, they had not been prejudiced as a result.[302]

---

[296] *Combe v Combe* [1951] 2 KB 215 (CA).
[297] *Combe v Combe*, 224 (Birkett LJ) (n 297).
[298] *Hughes v Metropolitan Rly* (1877) 2 App Cas 439 (HL) 448; see para 4.61.
[299] Carter, *Carter's Breach of Contract*, para 10-50 (n 15).
[300] (1879) 5 QBD 409 (CA).
[301] *Société Italo-Belge pour le Commerce et l'Industrie v Palm and Vegetable Oils (Malaysia) Sdn Bhd (The Post Chaser)* [1981] 2 Lloyd's Rep 695 (Robert Goff J).
[302] *The Post Chaser*, 701–2 (Robert Goff J) (n 301).

4.67   In a case of equitable estoppel, the party who makes the representation can generally resume his or her position by giving due notice to the other party.[303] This means that in the present context the innocent party can indicate that though he or she may have been willing to turn a blind eye to such breaches in the past, from now on he or she is going to insist on the contract being performed according to its terms, with a consequent right of termination if this is not done. However, in cases where it is impossible or impracticable to restore the representee to his or her original position, the doctrine may serve to extinguish the representor's rights altogether.[304] The reason for the general rule is said to be the discretionary nature of the equitable jurisdiction; the court is allowed to give such relief as is just and equitable in all the circumstances, and in most cases of this sort it would be neither just nor equitable to treat the representor's rights as being totally extinguished.[305]

(c) Relationship between the two doctrines

4.68   There is clearly a considerable overlap between waiver by election and equitable estoppel, and both doctrines share characteristics in common, most notably the requirement of clear and unequivocal words or conduct by the innocent party. However, as Lord Goff indicates in *The Kanchenjunga*, there are important differences as well.[306] In particular:[307]

- Waiver by election focuses on the conduct of the innocent party, who is not allowed to blow hot and cold, but must make up his or her mind as to which of two inconsistent rights to pursue. Equitable estoppel focuses on the conduct of the party in default.
- Waiver by election does not require proof of reliance by the party in default. Such reliance is of the very essence of equitable estoppel.
- Waiver by election requires knowledge of the right to terminate, or at the very least of the facts giving rise to that right. There is no such requirement for equitable estoppel.
- Waiver by election focuses on a decision by the innocent party as to what he or she is doing now. Equitable estoppel focuses on a decision as to what he or she will do in the future.
- Waiver by election is final in its effects. Equitable estoppel is generally only suspensory in its effects.

---

[303] *Tool Metal Manufacturing Co Ltd v Tungsten Electric Co Ltd* [1955] 1 WLR 561 (HL); *Ajayi v RT Briscoe (Nigeria) Ltd* [1964] 1 WLR 1326 (JCPC–Nigeria) 1330 (Lord Hodson).

[304] *Birmingham & District Land Co v London and North Western Rly* (1888) 40 Ch D 268 (CA); *Ogilvy v Hope-Davies* [1976] 1 All ER 683 (Ch D); *Nippon Yusen Kaisha v Pacifica Navegacion SA (The Ion)* [1980] 2 Lloyd's Rep 245 (QBD: Commercial Ct).

[305] Burrows et al, *Chitty on Contracts*, para 3-096 (n 3).

[306] *Motor Oil Hellas (Corinth) Refineries SA v Shipping Corp of India (The Kanchenjunga)* [1990] 1 Lloyd's Rep 391 (HL) 399; FMB Reynolds, 'The Notions of Waiver' [1990] LMCLQ 453; JW Carter, 'Waiver (of Contractual Rights) Distributed' (1990–91) 4 JCL 59; JW Carter, 'Problems in Enforcement' (1992) 5 JCL 199 and (1993) 6 JCL 1.

[307] See generally Carter, *Carter's Breach of Contract*, para 11-21 (n 15).

(2) 'Acceptance' of goods

Given that many cases of termination involve contracts for the sale of goods, men- **4.69**
tion must also be made in this context of loss of the right to terminate through
'acceptance'. This is covered by section 11(4) of the Sale of Goods Act 1979, which
uses the following words:

> Subject to section 35A below, where a contract of sale is not severable, and the
> buyer has accepted the goods, or part of them, the breach of a condition to be ful-
> filled by the seller can only be treated as a breach of warranty, and not as a ground
> for rejecting the goods and treating the contract as repudiated, unless there is an
> express or implied term of the contract to that effect.

What this does in effect is to provide, subject to provision in the contract to the
contrary, an extra[308] way in which the right to terminate can be lost in contracts for
the sale of goods. We shall now consider what amounts to acceptance,[309] before looking at how acceptance differs from the common law doctrines of waiver and equitable
estoppel.

(a) Elements of acceptance

Section 35 of the Sale of Goods Act 1979 gives three situations in which goods **4.70**
are deemed to have been 'accepted', namely: (1) where the buyer 'intimates' to the
seller that he or she has accepted them;[310] (2) by an act inconsistent with the seller's
ownership;[311] and (3) where after the lapse of a reasonable time the buyer retains
the goods without indicating to the seller that he or she has rejected them.[312]

(i) Express intimation Under section 35(1)(a) of the 1979 Act, a buyer is deemed **4.71**
to have accepted the goods 'when he intimates to the seller that he has accepted
them'.[313] The most obvious way in which this can be done is by express indication
to that effect, such as the signing of a delivery note,[314] but it has been said that
intimation can also be implied from conduct.[315] However, in either case the words
or conduct of the buyer must be unambiguous in this regard; merely complaining
about the defects and demanding that the seller do something about them is not
enough.[316] Problems may also arise where the buyer has had no chance to look at
the goods and where the 'intimation' in question is buried in the small print of a

---

[308] There is nothing in the Sale of Goods Act 1979, s 11(4) to prevent the seller from arguing that
the buyer's right to terminate has been lost in one of the other ways previously described.
[309] See generally Bridge, *Benjamin's Sale of Goods*, paras 12-040–12-062 (n 115).
[310] Sale of Goods Act 1979, s 35(1)(a).
[311] Sale of Goods Act 1979, s 35(1)(b).
[312] Sale of Goods Act 1979, s 35(4).
[313] *Saunders v Topp* (1849) 4 Exch 390, 154 ER 1264; Bridge, *Benjamin's Sale of Goods*, para
12-045 (n 115).
[314] *Hardy & Co (London) v Hillerns & Fowler* [1923] 2 KB 490 (CA) 498 (Atkin LJ).
[315] Bridge, *Benjamin's Sale of Goods*, para 12-047 (n 115).
[316] *Varley v Whipp* [1900] 1 QB 513 (QBD) (Channell and Bucknill JJ).

standard form contract.[317] For this reason, section 35(2) goes on to say that this will not apply unless either the buyer has examined the goods or at least had a reasonable opportunity to examine them in order to discover whether they are in conformity with the contract. This provision can be excluded by contrary agreement, but not as against a buyer who is dealing as consumer.[318] As well as this, buyers may be protected against unfair 'acceptance' clauses by the Unfair Contract Terms Act 1977[319] and the Unfair Terms in Consumer Contracts Regulations 1999.[320]

4.72 **(ii) Act inconsistent with seller's ownership** Section 35(1)(b) of the 1979 Act indicates that a buyer will be deemed to have accepted the goods 'when the goods have been delivered to him and he does any act in relation to them which is inconsistent with the ownership of the seller'.[321] The most obvious example of this used to be where the buyer had sold the goods on to a third party (so indicating that he or she, and not the seller, was now the owner),[322] but section 35(6)(b) now provides that the buyer is not deemed to have accepted the goods merely because the goods are delivered to another under a subsale or other disposition. However, this will not protect the buyer in relation to acts which do not involve delivering the goods to another at all, as where the buyer burns them or throws them in the sea. A buyer may also fall foul of section 35(1)(b) by making use of the goods for his or her own purposes in such a way that it is no longer possible to return them to the seller, as where perishable goods are consumed,[323] or raw materials are incorporated into a house or other structure.[324] However, section 35(1)(b) is subject to the same limitation as section 35(1)(a), namely that it does not apply unless the buyer has examined the goods or at least had a reasonable opportunity of examining them,[325] and making use of the goods may be the only way in which this can be done.

4.73 **(iii) Retention of goods for more than a reasonable time** The third situation where acceptance by the buyer is deemed to have taken place is 'where after the lapse of a reasonable time he retains the goods without intimating to the

---

[317] PS Atiyah, JN Adams and H McQueen, *The Sale of Goods* (12th edn, Pearson Longman, 2010) pp 508–9.

[318] Sale of Goods Act 1979, s 35(3).

[319] Most notably s 6 (see para 4.48) and s 13, which applies to clauses 'excluding or restricting any right or remedy in respect of the liability' and clauses 'excluding or restricting any rules of evidence or procedure'.

[320] See especially Sch 2 para 1(b), terms which have the effect of inappropriately excluding or limiting the legal rights of the consumer against the seller or supplier for total or partial non-performance or for inadequate performance by the seller or supplier of contractual obligations: Macdonald, *Exemption Clauses and Unfair Terms*, pp 252–3 (n 195).

[321] Bridge, *Benjamin's Sale of Goods*, paras 12-048–12-049 (n 115).

[322] Atiyah, Adams, and McQueen, *The Sale of Goods*, pp 512–13 (n 317).

[323] *Harnor v Groves* (1855) 15 CB 667, 135 ER 987.

[324] *Mechan & Sons Ltd v Bow, McLachan & Co Ltd* 1910 SC 758.

[325] Sale of Goods Act 1979, s 35(2). Once again this can be excluded by contrary provision, but not against a person dealing as consumer: s 35(3).

seller that he has rejected them'.[326] The question of whether a reasonable time has elapsed in this context is one of fact[327] depending on the circumstances of the case, in particular the extent to which the buyer had a reasonable opportunity to examine the goods to see whether they are in conformity with the contract.[328] Thus, for instance, the time for acceptance may be relatively short in relation to perishable goods, or where the defects were fairly obvious. On the other hand, in relation to complex items such as a car or other piece of machinery, a longer period may be appropriate. A buyer is not deemed to have accepted the goods merely because he or she asks for or agrees to their repair by or under arrangements with the seller,[329] but in a case where this allows the seller to tender goods that are fully in conformity with the contract, the right to reject would generally be lost.[330]

(b) Relationship of acceptance to other doctrines

At first sight there is some similarity between these rules and the general common law rules relating to waiver by election and equitable estoppel; in particular, the requirement that acceptance by intimation be unambiguous, and the rules relating to lapse of time. Acceptance, unlike waiver by election, does not require proof that the buyer was aware of the defect at the relevant time, and in that sense is akin to equitable estoppel, but unlike estoppel it does not require any act of reliance by the buyer. The policy behind waiver by election focuses on the innocent party, who cannot be allowed to blow hot and cold, but must make his or her mind up as to which of two or more inconsistent remedies to pursue. The policy behind equitable estoppel focuses on the party in default, the rationale being to protect that party where he or she has acted in reliance on a promise or representation by the innocent party. The policy behind acceptance would appear to be neither of these, but rather the need for finality in commercial affairs; in the end, in the words of Rougier J, the seller must be allowed to 'close his ledger'[331] reasonably soon after the transaction is complete without the threat of rejection hanging, like the sword of Damocles, over his head for an indefinite period. **4.74**

---

[326] Sale of Goods Act 1979, s 35(4); Bridge, *Benjamin's Sale of Goods*, paras 12-055–12-058 (n 115).

[327] Sale of Goods Act 1979, s 59.

[328] Sale of Goods Act 1979, s 35(5).

[329] Sale of Goods Act 1979, s 35(6).

[330] *J & H Ritchie Ltd v Lloyd Ltd* 2005 SLT 64; Atiyah, Adams, and McQueen, *The Sale of Goods*, p 518 (n 317); KK Low, 'Repair, Rejection and Rescission: an Uneasy Resolution' (2007) 123 LQR 536.

[331] *Bernstein v Pamson Motors (Golders Green) Ltd* [1987] RTR 384, 396; FMB Reynolds, (1988) 104 LQR 16; M Hwang, 'Time for Rejection of Defective Goods' [1992] LMCLQ 334.

(3) Judicial relief

4.75 Another way in which the right to terminate may be lost is as a consequence of the court's jurisdiction to grant relief in appropriate cases. This derives from a number of sources, but the main distinction that must be drawn in the present context is as between statutory relief and equitable relief against forfeiture.

(a) Statutory relief

4.76 There are various statutory provisions which have the effect of allowing the court to grant relief in circumstances where the normal rules of termination would produce unduly harsh consequences. For instance, there are various provisions allowing the courts to grant relief where a landlord seeks to forfeit the lease for breach of covenant; where the breach consists of non-payment of rent, there are various provisions the effect of which is to allow the court to grant relief to the tenant, if necessary subject to appropriate conditions including the payment of the outstanding arrears and costs,[332] while in other cases a more general jurisdiction is given by section 146(2) of the Law of Property Act 1925.[333] Again, in the context of consumer credit, the extent to which a creditor can reclaim the goods for arrears of instalments is restricted by statute,[334] and the debtor threatened with termination may apply for what is known as a 'time order', giving in effect extra time to pay.[335] A fuller explanation of these provisions can be found in the specialist works on the subject.[336]

(b) Equitable relief against forfeiture

4.77 There is also a long-standing equitable jurisdiction to grant relief in cases of this nature.[337] Prior to 1973 this was thought to be restricted to two cases, one being where the right of forfeiture was inserted by way of security for payment of a specific sum of money, and the other where the breach in question was occasioned by 'fraud, accident, mistake or surprise'.[338] However, a more general principle was enunciated by the House of Lords in *Shiloh Spinners Ltd v Harding*.[339] In the words of Lord Wilberforce:[340]

> ... it remains true today that equity expects men to carry out their bargains and will not let them buy their way out by uncovenanted payment. But it is

---

[332] Common Law Procedure Act 1852, ss 210–212; Senior Courts Act 1981, s 38; County Courts Act 1984, ss 138–140.

[333] Carter, *Carter's Breach of Contract*, para 10-61 (n 15).

[334] Consumer Credit Act 1974, ss 90–92.

[335] Consumer Credit Act 1974, s 129.

[336] M Pawlowski, *The Forfeiture of Leases* (Sweet & Maxwell, 1993) chs 9 and 10.

[337] Andrews et al, *Contractual Duties*, paras 10-068–10-072 (n 14); Carter, *Carter's Breach of Contract*, paras 10-61–10-73 (n 15).

[338] *Hill v Barclay* (1811) 18 Ves J 56, 34 ER 238.

[339] [1973] AC 691 (HL).

[340] *Shiloh Spinners v Harding*, 723–4 (n 339).

consistent with these principles that we should reaffirm the right of courts of equity in appropriate and limited cases to relieve against forfeiture for breach of covenant or condition where the primary object of the bargain is to secure a stated result which can effectively be attained when the matter comes before the court, and where the forfeiture provision is added by way of security for the production of that result. The word 'appropriate' involves consideration of the conduct of the applicant for relief, in particular whether his default was wilful, of the gravity of the breaches, and of the disparity between the value of the property of which the forfeiture is claimed as compared with the damage caused by the breach.

Though the words of Lord Wilberforce were expressed in general terms,[341] it **4.78** is now clear that the jurisdiction is confined to situations where the contract is one involving the transfer of possessory or proprietary rights. Thus in *The Scaptrade*,[342] the House of Lords refused to allow relief against the withdrawal of a time chartered ship for late payment of hire; the charter was an ordinary time charter which gave the charterer no interest in or right of possession to the vessel, but was in essence no more than a contract for services.[343] As Robert Goff LJ pointed out in the Court of Appeal,[344] such a charter was an ordinary commercial transaction carried out in the course of a trade between parties acting at arm's length; the possibility of withdrawal under these circumstances was well known to parties in the shipping world, and if a prospective time charterer was not happy with such a clause it was perfectly possible to exclude it by agreement with the owner.

There is some uncertainty as to what kind of possessory or proprietary rights can **4.79** be protected in this context. The doctrine is certainly not confined to cases involving the forfeiture of rights in land; thus, for instance, it has been applied to a charterparty by demise,[345] to a chattel lease,[346] and to an agreement involving the

---

[341] Lord Simon went even further, saying that the jurisdiction was 'unlimited and unfettered', and that what had been regarded in the past as fetters on the jurisdiction were more properly seen as mere considerations for the court to weigh in exercising that unfettered jurisdiction: *Shiloh Spinners v Harding*, 726–7 (n 339). However, those remarks were later described by Lord Diplock as a 'beguiling heresy' (*The Scaptrade*, p 700 (see n 342)) and can find no support in subsequent cases.

[342] *Scandinavian Trading Tanker Co A/B v Flota Petrolera Ecuatoriana* [1983] 2 AC 694 (HL).

[343] *The Scaptrade*, 700–1 (Lord Wilberforce) (n 342).

[344] [1983] 1 Lloyd's Rep 146 (CA) 153.

[345] *More Og Romsdal Fylkesbatar AS v Demise Charterers of the Ship 'Jotunheim'* [2004] EWHC 671 (Comm), [2005] 1 Lloyd's Rep 181.

[346] *Barton Thompson & Co Ltd v Stapling Machines Co* [1966] Ch 499; *Galbraith v Mitchenhall Estates* [1985] 2 QB 473, 482–4 (Sachs LJ); *Bristol Airport plc v Powdrill* [1990] Ch 744 (CA) 759; *On Demand Information plc v Michael Gerson (Finance) plc* [2001] 1 WLR 155 (CA). However, this will not apply in the case of a merely operational lease that only covers a small proportion of the economic life of the asset: *Celestial Aviation Trading 71 Ltd v Paramount Airways Pte Ltd* [2010] EWHC 185 (Comm), [2011] 1 Lloyd's Rep 9. See further L Smith, 'Relief against Forfeiture: a Restatement' [2001] CLJ 178.

transfer of patent rights.[347] A more controversial question is whether the doctrine can protect rights created by the very obligation that the innocent party is seeking to be discharged from by his or her election to terminate. In *Re Dagenham (Thames) Dock Co, ex parte Hulse*[348] a company agreed, in a contract signed in 1865, to purchase land for the construction of a dock, and were let into possession to undertake the works. The contract provided for the payment of the purchase price in two instalments, half in advance and the other half on completion. Time was stated to be of the essence, and the vendors were given the power in the event of default by the purchasers to re-enter and take possession of the land and of any works done thereon, and also to forfeit any instalments of the purchase price that may have been paid. The company failed to complete the works and was eventually wound up without the final instalment of the price ever having been paid. The purchasers then sought to exercise their power of re-entry and to forfeit the sums already paid, but this was disallowed by the court on the grounds that this would amount to the enforcement of a penalty. The case can easily be explained on the grounds of the well-established equitable jurisdiction to relieve against forfeiture of *instalments*,[349] but it has also been seen as one involving relief against the forfeiture of *the estate itself*.[350] But there is a certain circularity involved in this argument.[351] The only estate that the purchasers have in a case of this sort is the equitable interest arising out of the contract of sale. But this interest is founded on the willingness of the courts to grant specific performance of the vendor's obligation to convey the land—the very obligation that is at issue when termination is sought.

4.80 A similar line of reasoning was used by the High Court of Australia in *Legione v Hateley*,[352] where a contract for the sale of land provided for completion on a certain day and made time of the essence. The purchasers were allowed into possession,

---

[347] *BICC plc v Burndy Corp* [1985] Ch 232 (CA); C Harpum, 'Set-Off, Specific Performance and Relief against Forfeiture' [1985] CLJ 204. But relief was held not to be available where a similar agreement merely gave the defaulting party a contractual licence to use a certain trade mark: *Sport Intl Bussum BV v Inter-Footwear Ltd* [1984] 1 WLR 776 (CA); Peel, *Treitel*, para 18-064 (n 10). Harpum criticizes this case as unduly restrictive: C Harpum, 'Relief against Forfeiture in Commercial Cases—a Decision too Far' (1984) 100 LQR 369.

[348] (1872–73) LR 8 Ch App 1022; *Kilmer v British Columbia Orchard Lands Ltd* [1913] AC 319 (JCPC–Canada).

[349] *Cornwall v Henson* [1900] 2 Ch 298 (CA); *Kilmer v British Columbia Orchard Lands Ltd* (n 348); *Starside Properties v Mustapha* [1974] 1 WLR 816 (CA).

[350] This was the explanation given by the High Court of Australia in *Legione v Hateley* (discussed at para 4.80).

[351] See para 4.80.

[352] (1983) 152 CLR 406; Carter, *Carter's Breach of Contract*, para 10-73 (n 15): K Nicholson, 'Breach of an essential time stipulation and relief against forfeiture' (1983) 57 ALJ 632; AG Lang, 'Forfeiture of Interests in Land' (1984) 100 LQR 427; C Harpum, 'Relief against Forfeiture and the Purchaser of Land' [1984] CLJ 134; P Sparkes, 'Forfeiture of Equitable Leases' (1987) 16 Anglo-American L Rev 160; C Mitchell, 'The Equitable Doctrine of Relief against Forfeiture' (1987) 11 Sydney L Rev 387; K Nicholson, 'Relief against Forfeiture in Australia' (1990) 106 LQR 39; JW Carter, 'Problems of Enforcement' (1993) 6 JCL 1; KG Nicholson, 'Relief against Forfeiture in Australia' (1997–98) 12 JCL 189.

and even erected a building on the land, but in the end were unable to pay the price on time. The vendor's claim to terminate the contract and forfeit the deposit failed on the ground that this would involve an unjust forfeiture of the purchaser's equitable interest in the land,[353] but as was later pointed out this reasoning was 'bedevilled by circularity';[354] if the vendor was entitled to terminate, the purchaser had no equitable interest to protect in the first place. Whilst there can be no quarrel with the court's decision to grant relief in principle—after all, termination would have given the vendors an undue windfall by allowing them to claim ownership of the building that had been put up on the land by the purchasers—a better ground for such relief might have been the law of restitution for unjust enrichment.[355]

Whatever might be said about the present status of *Legione v Hateley*, the propos-   **4.81**
ition at stake there—namely that a court can prevent a purchaser of land from termination on the basis of relief against the forfeiture of his or her equitable interest
in the land—now appears to be untenable in the light of the decision of the Privy
Council in *Union Eagle Ltd v Golden Achievement Ltd*,[356] where the court refused
to give relief to a purchaser who had tendered the purchase money ten minutes late.
The contract had provided that time should be of the essence, and in giving the
judgment of the Board Lord Hoffmann stressed the need for commercial certainty
even in the context of contracts for the sale of land.[357] Turning to the reasoning
in *Legione v Hateley*, Lord Hoffmann cast doubt on the proposition that the very
fact of termination in a contract for the sale of land involved a forfeiture of the purchaser's equitable interest in the land. In the words of Lord Hoffmann:[358]

> When a vendor exercises his right to rescind, he terminates the contract. The pur-
> chaser's loss of the right to specific performance may be said to amount to a for-
> feiture of the equitable interest which the contract gave him in the land. But this
> forfeiture is different in its nature from, for example, the vendor's right to retain
> a deposit or part payments of the purchase price. So far as these retentions exceed
> a genuine pre-estimate of damage or a reasonable deposit they will constitute a
> penalty which can be said to be essentially to provide security for payment of the
> full price. No objectionable uncertainty is created by the existence of a restitution-
> ary form of relief against forfeiture, which gives the court a discretion to order

---

[353] [1983] 152 CLR 406, 423 (Gibbs CJ and Murphy J) and 445 (Mason and Deane JJ).

[354] *Stern v McArthur* (1988) 165 CLR 489 (HCA) 537 (Gaudron J); *Tanwar Enterprises Pty Ltd v Cauchi* (2003) 217 CLR 315 (HCA) 333 (Gleeson CJ and McHugh, Gummow, Hayne, and Heydon JJ); Carter, *Carter's Breach of Contract*, para 10-73 (n 15); GJ Tolhurst and JW Carter, 'Relief against Forfeiture in the High Court of Australia' (2004) 20 JCL 74.

[355] *Union Eagle Ltd v Golden Achievement Ltd* [1997] AC 514 (JCPC–Hong Kong) 522–3 (Lord Hoffmann). The problem was that no such claim had been made: see now *Pavey & Matthews Pty Ltd v Paul* (1987) 162 CLR 221 (HCA); Carter, *Carter's Breach of Contract*, para 10-73 (n 15).

[356] [1997] AC 514 (JCPC–Hong Kong); JD Heydon, 'Equitable Aid to Purchasers in Breach of Time-Essential Conditions' (1997) 113 LQR 385; H Abedian and MP Furmston, 'Relief against forfeiture for breach of essential time stipulation in the light of *Union Eagle Ltd v Golden Achievement Ltd*' (1997–98) 12 JCL 189.

[357] *Union Eagle Ltd v Golden Achievement Ltd* [1997] AC 514 (JCPC–Hong Kong), 519.

[358] *Union Eagle v Golden Achievement*, 520 (n 357).

repayment of all or part of the retained money. But the right to rescind the contract, though it involves termination of the purchaser's equitable interest, stands upon a rather different footing. Its purpose is, upon breach of an essential term, to restore to the vendor his freedom to deal with the land as he pleases. In a rising market, such a right may be valuable but volatile. Their Lordships think that in such circumstances a vendor should be able to know with reasonable certainty whether he may resell the land or not.[359]

Given that the reasoning in *Legione v Hateley* has now been doubted even in the jurisdiction in which it was formulated,[360] the better view now seems to be that the equitable doctrine does not apply in such cases. As the present author has stated in another context, while equity may protect the party in default from being summarily deprived by termination of the contract of a proprietary interest he or she already has, it will not go so far as to insist on that party being allowed by virtue of the contract to acquire a proprietary interest that he or she does not yet have.[361]

---

[359] *Union Eagle v Golden Achievement*, 520 (n 357).
[360] See n 354.
[361] JE Stannard, *Delay in the Performance of Contractual Obligations* (OUP, 2007) para 11.66.

PART III

THE RIGHT TO TERMINATE

5

BREACH OF CONDITION

The first situation in which termination will be available is where the other party **5.01** has broken a 'condition'. In this chapter we shall consider the nature of a condition and the ways in which it differs from other similar concepts before going on to outline the tests for determining whether a term of the contract amounts to a condition or not. After that we shall look at the rules for determining when timely performance is a condition, or as is generally said 'of the essence'.

A. What is a 'Condition'?

A good place to start in the present context[1] is with section 11(3) of the Sale of **5.02** Goods Act 1979. This corresponds to what was previously section 11(1)(b) of the Sale of Goods Act 1893, and reads as follows:

> Whether a stipulation in a contract of sale is a condition, the breach of which may give rise to a right to treat the contract as repudiated, or a warranty, the breach of

---

[1] Needless to say, it has other meanings in other contexts; in the words of Donaldson MR, it is 'a chameleon-like word that takes its meaning from its surroundings': *Skips A/S Nordheim v Syrian Petroleum Co Ltd* [1984] QB 599 (CA) 518; SJ Stoljar, 'The Contractual Concept of Condition' (1953) 69 LQR 485; JW Carter, *Carter's Breach of Contract* (Hart, 2012) para 4-10.

which may give rise to a claim for damages but not to a right to reject the goods and treat the contract as repudiated, depends in each case on the construction of the contract; and a stipulation may be a condition, though called a warranty in the contract.

On the basis of this definition a condition is a stipulation in a contract, be it a contract of sale or some other contract, the breach of which gives rise to the right to 'treat the contract as repudiated'. This formula also appears in section 11(2) and (4) of the 1979 Act.[2] But what do these words mean, and why does that right arise?

5.03 The matter is further explained in the celebrated dissenting judgment of Fletcher Moulton LJ in *Wallis, Son and Wells v Pratt & Haynes*,[3] the sentiments of which were subsequently adopted by the House of Lords on appeal:[4]

> A party to a contract who has performed, or is ready and willing to perform, his obligations under that contract is entitled to the performance by the other contracting party of all the obligations which rest on him. But from a very early period of our law it has been recognised that such obligations are not all of equal importance. There are some which go so directly to the substance of the contract or, in other words, are so essential to its very nature that their non-performance may fairly be considered by the other party as a substantial failure to perform the contract at all. On the other hand there are other obligations which, though they must be performed, are not so vital that a failure to perform them goes to the substance of the contract. Both classes are equally obligations under the contract, and the breach of any one of them entitles the other party to damages. But in the case of the former class he has the alternative of treating the contract as being completely broken by the non-performance and (if he takes the proper steps) he can refuse to perform any of the obligations resting upon himself and sue the other party for a total failure to perform the contract. Although the decisions are fairly consistent in recognizing this distinction between the two classes of obligations under a contract there has not been a similar consistency in the nomenclature applied to them. I do not, however, propose to discuss this matter, because later usage has consecrated the term 'condition' to describe an obligation of the former class and 'warranty' to describe an obligation of the latter class.[5]

So a 'condition' on this analysis is an obligation that 'goes directly to the substance of the contract', and is 'so essential to its very nature that [its] non-performance may fairly be considered by the other party as a substantial failure to perform the contract at all'; if such an obligation is broken, the other party can 'refuse to perform any of the obligations resting upon himself' and also 'sue the other party for a total failure to perform the contract', or in the words of the Sale of Goods Act, 'treat the contract as repudiated'. There are four aspects of this worth noting, these

---

[2] See also Sale of Goods Act 1979, s 11(2) and (4); Sale of Goods Act 1893, s 11(2)(a) and (c).
[3] [1910] 2 KB 1003.
[4] [1911] AC 394 (HL).
[5] [1910] 2 KB 1003 (CA) 1012.

being: (1) the notion of a conditional promise; (2) the condition as an obligation; (3) the condition as an essential obligation; and (4) the idea that breach of condition is equivalent in some sense to a repudiation of the contract.

(1) A conditional promise

If there is one idea that can be said to lie at the root of the doctrine of breach of **5.04** condition, it is that of a conditional promise by the innocent party.[6] A promise *to do X* is not the same as a promise *to do X if Y happens*. In the latter case, the promisor need not do X if Y does not happen; to put it another way, the occurrence of Y is an event on upon which the existence of the obligation depends.[7] That event can be of various sorts. For instance, it can be an external event of some sort, as in the case of an insurance policy, where the obligation of the insurer to pay up depends on the occurrence of the contingency insured against. Again, it can be something to be done by the promisee without the promisee being necessarily bound to do it, as in the case of a unilateral obligation. However, in the context of termination, the event on which the innocent party's obligation to perform is conditioned is neither of these things, but the performance of a counter-obligation by the party in default.

(2) The condition as an obligation

As we have seen in a previous chapter, the notion of a condition as an obligation **5.05** under the contract developed out of the old rules of pleading and the distinction between 'dependent' and 'independent' covenants.[8] In the former case A's obligation to perform covenant X would depend on prior performance by B of covenant Y, and B could not sue A for failing to perform X without averring that he or she had performed Y.[9] The upshot of this was that if B did not perform Y, A was effectively discharged from performing X; indeed, it would be better to say that A's obligation to perform X never arose in the first place.[10] It will be noted that in this

---

[6] AL Corbin, 'Conditions in the Law of Contracts' (1918) 28 Yale LJ 739, 742; FMB Reynolds, 'Discharge of Contract by Breach' (1981) 97 LQR 541.

[7] *Zhilka v Turney* [1959] SCR 578 (Supreme Court of Canada) 583 (Judson J); *Carlson, Carlson and Hettrick v Big Bud Tractor of Canada Ltd* (1981) 7 Sask R 337 (CA of Saskatchewan); Carter, *Carter's Breach of Contract*, para 4-12 (n 1). This is its normal meaning in the civilian context: EM Burchell, ' "Condition" and "Warranty" ' (1954) 71 SALJ 333.

[8] See Ch 2, paras 2.03–2.05.

[9] *Kingston v Preston* (1773) Lofft 194, cited in *Jones v Barkley* (1781) 2 Dougl 684, 690, 99 ER 434, 437; SJ Stoljar, 'Dependent and independent promises' (1957) 2 Sydney L Rev 217; SJ Stoljar, *A History of Contract at Common Law* (Australian National University Press, 1975) pp 147–63; J W Carter and C Hodgkiss, 'Conditions and Warranties: Forebears and Descendants' (1976) 8 Sydney L Rev 31; GH Treitel, ' "Conditions" and "conditions precedent" ' (1990) 106 LQR 185; O Black, 'Independent promises and the rescission of contracts' [2003] Legal Studies 555.

[10] This analysis works well for the older cases, but does not fit well with the modern idea that it is not the breach itself that discharges the innocent party from the obligation to perform but his or her election to terminate consequent on that breach: see Ch 4, para 4.13, and see AM Shea, 'Discharge of Performance of Contracts by Failure of Condition' (1979) 42 MLR 623.

analysis the condition for A's promise is not B's promise *as such*, but B's *performance* of that promise; be that as it may, the distinction was not always drawn,[11] and by the time of the Sale of Goods Act 1893 the word 'condition' had come to denote not the performance of the promise but the promise itself—hence the term often seen in this context, 'promissory condition'.[12]

(3) The condition as an essential obligation

5.06   Fletcher Moulton J refers to conditions as terms which go 'so directly to the substance of the contract or, in other words, are so essential to its very nature that their non-performance may fairly be considered by the other party as a substantial failure to perform the contract at all'.[13] Whether a term is to be classified as a condition or not depends in the main on the intention of the parties,[14] and ever since the seminal case of *Boone v Eyre*[15] the courts have taken the line that the parties are not likely to have intended to classify a term in this way unless that term is one of some significance in the context of the contract as a whole.[16] However, whereas this might be true as a general rule, the idea that all conditions are necessarily matters of importance is less compelling where the term in question is classified in that way by implication of law,[17] or on the basis of a standard form contract.[18] Indeed it can be argued that, given that a 'substantial failure to perform the contract at all' gives rise to a right of termination *irrespective of* whether the term broken is a condition or not,[19] the whole point of allowing the innocent party to terminate for breach of condition is to cover cases where the failure in performance does *not* have such drastic consequences, but where for other reasons (most notably the promotion of commercial certainty) the right to terminate should be granted.[20]

---

[11] See for instance *Glaholm v Hays* (1841) 2 M & G 257, 266, 133 ER 743, 746 (Tindal CJ); *Behn v Burness* (1863) 3 B & S 751, 755, 122 ER 281, 283 (Williams J); Carter and Hodgekiss, 'Conditions and Warranties' (n 9).

[12] HE Willis, 'Promissory and non-promissory conditions' (1941) 16 Ind LJ 349. A distinction is now sometimes drawn in the present context between 'contingent' and 'promissory' conditions; *Schuler AG v Wickman Machine Tool Sales Ltd* [1972] 1 WLR 840 (CA) 859 (Stephenson LJ), affd [1974] AC 235 (HL); Carter, *Carter's Breach of Contract*, para 4-12 (n 1).

[13] *Wallis, Son & Wells v Pratt & Haynes* [1910] 2 KB 1003 (CA) 1012; see para 5.02.

[14] Sale of Goods Act 1979, s 11(3); see para 5.14.

[15] (1777) 1 Hy Bl 273n, 126 ER 160; 2 Bl W 1313n, 96 ER 267.

[16] *Boone v Eyre* (Lord Mansfield) (n 15); *Glaholm v Hays* (1841) 2 M & G 257, 266, 133 ER 743, 746 (Tindal CJ); *Behn v Burness* (1863) 3 B & S 751, 755, 122 ER 281, 283 (Williams J); *Bentsen v Taylor, Sons & Co* [1893] 2 QB 274 (CA) 281 (Bowen LJ).

[17] See paras 5.35–5.37.

[18] As in *Lombard North Central plc v Butterworth* [1987] QB 527; see Ch 10, paras 10.15–10.17.

[19] *Hongkong Fir Shipping Co Ltd v Kawasaki Kisen Kaisha Ltd (The Hongkong Fir)* [1962] 2 QB 26 (CA); see Ch 6, paras 6.03–6.08.

[20] *Bunge Corp v Tradax Export SA* [1981] 1 WLR 711 (HL) 784–5 (Lord Roskill).

(4) Breach of condition and repudiation

If breach of a condition is indeed equivalent to a total failure to perform the **5.07** contract, then it follows, as night follows day, that any such breach is equivalent to a repudiation, and that the innocent party is entitled to treat it as such. This indeed seems to be the present state of the law; thus in *Lombard North Central plc v Butterworth*[21] it was decided by the Court of Appeal that late payment of hire in a contract where time was stated to be of the essence entitled the owners not only to terminate performance but also to recover damages on the footing of total repudiation, even though the court also decided on the facts that no such repudiation had taken place.[22] The court reached its decision with some reluctance,[23] and certainly this notion of what might be termed 'constructive repudiation' has its difficulties. In particular, by eliding what are in essence two distinct rationales for contractual discharge (failure of condition and failure of consideration)[24] it creates unnecessary inflexibility in the law.[25] Be that as it may, unless or until *Lombard North Central plc v Butterworth* is overruled, the doctrine of constructive repudiation must be taken to be part of English contract law.

B. Concepts Akin to Conditions

Before one can hope to understand the nature of a condition in the present con- **5.08** text, it is necessary to distinguish it from various other concepts with which it may appear to have similarities, but which work in different ways.

(1) Conditions precedent to the existence of a contract

The word 'condition' is sometimes used to denote not a term of the contract but an **5.09** event upon the occurrence of which the very existence of the contract depends.[26] The distinction was well drawn by Denning LJ (as he then was) in *Trans Trust SPRL v Danubian Trading Co*,[27] where the court had to consider the status of a stipulation that the defendant should organize a letter of credit. In the words of Denning LJ:[28]

> What is the legal position of such a stipulation? Sometimes it is a condition prece- dent to the formation of a contract, that is, it is a condition which must be fulfilled

---

[21] [1987] QB 527 (CA).
[22] *Lombard North Central v Butterworth*, 545 (Nicholls LJ) (n 21).
[23] *Lombard North Central v Butterworth*, 540 (Mustill LJ) and 546 (Nicholls LJ) (n 21).
[24] Reynolds, 'Discharge of Contract by Breach' (n 6).
[25] See further Ch 10, paras 10.15–10.17.
[26] MG Ferson, 'Conditions in the Law of Contracts' (1955) 8 Vand L Rev 537.
[27] [1952] 2 QB 297 (CA).
[28] *Trans Trust v Danubian Trading*, 304 (n 27).

before any contract is concluded at all. In those cases the stipulation 'subject to the opening of a credit' is rather like a stipulation 'subject to contract'. If no credit is provided, there is no contract between the parties. In other cases a contract is concluded and the stipulation for credit is a condition which is an essential term of the contract. In those cases the provision of the credit is a condition precedent, not to the formation of a contract, but to the obligation of the seller to deliver the goods. If the buyer fails to provide the credit, the seller can treat himself as discharged from any further performance of the contract and can sue the buyers for damages for not providing the credit.

An example of the first kind of condition is given by *Pym v Campbell*,[29] where the defendant agreed to invest in a machine invented by the plaintiff subject to the machine being approved by a third party. The third party not having approved of the agreement, it was held that no contract had come into existence at all. The distinction drawn by Denning LJ in this context may not be quite as stark as he makes it appear,[30] but in the present context the position is clear enough; before an event can qualify as a condition breach of which gives rise to the right to terminate, the party in default must have promised to bring that event about.

(2) Conditions precedent in unilateral contracts

5.10   Another possibility is that the contract may make the promisor's duty to perform conditional on the occurrence of a certain event, without the other party necessarily being under any obligation with regard to that event. In such a case the promisor's obligation is classified as unilateral, the rule being that if the event in question does not occur the obligation does not arise. The effect of this, as we have seen, is very similar to termination,[31] but the two are not the same.[32] In *Hare v Nicoll*[33] a seller of shares was held to be debarred from exercising an option to repurchase the shares when he has failed to come up with the price by the due date; here the seller's delay in paying the price discharged the buyer from having to resell the shares, but the seller was not bound to pay the price or indeed to exercise the option at all. In summary, the seller's payment of the price by the due date was a 'condition precedent' to the buyer's obligation to reconvey the shares, but it was not a 'condition' in

---

[29] (1856) 6 E & B 370, 119 ER 903; *Scott v Rania* [1966] NZLR 656.

[30] Treitel identifies a range of possibilities here: (1) there may be no contract at all pending the fulfilment of the condition; (2) the parties may be obliged to remain ready and willing to perform pending the fulfilment of the condition; (3) the parties may be under an obligation not to prevent the fulfilment of the condition; (4) one or other party may be obliged to take reasonable steps to bring about the fulfilment of the condition; and (5) one or other party may be obliged to bring about the fulfilment of the condition *simpliciter*: E Peel, *Treitel: The Law of Contract* (13th edn, Sweet & Maxwell, 2011) paras 2.111–2.117. There may indeed be further variations within this framework, but at the end of the day the only kind of condition we are interested in for the purposes of the present work is category number 5.

[31] See Ch 4, para 4.11.

[32] Carter, *Carter's Breach of Contract*, para 4-37 (n 1).

[33] [1966] 2 QB 130 (CA); *United Dominions Trust (Commercial) Ltd v Eagle Aircraft Services Ltd* [1968] 1 WLR 74 (CA).

the sense that the seller was bound to do it, or that the buyer could obtain damages for his failure to do it.

(3) Conditions subsequent

A 'condition subsequent' has been defined as 'an event the occurrence of which   **5.11** terminates a contractual relationship, or the obligation of one or both parties to perform'.[34] This is generally illustrated by the case of *Head v Tattersall*,[35] where a horse was sold with a warranty that it had been hunted with the Bicester hounds. The contract went on to provide that if the horse did not answer its description the buyer should have the right to return it by a certain day. Before removing the horse from the seller's stables the buyer was informed by the groom (who was not employed by the sellers) that the warranty was incorrect, but nevertheless decided to take the horse away, it being said that he did not require it for hunting purposes.[36] The horse was subsequently injured, and the buyer then decided to return it. It was held by the Court of Exchequer that this injury did not deprive the buyer of his right to return the horse, but the judges differed as to the legal effect of the information given by the groom. According to Kelly CB and Cleasby B, the buyer could not have been expected to make up his mind then and there whether or not to return the horse, as he was entitled to an opportunity to test the reliability of the information.[37] According to Bramwell B, the buyer would normally have been expected to reject the horse as soon as he learned that the warranty was incorrect, but this was overridden by the special condition in the contract allowing it to be returned at a later date.[38] This case was decided twenty years before the Sale of Goods Act, and is not easy to explain in terms of the current law. At one level it could be said that the buyer was entitled to reject the horse for failure to correspond with its description, and that his removal of the horse from the stables did not amount to a waiver by election as it was not done in the certain knowledge that the description was false.[39] On the other hand, Bramwell B at least seems to have thought that this was not a simple case of rejection, and there are certainly cases where a condition subsequent has been held to excuse performance by one or both parties without any suggestion of there having been any breach involved.[40] As Carter points out, the words 'precedent' and 'subsequent' in this context do no

---

[34] Carter, *Carter's Breach of Contract*, para 4-33 (n 1).

[35] (1871–72) LR 7 Ex 7.

[36] *Head v Tattersall*, 8 (n 35). The jury, however, found as a fact that the warranty had induced him to buy the horse (at 8).

[37] *Head v Tattersall*, 9 (Kelly CB) and 13 (Cleasby B) (n 35).

[38] *Head v Tattersall*, 11 (n 35).

[39] See Ch 4, para 4.56.

[40] In this context *Smith's Leading Cases* gives the example of an 'excepted risks' clause in a charterparty, and cites *Atlantic Maritime v Gibbon* [1954] 1 QB 88 (CA); AS Burrows et al (eds), *Chitty on Contracts* (31st edn, Sweet & Maxwell, 2012) para 12-030, and cf the 'implied term' theory of frustration set out in *Taylor v Caldwell* (1863) 3 B & S 826, 122 ER 309.

more than express contrasting relations in time,[41] and on this basis all 'conditions' (in the present sense of terms breach of which gives rise to a right to terminate) can also be classified as 'conditions subsequent',[42] though not all 'conditions subsequent' are necessarily 'conditions' in that sense.

(4) Express rights of termination

5.12 A contract will often contain provisions giving one or other of the parties an express right to terminate performance on the occurrence of certain contingencies.[43] Where such a contingency amounts to a breach of a term of the contract, it would be logical to conclude that the term in question was intended to be a condition, but this is not necessarily so.[44] On the contrary, as we shall see, the law draws a distinction between termination for breach of condition at common law and termination pursuant to a express right conferred by the contract; in particular, a party who exercises an express right of termination given in the contract may be entitled to less in damages than one who terminates for breach of condition at common law.[45]

5.13 That the law draws this distinction is not open to doubt, but the rationale for the distinction is not clear, nor is it always clear how to tell when a particular clause in the contract makes the relevant term a condition and when it merely confers an express right of termination.[46] This matter will be further explored later,[47] but in many cases the distinction will not be of any practical significance; if the only issue is whether the innocent party is entitled to terminate or not, it matters little whether that right arises from the contract alone or from the common law.[48] In the same way, given that the question whether the innocent party is entitled to terminate will generally be decided on the same basis whether it arises in the context of a contractual or common law right, it makes good sense to treat the two as the same for most purposes[49] whilst not forgetting that in some contexts the distinction can be crucial.

---

[41] Burrows et al, *Chitty on Contracts*, para 4-33 (n 40).

[42] DW McMorland, 'A New Approach to Precedent and Subsequent Conditions' (1980) 1 Otago L Rev 469, and see *Schuler AG v Wickman Machine Tool Sales Ltd* [1972] 1 WLR 840 (CA) 859 (Stephenson LJ).

[43] See Ch 8.

[44] See para 5.17.

[45] *Financings v Baldock* [1963] 2 QB 104 (CA); *Lombard North Central plc v Butterworth* [1987] QB 527 (CA).

[46] Thus Carter (*Carter's Breach of Contract*, para 5-51 (n 1)) says that the distinction is not always observed, and cites a dictum of Lord Diplock in *Scandinavian Trading Tanker Co AB v Flota Petrolera Ecuatoriana (The Scaptrade)* [1983] 2 AC 694 (HL) 703. In the context of termination for breach, a distinction that can confuse even Lord Diplock cannot be an easy one to draw!

[47] See Ch 8, paras 8.02–8.04.

[48] Carter, *Carter's Breach of Contract*, para 5-08 (n 1).

[49] Carter, *Carter's Breach of Contract*, para 3-08 (n 1).

C. Identifying a Condition

When is a term a 'condition' in this context?[50] The basic rule is as laid down by **5.14** Blackburn J in *Bettini v Gye*:[51]

> We think the answer to this question depends on the true construction of the contract taken as a whole. Parties may think some matter, apparently of very little importance, essential; and if they sufficiently express an intention to make the literal fulfilment of such a thing a condition precedent, it will be one; or they may think that the performance of some matter, apparently of essential importance and primâ facie a condition precedent, is not really vital, and may be compensated for in damages, and if they sufficiently expressed such an intention, it will not be a condition precedent.

Though Blackburn J uses the older terminology of 'condition precedent', his approach still represents the law;[52] deciding whether a term is a condition is a question of construction.[53] In this context we shall follow Carter in adopting the language of express and implied terms; hence a term can be made a condition either by express stipulation or by implication.[54]

(1) Condition by express stipulation

Given that a condition is a term of the contract breach of which gives rise to a right **5.15** of termination, the most obvious ways of making a term a condition might seem to be either: (1) to call it a 'condition', or (2) to provide that breach of the term will give rise to a right of termination. However, one of the curious features of the law in this area is that neither of these methods will suffice.

(a) Use of the word 'condition'

A party to a contract will not be entitled to terminate for breach of a term merely **5.16** because that term is called a 'condition' in the contract. In *Schuler AG v Wickman Machine Tool Sales Ltd*,[55] a contract gave the defendants the sole right to sell the plaintiff's products, and stated that it was a 'condition' that the defendant's representative visit certain firms at least once a week to solicit orders. Despite the use

---

[50] N Andrews, M Clarke, A Tettenborn, and G Virgo, *Contractual Duties: Performance, Breach, Termination and Remedies* (Sweet & Maxwell, 2011) paras 10-01–10-72; Carter, *Carter's Breach of Contract*, ch 5 (n 1).

[51] (1875–76) LR 1 QBD 183 (Divisional Ct) 187.

[52] *Bentsen v Taylor, Sons & Co* [1893] 2 QB 274 (CA) 281 (Esher MR); *Re Comptoir Commercial Anversois and Power, Son & Co* [1920] 1 KB 868 (CA) 899 (Scrutton LJ); *Schuler AG v Wickman Machine Tool Sales Ltd* [1974] AC 235 (HL); *Bunge Corp (New York) v Tradax Export SA* [1981] 1 WLR 711 (HL) 715 (Lord Wilberforce) and 725 (Lord Roskill); *Torvald Klaveness A/S v Arni Maritime Corp (The Gregos)* [1994] 1 WLR 1465 (HL) 1475 (Lord Mustill).

[53] Carter, *Carter's Breach of Contract*, para 4-06 (n 1).

[54] Carter, *Carter's Breach of Contract*, para 5-02 (n 1).

[55] [1974] AC 235 (HL); JH Baker, 'Contract—Construction of "Condition"' [1973] CLJ 196.

of this terminology, it was held by the House of Lords that the plaintiff could not terminate merely on the ground that some of the specified visits had not been made. As Lord Reid said, the more unreasonable a result the less likely that the parties could have intended it; if the plaintiffs' contention were right, failure to make even one visit would have entitled them to terminate no matter how blameless the defendant might be.[56] The word 'condition' can be used in many different senses, and what this case indicates is that it is not enough for the parties to *call* a term a condition; their intention must have been that, in the present sense, it should *be* one.

(b) Giving a right of termination

5.17   Nor will it be enough for the contract to specify a right of termination for breach of the term in question. Though it is assumed in some of the cases that the existence of such a right makes the term a condition,[57] this need not necessarily be so. Indeed, as we shall see, in some contexts the law draws a clear distinction between termination for breach of condition and termination under an express stipulation in the contract, and this it could not do if there was no difference between the two. That said, there is no easy test for distinguishing the former case from the latter, and the question has not often been litigated. No doubt this is because in most cases the only issue is whether the innocent party can terminate, and in this context it matters little whether the right arises from the contract or at common law.[58] The question has, however, been considered on a number of occasions by the High Court of Australia. In *Shevill v Builders Licensing Board*[59] a lease gave the landlords a power of re-entry for late payment of rent, but added that this was without prejudice to any other remedy they might have. The tenants having frequently failed to pay the rent on time, the landlords exercised the power of re-entry and then sought to recover as damages an amount equal to the rent payable over the balance of the term. The landlords argued that the effect of the contractual power of re-entry was

---

[56] [1974] AC 235, 251. This conclusion was supported by the inclusion of another term in the contract which entitled the plaintiffs in the event of any 'material breach' to call on the defendants to remedy it, and gave a right of termination if this was not done. It would have been odd to say the least if this coexisted with a right of summary termination for breaches that were *not* material. See, however, R Brownsword, 'L Schuler AG v Wickman Machine Tool Sales Ltd: a Tale of Two Principles' (1974) 37 MLR 104.

[57] Curiously enough even Lord Diplock seems to ignore the distinction: *Afovos Shipping Co SA v Pagnan & Flli* [1983] 1 WLR 195 (HL) 203; *Scandinavian Trading Tanker Co AB v Flota Petrolera Ecuatoriana (The Scaptrade)* [1983] 2 AC 694 (HL) 703. See also *BNP Paribas v Wockhardt EU Operation (Swiss) AG* [2009] EWHC 3116 (Comm), 132 Con LR 177, para 42 (Christopher Clarke J). The latter case is treated by Andrews et al, *Contractual Duties*, paras 10-42–10-46 (n 50) as one of breach of condition, but on the basis of the test suggested by Carter (see para 5.19) it looks more like a contractual right of termination.

[58] Carter, *Carter's Breach of Contract*, para 5-08 (n 1).

[59] (1982) 149 CLR 620 (HCA).

to make the prompt payment of rent a condition,[60] but this was rejected by the court. In the words of Gibbs J:

> In my opinion it does not follow from the fact that the contract gave the respondent the right to terminate the contract that it conferred on it the further right to recover damages as compensation for the loss it will sustain as a result of the failure of the lessee to pay the rent and observe the covenants for the rest of the term.[61]

Or, as Brennan J put it five years later in *Esanda Finance Corporation Ltd v Plessnig*: 'A stipulation which confers the right to terminate the hiring for any breach does not transform the non-essential terms into conditions.'[62] So it is not enough in this context for the contract to specify a right of termination for breach of the provision in question; something more is needed.

The converse of this can be seen in *Legione v Hateley*,[63] where a contract for the sale of   **5.18**
land made time of the essence and gave the vendor the right to rescind and forfeit the deposit in the event of the purchaser's default. However, it also specified that neither of the parties could enforce their rights without serving a notice giving the other party fourteen days to remedy the matter. The vendor having terminated for late completion, one of the key issues in the case was whether the court had jurisdiction to relieve the purchaser against forfeiture, and this depended to some extent on whether the vendor had terminated for breach of condition at common law or under an express contractual right. In the end it was decided that the effect of the clause making time of the essence was to elevate the duty of timely completion to the status of a condition, and that the effect of notice provision was merely to regulate this common law right.[64]

To what extent do these decisions provide us with a test for determining whether   **5.19**
a right of termination for breach set out in the contract makes the relevant term a condition or not? No doubt the court in all three cases was concerned to construe the contract in a way that was least onerous for the party in default, but what they do indicate is that merely providing a right of termination is not enough; rather, as Carter suggests,[65] the contract must say something about *the term itself* rather than merely setting out the consequences of its breach.

(c) Stating the importance of the term

The reason why labelling the term as a 'condition' is not enough is that the word   **5.20**
can be used in so many different senses;[66] it therefore need not necessarily indicate that the parties intended the term to be a condition in the sense used in the present context. However, there are other words that may be less ambiguous; thus,

---

[60] *Shevill v Builders Licensing Board*, 622–3 (n 59).
[61] *Shevill v Builders Licensing Board*, 627 (n 59).
[62] (1989) 166 CLR 131 (HCA) 144.
[63] (1982–83) 152 CLR 406 (HCA).
[64] *Legione v Hateley*, 445 (Mason and Deane JJ) (n 63).
[65] Carter, *Carter's Breach of Contract*, para 5-51 (n 1).
[66] See Ch 1, para 1.09.

for instance, it is clear that saying that time is 'of the essence' is enough to make timely performance a condition,[67] and Carter suggests that an express statement that some other term is 'essential' or words to that effect may bring about the same result.[68] Since the use of this sort of terminology puts the focus on the status of the term in question rather than on the consequences of its breach, there can be no question as to whether the intention was to make the term a condition in the full sense or merely to provide a contractual right of termination.

(2) Condition by implication

5.21 In the majority of cases the question whether a particular term of the contract is a condition or not will have to be decided by implication. As in the case of implied terms generally,[69] the implication can be in fact or in law.

(a) Condition implied in fact

5.22 A term is implied in fact when, in the words of Lord Denning MR, the implication is based on 'an intention imputed to the parties from their actual circumstances'.[70] In the present context this covers cases where it is clear from the circumstances that the parties must have intended the term to be a condition. There are a variety of factors that may point towards this conclusion, and the list is by no means closed, but several key pointers are worth highlighting in this regard.

5.23 **(i) What the parties said** In some cases the course of negotiations between the parties will make it clear that some particular term was regarded as of crucial importance. In *Bannerman v White*,[71] a case involving the sale of hops, the buyer asked the seller whether sulphur had been used in their cultivation, adding that if it had he would not even ask the price. The seller assured him that it had not, and the buyer bought the hops on this basis. It was then discovered that the seller's representation was inaccurate. The jury having found as a fact: (1) that the seller had not wilfully made a false representation at the time of the contract, but (2) that the buyer had purchased the hops on the faith of that representation,[72] the Court of Exchequer Chamber held that the buyer was entitled to reject the hops and sue for damages; in the words of Erle CJ, the intention of the parties was clearly that the contract should be 'null' if sulphur had been used.[73] Here the case

---

[67] *United Scientific Holdings v Burnley BC* [1978] AC 904 (HL) 907 (Lord Salmon); *Legione v Hateley* (1983) 152 CLR 406 (HCA) 445 (Mason and Deane JJ); *Lombard North Central plc v Butterworth* [1987] 1 QB 527 (CA) 535 (Mustill LJ) and 545 (Nicholls LJ).

[68] Carter, *Carter's Breach of Contract*, para 5-05 (n 1); see for instance *Gill & Duffus SA v Société pour l'Exportation des Sucres SA* [1986] 1 Lloyd's Rep 322 (CA) ('at latest').

[69] See Ch 3, para 3.11.

[70] *Shell (UK) Ltd v Lostock Garage Ltd* [1976] 1 WLR 1187 (CA) 1196.

[71] (1861) 10 CBNS 844, 142 ER 685.

[72] *Bannerman v White*, 846, 686 (n 71).

[73] *Bannerman v White*, 860, 692 (n 71). Though the word 'null' seems at first sight to indicate rescission rather than termination, the fact that damages were awarded, combined with the jury's finding that the misrepresentation was made in good faith, indicates that it must have been a case of termination.

turned on a statement by the innocent party, but the same principle can apply to a statement by the party in default. In *Harling v Eddy*[74] the defendant put his cow up for auction, but it was obviously in poor shape and nobody was willing to bid for it. The defendant then said that there was nothing wrong with the cow, that he would absolutely guarantee her in every respect, and that he would be willing to take her back if she turned out not to be what he stated she was, and on this basis the cow was sold to the plaintiff. However, the cow later turned out to be suffering from tuberculosis and died before the plaintiff could return it. It was held by the Court of Appeal that the defendant could not rely on a clause in the auctioneer's catalogue stating that no warranty was given; the circumstances clearly indicated that this was more than a mere warranty. In the words of Evershed MR:[75]

> The defendant's statement having, therefore, included words to the effect, 'If there is anything wrong I will take it back', it seems to me quite plain that the words which he used could not have been intended merely as a warranty; for a warranty would give no right of rejection to the purchaser. The final words involve necessarily a right in the purchaser to reject, that is, to return the animal; and they convert the statement, to my mind, from a warranty into a condition.

(ii) The importance of the term generally   It has been recognized from the   **5.24**
earliest days of the doctrine that a term is more likely to have been intended as a condition if it relates to a matter of importance. In the words of Lord Mansfield:[76]

> The distinction is very clear; where mutual covenants go to the whole of the consideration on both sides, they are mutual conditions, the one precedent to the other: but where they go only to a part, where a breach may be paid for in damages, there the defendant has a remedy on his covenant, and shall not plead it as a condition precedent.

Whether a term goes to the 'whole consideration', in this sense, is a matter of looking at its importance within the contract as a whole, or as Kerr LJ puts it 'making of what is in effect a value judgement about the commercial significance of the term in question'.[77] Thus in *Bentsen v Taylor, Sons & Co (No 2)*[78] a statement in a charterparty that the ship was 'sailed or about to sail' was held to be a condition, on the grounds that such a statement was of crucial importance in contracts of this kind. In the words of Bowen LJ:[79]

> ...the non-accuracy of such a statement is likely to affect the very foundation of the adventure, because its inaccuracy would displace the only basis, or one of the chief bases, of the calculation on which the parties would act. It is obvious that when you are dealing with a voyage, the contemplated date of its commencement

---

[74] [1951] 2 KB 739 (CA).
[75] *Harling v Eddy*, 742 (n 74).
[76] *Boone v Eyre* (1777) 1 Hy Bl 273n, 126 ER 160, 2 Bl W 1313n, 96 ER 267.
[77] *State Trading Corp of India Ltd v M Golodetz & Co Inc Ltd* [1989] 2 Lloyd's Rep 277 (CA) 263; J Beatson, AS Burrows, and J Cartwright, *Anson's Law of Contract* (29th edn, OUP, 2010) p 146.
[78] [1893] 2 QB 274 (CA).
[79] *Bentsen v Taylor, Sons & Co (No 2)*, 282 (n 78).

may be of the utmost importance. Having regard to the time of the year at which it is intended to prosecute the voyage, delay in its commencement, if it is protracted beyond a certain point, may in many cases be so vital a matter as to render the voyage impossible, or the risk may be so much increased as to make it no longer possible to have a voyage of the same kind.

5.25 **(iii) The importance of the term to the innocent party**   The key question in this context will often be the likely importance of the term to the other party. Thus in *Behn v Burness*[80] a stipulation in a charterparty as to the current location of the ship was held to be a condition on the basis that this might be the only datum on which the charterer could found his calculations of the time of the ship's arriving at the port of loading, and one of the reasons why time is generally held to be of the essence of delivery in a commercial contract for the sale of goods is that in such cases the buyer is likely to have arranged his or her affairs on the basis that the property would be delivered on the date specified.[81] In a contract for the sale of land, time is not so important,[82] but even here time will be of the essence if the vendor knows that the purchaser wants the property for immediate use.[83] In the same way, terms regarding the payment of deposits may be regarded as conditions on the basis that without the deposit the seller does not know where he stands, and has nothing to show for the contract except a fetter on his freedom to deal with his property.[84] According to Diplock LJ, a term will be a condition if it can be predicated that any breach will result in the innocent party being deprived of substantially the whole benefit which it was intended he should obtain from the contract,[85] but the likely effect of the breach does not have to be as extreme as this for a term to be classified in this way;[86] rather, it is a matter of degree to be taken into account by the court. The more serious the likely consequences for the innocent party, the more likely it is that the term will be classified as a condition on this basis.

5.26 **(iv) The balance of disadvantage**   Another way the courts have looked at the problem is by considering the balance of disadvantage, that is to say the disadvantage to the party in default if the term is construed as a condition as against the disadvantage to the innocent party if it is not. Thus in the early case of *Boone*

---

[80] (1863) 3 B & S 751, 122 ER 281.

[81] *Bunge Corp (New York) v Tradax Export SA* [1981] 1 WLR 711 (HL) 716 (Lord Wilberforce).

[82] See para 5.40.

[83] *Newman v Rogers* (1793) 4 Bro CC 391, 29 ER 950; *Spurrier v Hancock* (1799) 4 Ves J 667, 31 ER 344; *Wright v Howard* (1823) 1 Sim & St 190, 57 ER 76; *Levy v Stogdon* [1898] 1 Ch 478; *Bernard v Williams* (1928) 139 LT 22; see para 5.42.

[84] *Samarenko v Dawn Hill House Ltd* [2011] EWCA Civ 1445, [2013] Ch 36, [2012] 1 P & CR 14, para 24 (Lewison LJ).

[85] *Hongkong Fir Shipping Co Ltd v Kawasaki Kisen Kaisha Ltd (The Hongkong Fir)* [1962] 2 QB 26, 69.

[86] AC Hutchinson and JN Wakefield, 'Contracts—Innominate Terms: Contractual Encounters of the Third Kind' (1982) 60 Can BR 335.

v Eyre,[87] which involved the sale of a plantation with the slaves on it in return for an annuity, Lord Mansfield refused to allow the vendor's inability to make good title to all the slaves to prevent him from recovering the annuity, saying that if the purchaser's plea was allowed the seller's lack of title to a single slave would be a bar to the action;[88] in other words, such a finding would cause detriment to the vendor far in excess of any possible benefit to the purchaser. A similar approach can be seen in cases involving time limits in the context of rent review provisions; one of the reasons given for not treating time as of the essence of these provisions[89] is that, in the words of Slade LJ, 'the detriment to the landlord of losing his review altogether by failure to adhere strictly to the stipulated time limit will be wholly disproportionate to the disadvantage to the tenant of a delay in the assessment of the rent'.[90] It is, however, important to note the precise nature of the balancing exercise involved in this context. Slade LJ is not suggesting that a provision will only be construed as a condition if the disadvantage to the innocent party if the court does not do so outweighs the disadvantage to the party in default if it does. After all, the whole point of a condition is to allow the innocent party to terminate *without* having to show that he or she has been disadvantaged by the breach in the particular case.[91] Rather, it is a guide to the construction of the contract; to adapt the words of Slade LJ, is the proper intention to impute to the parties, from the words which they have used, the intention that the party in default should lose his or her right to enforce the contract for any and every breach of the term under consideration?[92] It is not a question of the *actual* effect of the breach, but of its *likely* effect at the time the contract was made.[93] As Carter points out, the application of this test is a matter of commercial judgment.[94] The fact that construing a term as a condition would cause a totally disproportionate disadvantage to the party in default may be a good indicator that he or she never agreed to such a construction in the first place,[95] but it is no more than an indicator, and ultimately other considerations, such as the need for commercial certainty, may outweigh the need to produce a result that is fair to the parties in the individual case.

---

[87] (1779) 1 Bl H 273n and 2 Bl W 1313n, 126 ER 148 and 96 ER 767.

[88] *Boone v Eyre* (n 87).

[89] *United Scientific Holdings Ltd v Burnley BC* [1978] AC 904 (HL); *Touche Ross & Co v Secretary of State for the Environment* (1983) 46 P & CR 187 (CA); *Metrolands Investments Ltd v JH Dewhurst Ltd* (1986) 52 P & CR 232 (CA).

[90] *Metrolands Investments v JH Dewhurst*, 244 (n 89); *McDonalds Property Co Ltd v HBSC Bank plc* [2002]1 P & CR 25 (Ch D) para 19 (Peter Leaver QC).

[91] *Bunge Corp New York v Tradax Export SA* [1981] 1 WLR 711 (HL) 715 (Lord Wilberforce), 718 (Lord Lowry), and 724–5 (Lord Roskill).

[92] *Metrolands Investments Ltd v JH Dewhurst Ltd* (1986) 52 P & CR 232 (CA) 243.

[93] *Bentsen v Taylor, Sons & Co (No 2)* [1893] 2 QB 274 (CA) 281 (Bowen LJ); Hutchinson and Wakefield, 'Contracts—Innominate Terms' (n 86).

[94] Carter, *Carter's Breach of Contract*, para 5-23 (n 1).

[95] As Carter says, the fact that a particular interpretation of a contractual term would lead to a commercially unreasonable result is an indication that the parties did not intend that construction: Carter, *Carter's Breach of Contract*, para 5-27 (n 1).

5.27   **(v) The nature of the subject matter**   Whether a term is construed as a condition may depend to some extent on the matters with which it deals. A good illustration of this is *Sharp v Christmas*,[96] where a buyer of a crop of potatoes agreed to take them by a certain date but failed to do so. The presumption that time was of the essence in the commercial context was held to be strengthened here on the grounds that the potatoes were a perishable commodity; in the words of Lord Esher MR, the buyer could not be allowed to leave them in the farmer's hands until they became rotten.[97] In a sale of land, time is generally not of the essence,[98] but it will be different if the obligation is to transfer property of a wasting or fluctuating value,[99] for in such cases the efficacy of the bargain depends on prompt performance by both transferor and transferee. Indeed, it has been argued that it is this principle which underlies the oft-cited presumption that time is of the essence in 'mercantile' or 'commercial' contracts, for when property is sold to be used in commerce or business rather than for private consumption or use, it is likely that the buyer will have arranged his or her affairs, and made other contracts, on the assumption that performance will be forthcoming.[100] This applies with particular force to the time of delivery in a commercial contract for the sale of goods, where the buyer may very well have made a subsale on the footing that he or she would have the goods at a certain time; hence the general rule that time is of the essence with regard to this obligation.[101]

5.28   **(vi) Interrelationship with other obligations**   A term of the contract is sometimes construed as a condition on the ground that the proper performance of other obligations in the same contract depends on it. Thus time will often be of the essence of an obligation where timely performance of that obligation is necessary to ensure timely performance by the other. In *Toepfer (Hamburg) v Lenersan Poortman NV (Rotterdam)*[102] a cif contract for the sale of rapeseed provided for 'payment net cash against documents and/or delivery order on arrival of the vessel at port of discharge but not later than 20 days after date of Bill of Lading'. The bill of lading was issued on 11 December 1974, but delivery orders were not tendered

---

[96] (1892) 8 TLR 687 (CA).
[97] *Sharp v Christmas*, 688 (n 96).
[98] See para 5.41.
[99] Such as the sale of a public house as a going concern (*Coslake v Till* (1826) 1 Russ 376, 38 ER 146; *Day v Luhke* (1867–68) LR 5 Eq 336; *Powell v Marshall, Parkes & Co* [1899] 1 QB 710 (CA); *Lock v Bell* [1931] 1 Ch 35 (Ch D) (Maugham J)); the transfer of a short lease (*Carter v Dean and Chapter of Ely* (1835) 7 Sim 211, 58 ER 817; *Southcomb v Bishop of Exeter* (1847) 16 LJ Ch 378; *Firth v Greenwood* (1855) 25 LTOS 51; *Hudson v Temple* (1860) 30 LJ Ch 251); or the sale of a reversion (*Newman v Rogers* (1793) 4 Bro CC 391, 29 ER 950; *Spurrier v Hancock* (1799) 4 Ves J 667, 31 ER 344; *Levy v Stogdon* [1898] 1 Ch 478 (CA)). See also *Withy v Cottle* (1823) Turn & R 78, 37 ER 1024 (annuity); *Doloret v Rothschild* (1824) 1 Sim & S 590, 57 ER 233 (government stock); *Pearson v London & Croydon Rly Co* (1845) 1 Holt Eq R 235, 71 ER 733 (sale of shares).
[100] K Lindgren, *Time in the Performance of Contracts* (2nd edn, Butterworths, 1982) pp 49–50.
[101] *Alewyn v Pryor* (1826) Ry & M 406, 171 ER 1065; *Plevins v Downing* (1876) 1 CPD 220; *Bowes v Shand* (1877) 2 App Cas 455 (HL); *Reuter, Hufeland & Co v Sala & Co* (1879) 4 CPD 239.
[102] [1980] 1 Lloyd's Rep 143 (CA); *McLeod Russel Ltd v Emerson* (1986) 51 P & CR 176 (CA).

to the buyer until the following February. It was held that the buyer was entitled
to reject the documents, since the clause concerning the time of tender was one
which bound both parties and time was of the essence; the buyer's obligation to
pay depended on prompt tender by the seller. Again, it was held in *Haugland
Tankers AS v RMK Marine*[103] that where a shipbuilding contract gave the buyer
an option to purchase an extra vessel on payment of a commitment fee, time was
of the essence of the payment no less than of the option. In the same way, clauses
relating to the time of nomination are often conditions, as important obligations
of the other party may depend on this being done promptly.[104] The same reasoning has been used in cases where a rent review mechanism is accompanied by a
'break' clause, which gives the tenant the right to surrender the lease by a certain
date if he or she does not wish to pay the revised rent. Obviously it would defeat
the purpose of such a clause if a landlord was allowed to have the rent reviewed
when it was too late for the tenant to exercise the break clause, and for this reason
it has been held that where rent review provisions contain such a clause, time will
be presumed to be of the essence with regard to the revision of the rent.[105]

(vii) Interrelationship with contractual rights of termination   Courts are   **5.29**
sometimes confronted with the question whether the provision of a contractual
right of termination excludes the right to terminate at common law for breach
of condition. As will be seen, the general rule is that it does not,[106] but the scope
of such a right may cast light on the issue whether a particular term in the contract was intended to be a condition in the first place. In *Schuler AG v Wickman
Machine Tool Sales Ltd*[107] the contract gave the plaintiffs sole selling rights in
relation to products manufactured by the defendants, clause 7 of the agreement
providing that it was a 'condition' of the agreement that the plaintiffs should send
salesmen to visit certain firms on a weekly basis. The contract also set out a procedure whereby in the event of any 'material breach' by either party the other could
call on the breach to be remedied, and terminate the contract if this was not done
within a certain time. The defendants sought to terminate on the grounds that
the plaintiffs had breached clause 7, but it was held by the House of Lords that
despite the terminology used to describe the clause in question it could not have
been intended to be a condition in the strict sense of the word. After all, it would

---

[103] [2005] EWHC 321 (Comm), [2005] 1 Lloyd's Rep 573.

[104] *Scandinavian Trading Co A/B v Zodiac Petroleum SA (The Al Hofuf)* [1981] 1 Lloyd's Rep 81
(QBD) (nomination of ship); *Gill & Duffus SA v Société pour l'Exportation des Sucres SA* [1986] 1
Lloyd's Rep 322 (nomination of port); *Warde v Feedex International Inc (No 2)* [1985] 2 Lloyd's Rep
290 (QBD: Commercial Ct) (nomination of bank).

[105] *Richards and Son v Karenita* (1971) 221 EG 25; *Coventry City Council v Hepworth & Son Ltd*
(1983) 46 P & CR 170 (CA); *Legal and General Assurance (Pension Management) Ltd v Cheshire
CC* (1983) 46 P & CR 160 (Ch D). The position may be different if the review process is not under
the control of the landlord: see *Metrolands Investments Ltd v JH Dewhurst Ltd* (1986) 52 P & CR
232 (CA).

[106] See Ch 8, para 8.20.

[107] [1974] AC 235 (HL); Carter, *Carter's Breach of Contract*, para 5-21 (n 1).

have been exceedingly odd if the parties had intended to allow material breaches to be remedied whilst giving a peremptory right of termination for breaches that were *not* material. In this context a lot depends on the ambit of the express right in question. In the case under discussion the limited ambit of the express right suggested that the parties did not intend it to coexist with a wider common law right, but different considerations will apply where the express right itself gives a wider power of termination than would have been available at common law. This will be so particularly where the express right of termination does not depend on proof of breach at all.[108]

5.30   **(viii) The breadth of the obligation**   The broader the ambit of the obligation in question, the less likely it is to be construed as a condition. Thus where a contractual provision embraces a wide variety of matters ranging from the critically important to the relatively trivial, it is difficult if not impossible to impute to the parties a common intention that any failure to carry out any of the obligations diligently and promptly, however insignificant the breach and however trivial the consequences, is to be treated without more as a repudiatory breach of an essential term.[109] In the same way, it has been said that time is more likely to be of the essence in relation to a term requiring a single act to be done than where it covers a variety of acts.[110] In *The Hongkong Fir*[111] the Court of Appeal was confronted with the issue whether a charterer could terminate the charter for delays caused by unseaworthiness. One of the arguments on behalf of the charterer was that the obligation to provide a seaworthy ship was a condition, but this was rejected by the court. In the words of Upjohn LJ:[112]

> Why is this apparently basic and underlying condition of seaworthiness not, in fact, treated as a condition? It is for the simple reason that the seaworthiness clause is breached by the slightest failure to be fitted 'in every way' for service. Thus, to take examples from the judgments in some of the cases...if a nail is missing from one of the timbers of a wooden vessel or if proper medical supplies or two anchors are not on board at the time of sailing, the owners are in breach of the seaworthiness stipulation. It is contrary to common sense to suppose that in such circumstances the parties contemplated that the charterer should at once be entitled to treat the contract as at an end for such trifling breaches.

This approach should be contrasted with the greater readiness of the courts to construe time stipulations as conditions. Indeed, an attempt to apply the reasoning in

---

[108] Carter, *Carter's Breach of Contract*, para 5-21 (n 1); *Maredelanto Compania Naviera SA v Bergbau-Handel GmbH (The Mihalis Angelos)* [1971] 1 QB 164 (CA); DW Greig, 'Condition—or Warranty?' (1973) 89 LQR 93.

[109] *Etzin v Reece* [2003] 1 P & CR DG9 (Ch D, Launcelot Henderson QC).

[110] *Bovis Homes Inc v Oakcliff Investment Corp* (Ch D, Harman J) 30 March 1994.

[111] *Hongkong Fir Shipping Co Ltd v Kawasaki Kisen Kaisha Ltd (The Hongkong Fir)* [1962] 2 QB 26 (CA).

[112] *The Hongkong Fir*, 62–3; MP Furmston, 'The Classification of Contractual Terms' (1962) 25 MLR 584.

The Hongkong Fir to such a stipulation was firmly rejected by the House of Lords in *Bunge Corporation (New York) v Tradax Export SA*.[113] In the words of Lord Wilberforce:[114]

> The fundamental fallacy of the appellants' argument lies in attempting to apply this analysis to a time clause such as the present in a mercantile contract, which is totally different in character. As to such a clause there is only one kind of breach possible, namely, to be late, and the questions which have to be asked are, first, what importance have the parties expressly ascribed to this consequence, and secondly, in the absence of expressed agreement, what consequence ought to be attached to it having regard to the contract as a whole.

The point here is not that time stipulations are necessarily more important than other stipulations. Rather, the point is that where the latter can be broken in a great many ways, a time stipulation can only be broken in one way.

(ix) Availability of other remedy   Termination for breach is a serious matter, **5.31** and the courts will be less likely to construe a term as a condition where the innocent party has some other remedy for the breach. Thus in *Lamprell v Billericay Union*[115] the provision of liquidated damages for delay was held to prevent time being of the essence with regard to the completion of the work, and in *Inman SS Co v Bischoff*[116] it was held by the House of Lords that the seaworthiness of the ship could not have been intended as a condition precedent to the right of the owner to recover freight under a charterparty, since the contract provided for deductions of freight in that instance. Indeed, in *Aktieselskabet v Arcos Ltd*[117] Sargant LJ observed that one of the functions of a demurrage clause in a charterparty was to prevent the owners from arguing that they had the right to withdraw the ship for delays by the charterer. On the other hand, one of the reasons why time is said to be of the essence in relation to unilateral contracts and options is that refusal to perform is the only remedy available to the promisor if the time limit is not kept.[118] Indeed, it has been argued that one of the reasons why termination is so often an issue in relation to time stipulations is that since delay will often cause no calculable economic loss the only possibilities are either to allow the innocent party to terminate or to ignore the time stipulation altogether.[119]

(x) Options   Strictly speaking, the discussion of unilateral obligations and options **5.32** is outside the remit of the present book;[120] though the principles governing the

---

[113] [1981] 1 WLR 711.
[114] *Bunge Corp v Tradax Export*, 715 (n 113).
[115] (1849) 3 Ex 283, 308, 154 ER 850, 861; *Platt v Parker* (1886) 2 TLR 786.
[116] (1881) 7 App Cas 670 (HL).
[117] [1927] 1 KB 352 (CA) 366.
[118] See para 5.32.
[119] SJ Stoljar, 'Untimely Performance in Contract' (1955) 71 LQR 527, 528–30.
[120] For a fuller account see JE Stannard, *Delay in the Performance of Contractual Obligations* (OUP, 2007) paras 11.32–11.37.

refusal of the promisor to perform in such cases are akin to termination,[121] such termination is not, *ex hypothesi*, termination for *breach* of contract. Nevertheless, the considerations taken into account by the courts are very similar, and for that reason options are worth discussing in the present context. The general rule is that any conditions precedent to the exercise of an option must be strictly complied with before the promisor can be called on to perform.[122] This is well illustrated by the early case of *Lock v Wright*,[123] where the defendant covenanted by deed poll to pay a sum of money to the plaintiff once the plaintiff had transferred certain stock to him. The court held that the plaintiff could not sue on the promise without averring tender or delivery, the reasoning being that since there was no counter-promise by the plaintiff to do this, refusal to perform was the only remedy available to the defendant. Again, in *United Dominions Trust (Commercial) Ltd v Eagle Aircraft Services Ltd*[124] the Court of Appeal drew a clear distinction between 'synallagmatic' contracts, where the right to terminate might depend on the effect of a failure in performance, and 'unilateral' contracts, where conditions precedent had to be strictly complied with before the promisor would be under any obligation at all.[125] The reasoning in these cases seems to be as given in the previous paragraph; whereas in the case of a bilateral or synallagmatic obligation damages are available for deficiencies in performance by the other party, termination (or rather refusal to perform) is the only remedy available in respect of one that is purely unilateral.[126]

5.33 **(xi) Commercial contracts** It has sometimes been said that terms are more likely to be construed as conditions in commercial contracts,[127] and that substantial and important provisions in a mercantile contract relating to the time, place, or mode of shipment of the goods are to be treated as conditions unless the contrary intention is manifest.[128] This is said in particular to apply to time stipulations,[129] a principle which 'may not be justifiable by any presumption of fact or rule of law', but is rather

---

[121] See Ch 4, para 4.11.

[122] *Hare v Nicoll* [1966] 2 QB 130 (CA); Carter, *Carter's Breach of Contract*, para 5-49 (n 1).

[123] (1720) 1 Stra 569, 93 ER 706.

[124] [1968] 1 WLR 74 (CA).

[125] *United Dominions Trust v Eagle Aircraft Services*, 80–1 (Denning MR), 82–4 (Diplock LJ), and 86–7 (Edmund Davies LJ) (n 124).

[126] Thus one reason why time is not generally of the essence of rent review provisions, though they are akin to options, may be that there are other remedies available to a party inconvenienced by delay, such as the service of a notice making time of the essence: *United Scientific Holdings Ltd v Burnley BC* [1978] AC 904 (HL); *London & Manchester Assurance Co v GA Dunn & Co* (1982) 265 EG 39 (CA); *Touche Ross & Co v Secretary of State for the Environment* (1983) 46 P & CR 187 (CA); *Amherst v James Walker Goldsmith & Silversmith Ltd* [1983] Ch 305; *Metrolands Investments Ltd v JH Dewhurst Ltd* (1986) 52 P & CR 232 (CA); *Idealview Ltd v Bello* [2009] EWHC 2828 (QB), [2010] 4 EG 118; Stannard, *Delay in the Performance of Contractual Obligations*, para 11-37 (n 120).

[127] Carter, *Carter's Breach of Contract*, para 5-29 (n 1).

[128] *Bowes v Chaleyer* (1923) 32 CLR 159 (HCA) 196 (Starke J); Carter, *Carter's Breach of Contract*, para 5-29 (n 1).

[129] *Sharp v Christmas* (1892) 8 TLR 687 (CA); *Bowes v Shand* (1877) 2 App Cas 455 (HL); *Reuter, Hufeland & Co v Sala & Co* (1879) 4 CPD 239; *Olearia Tirrena SpA v NV Algemeene Oliehandel*

'a practical expedient founded on and dictated by the experience of businessmen'.[130] This approach can be supported on the basis of the need for certainty in the commercial context, where the parties will frequently have entered into other transactions dealing with the same subject matter, and will need to know where they stand without having to engage in time-consuming and expensive litigation.[131] On the other hand, to label a contract 'commercial' or 'mercantile' and then to conclude that all the terms of that contract must be conditions is far too crude an approach;[132] after all, nothing could be more 'commercial' or 'mercantile' than a contract between businessmen for the sale of goods, but in relation to one very important obligation, that of payment, time is presumed *not* to be of the essence.[133] Rather, each contract, and indeed each obligation, must be considered on its own merits.

(xii) Executed and executory contracts   It was pointed out by Bridge in 1983[134]   **5.34** that ever since *Boone v Eyre*[135] the courts have been more willing to construe terms as conditions where the contract is purely executory than where the innocent party has received some kind of benefit under it. This result arises naturally from the approach adopted in that case; a covenant could hardly be said to go to the entire consideration where despite its breach the innocent party had received some if not all of the benefit of the contract.[136] This consideration may be another reason why the courts have taken a more strict approach in this respect to mercantile contracts—where any such benefits can often be returned to the party in default—than to building contracts or sales of land where there is a greater possibility of unjust enrichment. An obvious objection to this kind of 'execution analysis' is that a breach of condition need not necessarily have catastrophic effects,[137] and that in any event the question whether a term is a condition or

---

(The Osterbek) [1973] 2 Lloyd's Rep 86 (CA); *Bunge Corp (New York) v Tradax Export SA* [1981] 1 WLR 711 (HL).

[130]   *Bunge Corp (New York) v Tradax Export SA* [1981] 1 WLR 711 (HL) 719 (Lord Lowry).

[131]   *Bunge Corp v Tradax Export*, 720 (Lord Lowry) (n 130).

[132]   Thus the principle is no more than a presumption, and the courts are not absolved from making in effect a value judgment as to the significance of the term in the individual case: *State Trading Corp of India v Golodetz & Co Inc Ltd* [1989] 2 Lloyd's Rep 277, 283 (Kerr LJ); *Compagnie Commericale Sucres et Denrées v C Czarnikow Ltd (The Naxos)* [1990] 1 WLR 1337 (HL) 1347 (Lord Ackner); Treitel, ' "Conditions" and "Conditions Precedent" ' (n 9). This approach has been criticized as leading to unacceptable uncertainty in the commercial sphere: see M Clarke, 'Time and the Essence of Mercantile Contracts: the Law loses its Way' [1991] CLJ 29. However, it reflects the way in which the courts in the last forty years have adopted a less strict approach to terms concerning quality and description in the sale of goods: see in particular *Cehave NV v Bremer Handelsgesellschaft mbH (The Hansa Nord)* [1976] QB 44; *Reardon Smith Line Ltd v Hansen Tangen (The Diana Prosperity)* [1976] 1 WLR 989.

[133]   Sale of Goods Act 1979, s 10; *Martindale v Smith* (1841) 1 QB 389, 113 ER 1181.

[134]   MG Bridge, 'Discharge for Breach of the Contract of Sale of Goods' (1983) McGill LJ 867.

[135]   (1777) 1 Hy Bl 273n, 126 ER 160, 2 Bl W 1313n, 96 ER 267.

[136]   *Hall v Cazenove* (1804) 4 East 476, 102 ER 913; *Ellen v Topp* (1851) 6 Ex 424, 155 ER 609; *Graves v Legg* (1854) 9 Ex 709, 156 ER 304; *Inman SS Co v Bischoff* (1881) 7 App Cas 670 (HL).

[137]   *Bunge Corp New York v Tradax Export SA* [1981] 1 WLR 711 (HL) 715 (Lord Wilberforce), 718 (Lord Lowry), and 724–5 (Lord Roskill); see para 5.06.

not is one of construction,[138] and cannot therefore be affected by later events. However, the accrual of benefit to the innocent party can still detract from his or her right to termination in three ways. First of all, a party who voluntarily accepts the benefit of the other party's performance in the wake of a breach of condition may be held to have elected to affirm the contract.[139] Secondly, where the effect of termination would be to work a forfeiture on the party in default, relief may be granted by the courts.[140] Last but not least, the fact that construction of a term as a condition leads to unjust results may be an indication that such a construction was never intended in the first place.[141]

(b) Condition implied by law

5.35 A term is implied by law when, in the words of Lord Denning MR, the court imposes duties on one or other party in the context of 'relationships of common occurrence', such as buyer and seller, employer and employee, landlord and tenant, and so on.[142] These obligations differ from terms implied by fact in that they depend not on the intention of the parties in the particular case but on more general considerations.[143] In the present context, a condition is implied by law when it can be said that certain terms in certain types of contract are *always* conditions unless the parties provide otherwise.[144] Such implication can be by statute or by the common law.

5.36 (i) **Condition implied by statute**   Conditions implied by statute can be found in a number of contexts. Thus, for instance, section 42 of the Marine Insurance Act 1906 provides that in certain cases there is an implied condition that the adventure should be commenced within a reasonable time,[145] and section 8 of the Landlord and Tenant Act 1985 implies into certain leases a condition that the premises are fit for human habitation at the commencement of the term.[146] However, the most obvious examples of implied conditions of this sort are to be found in the obligations imposed on the seller with regard to title, correspondence with description, and quality in the Sale of Goods Act 1979.[147] Similar conditions have been implied by statute into other contracts involving the supply of

---

[138] See para 5.14.

[139] See Ch 4, para 4.57.

[140] See Ch 4, paras 4.77–4.81.

[141] Carter, *Carter's Breach of Contract*, para 5-27 (n 1).

[142] *Shell (UK) Ltd v Lostock Garage Ltd* [1976] 1 WLR 1187 (CA) 1196.

[143] *Shell (UK) v Lostock Garage* (n 142).

[144] Though in some cases this may not be allowed, especially in the consumer context: see Ch 4, para 4.48.

[145] Marine Insurance Act 1906, s 42(1).

[146] Landlord and Tenant Act 1985, s 8(1)(a).

[147] Sale of Goods Act 1979, ss 12(1) and (5A) (title), 13(1) and (1A) (correspondence with description), and 14(2), (3), and (6) (satisfactory quality and fitness for purpose).

goods and services.[148] In all of these cases the effect is the same; the provision in question is to be construed as a condition in all contracts of that nature, unless and so far as the parties are allowed to provide otherwise.[149]

(ii) Condition implied by common law A condition may also be implied into **5.37** contracts of a certain kind by the common law. This was the case prior to the Sale of Goods Act in relation to the implied terms regarding correspondence with description[150] and quality,[151] and similar examples can be seen in the present law. Thus in a contract for the carriage of goods by sea there is an implied condition that the ship will not deviate from the agreed voyage,[152] and in a lease there is an implied condition that the tenant shall not deny the landlord's title.[153] Again, it is now settled by authority that a statement in a charterparty that the ship is 'expected ready to load' on a certain day is a condition,[154] as is the time of delivery in a contract for the sale of goods.[155] No doubt the classification of these terms as conditions can often be justified in terms of their importance within the individual case, but with each succeeding decision on the point this factor becomes less important and the weight of previous authority more so;[156] where the term was

---

[148] Supply of Goods (Implied Terms) Act 1973, ss 8(1)(a) and (3), 9(1) and (1A), and 10(2), (3), and (7) (hire purchase); Supply of Goods and Services Act 1982, ss 2(1), 3(2), and 4(2) and (5) (contracts for transfer of property in goods); ss 7(1), 8(2), and 9(2) and (5) (hire).

[149] Unfair Contract Terms Act 1977, s 6; see Ch 4, para 4.48.

[150] *Bridge v Wain* (1816) 1 Stark 504, 171 ER 543; *Chanter v Hopkins* (1838) 4 M & W 399, 404, 150 ER 1484, 1486–7 (Lord Abinger); *Allan v Lake* (1852) 18 QB 560, 118 ER 212; *Nicol v Godts* (1854) 10 Ex 191, 156 ER 410; *Kirkpatrick v Gowan* (1875) IR 9 CL 521; Benjamin, *Sale of Goods* (6th edn, Sweet & Maxwell, 1920) pp 642–50.

[151] *Gardiner v Gray* (1815) 4 Camp 144, 171 ER 46; *Jones v Bright* (1829) 5 Bing 533, 130 ER 1167; *Shepherd v Pybus* (1842) 3 M & G 868, 130 ER 1167; *Jones v Just* (1868) LR 3 QB 197; *Gorton v Macintosh* [1883] WN 103 (CA).

[152] *Leduc v Ward* (1888) 20 QBD 475 (CA); *Joseph Thorley Ltd v Orchis SS Co Ltd* [1907] 1 KB 660 (CA); *Hain Steamship Co v Tate & Lyle Ltd* (1936) 41 Com Cas 350 (HL); Carter, *Carter's Breach of Contract*, para 5-37 (n 1).

[153] *Warner v Sampson* [1959] 1 QB 297 (CA); *WG Clark (Properties) Ltd v Dupre Properties Ltd* [1992] Ch 297 (Ch D) (Judge Thomas Morison QC); *Abidogun v Frolan Health Care Ltd* [2001] EWCA Civ 1821, [2002] L & TR 16 (CA).

[154] *Corkling v Massey* (1873) 8 CP 395; *Sanday v Keighley Maxsted & Co Ltd* (1922) 27 Com Cas 296 (CA); *Re Empire Shipping Co and Hall Bryan Ltd* [1940] 1 DLR 695 (Supreme Ct of British Columbia); *Maredelanto Compania Naviera SA v Bergbau-Handel GmbH (The Mihalis Angelos)* [1971] 1 QB 164 (CA); *Geogas SA v Trammo Gas Ltd (The Baleares)* [1993] 1 Lloyd's Rep 215 (CA).

[155] *Alewyn v Pryor* (1826) Ry & M 406, 171 ER 1065; *Wimshurst v Deeley* (1845) 2 CB 253, 135 ER 912; *Plevins v Downing* (1876) 1 CPD 220; *Harrington v Brown* (1917) 23 CLR 297; *Hartley v Hymans* [1920] 3 KB 475 (KBD); *Aron & Co Inc v Comptoir Wegimont* [1921] 3 KB 435; *Berg & Sons v Landauer* (1925) 42 TLR 142; *Finagrain SA Geneva v P Kruse Hamburg* [1976] 2 Lloyd's Rep 508 (CA); *Cerealmangimi SpA v Toepfer (The Eurometal)* [1981] 1 Lloyd's Rep 337; *Compagnie Commericale Sucres et Denrées v C Czarnikow Ltd (The Naxos)* [1990] 1 WLR 1337 (HL); *Phibro Energy AG v Nissho Iwai Corp (The Honam Jade)* [1991] 1 Lloyd's Rep 38 (CA); JW Carter, 'Two Cases on Time Stipulations in Commercial Contracts' (1992) 5 JCL 60.

[156] An example of this tendency can be seen in the line of nineteenth-century cases relating to the time of sailing in a charterparty: see *Glaholm v Hays* (1841) 2 M & G 257, 133 ER 743; *Ollive v Booker* (1847) 1 Ex 416, 154 ER 177; *Oliver v Fielden* (1849) 4 Ex 135, 154 ER 1155; *Behn v Burness* (1863) 3 B & S 751, 122 ER 281; *Smith v Dart & Son* (1884) 14 QBD 105; *Bentsen v Taylor, Sons & Co* [1893] 2 QB 274 (CA); *Engman v Palgrave* (1898) 4 Com Cas 75.

originally construed as a condition by implication of fact, it is now a condition by implication of law. The designation of terms as conditions on this basis without any reference to the particular contract in which they appear can be criticized on the ground that it enables the innocent party to terminate performance in cases where the breach has caused minimal or no loss, and where he or she is merely looking for an excuse to escape from an unprofitable bargain.[157] However, in cases of this sort these considerations are outweighed by the need for certainty;[158] in the commercial context parties need to know where they stand, and the classification of terms as conditions on this basis enables this end to be achieved.

D. Time Stipulations

5.38   Before leaving the topic of conditions, it is worth spending some time dealing with the special case of time stipulations. One reason for this is that a good many of the cases we have been considering involve such stipulations. The other is the divergent approaches of the common law and equity to time stipulations. As the ensuing discussion will show, attempts have been made to draw these together into a single body of doctrine, but these have not met with unqualified success.

(1) Time stipulations at common law and in equity

5.39   A good place to start is with Maitland's famous *Lectures on Equity*, where the learned author summarized the different approaches of the common law and equity to time stipulations in the following words:[159]

> As a general rule a man can not sue upon a contract at law if he himself has broken that contract, though of course, as you know, there are many exceptions to this statement. Now in contracts for the sale of land it very frequently happens that a breach of the terms of the contract has been committed by the person who wishes to enforce it. Such a contract will be full of stipulations that certain acts are to be done within certain times... Well you know that equity held as a general rule these stipulations as to time were not of the essence of the contract—that for example a purchaser might sue for specific performance although he had not in all respects kept the days assigned to him by the contract of sale for his various acts. This was the general rule—these stipulations as to time were not essential unless the parties declared them to be so.

---

[157] Law Commission, *Sale and Supply of Goods* (Law Com No 160) (Cmnd 137, 1987); *Reardon Smith Line Ltd v Hansen-Tangen (The Diana Prosperity)* [1976] 2 Lloyd's Rep 621 (HL) 626 (Lord Wilberforce). For this reason Brownsword considers whether the law should adopt the approach that termination is available only if the innocent party has good reason to do so rather than rely on damages alone, though he admits that this would cut across the grain of English contract law in a number of respects: R Brownsword, 'Retrieving Reasons, Retrieving Rationality? A New Look at the Right to Withdraw for Breach of Contract' (1992) 5 JCL 83.

[158] *Bunge Corp (New York) v Tradax Export SA* [1981] 1 WLR 711 (HL) 714 (Lord Wilberforce), 720 (Lord Lowry), and 725 (Lord Roskill).

[159] FW Maitland, *Lectures on Equity* (2nd revd edn by John Brunyate, CUP, 1947) p 307.

Hence the saying that time was generally of the essence at common law but not in equity.[160] But to what extent was that the case in the past, and to what extent is it the case today?

(2) The common law position

Maitland's assertion that as a general rule a man cannot sue on a contract at law **5.40** if he himself has broken that contract would seem to imply that all terms of the contract were effectively regarded by the common law as conditions, or were at least presumed to be conditions unless a contrary intention was shown. However, this was far from being the case; failure of performance by the party in default would excuse the innocent party from having to perform a dependent covenant, but not one that was independent or concurrent.[161] Indeed, far from there being a presumption of dependency, it seems that covenants were originally treated as independent unless a contrary intention was expressed.[162] Nor was there any general rule that time was of the essence at common law; while this may have been so in some cases (for instance the date of shipment in a contract for the sale of goods,[163] or the time of sailing in a charterparty)[164] it was not in others (for instance the time of payment,[165] or the time of completion in a building contract).[166] Indeed, time was not always of the essence at common law even in the conveyancing context.[167] However, that there was some difference of approach cannot be denied. If there had not been, the courts of equity would not have been in the practice of granting injunctions to prevent the innocent party taking proceedings at law on the footing that the contract had been terminated, or of granting specific performance in cases where such a decision had already been made.[168]

(3) The position in equity

Whatever the position of the common law may have been, there is no doubt that **5.41** the courts of equity were willing to take a more relaxed approach to the breach of

---

[160] *Hanslip v Padwick* (1850) 5 Ex 615, 623, 155 ER 269, 273 (Alderson B); *Parkin v Thorold* (1852) 16 Beav 59, 65, 51 ER 698, 701 (Romilly MR); *MacBryde v Weekes* (1856) 22 Beav 533, 544, 52 ER 1214, 1218 (Romilly MR); *Tilley v Thomas* (1867–68) LR 3 Ch App 61, 69 (Rolt LJ).

[161] *Kingston v Preston* (1773) Lofft 194, cited in *Jones v Barkley* (1781) 2 Dougl 684, 690, 99 ER 434, 437; Stoljar, 'Dependent and independent promises' (n 9).

[162] Stoljar, 'Dependent and independent promises' (n 9); Carter, *Carter's Breach of Contract*, para 1-21 (n 1).

[163] *Alewyn v Pryor* (1826) Ry & M 406, 171 ER 1065; *Plevins v Downing* (1876) 1 CPD 220; *Bowes v Shand* (1877) 2 App Cas 455 (HL); *Reuter, Hufeland & Co v Sala & Co* (1879) 4 CPD 239.

[164] *Glaholm v Hays* (1841) 2 M & G 257, 133 ER 743; *Ollive v Booker* (1847) 1 Ex 416, 154 ER 177; *Oliver v Fielden* (1849) 4 Ex 135, 154 ER 1155; *Behn v Burness* (1863) 3 B & S 751, 122 ER 281; *Smith v Dart & Son* (1884) 14 QBD 105; *Bentsen v Taylor, Sons & Co* [1893] 2 QB 274 (CA); *Engman v Palgrave* (1898) 4 Com Cas 75.

[165] *Martindale v Smith* (1841) 1 QB 389, 113 ER 1181.

[166] *Lamprell v Billericay Union* (1849) 3 Ex 283, 154 ER 850.

[167] See for instance *Lang v Gale* (1813) 1 M & S 111, 105 ER 42.

[168] See para 5.41.

time stipulations, at least in the conveyancing context. This equitable jurisdiction was exercised in two ways. The first was by granting a decree of specific performance to a party who was ready to proceed to completion even though he or she may have failed to meet the set completion date.[169] The other was by granting what was known as a 'common injunction' to prevent the other party bringing an action at law on the basis that the contract had been lawfully terminated.[170] In relation to time stipulations, as in relation to mortgages and penalties, equity looked to the substance rather than the form, and whatever the common law might say would not allow a party to withdraw from the contract simply for failure to meet the date set for completion.[171] Rather, a court would relieve against such failure provided that the other party was adequately compensated and that the damage caused by the delay was not great nor the substance of the covenant destroyed by it.[172]

5.42 However, this did not mean that equity was prepared to ignore time stipulations altogether, or that a decree of specific performance would be granted as a matter of course. The legal construction of the contract was the same in equity as it was at law,[173] which meant that time could be of the essence in equity no less than at law; in particular, this could be done by 'direct stipulation' (where the parties had expressly indicated an intention that this should be the case)[174] or by 'necessary implication' (where the surrounding circumstances showed that timely performance was essential).[175] In such cases equity would refuse to intervene, and the parties would be duly left to their position at common law.

(4) The Judicature Acts

5.43 A major sea change in the relationship between law and equity came with the passing of the Judicature Acts 1873 and 1875, the main purpose of which was to

---

[169] *Seton v Slade* (1784) 7 Ves J 265, 32 ER 108; *Milward v Earl Thanet* (1801) 5 Ves J 721n, 31 ER 823n; *Marquis of Hertford v Boore* (1801) 5 Ves 719, 31 ER 823; *Wynn v Morgan* (1802) 7 Ves J 202, 34 ER 979; *Hearne v Tenant* (1807) 13 Ves J 287 (High Ct of Chancery), 33 ER 301.

[170] Such as an action for the return of the deposit (*Levy v Lindo* (1817) 3 Mer 84, 36 ER 32), or for ejection (*Hearne v Tenant* (n 169)).

[171] *Parkin v Thorold* (1852) 16 Beav 59, 66–7, 51 ER 698, 702 (Romilly MR); *Roberts v Berry* (1853) De G, M & G 284, 291–2, 43 ER 112, 115 (Turner LJ); *Tilley v Thomas* (1867) LR 3 Ch App 61, 67 (Cairns LJ).

[172] J Fonblanque, *Treatise on Equity* (1793) p 387.

[173] *Parkin v Thorold* (1852) 16 Beav 59, 66–7, 51 ER 698, 702 (Romilly MR); *Tilley v Thomas* (1867) LR 3 Ch App 61, 67 (Cairns LJ).

[174] *Parkin v Thorold* (1852) 16 Beav 59, 65, 51 ER 698, 700 (Romilly MR); *Reynolds v Nelson* (1821) 6 Madd 18, 56 ER 995; *Hipwell v Knight* (1835) 1 Y & C Ex 400, 160 ER 163; *Hudson v Temple* (1860) 30 LJ Ch 251.

[175] *Parkin v Thorold* (1852) 16 Beav 59, 65, 51 ER 698, 700 (Romilly MR). This might be the case where the property sold was of a wasting nature, or subject to fluctuation in value: see *Newman v Rogers* (1793) 4 Bro CC 391, 29 ER 950 (reversion); *Withy v Cottle* (1823) Turn & R 78, 37 ER 1024 (annuity); *Doloret v Rothschild* (1824) 1 Sim & S 590, 57 ER 233 (government stock); *Coslake v Till* (1826) 1 Russ 376, 38 ER 146 (public house); *Carter v Dean and Chapter of Ely* (1835) 7 Sim 211, 58 ER 817 (concurrent lease); *Southcomb v Bishop of Exeter* (1847) 16 LJ Ch 378 (lease for lives); *Hudson v Temple* (1860) 30 LJ Ch 251 (lease).

amalgamate the superior courts into a single Supreme Court of Judicature which would administer both common law and equitable doctrine. As far as time stipulations were concerned, the key provision was section 25(7) of the Act of 1873, which read as follows:

> Stipulations in contracts, as to time or otherwise, which would not before the passing of this Act have been deemed to be or have become of the essence of such contracts in a Court of Equity, shall receive in all courts the same construction and effect as they would have heretofore received in equity.

On the face of it this seemed to prescribe for the courts a much more relaxed **5.44** approach to time stipulations, but in the end it made very little difference. As far as the 'construction' of such stipulations was concerned, equity had always followed the law in any event,[176] and when it came to the question of their 'effect' it was eventually affirmed by the House of Lords in *Stickney v Keeble*[177] that the key issue was the same as it had always been, namely whether the court would be ready to grant a decree of specific performance. In this case it was held that following protracted delays in completion by a vendor of land the purchaser was entitled to a declaration that the contract was at an end and to the recovery of his deposit with costs. At the time of the action, the vendor had put it out of his power to perform the contract by selling the land to a third party, and this was held to be fatal to his case, despite his argument that section 25(7) of the Judicature Act made the availability of specific performance irrelevant.[178] In the words of Lord Parker:[179]

> My Lords, I cannot give to the section in question the interpretation for which the respondents contend. It means, in my opinion, that where equity would prior to the Act have, for the purposes of decreeing its own remedies, disregarded a stipulation as to time and restrained an action at law based on the breach thereof, the Courts constituted by the Act are for the purpose of giving common law relief to disregard it in like manner. In considering whether it would give relief by restraining proceedings at law the Court of Chancery took cognizance of everything which had happened up to the date of the decree, and in applying s. 25, sub-s. 7, of the Act, everything up to the date of judgment ought, in my opinion, to be similarly taken into account. The section cannot in my opinion mean that the rules as to time laid down by Courts of Equity in certain cases, for certain purposes, and under certain circumstances only, shall be applied generally and without inquiry whether the particular case, purpose, or circumstances are such that equity would have applied the rules. If since the Judicature Acts the Court is asked to disregard a stipulation as to time in an action for common law relief, and it be established that equity would not under the then existing circumstances have prior to the Act granted specific performance or restrained the action, the section can, in my opinion, have no application, otherwise the stipulation in question would not, as

---

[176] *Parkin v Thorold* (1852) 16 Beav 59, 66, 51 ER 698, 702 (Romilly MR); *Tilley v Thomas* (1867) LR 3 Ch App 61, 67 (Cairns LJ).
[177] [1915] AC 386 (HL).
[178] *Stickney v Keeble*, 394 (n 177).
[179] *Stickney v Keeble*, 417 (n 177).

provided in the section, receive the same effect as it would prior to the Act have received in equity.

Lord Parker had already observed that, prior to the Judicature Acts, the vendor could only have obtained relief by filing a bill for specific performance and a common injunction to restrain the action. The injunction would only have been an adjunct to the main purpose of the action, namely the claim for specific performance. Since specific performance would not have been available to the vendor in the present case, he could not have the injunction either, and since prior to 1873 he would have been unable to restrain the purchaser's claim for the return of his deposit, that claim could not now be denied.[180]

5.45 The effect of all this was more or less to turn the clock back to where it was prior to the Judicature Acts. Though it was no longer necessary to go through the old procedure of filing a bill for specific performance and claiming for a common injunction, it still had to be asked what the result would have been if that procedure had been followed. This completely scotched any idea of the equitable rules having superseded those of the common law as to time stipulations; indeed, it ensured that those rules continued to be a specialized branch of the law mainly of interest to property lawyers.

(5) A unified approach?

5.46 Despite this setback, it could never be realistic to keep the equitable rules as to time stipulations indefinitely, as it were, in a sealed box, all the less so now all courts had to administer both common law and equitable rules. As well as that, the parallels between the two were plain for all to see; thus, for instance, equity no less than the common law allowed time to be made of the essence either by express stipulation or by implication, and the refusal by equity in such cases to grant specific performance was equivalent in effect to saying that the contract was terminated. A further attempt to consolidate the two sets of doctrines was made by the House of Lords in *United Scientific Holdings Ltd v Burnley Borough Council*, decided in 1977.[181] The issue in the case was whether time was of the essence for the exercise of a rent review clause in a commercial lease, and it was argued by the tenants on the basis of *Stickney v Keeble*[182] that equity had no jurisdiction in a case of this sort,[183] and that therefore the principles of the common law applied, whereby time was to be regarded as being of the essence in a unilateral option.[184]

---

[180] *Stickney v Keeble*, 416 (n 177).
[181] [1978] AC 904 (HL).
[182] See n 177.
[183] This was first because of the principle that equity would not perfect an imperfect, inchoate right (*Milroy v Lord* (1862) 4 De G M & G 264, 274, 45 ER 1185, 1189 (Turner LJ)), and secondly because equity had no appropriate remedy available in a case of this sort ([1978] AC 904 (HL) 915–17).
[184] *Hare v Nicoll* [1966] 2 QB 130 (CA); *United Dominions Trust (Commercial) Ltd v Eagle Aircraft Services Ltd* [1968] 1 WLR 74 (CA); see para 5.32.

The House of Lords held that the provisions in question were not options in the **5.47** true sense and that time was therefore not of the essence, but of more interest are the general observations made by members of the House on the scope of the equitable jurisdiction as to time. Thus care was taken to limit the observations of Lord Parker in *Stickney v Keeble* to the facts of the case, Lord Diplock saying that they were not to be taken as determining the question as to when time stipulations were to be regarded as of the essence of the contract. He then went on to suggest that following the Judicature Acts the two systems of substantive and adjectival law formerly administered by the common law courts and the Courts of Chancery had been effectively 'fused', and that whilst it might have been true for a while to say that the two streams of jurisdiction ran side by side and did not mingle their waters, this had long since ceased to be the case. In the same vein, Lord Simon suggested that the time had come to restate the equitable principles relating to time stipulations in the language of the common law. In the words of Lord Simon:

> Discussion of stipulations as to time has generally turned on the historic distinction between time being or not being of the 'essence' of a contract... But the fused law has continued to evolve since 1875; and it has developed a more sophisticated approach to contractual terms... The law may well come to inquire whether a contractual stipulation as to time is (a) so fundamental to the efficacy of the contract that any breach discharges the other party from his contractual obligations ('essence'), or (b) such that a serious breach discharges the other party, a less serious breach giving a right to damages (if any)... or (c) such that no breach does more than give a right to damages (if any)... ('non-essential'). If this sort of analysis falls to be made, I see no reason why any type of contract should, because of its nature, be excluded.

What Lord Simon was essentially trying to do here was to restate the equitable rules as to time in the common law language of 'condition', 'warranty', and 'innominate term'. To what extent, then does it still make sense to talk about an equitable jurisdiction in this context?

(6) The modern law

Whatever one's views may be on the extent of the so-called 'fusion' between law **5.48** and equity,[185] there is no doubt that Lord Simon's restatement holds true for the vast majority of cases.[186] The construction of contracts is and always has been the

---

[185] JM Martin, *Hanbury and Maudsley's Modern Equity* (19th edn, Sweet & Maxwell, 2012) paras 1-020–1-023; RP Meagher, JD Heydon, and MJ Leeming, *Meagher, Gummow and Lehane's Equity: Doctrines and Remedies* (4th edn, Butterworths LexisNexis, 2002) paras 2.100–2.110 (the 'fusion fallacy'); A Burrows, 'We do this at Common Law but that in Equity' (2002) 22 OJLS 1.

[186] Thus it has been said that the main difference between the historic approach of equity and the current approach is largely one of perspective, the former concentrating on the right of the party in default to enforce the contract and the latter on the right of the innocent party to terminate: Carter, *Carter's Breach of Contract*, para 5-48 (n 1).

same at law and in equity;[187] to say that time has been made expressly of the essence is more or less the same as saying that timely performance is a condition of the contract;[188] for it to be made so by implication involves consideration of the same factors as apply in relation to any other kind of term.[189] However, there are still some situations where the law is somewhat more complicated, and Lord Simon's formulation therefore needs to be treated with care.

(a) Time of the essence in the commercial context

5.49 There is nothing in *United Scientific Holdings Ltd v Burnley Borough Council*[190] to prevent the court treating time as of the essence in the commercial context. In *Bunge Corporation (New York) v Tradax Export SA*[191] the question arose before the House of Lords as to the status of a term in an fob contract requiring the buyers to give at least 15 days' notice of readiness to load. The buyers argued on the basis of *United Scientific Holdings Ltd v Burnley Borough Council* that time was no longer presumed to be of the essence in cases of this sort,[192] but the House of Lords were having none of it. Whilst time might not always be of the essence in the commercial context, there were clearly cases where the need for certainty and the interdependence of other obligations on the prompt performance of the term in question required a term to be construed in such a way.[193] In particular, there was no presumption against time being of the essence where the courts could infer from the nature of the contract or the surrounding circumstances that the parties regarded time stipulations as of the essence of their bargains, most notably in mercantile contracts.[194] Whilst it was not necessarily helpful in determining whether a particular term was to be construed as a condition by attaching a particular label to the contract, the need for certainty in mercantile contracts was often of great importance and sometimes might well be a determining factor in deciding the true construction of a particular term in such a contract.[195] That was certainly the case before *United Scientific Holdings Ltd v Burnley Borough Council*, and it remains the case at the present day.[196]

(b) Time of the essence and express rights of termination

5.50 While it seems clear that timely performance will be made a condition by use of the actual formula 'time is [or shall be] of the essence',[197] giving the innocent party

---

[187] See para 5.42.
[188] See para 5.19.
[189] See paras 5.22–5.34.
[190] [1978] AC 904 (HL).
[191] [1981] 1 WLR 711 (HL).
[192] *Bunge Corp v Tradax Export*, 727–8 (n 191).
[193] *Bunge Corp v Tradax Export*, 729 (Lord Roskill) (n 191).
[194] *Bunge Corp v Tradax Export*, 728 (Lord Roskill) (n 191).
[195] *Bunge Corp v Tradax Export*, 729 (Lord Roskill) (n 191).
[196] See further para 5.33.
[197] *Lombard North Central plc v Butterworth* [1987] 1 QB 527 (CA).

the right to terminate in the event of late performance by the party in default will not necessarily have this effect. As we have seen, the granting of a contractual right of termination for breach of a particular term does not necessary make that term a condition in the full sense,[198] and this applies to time stipulations no less than to any other kind of stipulation.[199]

(c) Time of the essence and specific performance

The key to the old equitable jurisdiction to time was, as already indicated, the **5.51** granting of specific performance to a party in default despite the fact that he or she had failed to perform on time.[200] Where such a decree is granted we can still say that time is not of the essence, for the fact that the innocent party is still under a duty to perform his or her primary obligations necessarily excludes termination for breach of condition.[201] However, the converse is not so; the fact that time is not of the essence does not necessarily mean that specific performance will be available, for it may be withheld on other grounds.[202] To put it another way, the availability of specific performance in cases of this sort is a *sufficient* indication that time is not of the essence, but not a *necessary* one.

(d) Time of the essence and relief against forfeiture

Another relevant factor in the present context is the jurisdiction of equity to grant **5.52** relief against forfeiture.[203] As indicated in Chapter 4, the extent to which this can be given to a party in breach of an essential time stipulation is open to doubt,[204] but it is clear that the jurisdiction only applies to contracts involving the transfer of proprietary or possessory rights.[205] The cases also seem to indicate that such rights must be in existence at the time when the relief is sought; the position being that whereas equity may protect a party in breach of an essential time stipulation from being deprived of a possessory or proprietary interest that he or she already has, it will not go so far as to insist on that party being allowed to acquire such an interest that he or she does not yet have.[206] However, where these conditions are met there is nothing to prevent the court from granting relief in appropriate

---

[198] See para 5.17.

[199] *Financings v Baldock* [1963] 2 QB 104 (CA).

[200] See para 5.41.

[201] *Moschi v Lep Air Services* [1973] AC 331 (HL) 350 (Lord Diplock). This was not so prior to the Judicature Acts, when a decree of specific performance might frequently be accompanied by a 'common injunction' to prevent the innocent party bringing proceedings at common law on the footing that the contract had been validly terminated, or even after such proceedings had taken place; see para 5.41.

[202] In particular, damages will normally be an adequate remedy in the commercial context: Peel, *Treitel*, para 21-018 (n 30).

[203] *Shiloh Spinners v Harding* [1973] AC 691 (HL).

[204] See Ch 4, para 4.80–4.81.

[205] *Scandinavian Trading Tanker Co AB v Flota Petrolera Ecuatoriana (The Scaptrade)* [1983] 2 AC 694 (HL).

[206] See Ch 4, para 4.81.

cases,[207] and where it does so the position is not dissimilar to that which prevailed prior to the Judicature Acts, the right of the innocent party to terminate being limited or even excluded in so far as it would be unconscionable for him or her to insist on it. To that extent it may still make sense to say that time is of the essence at common law, but not in equity.

---

[207] See Ch 4, paras 4.77–4.79.

6

FUNDAMENTAL BREACH

6.01 The right of the innocent party to terminate is not limited to cases of breach of condition. Termination is also available in other cases of very serious breach. A number of different labels are used in the cases and commentaries to denote breaches of this character, but they all boil down to the saying that the breach is sufficiently serious to deprive the innocent party of most if not all of the benefit of the contract. In this chapter we shall follow the lead of Cheshire, Fifoot and Furmston by referring to such breaches as 'fundamental'.[1]

6.02 In the pages which follow we shall begin by looking at the general doctrine of fundamental breach in the light of the leading decision of the Court of Appeal in *The Hongkong Fir*,[2] before going on to look at the scope of the principle, the terminology used to describe it, and the way in which it relates to other similar legal doctrines. We shall then consider the factors used by the courts in deciding whether a breach is sufficiently serious to justify termination under this principle.

---

[1] MP Furmston, CHS Fifoot, and AWB Simpson, *Cheshire, Fifoot and Furmston's Law of Contract* (16th edn, OUP, 2012) p 678; see also *Suisse Atlantique Société d'Armement Maritime SA v NV Rotterdamsche Kolen Centrale* [1967] 1 AC 361 (HL) 421 (Lord Upjohn); *Great Peace Shipping Ltd v Tsavrilis Salvage International Ltd (The Great Peace)* [2002] EWCA Civ 1407, [2003] QB 679, para 82 (Lord Phillips MR).

[2] *Hongkong Fir Shipping Co Ltd v Kawasaki Kisen Kaisha Ltd (The Hongkong Fir)* [1962] 2 QB 26 (CA).

A. *The Hongkong Fir*

6.03   The question posed to the Court of Appeal in *The Hongkong Fir* was a simple one: whether and to what extent a charterer could terminate on account of delays caused by the unseaworthiness of the chartered vessel. The case involved a twenty-four month time charter of a rather elderly ship, formerly known as the *Antrim*.[3] The ship was put at the disposal of the charterers at the beginning of February 1957, and duly sailed from Liverpool on that very day for a port in Virginia where she was due to pick up a cargo for Osaka. However, the voyage out to Osaka was bedevilled by frequent delays due to the condition of the engines, the ship was off hire for repairs for over a month, and when she finally arrived at Osaka at the end of May it was found that further major repairs were needed, and that she would not be ready until September at the earliest. In the meantime freight rates had dropped considerably, and the charterers therefore decided to throw up the charter and sue for damages. In their turn the owners counterclaimed for wrongful repudiation. It was found by Salmon J at first instance that though the engines were in reasonably good condition at the commencement of the charter, due to their age they required the attention of a competent and adequate engine room staff, and that this the owners had failed to provide.[4] There had therefore been a clear breach of their obligation under the charterparty to provide a seaworthy ship.[5] But to what extent did this give the charterers the right to terminate?

6.04   The first argument put forward by the charterers was that the obligation to supply a seaworthy ship was a condition, and that they therefore had the right to terminate for any breach of it. But this was rejected as contrary to long-standing authority[6] both by Salmon J and by the Court of Appeal. Though seaworthiness was an important obligation, it could be broken in a multitude of ways, ranging from a hole in the bottom of the ship to a failure to provide the proper medical kit,[7] and this made it very unlikely that the parties could have intended that any breach whatsoever should give rise to a right to terminate.[8] In the words of Sellers LJ:[9]

> It would be unthinkable that all the relatively trivial matters which have been held to be unseaworthiness could be regarded as conditions of the contract or conditions

---

[3] The facts are taken from *The Hongkong Fir*, 28–31 (n 2).

[4] *The Hongkong Fir*, 34–5 (n 2).

[5] *The Hongkong Fir*, 34 (n 2). Failure to provide an adequate crew can make a ship unseaworthy, the test being whether a reasonably prudent owner, knowing the relevant facts, would have allowed the vessel to put to sea with that crew: *Clifford v Hunter* (1827) 3 C & P 16, 172 ER 303; *Rio Tinto Co Ltd v Seed Shipping Co* (1926) 24 Ll L R 316 (KBD).

[6] *Havelock v Geddes* (1809) 10 East 555, 103 ER 886; *Tarrabochia v Hickie* (1856) 1 H & N 183, 156 ER 1168; *Stanton v Richardson* (1873–74) LR 9 CP 390 (Exchequer Chamber); *J & E Kish v Charles Taylor & Sons & Co* [1912] AC 604 (HL).

[7] *Hongkong Fir Shipping Co Ltd v Kawasaki Kisen Kaisha Ltd (The Hongkong Fir)* [1962] 2 QB 26, 62 (Upjohn LJ).

[8] See Ch 5, para 5.30.

[9] *The Hongkong Fir*, 56 (n 7).

precedent to a charterer's liability and justify in themselves a cancellation or refusal to perform on the part of the charterer.

However, this was not the end of the matter. Though the charterer could not ter- **6.05** minate on the basis of unseaworthiness per se, this did not mean that delays caused by unseaworthiness could never gave rise to a right of termination. On the contrary, the law clearly allowed for termination in such cases provided that the delay was sufficiently serious. The question for the court was therefore how serious the delay had to be. On the basis of past authority[10] it was held by Salmon J at first instance that the test was akin to that for frustration; namely whether the delay was or appeared likely at the date of the repudiation to be so great as to frustrate the commercial object of the charter.[11] It was argued by the charterers on appeal that this test was too restrictive, and that the court should rather apply a yardstick of reasonableness,[12] but it was held by the Court of Appeal that Salmon J had applied the correct test, and that the yardstick was one of frustration. In the words of Sellers LJ:[13]

> If what is done or not done in breach of the contractual obligation does not make the performance a totally different performance of the contract from that intended by the parties, it is not so fundamental as to undermine the whole contract. Many existing conditions of unseaworthiness can be remedied by attention or repairs, many are intended to be rectified as the voyage proceeds, so that the vessel becomes seaworthy; and, as the judgment points out, the breach of a shipowner's obligation to deliver a seaworthy vessel has not been held by itself to entitle a charterer to escape from the charterparty. The charterer may rightly terminate the engagement if the delay in remedying any breach is so long in fact, or likely to be so long in reasonable anticipation, that the commercial purpose of the contract would be frustrated.

On the facts, it was found that this test had not been satisfied in the present case; whilst the delays had undoubtedly caused inconvenience to the charterers, the charter had still over seventeen months to run at the relevant time and the defects in the ship and crew had in the event been fully cured.[14] This fell well short of a situation where it could be said that the charterers had substantially been deprived of the entire benefit of the contract.

So far the analysis of the law was largely of relevance to the law of charterparties, but **6.06** Diplock LJ sought to locate it within a broader context. In the words of Diplock LJ:[15]

> Every synallagmatic contract contains in it the seeds of the problem: in what event will a party be relieved of his undertaking to do that which he has agreed to do but has not

---

[10] *Clipsham v Vertue* (1843) 5 QB 625, 114 ER 1429; *Tarrabochia v Hickie* (1856) 1 H & N 183, 156 ER 1168; *Stanton v Richardson* (1873–74) LR 9 CP 390 (Exchequer Chamber); *Universal Cargo Carriers Corp v Citati* [1957] 2 QB 401 (Devlin J).
[11] [1962] 2 QB 26, 39.
[12] *The Hongkong Fir*, 41–3 (n 7).
[13] *The Hongkong Fir*, 57 (n 7).
[14] *The Hongkong Fir*, 40 (Salmon J) (n 7).
[15] *The Hongkong Fir*, 65–6 (n 7).

yet done? The contract may itself expressly define some of these events, as in the cancellation clause in a charterparty; but, human prescience being limited, it seldom does so exhaustively and often fails to do so at all. In some classes of contracts such as sale of goods, marine insurance, contracts of affreightment evidenced by bills of lading and those between parties to bills of exchange, Parliament has defined by statute some of the events not provided for expressly in individual contracts of that class; but where an event occurs the occurrence of which neither the parties nor Parliament have expressly stated will discharge one of the parties from further performance of his undertakings, it is for the court to determine whether the event has this effect or not. The test whether an event has this effect or not has been stated in a number of metaphors all of which I think amount to the same thing: does the occurrence of the event deprive the party who has further undertakings still to perform of substantially the whole benefit which it was the intention of the parties as expressed in the contract that he should obtain as the consideration for performing those undertakings?

6.07 What was crucial in this context was the event itself rather than the factors which gave rise to the event. This being so:[16]

> Once it is appreciated that it is the event and not the fact that the event is a result of a breach of contract which relieves the party not in default of further performance of his obligations, two consequences follow. (1) The test whether the event relied upon has this consequence is the same whether the event is the result of the other party's breach of contract or not... (2) The question whether an event which is the result of the other party's breach of contract has this consequence cannot be answered by treating all contractual undertakings as falling into one of two separate categories: 'conditions' the breach of which gives rise to an event which relieves the party not in default of further performance of his obligations, and 'warranties' the breach of which does not give rise to such an event.

From this we can see that the principle set out by Diplock LJ is not confined to cases of termination for breach, but also encompasses parts of what would now be classified as the doctrine of discharge by frustration. This means that where a breach of contract is involved, termination on this ground, unlike breach of condition, does not depend on the classification of the term broken, but rather on the consequences of the 'event' brought about by the breach in question.

6.08 In a sense *The Hongkong Fir* laid down no new doctrine, but it was a seminal case none the less.[17] What made it seminal was the way in which it elevated what might have been an arcane point of maritime law of interest only to specialists in the field

---

[16] *The Hongkong Fir*, 69 (n 7).

[17] *Bunge Corp (New York) v Tradax Export SA* [1981] 1 WLR 711, 714 (Lord Wilberforce) and 725 (Lord Roskill); B Dickson, 'The Contribution of Lord Diplock to the General Law of Contract' (1989) 9 OJLS 441, 447; D Nolan, 'Hongkong Fir Shipping Co v Kawasaki Kisen Kaisha Ltd, The Hongkong Fir (1961)' in C Mitchell and P Mitchell (eds), *Landmark Cases in the Law of Contract* (Hart Publishing, 2008) p 269. For the application of the case in other jurisdictions: see *Ankar Pty Ltd v National Westminster Finance (Australia) Ltd* (1987) 61 ALJR 245; *Koompahtoo Local Aboriginal Land Council v Sanpine Pty Ltd* [2007] HCA 61, (2007) 233 CLR 115, (2008) 241 ALR 88; *RDC Concrete (Pte) Ltd v Sato Kogyo (S) Pte Ltd* [2007] SGCA 39, [2007] 4 SLR 413; JW

into a key principle regarding termination. The result of that case was to affirm that there were not one but two bases on which termination could be allowed;[18] one being because of a breach of condition, and the other because the breach had the effect (in the words of Sellers LJ) of frustrating the commercial purpose of the contract, or (in the words of Diplock LJ) of depriving the innocent party of substantially the whole of the anticipated benefit of it. It is this second basis for termination—fundamental breach—with which this chapter is concerned.

B. The Scope of the Principle

In this section we shall consider the scope of the fundamental breach principle **6.09** in two contexts, the first being its relationship to the classification of contractual terms, and the second its application to past and future events.

(1) Fundamental breach and the classification of contract terms

Prior to *The Hongkong Fir* a twofold classification of contract terms was adopted **6.10** based on the Sale of Goods Act 1893; a term was either 'a condition, the breach of which may give rise to a right to treat the contract as repudiated', or 'a warranty, the breach of which may give rise to a claim for damages but not to a right to . . . treat the contract as repudiated'.[19] However Diplock LJ found this classification inadequate, and said that not all terms could be classified in this way. In the words of Diplock LJ:[20]

> No doubt there are many simple contractual undertakings, sometimes express but more often because of their very simplicity ('It goes without saying') to be implied, of which it can be predicated that every breach of such an undertaking must give rise to an event which will deprive the party not in default of substantially the whole benefit which it was intended that he should obtain from the contract; and such a stipulation, unless the parties have agreed that breach of it shall not entitle the non-defaulting party to treat the contract as repudiated, is a 'condition.' So too there may be other simple contractual undertakings of which it can be predicated that no breach can give rise to an event which will deprive the party not in default

---

Carter and JC Phillips 'Construction of Contracts of Guarantee and the Hongkong Fir Case' (1988–89) 1 JCL 70; JW Carter, 'Intermediate Terms Arrive in Australia and Singapore' (2008) 24 JCL 226; PG Turner, 'The *Hongkong Fir* Docks in Australia' [2008] LMCLQ 432.

[18] For a while it was thought by some that the test propounded in *The Hongkong Fir* had effectively rendered the traditional condition/warranty classification redundant; see JW Carter and C Hodgekiss, 'Conditions and Warranties: Forebears and Descendants' (1977) 8 Sydney L Rev 31. However, this was firmly rejected by the House of Lords in *Bunge Corp (New York) v Tradax Export SA* [1981] 1 WLR 711. In effect, it is not a case of either/or but of both/and; see Lord Devlin, 'The Treatment of Breach of Contract' [1966] CLJ 192.

[19] Sale of Goods Act 1893, s 11(2)(b).

[20] [1962] 2 QB 26, 69–70.

of substantially the whole benefit which it was intended that he should obtain from the contract; and such a stipulation, unless the parties have agreed that breach of it shall entitle the non-defaulting party to treat the contract as repudiated, is a 'warranty.' There are, however, many contractual undertakings of a more complex character which cannot be categorised as being 'conditions' or 'warranties'... Of such undertakings all that can be predicated is that some breaches will and others will not give rise to an event which will deprive the party not in default of substantially the whole benefit which it was intended that he should obtain from the contract; and the legal consequences of a breach of such an undertaking, unless provided for expressly in the contract, depend upon the nature of the event to which the breach gives rise and do not follow automatically from a prior classification of the undertaking as a 'condition' or a 'warranty.'

This suggested a threefold classification of terms: (1) 'conditions' (breach of which would *always* give rise to a right to terminate); (2) 'warranties' (breach of which would *never* give rise to a right to terminate); and (3) other terms (breach of which would *sometimes* give rise to a right to terminate). Though Diplock LJ gave no label to terms in this third category, at least in any of his judgments,[21] it has since become customary to refer to them as 'innominate'[22] or 'intermediate'[23] terms. However, as we shall now see, the picture is not quite so straightforward as this threefold classification might suggest.

(a) Fundamental breach and conditions

6.11   Where a term is classified as a condition, there is no need to investigate the consequences of the breach, as the innocent party can terminate in any event. However, the concept of fundamental breach is not entirely irrelevant in relation to conditions, as the likely effect of the breach of a given term may impact on the decision of the court as to whether that term should be classified as a condition or not in the first place.[24] Thus in his famous dissenting judgment in *Wallis, Son and Wells v Pratt & Haynes*,[25] Fletcher Moulton LJ described conditions as terms which 'go so directly to the substance of the contract or, in other words, are so essential to its very nature that their non-performance may fairly be considered by the other party as a substantial failure to perform the contract at all'.[26] In the same way Diplock LJ, in *The Hongkong Fir* itself, referred to terms 'of which it can be predicated that

---

[21] But twenty years later in an extra-judicial capacity he adopted the label 'innominate' for terms of this kind: Lord Diplock, 'The Law of Contract in the Eighties' (1981) 15 University of British Columbia Law Review 371, 376–7; Dickson, 'The Contribution of Lord Diplock' (n 17).

[22] Though later adopted by Lord Diplock himself, the term seems to have been coined by the then editor of *Anson's Law of Contract*: see *Wickman Machine Tool Sales Ltd v Schuler AG* [1972] 1 WLR 840 (CA) 860 (Stephenson LJ). Although Stephenson LJ does not specify who this was, it must have been AG Guest, who was editor from 1959 to 1984.

[23] This seems to have originated in *Cehave NV v Bremer Handelsgesellschaft mbH (The Hansa Nord)* [1976] QB 44 (CA) 60 (Denning MR); Dickson, 'The Contribution of Lord Diplock' (n 17).

[24] See Ch 5, para 5.24.

[25] [1910] 2 KB 1003 (CA).

[26] *Wallis, Son and Wells v Pratt & Haynes*, 1012: see Ch 5, para 5.02.

every breach of such an undertaking must give rise to an event which will deprive the party not in default of substantially the whole benefit which it was intended that he should obtain from the contract'.[27] However, whilst it may be true to say that such terms will be classified as conditions, it is quite possible as we have seen to have conditions which do not satisfy this test;[28] indeed, the whole point of construing a term as a condition is to give the innocent party a right of termination which does *not* depend on the consequences of the breach.[29] This means that whilst a breach of condition may be 'fundamental' in the present sense, it need not necessarily be so.[30]

(b) Fundamental breach and warranties

Section 61(1) of the Sale of Goods Act 1979[31] refers to a warranty as 'an agreement with reference to goods which are the subject of a contract of sale, but collateral to the main purpose of such contract, the breach of which gives rise to a claim for damages, but not to a right to reject the goods and treat the contract as repudiated', and in *The Hongkong Fir* itself Diplock LJ refers to terms 'of which it can be predicated that no breach can give rise to an event which will deprive the party not in default of substantially the whole benefit which it was intended that he should obtain from the contract',[32] and goes on to say that such terms will be construed as warranties.[33] The obvious implication of this is that breach of warranty can never give rise to a right of termination, but in fact the courts have been prepared to allow this to be done where the breach in question has had serious consequences. In *Rubicon Computer Systems Ltd v United Paints Ltd*[34] the buyers of a computer system withheld part of the purchase price following a dispute with the sellers; the sellers, who still had access to the system, then installed a piece of software which denied the buyers access to their data, so effectively rendering the system useless, and intimated that they would not remove the device until the price was paid in full. This was held by the Court of Appeal to be a repudiatory breach of the implied obligation under section 12(2)(b) of the Sale of Goods Act 1979 to give the buyer quiet possession of the goods, and damages were awarded on that basis.[35] As we shall see, a 'repudiatory' breach can be used to mean a fundamental breach,[36] that

6.12

---

[27] [1962] 2 QB 26, 69.

[28] See Ch 5, para 5.06; JW Carter, *Carter's Breach of Contract* (Hart, 2012) para 5-12.

[29] See Ch 5, para 5.06.

[30] *Re Moore & Co Ltd and Landauer & Co* [1921] 2 KB 519 (CA); *Arcos Ltd v EA Ronaasen & Son* [1933] AC 470 (HL); *Union Eagle Ltd v Golden Achievement Ltd* [1997] AC 514 (JCPC–Hong Kong).

[31] This reproduces in all relevant respects the definitions given in the Sale of Goods Act 1893, ss 11(2)(b) and 62(1): see Ch 2, para 2.11.

[32] [1962] 2 QB 26, 70.

[33] *The Hongkong Fir*, 70.

[34] (2000) 2 TCLR 453 (CA); cf *Healing (Sales) Property Ltd v Inglis Electrix Property Ltd* (1968) 121 CLR 584.

[35] *Rubicon Computer Systems v United Paints*, 457–8 (Mantell LJ).

[36] See n 59.

is to say one which gives rise to a right to terminate under the *Hongkong Fir* doctrine,[37] and given that the implied term in question is specifically classified in the Act as a warranty,[38] the notion of a repudiatory breach of such a term seems at first sight to be an oxymoron. However, the court could hardly have come to any other decision in the circumstances; it would have been monstrous if the sellers, who had quite deliberately rendered the goods totally useless,[39] could have been allowed to shelter behind the argument that this was only a breach of warranty and that therefore the right to terminate was *ipso facto* excluded.[40]

6.13 The application of the *Hongkong Fir* doctrine to breaches of warranty lends support to the view that there are in fact not three but only two classes of contractual term: conditions (breach of which *always* gives the innocent party the right of termination) and warranties (breach of which *sometimes* gives the innocent party the right of termination—that is to say, where the breach is sufficiently serious).[41] However, the orthodox view seems to be that there are three categories of term,[42] and this allows for the possibility that there may be terms the breach of which will *never* in any circumstances give rise to a right of termination.[43] One possibility may

---

[37] Indeed, that case was specifically applied by the Court of Appeal: (2000) 2 TCLR 453, 457–8.

[38] Sale of Goods Act 1979, s 12(5A).

[39] Indeed, this conduct clearly amounted to a tort on the part of the sellers, and it could even have been a criminal offence under the Computer Misuse Act 1990: T Sewart, 'Time to drop the bomb' (2003) 14 Computers and Law 22.

[40] In fact this argument does not even seem to have been raised in the case. Given that the *Hongkong Fir* doctrine had not developed at the time the Sale of Goods Act was first enacted, it is not surprising that the Act proceeds on the assumption that all terms are either conditions or warranties, and perhaps the definition in s 61(1) might best be interpreted as meaning that a warranty is a term 'the breach of which gives rise to a claim for damages, but not *necessarily* to a right to reject the goods and treat the contract as repudiated'.

[41] This was the view of Ormrod LJ in *Cehave NV v Bremer Handelsgesellschaft mbH (The Hansa Nord)* [1976] QB 44, 84, and was adopted by Kirby J in *Koompahtoo Local Aboriginal Land Council v Sanpine Pty Ltd* [2007] HCA 61, (2007) 233 CLR 115, (2008) 241 ALR 88, paras 98–99; see E Peel, *Treitel: The Law of Contract* (13th edn, Sweet & Maxwell, 2011) para 18-048; FMB Reynolds, 'Discharge of Contracts by Breach' (1976) 92 LQR 17; K Dharmananda and A Papamatheos, 'Termination and the Third Term: Discharge and Repudiation' (2008) 124 LQR 373.

[42] This approach was adopted by the majority (Gleeson CJ and Gummow, Heydon, and Crennan JJ) in the *Koompahtoo* case at para 52 (see n 41); see also JW Carter, 'Classification of Contractual Terms: the New Orthodoxy' [1981] CLJ 209, JW Carter, GJ Tolhurst, and E Peden, 'Developing the Intermediate Term Concept' (2006) 22 JCL 268, 271–2; Peel, *Treitel*, para 18-048 (n 41); N Andrews, M Clarke, A Tettenborn, and G Virgo, *Contractual Duties: Performance, Breach, Termination and Remedies* (Sweet & Maxwell, 2011) ch 12; Carter, *Carter's Breach of Contract*, ch 6 (n 28); J Beatson, AS Burrows, and J Cartwright, *Anson's Law of Contract* (29th edn, OUP, 2010) pp 145–6. In *RDC Concrete (Pte) Ltd v Sato Kogyo (S) Pte Ltd* [2007] SGCA 39, [2007] 4 SLR 413, para 109 the Singapore Court of Appeal opted for an 'integrated' approach; Y Goh, 'Towards a Consistent Approach in Breach and Termination of Contract at Common Law' (2008) 24 JCL 251. See generally JW Carter, 'Intermediate Terms' (n 17), and cf Furmston, Fifoot, and Simpson, *Cheshire, Fifoot and Furmston's Law of Contract*, pp 201–5 (n 1).

[43] Carter, *Carter's Breach of Contract*, para 6-18 (n 28), citing *Friends Provident Life & Pensions Ltd v Sirius International Insurance* [2005] EWCA Civ 601, [2005] 2 Lloyd's Rep 517. In *Wuhan Ocean Ecomomic & Technical Co-operation Co Ltd v Schiffahrts-Gesellschaft 'Hansa Murcia' mbH & Co KG* [2012] EWHC 3104 (Comm), [2013] 1 Lloyd's Rep 273, para 35 Cooke J refused to construe

be the sort of term envisaged by Diplock LJ in *The Hongkong Fir*; that is to say a term so trivial that it can be predicated that no breach of it could ever be serious enough to trigger a right to termination.[44] Another may be where the parties have expressly provided that a particular term should be construed in this way;[45] after all, it is perfectly possible in principle for the right of termination to be excluded by contrary agreement,[46] and where this is done the term in question is effectively relegated to the status of a warranty as envisaged by the traditional threefold classification.

(c) Fundamental breach and intermediate terms

In the light of the previous discussion, it goes without saying that termination **6.14** for fundamental breach is available for breach of an intermediate or innominate term; indeed, this is the paradigm case to which the *Hongkong Fir* doctrine applies. However, though true, this proposition is somewhat misleading in so far as it suggests that the availability of termination on this ground depends on the prior classification of the term broken. Whilst there may be some terms, as we have seen in the previous paragraph, to which the doctrine will not apply, that doctrine is ultimately based not on the parties' intentions[47] but on the principle that a party should not be expected to perform the contract in a case where he or she has been substantially deprived—whether by breach or otherwise—of the expected benefit of the contract. In the end, as Diplock LJ says, 'it is the event and not the fact that the event is a result of a breach of contract which relieves the party not in default of further performance of his obligations'.[48]

(2) Past and future events

When deciding whether a fundamental breach has occurred it is necessary to look **6.15** not only at what has happened in the past as a result of the breach but at what is likely to happen in the future. Thus in *The Hongkong Fir* itself the court had to take into account not only the delay that had already accrued at the time the charterers purported to terminate, but also at how much delay was likely to occur during the remainder of the charter. In the words of Sellers LJ: 'the charterer may rightly terminate the engagement if the delay in remedying any breach is so long in fact, *or likely to be so long in reasonable anticipation*, that the commercial purpose of the

---

a term as a warranty on the basis that a breach might in certain circumstances have serious consequences, adding that such terms were likely to be rare.

[44] See para 6.10.

[45] Carter, *Carter's Breach of Contract*, para 6-17 (n 28). Needless to say, merely labelling a term a 'warranty' will not necessarily have this effect, any more than labelling it as a 'condition' will have the opposite effect; the word 'warranty', no less than the word 'condition', has a wide range of meanings in the law of contract (Carter, para 4-16).

[46] See Ch 4, para 4.40.

[47] *Hongkong Fir Shipping Co Ltd v Kawasaki Kisen Kaisha Ltd (The Hongkong Fir)* [1962] 2 QB 26 (CA) 70–1 (Diplock LJ).

[48] *The Hongkong Fir*, 69 (n 47).

contract would be frustrated'.[49] Thus in a sale of goods by instalments it has been held that if the breach is of such a kind as reasonably to lead to the inference that similar breaches will occur in the future, the contract can be terminated,[50] and wilful disobedience on the part of an employee may justify dismissal in so far as it indicates a refusal to be bound by the contract.[51] The rationale for all this is the need for certainty; as was said in another context, commercial men must be entitled to act on reasonable commercial probabilities at the time when they are called upon to make up their minds.[52]

C. Terminology

6.16 According to the late Lord Upjohn there is no magic in the words 'fundamental breach'; the expression is[53] 'no more than a convenient shorthand expression for saying that a particular breach or breaches of contract by one party is or are such as to go to the root of the contract which entitles the other party to treat such breach or breaches as a repudiation of the whole contract'. The question whether a breach is sufficiently serious to have this effect is often framed in the following terms, as set out by Diplock LJ in *The Hongkong Fir*:[54]

> Does the occurrence of the event deprive the party who has further undertakings to perform of substantially the whole benefit which it was the intention of the parties as expressed in the contract that he should obtain as the consideration for performing those undertakings?

Such breaches are said to 'affect the very substance of the contract',[55] or go to the 'foundation of the adventure',[56] or to 'the root of the contract'.[57] Other terms

---

[49] *The Hongkong Fir*, 57 (emphasis added) (n 47).

[50] *Millar's Karri and Jarrah Co (1902) v Weddell Turner & Co* (1908) 14 Com Cas 25 (DC) 29 (Bigham J); *Maple Flock Co Ltd v Universal Furniture Products (Wembley) Ltd* [1934] 1 KB 148 (CA) 157 (Lord Hewart CJ).

[51] *Gorse v Durham County Council* [1971] 1 WLR 775 (QBD), 781 (Cusack J).

[52] *Embiricos v Sydney Reid & Co* [1914] 3 KB 45, 59 (Scrutton J). This was a case of frustration, but the same principle applies to cases of fundamental breach, at least where the breach is actual rather than anticipatory: see Ch 7, para 7.22.

[53] *Suisse Atlantique Société d'Armement Maritime SA v NV Rotterdamsche Kolen Centrale* [1967] 1 AC 361 (HL) 421.

[54] [1962] 2 QB 26, 66; *Ampurius Nu Homes Holdings Ltd v Telford Homes (Creekside) Ltd* [2012] EWHC 1820, para 104 (Roth J).

[55] *Ritchie v Atkinson* (1808) 10 East 295, 306, 103 ER 787, 791 (Littledale, *arguendo*); *Eaton v Lyon* (1817) 1 Ves J Supp 416, 417, 34 ER 853; *Thompson v Corroon* (1993) 66 P & Cr 445 (JCPC–West Indies) 459; AS Burrows et al (eds), *Chitty on Contracts* (31st edn, Sweet & Maxwell, 2012) para 24-039.

[56] *Bentsen v Taylor, Sons & Co (No 2)* [1893] 2 QB 274, 281 (Bowen LJ).

[57] *Fillieul v Armstrong* (1837) 7 A & E 557, 563, 112 ER 580, 582 (Cresswell and WH Watson, *arguendo*); *Clipsham v Vertue* (1843) 5 QB 265, 271, 114 ER 1249, 1251 (WH Watson, *arguendo*); *Graves v Legg* (1854) 9 Ex 709, 712, 156 ER 304, 305 (Blackburn, *arguendo*); *Roberts v Brett* (1859) 6 CB (NS) 611, 635, 141 ER 595, 604 (Watson B); *Bradford v Williams* (1871–72) LR 7 Ex 259,

commonly used are 'frustrating' breaches,[58] 'repudiatory' breaches,[59] and 'fundamental' breaches.[60] Though the formulation in terms of a breach 'going to the root of the contract' has the weight of tradition behind it, it is somewhat cumbersome to

---

262 (Piggott B); *Mersey Steel and Iron Co Ltd v Naylor, Benzon & Co* (1884) 9 App Cas 434 (HL) 443 (Lord Blackburn); *Joseph Thorley Ltd v Orchis SS Co Ltd* [1907] 1 KB 660 (CA) 667 (Collins MR); *Morris v Baron* [1918] AC 1 (HL) 9 (Lord Finlay LC); *Dies and anor v British and International Mining and Finance Co Ltd* [1939] 1 KB 724 (KBD) 732 (Stable J); *Cooden Engineering Co Ltd v Stanford* [1953] 1 QB 86 (CA) 96 (Somervell MR); *Financings Ltd v Baldock* [1963] 2 QB 104 (CA) 113, 118, 120, and 121 (Lord Denning MR); *Maredelanto Compania Naviera SA v Bergbau-Handel GmbH (The Mihalis Angelos)* [1971] 1 QB 164 (CA) 205 (Lord Denning MR); *Woodar Investment Development Ltd v Wimpey Construction UK Ltd* [1980] 1 WLR 277 (HL) 286 (Lord Wilberforce); *FC Shepherd & Co Ltd v Jerrom* [1987] QB 301 (CA) 323 (Mustill LJ); *Gunatunga v DeAlwis* (1996) 72 P & CR 161 (CA) 171 (Sir Christopher Slade); *McCabe v London Borough of Greenwich* [2005] EWCA Civ 1364, para 9 (Maurice Kay LJ).

58 *Suisse Atlantique Société d'Armement Maritime SA v NV Rotterdamsche Kolen Centrale* [1967] 1 AC 361 (HL) 436 (Lord Wilberforce); *Trade and Transport Inc v Iino Kaiun Kaisha (The Angelia)* [1973] 1 WLR 210 (QBD) 221 (Kerr J).

59 *Suisse Atlantique Société d'Armement Maritime SA v NV Rotterdamsche Kolen Centrale* (n 58) 409 (Lord Hodson) and 434 (Lord Wilberforce); *Johnson v Agnew* [1980] AC 367, 393 (Lord Wilberforce); *Antaios Compania Naviera SA v Salen Rederierna AB (The Antaios)* [1985] AC 191 (HL) 200, 203, and 205 (Lord Diplock), and 209 (Lord Roskill); *Lister and ors v Forth Dry Dock & Engineering Co Ltd* [1990] 1 AC 546 (HL) 568 (Lord Oliver); *Linden Gardens Trust Ltd v Lenesta Sludge Disposal Ltd* [1994] 1 AC 85 (HL) 104 (Lord Browne-Wilkinson); *E Johnson & Co (Barbados) Ltd v NSR Ltd* [1997] AC 400 (JCPC–Barbados) 411 (Lord Jauncey); *Malik v Bank of Credit and Commerce International SA* [1998] AC 20 (HL) 35 (Lord Nicholls); *Stocznia Gdanska SA v Latreefers Inc* [2001] BCC 174 (CA) 191; *Maridive & Oil Services (SAE) v CNA Insurance Co (Europe) Ltd* [2002] CP Rep 45 (CA) para 4 (Mance LJ); *Brotherton and ors v Asegudora Colseguras SA and anor* [2003] 2 CLC 629 (CA) 657 (Mance LJ); *Item Software (UK) Ltd v Fassihi and ors* [2004] EWCA Civ 1244, [2005] ICR 450, para 33 (Arden LJ); *Melia v Magna Kansei Ltd* [2005] EWCA Civ 1547, [2006] ICR 410, para 46 (Smith LJ); *Vertex Data Science Ltd v Powergen Retail Ltd* [2006] EWHC 1340 (Comm) para 6 (Tomlinson J); *Reinwood Ltd v L Brown & Sons Ltd* [2007] EWCA Civ 601, [2007] 1 CLC 959, para 10 (Dyson LJ); *Leofelis SA v Lonsdale Sports Ltd* [2008] EWCA Civ 640, [2008] ETMR 63, para 47 (Lloyd LJ); *Mansel Oil Ltd and anor v Troon Storage Tankers AG (The Ailsa Craig)* [2009] EWCA Civ 425, [2009] 1 CLC 782, para 10 (Longmore LJ); *Geldof Metaalconstructie NV v Simon Carves Ltd* [2010] EWCA Civ 667, [2010] 1 CLC 895, para 28 (Rix LJ); *Willoughby v CF Capital plc* [2011] EWCA Civ 1115, [2012] ICR 1038, para 21 (Rimer LJ); *Geys v Société Générale* [2012] UKSC 63, para 13 (Lord Hope), para 42 (Lady Hale), para 93 (Lord Wilson), para 102 (Lord Carnwath), and para 109 (Lord Sumption).

60 *Johnson v Taylor Bros & Co* [1920] AC 144 (HL) 150 (Lord Birkenhead LC); *Compagnie Primera de Navagaziona Panama v Compania Arrendataria de Monopolio de Petroleos SA* [1940] 1 KB 362 (CA) 375 (Mackinnon LJ); *Commissioners of Crown Lands v Page* [1960] 2 QB 274 (CA) 290 (Devlin J); *Denmark Productions Ltd v Boscobel Productions Ltd* [1969] 1 QB 699 (CA) 721–2 (Salmon LJ); *Moschi v Lep Air Services Ltd* [1973] AC 331 (HL) 344 (Lord Reid) and 353 (Lord Simon); *Miller v Hamworthy Engineering Ltd* [1986] ICR 846 (CA) 854 (Ewbank J); *Behzadi v Shaftesbury Hotels Ltd* [1992] Ch 1 (CA) 32 (Purchas LJ); *Rubicon Computer Systems Ltd v United Paints Ltd* (2000) 2 TCLR 453 (CA) 458 (Mantell LJ); *Chambers v Hartwell Services Ltd* [2001] EWCA Civ 774, para 14 (Clarke LJ); *Great Peace Shipping Ltd v Tsavliris Salvage (International) Ltd (The Great Peace)* [2002] EWCA Civ 1407, [2003] 2 CLC 16, para 82 (Lord Phillips MR); *Grady v Prison Service* [2003] EWCA Civ 527, [2003] ICR 753, para 22 (Sedley LJ); *Cooper and ors v Pure Fishing (UK) Ltd* [2004] EWCA Civ 375, [2004] 2 CLC 412, para 2 (Tuckey LJ); *Ryan v Jarvis* [2005] UKPC 27, para 6 (Lord Hoffmann); *BP plc v Aon Ltd and anor (No 2)* [2006] EWHC 424 (Comm), [2006] 1 CLC 881, para 274 (Colman J); *Basingstoke Press Ltd v Clarke* [2007] ICR 1284 (EAT) para 3 (Judge McMullen QC); *Collidge v Freeport plc* [2008] EWCA Civ 485, [2008] IRLR 697, para 18 (Sedley LJ); *Woodhouse School v Webster* [2009] EWCA Civ 91, [2009] ICR 818, para 15 (Mummery LJ); *Mayhaven Healthcare Ltd v Bothma (T/A Dab Builders)* [2009] EWHC 2634 (TCC), [2010] BLR

use, and the term 'repudiatory', though even more widely used in the cases, carries a suggestion of an element of refusal to be bound by the contract on the part of the party in default, and is therefore best reserved for breaches of that character.[61] For this reason we shall follow Lord Upjohn in using the term 'fundamental breach' to describe breaches that satisfy Lord Diplock's test;[62] after all, this is just another way of saying that the breach goes to the root of the contract without using so many words.

D. Types of Fundamental Breach

6.17 The traditional classification of fundamental breach is as formulated by Anson[63] and set out by Lord Porter in *Heyman v Darwins*:[64]

> The three sets of circumstances giving rise to a discharge of contract are . . . (1) renunciation by a party of his liabilities under it; (2) impossibility created by his own act; and (3) total or partial failure of performance. In the case of the first two, the renunciation may occur or impossibility be created either before or at the time for performance. In the case of the third, it can occur only at the time or during the course of performance.

However, these categories overlap to a large extent,[65] and the labels attached to them can sometimes be rather misleading. In particular: (1) though the term 'renunciation' suggests an express refusal to perform, renunciation can also be implied from conduct;[66] (2) the term 'repudiation' can be used in a wider sense to encompass cases of impossibility as well as renunciation;[67] and (3) most cases of self-induced impossibility are dealt with as cases of implied renunciation rather than under the express heading of impossibility as such.[68] In the present work we shall follow Carter[69] by using the term 'repudiation' to cover any breaches involving a prospective failure of performance, whether or not they also involve an existing or actual breach, and whether they are based on renunciation or on impossibility. Though this may involve a certain degree of repetition, we shall therefore postpone discussion of such cases until Chapter 7, leaving the present chapter to concentrate on

---

154, para 18 (Ramsey J); *Lowe v W Machell Joinery Ltd* [2011] EWCA Civ 794, [2011] BLR 591, para 18 (Lloyd LJ); *Geys v Société Générale* [2012] UKSC 63, para 96 (Lord Wilson).

[61] See Ch 7, para 7.02.

[62] In the past this might have caused confusion with the doctrine whereby a fundamental breach of contract disentitled the party in default from relying on an exemption clause, but this doctrine is now long since discredited, and we need no longer concern ourselves with it: see Ch 4, para 4.45.

[63] See now Beatson, Burrows, and Cartwright, *Anson's Law of Contract*, pp 512–24 (n 42).

[64] [1942] AC 356 (HL) 397.

[65] Thus as we shall see in Ch 7, self-induced impossibility can often be construed as an implied renunciation, and renunciation can take place during the course of performance as well as before performance is due: see Ch 7, para 7.34.

[66] Beatson, Burrows, and Cartwright, *Anson's Law of Contract*, pp 512–13 (n 42); Peel, *Treitel*, para 18-023 (n 41); see Ch 7, para 7.34.

[67] As in Carter, *Carter's Breach of Contract*, paras 9-03–9-04 (n 28).

[68] Carter, *Carter's Breach of Contract*, para 9-04 (n 28).

[69] Carter, *Carter's Breach of Contract*, chs 8 and 9 (n 28).

cases where the focus is on the failure of performance that has actually occurred rather than on what might happen in the future.

E. Concepts Akin to Fundamental Breach

As with breach of condition, there are a number of concepts akin to fundamental **6.18** breach that overlap with it to a greater or lesser extent, but which need to be distinguished from it. In the pages which follow we shall look at four such concepts, namely: (1) breach of condition; (2) the doctrine of frustration; (3) the doctrine of substantial performance; and (4) the doctrine whereby time may be made of the essence by notice.

(1) Breach of condition

If a fundamental breach is one that 'goes to the root of the contract' and 'entitles **6.19** the other party to treat such breach or breaches as a repudiation of the whole contract',[70] how is it to be distinguished from a breach of condition? After all, has this too not been described in terms of 'a substantial failure to perform the contract at all',[71] and as something which gives rise to 'a right to treat the contract as repudiated'?[72] There are two answers to this. The first is that even if breaches of condition are correctly regarded as a species of fundamental breach, not all fundamental breaches are necessarily breaches of condition, the whole point of the doctrine being to allow termination for breaches of terms that are not classified as such.[73] The second is that while many breaches of condition may also be categorized as 'fundamental' on this test, not all do so by any means; indeed, there are instances where termination has been allowed for breaches of condition which have resulted in little or no detriment to the innocent party.[74] This point has been dealt with previously,[75] and there is no need to say more about it in the present context.[76]

---

[70] *Suisse Atlantique Société d'Armement Maritime SA v NV Rotterdamsche Kolen Centrale* [1967] 1 AC 361 (HL) 421 (Lord Upjohn).

[71] By Fletcher Moulton LJ in his celebrated dissenting judgment in *Wallis, Son and Wells v Pratt & Haynes* [1910] 2 KB 1003 (CA) 1012: see Ch 5, para 5.03.

[72] Sale of Goods Act 1893, s 11(2)(a) and (c); Sale of Goods Act 1979, s 11(2) and (4); see Ch 5, para 5.02.

[73] Thus the decision in *The Hongkong Fir* (see paras 6.03–6.08) was that the stipulation as to seaworthiness was not a condition, but that nevertheless the charterer could have terminated if the consequences of the breach had been sufficiently grave.

[74] *Re Moore & Co Ltd and Landauer & Co* [1921] 2 KB 519 (CA); *Arcos Ltd v EA Ronaasen & Son* [1933] AC 470 (HL); *Union Eagle Ltd v Golden Achievement Ltd* [1997] AC 514 (JCPC–Hong Kong); see generally Law Commission Report, *Sale and Supply of Goods* (Law Com No 160) (Cmnd 137, 1987); *Reardon Smith Line Ltd v Hansen-Tangen (The Diana Prosperity)* [1976] 2 Lloyd's Rep 621 (HL) 626 (Lord Wilberforce).

[75] See Ch 5, para 5.06.

[76] Ultimately, though there is an obvious overlap between breach of condition and fundamental breach, the theoretical justification for termination is not the same, the former being predicated

(2) Doctrine of frustration

6.20 One thing made very clear by *The Hongkong Fir* is the close relationship between discharge for fundamental breach and discharge under the doctrine of frustration. Both doctrines share common roots,[77] and the degree of detriment needed to trigger discharge is said to be the same under both doctrines.[78] As well as this, there are many cases which sit on the borderline between the two,[79] and where only a very slight change of facts is needed to take the case across that line.[80] However, there are still several important distinctions between the two doctrines which cannot be ignored.[81] The first is that frustration operates automatically, and does not depend on the choice of the party affected.[82] The second is that frustration discharges both parties from their primary obligations in so far as they remain unperformed, and does not give rise to any secondary obligation to pay damages.[83] The third is that frustration presupposes a lack of fault on the part of either party to the contract.[84]

---

on 'failure of condition' and the latter on 'failure of consideration': FMB Reynolds, 'Discharge of Contract by Breach' (1981) 97 LQR 541.

[77] *Hongkong Fir Shipping Co Ltd v Kawasaki Kisen Kaisha Ltd (The Hongkong Fir)* [1962] 2 QB 26 (CA) 66–9 (Diplock LJ); GH Treitel, *Frustration and Force Majeure* (2nd edn, Sweet & Maxwell, 2004) ch 2.

[78] *Universal Cargo Carriers Corp v Citati* [1957] 2 QB 401, 434 (Devlin J); *The Hongkong Fir* [1962] 2 QB 26 (CA) 69 (Diplock LJ); *Chilean Nitrate Sales Corp v Marine Transportation Co Ltd (The Hermosa)* [1980] 1 Lloyd's Rep 638 (QBD: Commercial Ct), 648 (Mustill J) (affd [1982] 1 Lloyd's Rep 570 (CA)).

[79] See for instance *Poussard v Spiers & Pond* (1876) 1 QBD 410 (DC), where the sickness of the plaintiff was held to justify the defendants in terminating her engagement to sing in an opera; this would now be considered a case of frustration, but the reasoning of the court was on the basis of termination.

[80] As in *Jackson v Union Marine Insurance Co Ltd* (1874–75) LR 10 CP 125 (Exchequer Chamber), where a charterparty was held to be frustrated following delays to the voyage resulting from an excepted peril. Had the delay not been within the scope of the exceptions clause, it would have been a case of termination not frustration.

[81] Treitel, *Frustration and Force Majeure*, para 15-004 (n 77); *Paal Wilson & Co A/S v Partenreederei Hannah Blumenthal (The Hannah Blumenthal)* [1983] 1 AC 854 (CA) 881–2 (Griffiths LJ (dissenting)). The decision of the Court of Appeal was reversed, and the judgment of Griffiths LJ affirmed, by the House of Lords: see especially at 909–10 (Lord Brandon) and 919–20 (Lord Diplock).

[82] Treitel, *Frustration and Force Majeure*, para 15-002 (n 77); *Hirji Mulji v Cheong Yue SS Co* [1926] AC 497 (JCPC–Hong Kong) 505 (Lord Sumner); *Joseph Constantine SS Line Ltd v Imperial Smelting Co* [1942] AC 154 (HL) 170 (Viscount Maugham); *Fibrosa Spolka Akcynja v Fairbairn Lawson Combe Barbour Ltd* [1943] AC 32 (HL) 70 (Lord Wright); *Denny, Mott & Dickson Ltd v James B Fraser & Co Ltd* [1944] AC 265 (HL) (Sc) 274 (Lord Wright); *Islamic Republic of Iran Shipping Lines v Steamship Mutual Underwriting Association (Bermuda) Ltd* [2010] 2 EWHC 2661 (Comm), [2010] 2 CLC 534, para 119 (Beatson J).

[83] Treitel, *Frustration and Force Majeure*, para 15-009 (n 77); *Taylor v Caldwell* (1863) 3 B & S 826, 840, 122 ER 309, 315 (Blackburn J); *Joseph Constantine SS Line Ltd v Imperial Smelting Co* [1942] AC 154 (HL) 187 (Lord Wright); *National Carriers Ltd v Panalpina (Northern) Ltd* [1981] AC 675 (HL) 689 (Lord Hailsham).

[84] Treitel, *Frustration and Force Majeure*, para 14-001 (n 77); *Taylor v Caldwell* (1863) 3 B & S 826, 834, 122 ER 309, 312 (Blackburn J); *Bank Line Ltd v Arthur Capel and Co* [1919] AC 435 (HL) 452 (Lord Sumner); *Denny, Mott & Dickson Ltd v James B Fraser & Co Ltd* [1944] AC 265 (HL) (Sc) 272 (Lord Macmillan); *Davis Contractors Ltd v Fareham UDC* [1956] AC 696 (HL) 729 (Lord Radcliffe); *Paal Wilson & Co A/S v Partenreederei Hannah Blumenthal (The Hannah Blumenthal)* [1983] 1 AC 854 (CA and HL) 881–2 (Griffiths LJ) and 909 (Lord Brandon).

As well as this, frustration encompasses not only cases of failure of consideration (where the catastrophic event has deprived one or both parties of the benefit of the contract) but also cases of impossibility of performance, which has nothing to do with termination for breach.[85] The two doctrines may merge into one another at some points, but ultimately they still need to be kept apart.

(3) Doctrine of substantial performance

The law regarding the so-called doctrine of 'substantial performance'[86] has some **6.21** similarities to that regarding fundamental breach. In *Hoenig v Isaacs*[87] the plaintiff contractor agreed to do some work on the defendant's property for a lump sum of £750, the terms being 'net cash as the work proceeds, and balance on completion'. The defendant refused to pay the final balance on the ground that the plaintiff had not completed the work fully in accordance with the contract. It was held, however, by the Court of Appeal that in a lump sum contract of this sort, precise fulfilment of every term was not necessarily a condition precedent to the recovery of the price, and on this basis the plaintiff was allowed to recover the sum claimed less a deduction for the cost of making good the defects. In *Bolton v Mahadeva*,[88] however, a similar claim by a contractor for the price of a central heating system was rejected on the ground of major defects in the system which meant that the contract had been far from substantially performed. At first sight these cases look very much like cases of termination for breach,[89] but this is not necessarily so; what was in issue here was not the right to terminate but the right to withhold performance,[90] and indeed cases of this sort need not even involve a breach by the party in default at all.[91] The two

---

[85] Treitel, *Frustration and Force Majeure*, chs 1–6 (n 77).

[86] JW Fischer, 'Rights of recovery by a building contractor on contracts partially or substantially performed' (1937) 11 University of Cincinnati Law Review 379; R Childres, 'Conditions in the law of contracts' (1970) 45 NYU L Rev 33; A Beck, 'The doctrine of substantial performance' (1975) 38 MLR 413.

[87] [1952] 2 All ER 176 (CA).

[88] [1972] 1 WLR 1009 (CA).

[89] Indeed, Denning MR in *Hoenig v Isaacs* specifically said that the contractor would have been disentitled to recover only if his 'breach' had gone to the 'root of the contract' [1953] 2 All ER 176, 181. Carter sees this as a mirror of the *Hongkong Fir* doctrine, but says that it remains unclear whether the proper rationale of the claimant's inability to recover in cases of this sort is that the other party has terminated the contract: Carter, *Carter's Breach of Contract*, paras 6-91 and 6-92 (n 28).

[90] H Beale, *Remedies for Breach of Contract* (Sweet & Maxwell, 1980) pp 20–1. Thus for instance the contractor may be entitled to be given the opportunity to remedy the defects in performance: *Tetley v Shand* (1871) 25 LT 658; *Borrowman, Phillips & Co v Free & Hollis* (1878) 4 QBD 500 (CA); *Motor Oil Hellas (Corinth) Refineries SA v Shipping Corp of India (The Kanchenjunga)* [1990] 1 Lloyd's Rep 391 (HL) 399 (Lord Goff); *Hyundai Merchant Marine Co Ltd v Karanda Maritime Inc (The Niizuru)* [1996] 2 Lloyd's Rep 66 (QBD: Commercial Ct); A Apps, 'The right to cure defective performance' [1994] LMCLQ 525.

[91] This will only be the case if the time for performance has passed. However, given the delays in litigation this will almost inevitably be the case if the matter ever comes to court: HG Beale, WD Bishop, and MP Furmston, *Contract: Cases and Materials* (5th edn, OUP, 2007) 551.

doctrines share a common root,[92] and a right to withhold performance may often mature into a right to terminate,[93] but once again it may still sometimes be necessary to distinguish between them.

(4) Notice making time of the essence

6.22 Where a party to a contract seeks to terminate for breach of a time stipulation, the rules are basically the same as for stipulations of other kinds; if timely performance is a condition of the contract, then any delay in performance will give rise to a right of termination,[94] but if not, termination will only be allowed if the delay is such as to amount to a fundamental breach under the principles set out earlier.[95] However, in cases where a time stipulation had been broken, the courts of equity also allowed the innocent party to serve a 'notice making time of the essence' on the party in default, setting a final deadline for performance.[96] If this deadline was not met, then the innocent party could terminate. Historically this procedure was treated as something *sui generis* and of relevance only in the conveyancing context,[97] but in *United Scientific Holdings Ltd v Burnley Borough Council*[98] an attempt was made by the House of Lords to restate it in traditional common law terms by suggesting that a defaulting party who failed to comply with such a notice could be seen as having repudiated the contract. If that is right, failure to comply with a notice making time of the essence can be seen as a species of fundamental breach, the reasoning presumably being that a party in this position indicates that he or she has a cavalier attitude towards the obligations under the contract, and is unlikely to perform them in the future.[99] Since, however, the issue is one of repudiation rather than fundamental breach *simpliciter*, it will be discussed more fully in Chapter 7.[100]

F. When is a Breach Fundamental?

6.23 As we have seen, the traditional test for fundamental breach, as stated by Diplock LJ in *The Hongkong Fir*, is whether its effect is to 'deprive the party who has further

---

[92] Namely, Lord Mansfield's observation in *Boone v Eyre* that a covenant should be construed as a condition precedent only where it 'goes to the whole consideration': (1777) 1 Hy Bl 273n, 126 ER 160; 2 Bl W 1313n, 96 ER 267; Carter, *Carter's Breach of Contract*, para 6-91 (n 28).

[93] This will be the case where the other party can no longer put the defects right, or where the defective performance is so bad as to amount to a repudiation of the entire contract: Beale, *Remedies for Breach of Contract*, p 91 (n 90).

[94] JE Stannard, *Delay in the Performance of Contractual Obligations* (OUP, 2007) ch 11.

[95] Stannard, *Delay in Performance*, ch 12 (n 94).

[96] Stannard, *Delay in Performance*, ch 8 (n 94).

[97] The procedure also applied in cases where time had originally been of the essence but there had been a waiver by the innocent party, as in *Charles Rickards Ltd v Oppenhaim* [1950] 1 KB 616 (CA).

[98] [1978] AC 904 (HL): see Ch 5, para 5.51.

[99] *BNP Paribas v Wockhart EU Operations (Swiss) AG* [2009] EWHC 3116 (Comm), 132 Con LR 177, para 40 (Christopher Clarke J); Andrews et al, *Contractual Duties*, para 11-024 (n 42).

[100] See Ch 7, paras 7.39–7.44.

undertakings to perform of substantially the whole benefit which it was the intention of the parties as expressed in the contract that he should obtain as the consideration for performing those undertakings'.[101] Diplock LJ goes on to say that the test is the same as that for the doctrine of frustration,[102] and if that is the case the availability of termination in cases such as this would seem to be very limited indeed. However, the courts do not seem to apply such a strict test in practice, and it has been suggested that it would be more appropriate to reformulate the test in terms of whether the breach was 'serious as opposed to trivial in its impact',[103] or 'serious and substantial',[104] or 'sufficiently serious so as to permit the innocent party to terminate the contract',[105] or even whether it would be 'unfair' on the innocent party to confine him or her to a remedy in damages.[106] In the end, what is important in this context is not so much the way the test is formulated[107] but the factual matrix of the case itself,[108] and this means that no watertight definition of a fundamental breach is possible. However, there are a number of factors which crop up in the cases, and which at least can be said to provide useful guidance for the courts in approaching questions of this sort.

(1) Performance totally worthless

It goes without saying that where the effect of the breach is to deprive the contractual performance of the party in default of all value to the innocent party, the test for fundamental breach is likely to be satisfied. Thus in *Vigers v Cook*[109] an undertaker who had constructed the coffin so negligently that it leaked and could not be taken into the chuch was held to be unable to recover any of the contract price; it was an essential part of the funeral that the body should be taken into the church so

6.24

---

[101] *Hongkong Fir Shipping Co Ltd v Kawasaki Kisen Kaisha Ltd (The Hongkong Fir)* [1962] 2 QB 26 (CA) 66 (Diplock LJ); see para 6.06; Carter, Tolhurst, and Peden, 'Developing the Intermediate Term Concept' pp 272–3 (n 42). This is sometimes referred to as the 'total wipeout' test: Andrews et al, *Contractual Duties*, para 12-009 (n 42).

[102] *Universal Cargo Carriers Corp v Citati* [1957] 2 QB 401, 434 (Devlin J); *The Hongkong Fir* [1962] 2 QB 26 (CA) 69 (Diplock LJ); *Chilean Nitrate Sales Corp v Marine Transportation Co Ltd (The Hermosa)* [1980] 1 Lloyd's Rep 638 (QBD: Commercial Ct), 648 (Mustill J) (affd [1982] 1 Lloyd's Rep 570 (CA)).

[103] Andrews et al, *Contractual Duties*, para 12-010 (n 42).

[104] This is the approach taken by the High Court of Australia in *Koompahtoo Local Aboriginal Land Council v Sanpine Pty Ltd* [2007] HCA 61, (2007) 233 CLR 115, (2008) 241 ALR 88, paras 54 and 71; Andrews et al, *Contractual Duties*, para 12-010 (n 42).

[105] And this is the approach of the Singapore Court of Appeal: *Sports Connection Pte Ltd v Deuter Sports GmbH* [2009] SGCA 22, [2009] 3 SLR 883, para 64; Andrews et al, *Contractual Duties*, para 12-010 (n 42).

[106] *Decro-Wall International SA v Practitioners in Marketing* [1971] 1 WLR 361 (CA) 380 (Buckley LJ).

[107] Though the question whether a breach is serious enough to justify termination is said to be an issue of fact (Carter, *Carter's Breach of Contract*, para 6-49 (n 28)), it will still be decided by the judge. Were it still necessary to direct a jury on the matter, the correct formulation of the test would of course be crucial.

[108] Carter, *Carter's Breach of Contract*, para 6-49 (n 28).

[109] [1919] 2 KB 475 (CA).

that the service might be read in its presence, and in effect the plaintiff had totally failed to perform the contract.[110] Again, in *Aerial Advertising Co v Batchelor's Peas (Manchester) Ltd*[111] the defendants hired the plaintiffs to advertise their wares by towing a banner across the sky marked 'Eat Batchelor's Peas', but the plaintiffs made the mistake of doing so over the middle of Salford on Armistice Day where there was a large crowd observing the two minutes' silence; the effect of this blunder on the standing of the defendants was held to justify them in terminating the contract forthwith. In the same way, where in *Rubicon Computer Systems Ltd v United Paints Ltd*[112] the sellers of a computer system put a lock in place preventing the buyers from accessing their data, the buyers were held to be entitled to treat the contract as having been repudiated. Similarly, a breach may be treated as fundamental where it completely destroys the subject matter of the contract, as in *Harbutt's Plasticine Ltd v Wayne Tank & Pump Co Ltd*,[113] or where goods delivered under the contract are totally useless to the buyer, as in *W & S Pollock Ltd v Macrae*.[114] In all of these cases the innocent party has in effect received nothing from the contract, and it is therefore not difficult for the court to categorize the breach as fundamental. But to what extent can less serious breaches be categorized in this way?

(2) Degree of failure in performance

6.25 The basic starting point here is the degree of failure in performance by the party in default. The leading authority here is *Maple Flock Co Ltd v Universal Furniture Products (Wembley) Ltd*[115] where the two crucial questions in cases of this sort were said to be first the ratio quantitatively which the breach bears to the contract as a whole, and secondly the degree of probability or improbability that such a breach will be repeated.[116] It is the first of these criteria that is of particular interest in this context. In the *Maple Flock* case itself, the buyers of a consignment of flock deliverable by instalments sought to terminate the whole contract on the ground that one of the deliveries contained an excessive amount of chlorine. However, the Court of Appeal refused to allow termination on this ground, one key consideration being that this was the sixteenth instalment and that there had been no complaint about any of the previous ones. Only one and a half tons out of a total of a hundred tons

---

[110] *Vigers v Cook*, 479 (AT Lawrence LJ) (n 109).

[111] [1938] 2 All ER 788 (KBD, Atkinson J).

[112] (2000) 2 TCLR 453 (CA).

[113] [1970] 1 QB 447 (CA) (innocent party's factory destroyed by fire). The case was later disapproved of by the House of Lords in *Photo Production Ltd v Securicor Transport Ltd* [1980] AC 827 (HL) in relation to the applicability of the limitation clause, but the court's finding that there had been a fundamental breach was obviously correct.

[114] 1922 SC (HL) 192, 200 (Lord Dunedin).

[115] [1934] 1 KB 148 (CA); *Tradax Internacional SA v Goldschmidt SA* [1977] 2 Lloyd's Rep 604 (Slynn J); Carter, *Carter's Breach of Contract*, para 6-60 (n 28).

[116] *Maple Flock Co Ltd v Universal Furniture Products (Wembley) Ltd* [1934] 1 KB 148, 157 (Lord Hewart CJ).

had been found to be defective, and whilst the buyers might have been justified in rejecting the consignment in question,[117] this was very far from amounting to a repudiation of the contract as a whole.[118] In the same way, in *The Hongkong Fir* itself,[119] the delays caused by the unseaworthiness of the ship were held not to be sufficient to justify the charterers in terminating; though the delays had been substantial, the ship had been off hire for a lot of the time, and at the end of the day she was still available for well over half of the chartered period.[120] These cases can be contrasted with *Millar's Karri and Jarrah Co (1902) v Weddell Turner & Co*,[121] where the contract provided for the sale of 1,100 pieces of timber. The first instalment, consisting of 750 pieces, was defective, and it was held that the buyers were entitled not merely to reject that consignment but to terminate the entire contract. What was of significance here was not only the fact that nearly three-quarters of the goods delivered under the contract were not up to scratch, but that the buyers had good reason to suspect that the remaining instalments would be equally unsatisfactory;[122] taken together, these factors entitled the buyers to walk away from the contract.[123]

(3) Adequacy of damages

Termination is a drastic step to take, and will not be allowed where the breach can perfectly well be compensated for in damages. The leading case here is *Decro-Wall International SA v Practitioners in Marketing*,[124] where the buyers under a sole agency agreement contracted to pay for the goods by bills of exchange due 90 days from the submission of the invoice. Due to a shortage of working capital, the buyers were constantly between two and twenty days late in paying for the goods. In the end the sellers purported to terminate the contract, but it was held by the Court of Appeal that this was unjustified, despite the fact that the buyers had only paid on time once and were unlikely to do so in the future. No doubt the delays in payment were a source of irritation to the sellers, but payment had always been forthcoming in the end. Though the sellers might be out of pocket as a result of the delay, this could always be recovered from the buyers in compensation.[125] For this reason, it

6.26

---

[117] Sale of Goods Act 1893, s 14(2); Sale of Goods Act 1979, s 14(2).

[118] [1934] 1 KB 148, 157 (Lord Hewart CJ); Sale of Goods Act 1893, s 31(2); Sale of Goods Act 1979, s 31(2).

[119] *Hongkong Fir Shipping Co Ltd v Kawasaki Kisen Kaisha Ltd (The Hongkong Fir)* [1962] 2 QB 26 (CA) 40 (Salmon J).

[120] *The Hongkong Fir*, 40 (Salmon J at first instance) (n 119); Peel, *Treitel*, para 18-031 (n 41).

[121] (1908) 14 Com Cas 25 (DC); cf *Warinco AG v Samor SpA* [1979] 1 Lloyd's Rep 450 (CA).

[122] See further para 6.31.

[123] (1908) 14 Com Cas 25, 29 (Bigham J).

[124] [1971] 1 WLR 361 (CA); Peel, *Treitel*, para 18-028 (n 41).

[125] *Decro-Wall International v Practitioners in Marketing*, 366 (Salmon LJ) (n 124); cf *Koompahtoo Local Aboriginal Land Council v Sanpine Pty Ltd* [2007] HCA 61, (2007) 233 CLR 115, (2008) 241 ALR 88, para 54. Peel, *Treitel*, para 18-029 (n 41) compares this to the equitable principle allowing a court to order specific performance of contracts for the sale of land with compensation in cases of

is suggested that termination for fundamental breach is less likely to be allowed in cases where the loss to the innocent party is purely financial than in relation to other kinds of loss.[126] Thus in *Vigers v Cook*,[127] where defects in a coffin supplied by the undertaker meant that the body could not be taken into church for the funeral, it was held by the Court of Appeal that the undertaker could recover nothing for his services; this was not a case where the defects in performance were capable of being remedied by a money payment.[128] In the same way, a breach which seriously damages or threatens to damage the commercial reputation of the innocent party may also be sufficient to justify termination,[129] as this sort of loss is very difficult to quantify in money terms.

(4) Motives of innocent party

6.27 Where the party in default has committed a breach of condition, the motives of the innocent party in electing to terminate are irrelevant; indeed, his or her reasons may have nothing whatever to do with the loss caused by the breach and everything to do with the desire to get out of a contract that has become unprofitable.[130] However, given that termination for fundamental breach requires proof of serious loss to the innocent party, the opportunity to make strategic decisions of this sort is considerably less in that context.[131]

6.28 In *The Hansa Nord*[132] the buyers of a consignment of citrus pulp sought to reject the goods on a falling market, ostensibly on the ground that they had not been shipped 'in good condition' as stipulated by the contract. However, they then bought the very same goods at a reduced price and proceeded to use them for the manufacture of cattle feed in accordance with their original intentions. The Court of Appeal rejected the buyers' contention that the breach had gone to the root of the contract.[133] As Lord Denning MR pointed out, it often happened that the market price falls between the making of the contract and the time for delivery, but in such a situation it was not fair that a buyer should be allowed to reject a whole

---

misdescription, but as Carter points out, cases of termination do not involve the exercise of discretion by the court: Carter, *Carter's Breach of Contract*, para 6-83 (n 28).

[126] Carter, *Carter's Breach of Contract*, para 6-62 (n 28).

[127] [1919] 2 KB 475 (CA): see para 6.24.

[128] *Vigers v Cook*, 479 (AT Lawrence J) (n 127).

[129] *Aerial Advertising Co v Batchelor's Peas (Manchester) Ltd* [1938] 2 All ER 788 (KBD, Atkinson J); *Federal Commerce and Navigation Co Ltd v Molena Alpha Inc (The Nanfri)* [1979] AC 757 (HL); Carter, *Carter's Breach of Contract*, para 6-62 (n 28).

[130] *Cunliffe v Harrison* (1851) 6 Ex 901, 155 ER 813; *Arcos Ltd v Ronaasen* [1933] AC 470 (HL); Carter, *Carter's Breach of Contract*, para 5-72 (n 28); Peel, *Treitel*, para 18-045 (n 41); Law Commission, *Sale and Supply of Goods* (Law Com No 196, 1987).

[131] Peel, *Treitel*, para 18-033 (n 41).

[132] *Cehave NV v Bremer Handelsgesellschaft mbH (The Hansa Nord)* [1976] QB 44 (CA); T Weir, 'Contract—the Buyer's Right to Reject Defective Goods' [1976] CLJ 33.

[133] *The Hansa Nord*, 61 (Lord Denning MR), 73 (Roskill LJ), and 84 (Ormrod LJ) (n 132).

consignment of goods just because a small quantity were not up to the contract quality or condition.[134]

A similar result was reached in *Dakin v Oxley*,[135] where a charterer sought to ter- **6.29** minate on the grounds of damage to the cargo caused by the negligence of the shipowner. The market had fallen considerably since the contract was signed, and the cargo was now worth less than the freight payable. It was held that the charterer was not entitled to walk away from the contract; in the words of Willes CJ:[136]

> It would be unjust, and almost absurd that, without regard to the comparative value of the freight and cargo when uninjured, the risk of a mercantile adventure should be thrown upon the ship-owner by the accident of the value of the cargo being a little more than the freight; so that a trifling damage, much less than the freight, would reduce the value to less than the freight; whilst, if the cargo had been much more valuable and the damage greater, or the cargo worth a little less than the freight and the damage the same, so as to bear a greater proportion to the whole value, the freight would have been payable, and the merchant have been put to his cross-action.

Whatever the position may be in relation to breaches of condition, the general **6.30** principle to be applied here is as Roskill LJ said in *The Hansa Nord*, namely that contracts are made to be performed and not to be avoided according to the whims of market fluctuation.[137]

(5) Uncertainty as to future performance

So far our focus has been on the adverse effects of the breach on the innocent party **6.31** that have already occurred at the time of termination. However, what are equally if not more important in most cases of termination for fundamental breach are the projected consequences of the breach in the future. Thus in *The Hongkong Fir* itself, as we have seen, Sellers LJ speaks of termination for delay that is so long in fact, or likely to be so long in reasonable anticipation, that the commercial purpose of the contract would be frustrated,[138] and in *Maple Flock Co Ltd v Universal Furniture Products (Wembley) Ltd* Lord Hewart CJ speaks not only of the ratio quantitatively which the breach bears to the contract as a whole, but also of the degree of probability or improbability that such a breach will be repeated in the future.[139] It is not too difficult for the victim of a breach of contract to assess the losses that have

---

[134] *The Hansa Nord*, 63 (n 132).
[135] (1864) 16 CB(NS) 646, 143 ER 938.
[136] *Dakin v Oxley*, 667–8 and 947 (n 135). Another illustration of the same principle may be *The Hongkong Fir* itself, where the charterer's motive for termination may have been that freight rates had fallen catastrophically since the contract was signed: [1962] 2 QB 26, 39 (Salmon J); Peel, *Treitel*, para 18-033 (n 41).
[137] [1976] QB 44 (CA) 71; Peel, *Treitel*, para 18-033 (n 41).
[138] [1962] 2 QB 26 (CA) 57.
[139] [1934] 1 KB 148 (CA) 157.

already occurred as a result of the breach; what is much more difficult is to assess the losses that may occur in the future as a result of that breach, and those that may occur as a result of future breaches of the same sort. Where the right of the innocent party to terminate depends in whole or in part on the projected consequences of the breach in the future, we have a case of repudiation, and it is to this that we must now turn.

7

REPUDIATION AND
ANTICIPATORY BREACH

We have seen how in *The Hongkong Fir* Sellers LJ spoke in terms of the charterer **7.01**
being entitled to terminate the engagement if the delay in remedying any breach
was so long in fact, or likely to be so long in reasonable anticipation, that the
commercial purpose of the contract would be frustrated.[1] In some cases it will
be possible to say that a breach is serious enough to justify termination on this
ground purely on the basis of its effect in the past, and these have been dealt with
in Chapter 6. In others, however, it will also be necessary to take into account its
likely effects in the future, and where this is so we have a case of repudiation. And
where such a breach occurs before the time of performance has arrived, we have a
case of 'anticipatory' breach.

A. Terminology

The essence of repudiation, according to Carter, is the absence of readiness and **7.02**
willingness by the defaulting party to perform his or her obligations under the

---

[1] *Hongkong Fir Shipping Co Ltd v Kawasaki Kisen Kaisha Ltd (The Hongkong Fir)* [1962] 2 QB
26 (CA) 57.

contract.[2] This is a useful and a helpful definition to bear in mind. The word 'repudiation' is an ambiguous one,[3] and is used in a variety of senses.[4] In particular, it is sometimes used to denote fundamental breach generally, as in the case of the term 'repudiatory breach',[5] and is sometimes even used in connection with breaches of condition.[6] However, whilst the use of the term 'repudiation' in this broad sense is probably too well ingrained among lawyers to be abandoned, it is not a helpful use of the term. There are other equally suitable ways of describing such breaches, and in any event the English word 'repudiation'[7] is not really appropriate to describe a situation where the party in default has committed a breach of contract that is serious enough to justify termination without necessarily indicating any unwillingness or inability to perform his or her contractual obligations as they arise in the future. For this reason we shall in the present work use the word 'repudiation' to describe serious breaches with such a future element. However, this must be read subject to two qualifications.

7.03 The first is that though the word 'repudiation' suggests an unwillingness or refusal to perform—what is sometimes termed 'renunciation'[8]—it can also include the situation in which the defaulting party, though perfectly willing to perform when the time comes, is incapable of doing so.[9] In this situation, where the party in question is said to be 'totally and finally disabled' from performing,[10] the other party may terminate on the grounds of anticipatory breach. This will be discussed later.[11]

7.04 Nor is it clear to what extent a renunciation will amount to a repudiation in the sense of a fundamental breach or one going to the root of the contract. According to Lord Diplock in *The Afovos*[12] a renunciation will only give rise to a right of termination if the threatened non-performance would, in his words, 'have the effect

---

[2] JW Carter, *Carter's Breach of Contract* (Hart, 2012) para 7.03.

[3] *Heyman v Darwins Ltd* [1942] AC 356 (HL) 378 (Lord Wright).

[4] Thus, as Lord Wright points out, it can also be used to mean: (1) a denial that any contract was made in the first place; (2) a claim that the contract was vitiated by duress, mistake, or illegality; and (3) a claim that the contract is no longer binding because of 'the failure of some condition or the infringement of some duty fundamental to the enforcement of the contract': [1942] AC 356, 378. As well as this, the term has been used to denote lawful termination, as in *Behn v Burness* (1863) 3 B & S 751, 755, 122 ER 281, 283 (Williams J) ('...may, if he is so minded, repudiate the contract in toto...').

[5] See Ch 1, para 1.12 and Ch 6, para 6.16 n 59.

[6] As in *Wallis, Son and Wells v Pratt & Haynes* [1910] 2 KB 1003 (CA) 1012 (Fletcher Moulton LJ, dissenting): see Ch 5, para 5.03.

[7] This has been defined in general terms as 'the action of rejecting, disowning, or disavowing something': *Oxford English Dictionary Online* <http://www.oed.com> (accessed 26 February 2013).

[8] See Ch 1, para 1.12; and para 7.31.

[9] See paras 7.35–7.36.

[10] *British & Beningtons Ltd v NW Cachar Tea Co Ltd* [1923] AC 48 (HL) 71 (Lord Sumner); *Universal Cargo Carriers Corp v Citati* [1957] 2 QB 401, 446 (Devlin J); *Trade and Transport Inc v Iino Kaiun Kaisha Ltd (The Angelia)* [1973] 1 WLR 210, 219 (Kerr J).

[11] See paras 7.35–7.36.

[12] *Afovos Shipping Co SA v Pagnan & Flli (The Afovos)* [1983] 1 WLR 195 (HL) 203: Carter, *Carter's Breach of Contract*, para 7-37 (n 2).

of depriving that other party of substantially the whole benefit which it was the intention of the parties that he should obtain from the primary obligations of the parties under the contract then remaining unperformed'; in other words, the non-performance must itself satisfy the criteria of a fundamental breach. However, this is by no means clear from the cases, some of which suggest a less stringent test. Say, for instance, a buyer of goods were to declare his or her intent to pay the price a day late. In the case of actual breach this would not give rise to a right of termination, as the time of payment is a mere warranty,[13] and breach of warranty does not of itself give rise to a right of termination. On the other hand, such a declaration might in certain circumstances entitle the innocent party to terminate on the basis that it called into question the readiness and willingness of the defaulting party to perform other more important terms in the future.[14] This matter is discussed more fully later,[15] but as the law stands the precise relationship between the doctrines of fundamental breach, repudiation, renunciation, and anticipatory breach has still not been entirely worked out.

B. Concepts Akin to Repudiation

As in relation to breach of condition and fundamental breach generally, there are a number of legal concepts closely akin to repudiation but which must nevertheless be distinguished from it.   **7.05**

(1) Breach of condition

Breaches of condition are sometimes discussed in terms of repudiation; thus, for instance, section 11(3) of the Sale of Goods Act 1979 describes a breach of condition as giving rise to the right to 'treat the contract as repudiated', and similar terminology can be found in the cases.[16] However, the analogy is an unhelpful one for a number of reasons; for one thing, the theoretical basis of discharge for breach of condition is very different from that for repudiation,[17] and in any event not all breaches of condition necessarily indicate any lack of readiness and willingness by the party in default to perform in the future, still less to the necessary degree of seriousness.[18] It has been said that the reference to repudiation in this context is no more than contractual shorthand for the right to terminate,[19] and this is in   **7.06**

---

[13] Sale of Goods Act 1979, s 10(1).

[14] Carter, *Carter's Breach of Contract*, para 7-41 (n 2).

[15] See para 7.16.

[16] As in *Wallis, Son and Wells v Pratt & Haynes* [1910] 2 KB 1003 (CA) 1012 (Fletcher Moulton LJ, dissenting).

[17] See Ch 5, para 5.04.

[18] See Ch 5, para 5.06.

[19] M Bridge, 'Discharge for Breach of the Contract of Sale of Goods' (1983) 28 McGill LJ 867, 869–70.

accordance with the proposition that though breach of condition and repudiation both give rise to the right to terminate, they do so on different grounds.

(2) Fundamental breach generally

7.07 As we have seen, Lord Diplock in *The Afovos* confines repudiation to cases where 'the threatened non-performance would have the effect of depriving that other party of substantially the whole benefit which it was the intention of the parties that he should obtain from the primary obligations of the parties under the contract then remaining unperformed',[20] or to put it more briefly, goes to the root of the contract or amounts to a fundamental breach on the basis of the criteria set out in Chapter 6.[21] However, the precise relationship between repudiation and fundamental breach is not as clear as it might be. Clearly not all fundamental breaches involve repudiation in the sense of an absence of readiness and willingness to perform the contract in the future, as the innocent party may be entitled to terminate purely on the basis of the effects of the breach that have already occurred in the past.[22] So not all fundamental breaches involve repudiation, but do all repudiations involve fundamental breach? Certainly Lord Diplock suggests that they do, but this has been disputed. Thus, for instance, repudiation may encompass not only cases of prospective breach of condition[23]—for instance, a declaration that the party in default is going to perform late in cases where time is of the essence— but even a refusal to perform obligations the actual breach of which would not give rise to a right of termination at all.[24] This question is discussed more fully later.[25]

(3) Frustration

7.08 As with its sister doctrine of fundamental breach, the doctrine of repudiation bears close affinities with the doctrine of frustration, with which it shares a common root.[26] In particular frustration, no less than repudiation, looks forward as well as backward, in that an event may frustrate the contract not only on the basis of its effects in the past but also on the basis of its likely effects in the future.[27] However, there are clear differences between the two doctrines, the most obvious being that frustration, unlike repudiation, discharges both parties from their primary obligations and does not give rise to any secondary obligation to pay damages.[28] Another more subtle difference is in relation to the doctrine of anticipatory breach, where

---

[20] See para 7.04.

[21] See Ch 6, paras 6.23–6.31.

[22] See for instance the cases discussed at Ch 6, para 6.24.

[23] See para 7.15; Carter, *Carter's Breach of Contract*, paras 7-37 and 7-38 (n 2).

[24] See para 7.16.

[25] See para 7.16.

[26] See Ch 6, para 6.20.

[27] *Embiricos v Sydney Reid & Co* [1914] 3 KB 45 (CA).

[28] See Ch 1, para 1.03.

the cases establish that in the case of a non-performance that is purely prospective and involves no express or implied renunciation of contractual liability, it is not enough to show that the defaulting party was unlikely to perform in the future, but that he or she was totally and finally disabled from doing so.[29] Given the close affinity between the two doctrines, and given that in certain cases the line between them is a very fine one,[30] these distinctions can give rise to difficulties in the application of the law.[31]

(4) Notice making time of the essence

In cases where time was not originally of the essence, or where an essential time **7.09** stipulation had been waived, the courts of equity allowed the innocent party to serve a notice on the party in default setting a deadline for performance, on the basis that if this deadline was not met the contract would then be terminated. For many years this doctrine was treated as being distinct from the ordinary common law rules of termination, but in *United Scientific Holdings Ltd v Burnley Borough Council*[32] Lord Simon sought to reformulate the doctrine in common law terms by declaring that failure to comply with a notice of this nature could be taken as evidence of repudiation, so that the contract could be terminated on that basis.[33] Though this analysis has more recently been reaffirmed in the Commercial Court,[34] it is not without its difficulties; be that as it may, the question is more fully discussed later.[35]

C. Modes of Repudiation

Repudiation can occur in different ways, and it is sometimes important to know **7.10** the way in which it is alleged to have occurred, as this may make a difference to the rules for determining whether a right to terminate arises. The basic idea behind repudiation is, in the words of Lord Coleridge CJ, an intention to abandon and altogether to refuse performance of the contract,[36] but neither of these factors is

---

[29] *British & Beningtons Ltd v NW Cachar Tea Co Ltd* [1923] AC 48 (HL) 71 (Lord Sumner); *Universal Cargo Carriers Corp v Citati* [1957] 2 QB 401, 446 (Devlin J); *Trade and Transport Inc v Iino Kaiun Kaisha Ltd (The Angelia)* [1973] 1 WLR 210, 219 (Kerr J).

[30] For instance where what would normally be a breach of contract is covered by an exemption clause (as in *Jackson v Union Marine Insurance Co Ltd* (1874–75) LR 10 CP 125 (Exchequer Chamber)), or where a frustrating event is caused partly by a breach of contract and partly by other factors (as in *Chilean Nitrate Sales Corp v Marine Transportation Co Ltd (The Hermosa)* [1980] 1 Lloyd's Rep 638 (QBD: Commercial Ct)).

[31] See further paras 7.35–7.36.

[32] [1978] AC 904 (HL).

[33] *United Scientific Holdings v Burnley BC*, 906 (n 32).

[34] *Dalkia v Utilities Services plc v Celtech International Ltd* [2006] EWHC 63, [2006] 1 Lloyd's Rep 599, para 131.

[35] See paras 7.39–7.44.

[36] *Freeth v Burr* (18740 LR 9 CP 208, 213: Carter, *Carter's Breach of Contract*, para 8-04 (n 2).

essential; thus no subjective intention need be shown,[37] nor need a refusal to perform the contract in its entirety.[38] In fact, there are two variables here, the first relating to the conduct of the defaulting party and the second relating to whether this is or is not accompanied by an actual failure in performance. As far as the first of these is concerned, there are three possibilities, the first being where the defaulting party expressly refuses to perform in so many words (express refusal), the second where such a refusal is inferred from the circumstances (implied refusal), and the third where, without there being any absence of willingness to perform, the party in question has become unable to do so (inability). As far as the second variable is concerned, there may be an actual breach involved, or it may be a case of anticipatory breach. This gives us six possibilities in all:

(1) express refusal accompanied by actual breach;
(2) implied refusal accompanied by actual breach;
(3) inability accompanied by actual breach;
(4) express refusal without actual breach;
(5) implied refusal without actual breach; and
(6) inability without actual breach.

As we shall see, the sixth and last of these is the odd man out, repudiation being harder to establish in this case than in the other five.[39]

D. What Amounts to Repudiation?

7.11 According to the Court of Appeal in *Maple Flock Co Ltd v Universal Furniture Products (Wembley) Ltd*[40] the two key questions in deciding whether repudiation has taken place are: (1) the ratio quantitatively which the breach bears to the contract as a whole, and (2) the degree of probability or improbability that such a breach will be repeated.[41] As well as this, there is another key factor in the equation, namely the attitude of the party in default. These factors will now be considered in more detail.

(1) Degree of prospective failure

7.12 As a general rule a contracting party who indicates that he or she will not perform the contract *at all* will be held to have repudiated it.[42] However, there may be

---

[37] See paras 7.21 and 7.32; Q Liu, 'The Pitfall of Subjective Renunciation' [2010] LMCLQ 359.
[38] See paras 7.12–7.15.
[39] See paras 7.35–7.36.
[40] [1934] 1 KB 148 (CA); *Tradax Internacional SA v Goldschmidt SA* [1977] 2 Lloyd's Rep 604 (Slynn J); Carter, *Carter's Breach of Contract*, para 6-60 (n 2).
[41] [1934] 1 KB 148, 157 (Lord Hewart CJ).
[42] *Hochster v de la Tour* (1853) 2 E & B 678, 118 ER 922; *Frost v Knight* (1871–72) LR 7 Ex 111 (Exchequer Chamber). But in some cases a refusal to perform may not be a repudiation if it derives from a bona fide misinterpretation of the contract: see further paras 7.23–7.26.

repudiation even in the absence of such an indication. In particular, a party may, in the words of Lord Wright, intend to fulfil the contract, but may be determined to do so only in a manner substantially inconsistent with his obligations and not in any other way.[43] One obvious way of doing this is for the defaulting party to indicate that he or she will only perform in part, as where an employer seeks to reduce the wages payable to an employee,[44] or where a buyer of goods seeks to reduce or withhold the price.[45] As a general rule, the principles for determining whether a prospective failure of performance will amount to repudiation are said to be the same as in the case of fundamental breach,[46] but there are three issues which call for further examination in the present context, these being: (1) cases where the defaulting party seeks to attach conditions to his or her agreement to perform; (2) whether a prospective breach of condition amounts to a repudiation; and (3) whether it is easier or harder to establish repudiation than it is to establish fundamental breach generally.

(a) Attaching conditions

In some cases a party may repudiate the contract by saying that he or she will **7.13** only perform if certain conditions are met. Thus, for instance, in *The Apollonius* a charterer was held to have repudiated the contract by refusing to pay hire unless the owners complied with an unwarranted demand to do certain repairs to the ship.[47] A similar result was reached in *The Nanfri*,[48] where the owners under a charterparty involving three ships became involved in a dispute with the charterers over deductions from hire. As a consequence the owners threatened to discontinue normal performance by instructing their masters not to sign 'freight pre-paid' bills of lading, insisting instead that they should all be 'claused' so as to incorporate the terms of the charters. This was held to be a repudiation, since the consequences for the charterers would have been catastrophic, and it was held to be no defence for the owners to say that their threats would not be carried out if the charterers stopped withholding hire.[49] On the other hand, where in *Johnstone v Milling*[50] a lessor indicated that he would not be able to raise the money to rebuild

---

[43] *Ross T Smyth & Co Ltd v TD Bailey Son & Co* [1940] 3 All ER 60 (HL) 72; Carter, *Carter's Breach of Contract*, para 8-08 (n 2).

[44] *Rigby v Ferodo Ltd* [1988] ICR 29 (HL) 33 (Lord Oliver).

[45] *Withers v Reynolds* (1831) 2 B & Ad 882, 109 ER 1370; cf *PD Berlian Laju Tanker TBK v Nuse Shipping Ltd (The Aktor)* [2008] EWHC 1330 (Comm), [2008] 2 Lloyd's Rep 246 (insistence on payment at a place different from that specified in contract).

[46] *Afovos Shipping Co SA v Pagnan & Flli (The Afovos)* [1983] 1 WLR 195 (HL) 903 (Lord Diplock) see para 7.04.

[47] *Mafracht v Parnes Shipping Co SA (The Apollonius)* [1986] 2 Lloyd's Rep 405 (QBD: Commercial Ct) 415 (Bigham J); cf *Kuwait Rocks Co v AMN Bulkcarriers Inc (The Astra)* [2013] EWHC 865 (Comm), [2013] 2 Lloyd's Rep 69.

[48] *Federal Commerce & Navigation Co Ltd v Molena Alpha Inc (The Nanfri)* [1979] AC 757 (HL): see further para 7.25.

[49] [1979] AC 757 (HL) 786–7 (Lord Russell).

[50] (1886) 16 QBD 460 (CA).

the premises as required by the lease, it was held that no repudiation had occurred, since the lessor was clearly willing to perform if he could.[51] The difference between this and the other two cases seems to be the nature of the condition attached to the promisor's performance. In the first two cases the promisor was seeking to impose as a condition of his or her own performance something to be done by the promisee, so effectively putting unlawful pressure on the promisee to agree to an alteration in the terms of the contract.[52] In the last case, however, the condition concerned something to be done by the promisor, and there was no indication that the promisor was not willing to do his or her best to ensure that that condition was fulfilled.[53]

7.14 Another way in which the defaulting party can perform in a manner inconsistent with his or her obligations under the contract is to impose extra burdens on the promisee that are not warranted by that contract. In *Total Oil Great Britain Ltd v Thompson Garages (Biggin Hill) Ltd*[54] a contract for the supply of petrol stipulated that payment was to be made on delivery, but after two of the defendants' cheques had been dishonoured the suppliers indicated that from now on they would only supply petrol upon presentation of a bankers' draft. This was held to be a repudiation of the supply contract;[55] in effect, the suppliers had evinced an intention no longer to be bound by the agreement by demanding cash where the contract provided for credit. Similarly in *Metro Meat Ltd v Fares Rural Co Pty Ltd*[56] a seller of meat who indicated that no more instalments would be provided unless a bonus was paid for prompt delivery was held to have repudiated the contract thereby. A different result was reached in *Vaswani v Italian Motors (Sales and Services) Ltd*,[57] where a contract for the sale of a car provided for the payment of a deposit followed by the balance of the price on delivery. A clause in the contract provided that in certain circumstances the price could be increased. Following the payment of the

---

[51] *Johnstone v Milling*, 468 (Lord Esher MR) (n 50); Carter, *Carter's Breach of Contract*, para 8-14 (n 2).

[52] Hence a threat to break the contract unless the other party agrees to vary its terms may amount to economic duress: *North Ocean Shipping Co Ltd v Hyundai Construction Co Ltd (The Atlantic Baron)* [1979] 2 QB 705 (QBD: Commercial Ct); *Atlas Express Ltd v Kafco (Importers and Distributors) Ltd* [1989] QB 833 (QBD: Commercial Ct).

[53] But this will be no excuse if the promisor is 'wholly and finally disabled' from performing at the relevant time: see para 7.35. For this reason Carter prefers to treat the case as one where the prospective breach was not serious enough: the tenant's inability to rebuild the premises was not sufficient to amount to a repudiation of the lease as a whole (Carter, *Carter's Breach of Contract*, para 8-14 (n 2)).

[54] [1972] 1 QB 318 (CA) 322 (Lord Denning MR); *BV Oliehandel Jongkind v Coastal Intl Ltd* [1983] 2 Lloyd's Rep 463 (QBD: Commercial Ct).

[55] However, it could not be taken as a repudiation of the lease as a whole, since it was held in that case that a lease could not be brought to an end by repudiation and acceptance: [1972] 1 QB 318, 324 (Lord Denning MR). However, this view is now taken as being misconceived: see further Ch 4, para 4.16.

[56] [1985] 2 Lloyd's Rep 13 (JCPC–Australia) 17 (Lord Diplock).

[57] [1996] 1 WLR 270 (JCPC–Hong Kong); E Peel, 'Misinterpretation of Contractual Rights and Repudiation' [1996] LMCLQ 309; see further paras 7.23–7.26.

deposit by the buyer, the sellers sought to demand an increased price under the provisions of this clause, and when this was not forthcoming claimed to be entitled to forfeit the deposit. It was held by the Privy Council that in the circumstances the demand for the increased price, though not in conformity with the relevant clause, did not amount to a repudiation. The demand was made in good faith, the sellers had not made delivery of the car conditional on payment of the increased price,[58] and indeed there was no indication that the buyers would have come up with the balance even if the sellers had asked for the price as originally agreed.[59]

(b) Prospective breach of condition

In all of the cases discussed so far the issue has been couched in terms of fundamen- **7.15**
tal breach, the question being whether the prospective failure of performance 'goes to the root of the contract', or in the words of Diplock LJ deprives the party who has further undertakings to perform of 'substantially the whole benefit which it was the intention of the parties as expressed in the contract that he should obtain as the consideration for performing those undertakings'.[60] What if the defaulting party indicates in advance that he or she will not perform a condition? In many cases, of course, the condition will be construed as such because the term is so important that, in the words of Fletcher Moulton LJ, its non-performance 'may fairly be considered by the other party as a substantial failure to perform the contract at all',[61] and in such cases any refusal to perform will qualify as a repudiation under the ordinary principles set out previously. However, we have already seen that not all conditions can be described in this way,[62] and the question then arises as to whether a prospective refusal or inability to perform such a condition could give rise to the right to terminate. Say, for instance, a contract makes time of the essence, and the defaulting party indicates in advance that he or she will perform a day, or even an hour late.[63] Can the innocent party terminate in the absence of any indication that the delay will cause him or her any real prejudice? There are dicta in the cases which suggest that the innocent party has a general right to terminate for a prospective breach of condition,[64] and this is borne out by the decision of the Commercial Court in *The*

---

[58] Contrast *Owners of The Norway v Ashburner (The Norway)* (1865) 3 Moo PC (NS) 245, 16 ER 92 (indication by the ship's master that unless an excessive sum was paid cargo would not be released).

[59] [1996] 1 WLR 270 (JCPC–Hong Kong), 277 (Lord Woolf).

[60] *Hongkong Fir Shipping Co Ltd v Kawasaki Kisen Kaisha Ltd (The Hongkong Fir)* [1962] 2 QB 26 (CA) 66 (Diplock LJ); see Ch 6, para 6.06.

[61] *Wallis, Son and Wells v Pratt & Haynes* [1910] 2 KB 1003 (CA) 1012; see Ch 5, para 5.03.

[62] See Ch 5, para 5.06; E Peel, *Treitel: The Law of Contract* (13th edn, Sweet & Maxwell, 2011) para 18-042.

[63] cf *Union Eagle Ltd v Golden Achievement Ltd* [1997] AC 514 (JCPC–Hong Kong).

[64] *McDougall v Aeromarine of Emsworth Ltd* [1958] 1 WLR 1126 (QBD) 1133 (Diplock J); *Metro Meat Ltd v Fares Rural Co Pty Ltd* [1985] 2 Lloyd's Rep 13 (JCPC–Australia) (Bigham J); *Federal Commerce & Navigation Co Ltd v Molena Alpha Inc (The Nanfri)* [1979] AC 757 (HL) 778 (Lord Wilberforce) and 783 (Viscount Dilhorne); Carter, *Carter's Breach of Contract*, para 7-38 (n 2).

Aktor.[65] Here it was decided by Christopher Clarke J that the sellers of a ship were entitled to terminate when the buyers insisted that they would pay the balance of the purchase price in Singapore rather than in Greece as stipulated by the contract. What is interesting here is that the term in question was construed as a condition purely on the grounds of commercial certainty,[66] and if this is right,[67] termination in these cases may take place irrespective of any prejudice caused by the prospective breach. This of course is at odds with the general requirement that repudiation should amount to 'an intention to abandon and altogether to refuse performance of the contract'.[68] A contractual right of termination cannot be exercised before it accrues,[69] and it could be argued in this as in other contexts[70] that to allow this to be done in cases of prospective breach of condition places undue weight on the admittedly tricky and fine distinction between conditions and contractual rights of termination.[71]

(c) Repudiation and fundamental breach

7.16 According to Lord Wilberforce, repudiation is 'a drastic conclusion which should only be held to arise in clear cases of a refusal, in a matter going to the root of the contract, to perform contractual obligations',[72] and the orthodox view is that a prospective breach will not amount to repudiation in circumstances where the actual breach of the same sort would not be sufficiently serious to justify termination;[73] in the words of Lord Diplock, the non-performance threatened must itself satisfy the criteria of a fundamental breach.[74] That said, not all of the cases on the topic are easy to reconcile with this test. In *Withers v Reynolds*,[75] a case involving the sale of straw by instalments, the buyer intimated that he would no longer pay

---

[65] *PD Berlian Laju Tanker TBK v Nuse Shipping Ltd (The Aktor)* [2008] EWHC 1330 (Comm), [2008] 2 Lloyd's Rep 246.

[66] *The Aktor*, para 66 (n 65).

[67] It is argued in N Andrews, M Clarke, A Tettenborn, and G Virgo, *Contractual Duties: Performance, Breach, Termination and Remedies* (Sweet & Maxwell, 2011) paras 7-014–7-018, that the decision is consistent with the requirement that the anticipation should be a 'serious default', but it is not entirely clear from the context whether this is thought to include breaches of condition.

[68] *Freeth v Burr* (1874) LR 9 CP 208, 213 (Lord Coleridge CJ); *Afovos Shipping Co SA v Pagnan & Flli (The Afovos)* [1983] 1 WLR 195 (HL) 203 (Lord Diplock); see para 7.04. It is therefore argued by Liu that a threatened or apprehended breach of condition should not be enough: see Q Liu, *Anticipatory Breach* (Hart, 2010) pp 79–85, as cited by Andrews et al, *Contractual Duties*, para 7-019 (n 67).

[69] *Maredelanto Compania Naviera SA v Bergbau-Handel GmbH (The Mihalis Angelos)* [1971] 1 QB 164 (CA); *Afovos Shipping Co SA v Pagnan & Flli (The Afovos)* [1983] 1 WLR 195 (HL); Carter, *Carter's Breach of Contract*, para 10-14 (n 2).

[70] See Ch 10, para 10.17.

[71] See Ch 8, paras 8.02–8.04.

[72] *Woodar Investment Development Ltd v Wimpey Construction (UK) Ltd* [1980] 1 WLR 277 (HL) 283; *Chilean Nitrate Sales Corp v Marine Transportation Co Ltd (The Hermosa)* [1982] 1 Lloyd's Rep 570 (CA) 572 (Donaldson LJ).

[73] Carter, *Carter's Breach of Contract*, para 7-37 (n 2).

[74] *Afovos Shipping Co SA v Pagnan & Flli (The Afovos)* [1983] 1 WLR 195 (HL) 203.

[75] (1831) 2 B & Ad 882, 109 ER 1370.

for each instalment on delivery as agreed, but would henceforth pay one instalment in arrear. This was held to be a clear repudiation, but it is by no means evident that if the buyer had actually done this without indicating in advance that he would do so the breach would necessarily have given rise to a right of termination;[76] as has been said, the breach of an intermediate term cannot be regarded as sufficiently serious merely because of prior breaches.[77] Similarly, in *Rigby v Ferodo Ltd*,[78] where an employer announced a 5 per cent cut in wages, this was said to amount to a repudiation,[79] but it is by no means clear how such a reduction could be said to satisfy the test for fundamental breach put forward by Diplock LJ, which requires proof that the breach would deprive the innocent party of substantially the *whole* benefit of the contract. Perhaps the answer may lie in the notion that an outright refusal to perform one's contractual obligations in the future is, in some sense, more serious than actual failure to do so, in so far as it may demonstrate a cavalier disregard of those obligations.[80] In this connection it is perhaps also significant that whereas an actual breach can be remedied in damages without recourse to termination, an unaccepted repudiation, in the famous words of Asquith LJ, is a thing 'writ in water';[81] so unless the innocent party is allowed to terminate in these circumstances, he or she will have no remedy at all.

(2) Risk of future breaches

The second key factor identified by the Court of Appeal in the *Maple Flock* case **7.17** was the risk of the breach occurring in the future.[82] This is a crucial factor; since English law provides no mechanism allowing a promisee to demand an assurance

---

[76] cf for instance *Decro-Wall Intl SA v Practitioners in Marketing* [1971] 1 WLR 361 (CA). It was suggested by Sellers LJ in *The Hongkong Fir* that if the owners had known the ship was unseaworthy and had refused to put it right, that would have amounted to a repudiation: [1962] 2 QB 26, 56; see also *Bowmakers (Commercial) Ltd v Smith* [1965] 1 WLR 855 (CA) 859; H Beale, *Remedies for Breach of Contract* (Sweet & Maxwell, 1980) p 70.

[77] Carter, *Carter's Breach of Contract*, para 6-82 (n 2).

[78] [1988] ICR 29 (HL); cf *Morris v CH Bailey Ltd* [1969] 2 Lloyd's Rep 215 (CA) 219 (Salmon LJ); *PD Berlian Laju Tanker TBK v Nuse Shipping Ltd (The Aktor)* [2008] EWHC 1330 (Comm), [2008] 2 Lloyd's Rep 246.

[79] *Rigby v Ferodo*, 33 (Lord Oliver) (n 78).

[80] See para 7.21. Thus, according to Carter, a refusal to perform may be established on the basis of a professed or inferred absence of readiness whether or not the actual failure to perform which it implies would confer a right to terminate: Carter, *Carter's Breach of Contract*, para 8-05 (n 2); *Dymocks Franchise Systems (NSW) Pty Ltd v Todd* [2002] UKPC 50, [2004] 1 NZLR 289, and see GH Treitel, *Remedies for Breach of Contract: a Comparative Perspective* (OUP, 1988) p 380. The Court of Appeal has recently drawn attention to these different approaches in *Ampurius Nu Homes Holdings Ltd v Telford Homes (Creekside) Ltd* [2013] EWCA Civ 577, [2013] BLR 400, paras 51–57; but concluded that whatever test was applied in that case the breach was not serious enough to justify termination.

[81] *Howard v Pickford Tool Co* [1951] 1 KB 417 (CA) 421; see para 7.34.

[82] *Maple Flock Co Ltd v Universal Furniture Products (Wembley) Ltd* [1934] 1 KB 148 (CA) 157 (Lord Hewart CJ). In the same way, a breach which is capable of remedy is less likely to be classified as repudiatory than one which is not: *Ampurius Nu Homes Holdings Ltd v Telford Homes (Creekside) Ltd* [2013] EWCA Civ 577, [2013] BLR 400, para 63.

of future performance,[83] termination may be the only way of resolving an uncertainty in this regard.[84] In the *Maple Flock* case itself it was held that no repudiation had occurred, one of the reasons being that the chance of the breach being repeated in the future was 'practically negligible'.[85] This case can be contrasted with *Warinco AG v Samor SpA*,[86] where a contract for the sale of rapeseed oil provided for delivery in two instalments. The buyers refused to accept the first instalment on the ground that it was not of merchantable quality, and when the sellers asked whether the second instalment would be accepted, said that they would do so only if it was in accordance with the contract. It was held by the Court of Appeal that the sellers were entitled to infer that the second instalment would also be rejected and to terminate on that footing. Obviously the question of whether the risk of future non-performance is sufficiently serious to justify termination in any individual case depends very much on the circumstances of that case, but there are three situations which deserve particular comment in this connection, the first of these being the relevance of repeated breaches, the second is the issue of early breaches in instalment contracts, and the third the degree of likelihood that has to be shown in cases of this sort.

(a) More than one breach

7.18 A breach cannot be classified as fundamental merely because similar breaches have occurred in the past,[87] but repeated breaches of the same obligation may entitle the innocent party to conclude that such breaches will continue to occur in the future, and to terminate on that basis. In *Robert A Munro & Co Ltd v Meyer*[88] a contract for the sale of bonemeal provided for delivery in twelve monthly instalments. The first four instalments were all subsequently found to be adulterated, and it was held that the buyer would have been entitled on this basis not only to reject the bad instalments but to terminate the contract as a whole.[89] A similar result was reached by the High Court of Australia in *Associated Newspapers Ltd v Bancks*,[90] where the plaintiffs on several occasions published the defendant's cartoon inside the comic section rather than on the front as stipulated by the contract; such conduct was held to evince a refusal to be bound by the contract. In *Rice (t/a Garden Guardian) v Great Yarmouth Borough Council*,[91] a case involving numerous breaches by the

---

[83] Carter, *Carter's Breach of Contract*, para 7-32 (n 2).

[84] *Bradford v Williams* (1871–72) LR 7 Ex 259; Peel, *Treitel*, para 18-032 (n 62). However, in some circumstances the service of a notice making time of the essence may help in this regard: see paras 7.39–7.44.

[85] [1934] 1 KB 148 (CA) 157 (Lord Hewart CJ).

[86] [1979] 1 Lloyd's Rep 450 (CA).

[87] *Financings Ltd v Baldock* [1963] 2 QB 104 (CA); *Decro-Wall International SA v Practitioners in Marketing* [1971] 1 WLR 361 (CA); Carter, *Carter's Breach of Contract*, para 8-17 (n 2).

[88] [1930] 1 KB 312 (KBD).

[89] *Robert A Munro & Co v Meyer*, 330 (Wright J) (n 88).

[90] (1951) 83 CLR 322; Carter, *Carter's Breach of Contract*, para 8-17 (n 2).

[91] [2003] TCLR 1 (CA); *Alan Auld Associates Ltd v Rick Pollard Associates and anor* [2008] EWCA Civ 655, [2008] BLR 419.

claimant over the first year of a four-year contract to maintain parks and gardens owned by the council, the issue was said to be whether the cumulative effect of the breaches in question was sufficient to justify the defendants bringing the contract to a premature end. In the words of Hale LJ:[92]

> These contracts are…like building contracts in that the accumulation of past breaches is relevant, not only for its own sake, but also for what it shows about the future. In my view, the judge was right to ask himself whether the cumulative breaches were such as to justify an inference that the contractor would continue to deliver a substandard performance.

What is significant here is not so much that the breach has occurred on more than one occasion, but that every repeated breach increases the risk of the innocent party ultimately being deprived of the benefit of the contract as a whole.[93]

(b) Early breach

Another key factor in this context is the time when the breach takes place, the principle being that early breaches are more likely to constitute repudiation than later ones. Most of the cases on this point relate to instalment contracts,[94] the question being whether default on one or more instalments is enough to constitute repudiation of the contract as a whole.[95] Particular issues arise where the default relates to the very first instalment, and some of the older authorities seem to indicate that such a default will always amount to a repudiation as a matter of law.[96] However, in *Mersey Steel and Iron Co Ltd v Naylor, Benzon & Co*[97] the question was said by the House of Lords to be one of degree, and the better view now is that it depends on the circumstances of the individual case.[98] In *Millar's Karri and Jarrah Co (1902) v Weddell Turner & Co*,[99] a case involving a contract for the sale of timber, the first delivery was found to be defective. It was held that the buyers were entitled not merely to reject that consignment but to terminate the entire contract. In the words of Bigham J:[100]

7.19

> If the breach is of such a kind, or takes place in such circumstances as reasonably to lead to the inference that similar breaches will be committed in relation

---

[92] [2003] TCLR 1.

[93] Carter, *Carter's Breach of Contract*, para 8-17 (n 2).

[94] But not all by any means; see for instance *Myton v Schwab-Morris* [1974] 1 WLR 331 (Ch D) (failure by a purchaser of land to pay the initial deposit).

[95] Where the contract is one for the sale of goods, the position is governed by the Sale of Goods Act 1979, s 31(2) but this does no more than codify the common law: Carter, *Carter's Breach of Contract*, para 8-33 (n 2).

[96] *Hoare v Rennie* (1859) 5 H & N 19, 157 ER 1083; *Honck v Muller* (1881) 7 QBD 92.

[97] (1884) 9 App Cas 434.

[98] *Mersey Steel and Iron v Naylor, Benzon*, 438 (Lord Selborne LC) (n 97); Carter, *Carter's Breach of Contract*, para 8-32 (n 2).

[99] (1908) 14 Com Cas 25 (DC).

[100] *Millar's Karri and Jarrah v Weddell Turner*, 29 (n 99).

to subsequent deliveries, the whole contract may then and there be regarded as repudiated and may be rescinded.

Clearly this inference will, other things being equal,[101] be much stronger in relation to early instalments than in relation to subsequent ones.[102] However, a lot will depend on the facts of the given case; in particular, whether the defaulting party is aware of the breach or not, and whether, if so aware, he or she demonstrates a willingness to remedy it in relation to future instalments.

(c) Degree of likelihood

7.20 Does it have to be shown that the future breach is certain to occur, or will some lesser degree of likelihood suffice? The answer differs here depending on the way the repudiation is alleged to have taken place, and in particular whether or not it is accompanied by an actual breach. Where an actual breach has occurred, the rule is stated in terms of degrees of probability or likelihood,[103] the idea being that, as in the case of frustration,[104] the innocent party is entitled to act on the basis of reasonable commercial probabilities. Where there is no actual breach—that is to say in cases of anticipatory breach—the position is more complicated. Where there has been an express or implied refusal to perform or 'renunciation', the rule is the same as for cases of actual breach,[105] but where the alleged repudiation is based on impossibility, it seems that the innocent party cannot proceed on the basis of mere probability or likelihood; rather, he or she must establish that the party in default was 'wholly and finally disabled' from performing.[106] This curious anomaly will be discussed later in the context of a discussion of anticipatory breach.[107]

(3) Attitude of defaulting party

7.21 The third crucial factor to consider is the attitude of the defaulting party to the contract and to its future performance. In cases where there is no express refusal to perform, the question that the court must ask is an objective one, in that what does or does not amount to a sufficient refusal is to be judged in the light of whether a reasonable person in the position of the party claiming to be freed from the

---

[101] Thus in the *Mersey Steel and Iron Co* case itself the inference was rebutted by the bona fides of the defaulting party: see further para 7.23.

[102] See for instance *Cornwall v Henson* [1900] 2 Ch 298 (CA) (protracted failure to pay final instalment was not repudiation).

[103] *Millars Karri and Jarrah Co Ltd v Weddell Turner & Co* (1908) 14 Com Cas 25 (DC) 29 (Bigham J); *Maple Flock Co Ltd v Universal Furniture Products (Wembley) Ltd* [1934] 1 KB 148 (CA) 157 (Lord Hewart CJ); *Hongkong Fir Shipping Co Ltd v Kawasaki Kisen Kaisha Ltd (The Hongkong Fir)* [1962] 2 QB 26, 38 (Salmon J), 57 (Sellers LJ), 64 (Diplock LJ), and 72 (Upjohn LJ).

[104] *Embiricos v Sydney Reid & Co* [1914] 3 KB 45 (CA) 54 (Scrutton J).

[105] *Robert A Munro & Co Ltd v Meyer* [1930] 2 KB 312, 331 (Wright J); *Warinco AG v Samor SpA* [1979] 1 Lloyd's Rep 450 (CA) 451; *Ampurius Nu Homes Holdings Ltd v Telford Homes (Creekside) Ltd* [2013] EWCA Civ 577, [2013] BLR 400, paras 62–63; *Satellite Estate Pty Ltd v Jaquet* (1968) SR (NSW) 126, 150 (Asprey JA); Carter, *Carter's Breach of Contract*, para 8-15 (n 2).

[106] *Universal Cargo Carriers Corp v Citati* [1957] 2 QB 401, 450 (Devlin J).

[107] See paras 7.35–7.36.

contract would regard the refusal as being clear and absolute.[108] There are two key aspects to this, one being whether the breach itself was deliberate or accidental, and the other being whether it was committed in good faith.

(a) Deliberate breaches

7.22 The mere fact that a breach was deliberate will not of itself justify termination;[109] as Lord Wilberforce pointed out when discussing the issue in the *Suisse Atlantique* case,[110] some deliberate breaches may be of a minor character that can appropriately be sanctioned by damages.[111] However, as Lord Wilberforce went on to say, such a breach may give rise to a right for the innocent party to refuse further performance because it indicates the other party's attitude towards future performance.[112] This will be particularly so where the contract is one which involves a relationship of trust and confidence between the parties, such as a contract of agency[113] or of partnership[114] or employment,[115] though the fact that the breach was deliberate may be of relevance in other contexts as well.[116] Even so, a deliberate breach—indeed a deliberate refusal to perform the contract at all—will not necessarily amount to repudiation even in these circumstances. Whether it does so may depend on the reason for the breach, and on the motives of the party in default in committing it.

(b) Good faith of party in default

7.23 Even a deliberate refusal to perform will not necessarily amount to repudiation if it is done in good faith.[117] This was established by the House of Lords in *Mersey Steel*

---

[108] *Chilean Nitrate Sales Corp v Marine Transportation Co Ltd (The Hermosa)* [1982] 1 Lloyd's Rep 570 (CA) 573 (Donaldson LJ); *Seadrill Management Services Ltd v OAO Gazprom (The Ekha)* [2009] EWHC 1530 (Comm), [2010] 1 Lloyd's Rep 543, para 249 (Flaux J).

[109] A Burrows et al (eds), *Chitty on Contracts* (31st edn, Sweet & Maxwell, 2012) para 24-018; Peel, *Treitel*, para 18-034 (n 62); Carter, *Carter's Breach of Contract*, para 8-09 (n 2). It may, however, be relevant to other issues, for instance the grant of relief against forfeiture (*Shiloh Spinners Ltd v Harding* [1973] AC 691 (HL) 724 (Lord Wilberforce)), or the quantum of damages (*Experience Hendrix LLC v PPX Enterprises Inc* [2003] EWCA Civ 323, [2003] EMLR 25, para 58 (Peter Gibson LJ)), or the applicability of an exemption clause (*Internet Broadcasting Corp Ltd v Mar LLC* [2009] EWHC 844 (Ch), [2009] 2 Lloyd's Rep 295 (Gabriel Moss QC)).

[110] *Suisse Atlantique Société d'Armement Maritime SA v NV Rotterdamsche Kolen Centrale* [1967] 1 AC 361.

[111] *Suisse Atlantique v NV Rotterdamsche Kolen Centrale*, 435 (n 110).

[112] *Suisse Atlantique v NV Rotterdamsche Kolen Centrale*, 435 (n 110).

[113] *Gledhill v Bentley Designs (UK) Ltd* [2010] EWHC 1965 (QB), [2011] 1 Lloyd's Rep 270 (HH Judge Simon Brown QC).

[114] *Wilson v Johnstone* (1873) LR 16 Eq 606, 611 (Sir John Wickens V-C).

[115] *Turner v Mason* (1845) 14 M & W 112, 153 ER 411; *Adami v Maison de Luxe Ltd* (1924) 35 CLR 143 (HCA); cf *Evans v SMG TV Ltd* [2003] EWHC 1423 (Ch) (deliberate and flagrant disregard of obligations by radio presenter).

[116] As in *Mafracht v Parnes Shipping Co SA (The Apollonius)* [1986] 2 Lloyd's Rep 405 (Bingham J) (deliberate refusal by charterer to pay hire unless an unjustified demand was met).

[117] The position is different for breach of condition; here good faith on the part of the defaulting party is no defence: *Luna Park (NSW) Ltd v Tramways Advertising Pty Ltd* (1938) 61 CLR 286; Carter, *Carter's Breach of Contract*, para 8-20 (n 2).

and Iron Co Ltd v Naylor, Benzon & Co,[118] where the crucial issue was whether the refusal by the defendants to pay for a quantity of steel delivered by the plaintiffs entitled the latter to terminate performance. The facts were that shortly before payment became due a petition had been brought before the court to wind up the plaintiffs' company, and the defendants were then advised by their solicitors that it would not be safe for payment to be made without the sanction of the court. The defendants therefore suggested to the plaintiffs that this should be obtained, but indicated that they would not pay the money over until this was done. The plaintiffs then sought to cancel the contract, but it was held by the House of Lords that in the special circumstances of the case no repudiation had taken place. In the words of the Lord Chancellor:

> I cannot ascribe to their conduct, under these circumstances, the character of a renunciation of the contract, a repudiation of the contract, a refusal to fulfil the contract. It is just the reverse; the purchasers were desirous of fulfilling the contract; they were advised that there was a difficulty in the way, and they expressed anxiety that that difficulty should be as soon as possible removed, by means which were suggested to them, and which they pointed out to the solicitors of the company.[119]

A similar result was reached by the Court of Appeal in *Laws v London Chronicle (Indicator Newspapers) Ltd,*[120] where the plaintiff was dismissed from her employment for refusing to obey an order by the managing director. A heated argument had taken place at a meeting between the director and the plaintiff's immediate superior, and the latter had left the room, instructing his assistants to accompany him. The plaintiff then did so, despite an order by the director that she should stay, and was then summarily dismissed. In a claim by the plaintiff for wrongful dismissal it was argued by the defendants that a deliberate refusal by an employee to obey orders was tantamount to a repudiation,[121] but it was held that in the special circumstances of this case no repudiation had taken place. The plaintiff had been put in an impossible position, and it could not be said that her conduct amounted to such a deliberate disregard of the conditions of service as justified the employer in summarily dismissing her.[122]

7.24 Neither of these cases involved a complete refusal to perform the contract in its entirety, but even where this is so the good faith of the party in default may sometimes negative repudiation, as is shown by the decision of the House of Lords in *Woodar Investment Development Ltd v Wimpey Construction (UK) Ltd.*[123] In this

---

[118] (1884) 9 App Cas 434 (HL); *Vaswani v Italian Motors (Sales and Services) Ltd* [1996] 1 WLR 270 (JCPC–Hong Kong); see para 7.16.

[119] *Mersey Steel and Iron v Naylor, Benzon*, 441 (Lord Selborne LC) (n 118).

[120] [1959] 1 WLR 698 (CA).

[121] On the basis of *Turner v Mason* (1845) 14 M & W 112, 153 ER 411; see para 7.22.

[122] [1959] 1 WLR 698, 701 (Lord Evershed MR).

[123] [1980] 1 WLR 277; P Butt, Note (1981) 55 ALJ 231; AG Guest, Note (1980) 96 LQR 321; A Nicol and N Rawlings, 'Changing Attitudes to Anticipatory Breach and Third Party Beneficiaries'

case a contract for the sale of land provided a right of rescission if prior to the date of completion compulsory purchase procedures should have been initiated. In fact, as both parties were aware, such procedures had already been initiated at the time the contract was signed. Land values having fallen, the purchasers subsequently sought to get out of the contract, and told the vendors that they intended to invoke the clause in question. The vendors said that if that were done they would take the matter to court. The purchasers then having purported to rescind the contract, the vendors brought an action for a declaration that they were not entitled to do so. However, when the purchasers sought to defend the action, the vendors then brought further proceedings claiming that the contract had been repudiated. It was subsequently admitted by the purchasers that no right of rescission had arisen. As a general rule such conduct would amount to an unlawful repudiation,[124] but it was held by the House of Lords, by a majority of three to two,[125] that in the circumstances of the case no repudiation had taken place; though the vendors had sought to exercise a right of rescission to which they were not entitled, their conduct taken as a whole did not demonstrate the necessary refusal to be bound by the contract.[126] In the words of Lord Wilberforce:[127]

> ... [It] would be a regrettable development of the law of contract to hold that a party who bona fide relies on an express stipulation in a contract in order to rescind or terminate a contract should, by that fact alone, be treated as having repudiated his contractual obligations if he turns out to be mistaken as to his rights. Repudiation is a drastic conclusion which should only be held to arise in clear cases of a refusal, in a matter going to the root of the contract, to perform contractual obligations. To uphold the respondents' contentions in this case would represent an undesirable extension of the doctrine.

7.25 The proposition that a party can purport to rescind a contract without indicating a refusal to be bound by it is at first sight odd to say the least,[128] but *Woodar Investment Development Ltd v Wimpey Construction (UK) Ltd* has been explained on the ground that the vendors did not have to act at once; given that the date for completion was still some time in the future, and legal proceedings were still pending, they could have waited for the conclusion of those proceedings before deciding what to do.[129] In most cases, however, this will not be a realistic option.

(1980) 43 MLR 696; RC Nicholls, 'Conduct after Breach: the Position of the Party in Breach' (1990–91) 3 JCL 132, 163.

[124] See para 7.12.

[125] Lords Wilberforce, Keith, and Scarman, with Lords Salmon and Russell dissenting.

[126] *Freeth v Burr* (1874) LR 9 CP 208, 213 (Lord Coleridge CJ).

[127] *Freeth v Burr*, 283 (n 126).

[128] As Lord Salmon said in his dissent, if such conduct does not amount to a repudiation, it is difficult to see what will: [1980] 1 WLR 277, 286–7.

[129] MP Furmston, CHS Fifoot, and AWB Simpson, *Cheshire, Fifoot and Furmston's Law of Contract* (16th edn, OUP, 2012) p 676. Carter, however, argues that since it was the purchasers who wanted to get out of the contract, they were the ones who should have been expected to have the matter clarified by the court: Carter, *Carter's Breach of Contract*, para 8-29 (n 2).

In *The Nanfri* [130] the shipowners under a time charterparty involving three ships became involved with a dispute with the charterers with regard to deductions made from the hire by way of purported set-off. Having taken legal advice with regard to the matter, they gave instructions to the masters to refuse to sign bills of lading marked 'freight pre-paid' and to insist that all bills of lading should be 'claused' so as to incorporate the terms of the charters. On the facts found by the umpire, the consequences of this move would have been catastrophic to the charterers; not only would they have been unable to carry out their normal trade, but they risked being blacklisted by the relevant trade association. [131] The charterers therefore entered into a 'without prejudice' agreement whereby in the interim the vessels remained in service, the deductions from hire were discontinued, and the owners' instructions suspended. However, in subsequent legal proceedings it was contended by the charterers that the owners had repudiated the contract. The owners argued that, so far from this being the case, there had not been a breach of contract at all; their instructions to the masters had been fully within the terms of the charterparty. In any event, it was argued, their action should not be taken to be repudiatory in the circumstances of the case; the question had been referred to arbitration, and once the issue had been cleared up the charters would continue to be operated in accordance with the arbitrators' decision. This argument, however, was rejected by the House of Lords. As Lord Wilberforce said: [132]

> Even if I were prepared to accept the assumption that arbitration proceedings...would be rapidly concluded...even so the owners' action must be regarded as going to the root of the contract. The issue of freight pre-paid bills of lading in respect of each of the three vessels was an urgent, indeed an immediate, requirement...the resolution of the deductions issue by arbitration, however soon this might be achieved, would still have left the charterers in a position where they might have lost the whole benefit of the time charters. That a 'without prejudice' agreement was in fact entered into which averted these consequences is of course irrelevant though the fact that it was made does underline the extent of the pressure on the charterers. It is also irrelevant that the steps the charterers were being compelled, under threat of a breach of contract, to take were not very serious for them. A threat to commit a breach, having radical consequences, is nonetheless serious because it is disproportionate to the intended effect. It is thirdly irrelevant that it was in the owners' real interest to continue the charters rather than to put an end to them. If a party's conduct is such as to amount to a threatened repudiatory breach, his subjective desire to maintain the contract cannot prevent the other party from drawing the consequences of his actions.

7.26 It seems that only in exceptional cases will a party be able to rely on a claim of good faith misconstruction as a defence to repudiation. In particular, it seems that: (1) the party seeking to raise such a defence must at least be able to identify the provision in

---

[130] *Federal Commerce & Navigation Co Ltd v Molena Alpha Inc (The Nanfri)* [1979] AC 757.
[131] *The Nanfri*, 775 (n 130).
[132] *The Nanfri*, 779 (n 130).

the contract upon which he or she is seeking to rely; (2) that provision must at least on the face of it purport to grant a right of termination; and (3) he or she must be able to show a readiness and willingness to perform the contract in the event of the provision being held to be inapplicable.[133] In *Dalkia Utilities Services plc v Celtech International Ltd*[134] a firm of energy suppliers sought to terminate the contract for failure to pay outstanding charges on the footing of an express clause in the contract. The question arose whether, assuming that the termination was wrongful,[135] it could be construed as a repudiation. It was held by the court that it could, and that *Woodar Investment Development Ltd v Wimpey Construction (UK) Ltd* could be distinguished on four grounds: (1) the time of performance in that case had not arrived; (2) the innocent party needed to serve a notice of termination in order to reserve its position; (3) the discussions between the parties had proceeded on the basis that the service of a notice was not to be regarded as a hostile act; and (4) it was accepted by both parties that once the matter had been decided by the court they would both abide by it.[136] In the present case, however, the position was very different; the time for performance had arrived, there were no ongoing discussions, the suppliers were continuing to insist on the validity of their notice of termination and to claim damages on that basis, and there was no understanding that they would be ready to continue performance should their interpretation of the contract turn out to be wrong.[137]

E. Anticipatory Breach

In most cases a repudiation, though relating to future obligations, will also involve **7.27** breach of an existing obligation by the defaulting party. In some cases, however, the repudiation will relate entirely to the future, and where this occurs we have a case of 'anticipatory' breach. The leading case here is *Hochster v de la Tour*,[138] where the plaintiff agreed to serve as a courier for the defendant on a forthcoming tour of the Continent. Some weeks before the tour was due to begin, the defendant wrote to the plaintiff cancelling the engagement. It was held that the plaintiff was entitled to sue at once for damages, even though the date for performance had not arrived. In the words of Lord Campbell CJ:[139]

> If the plaintiff has no remedy for breach of the contract unless he treats the contract as in force, and acts upon it down to the 1st June 1852, it follows that, till then, he

---

[133] *Zodiac Maritime Agencies Ltd v Fortescue Metals Group Ltd (The Kildare)* [2010] EWHC 903 (Comm); [2011] 2 Lloyd's Rep 360 (David Steel J).

[134] [2006] EWHC 63 (Comm); [2006] 2 P & CR 9 (Christopher Clarke J).

[135] On the facts it was held that the suppliers were entitled to terminate under the clause in question: [2006] EWHC (Comm) para 102.

[136] *Dalkia Utilities v Celtech Intl*, para 148 (n 134).

[137] *Dalkia Utilities v Celtech Intl*, para 149 (n 134).

[138] (1853) 2 E & B 678, 118 ER 922.

[139] *Hochster v de la Tour*, 689–90 and 926 (n 138).

must enter into no employment which will interfere with his promise 'to start with the defendant on such travels on the day and year,' and that he must then be properly equipped in all respects as a courier for a three months' tour on the continent of Europe. But it is surely much more rational, and more for the benefit of both parties, that, after the renunciation of the agreement by the defendant, the plaintiff should be at liberty to consider himself absolved from any future performance of it, retaining his right to sue for any damage he has suffered from the breach of it.

7.28   Likewise, in *Frost v Knight*,[140] where the defendant promised to marry the plaintiff as soon as his father died, and then called off the engagement, it was held that the plaintiff could bring an action at once without having to wait until the death took place. In cases of this sort, in the words of Cockburn CJ:[141]

> The promisee, if he pleases, may treat the notice of intention as inoperative, and await the time when the contract is to be executed, and then hold the other party responsible for all the consequences of non-performance: but in that case he keeps the contract alive for the benefit of the other party as well as his own; he remains subject to all his own obligations and liabilities under it, and enables the other party not only to complete the contract, if so advised, notwithstanding his previous repudiation of it, but also to take advantage of any supervening circumstance which would justify him in declining to complete it. On the other hand, the promisee may, if he thinks proper, treat the repudiation of the other party as a wrongful putting an end to the contract, and may at once bring his action as on a breach of it; and in such action he will be entitled to such damages as would have arisen from the non-performance of the contract at the appointed time, subject, however, to abatement in respect of any circumstances which may have afforded him the means of mitigating his loss.

7.29   For the most part cases of anticipatory breach are governed by the general law of repudiation,[142] but there are five topics that further attention in this context, namely: (1) the justification for the doctrine; (2) its theoretical basis; (3) the ways in which anticipatory breach may be proved; (4) the effect of such a breach; and (5) the problem of substantially executed contracts.

(1) Justification for the doctrine

7.30   Where one party indicates to the other in advance that he or she will not perform, it clearly makes good sense to allow him or her to terminate and sue for damages at once without having to wait until the due date. Various justifications for this are set out by Campbell CJ in *Hochster v de la Tour*:[143] the defaulting party has rendered it impossible for him or her to perform on the day; the parties having entered into a contractual relationship, there is a breach of an implied promise that neither of

---

[140] (1871–72) LR 7 Ex 111 (Exchequer Chamber).
[141] *Frost v Knight*, 112–13 (n 140).
[142] See, however, Nicholls, 'Conduct after Breach', pp 141–6 (n 123).
[143] (1853) E & B 678, 689–690, 118 ER 922, 926.

them will do anything to the prejudice of the other inconsistent with that relationship; allowing an immediate cause of action spares the innocent party from having to waste time and effort preparing to perform; the defaulting party having represented that he or she is not going to perform, the innocent party is entitled to act on that representation. One justification for the doctrine is that it protects the legitimate expectation of the innocent party in receiving the performance of the other—an expectation on the basis of which he or she may have incurred expenses, say in making contracts with third parties relating to the same subject matter.[144] Another is based on economic efficiency; by allowing the innocent party to cut loose at once without waiting for performance, both parties are left at liberty to use their resources to more productive ends.[145]

(2) Theoretical basis of the doctrine

Whatever the practical justification for the doctrine may be, its theoretical basis **7.31** is a matter of dispute.[146] The label 'anticipatory breach' clearly suggests that the effect of the doctrine is to bring forward a future liability by deeming a prospective breach to have taken place already. This position is reflected in the words of Cockburn CJ to the effect that the eventual non-performance is, by anticipation, treated as a cause of action.[147] The main advantage of this theory is that it reflects the difference between an actual breach (which gives rise to a right of damages as of right) and an anticipatory breach (which only does so if and when it is 'accepted' by the innocent party).[148] The difficulty here lies in explaining why the law should allow a party to sue on the basis of a breach which in fact may never take place.[149] As well as this, the theory looks rather contrived, and it does not tally either with the rules for the assessment of damages[150] nor with a line of cases suggesting that the breach occurs at the place of the repudiation rather than at the place where performance was due.[151] As against this, Carter and others have argued that the essence of these cases is a breach by the party in default of his or her obligation to

---

[144] Peel, *Treitel*, para 17-081 (n 62).

[145] Peel, *Treitel*, para 17-081 (n 62); Beale, *Remedies for Breach of Contract*, pp 68–77 (n 76); Andrews et al, *Contractual Duties*, para 7-009 (n 67).

[146] E Tabachnik, 'Anticipatory Breach of Contract' [1972] CLP 149.

[147] *Frost v Knight* (1871–72) LR 7 Ex 111 (Exchequer Chamber), 114.

[148] See para 7.37. But it has been argued that in some cases the law should allow damages to be claimed for anticipatory breach without the necessity of termination: see Andrews et al, *Contractual Duties*, paras 7-025–7-038 (n 67). For other approaches to the problem see HR Limburg, 'Anticipatory Repudiation of Contracts' (1925) 10 Cornell L Rev 135; JC Gulotta, 'Anticipatory Breach: a Comparative Analysis' (1976) 50 Tulane L Rev 927.

[149] This difficulty is specifically alluded to by Campbell CJ in *Hochster v de la Tour* (1853) E & B 678, 688–9, 118 ER 922, 926.

[150] See Ch 10, para 10.05.

[151] *Cherry v Thompson* (1872) LR 7 QB 573; *Holland v Bennett* [1902] 1 KB 867 (CA); *Martin v Stout* [1925] AC 359 (JCPC–Egypt); *Atlantic Underwriting Agencies Ltd v Compagnia di Assicurazione di Milano SpA* [1979] 2 Lloyd's Rep 240 (QBD: Commercial Ct); all cited by Carter, *Carter's Breach of Contract*, para 7-23, note 134 (n 2).

be ready and willing to perform.[152] This is certainly a much more satisfying and elegant approach, but it is hard to reconcile with the 'acceptance' requirement. A third possibility is canvassed by Liu, who argues that though all anticipatory breaches must be serious enough to justify termination, the breach itself is essentially free-standing in nature and should not depend on that right of termination actually being exercised by the innocent party.[153] In the end, as Carter says, it may be that no one theory can account for all the different ramifications of the doctrine;[154] perhaps it is better to admit that it is essentially an artificial construct[155] based not so much on a coherent conceptual framework as on considerations of commercial convenience.[156]

(3) Modes of anticipatory breach

7.32 According to the traditional classification as set out by Lord Porter, an anticipatory breach can be established either by renunciation or by prospective impossibility.[157] Renunciation occurs when the defaulting party, in advance of the time of performance, evinces a clear and absolute refusal to go on with the contract. Prospective impossibility occurs when that party disables himself or herself from performing. Though these two modes of anticipatory breach are said to be difficult to disentangle,[158] it is nevertheless essential that they be disentangled,[159] as the former is much easier to establish than the latter. The leading case here is *Universal Cargo Carriers Corporation v Citati*,[160] which concerned a voyage charterparty for the carriage of a cargo of scrap iron from Basrah to Buenos Aires. Under the terms of the contract the charterers were bound to complete loading by 21 July 1951. The ship arrived at

---

[152] Carter, *Carter's Breach of Contract*, para 7-24; F Dawson, 'Metaphors and Anticipatory Breach of Contract' [1981] CLJ 83.

[153] Q Liu, 'Claiming Damages upon an Anticipatory Breach: why should an Acceptance be Necessary?' (2005) 25 LS 557; Liu, *Anticipatory Breach*, p 30 (n 68); Andrews et al, *Contractual Duties*, para 7-032 (n 67).

[154] Andrews et al, *Contractual Duties*, para 7-17 (n 67).

[155] *Maredelanto Compania Naviera SA v Bergbau-Handel GmbH (The Mihalis Angelos)* [1971] 1 QB 164, 182 (Mocatta J) (reversed on the merits of the case).

[156] *Danube and Black Sea Rly v Xenos* (1861) 11 CBNS 152, 177, 142 ER 753, 763 (Erle CJ); *Woodar Investment Development Ltd v Wimpey Construction UK Ltd* [1980] 1 WLR 277 (HL) 296–7 (Lord Keith); Carter, *Carter's Breach of Contract*, para 7-17 (n 2).

[157] *Heyman v Darwins* [1942] AC 356 (HL) 397.

[158] *Universal Cargo Carriers Corp v Citati* [1957] 2 QB 401, 437 (Devlin J); *Chilean Nitrate Sales Corp v Marine Transportation Co Ltd (The Hermosa)* [1982] 1 Lloyd's Rep 570 (CA) 572–3 (Donaldson LJ).

[159] Liu, however, argues for what has been called a 'unitary' theory of anticipatory breach, whereby in all cases the ultimate question is whether the conduct of the defaulting party justifies the inference that he or she is likely to commit a fundamental breach when the time for performance arrives. However, though this theory fits well with the law on renunciation, it does not fit with the orthodox approach to impossibility, under which mere inferences of this sort are not enough. See further Liu, *Anticipatory Breach*, p 37 (n 68); Q Liu, 'Inferring Future Breach: towards a Unifying Test of Anticipatory Breach of Contract' [2007] CLJ 574; Andrews et al, *Contractual Duties*, paras 7-084–7-091 (n 67); see paras 7.35–7.36.

[160] [1957] 2 QB 401.

the loading port on 12 July, but no cargo was ready, nor was there any reasonable prospect of one being made available in the foreseeable future. On 18 July, three days before the expiry of the lay days, the owners decided to throw up the charter and claimed damages from the charterers on the grounds of repudiation. The case went to arbitration, the key issue being whether, assuming the charterers' breach to be anticipatory,[161] the owners were entitled to terminate. The arbitrators having found for the shipowners both on the grounds of renunciation and on the grounds of impossibility, the court then had to decide whether the arbitrators had adopted the correct approach.

(a) Anticipatory breach by renunciation

The first possibility canvassed by Devlin J was an anticipatory breach by renunci- **7.33** ation. The essence of renunciation, as previously stated, is an absence of willingness to perform the contract. In the words of Devlin J:[162]

> A renunciation can be made either by words or by conduct, provided it is clearly made. It is often put that the party renunciating must 'evince an intention' not to go on with the contract. The intention can be evinced either by words or by conduct. The test of whether an intention is sufficiently evinced by conduct is whether the party renunciating has acted in such a way as to lead a reasonable person to the conclusion that he does not intend to fulfil his part of the contract.

Where this happens, there is no need for the innocent party to show that the con- **7.34** tract would not, in fact, be fulfilled. Rather, as Devlin J said, if a man proclaimed by words or conduct an inability to perform, the other party could safely act upon it without having to prove that when the time for performance came the inability was still effective.[163] As we have seen, the owners succeeded before the arbitrators on this ground, and there was good evidence to back up this finding. As Devlin J put it:[164]

> Since a man must be both ready and willing to perform, a profession by words or conduct of inability is by itself enough to constitute renunciation. But unwilling- ness and inability are often difficult to disentangle, and it is rarely necessary to make the attempt. Inability often lies at the root of unwillingness to perform. Willingness in this context does not mean cheerfulness; it means simply an intent to perform. To say: 'I would like to but I cannot' negatives intent just as much as 'I will not'.

Thus a renunciation may be found to have occurred whether the defaulting party declares in so many words that he or she is unable to perform[165] or whether such

---

[161] Arguably the charterer was in actual breach here both for failing to provide a cargo and for failing to nominate a berth: [1957] 2 QB 401, 429, and see Peel, *Treitel*, para 17-086 (n 62).

[162] [1957] 2 QB 401, 436; *SK Shipping (S) Pte Ltd v Petroexport Ltd (The Pro Victor)* [2009] EWHC 2974 (Comm), [2010] 2 Lloyd's Rep 158, para 84.

[163] *Universal Cargo Carriers Corp v Citati*, 437 (n 162).

[164] *Universal Cargo Carriers Corp v Citati*, 437 (n 162). Thus, as a matter of principle, the subjec- tive intent of the party in default should be irrelevant: Liu, 'The Pitfall of Subjective Renunciation' (n 37).

[165] *Anchor Line Ltd v Keith Rowell Ltd (The Hazelmoor)* [1980] 2 Lloyd's Rep 351 (CA) 353 (Megaw LJ).

inability is manifested by conduct on his or her part, as where A agrees to sell land to B and then sells the very same land to C.[166] However, that was not the end of the matter. Unfortunately for the owners, the arbitrators were held to have misdirected themselves on the point by taking irrelevant factors into consideration.[167] It was therefore necessary to see whether the owners were entitled to succeed on the second issue, that of impossibility.

(b) Anticipatory breach by prospective impossibility

7.35 Impossibility is far more difficult to establish, the test here being whether the innocent party can prove that at the relevant time the defaulting party was 'wholly and finally disabled' from performing.[168] This is in stark contrast not only to the position with regard to repudiation generally,[169] but to the law of frustration where, according to Scrutton J in *Embiricos v Sydney Reid & Co*:[170] 'Commercial men must not be asked to wait until the end of a long delay to find out from what in fact happens whether they are bound by a contract or not; they must be entitled to act on reasonable commercial probabilities at the time when they are called on to make up their minds.' However, Devlin J went on to say that the *Embiricos* principle had no application to cases of anticipatory breach,[171] the reason being that it would be unjust to subject a party to damages[172] in the absence of proof either that he or she was unwilling to perform or that the breach was inevitable.[173] In the words of Devlin J, an anticipatory breach must be proved in fact and not in supposition.[174]

---

[166] Carter, *Carter's Breach of Contract*, para 9-11 (n 2); *Duke of St Albans v Shore* (1879) 1 Bl H 270, 126 ER 158; *Synge v Synge* [1894] 1 QB 466 (CA); *Omnium d'Enterprises v Sutherland* [1919] 1 KB 618 (CA); *Wright v Dean* [1948] Ch 686 (Ch D); *J Lauritzen AS v Wijsmuller BV (The Super Servant Two)* [1990] 1 Lloyd's Rep 1 (CA).

[167] *Universal Cargo Carriers Corp v Citati*, 440–1 (n 162).

[168] *Universal Cargo Carriers Corp v Citati*, 446 (n 162); *British & Beningtons Ltd v NW Cachar Tea Co Ltd* [1923] AC 48 (HL) 72 (Lord Sumner); *Continental Contractors Ltd and Ernest Beck & Co Ltd v Medway Oil & Storage Co Ltd* (1926) 25 Ll L Rep 288 (HL); *Trade and Transport Inc v Iino Kaiun Kaisha Ltd (The Angelia)* [1973] 1 WLR 210, 219 (Kerr J); *Alfred Toepfer International GmbH v Itex Italgrani Export SA* [1993] 1 Lloyd's Rep 360 (QBD: Commercial Ct) 362 (Saville J); *SK Shipping (S) Pte Ltd v Petroexport Ltd (The Pro Victor)* [2009] EWHC 2974, [2010] 2 Lloyd's Rep 158, para 123 (Flaux J); Andrews et al, *Contractual Duties*, paras 7-059–7-070 (n 67).

[169] See para 7.20.

[170] [1914] 3 KB 45 (CA) 54; *Watts, Watts & Co Ltd v Mitsui & Co Ltd* [1917] AC 227 (HL) 246 (Lord Dunedin).

[171] [1957] 2 QB 401, 449. A different approach was taken by Macdonald J in the Supreme Court of British Columbia in *Sanko Steamship Co Ltd v Eacom Timber Sales Ltd (The Sanko Iris)* [1987] 1 Lloyd's Rep 487, but this seems contrary to principle: see JW Carter, 'Anticipating Confusion' [1988] LMCLQ 21.

[172] This is a fair enough point, but as Treitel says it does not necessarily follow that he or she should not be entitled to terminate in these circumstances: Peel, *Treitel*, para 17-086 (n 62); and see M Mustill, 'The Golden Victory—Some Reflections' (2008) 124 LQR 569, 572–3.

[173] *Grace & Co Ltd v General Steam Navigation Co Ltd* [1950] 2 KB 383 (KBD), 393 (Devlin J); Carter, *Carter's Breach of Contract*, para 9-25 (n 2).

[174] [1950] 2 QB 401, 450.

The approach of Devlin J in the *Citati* case has been subjected to criticism on a   **7.36**
number of grounds; in particular, it is said to impose too heavy a burden on the
innocent party, who runs the risk of being held to have repudiated the contract by
terminating even though any sensible businessman would have concluded that
performance by the party in default was very unlikely to be forthcoming.[175] For
this reason it is argued by Liu and others that a reasonable inference should be
enough to justify termination in this context as well,[176] though not necessarily a
claim for damages.[177] However, the problem is perhaps more apparent than real;
given that virtually all cases of impossibility can also be construed in terms of
implied renunciation, cases where the former has to be relied on are likely to be few
and far between.[178]

(4) Effect of anticipatory breach

Where an anticipatory breach occurs, the innocent party has the same choice as   **7.37**
exists in the case of breach of condition and fundamental breach generally, namely
either to terminate performance by 'accepting' the breach or to affirm the contract.[179] If the innocent party terminates, the result is the same as in other cases
of termination, in that the primary obligations of both parties, in so far as they
are still outstanding, need generally no longer be performed.[180] In the same way,
the party in default now has a secondary obligation—the so-called 'anticipatory
secondary obligation'[181]—to pay damages to compensate the innocent party for
loss in respect of his or her non-performance of the primary obligation. If the
innocent party affirms, the primary obligations of each party remain binding,
but here in contrast to cases of actual breach, there is no secondary obligation, the
general rule being that an unaccepted repudiation is a thing 'writ in water',[182] and

---

[175] Carter, *Carter's Breach of Contract*, para 9-27 (n 2). Another approach is to allow the innocent
party in this situation to suspend his or her own performance pending an adequate assurance of
due performance from the party in default, and to allow termination if this is not forthcoming, as
in the Uniform Commercial Code, para 2-609, the American Law Institute, Restatement Second,
s 251, and the UNIDROIT Principles for International Contracts, Art 7.3.4; AI Rosett, 'Contract
Performance: Promises, Conditions and the Obligation to Communicate' (1975) 22 UCLA L Rev
1083; RJ Robertson, 'The Right to Demand Adequate Assurance of Due Performance' (1988–89)
38 Drake L Rev 305; JW Carter, 'Adequate Assurance of Due Performance' (1995) 9 JCL 1.

[176] Liu, *Anticipatory Breach*, p 77 (n 68); JE Stannard, 'Frustrating Delay' (1983) 46 MLR 738;
JW Carter, 'The Embiricos Principle and the Law of Anticipatory Breach' (1984) 47 MLR 422. For
a contrary view see Andrews et al, *Contractual Duties*, para 7-077 (n 67).

[177] Peel, *Treitel*, para 17-086 (n 62).

[178] Indeed, according to Carter there appears to be no recorded case in which anticipatory breach
has been successfully proved on this basis: Carter, *Carter's Breach of Contract*, para 9-24 (n 2).

[179] See Chs 9–12.

[180] *Moschi v Lep Air Services Ltd* [1973] AC 331 (HL) 350 (Lord Diplock); see Ch 9, para 9.02.

[181] *Photo Production Ltd v Securicor Transport Ltd* [1980] AC 827 (HL) 849 (Lord Diplock). This
is to be contrasted with the 'general secondary obligation' to pay damages for breach in cases where
the contract is not terminated: see further Ch 10, para 10.02.

[182] *Howard v Pickford Tool Co* [1951] 1 KB 417 (CA) 421 (Asquith LJ).

that damages for an anticipatory breach only accrue in the event of termination.[183] However, even an unaccepted repudiation may have *some* effect in cases of this sort; in particular, where the innocent party changes his or her position in reliance on the repudiation, the party in default may not be allowed to retract it.[184]

(5) Substantially executed contracts

7.38 In some cases renunciation by the defaulting party may occur before any performance at all on his or her part takes place, but in others this may happen at a later stage. Particular problems arise in this context where the defaulting party has largely completed his or her performance under the contract but then indicates that he or she is not going to finish the job.[185] To take an example given by the Law Commission,[186] say a painter agrees to decorate a house and then return a year later to do any necessary touching up. The main part of the work is duly completed, but the painter then indicates that he will not come back to do the touching up. According to the law as it stands, there is nothing the customer can do except wait until the twelve months has passed, since taken in the context of the contract as a whole the painter's default would not be serious enough to justify termination. This seems unfair to the customer, who may wish to get someone else in to do the job. One way round this conundrum would be to allow the innocent party to claim damages in this sort of case without termination of the contract as a whole, but as stated previously, this does not fit in with the present state of the law. As Andrews points out, there seems to be a gap in the law here.[187]

F. Notices Making Time of the Essence

7.39 The main practical advantage in commercial terms of allowing termination for repudiation is that it enables the innocent party to deal with the problem of uncertainty as to future performance; rather than having to waste time and expense waiting for the other party to render a performance which may never be forthcoming, the innocent party can 'cut loose', as it were, and use his or her resources for more profitable ends. However, this is not the only way in which the law deals with this problem. Another way is to allow the innocent party to give the party in default one last chance to perform, and to say that if this chance is not taken then

---

[183] Liu, however, argues that, although damages for anticipatory breach depend on the breach being serious enough to *justify* termination, termination need not actually have *occurred* in such cases for the breach to be actionable; Liu, *Anticipatory Breach*, pp 29–30 (n 68); Andrews et al, *Contractual Duties*, paras 7-032–7-038 (n 67).

[184] Carter, *Carter's Breach of Contract*, para 7-57 (n 2).

[185] Andrews et al, *Contractual Duties*, paras 7-025–7-031 (n 67).

[186] Contract Code: Drawn up on behalf of the English Law Commission (Milano, 1993) pp 74–5; Andrews et al, *Contractual Duties*, para 7-029 (n 67).

[187] Andrews et al, *Contractual Duties*, para 7-025 (n 67).

the contract will be terminated. In the common law this can be done, at least in certain cases, by issuing a notice making time of the essence.[188] In the remaining pages of this chapter we shall consider the law regarding the issue of such notices before looking at how the procedure relates to the principles discussed earlier.

(1) The notice procedure

The procedure whereby a notice of this sort may be issued was developed by the old **7.40** court of Chancery at the beginning of the nineteenth century,[189] and was conveniently summarized by Clarke J in *Dalkia Utilities Services plc v Celtech International Ltd*.[190] The law may be outlined under three headings: (1) the requirements for the issue of a notice; (2) the content of the notice; and (3) the effect of the notice.

(a) Requirements for issue of notice

There are two basic requirements for the service of a notice of this kind, the first **7.41** being that the party who wishes to serve the notice must be fully 'able, ready and willing' to perform, and the second undue delay by the party in default.[191] The first requirement involves showing that the party serving the notice is not presently guilty of any significant outstanding default on his or her contractual obligations,[192] and that he or she is ready and willing to perform his or her future obligations as and when they arise.[193] The second requirement involves showing that the defaulting party has failed to perform on time, either by breaching an express time stipulation[194] or, in cases where the contract is silent as to time, by failure to perform within a reasonable time.[195] As well as this, it may be possible in some cases to serve a notice even before the time for performance arrives; in particular, where no time for performance is set, but where such time would have been of the essence if set, the promisee may effectively set such a time by serving a

---

[188] P Butt, 'The Modern Law of Notices to Complete' (1985) 59 ALJ 260; P Butt, 'Notices to Perform Obligations in Conveyancing Contracts—a View from Down Under' [1991] Conveyancer 94; JE Stannard, *Delay in the Performance of Contractual Obligations* (OUP, 2007) para 8.02.

[189] *Reynolds v Nelson* (1821) 6 Madd 18, 56 ER 995; *Heaphy v Hill* (1824) 2 Sim & St 29, 57 ER 255; *Watson v Reid* (1830) 1 Russ & My 236, 39 ER 91; *Taylor v Brown* (1839) 2 Beav 180, 48 ER 1149; Stannard, *Delay in Performance*, para 8.05 (n 188).

[190] [2006] EWHC Civ 63, [2006] 2 P & CR 9, para 131; *Re Olympia & York Canary Wharf Ltd (No 2)* [1993] BCC 159 (Ch D: Companies Ct) 168–73 (Morritt J); JE Stannard, 'In the Contractual Last Chance Saloon' (2004) 120 LQR 137.

[191] Stannard, *Delay in Performance*, paras 8.07–8.19 (n 188).

[192] Stannard, *Delay in Performance*, para 8.10 (n 188); *Pagebar Properties Ltd v Derby Investments (Holdings) Ltd* [1972] 1 WLR 1500 (Ch D); *Wood v Berkeley Homes (Sussex) Ltd* (1992) 64 P & CR 311 (CA); P Butt, 'Notices to Complete: "Ready, Able and Willing"' [1982] Conveyancer 62.

[193] *Re Barr's Contract* [1956] Ch 551, 556 (Danckwerts J); *Neeta (Epping) Pty v Phillips* (1974) 131 CLR 286 (High Ct of Australia) 299 (Barwick CJ and Jacobs J); *Ramlal v Chaitlal* [2003] UKPC 12, [2004] 1 P & CR 1 (JCPC–Trinidad and Tobago); Stannard, *Delay in Performance*, paras 8.08–8.09 (n 188).

[194] *Behzadi v Shaftesbury Hotels* [1992] Ch 1 (CA); Stannard, *Delay in Performance*, para 8.16 (n 188); C Harpum, 'Conveyancing: Notices to Fulfil Contractual Obligation' [1991] CLJ 40.

[195] *Hick v Raymond and Reid* [1893] AC 22 (HL); *Barclays Bank plc v Savile Estates Ltd* [2002] EWCA Civ 589, [2003] P & CR 28; Stannard, *Delay in Performance*, para 8.15 (n 188).

notice to that effect. This gives the promisor due warning that if he or she does not perform at that time, the contract will be terminated.[196]

(b) Content of notice

7.42 Even if a notice is validly served, it may still fail because of inherent defects. This has a number of aspects to it.[197] First of all, the notice must set out clearly what has to be done, no more and no less.[198] Secondly, it must give the other party a reasonable time to do it,[199] though this may not be the case in instances where the delay has been very protracted,[200] since, as Lord Parker said, a party cannot claim as a result of his or her own past delay to be entitled to a longer period of notice than would otherwise have been the case.[201] Finally, it must set out the consequences of default in clear and unambiguous terms;[202] it has been suggested that this is best done by saying in so many words that time is now of the essence, and that if the notice is not complied with the promisee reserves the right to terminate the contract.[203]

(c) Effect of notice

7.43 If, having been served with a valid notice, the promisor fails to comply with it, the promisee has the same choice as in cases of breach of condition or fundamental breach;[204] that is to say, he or she can either terminate performance[205] or affirm the

---

[196] *British and Commonwealth Holdings plc v Quadrex Holdings Inc* [1989] QB 842 (CA); Stannard, *Delay in Performance*, para 8.17 (n 188).

[197] *O'Brien v Dawson* (1941) 42 SR (NSW) 295, 304 (Jordan CJ); Stannard, *Delay in Performance*, para 8.20 (n 188).

[198] *Babacomp Ltd v Rightside Properties Ltd* (1973) 26 P & CR 26 (CA); *Hanson v Cameron* [1949] 1 DLR 16 (Supreme Court of Canada) 16; *Neeta (Epping) Co v Phillips* (1974) 131 CLR 286 (High Court of Australia); Stannard, *Delay in Performance*, para 8.27 (n 188).

[199] *Wells v Maxwell* (1863) 33 LJ Ch 44; *McMurray v Spicer* (1868) LR 5 Eq 527; *Crawford v Toogood* (1879) 13 Ch D 153; *Green v Sevin* (1879) 13 Ch D 589; *Compton v Bagley* [1892] 1 Ch 313; *Re Barr's Contract* [1956] Ch 551; *Ajit v Sammy* [1967] 1 AC 255 (JCPC–British Guiana); Stannard, *Delay in Performance*, para 8.22 (n 188).

[200] *MacBryde v Weekes* (1856) 22 Beav 533, 52 ER 1214; *Stickney v Keeble* [1915] AC 386 (HL); *Ajit v Sammy* [1967] 1 AC 255 (JCPC–British Guiana); Stannard, *Delay in Performance*, para 8.23 (n 188). Arguably these are cases where the party could have terminated even without serving a notice: A Sydenham, 'Unreasonable Delay' [1980] Conveyancer 19.

[201] *Stickney v Keeble* [1915] AC 386 (HL) 418.

[202] *Reynolds v Nelson* (1821) 6 Madd 18, 56 ER 995; *Smith v Hamilton* [1951] Ch 174; *Balog v Crestani* (1975) 132 CLR 289 (High Court of Australia); Stannard, *Delay in Performance*, paras 8.28–8.29 (n 188).

[203] K Lindgren, *Time in the Performance of Contracts* (2nd edn, Butterworths, 1982) p 102. The House of Lords in *Mannai Investment Co Ltd v Eagle Star Life Assurance Co* [1997] AC 749 suggested a less demanding approach to contractual notices generally, saying that the crucial question was the effect of the notice on a reasonable person in the position of the recipient. However, the extent to which these principles apply in the present context is open to doubt: *Western Bulk Carriers K/S v Li Hai Maritime Inc (The Li Hai)* [2005] EWHC 735 (Comm), [2005] 1 CLC 704, and see further Ch 8, paras 8.07–8.10.

[204] Stannard, *Delay in Performance*, paras 8.30–8.32 (n 188).

[205] *Whitbread and Co Ltd v Watt* [1902] 1 Ch 835 (CA); *Harold Wood Brick Co v Ferris* [1935] 2 KB 198 (CA); *Buckland v Farmar and Moody* [1979] 1 WLR 221 (CA).

contract, say by serving further notices to the same effect.[206] However, once served the notice binds the promisee no less than the promisor, so that if the giver of the notice subsequently refuses to perform or fails to do so without good reason, the recipient may in turn be entitled to terminate.[207]

(2) Relationship with repudiation

What has all of this got to do with repudiation? Traditionally, as we have seen,[208] **7.44** the equitable doctrines relating to time were thought to operate entirely independently of the common law of termination, but in 1978 an attempt was made by the House of Lords to bring the two together in *United Scientific Holdings Ltd v Burnley Borough Council*.[209] In this context Lord Simon sought to reinterpret the notice procedure in terms of repudiation, saying:[210]

> The notice operates as evidence that the promisee considers that a reasonable time for performance has elapsed by the date of the notice and as evidence of the date by which the promisee now considers it reasonable for the contractual obligation to be performed. The promisor is put on notice of these matters. It is only in this sense that time is made of the essence of a contract in which it was previously non-essential. The promisee is really saying, 'Unless you perform by such-and-such a date, I shall treat your failure as a repudiation of the contract'.

The difficulty with this approach is that the ordinary principles of repudiation do not allow the innocent party to put the defaulting party 'on the spot' in this way; as Lord Denning pointed out, one party cannot seek to put on the other a repudiation where he or she has not actually repudiated.[211] Whereas failure by the defaulting party to meet the set deadline under the notice procedure gives the innocent party a clear right of termination, such failure can only be regarded by the common law as 'evidence' of repudiation and no more.[212] It has been argued for this reason that the new interpretation is too vague, and that a 'bright line' approach would be preferable,[213] though bringing such an approach in line with the general principles of repudiation would be a different matter.

---

[206] *Charles Rickards Ltd v Oppenhaim* [1950] 1 KB 616 (CA); *Afford v Till* [1990] 35 EG 56 (CA).
[207] *Upperton v Nickolson* (1871) LR 6 Ch App 436; *Finkielkraut v Monahan* [1949] 2 All ER 234; *Quadrangle Development and Construction Co v Jenner* [1974] 1 WLR 68 (CA); Stannard, *Delay in Performance*, para 8.32 (n 188).
[208] See Ch 5, paras 5.41–5.42.
[209] [1978] AC 904 (HL).
[210] *United Scientific Holdings Ltd v Burnley BC*, 946–7 (n 209).
[211] *Eshun v Moorgate Mercantile Credit Co* [1971] 1 WLR 722 (CA) 726.
[212] *Re Olympia & York Canary Wharf Ltd (No 2)* [1993] BCC 159 (Ch D: Companies Ct) 171–2 (Morritt J); *Ocular Sciences Ltd v Aspect Vision Care Ltd* [1997] RPC 289 (Ch D: Patents Ct), 442 (Laddie J); *Dalkia Utilities Services plc v Celtech International Ltd* [2006] EWHC Civ 63, [2006] 2 P & CR 9, para 131 (Clarke J); *BNP Paribas v Wockhardt EU Operations (Swiss) AG* [2009] EWHC (Comm) para 40 (Clarke J); Andrews et al, *Contractual Duties*, paras 11-024–11-031 (n 67).
[213] Andrews et al, *Contractual Duties*, para 11-034 (n 67).

8

EXPRESS RIGHTS OF TERMINATION

The previous three chapters have shown us that it is not always easy for a party to **8.01** know for certain whether he or she is entitled to terminate or not. This is particularly so where the right in question depends on proof of fundamental breach or repudiation, yet the consequences of error can be catastrophic.[1] For this reason parties to a contract frequently, in the interests of certainty,[2] make express provision for this by agreeing in advance that one or both of them may terminate if certain conditions are met.[3] Such express rights of termination can depend on a wide variety of contingencies, but very frequently these will include a breach by the other party. Where this is the case, it is often difficult to distinguish termination under the express right from termination under the general law, in particular where the latter involves termination for breach of condition. In the pages which follow we shall consider four key issues with regard to express rights of this sort, most notably: (1) the relationship between express rights of termination and conditions at common law; (2) the requirements for the exercise of such rights; (3) the

---

[1] As Carter says, parties who wrongfully terminate a contract do so at their peril: JW Carter, *Carter's Breach of Contract* (Hart, 2012) para 8-23. This is because, as we have seen, wrongful termination will generally itself amount to repudiation: see Ch 7, para 7.14.

[2] Carter, *Carter's Breach of Contract*, para 3-09 (n 1).

[3] JW Carter, 'Termination Clauses' (1990–91) 3 JCL 90; N Andrews, M Clarke, A Tettenborn, and G Virgo, *Contractual Duties: Performance, Breach, Termination and Remedies* (Sweet & Maxwell, 2011) ch 9; Carter, *Carter's Breach of Contract*, paras 3-07–3-10 (n 1); E Peel, *Treitel: The Law of Contract* (13th edn, Sweet & Maxwell, 2011) para 18-061.

Chapter 8: Express Rights of Termination

effect of termination under such a right; and (4) the problem of concurrent rights of termination.

A. Express Rights of Termination and Conditions

8.02 Given that the essence of a condition is that the innocent party may terminate if it is broken, it is very difficult to see how making a term a condition at common law differs from granting an express right of termination for breach of that term. Indeed, it can be argued that there is no difference of substance at all between the two cases, and this view seems to have been shared by Lord Diplock, at least in his later pronouncements on the topic.[4] This can be seen from *The Afovos*,[5] where the question concerned a clause in a charterparty (clause 5 of the New York Produce Exchange form) allowing the owners to withdraw the ship for late payment of hire. Commenting on this clause, Lord Diplock said:[6]

> The second part of clause 5....goes on to provide expressly what the rights of the owners are to be in the event of any such breach by the charterers of their primary obligation to make punctual payment of an instalment. The owners are to be at liberty to withdraw the vessel from the service of the charterers; in other words they are entitled to treat the breach when it occurs as a breach of condition and so giving them the right to elect to treat it as putting an end to all their own primary obligations under the charterparty then remaining unperformed.

This, however, is clearly at odds with his earlier pronouncements on the subject, which indicate a clear distinction between the two cases.[7] Indeed, since both the requirements and the consequences of termination may differ depending on whether it is done for breach of condition or under an express right,[8] *some* distinction there must be, otherwise the law in this area would be totally incoherent.

8.03 The question has received surprisingly little attention in the courts, no doubt because if the only issue is whether the innocent party is entitled to terminate or not, it matters little whether this is done under the common law or under an express contractual right.[9] The matter did, however, come up for consideration in

---

[4] See also *Scandinavian Tanker Co AB v Flota Petrolera Ecuatoriana (The Scaptrade)* [1983] 2 AC 694 (HL) 703, where the dispute concerned clause 3 of the standard 'Shelltime' charterparty, which allowed the charterers to withdraw the ship for non-payment of hire. In his opinion Lord Diplock suggested that the House of Lords had in a previous decision (*Tankexpress A/S v Compagnie Financière Belge des Petroles SA (The Petrofina)* [1949] AC 76) construed the clause in question as a condition making time of the essence, but there is no indication of that in the case in question.

[5] *Afovos Shipping Co SA v Pagnan & Flli (The Afovos)* [1983] 1 WLR 195 (HL).

[6] *The Afovos*, 203 (n 5).

[7] See in particular *Financings v Baldock* [1963] 2 QB 104 (CA) at 120–1; discussed further Ch 10, para 10.10.

[8] Thus for instance the doctrine of anticipatory breach does not apply to express rights of termination (see para 8.06), and the measure of damages following termination may differ depending on whether it took place at common law or under an express right (see Ch 10, paras 10.07–10.18).

[9] Carter, *Carter's Breach of Contract*, para 5-08 (n 1).

the High Court of Australia in *Legione v Hateley*,[10] where a contract for the sale of land contained a provision stating that 'time shall be of the essence of this contract in all respects', but then went on to specify that neither party should be allowed to enforce any rights granted under the contract or at common law without service of a default notice giving the defaulting party the opportunity of making good the default in question. According to Mason and Deane JJ, in so far as the effect of this provision was to work a forfeiture,[11] it did so not under the contract but under the common law. In the words of Mason and Deane JJ:[12]

> Forfeiture of the purchaser's interest, usually the consequence of the vendor's rescission for breach of an essential term, occurs under the general law regulating the rights of vendor and purchaser. Such a forfeiture is to be distinguished from a contractual forfeiture which is designed to ensure performance of a contractual obligation. True it is that [the relevant provision] expressly regulated the vendor's right of rescission in the present case and provided for rescission on non-compliance with the prescribed notice on expiration of the time limited. However, the presence of this contractual stipulation, which merely regulates the vendor's common law right to rescind, does not alter the essential character of the forfeiture of the purchaser's interest which occurs when rescission takes place.

Though Mason and Deane JJ did not say so in so many words, the crucial factor seems to have been that, in providing that 'time shall be of the essence in all respects', the contract did more than just give a right of termination for late performance. Rather, it said something not only about the *consequences of the breach* but also about *the term itself*.[13]

This analysis of course tallies with the traditional understanding of a condition as an **8.04** essential term of the contract, breach of which is, in the words of Fletcher Moulton LJ, equivalent to 'a substantial failure to perform the contract at all'.[14] However, as we have already argued,[15] not all conditions can necessarily be described in this way; sometimes a term is classified as a condition not on the grounds of its intrinsic importance, or even because the parties have chosen to make it important, but merely on the grounds of commercial certainty. Where we have a condition of this sort, its relation to an express right of termination is much more problematic; indeed, it can be argued that for some purposes at least this sort of condition has more in common with an express right than with conditions of the previous type. This matter will be further explored in due course.[16]

---

[10] (1983) 152 CLR 406.

[11] The extent to which the equitable jurisdiction to relieve against forfeiture applies to cases such as this is now open to doubt; see further Ch 4, paras 4.80–4.81.

[12] *Legione v Hateley*, 445 (n 10).

[13] cf *Lombard North Central plc v Butterworth* [1987] 1 QB 527 (clause making time of the essence a condition rather than conferring a mere contractual right of termination).

[14] *Wallis, Son and Wells v Pratt & Haynes* [1910] 2 KB 1003 (CA) 1012; see Ch 5, para 5.03.

[15] See Ch 5, para 5.06.

[16] JE Stannard, 'Delay, Damages and the Doctrine of Constructive Repudiation' (2013) 29 JCL 178.

B. Exercise of the Right

8.05 Where a right of termination arises under the general law, the conditions for its exercise are as set out in the general law. But where such a right arises under an express term of the contract, the conditions for its exercise are as set out in the contract. This means that an express right of termination can only be exercised in accordance with its terms, and not otherwise. This has a number of consequences, the first relating to the time when the right may be exercised, the second relating to the way in which it may be exercised, and the third relating to the nature of the breach giving rise to the exercise of the right.

(1) Time of exercise

8.06 The doctrines of repudiation and anticipatory breach, as we have seen,[17] allow the innocent party to terminate before any actual breach takes place. This applies not only to cases of prospective fundamental breach, but also possibly even to prospective breaches of condition.[18] However, an express right to terminate for breach cannot be exercised before the breach has taken place; it is not enough to show that it was bound to take place at some future date. In *The Mihalis Angelos*[19] a charterparty contained a clause in the following terms:[20]

> Should the vessel not be ready to load (whether in berth or not) on or before July 20, 1965, charterers have the option of cancelling this contract, such option to be declared, if demanded, at least 48 hours before vessel's expected arrival at port of loading.

Three days before the deadline, the charterers purported to terminate the contract for *force majeure*, claiming that there was no cargo available, and this was then accepted by the owners as a repudiation of the contract. In subsequent proceedings it was found by the arbitrators that at the relevant time there was no prospect of the vessel being ready to load by the set date, and that if there had been no repudiation the charterers would inevitably have exercised their right of cancellation under the clause in question.[21] Nevertheless, the Court of Appeal held by a majority[22] that this could not avail the charterers.[23] In this context, reference was made to

---

[17] See Ch 7.

[18] See Ch 7, para 7.15.

[19] *Maredelanto Compania Naviera SA v Bergbau-Handel GmbH (The Mihalis Angelos)* [1971] 1 QB 164 (CA).

[20] *The Mihalis Angelos*, 194–5 (n 19).

[21] *The Mihalis Angelos*, 171 (n 19).

[22] Edmund Davies and Megaw LJJ, Lord Denning MR dissenting.

[23] However, the charterers were held to have had the right to terminate on the alternative ground that the owners had already broken a condition of the contract, namely the provision that the vessel be 'expected ready to load' on 1 July: [1971] 1 QB 164, 193–4 (Denning MR), 200 (Edmund Davies LJ), and 205 (Megaw LJ). For the right to terminate on a ground other than that originally specified, see Ch 4, paras 4.37–4.41.

The Madeleine,[24] in which it was held by Roskill J in the Commercial Court that a clause allowing the charterers of a ship to cancel if the ship was not delivered by 10 May could not be exercised on the previous day. In the words of Roskill J:[25]

> For my part, I have great difficulty in seeing how, where there is an express right given to cancel if the vessel is not delivered by May 10, an implied right can concurrently exist to cancel under the clause at some earlier point of time, namely, when it becomes inevitable that the stated cancelling date will not be able to be attained by the ship...I would say that however reasonable it might be to imply [such] a term...it cannot be said to be necessary so to do for the purpose of giving business efficacy to the contract because the contract gives an express right to cancel at a certain date and not at any earlier time.

(2) Mode of exercise

In some cases the clause may provide for automatic termination in the event of a **8.07** relevant breach,[26] but normally the innocent party will at least be obliged to give notice of termination to the party in default, and may also require that the party in default be given the opportunity of remedying the breach in question.[27] In the past the courts have tended to construe these clauses strictly as against the party seeking to terminate.[28] In *The Pamela*[29] a charterparty provided for the payment of hire every fifteen days, and stated that in default of prompt payment the owners could give the charterers 48 hours' notice of withdrawal if payment was not received by the expiry of the deadline.[30] An instalment of hire that fell due on 6 November 1994 was not paid, and the owners duly served a notice in accordance with the contract, which the charterers complied with.[31] On 2 December 1994 a further instalment was not paid, and the owners served another notice, this time simply stating that the hire had not been paid and giving 48 hours' notice of withdrawal.[32] It was found by the arbitrators that though this second notice did not expressly give

---

[24] *Cheikh Boutros Selim El-Khoury v Ceylon Shipping Lines (The Madeleine)* [1967] 2 Lloyd's Rep 224 (QBD: Commercial Ct).

[25] *The Madeleine*, 241 (n 24); *Christie & Vesey Ltd v Maatschappij Tot Exploitatie van Schepen en Andere Zaken, Helvetia NV (The Helvetia-S)* [1960] 1 Lloyd's Rep 540 (QBD: Commercial Ct) 551 (Pearson J); *Afovos Shipping Co SA v R Pagnan & Flli (The Afovos)* [1983] 1 WLR 195 (HL) 199–201 (Lord Hailsham LC).

[26] See Carter, *Carter's Breach of Contract*, para 10-03 (n 1). Such clauses will not be applied literally unless very clear words are used, the reason being that otherwise the innocent party would be deprived of his or her right of affirmation, and the defaulting party would be entitled to take advantage of his or her own wrong; see *Kilmer v British Columbia Orchard Lands Ltd* [1913] AC 319 (JCPC–Canada); *Cheall v Association of Professional, Executive and Computer Staff* [1983] 2 AC 180 (HL); *More OG Romsdal Fylkesbatar AS v Demise Charterers of the Ship 'Jotunheim'* [2004] EWHC 671 (Comm), [2005] 1 Lloyd's Rep 181, para 30.

[27] As in *Gesner Investments Ltd v Bombadier Inc* [2011] EWCA Civ 1118.

[28] As in *Italmare Shipping Co v Oceantanker Co Inc (The Rio Sun)* [1981] 2 Lloyd's Rep 489 (CA).

[29] *Schelde Delta Shipping BV v Astarte Shipping BV (The Pamela)* [1995] CLC 1011 (QBD: Commercial Ct).

[30] *The Pamela*, 1012 (n 29).

[31] *The Pamela*, 1013 (n 29).

[32] *The Pamela*, 1013 (n 29).

the charterers the opportunity to remedy the breach, and therefore did not comply precisely with the requirements of the contract, the charterers must have realized its significance in the light of the previous dealings between the parties.[33] However, this was held by Gatehouse J to be neither here nor there.[34] In this connection reference was made to *The Afovos*,[35] where the importance of complying in these cases precisely with the contractual procedure was stressed by the Court of Appeal. In the words of Griffiths LJ:[36]

> Withdrawal is so serious a matter for the charterer that it is the duty of the owner to give a clear and unambiguous notice of his intention to withdraw the ship. It should state that payment has not been received and give the charterer 48 hours to pay or lose the ship...Of course no special wording is required but it is surely not too much to expect men of commerce dealing in huge sums to make their meaning clear.

8.08 A rather more relaxed approach to notices of this kind was taken by the House of Lords in *Mannai Investment Co Ltd v Eagle Star Life Assurance Co*,[37] where the crucial question was said to be the effect of the notice on a reasonable person in the position of the recipient. Though this case concerned a break clause in a lease rather than a termination clause as such, the principle was said to apply to notices of all kinds. In the words of Lord Steyn:[38]

> There is no justification for placing notices under a break clause in leases in a unique category. Making due allowance for contextual differences, such notices belong to the general class of unilateral notices served under contractual rights reserved, e.g. notices to quit, notices to determine licences and notices to complete... To those examples may be added notices under charter parties, contracts of affreightment, and so forth. Even if such notices under contractual rights reserved contain errors they may be valid if they are sufficiently clear and unambiguous to leave a reasonable recipient in no reasonable doubt as to how and when they are intended to operate. That test postulates that the reasonable recipient is left in no doubt that the right reserved is being exercised. It acknowledges the importance of such notices. The application of that test is principled and cannot cause any injustice to a recipient of the notice. I would gratefully adopt it.

8.09 However, the extent to which this heralds a different approach to termination clauses is open to doubt. In *The Li Hai*,[39] the question for the court was the effect of a notice served on the charterers telling them that hire had not been paid and that the ship would be withdrawn after the period specified. Once again the contract provided

---

[33] *The Pamela*, 1016 (n 29).
[34] *The Pamela*, 1017 (n 29).
[35] *Afovos Shipping Co SA v R Pagnan & Flli* [1982] 1 Lloyd's Rep 562 (CA).
[36] *Afovos Shipping v Pagnan & Flli*, 568 (n 35).
[37] [1997] AC 749 (HL) (Lord Steyn, Lord Hoffmann, and Lord Clyde, Lord Goff and Lord Jauncey dissenting); PV Baker, 'Reconstructing the Rules of Construction' (1998) 114 LQR 55.
[38] *Mannai Investment v Eagle Star*, 768 (n 37).
[39] *Western Bulk Carriers K/S v Li Hai Maritime Inc (The Li Hai)* [2005] EWHC 735 (Comm), [2005] 1 CLC 704.

that the charterers should be given the chance to rectify the breach,[40] and the question arose whether the notice was invalidated by its failure to refer to this possibility.[41] It was argued by the owners, on the basis of the *Mannai* case,[42] that all that was required was that the notice be sufficiently clear and unambiguous as to leave a reasonable recipient in no reasonable doubt as to how and when it was intended to operate, and that what mattered was how the notice would be understood by a reasonable person in the position of the charterers, not the precise wording of the notice.[43] However, the court held that though the rather 'formulaic' approach of Gatehouse J in *The Pamela* could no longer be upheld,[44] the notice still had to comply with the requirements of the contract. In the words of Jonathan Hirst QC:[45]

> The starting point must be the anti-technicality clause itself. What did it require? In this case the requirement was that the Owners gave '72 hours…official notice in writing and will not withdraw the vessel if the hire is paid or the alleged breach is rectified within the 72 hours allowed for notice from time the Charterers served such notice'. The language of the clause is somewhat foreshortened but its sense is clear enough. The notice must be official, that is formal, and in writing and it must put the charterers on notice that, unless they rectify their failure to pay hire within 72 hours, the vessel will be withdrawn…

In the present case, he concluded, the notice came nowhere near to complying with the contractual requirement for an ultimatum.[46] It simply stated that the vessel would be withdrawn and did not state how this consequence could be avoided. This was not enough to satisfy the requirements laid down by the contract. The moral of all this would seem to be clear; a party who wishes to rely on a notice of this sort should make sure that it complies with the contract to the letter, rather than relying on *Mannai Investment Co Ltd v Eagle Star Life Assurance Co* to cover up for any mistakes or omissions.

(3) Nature of breach

Where the contract gives a right to terminate for breaches of a certain description, it **8.10** will have to be shown that the breach meets that description for the right of termination to be exercised. Obviously it is up to the parties to decide what this should involve, and in theory at any rate the possibilities are unlimited. However, there are three situations here that deserve closer examination, the first being clauses which allow a general right of termination for breach, the second being clauses that allow termination for 'material' breach, and the third clauses which allow termination only if the breach is not remedied by the defaulting party.

---

[40] *The Li Hai*, para 3 (n 39).
[41] *The Li Hai*, para 70 (n 39).
[42] See para 8.08.
[43] [2005] EWHC 735 (Comm), [2005] 1 CLC 704, paras 84 and 86.
[44] *The Li Hai*, para 88 (n 39).
[45] *The Li Hai*, para 87 (n 39).
[46] *The Li Hai*, para 91 (n 39).

(a) General right of termination for breach

8.11   In some cases the contract may contain a clause which purports to allow termination for any breach whatsoever. The courts are obviously reluctant to take such clauses at their face value, as is seen in *The Athos*,[47] where a charterparty contained a standard form clause allowing termination failing regular and punctual payment of hire 'or on any breach of this charterparty'.[48] The Court of Appeal held that there had been no breach by the charterers on the facts, but went on to consider whether in any event the clause allowed the owners to terminate for any breach whatever, however trivial. The court held by a majority[49] that the clause could not be construed in such a way. As Stephenson LJ said, this was so unreasonable a construction that the court had to search for some other meaning, in order to avoid the clause being made 'arbitrary, capricious or fantastic'.[50] The words in question were subsequently interpreted by the House of Lords in *The Antaios*[51] as allowing termination only for *repudiatory* breach, Lord Diplock stating that if detailed semantic and syntactical analysis of words in a commercial contract was going to lead to a conclusion that flouts business commonsense, it must be made to yield to business commonsense.[52] Or, as Lord Reid said in another context, the more unreasonable a result the less likely that the parties intended it, and if they do intend it the more necessary it is that they make that intention abundantly clear.[53]

(b) Right of termination for 'material' breach

8.12   Another commonly used formula allows termination for 'material' breach.[54] A material breach in English law[55] is, in the words of Jackson LJ, 'more than trivial but need not be repudiatory'.[56] According to Neuberger J:[57] 'Whether a breach of

---

[47] *Telfair Shipping Corp v Athos Shipping Co SA (The Athos)* [1983] 1 Lloyd's Rep 127 (CA): Carter, *Carter's Breach of Contract*, para 3-10 (n 1).

[48] This was clause 5 of New York Produce Exchange Form.

[49] Kerr and Stephenson LJJ, Purchas LJ dissenting.

[50] [1983] 1 Lloyd's Rep 127, 145.

[51] *Antaios Compania Naviera SA v Salen Rederierna AB (The Antaios)* [1985] AC 191 (HL); Carter, *Carter's Breach of Contract*, para 3-10 (n 1).

[52] [1985] AC 191, 201; *Rice (t/a Garden Guardian) v Great Yarmouth LBC* [2003] TCLR 1 (CA); *Dominion Corporate Trustees Ltd v Debenhams Properties Ltd* [2010] EWHC 1193 (Ch), [2010] 23 EG 106; Peel, *Treitel*, para 18-062 (n 3).

[53] *L Schuler AG v Wickman Machine Tool Sales Ltd* [1974] AC 235 (HL) 251.

[54] Andrews et al, *Contractual Duties*, paras 9-018–9-028 (n 3).

[55] In Scots law, material breach is broadly equivalent to fundamental breach in that it gives rise to a right of termination or 'rescission' at common law: *Davie v Stark* (1876) 3 R 1114 (Court of Session), 1119; Scottish Law Commission, *Discussion Paper on Remedies for Breach of Contract* (No 109, 1999) para 2.9.

[56] *Mid Essex Hospital Services NHS Trust v Compass Group and Ireland Ltd (t/a Medirest)* [2013] EWCA Civ 200, para 126; *Crosstown Music Co 1 LLC v Rive Droite Music Ltd* [2009] EWHC 600 (Ch) para 99 (Mann J).

[57] *Glolite Ltd v Jasper Conran Ltd*, The Times, 28 January 1998, quoted by Andrews et al, *Contractual Duties*, para 9-024 (n 3). See also the dictum of the same judge in *Phoenix Media Ltd v Cobweb Information Ltd* (unreported, 16 May 2000) para 61; *Gallaher Intl Ltd v Tlais Enterprises Ltd* [2008] EWHC 804 (Comm) para 764 (Christopher Clarke J).

an agreement is "material" must depend on the facts of the particular case, including the nature of the terms and duration of the agreement in question, the nature of the breach and the consequences of the breach...' Again, according to Christopher Clarke J:[58] 'In assessing the materiality of any breach it is relevant to consider not only of what the breach consists but also the circumstances in which the breach arises, including any explanation given or apparent as to why it has occurred.' In this context the cases reveal a variety of factors at play, including not only the degree of the breach in the context of the contract as a whole,[59] but also the length of time the breach has persisted,[60] whether the breach was accidental or deliberate,[61] whether there has been a pattern of default in the past,[62] the reasons for the breach,[63] and its effect on the innocent party.[64] At the same time, the courts will consider whether the loss caused to the defaulting party by allowing termination is disproportionate to that caused to the innocent party by the breach in question.[65] As in the case of fundamental breach, there are no hard and fast rules of thumb in this context; as Neuberger J says, ultimately, all must depend on the facts of the particular case.[66]

(c) Opportunity to remedy breach

In many cases the right of termination will be made subject to a requirement that   **8.13**
the innocent party first give notice of the breach to the party in default, giving him or her the chance to remedy it within a certain period of time, if indeed it is capable of being remedied. For the defaulting party to take advantage of this, two requirements must be met; the breach must be remediable to start with, and the notice must be complied with within the time permitted.

---

[58] *Dalkia Utilities Services plc v Celtech International Ltd* [2006] EWHC 63 (Comm), [2006] 1 Lloyd's Rep 599, para 102; Andrews et al, *Contractual Duties*, para 9-020 (n 3).

[59] *Phoenix Media Ltd v Cobweb Information Ltd*, para 71 (n 57); *Fortman Holdings Ltd v Modem Holdings Ltd* [2001] EWCA Civ 1235, para 21; *Dalkia Utilities Services v Celtech Intl*, para 98 (n 58); *Crosstown Music Co 1 v Rive Droite Music*, paras 105, 106, 116, 122, and 130 (n 56); *VLM Holdings Ltd v Ravensworth Digital Services Ltd* [2013] EWHC 228 (Ch) para 89.

[60] *Phoenix Media v Cobweb Information*, para 71 (n 57); *Gallaher Intl v Tlais Enterprises*, para 644 (n 57); *Crosstown Music Co 1 v Rive Droite Music*, para 105 (n 56).

[61] *Phoenix Media v Cobweb Information*, para 67 (n 57); *Dalkia Utilities Services v Celtech Intl*, para 102 (n 58).

[62] *Crosstown Music Co 1 v Rive Droite Music*, para 116 (n 56).

[63] *Crosstown Music Co 1 v Rive Droite Music*, para 106 (n 56).

[64] *Phoenix Media v Cobweb Information*, 66 (n 57); *Tele2 International Card Co SA v Post Office Ltd* [2008] EWHC 158 (QB) para 79; *Force India Formula One Team Ltd v Etihad Airways PJSC* [2010] EWCA Civ 1051, [2011] ETMR 10; *Group Lotus plc and Lotus Cars Ltd v 1Malaysia Racing Team Sdn Bhd* [2011] EWHC 1366 (Ch), [2011] ETMR 62, para 357. This is particularly important where the parties are in a relationship of trust and confidence: *Phoenix Media Ltd v Cobweb Information Ltd*, para 60 (n 57); *Gallaher Intl v Tlais Enterprises*, para 644 (n 57); *Crosstown Music Co 1 v Rive Droite Music*, para 105 (n 56).

[65] *National Power plc v United Gas Co Ltd* (unreported, 3 July 1998 (Colman J)), cited by Andrews et al, *Contractual Duties* at para 9-025 (n 3); *Phoenix Media Ltd v Cobweb Information Ltd*, para 69 (n 57); *Gallaher Intl v Tlais Enterprises*, para 765 (n 57).

[66] See n 57.

8.14 **(i) Breach remediable** It can be argued at one level that a breach can never be remedied, for even if the failure is rectified, this cannot be done within the time stipulated for performance;[67] if it can, there is no breach to begin with. What the defaulting party can do, however, is to remedy the damage or loss caused by the breach. What precisely this involves was discussed at some length by Lord Reid in *L Schuler AG v Wickman Machine Tool Sales Ltd*:[68]

> The question then is what is meant in this context by the word 'remedy.' It could mean obviate or nullify the effect of a breach so that any damage already done is in some way made good. Or it could mean cure so that matters are put right for the future. I think that the latter is the more natural meaning. The word is commonly used in connection with diseases or ailments and they would normally be said to be remedied if they were cured although no cure can remove the past effect or result of the disease before the cure took place, and in general it can only be in a rare case that any remedy of something that has gone wrong in the performance of a continuing positive obligation will, in addition to putting it right for the future, remove or nullify damage already incurred before the remedy was applied. To restrict the meaning of remedy to cases where all damage past and future can be put right would leave hardly any scope at all for this clause. On the other hand, there are cases where it would seem a misuse of language to say that a breach can be remedied. For example, a breach . . . by disclosure of confidential information could not be said to be remedied by a promise not to do it again.

8.15 The question of whether a breach is remediable has often been discussed in the context of section 146(1) of the Law of Property Act 1925, which, as seen previously, provides that a lease cannot be forfeited for a breach of covenant without first serving a notice on the tenant specifying the breach, and requiring him or her to remedy it (if it is capable of remedy) or pay compensation (if it is not).[69] It was said by the Court of Appeal in *Expert Clothing Service & Sales Ltd v Hillgate House Ltd*[70] that the breach of a positive covenant, whether a continuing breach or a once-for-all breach, was ordinarily remediable by the performance of the covenant in question and the payment of compensation,[71] but breaches of negative covenants are more problematic. Indeed in *Governors of Rugby School v Tannahill*[72] MacKinnon J went so far as to suggest that such breaches could not be remedied as a matter of principle. In this case the breach consisted of allowing the premises to be used as a brothel. In the words of MacKinnon J:[73]

> I think there is a radical distinction between the two sorts of covenant. A promise to do a thing, if broken, can be remedied by the thing being done. But breach of

---

[67] *Hoffmann v Fineberg and ors* [1949] Ch 245 (Ch D), 253 (Harman J).
[68] [1974] AC 235 (HL) 248–50; Andrews et al, *Contractual Duties*, para 9-033 (n 3).
[69] See Ch 4, para 4.76.
[70] [1986] Ch 340 (CA).
[71] *Expert Clothing Service & Sales v Hillgate House*, 355 (Slade LJ) and 362 (O'Connor LJ) (n 70); *Peregrine Systems Ltd v Steria Ltd* [2004] EWHC 275, para 172 (Richard Seymour QC).
[72] [1934] KB 695; *Egerton v Esplanade Hotels Ltd* [1947] 2 All ER 88 (KBD); *Hoffmann v Fineberg and ors* [1949] Ch 245 (Ch D).
[73] [1934] KB 695, 701.

a promise not to do a thing cannot in any true sense be remedied; that which was done cannot be undone.

Whilst the Court of Appeal was not prepared to go this far,[74] the decision of MacKinnon J was upheld on the grounds that the effects of the breach could not be undone; as a result of the tenants' conduct, the premises had now acquired a bad name and their value had been considerably reduced as a result.[75] Similarly, where in *Force India Formula One Team Ltd v Etihad Airways PJSC*[76] a racing team had broken a sponsorship agreement by changing its name and the logo of its cars, it was held by the Court of Appeal that it was too late to remedy the breach; in the words of Rix LJ, the marketing genie could not be put back into the bottle![77]

(ii) **Remedying the breach**   Assuming the breach to be remediable in principle,   **8.16** it is up to the defaulting party to take whatever steps are necessary to comply with the notice and so avoid termination. Whether this has been done is said to be a question of fact.[78] If the notice is complied with, all well and good. If not, the consequences will depend on the procedure specified in the contract. In some cases termination may follow without further ado,[79] but in others further steps by the innocent party may be necessary;[80] for instance, the contract may allow him or her to deal with the subject matter of the contract in a specified way (say, for instance, by repossessing goods, or forfeiting a deposit) or may even require service of a further notice of some kind.

C. Multiple Termination Rights

Difficult problems can arise in this area of the law where a party enjoys the bene-   **8.17** fit of multiple termination rights; in particular, where he or she has the choice between express rights of termination and those which arise at common law.[81] In particular, the innocent party may seek to terminate but will not make it clear whether he or she is doing so under the express right or under the common law. Alternatively, he or she may purport to terminate under the express right, and when this is unsuccessful, may seek to rely on the common law as a backup. In the final

---

[74] [1935] 1 KB 87 (CA) 90 (Greer LJ), 92 (Maugham LJ), and 94 (Roche LJ).

[75] *Governors of Rugby School v Tannahill*, 91 (Greer LJ), 93 (Maugham LJ), and 94 (Roche LJ) (n 74). It would be different if the tenants neither knew nor had reason to know of the immoral user, and on being so apprised had immediately taken action to deal with it: *Glass v Kencakes* [1966] 1 QB 611 (QBD) (Paull J); *Patel v K & J Restaurants Ltd* [2010] EWCA Civ 1211, [2011] L & TR 6.

[76] [2010] EWCA Civ 1051, [2011] ETMR 10.

[77] *Force India Formula One Team v Etihad Airways*, para 108 (n 76); Andrews et al, *Contractual Duties*, para 9-029 (n 3).

[78] Carter, *Carter's Breach of Contract*, para 10-13 (n 1).

[79] Carter, *Carter's Breach of Contract*, para 10-15 (n 1); Carter calls this a 'self-executing' notice.

[80] Carter, *Carter's Breach of Contract*, para 10-15 (n 1).

[81] See JW Carter and Y Goh, 'Concurrent and Independent Rights to Terminate for Breach of Contract' (2010) 26 JCL 103. The discussion which follows is largely indebted to the analysis set out in this most valuable article, though it seeks to build on it in a number of respects.

pages of this chapter, the different ways in which multiple termination rights can coexist and the legal consequences to which this gives rise will be considered.

8.18 Express rights and common law rights may relate to one another in various different ways, for instance: (1) they may be mutually exclusive or mutually inclusive; (2) they may be available against the same promisor or against different promisors; (3) they may exist in series or in parallel; (4) they may relate to the same event or to different events; (5) they may be exercised in the same way or in different ways; and (6) they may have consistent or inconsistent consequences.

(1) Exclusive and inclusive rights

8.19 It is perfectly possible for a contract to set out an exhaustive code dealing with the circumstances in which termination may take place. Where this is done, the problem of multiple termination rights does not arise; the innocent party can only terminate under the express right and not otherwise. Given the need for certainty in the present context and the importance of contract planning, one would expect this situation to arise much more often than it does,[82] but the courts have been reluctant to conclude that express rights of termination were intended to exclude common law rights even where this was suggested by the contract. In *Dalkia Utilities Services plc v Celtech International Ltd*,[83] for instance, a contract for the construction of a power plant contained detailed terms allowing termination for material breach, including the following provision:[84] 'The consequences of termination set out in this clause represent the full extent of the parties' respective rights and remedies arising out of any termination save for those rights remedies and liabilities which arise prior to termination.' Despite this, it was held that the clause in question did not provide a 'complete code' as to the rights and remedies enjoyed by the parties in the event of termination, but only related to the express rights mentioned in the clause.[85] In particular, the clause was not sufficient to exclude the right of the parties to terminate for repudiation.[86] In this context reference was made to *Gilbert Ash (Northern) Ltd v Modern Engineering (Bristol) Ltd*,[87] where Lord Diplock set out his view in the following words:[88]

> It is, of course, open to parties to a contract for sale of goods or for work and labour or for both to exclude by express agreement a remedy for its breach which

---

[82] The attitude of the courts to this issue is criticized by Carter and Goh, who say that parties to a commercial contract do not go to all the bother of drawing up complex regimes for termination merely to supplement common law rights, and that this is one area in which the so-called presumption in favour of common law rights has been taken too far: Carter and Goh, 'Concurrent and Independent Rights', p 132 (n 81), and see para 8.27.

[83] [2006] EWHC 63 (Comm), [2006] 1 Lloyd's Rep 599.

[84] *Dalkia Utilities Services v Celtech Intl*, para 19 (n 83).

[85] *Dalkia Utilities Services v Celtech Intl*, para 20 (n 83).

[86] *Dalkia Utilities Services v Celtech Intl*, para 20 (n 83).

[87] [1974] AC 689 (HL).

[88] *Gilbert Ash v Modern Engineering*, 717 (n 87).

would otherwise arise by operation of law or such remedy may be excluded by usage binding upon the parties... But in construing such a contract one starts with the presumption that neither party intends to abandon any remedies for its breach arising by operation of law, and clear express words must be used in order to rebut this presumption.

The moral of this is that if the parties wish to make exhaustive provision in the contract for the circumstances in which termination may take place and to exclude the equivalent common law rights, this must be done in unambiguous terms.

(2) Same promisor or different promisors

Sometimes a contract involves more than two parties, and here the question can **8.20** arise of the extent to which termination in relation to one affects the other.[89] Here the general rule is that where parties enter into a contract involving different termination rights against different promisors, the fact that the innocent party enjoys a right of termination against one does not necessarily allow him or her to terminate as against the other.[90] Indeed, even where the innocent party is entitled to terminate against both parties in this scenario, he or she may prefer to terminate against one and affirm against the other, as for instance where the latter is the guarantor of the former's performance.[91] Though these cases may be extremely complex, they do not raise significant issues in the present context; rather, as will now be seen, the problems arise where the innocent party enjoys multiple rights against the *same* promisor.

(3) Rights of termination in series or in parallel

Where a contract runs over an extended period, it is quite possible for different **8.21** rights of termination to arise at different times, or, to adopt an electrical metaphor, in series.[92] The obvious example of this is an instalment contract for the sale of goods in which the buyer has the right to terminate for late delivery; if the seller delivers late on more than one occasion, each late delivery will give rise to a separate right of termination. This type of case gives rise to no particular problem in the

---

[89] Carter and Goh call these 'several' rights, that is to say, concurrent or independent termination rights available against different promisors or in relation to several parts of a contract: Carter and Goh, 'Concurrent and Independent Rights', p 109 (n 81).

[90] Carter and Goh, 'Concurrent and Independent Rights', p 109 (n 81), citing *Bank of NSW v Commonwealth Savings Bank of Australia* (1985) 6 FCR 524.

[91] As in *Moschi v Lep Air Services Ltd* [1973] AC 331; Carter and Goh, 'Concurrent and Independent Rights' (n 81).

[92] In this connection Carter and Goh refer to 'independent' and 'concurrent' rights, but go on to say that concurrent rights must arise from the same event: Carter and Goh, 'Concurrent and Independent Rights', p 108 (n 81). The electrical metaphor is adopted here as we need a different label so as to reflect the fact that a party can at the same time enjoy multiple termination rights related to different events: see para 8.22.

present context; though the buyer may enjoy multiple rights of termination, he or she never has more than one such right at any given time. In some cases, however, the innocent party enjoys two or more rights of termination at the same time; for instance a failure by the party in default to pay instalments may both give rise to a right of termination for repudiation and a right to terminate under an express clause. Here the rights are held concurrently, or as one might say, in parallel, and questions may then arise as to which right has been exercised, and as to whether the exercise of one right excludes the other.

(4) Same event or different events

8.22 Rights of termination that are independent or in series will necessarily arise from different events, but the converse is not necessarily the case; rights can be held in parallel both in relation to the same event and in relation to different events. An example of parallel rights being held in relation to the same event is given by Carter and Goh, where a buyer under a shipbuilding contract is given an express right to terminate if the builder fails to achieve two consecutive construction milestones on time; this may allow the buyer to invoke not only the express right but also the right to terminate for repudiation at common law.[93] An example of parallel rights in relation to different events is suggested by the facts of *The Mihalis Angelos*,[94] where a charterparty contained a clause stating that the ship was *expected* ready to load at the beginning of July 1965, and giving the charterers the right to cancel if the ship was not *actually* ready to load by 20 July. On 17 July the charterers purported to terminate the contract on the ground of *force majeure*, and when the owners claimed damages for unlawful repudiation sought to rely on the cancellation clause. It was held by the Court of Appeal that the charterers could not do this, as the right of cancellation had not yet accrued,[95] but that the charterers could justify their termination on a different ground, namely that the owners were already in breach of the 'expected ready to load' stipulation, which was a condition of the contract.[96] In the event, it was held here that the charterers had only one right of termination, but if they had waited three more days they would have had two, one in relation to the breach of condition and the other under the express clause. Indeed, given that the innocent party in these cases does not have to stipulate which right of termination he or she is relying on,[97] this is a matter of some importance; it is by no means unknown, as previously seen, for a party who purports to terminate on one ground to then justify their termination upon a totally different ground.[98]

---

[93] Carter and Goh, 'Concurrent and Independent Rights', pp 103–4 (n 81).

[94] *Maredelanto Compania Naviera SA v Bergbau-Handel GmbH (The Mihalis Angelos)* [1971] 1 QB 164 (CA).

[95] See para 8.06.

[96] [1971] 1 QB 164 (CA) 193–4 (Lord Denning MR), 200 (Edmund Davies LJ), and 205 (Megaw LJ).

[97] See para 8.24.

[98] See Ch 4, paras 4.39–4.41.

(5) Modes of exercise

As has been seen, the exercise of a common law right of termination requires no **8.23** more than the doing of some act inconsistent with the continuance of the contract;[99] no actual notice of termination need be served on the party in default, still less a notice in any particular form. There is nothing to prevent the parties to a contract from drafting an express right of termination in such terms, but more often, as previously seen, the exercise of such rights requires at least the giving of notice to the party in default, and quite possibly the chance to remedy the breach as well.[100] The question then arises of whether a party who serves such a notice can then turn round and rely on his or her common law rights. In principle, the law does seem to allow this. In *L Schuler AG v Wickman Machine Tool Sales Ltd*[101] the contract gave the defendants sole selling rights in relation to the claimants' machinery. The contract further provided: (1) a clause described as a 'condition' stating that the defendants should send representatives to key customers on a weekly basis, and (2) a clause allowing termination in relation to 'material' breaches which the defendants failed to remedy within sixty days. Following numerous breaches of the former, the claimants sought to exercise their right of termination under the latter, and when this was rejected by the arbitrators sought to argue that in any event they could terminate for breach of condition at common law. In the event it was held by the House of Lords that the term in question was not a condition at all,[102] but there was no suggestion that if it had been the common law right of termination would have been excluded merely by the purported exercise of the contractual right. However, an innocent party who serves a notice of this sort must at least give the party in default a reasonable opportunity to comply with it; and to that extent the exercise of the contractual right will exclude the common law right. If, however, the attempt to invoke the express right is unsuccessful, there is nothing to stop the innocent party then falling back on the common law right. [103]

(6) Consequences of exercise

Particular problems arise when parallel rights of termination against the same **8.24** promisor involve different remedial consequences. The most obvious example of this is where an express right of termination also provides for the payment of liquidated damages. Assuming that the innocent party is in a position to terminate either under the express right or at common law, to what extent does the exercise of one right rule out the other? On one hand, the innocent party can clearly terminate on either ground, but on the other there can be no question of him or her securing

---

[99] See Ch 4, para 4.19.
[100] See para 8.13.
[101] [1974] AC 235 (HL).
[102] See Ch 5, para 5.29.
[103] Carter and Goh, 'Concurrent and Independent Rights', p 112 (n 81).

both liquidated damages *and* the damages for loss of bargain that are allowed for termination at common law! At some stage a choice must be made, but where is the point of no return? Unfortunately the cases on this point are not at all consistent in their approach.

8.25 On one hand, there are cases which suggest that the exercise of the express right rules out the common law right; indeed, that that exercise amounts in some sense to an affirmation of the contract.[104] In *United Dominions Trust (Commercial) Ltd v Ennis*[105] a hire purchase contract contained a term allowing the hirer to terminate on payment of a substantial agreed sum. The hirer was unable to keep up his payments, and decided to exercise his right of termination by returning the car to the dealer from which he had obtained it. In fact this was the worst thing he could possibly have done, since this triggered an obligation to pay the agreed sum, and in the absence of any breach on his part the doctrine of penalties could give him no protection.[106] The claimants duly sued for the agreed sum, but the court managed to avoid awarding this by saying that the hirer had not terminated properly;[107] on the contrary, by returning the car to the dealer rather than to the finance company, as required by the literal words of the clause in question, he had repudiated the contract![108] However, this was not the end of the matter, since this conclusion in turn entailed the recovery of loss of bargain damages by the finance company, which they duly proceeded to claim. However, the Court of Appeal managed to avoid this consequence too by saying that though the hirer had indeed repudiated the contract the repudiation had not been accepted by the finance company; on the contrary, by suing for the agreed sum they had in essence elected to keep the contract on foot.[109] As Carter and Goh point out, this makes no sense, since it was only by purporting to terminate the contract that the finance company could claim the agreed sum in the first place.[110] Nevertheless, a similar result was reached in *Dalkia Utilities Services plc v Celtech International Ltd*,[111] where it was held that

---

[104] Certainly the courts will not be slow to hold that this is the case where a party relies on a right of termination not based on breach: see *Shell Egypt West Manzala GmbH v Dana Gas Egypt Ltd* [2010] EWHC 465 (Comm); *Cavenagh v William Evans Ltd* [2012] EWCA Civ 697, [2013] 1 WLR 238; Q Liu, 'The Puzzle of Unintended Acceptance of Repudiation' [2011] LMCLQ 4.

[105] [1968] 1 QB 54 (CA); Carter and Goh, 'Concurrent and Independent Rights', pp 115–17 (n 81).

[106] This was the consequence of the decision of the Court of Appeal in *Associated Distributors Ltd v Hall* [1938] 2 KB 83, which gave rise to the curious paradox that the person who kept the contract was worse off than the one who broke it.

[107] cf *Bridge v Campbell Discount Co Ltd* [1962] AC 600.

[108] [1968] 1 QB 54, 68 (Harman LJ) and 71 (Salmon LJ).

[109] *United Dominions Trust v Ennis*, 65–6 (Lord Denning MR), 68 (Harman LJ), and 71 (Salmon LJ) (n 108).

[110] Carter and Goh, 'Concurrent and Independent Rights', p 116 (n 81); *Stocznia Gdynia SA v Gearbulk Holdings Ltd* [2009] EWCA Civ 75, [2010] QB 27, [2009] 1 Lloyd's Rep 461, para 35 (Moore-Bick LJ); E Peel, 'Affirmation by Termination' (2009) 125 LQR 378.

[111] [2006] EWHC 63 (Comm), [2006] 1 Lloyd's Rep 599; Carter and Goh, 'Concurrent and Independent Rights', pp 120–2 (n 81).

the claimants had, by invoking an express right to terminate for material breach, barred themselves from claiming that the contract had been repudiated, it being said that the issue of a notice of termination under the express clause could not at the same time amount to the acceptance of a repudiation.[112] Again, this seems to put the point of no return too early. There is no reason in principle why the courts should not have held that the claimants were entitled to exercise both *rights* of termination, so long as they did not end up obtaining both of the *remedies* consequent on those rights.

On the other hand, there are cases which seem to give the innocent party much **8.26** more latitude. In *Stocznia Gdanska SA v Latvian Shipping Co (No 2)*[113] a shipbuilding contract for the construction of six vessels contained a clause allowing the builders, in the event of any instalment of the price remaining unpaid for twenty-one days, (a) to 'rescind' the contract, and (b) to complete the vessel and sell it off.[114] The buyers having subsequently repudiated the contract, the builders went ahead, completed the first two vessels, and sold them to a third party, but then sought to recover damages for loss of bargain on the contract as a whole. It was held by the Court of Appeal that whilst the buyers clearly could not be allowed to be compensated twice over, they could claim loss of bargain damages subject to the provisions of the clause.[115] Again, in *Stocznia Gdynia SA v Gearbulk Holdings Ltd*,[116] another shipbuilding case, the builders agreed to construct three ships for the buyers subject to (a) a clause allowing termination if the vessel was not completed 150 days after the delivery date, and (b) a 'refund guarantee' under which the builders agreed to refund all previous instalments of the purchase price.[117] When the builders failed to complete the ships, the buyers issued notices of termination and duly received payment under the refund guarantee. The question then arose of whether they could top this up, as it were, by claiming damages at common law. This in turn involved the question whether they had terminated under the express right or at common law.[118] It was held by the Court of Appeal that there was nothing in the contract to show that the parties intended to displace the right to terminate for breach at common law,[119] that the refund guarantee was not intended to operate in isolation or in a manner inconsistent with common law

---

[112] *Dalkia Utilities Services v Celtech Intl*, para 144 (Christopher Clarke J) (n 111).
[113] [2002] EWCA Civ 889, [2002] 2 Lloyd's Rep 436; Carter and Goh, 'Concurrent and Independent Rights', pp 117–20 (n 81).
[114] *Stocznia Gdanska v Latvian Shipping (No 2)*, para 58 (n 113).
[115] *Stocznia Gdanska v Latvian Shipping (No 2)*, para 83 (n 113).
[116] [2009] EWCA Civ 75, [2010] QB 27; Carter and Goh, 'Concurrent and Independent Rights', pp 122–5 (n 81).
[117] *Stocznia Gdynia v Gearbulk Holdings*, para 5 (n 116).
[118] In two cases the notices of termination referred specifically to the express clause, whilst in the third they purported to relate both to the express right and the common law right; *Stocznia Gdynia v Gearbulk Holdings*, para 45 (n 116).
[119] *Stocznia Gdynia v Gearbulk Holdings*, paras 18–20 (n 116).

rights,[120] and that the buyers' invocation of the express termination clause did not debar them from exercising those rights.[121] Whilst at first sight these cases seem to take a different approach from those discussed in paragraph 8.25, this can perhaps be explained on the ground that the remedies involved were not fundamentally inconsistent, and that therefore there was no need to choose between them.

8.27 While this is clearly a very complex area of the law, a lot of the complexity seems unnecessary, and it is hard to disagree with the criticism that the courts have got their emphasis wrong in allowing common law rights of termination to be exercised alongside those provided for in the contract. As Carter and Goh say, why should the parties go to all the bother of drawing up complex termination rules if the courts are then going to allow them to be circumvented in this way?[122] It is all very well to talk in terms of a presumption in favour of common law rights, but perhaps, at least in the commercial context, the presumption should be the other way round.

---

[120] *Stocznia Gdynia v Gearbulk Holdings*, paras 21–25 (n 116).
[121] *Stocznia Gdynia v Gearbulk Holdings*, paras 26–42 (n 116).
[122] Carter and Goh, 'Concurrent and Independent Rights', p 132 (n 81).

PART IV

TERMINATION AND AFFIRMATION

9

DISCHARGE OF PRIMARY OBLIGATIONS

The main effect of termination, broadly speaking, is as the word suggests; the con‑ **9.01**
tract is brought to an end, or cancelled, or discharged. However, these metaphors
cannot be carried too far.[1] As Lord Porter said, whilst it might be accurate to say
in some cases that the contract has come to an end or ceased to exist, a fuller and
more precise description is to say that the injured party is absolved from the future
performance of his obligations under the contract.[2] In the present chapter we shall
look more closely at what this involves.

A. Lord Diplock's Analysis

A useful starting point for the discussion is Lord Diplock's classic analysis of the ter‑ **9.02**
mination process in *Moschi v Lep Air Services Ltd*.[3] The main issue in this case con‑
cerned the extent to which a guarantor could be held liable for instalments payable
by the principal debtor after the contract had been terminated for repudiation,[4] but
in the course of his opinion Lord Diplock set out the basic contractual framework
within which this operated. In the words of Lord Diplock:[5]

> It is no doubt convenient to speak of a contract as being terminated or coming to an
> end when the party who is not in default exercises his right to treat it as rescinded.

---

[1] See Ch 1, para 1.36.
[2] *Heyman v Darwins Ltd* [1942] AC 356 (HL) 399; JW Carter, *Carter's Breach of Contract* (Hart, 2012) para 12-01.
[3] [1973] AC 331 (HL).
[4] For the extent to which such obligations survive termination, see further para 9.06.
[5] [1973] AC 331, 350.

But the law is concerned with the effect of that election upon those obligations of the parties of which the contract was the source, and this depends upon the nature of the particular obligation and upon which party promised to perform it. Generally speaking, the rescission of the contract puts an end to the primary obligations of the party not in default to perform any of his contractual promises which he has not already performed by the time of the rescission. It deprives him of any right as against the other party to continue to perform them. It does not give rise to any secondary obligation in substitution for a primary obligation which has come to an end. The primary obligations of the party in default to perform any of the promises made by him and remaining unperformed likewise come to an end as does his right to continue to perform them. But for his primary obligations there is substituted by operation of law a secondary obligation to pay to the other party a sum of money to compensate him for the loss he has sustained as a result of the failure to perform the primary obligations.

9.03 Though Lord Diplock speaks here in terms of 'rescission', his analysis clearly shows that he was not speaking of this in its narrow sense of rescission *ab initio*,[6] but of termination for breach.[7] The basic effect of this, in his analysis, is that both parties are discharged from their 'primary' obligations—that is to say, their outstanding obligations under the contract—but that in the case of the party in default this is replaced by a 'secondary' obligation to pay damages.

9.04 Whilst this certainly gives a better picture than does the crude metaphor of the contract 'coming to an end', it is still not entirely accurate. Thus, for instance, as Lord Diplock goes on to say, there may be exceptional primary obligations which continue to exist, namely obligations that are 'ancillary to the main purpose of the contract', such as arbitration clauses.[8] Indeed, even in relation to primary obligations that do not fall into this category, the rule is by no means absolute; in particular, as will be seen, such obligations will remain binding in so far as they have accrued at the time of termination.[9] However, Lord Diplock's analysis of termination in terms of primary and secondary obligations is nevertheless a sound one, and provides a useful basis on which to build the discussion which follows. In the remainder of this chapter we shall consider the effect of termination in so far as it applies to the primary obligations of the parties, including ancillary obligations. Then in Chapter 10 the secondary obligation which attaches to the party in default—that is to say, the obligation to compensate the innocent party for his or her loss—will be considered.

---

[6] See Ch 4, para 4.07; *McDonald v Dennys Lascelles Ltd* (1933) 48 CLR 457, 476–7 (Dixon J); *Johnson v Agnew* [1980] AC 367 (HL) 392–3 (Lord Wilberforce).

[7] Though Lord Diplock was here referring to termination at common law, he applies the same analysis to termination under an express contractual right: see *Stellar Chartering & Brokerage Inc v Efibanca-Ente Finanziario Interbancario SpA (The Span Terza (No 2))* [1984] 1 WLR 27 (HL) 33.

[8] [1973] AC 331 (HL) 350.

[9] See paras 9.07–9.18.

B. Primary Obligations in General

The first and most important consequence of termination is that both parties are, **9.05** as a general rule, discharged from their outstanding primary obligations under the contract. This applies both to the innocent party and to the party in default.

(1) Discharge of innocent party

According to Lord Diplock, termination 'puts an end to the primary obligations **9.06** of the party not in default to perform any of his contractual promises which he has not already performed by the time of the rescission',[10] or as he put it subsequently, 'the unperformed primary obligations of that…party are discharged'.[11] This has two aspects to it, one being that the innocent party is absolved from any obligation to perform his or her outstanding obligations in the future,[12] and the other that he or she is no longer bound to accept or to pay for future performance by the party in default.[13] This is well illustrated by *Cort and Gee v Ambergate Railway Company*,[14] where the plaintiffs agreed with the defendant company to manufacture and deliver a quantity of iron chairs on a monthly basis as specified by the contract. After about half the chairs had been delivered, the defendants indicated that they did not want any more. It was held that the plaintiffs could recover damages for non-acceptance without having to show that the balance of the chairs had been manufactured and tendered. In the words of Lord Campbell CJ:[15]

> We are of the opinion…that the jury were fully justified upon the evidence in finding that the plaintiffs were ready and willing to perform the contract, although they never made and tendered the residue of the chairs…What more can reasonably be required by the parties for whom the goods are to be manufactured? If, having accepted a part, they are unable to pay for the residue, and have resolved not to accept them, no benefit can accrue to them from a useless waste of materials and labour, which might possibly enhance the measure of damages to be awarded against them.

---

[10] [1973] AC 331 (HL) 350.

[11] *Photo Production Ltd v Securicor Transport Ltd* [1980] AC 827 (HL) 849; *Howard-Jones v Tate* [2011] EWCA Civ 1330, [2012] 1 P & CR 11, paras 15–16.

[12] *General Billposting Co Ltd v Atkinson* [1909] AC 118 (HL); *Afovos Shipping Co SA v Pagnan & Flli (The Afovos)* [1983] 1 WLR 195 (HL) 203 (Lord Diplock); *Rock Refrigeration Ltd v Jones* [1997] ICR 938 (CA); *Dalkia Utilities Services plc v Celtech Intl Ltd* [2006] EWHC 63 (Comm), [2006] 1 Lloyd's Rep 599, para 143 (Clarke J); *SCI (Sales Curve Interactive) Ltd v Titus Sarl* [2001] EWCA Civ 591, [2001] 2 All ER (Comm) 416; *Geys v Société Générale* [2012] UKSC 63, [2013] 1 AC 523, para 113 (Lord Sumption).

[13] E Peel, *Treitel: The Law of Contract* (13th edn, Sweet & Maxwell, 2011) para 18-010; *Protea Leasing Ltd v Royal Air Cambodge Co Ltd* [2002] EWHC 2731 (Comm) para 30; *Howard-Jones v Tate* [2011] EWCA Civ 1330, [2012] 1 P & CR 11, para 30.

[14] *Cort and Gee v Ambergate, Nottingham and Boston and Eastern Junction Rly Co* (1851) 17 QB 127, 117 ER 1229.

[15] (1851) 17 QB 127, 144, 117 ER 1229, 1236.

Again, in *Thompson v Corroon*[16] the defendants granted the plaintiffs an option to purchase land and to construct houses on it. It was held by the Privy Council that the plaintiffs could not exercise the option to purchase when they had failed to construct any of the houses. In the words of Lord Lowry:[17]

> A breach, no matter what form it takes, always entitles the innocent party to maintain an action for damages, but the breach does not always discharge the contract. One result which follows from a breach which is sufficiently serious to amount to a discharge is that the party not in default, in addition to suing for damages, may refuse to perform the obligations that he has undertaken.

(2) Discharge of party in default

9.07 However, that is not all. Though dicta in some of the cases tend, for obvious reasons, to lay stress on termination as discharging the primary obligations of the innocent party,[18] the same applies no less to the party in default,[19] the only difference being that in the latter case there is substituted a secondary obligation to pay damages. This is well illustrated by *Ward v Bignall*,[20] a case involving the sale of two cars. The buyer having repudiated the contract, the seller exercised his right of resale under section 48 of the Sale of Goods Act 1893 and then sought to claim from the buyer a sum equivalent to the contract price less the money realized from the resale. However, it was held by the Court of Appeal that this claim was misconceived. By reselling the goods under section 48 the seller had effectively elected to terminate the contract, and in doing so had discharged the buyers from any obligation to pay the price; rather, the appropriate claim would be one for damages for non-acceptance. In the words of Diplock LJ:[21]

> ...[An] unpaid seller who resells the goods before the property has passed puts it out of his power to perform his primary obligation to the buyer to transfer the property in the goods to the buyer and, whether or not the property has already passed, to deliver up possession of the goods to the buyer. By making the act of resale one which the unpaid seller is entitled to perform, the subsection empowers the seller by his conduct in doing that act to exercise his right to treat the contract as repudiated by the buyer...with the consequence that the buyer is discharged from any further liability to perform his primary obligation to pay the purchase price, and becomes subject to the secondary obligation to pay damages for the non-acceptance of the goods.

---

[16] (1993) 66 P & CR 445 (JCPC–West Indies).

[17] *Thompson v Corroon*, 459 (n 16).

[18] *General Billposting Co Ltd v Atkinson* [1909] AC 118 (HL) 122 (Lord Collins); *Heyman v Darwins* [1942] AC 356 (HL) 399 (Lord Porter); *Fibrosa Spolka Ackynja v Fairbairn Lawson Combe Barbour Ltd* [1943] AC 32 (HL) 53 (Lord Atkin); Carter, *Carter's Breach of Contract*, para 12-02 (n 2).

[19] *Moschi v Lep Air Services* [1973] AC 331 (HL) 350 (Lord Diplock); *Photo Production Ltd v Securicor Transport Ltd* [1980] AC 827 (HL) 849 (Lord Diplock); *Hurst v Bryk* [1999] Ch 1 (CA) 21 (Hobhouse LJ).

[20] [1967] 1 QB 534 (CA).

[21] *Ward v Bignall*, 550 (n 20).

A similar result was reached in *FJ Bloemen Pty Ltd v Council of the City of Gold Coast*,[22] where the defendant council purported to terminate a contract with the claimants for the construction of a sewage plant. The dispute went to arbitration, where an award was made in favour of the claimants. The claimants then sought to recover interest on the award on the basis of a provision in the contract. Once again it was held by the Privy Council that the claim was misconceived. It was clear from the facts not only that the defendants had repudiated the contract, but that the claimants had accepted the repudiation. Since the clause providing for interest was essentially a primary obligation of the contract, the defendants could no longer be obliged to perform it.[23] The innocent party cannot have it both ways by terminating the contract but still demanding performance from the party in default.

C. Accrued Obligations

Though Lord Diplock speaks in terms of the primary obligations of both parties **9.08** being discharged in so far as they are not already performed at the time of termination,[24] this is not always the case. On the contrary, such obligations can still remain binding in so far as they have already accrued.[25] Given that most of the cases on this point concern obligations to pay money,[26] the issue here is the extent to which either party can sue for the relevant sum as a liquidated debt despite termination having taken place.[27] The law on this point is somewhat complex and uncertain, but a number of principles emerge.

(1) Time for performance irrelevant

The first point to note is that it is of no consequence in this connection whether or **9.09** not the time for performance of the obligation has arrived.[28] Thus in some cases the obligation may be discharged even though the time for performance may have passed. Say, for instance, a contract for the sale of land provides for payment of the purchase price on a certain day prior to conveyance. If the vendor terminates, there can be no question of him or her suing for the price even though the relevant date may have passed; were it otherwise, the vendor would end up with the land and the price as well.[29] On the other hand, there are cases where a future obligation

---

[22] [1973] AC 115 (JCPC–Australia).

[23] *Bloemen Pty v Council of the City of Gold Coast*, 126–7 (n 22).

[24] See para 9.02.

[25] N Andrews, M Clarke, A Tettenborn, and G Virgo, *Contractual Duties: Performance, Breach, Termination and Remedies* (Sweet & Maxwell, 2011) para 13-010.

[26] Carter, *Carter's Breach of Contract*, para 13-15 (n 2); for an exception to this, see *Government of Newfoundland v Newfoundland Rly Co* (1888) 13 App Cas 199 (JCPC–Canada).

[27] JW Carter and GJ Tolhurst, 'Recovery of Contract Debts following Termination for Breach' (2009) 25 JCL 191.

[28] Carter, *Carter's Breach of Contract*, para 13-16 (n 2).

[29] *McDonald v Dennys Lascelles* (1933) 48 CLR 457.

will survive termination. Say, for instance, a contract of employment provides for the payment of wages on a weekly basis, with the employer keeping one week's wages in hand. This means that the employee will be paid for a week's work not at the end of that week, but at the end of the following week. If the employee is dismissed at the end of the first week, this will not prevent him or her recovering the outstanding wages a week later. The issue in these cases is not whether the time for performance has passed or not, but whether the party in question has furnished the agreed return for the obligation in question. As Dixon and Evatt JJ put it in *Westralian Farmers Ltd v Commonwealth Agricultural Service Engineers Ltd*:[30]

> In general the termination of an executory agreement out of the performance of which pecuniary demands may arise imports that, just as on the one side no further acts of performance can be required, so, on the other side, no liability can be brought into existence if it depends upon a further act of performance. If the title to rights consists of vestitive facts which would result from the further execution of the contract but which have not been brought about before the agreement terminates, the rights cannot arise. But if all the facts have occurred which entitle one party to such a right as a debt, a distinct chose in action which for many purposes is conceived as possessing proprietary characteristics, the fact that the right to payment is future or is contingent upon some event, not involving further performance of the contract, does not prevent it maturing into an immediately enforceable obligation.

In other words, the key question is not whether the *time* for the performance has *arrived*; it is whether the *right* to the performance has been *earned*.

(2) Right to performance earned

9.10 The crucial question is therefore whether, in the words of Carter, the agreed return for payment has been provided prior to termination.[31] The classic statement of the law here is from the judgment of Dixon J in *McDonald v Dennys Lascelles*:[32]

> When a party to a simple contract, upon a breach by the other contracting party of a condition of the contract, elects to treat the contract as no longer binding upon him, the contract is not rescinded as from the beginning. Both parties are discharged from further performance of the contract, but rights are not divested or discharged which have already been unconditionally acquired. Rights and obligations which arise from the partial execution of the contract and causes of action which have accrued from its breach alike continue unaffected.

Whether rights have been 'unconditionally acquired' in this sense depends on a number of factors, with the cases on the point falling into a number of different categories.

---

[30] (1936) CLR 361, 380; Carter, *Carter's Breach of Contract*, para 13-27 (n 2).
[31] Carter, *Carter's Breach of Contract*, para 13-15 (n 2).
[32] (1933) CLR 457, 476–7; *Johnson v Agnew* [1980] AC 367 (HL) 396 (Lord Wilberforce); *Bank of Boston Connecticut v European Grain and Shipping Ltd (The Dominique)* [1989] AC 1056 (HL) 1099 (Lord Brandon); *Hurst v Bryk* [2002] 1 AC 185 (HL) 193 (Lord Millett); *Collidge v Freeport plc* [2007] EWHC 1216 (QB) para 9 (Jack J) affd [2008] EWCA Civ 485, [2008] IRLR 697.

(a) Periodical payments for services rendered

The simplest category of cases is where the contract provides for a periodical pay- **9.11** ment in return for a service to be rendered by the other party.[33] Thus, for instance, a lease or licence may provide for periodic payments of rent in return for the right to occupy the property; a contract of hire or hire purchase may provide for periodic payments of hire in return for the possession and use of the goods; a contract of employment may provide for periodic payments of wages in return for the work done. Where such a contract is terminated by either party the landlord, or owner, or employee as the case may be, is entitled to recover any outstanding payments for which the agreed return has been furnished. In *Taylor v Laird*[34] the plaintiff contracted to serve the defendant as captain of his ship for an expedition to explore the River Niger at a rate of £50 per month, but after sailing some way up the river refused to go any further and abandoned his command. It was held nevertheless that he was entitled to recover his arrears of wages in respect of the time served, and that any loss sustained by the defendants could only sound in damages. In the words of Pollock CB, the contract gave a cause of action as each month accrued, which, once vested, was not subsequently lost or divested by the plaintiff's desertion or abandonment of his contract.[35] Similarly, in *Brooks v Beirnstein*[36] it was held that the repossession of goods by the owner under a contract of hire purchase did not destroy his right to recover arrears of hire outstanding at the time of termination; since in essence the contract was one of hire coupled with an option to purchase at the end of the relevant period, the hirer was bound to pay for the use of the goods during the time he had them in his possession. Similar principles apply in the context of time charterparties,[37] leases,[38] and other contracts of this sort.[39] Since termination is not retrospective, this applies even where the person claiming payment was in default at the time when the payment was earned,[40] though obviously in such cases the other party will have a counterclaim in damages.

---

[33] Carter, *Carter's Breach of Contract*, para 13-34 (n 2).

[34] (1856) 1 H & N 266, 156 ER 1203; *Hartley v Harman* (1840) 11 A & E 798, 113 ER 617; *Button v Thompson* (1869) LR 4 CP 330; *Healey v Société Anonyme Française Rubastic* [1917] 1 KB 946; *Fassihi and ors v Item Software UK Ltd* [2004] EWCA Civ 1244, [2004] BCC 994 (CA).

[35] (1856) 1 H & N 266, 273, 156 ER 1203, 1206.

[36] [1909] 1 KB 98; *Financings Ltd v Baldock* [1963] 2 QB 104 (CA) 111 (Lord Denning MR).

[37] *Leslie Shipping Co v Welstead (The Raithwaite)* [1921] 3 KB 420 (KBD).

[38] *Jones v Carter* (1846) 15 M & W 718, 153 ER 1040; *Canas Property Co Ltd v KL Television Services Ltd* [1970] 2 QB 433 (CA) 442 (Lord Denning MR); *Zea Star Shipping Co SA v Parley Augustsson* [1984] 2 Lloyd's Rep 605n (QBD: Admin Ct) 607 (Sheen J).

[39] *Odffell Seachem A/S v Continental des Petroles et D'Investissements* [2004] EWHC 2929 (Comm), [2005] 1 Lloyd's 275 (accrued claim for demurrage). In *Hurst v Bryk* [2002] AC 185 (HL) it was held that, assuming a partnership could be terminated by repudiation and acceptance, the partner in question still remained liable to contribute towards any liabilities of the firm incurred or assumed prior to termination, as these had already accrued at the relevant time. This assumption was held to be wrong in *Mullins v Lawton* [2002] EWHC 2761 (Ch), [2003] Ch 250, but this does not affect the point presently at issue; see Andrews et al, *Contractual Duties*, para 13-010 (n 25).

[40] AS Burrows et al (eds), *Chitty on Contracts* (31st edn, Sweet & Maxwell, 2012) para 39-191; *Ramsden v David Sharratt & Sons Ltd* (1930) 35 Com Cas 314 (HL).

(b) Other severable contracts

9.12 Similar rules apply to other kinds of severable contract where the payment is in return for a given quantity of goods supplied or a given amount of work done.[41] Thus in the context of a sale of goods by instalments, section 31(2) of the Sale of Goods Act 1979 draws a distinction between 'severable' breaches giving rise to a claim for damages, and breaches that constitute 'a repudiation of the whole contract'. In the latter case the innocent party may terminate, but the buyer remains liable to pay for any instalments that have been delivered and accepted. This is illustrated by *Mersey Steel & Iron Co Ltd v Naylor, Benzon & Co*,[42] which involved a contract for the sale of steel in five monthly instalments. After the sellers had delivered some of the goods a winding-up petition was brought, and the buyers—who were acting on erroneous legal advice—refused to pay the price due without the sanction of the court. The sellers then treated this as an unlawful repudiation of the contract and refused to make any further deliveries. As we have seen, the court decided that the buyers' conduct did not amount to unlawful repudiation,[43] but they still remained liable to pay the price for the goods delivered subject to the right to set off the damages due to them.[44] In the same way, an agent who is lawfully dismissed from employment may nevertheless recover commission earned on business done prior to his or her dismissal,[45] and an employee who is paid on a piecework basis may recover for work done in the same manner.[46] Indeed, the principle is not confined to payments of money; thus where in *Government of Newfoundland v Newfoundland Railway Co*[47] the government agreed to transfer a certain amount of land to the defendants in return for every mile of railway constructed, the obligation to do so remained even though the defendants were unable to complete the full distance contracted for.

(c) Instalments of purchase price

9.13 Sometimes a contract provides for the payment of advance instalments of the purchase price. Where the contract is severable, in the sense that a particular part of the consideration is supplied for each instalment, there is no problem. However, what if it is not? The general rule for non-severable contracts is that the contract price is only earned by complete performance,[48] or at any rate by substantial

---

[41] Carter, *Carter's Breach of Contract*, paras 13-20 and 13-32–13-33 (n 2).

[42] (1884) 9 App Cas 434 (HL).

[43] See Ch 7, para 7.23.

[44] (1882) 9 QBD 648 (CA); affd (1884) 9 App Cas 434 (HL).

[45] *Boston Deep Sea Fishing & Ice Co v Ansell* (1889) 39 Ch D 339 (CA) 352 (Cotton LJ) and 366–7 (Bowen LJ).

[46] *Steele v Tardiani* (1946) 72 CLR 386; Carter, *Carter's Breach of Contract*, para 13-20 (n 2); cf *And So to Bed Ltd v Dixon* (Ch D, 21 November 2000) (Official Transcript) para 28 (David Donaldson QC) (payment of outstanding royalties).

[47] (1888) 13 App Cas 199 (JCPC–Canada); Carter, *Carter's Breach of Contract*, para 13-32 (n 2).

[48] *Cutter v Powell* (1795) 6 TR 320, 101 ER 573; *Sumpter v Hedges* [1898] 1 QB 673 (CA).

performance,[49] so on the basis of the principles discussed previously, the party concerned should not be able to recover anything at all. This was certainly the approach of the High Court of Australia in *McDonald v Dennys Lascelles* itself,[50] where the assignees of the vendors under a contract of sale sued a guarantor following the failure of the purchasers to pay an advance instalment of the purchase price. The contract was subsequently repudiated by the purchasers, and the question then arose as to what effect this had on the obligations of the purchasers, and of the guarantor, to pay the outstanding instalment. The court held by a majority[51] that the vendors could not recover the sum in question as an accrued debt. Whether or not the purchasers' repudiation had been justified, that repudiation had been accepted by the vendors and their assignees.[52] Though some of the price may have been payable in advance, this was only on the basis that title to the property would eventually be conveyed, and having accepted the repudiation the vendors were no longer ready or willing to do this.[53] In the words of Parke B, they could not have both the land and its value too.[54]

This decision was subsequently cited by the House of Lords in the difficult case **9.14** of *Hyundai Heavy Industries Ltd v Papadopoulos*,[55] where, however, the builders of a ship were held entitled to recover an outstanding instalment of the price from guarantors even though they had already terminated the contract with the buyers for failure to pay that very instalment. The House of Lords held unanimously that the guarantors remained liable for the instalment in question even if the buyers of the ship were not,[56] but three members of the Committee were of the opinion that the buyers themselves were not discharged either.[57] According to Viscount Dilhorne and Lord Fraser, this was not merely a contract for the sale of the ship, but was more akin to a building contract or a contract for the supply of a service,[58] where the consideration for the payment had already been provided before the payment in

---

[49] *Hoenig v Isaacs* [1952] 2 All ER 176 (CA); *Bolton v Mahadeva* [1972] 1 WLR 1009 (CA).

[50] (1933) 48 CLR 457.

[51] Rich, Starke, Dixon, and McTiernan JJ, Evatt J dissenting.

[52] (1933) 48 CLR 457, 469 (Starke J) and 479 (Dixon J).

[53] (1933) 48 CLR 457, 469 (Starke J) and 479 (Dixon J).

[54] *Laird v Pim* (1841) 7 M & W 478, 480, 151 ER 854, 855.

[55] [1980] 1 WLR 1129 (HL); *Brown v Langwoods Photo Stores* [1991] 1 NZLR 173; *Azimut-Benetti SpA v Healey* [2010] EWHC 2234 (Comm), [2011] 1 Lloyd's Rep 43, para 34 (Blair J).

[56] *Hyundai v Papadopoulos*, 1137–8 (Viscount Dilhorne), 1141–2 (Lord Edmund-Davies), 1148–9 (Lord Fraser), 1153 (Lord Russell), and 1153 (Lord Keith) (n 55).

[57] *Hyundai v Papadopoulos*, 1134–7 (Viscount Dilhorne), 1140–1 (Lord Edmund-Davies), and 1145–8 (Lord Fraser) (n 55). Lord Russell (1152–3) and Lord Keith (1153) were unpersuaded on the matter. It is perhaps significant that Lord Diplock did not sit on this case; if he had done so, the analysis of the issues might have been more precise.

[58] *Hyundai v Papadopoulos*, 1134 (Viscount Dilhorne) and 1148 (Lord Fraser) (n 55); J Beatson, 'Discharge for Breach: the Position of Instalments, Deposits and other Payments due before Completion' (1981) 97 LQR 389, 397.

question became due.[59] Lord Edmund-Davies went even further, suggesting that whether or not consideration had been provided, the termination of the contract did not affect rights that had already accrued.[60] These differences of approach, combined with the reasoning of the High Court of Australia in *McDonald v Dennys Lascelles*,[61] make the law difficult to state with any precision, but there are two crucial questions that have to be asked in cases of this sort.

9.15 (i) **Total failure of consideration** The first is whether or not the termination of the contract has given rise to a total failure of consideration for the party from whom the payment is due. Thus, for instance, a seller of goods or of land who terminates will get his or her property back, and it would therefore on the face of it be inconsistent if he or she could also recover part of the price. Indeed, in such circumstances the law certainly allows for the recovery of such a payment where it has been made,[62] and it would therefore be odd to say the least if the other party could sue for it where it had not.[63] Whether a total failure of consideration has occurred in this context depends on whether the party claiming payment has received any part of the benefit bargained for.[64] The fact that he or she may have received some other benefit is neither here nor there.[65] On the other hand, where the contract on its proper construction so provides, the relevant benefit can include steps taken towards performing the contract, whether or not these were, in fact, of any value to the party from whom the payment is claimed. This was the approach adopted by the House of Lords in *Stocznia Gdanska SA v Latvian Shipping Co*,[66] another case involving the recovery of instalments of the purchase

---

[59] Indeed, Lord Fraser made a point of saying (*Hyundai v Papadopoulos*, 1148 (n 55)) that though the buyer had not actually enjoyed any benefit from the work done by the builders, it had to be assumed in the absence of evidence to the contrary that such work had been done on the faith of the buyer's promise to pay the instalments on the due dates. This reasoning has been criticized on the grounds that this was essentially an entire contract, that the consideration for the price was not furnished until the ship was complete, and that the builders should therefore have been left to their claim in damages: Carter, *Carter's Breach of Contract*, para 13-37 (n 2). However, a similar line of argument was followed by the House of Lords in *Stocznia Gdanska SA v Latvian Shipping Co* [1998] 1 WLR 574, discussed at para 9.15.

[60] *Hyundai v Papadopoulos*, 1142 (Lord Edmund-Davies) (n 55); Beatson, 'Discharge for Breach' (n 58).

[61] (1933) 48 CLR 457; see para 9.09.

[62] *Palmer v Temple* (1839) 9 A & E 508, 520, 112 ER 1304, 1308 (Lord Denman); *Dies v British and Intl Mining and Finance Co Ltd* [1939] 1 KB 724, 742 (Stable J); *Mayson v Clouet* [1924] AC 980 (JCPC–Singapore); *Stockloser v Johnson* [1954] 1 QB 476 (CA) 489–90 (Denning LJ). The position is different if the contract specifically provides for forfeiture of the advance payment: *Cadogan Petroleum Holdings Ltd v Global Process Systems LLC* [2013] EWHC 241 (Comm), but even here the courts have jurisdiction to grant relief against the forfeiture in appropriate cases: *Re Dagenham (Thames) Dock Co, ex p Hulse* (1872–73) LR 8 Ch App 1022; see Ch 4, para 4.79.

[63] Carter, *Carter's Breach of Contract*, para 13-39 (n 2).

[64] *Rover Intl Film Sales Ltd v Cannon Film Sales Ltd* [1989] 1 WLR 912 (CA).

[65] *Rowland v Divall* [1923] 2 KB 500 (CA); *Comptoir d'Achat et de Vente du Boerenbond Belge SA v Luis de Ridder Limitada (The Julia)* [1949] AC 293 (HL).

[66] [1998] 1 WLR 574 (HL); G McMeel, 'Construction and Failure of Consideration—the Primacy of Contract' [1998] LMCLQ 308; J Beatson and GJ Tolhurst, 'Debt, Damages and

price in relation to a shipbuilding contract which had been subsequently terminated. There Lord Goff drew a distinction between simple contracts of sale, where the sole consideration for the payment was the transfer of property in the goods, and contracts for work and materials, where the consideration included the carrying out of preparatory work.[67] Since the case in question fell into the latter category rather than the former, it was held that the outstanding instalments could be recovered. In the words of Lord Goff:[68]

> ...failure of consideration does not depend upon the question whether the promisee has or has not *received* anything under the contract...Indeed, if that were so, in cases in which the promisor undertakes to do work or render services which confer no direct benefit on the promisee, for example where he undertakes to paint the promisee's daughter's house, no consideration would ever be furnished for the promisee's payment. In truth, the test is not whether the promisee has received a specific benefit, but rather whether the promisor has performed any part of the contractual duties in respect of which the payment is due.

(ii) Express provision in contract This principle is, however, subject to one key **9.16** qualification. Even where there would appear to have been a total failure of consideration, the outstanding sums may still be recoverable if the contract contains an express provision to that effect. In *Cadogan Petroleum Holdings Ltd v Global Process Systems LLC*[69] a settlement agreement made in relation to the sale of two gas stripping plants provided for payment of the price in instalments. The agreement also included a provision (clause 22) allowing the sellers to terminate for default, which was expressed to be without prejudice to any accrued rights. The sellers having terminated under this clause, the question then arose of whether they could recover the arrears of instalments outstanding at the relevant time. It was held that any claim based on failure of consideration was excluded here by the express words of the contract, and that any unconscionability that might arise should be addressed in the context of the power of the courts to relieve against forfeiture.[70] In the words of Eder J:[71]

> ...I am prepared to assume (without deciding the point) that this is a case where it might be said that there was here a failure of consideration in the nature of part performance for which the particular instalments were payable. Nevertheless...in a contractual case, if a contract provides that one party can obtain or retain a benefit even if a contractual provision for termination is exercised, there has been no relevant failure of consideration...Further, in any event, where the contract has explicitly provided for the circumstances in which benefits will be or will not be

---

Restitution' [1998] CLJ 253; JW Carter, 'Shipbuilding Contracts—not Quite the Final Chapter' (1998) 13 JCL 156.

[67] *Stocznia Gdanska v Latvian Shipping*, 588 (n 66).

[68] *Stocznia Gdanska v Latvian Shipping*, 588 (emphasis in original) (n 66).

[69] [2013] EWHC 241 (Comm).

[70] *Cadogan v Global Process Systems*, para 20 (n 69).

[71] *Cadogan v Global Process Systems*, para 27 (emphasis in original) (n 69).

returned, its provisions govern...Here, for the reasons given above, it is my conclusion that the contract expressly governed the matter and provided that accrued rights should *not* be affected by rescission under clause 22. Accordingly, if I am right with regard to the proper construction of the Sale Agreement, there is no room for the actual or putative restitutionary claim on which [the defendant] relies.

Though this might on the face of it seem counter-intuitive, it made good commercial sense in the context of a situation where the parties enjoyed an ongoing business relationship despite the exercise of the termination right.[72] In the light of this, in the words of Eder J, it would be 'uncommercial in the extreme' that the seller's accrued rights to the monies paid and outstanding immediately prior to termination should in effect self-destruct and be replaced with a claim in damages when the right to terminate was exercised.[73]

(d) Deposits

9.17   Different considerations apply where the contract provides for a deposit which is due but unpaid at the time of termination. The law treats deposits differently from advance payments of the price, the reason being that a deposit is intended by its very nature to be an earnest of performance.[74] This means that as a general rule the innocent party following termination may forfeit a deposit that has already been paid,[75] not only where the contract provides to this effect[76] but even where it does not.[77] Whether the innocent party may recover an unpaid deposit in such circumstances is less clear. In *Dewar v Mintoft*[78] a contract for the sale of land provided for the payment of a deposit which was to be forfeited in the event of default. The purchaser then repudiated the contract before paying the deposit. The main issue in the case was whether a sufficient memorandum existed for the purpose of the Statute of Frauds, but it was held by Horridge J that the vendor could recover the sum in question as a contract debt, the reasoning being that the purchaser could not put himself in a better position by refusing to pay the deposit than if the deposit had in fact been paid.[79] In *Lowe v Hope*,[80] however, Pennycuick J refused to follow

---

[72] *Cadogan v Global Process Systems*, para 20 (n 69).

[73] *Cadogan v Global Process Systems*, para 20 (n 69).

[74] *Howe v Smith* (1884) 27 Ch D 89 (CA) 94 (Cotton LJ) and 101 (Fry LJ); *Soper v Arnold* (1889) 14 App Cas 429 (HL), 435 (Lord Macnaghten).

[75] *Howe v Smith* (1884) 27 Ch D 89 (CA); *Smith v Butler* [1900] 1 QB 694 (CA); *Mayson v Clouet* [1924] AC 980 (JCPC–Singapore).

[76] *Kingdon v Kirk* (1887) 37 Ch D 141; *Lock v Bell* [1931] 1 Ch 35 (Ch D); *Union Eagle Ltd v Golden Achievement Ltd* [1997] AC 514 (JCPC–Hong Kong); *Urban Manor Ltd v Sadiq* [1997] 1 WLR 1016 (CA); *Velmore Estates v Roseberry Homes Ltd* [2005] EWHC 3061 (Ch), [2006] 2 P & CR 10.

[77] *Workers Trust and Merchant Bank Ltd v Dojap Investments Ltd* [1993] AC 573 (JCPC–Jamaica) 578–9 (Lord Browne-Wilkinson); *Midill (97PL) Ltd v Park Lane Estates Ltd* [2008] EWCA Civ 1227, [2009] 1 WLR 2460, para 32 (Carnwath LJ); *Omar v El Wakil* [2001] EWCA Civ 1090, [2002] 2 P & CR 3, para 36 (Arden LJ).

[78] [1912] 2 KB 373; *Hinton v Sparkes* (1868) LR 3 CP 161.

[79] [1912] 2 KB 373, 387–8.

[80] [1970] 1 Ch 94 (Ch D).

this decision, saying that once the vendor had elected to 'bring the contract to an end' he could no longer enforce its provisions.[81] This decision has in turn been criticized on the ground that it confuses termination with rescission *ab initio*,[82] and that since the time for the payment of the deposit had already arrived prior to termination, the accrued right should have been enforceable by the vendor.[83] However, as has been seen, the fact that the time for performance has arrived is not normally conclusive in these cases; what matters is whether the right to performance has been earned.[84] In particular, where termination gives rise to a total failure of consideration the defaulting party should not have to pay something for nothing,[85] at least in cases where the contract does not specifically provide to that effect.[86] As against this, it is argued that the 'total failure of consideration' principle is excluded by the rule allowing the forfeiture of deposits that have already been paid in this sort of case.[87]

The matter was further considered by the Court of Appeal in *The Blankenstein*,[88] **9.18** where a contract was concluded for the sale of three ships, and provided for the payment of a deposit when the contract was formally signed. The buyers repudiated the contract before signature took place, which meant that the deposit never became payable. It was nevertheless held by a majority[89] that the buyers had been under an obligation at the relevant time to sign the contract and then pay the deposit, and that since the sellers would have been entitled to forfeit the deposit if it had been paid, the measure of damages payable by the buyers should be based on the amount of that deposit. Though no view was expressed by the majority as to whether the sellers could have recovered the deposit as a debt once it became payable,[90] Fox LJ doubted the soundness of the decision in *Lowe v Hope* and said that the reasoning in *Dewar v Mintoft* was to be preferred.[91] In the end, the matter is a moot point, but on balance the better view would seem to be to allow the recovery of an unpaid deposit in this sort of case,[92] if only to preserve some degree of symmetry with the

---

[81] *Lowe v Hope*, 98 (n 80).

[82] M Albery, 'Cyprian Williams' Great Fallacy' (1975) 90 LQR 337; *Johnson v Agnew* [1980] AC 367 (HL); see Ch 4, para 4.07.

[83] Carter, *Carter's Breach of Contract*, para 13-43 (n 2).

[84] See para 9.09.

[85] See para 9.14.

[86] See para 9.15.

[87] Carter, *Carter's Breach of Contract*, para 13-43 (n 2).

[88] *Damon Compania Naviera SA v Hapag-Lloyd Intl SA (The Blankenstein)* [1985] 1 WLR 435 (CA); MP Thompson, 'Deposits and Penalties' [1985] Conveyancer 286; JW Carter, 'Deposits, Accrued Rights and Damages' (1988) 101 LQR 207; Carter, *Carter's Breach of Contract*, para 13-44 (n 2).

[89] Fox and Stephenson LJJ, Robert Goff LJ dissenting.

[90] *The Blankenstein*, 449 (Fox LJ) (n 88).

[91] *The Blankenstein*, 449 (n 88).

[92] See *Barnard v Zarbafi* [2010] EWHC 3256 (Ch) (Newey J); *Griffon Shipping LLC v Firodi Shipping Co Ltd (The Griffon)* [2013] EWHC 593 (Comm), [2013] 2 Lloyd's Rep 50 (Teare J).

law relating to forfeiture and to prevent the defaulting party from benefiting from his or her own breach.

9.19 Even if the innocent party does have the right to sue for an unpaid deposit in cases of this sort, this has to be read subject to the power of the court to relieve against forfeiture in appropriate cases.[93] This has already been discussed,[94] but there are some powers that are of particular relevance to deposits. One is section 49(2) of the Law of Property Act 1925, which deals with contracts for the sale or exchange of any interest in land,[95] and allows the court in any action where specific performance is refused, or in any action for the return of a deposit, to order the deposit to be repaid.[96] Another is the general power of equity to relieve a purchaser against forfeiture to the extent of giving extra time to pay, provided he or she is ready and willing to do so.[97] As well as this, it has been held by the Privy Council that the general power of the courts to relieve against penalties applies equally to deposits,[98] at least where they are set at an excessively high level,[99] though whether this decision reflects English law has been doubted.[100] Though all of these powers relate to the forfeiture of a deposit that has already been paid rather than to a claim for the payment of one that has not, they are still of relevance in the present context; as Carter points out, the sole purpose of claiming payment of the deposit in these cases is so

---

[93] C Harpum, 'Relief against Forfeiture and the Purchaser of Land' [1984] CLJ 134; C Mitchell, 'Equitable Doctrine of Relief against Forfeiture' (1987) 11 Sydney L Rev 387.

[94] See Ch 4, paras 4.76–4.81.

[95] Law of Property Act 1925, s 49(3).

[96] Burrows et al, *Chitty on Contracts*, para 26-199 (n 40). The court has a wide discretion with regard to the matter: *Schindler v Pigault* (1975) 30 P & CR 328 (Ch D); *Universal Corp v Five Ways Properties Ltd* (1979) 38 P & CR 687 (CA). However, where a purchaser reneges on a conveyancing transaction, the court's discretion will only be exercised in exceptional circumstances, since inability to complete is the very risk that the deposit is intended to guard against: *Omar v El Wakil* [2001] EWCA Civ 1090, [2002] 2 P & CR 3.

[97] *Re Dagenham (Thames) Dock Co, ex p Hulse* (1872–73) LR 8 Ch App 1022; *Kilmer v British Columbia Orchard Lands Ltd* [1913] AC 319 (JCPC–Canada); *Steedman v Drinkle* [1916] 1 AC 275 (JCPC–Canada); *Starside Properties v Mustapha* [1974] 1 WLR 816 (CA); Burrows et al, *Chitty on Contracts*, para 26-196 (n 40); Harpum, 'Relief against Forfeiture', 143–4 (n 93).

[98] *Workers Trust & Merchant Bank Ltd v Dojap Investments Ltd* [1993] AC 573 (JCPC–Jamaica); H Beale, 'Unreasonable Deposits' (1993) 109 LQR 524; C Harpum, 'Deposits as Penalties' [1993] CLJ 389; JW Carter, 'Two Privy Council Cases' (1993) 6 JCL 266.

[99] *Workers Trust & Merchant Bank Ltd v Dojap Investments Ltd* [1993] AC 573 (JCPC–Jamaica), 578 (Lord Browne-Wilkinson). The jurisdiction to relieve against penalties will not apply to the normal 10% deposit, which the courts will allow to be forfeited save in exceptional circumstances: *Bidaisee v Dorinsa Yusidai Sampath and ors* [1995] NPC 59 (JCPC–Trinidad and Tobago); *Omar v El Wakil* [2001] EWCA Civ 1090, [2002] 2 P & CR 3, para 35–37 (Arden LJ); *Tennaro Ltd v Majorarch Ltd* [2003] EWHC 2601 (Ch), [2003] 47 EG 154 (CS) para 84 (Neuberger J); *Midill (97PL) Ltd v Park Lane Estates Ltd* [2008] EWCA Civ 1227, [2009] 1 WLR 2460, para 52 (Carnwath LJ); *Barnard v Zarbafi* [2010] EWHC 3256 (Ch) (Newey J). Nor does it apply to instalments of the purchase price which a seller is entitled to claim on termination, as these are not sums payable on breach: *Cadogan Petroleum Holdings Ltd v Global Process Systems LLC* [2013] EWHC 214 (Comm), [2013] 2 Lloyd's Rep 26.

[100] Beale, 'Unreasonable Deposits' (n 98); Burrows et al, *Chitty on Contracts*, para 26-198 (n 40); Carter, *Carter's Breach of Contract*, para 13-54 (n 2). Treitel, however, supports the decision: Peel, *Treitel*, para 20-137 (n 13).

that it may then be forfeited, and there is therefore no reason why a claim for relief should be made as a defence in the context of an action of this sort.[101]

D. Ancillary Terms

According to Lord Diplock's analysis, there are some primary obligations which, **9.20** while not actually requiring the party concerned to *do* anything, nevertheless form an important part of the contractual matrix. In the pages which follow we shall be looking at the effect of termination on what Lord Diplock refers to as 'ancillary' terms of this sort,[102] most notably dispute resolution clauses and clauses excluding or limiting the liability of one or other of the parties.

(1) Dispute resolution clauses

Contracts frequently contain clauses relating to the resolution of disputes arising, **9.21** arbitration clauses being an obvious example of this. In the past it was thought that such clauses could not survive termination, the argument being that since the contract was at an end its provisions could no longer apply.[103] Thus in *Hirji Mulji v Cheong Yue SS Co*[104] it was held by the Privy Council that a clause in a charterparty requiring 'all disputes under this charter' to be submitted to arbitration in Hong Kong could not survive the frustration of the charterparty by the requisition of the ship. In the words of Lord Sumner:[105]

> The ship was requisitioned before she was placed at the charterers' disposal; the performance of the charter never began, and the failure to begin it by tendering the ship at Singapore was excused in the owners' favour by the excepted restraints of princes. Under these circumstances, by the year 1919, when a dispute first arose, 'this charter' no longer existed. The dispute was not one, of which it could be predicated that it was one arising under 'this charter,' since that had terminated by frustration a year before. An arbitration clause is not a phoenix, that can be raised again by one of the parties from the dead ashes of its former self.

Whatever the position may be in regard to frustration,[106] this line of reasoning was **9.22** decisively rejected by the House of Lords in the context of termination twenty-five

---

[101] Carter, *Carter's Breach of Contract*, para 13-43 (n 2).

[102] *Moschi v Lep Air Services Ltd* [1973] AC 331 (HL) 350; Carter, *Carter's Breach of Contract*, para 12-24 (n 2).

[103] *Johannesburg Municipal Council v D Stewart & Co* (1902) Ltd 1909 SC (HL) 53, 54 (Lord Loreburn LC) and 56 (Lord Shaw); *Jureidini v National British and Irish Millers Insurance Co Ltd* [1915] AC 499 (HL) 505 (Viscount Haldane LC).

[104] [1926] AC 497 (JCPC–Hong Kong).

[105] *Hirji Mulji v Cheong Yue SS*, 510–11 (n 104).

[106] Though the case has never been overruled, Lord Sumner's reasoning was criticized in later cases, most notably *Heyman v Darwins Ltd* [1942] AC 356 (HL) 365–6 (Viscount Simon LC), 369 (Lord Russell), 375 (Lord Macmillan), 382–3 (Lord Wright), and 401 (Lord Porter); *Charles Mauritzen v Baltic Shipping Co* 1948 SC 646, 650 (Lord Blades). The case has not been followed

years or so later. In *Heyman v Darwins Ltd*[107] a sole agency contract for the sale of tool steel contained a clause stating that disputes arising out of the contract should be submitted to arbitration. A dispute having arisen between the parties, the agents issued a writ for a declaration to the effect that the manufacturers had repudiated the contract. The manufacturers then sought to have the proceedings stayed on the basis of the arbitration clause, but the agents claimed, on the basis of *Hirji Mulji v Cheong Yue SS Co* and other cases,[108] that their acceptance of the repudiation had brought the contract to an end, and so the clause had ceased to apply. However, this the House of Lords would not have. Though it might be accurate in some sense to say that the contract was brought to an end, this did not mean that all of its provisions automatically ceased to apply. Rather, the matter was to be determined as a matter of construction.[109] In the words of Lord Macmillan:[110]

> I am, accordingly, of opinion that what is commonly called repudiation or total breach of a contract, whether acquiesced in by the other party or not, does not abrogate the contract, though it may relieve the injured party of the duty of further fulfilling the obligations which he has by the contract undertaken to the repudiating party. The contract is not put out of existence, though all further performance of the obligations undertaken by each party in favour of the other may cease. It survives for the purpose of measuring the claims arising out of the breach, and the arbitration clause survives for determining the mode of their settlement. The purposes of the contract have failed, but the arbitration clause is not one of the purposes of the contract.

9.23 The upshot of all this is that whether terms of this sort apply following termination is purely a question of construction. If this is what the parties intended, so be it; it makes no sense to disregard their intentions in deference to a mere metaphor, namely that the contract has 'come to an end'. Indeed, it has been said that although such terms are promissory in nature, an intention that they are to remain enforceable in any proceedings which occur after termination of the contract is easily inferred;[111] an agreement to settle disputes in a particular way is essentially distinct from the main contract to which it relates,[112] and will normally be taken to encompass all disputes relating to the contract, whatever their nature may be.[113]

---

either in England (*Kruse v Questier & Co Ltd* [1953] 1 QB 669 (QBD) (Pilcher J)) or in Australia (*Codelfa Construction Pty Ltd v State Rail Authority of New South Wales* (1982) 149 CLR 337 (HCA)).

[107] [1942] AC 356 (HL).
[108] See para 9.20.
[109] [1942] AC 356 (HL) 366 (Viscount Simon LC), 389 (Lord Wright), and 392 (Lord Porter).
[110] *Heyman v Darwins*, 374 (n 109).
[111] Carter, *Carter's Breach of Contract*, para 12-24 (n 2).
[112] *Paul Smith Ltd v H & S Intl Holding Inc* [1991] 2 Lloyd's Rep 127 (QBD: Commercial Ct) 130 (Steyn J); *Beijing Jianlong Heavy Industry Group v Golden Ocean Group Ltd* [2013] EWHC 1063.
[113] Thus an arbitration clause can even apply to issues such as rectification (*Ashville Investments Ltd v Elmer Contractors Ltd* [1989] QB 488 (CA)), illegality (*Harbour Assurance Co (UK) Ltd v Kansa General Intl Insurance Ltd* [1993] QB 701 (CA)), and rescission for fraud (*Fiona Trust & Holding Corp v Privalov* [2007] UKHL 40, [2008] 1 Lloyd's Rep 254). Doubts have, however, been expressed as to whether such a clause can apply to a dispute regarding whether a contract has

(2) Exemption clauses

9.24 The effect of termination on exemption clauses and other limitation provisions has been and continues to be somewhat controversial, not least because of the tendency of courts in the past century to twist the principles of termination for breach in order to protect the weaker party against exploitation. In the passage which follows we shall examine the maritime doctrine of deviation and its offspring, the now discredited substantive law of fundamental breach,[114] before considering to what extent the relevant principles survive into the modern law.

(a) Deviation

9.25 One of the key obligations of a shipowner under a charterparty is to sail direct to the contract destination without departing or deviating from the agreed route.[115] Any deviation of this sort by the owner will amount to a fundamental breach in the sense that it will entitle the charterer to terminate and claim damages.[116] Though a deviation might be better described as a breach of condition in this context—there is no requirement that a deviation have serious consequences for the charterer[117]— the use of the term 'fundamental breach' in this sense is relatively uncontroversial, and represents a well-settled principle of maritime law.[118]

9.26 However, the cases go further than this. Not only did a deviation entitle the charterer to terminate, it also had the effect of depriving the shipowner of the protection of any exemption clauses in the contract.[119] Thus in *Joseph Thorley Ltd v Orchis SS Co SA*[120] a cargo of goods was shipped under a bill of lading which contained a clause excluding the shipowners from any liability for loss caused by the negligence of the stevedores in discharging the ship. The ship having deviated significantly on the course of the voyage, it was held that the shipowners had lost the right to rely on the exemption clause as a defence irrespective of whether the loss in question had resulted from the deviation. In the words of Fletcher Moulton LJ:[121]

> The cases shew that, for a long series of years, the Courts have held that a deviation
> is such a serious matter, and changes the character of the contemplated voyage so

---

been concluded in the first place: *Paul Smith Ltd v H & S Intl Holding Inc* [1991] 2 Lloyd's Rep 127 (QBD: Commercial Ct) 130 (Steyn J).

[114] See further D Yates, *Exclusion Clauses in Contracts* (2nd edn, Sweet & Maxwell, 1982) ch 6; Richard Lawson, *Exclusion Clauses and Unfair Contract Terms* (10th edn, Sweet & Maxwell, 2011) para 3.09.

[115] *Davis v Garrett* (1830) 6 Bing 716, 130 ER 1456; *Scaramanga v Stamp* (1880) 5 CPD 295 (CA).

[116] Sir Bernard Eder et al, *Scrutton on Charterparties and Bills of Lading* (22nd edn, Sweet & Maxwell, 1996) para 12-013; *Compagnie Primera de Navagaziona Panama v Compania Arrendataria de Monopolio de Petroleos SA* [1940] 1 KB 362 (CA) 375 (MacKinnon LJ).

[117] See Ch 5, para 5.06.

[118] Eder et al, *Scrutton on Charterparties*, art 140 (n 116).

[119] *Balian v Joly, Victoria & Co* (1890) 6 TLR 345 (CA).

[120] [1907] 1 KB 660 (CA); *Morrison & Co Ltd v Shaw, Savill & Albion Co Ltd* [1916] 2 KB 783 (CA); *Hain Steamship Co v Tate & Lyle Ltd* (1936) 55 Ll L R 159 (HL).

[121] *Joseph Thorley v Orchis SS*, 669 (n 120).

essentially, that a shipowner who has been guilty of a deviation cannot be considered as having performed his part of the bill of lading contract, but something fundamentally different, and therefore he cannot claim the benefit of stipulations in his favour contained in the bill of lading.

9.27 Though having its origins in maritime law, the same principle was applied in other areas. Thus, for instance, a carrier of goods by land who conveyed them to the wrong destination was held to have lost the protection of exemption clauses in the contract,[122] as was a bailee who stored the goods in the wrong place.[123] The idea was that a party who stepped out of the 'four corners' of the contract could not at the same time rely on limitations and exceptions inserted into that contract for his or her benefit.[124] In the words of Scrutton LJ:[125]

> If you undertake to do a thing in a certain way, or to keep a thing in a certain place, with certain conditions protecting it, and have broken the contract by not doing the thing contracted for, or not keeping the article in the place where you have contracted to keep it, you cannot rely on the conditions which were only intended to protect you if you carried out the contract in the way in which you had contracted to do it.

(b) Doctrine of 'fundamental breach'

9.28 During the 1950s these strands were drawn together by the formulation of the so-called 'substantive law' doctrine of fundamental breach. The essence of this was that a party who committed a fundamental breach of the contract brought the contract to an end, and as a result could not rely on exemptions inserted for his or her benefit into that contract. Thus in *Alexander v Railway Executive*[126] it was held by Devlin J that the defendants could not rely on an exemption clause when they had permitted a third party to remove luggage deposited by the plaintiff at their station. There had been a fundamental breach of the contract, the effect of which was to determine the bailment and to render the exemption clauses inapplicable. In the words of Devlin J:[127]

> The ordinary law of contract, quite apart from the law of bailment... involves that, where there has been a breach of a fundamental term of a contract giving the other party the right to rescind it, then, unless and until, with full knowledge of all the facts, he elects to affirm the contract and not to rescind it, the special terms of the contract go and cannot be relied upon by the defaulting party. There

---

[122] *Mallet v Great Eastern Rly Co* [1899] 1 QB 309; *London & North Western Rly Co v Neilson* [1922] 2 AC 263 (HL).

[123] *Lilley v Doubleday* (1881) 7 QBD 510; *Gibaud v Great Eastern Rly Co* [1921] KB 426 (CA) 431–2 (Lord Sterndale MR) and 435 (Scrutton LJ); *Woolmer v Delmer Price LD* [1955] 1 QB 291 (QBD).

[124] *Alderslade v Hendon Laundry Ltd* [1945] 1 KB 189 (CA) 192 (Lord Greene MR); *Hunt & Winterbotham (West of England) Ltd v BRS (Parcels) Ltd* [1962] 1 QB 617 (CA) 626 (Donovan LJ).

[125] *Gibaud v Great Eastern Rly Co* [1921] KB 426 (CA) 435; *Future Publishing Ltd v Edge Interactive Media Ltd* [2011] EWHC 1489 (Ch), [2011] ETMR 50, para 63 (Proudman J).

[126] [1951] 2 KB 882.

[127] *Alexander v Rly Executive*, 889–90 (n 126).

is no question that the plaintiff ever knew of the circumstances in this case which entitled him to rescind or that he ever elected to affirm the contract. This point therefore succeeds and provides a good answer to the executive's reliance upon the conditions.

A similar result was reached by the Court of Appeal in *Karsales (Harrow) Ltd v* **9.29** *Wallis*,[128] a case involving the hire purchase of a car. The defendant inspected the car, which appeared to be in good condition, and then signed a contract agreeing to take it on hire purchase terms. The contract contained a clause excluding liability for all express or implied conditions relating to the roadworthiness of the car or its fitness for purpose. The car was subsequently towed out to the defendant's house late one night in a deplorable state; new parts had been replaced by old, other parts had been removed altogether, the engine was totally burnt out, and the car would not even go. The defendant having refused to accept the car, it was held that the dealers could not rely on the exemption clause, since what had been delivered was not what had been contracted for.[129] In the words of Denning LJ:[130]

> The thing to do is to look at the contract apart from the exempting clauses and see what are the terms, express or implied, which impose an obligation on the party. If he has been guilty of a breach of those obligations in a respect which goes to the very root of the contract, he cannot rely on the exempting clauses.

As was pointed out by Yates, there were two separate notions involved here.[131] **9.30** The first was the ordinary doctrine of fundamental breach, that is to say a breach which goes to the root of the contract or substantially deprives the other party of the benefit of its performance.[132] The reasoning here was that once the contract was terminated by the innocent party the exemption clauses ceased to apply.[133] The other was the so-called 'breach of a fundamental term', or in the words of Devlin J, something which underlay the whole contract so that, if it was not complied with, the performance became something totally different from that which the contract contemplated.[134] Such a breach went beyond a mere breach of condition, in that it amounted in essence to a total failure to perform the contract in any respect, as

---

[128] [1956] 1 WLR 936 (CA).

[129] In the words of Birkett LJ, a car which would not go was 'not a car at all'; [1956] 1 WLR 936, 942.

[130] *Karsales v Wallis*, 940 (n 128).

[131] Yates, *Exclusion Clauses in Contracts*, ch 6 (n 114); *Suisse Atlantique Société d'Armement Maritime SA v NV Rotterdamsche Kolen Centrale* [1967] 1 AC 361 (HL) 421–2 (Lord Upjohn).

[132] See Ch 6.

[133] *Alexander v Rly Executive* [1951] 2 KB 882, 889–90 (Devlin J); *Suisse Atlantique Société d'Armement Maritime SA v NV Rotterdamsche Kolen Centrale* [1967] 1 AC 361 (HL) 398 (Lord Reid); *Harbutt's 'Plasticine' Ltd v Wayne Tank and Pump Co Ltd* [1970] 1 QB 447 (CA); *Farnworth Finance Facilities Ltd v Attryde* [1970] 1 WLR 1053 (CA).

[134] *Smeaton Hanscomb v Sassoon I Setty* [1953] 1 WLR 1468 (QBD), 1470; FMB Reynolds, 'Warranty, Condition and Fundamental Term' (1963) 79 LQR 534, 540–4.

where a seller agreed to supply peas and then delivered beans.[135] The idea behind fundamental breach was that the exemption clauses did not apply because the contract was terminated, but breach of a fundamental term involved in essence a special rule of law,[136] which could apply not only where the contract was terminated but even in cases where it was affirmed.[137]

(c) A matter of construction

9.31 Though the substantive law doctrine of fundamental breach proved to be a useful tool in the context of consumer protection,[138] its doctrinal basis was decidedly suspect, and it was somewhat crude in its effects, striking down bargains that were commercially unimpeachable alongside those that were not. A number of cases had sought to define the fundamental breach principle in terms of a rule of construction,[139] and ultimately that was the approach that won the day. In *Photo Production Ltd v Securicor Transport Ltd*[140] the House of Lords was faced with a case where an employee of the defendants, who had been engaged to guard their factory, deliberately burnt it to the ground. Could the defendants rely on an exemption clause limiting their liability to cases where the company itself could be shown to have been negligent in some way? The Court of Appeal had held that since this was a fundamental breach the defendants could not rely on the clause,[141] but the House of Lords held that this approach was incorrect, and that the application of exemption clauses in cases of this sort was a matter of construction. The problem that the substantive law doctrine was intended to address was now adequately dealt with by legislation,[142] and as a general rule the parties should be free to allocate the risks in the contract as and where they chose. In the words of Lord Diplock:[143]

> A basic principle of the common law of contract, to which there are no exceptions that are relevant in the instant case, is that parties to a contract are free to determine for themselves what primary obligations they will accept. They may state these in express words in the contract itself and, where they do, the statement is

---

[135] *Chanter v Hopkins* (1838) 4 M & W 399, 404, 150 ER 1484, 1487 (Lord Abinger CJ); *Pinnock Bros v Lewis & Peat Ltd* [1923] 1 KB 690 (KBD), 696 (Roche J); *Karsales (Harrow) Ltd v Wallis* [1956] 1 WLR 936, 942 (Birkett LJ).

[136] *Yeoman Credit Ltd v Apps* [1962] 2 QB 508 (CA) 520 (Holroyd Pearce LJ).

[137] As in *Charterhouse Credit Co Ltd v Tolly* [1963] 2 QB 683 (CA) and in *Wathes (Western) Ltd v Austins (Menswear) Ltd* [1976] 1 Lloyd's Rep 14 (CA).

[138] *Photo Production Ltd v Securicor Transport Ltd* [1980] AC 827 (HL) 843 (Lord Wilberforce).

[139] *Glynn v Margetson & Co* [1893] AC 351 (HL); *The Cap Palos* [1921] P 458 (CA) 467–8 (Lord Sterndale MR) and 471–2 (Atkin LJ); *Sze Hai Tong Bank v Rambler Cycle Co Ltd* [1959] AC 576 (JCPC–Singapore) 587 (Lord Denning); *UGS Finance Ltd v National Mortgage Bank of Greece and National Bank of Greece SA* [1964] 1 Lloyd's Rep 446 (CA) 453 (Pearson LJ); *Suisse Atlantique Société d'Armement Maritime SA v NV Rotterdamsche Kolen Centrale* [1967] 1 AC 361 (HL).

[140] [1980] AC 827 (HL); AG Guest (1980) 96 LQR 324; A Nicol and N Rawlings, 'Substantive Fundamental Breach Burnt Out' (1980) 43 MLR 567; LS Sealy, 'Contract—Farewell to the Doctrine of Fundamental Breach' [1980] CLJ 252.

[141] [1978] 1 WLR 856 (CA).

[142] Namely, the Unfair Contract Terms Act 1977.

[143] [1980] AC 827 (HL) 848.

determinative; but in practice a commercial contract never states all the primary obligations of the parties in full; many are left to be incorporated by implication of law from the legal nature of the contract into which the parties are entering. But if the parties wish to reject or modify primary obligations which would otherwise be so incorporated, they are fully at liberty to do so by express words.

(d) The effect of termination

The House of Lords was equally dismissive of the doctrine propounded by Devlin J **9.32** and others to the effect that termination by the innocent party brought the contract to an end and the exemption clauses with it.[144] As we have seen, that very same doctrine had been exploded in relation to an arbitration clause nearly forty years previously in *Heyman v Darwins*,[145] and *Photo Productions Ltd v Securicor Transport Ltd* held it to be equally fallacious when applied to exemption clauses. As Lord Wilberforce put it:[146]

> I have, indeed, been unable to understand how the doctrine can be reconciled with the well accepted principle of law, stated by the highest modern authority, that when in the context of a breach of contract one speaks of 'termination', what is meant is no more than that the innocent party or, in some cases, both parties, are excused from further performance. Damages, in such cases, are then claimed under the contract, so what reason in principle can there be for disregarding what the contract itself says about damages—whether it 'liquidates' them, or limits them, or excludes them? These difficulties arise in part from uncertain or inconsistent terminology. A vast number of expressions are used to describe situations where a breach has been committed by one party of such a character as to entitle the other party to refuse further performance: discharge, rescission, termination, the contract is at an end, or dead, or displaced; clauses cannot survive, or simply go... To plead for complete uniformity may be to cry for the moon. But what can and ought to be avoided is to make use of these confusions in order to produce a concealed and unreasoned legal innovation: to pass, for example, from saying that a party, victim of a breach of contract, is entitled to refuse further performance, to saying that he may treat the contract as at an end, or as rescinded, and to draw from this the proposition, which is not analytical but one of policy, that all or (arbitrarily) some of the clauses of the contract lose, automatically, their force, regardless of intention.

(e) The current position

The upshot of all this is that whether the defaulting party can rely on an exemp- **9.33** tion clause following termination is, as with the question whether he or she can rely on it to cover a fundamental breach, a matter of construction.[147] However, two questions still remain, one relating to breach of a fundamental term, and the other relating to the deviation principle.

---

[144] See para 9.27.
[145] [1942] AC 356 (HL); see para 9.21.
[146] [1980] AC 827 (HL) 844.
[147] *George Mitchell (Chesterhall) Ltd v Finney Lock Seeds Ltd* [1983] 2 AC 803 (HL).

9.34 **(i) Breach of fundamental term**   As has been seen, the courts in the past have used the notion of breach of fundamental term to denote a total failure to perform, as where a party delivers beans instead of peas.[148] Obviously there may be cases where a so-called exemption clause serves the function of defining the primary obligations of the party in question,[149] but leaving that aside, to what extent can a defaulting party use such a clause to cover breaches of this nature? No doubt this is now possible in theory, but to what extent is it a realistic possibility in practice? Certainly the courts have been reluctant in the past to construe exemption clauses in such a way as to cover a complete disregard by a party of his or her contractual obligations.[150] To do so would be to deprive the contract, on which the exemption clause depends for its validity, of all content. As Lord Wilberforce put it:[151]

> One may safely say that the parties cannot, in a contract, have contemplated that the clause should have so wide an ambit as in effect to deprive one party's stipulations of all contractual force: to do so would be to reduce the contract to a mere declaration of intent. To this extent it may be correct to say that there is a rule of law against the application of an exceptions clause to a particular type of breach.

9.35 **(ii) Deviation**   The other question relates to the present status of the deviation doctrine, in which the substantive law doctrine of fundamental breach was rooted.[152] Now that the latter has been discredited, does the former still hold good?[153] It was suggested by Lord Wilberforce in *Photo Production Ltd v Securicor Transport Ltd* that the deviation cases should be considered as a separate body of doctrine *sui generis* with special rules derived from historical and commercial reasons,[154] but others have argued that there are no longer any special rules applying to deviation and

---

[148] See para 9.29.

[149] In the words of Lord Wilberforce, an act which, apart from the exceptions clause, might be a breach sufficiently serious to justify refusal of further performance, may be reduced in effect, or made not a breach at all, by the terms of the clause: *Suisse Atlantique Société d'Armement Maritime SA v NV Rotterdamsche Kolen Centrale* [1967] 1 AC 361 (HL) 431.

[150] *The Cap Palos* [1921] P 458 (CA) 471–2 (Atkin LJ) (deliberate abandonment of tow by tug owner); *Sze Hai Tong Bank v Rambler Cycle Co Ltd* [1959] AC 576 (JCPC–Singapore) 587 (Lord Denning) (goods given away to thief or burnt or thrown in the sea); *Kamil Export (Australia) Pty Ltd v NPL (Australia) Pty Ltd* [1996] 1 VR 538 (deliberate misdelivery by carrier); *Motis Exports Ltd v Dampskibsselskabet AF 1912* [2000] 1 Lloyd's Rep 211 (CA) (delivery of goods on production of forged bill of lading); B Coote, 'Exception Clauses, Deliberate Acts and the Onus of Proof in Bailment Cases' (1997–98) 12 JCL 169; BJ Davenport, 'Misdelivery: a Fundamental Breach' [2000] LMCLQ 455.

[151] *Suisse Atlantique Société d'Armement Maritime SA v NV Rotterdamsche Kolen Centrale* [1967] 1 AC 361 (HL) 432; *Tor Line AB v Alltrans Group of Canada Ltd* [1984] 1 WLR 48 (HL) 58–9 (Lord Roskill); *Internet Broadcasting Corp Ltd v Mar LLC* [2009] EWHC 844 (Ch), [2009] 2 Lloyd's Rep 295, para 33 (G Moss QC); *Kudos Catering (UK) Ltd v Manchester Central Convention Complex Ltd* [2013] EWCA Civ 38, para 19; J Wade, 'Fundamental Breach as a Rule of Law—Battered but still Breathing' [1981] Conveyancer 306; M Clarke, 'Fundamental Breach is Dead! Long Live...the Rule against Absurdity!' [1984] CLJ 32.

[152] See para 9.24.

[153] See Burrows et al, *Chitty on Contracts*, para 14-029 (n 40); Peel, *Treitel*, para 7-032 (n 13).

[154] [1980] AC 827 (HL) 845; Eder et al, *Scrutton on Charterparties*, para 12-014 (n 116); M Dockray, 'Deviation: a Doctrine all at Sea' [2000] LMCLQ 76.

that the relevant cases should be assimilated into the general law of contract.[155] In *The Kapitan Petko Voivoda*[156] the question arose of whether a shipowner who had carried the cargo on deck in breach of a contract of carriage governed by the Hague Rules could take advantage of those rules so as to limit his liability when some of it was washed overboard in a storm. The cargo owners sought to argue that carriage of the cargo on deck instead of in the hold was akin to deviation, but it was held by the Court of Appeal that in so far as the doctrine still survived in the modern law it had no application to the facts of the given case. In the words of Longmore LJ, it had not been conclusively decided whether the deviation cases and others akin to them must be regarded as 'dead and buried' along with the doctrine of fundamental breach,[157] but on any showing they were a 'peculiar creature of the common law' without parallel in many other jurisdictions,[158] and it would not be appropriate to extend them any further than was strictly necessary.

(3) Other provisions

There are other obligations that may survive termination. This will certainly be **9.36** the case where the obligation in question arises quite apart from the contract, as in the case of bailment,[159] agency,[160] and other relationships of a fiduciary nature.[161] The position is less clear where the obligation depends on the contract for its validity. In *General Billposting Co Ltd v Atkinson*[162] it was held by the House of Lords that following wrongful dismissal, an employee could not be held bound by a covenant in restraint of trade, since once he had accepted the repudiation the contract came to an end and the covenant with it. However, the discussion of the issue was perfunctory in the extreme,[163] and the reasoning is difficult to reconcile with the more nuanced analysis of the effects of termination now used by the courts. In *Yasuda Fire & Marine Insurance Co of Europe Ltd v Orion Marine Insurance Underwriting Agency Ltd*[164] the High Court had to decide the effect

---

[155] *Kenya Rlys v Antares Co Pte Ltd (The Antares)* [1987] 1 Lloyd's Rep 424 (CA) 430 (Lloyd LJ); *State Trading Corp of India Ltd v M Golodetz & Co Inc Ltd* [1989] 2 Lloyd's Rep 277 (CA) 289 (Lloyd LJ); Eder et al, *Scrutton on Charterparties*, para 12-015 (n 116); J Livermore, 'Deviation, Deck Cargo and Fundamental Breach' (1989–90) 2 JCL 241, 263.

[156] *Daewoo Heavy Industries Ltd v Klipriver Shipping Ltd (The Kapitan Petko Voivoda)* [2003] EWCA Civ 451, [2003] 2 Lloyd's Rep 1.

[157] *The Kapitan Petko Voivoda*, para 10 (n 156).

[158] *The Kapitan Petko Voivoda*, para 14 (n 156).

[159] *Gaudet v Brown* (1873–74) LR 5 PC 134; *Great Northern Rly Co v Swaffield* (1873–74) LR 9 Ex 132; *China-Pacific SA v Food Corp of India (The Winson)* [1982] AC 939 (HL); *ENE 1 Kos Ltd v Petroleo Brasileiro SA (The Kos)* [2012] UKSC 17, [2012] 2 AC 164.

[160] *Pearse v Green* (1819) 1 Jac & W 135, 37 ER 327; *Gray v Haig & Sons* (1855) 20 Beav 219, 52 ER 587; *Yasuda Fire & Marine Insurance Co of Europe Ltd v Orion Marine Insurance Underwriting Agency Ltd* [1995] QB 174 (QBD: Commercial Ct).

[161] *Longstaff v Birtles* [2001] EWCA Civ 1219, [2002] 1 WLR 470, para 35 (Mummery LJ).

[162] [1909] AC 118 (HL).

[163] The whole case takes up only four pages of the Reports.

[164] [1995] QB 174 (QBD: Commercial Ct).

of termination of an agency contract on a provision entitling the principal to inspect 'books, accounts, records and other documentation' held by the agent. It was argued on the part of the agent that since the main contract had been terminated the provision in question could no longer apply,[165] but this argument was rejected by the court on the ground that the obligation in question was inherent in the relationship of principal and agent, and so did not depend purely on the contract.[166] However, the court then went on to discuss whether the contractual obligation itself survived termination, and concluded that it did, on the ground that it was, like an arbitration clause, purely ancillary to the main purpose of the contract. In the words of Colman J:[167]

> I have already considered the contractual function of the inspection facility under clause 4.2 of the agreements. That function was, in my judgment, wholly ancillary to the subject matter of the agency agreements. Its purpose was solely to provide the plaintiff with information as to transactions binding on them which was exclusively within the defendants' knowledge. It was, however, the entering into and administration of those transactions by the defendants which was the subject matter of the agency agreements. Therefore, for the reasons which I have explained, that part of clause 4.2 which entitled the plaintiff to inspect all the relevant records of the defendants at any reasonable time upon notice remained in full effect in spite of the accepted repudiation of the agency agreements.

The question whether the parties can insert provisions of this sort that are, in the words of Colman J, 'discharge-proof'[168] would therefore seem to be essentially one of construction. On this basis it has been suggested that any terms which by their very nature can be assumed to apply following termination, such as terms imposing a duty of good faith or prohibiting the disclosure of confidential information,[169] will do so unless the contract provides to the contrary.[170] As things stand, covenants in restraint of trade must be an exception to this principle on the basis of *General Billposting Co Ltd v Atkinson*,[171] but that case may be open to reconsideration by the House of Lords in the light of more recent thinking on the topic.

---

[165] *Yasuda Fire & Marine v Orion Marine*, 177–8 (n 164).
[166] *Yasuda Fire & Marine v Orion Marine*, 184–6 and 187 (n 164).
[167] *Yasuda Fire & Marine v Orion Marine*, 191 (n 164).
[168] *Yasuda Fire & Marine v Orion Marine*, 187 (n 164).
[169] *Faccenda Chicken Ltd v Fowler* [1987] Ch 117 (CA); *Thomas Marshall (Exports) Ltd v Guinle* [1979] Ch 227 (Ch D).
[170] Carter, *Carter's Breach of Contract*, para 12-23 (n 2).
[171] [1909] AC 118 (HL); *Strange (SW) v Mann* [1965] 1 WLR 629 (Ch D); *Rock Refrigeration Ltd v Jones* [1997] ICR 938 (CA); C Wynn-Evans, 'Restrictive Covenants, Reasonableness and Wrongful Dismissal' (1997) 113 LQR 377.

10

DAMAGES ON TERMINATION

We have seen from the previous chapter that the main effect of termination is **10.01** as a general rule to bring to an end the duty of either party to perform his or her 'primary' obligations under the contract in so far as they remain outstanding at the relevant date.[1] However, in the case of the party in default this is replaced by a 'secondary' obligation to pay damages. This is explained by Lord Diplock in his classic analysis as set out in *Moschi v Lep Air Services Ltd*:[2]

> Generally speaking, the rescission of the contract puts an end to the primary obligations of the party not in default to perform any of his contractual promises which he has not already performed by the time of the rescission. It deprives him of any right as against the other party to continue to perform them. It does not give rise to any secondary obligation in substitution for a primary obligation which has come to an end. The primary obligations of the party in default to perform any of the promises made by him and remaining unperformed likewise come to an end as does his right to continue to perform them. But for his primary obligations there is substituted by operation of law a secondary obligation to pay to the other party a sum of money to compensate him for the loss he has sustained as a result of the failure to perform the primary obligations.

Though Lord Diplock speaks here in terms of 'rescission', it is clear from the con- **10.02** text that he is speaking not of rescission in terms of rescission *ab initio*,[3] but of termination. This analysis was further refined in *Photo Productions Ltd v Securicor Transport Ltd*,[4] where Lord Diplock drew a distinction between damages in general

---

[1] See Ch 9, para 9.02.
[2] [1973] AC 331 (HL) 350.
[3] See Ch 4, para 4.07.
[4] [1980] AC 827 (HL).

(the 'general secondary obligation') and damages awarded following termination (the 'anticipatory secondary obligation'):[5]

> Every failure to perform a primary obligation is a breach of contract. The second-ary obligation on the part of the contract breaker to which it gives rise by implica-tion of the common law is to pay monetary compensation to the other party for the loss sustained by him in consequence of the breach; but, with two exceptions, the primary obligations of both parties so far as they have not yet been fully per-formed remain unchanged. This secondary obligation to pay compensation (dam-ages) for non-performance of primary obligations I will call the 'general secondary obligation.' It applies in the cases of the two exceptions as well. The exceptions are: (1) Where the event resulting from the failure by one party to perform a pri-mary obligation has the effect of depriving the other party of substantially the whole benefit which it was the intention of the parties that he should obtain from the contract, the party not in default may elect to put an end to all primary obliga-tions of both parties remaining unperformed... (2) Where the contracting parties have agreed, whether by express words or by implication of law, that *any* failure by one party to perform a particular primary obligation... irrespective of the grav-ity of the event that has in fact resulted from the breach, shall entitle the other party to elect to put an end to all primary obligations of both parties remaining unperformed...
>
> Where such an election is made (a) there is substituted by implication of law for the primary obligations of the party in default which remain unperformed a second-ary obligation to pay monetary compensation to the other party for the loss sus-tained by him in consequence of their non-performance in the future and (b) the unperformed primary obligations of that other party are discharged. This second-ary obligation is additional to the general secondary obligation; I will call it 'the anticipatory secondary obligation.'

10.03   It is this 'anticipatory secondary obligation' with which the present chapter is con-cerned.[6] It is 'anticipatory', in the sense that the obligation relates to matters in the future, namely the unperformed primary obligations of the party in default. It is 'secondary', in that it applies in lieu of the main obligations of the defaulting party, from which he or she has been discharged by the process of termination. It is an 'obligation', in that it arises from the contract no less than do the relevant primary obligations. In the words of Lord Diplock:[7] 'This secondary obligation is just as much an obligation arising from the contract as are the primary obligations it replaces.'

10.04   How is this obligation calculated? Generally speaking, the obligation is, in the words of Lord Diplock quoted previously, to pay monetary compensation to the other party 'for the loss sustained by him in consequence of their non-performance

---

   [5] *Photo Productions Ltd v Securicor Transport*, 849.
   [6] See generally JW Carter, 'The Effect of Discharge of a Contract on the Assessment of Damages for Breach or Repudiation' (1988–89) 1 JCL 113 and 249.
   [7] *Moschi v Lep Air Services* [1973] AC 331 (HL) 350; F Dawson, 'Reflections on Certain Aspects of the Law of Damages for Breach of Contract' (1995) 9 JCL 125.

in the future',[8] that is to say, the non-performance of the outstanding primary obligations of the party in default. This is normally done by making the defaulting party in these cases pay damages for 'loss of bargain'.[9] Though there may be other measures used,[10] loss of bargain damages is the normal rule in cases of termination.

A. Loss of Bargain Damages

According to the classic statement of the law by Lord Blackburn in *Livingstone v Rawyards Coal Co*,[11] the purpose of damages is to put the injured party 'in the same position as he would have been in if he had not sustained the wrong for which he is now getting his compensation or reparation'.[12] In the contractual context this can be approached in a number of ways, but the normal starting point, as stated by Parke B in *Robinson v Harman*,[13] is to place the claimant, so far as money can do it, in the same position as he would have been in if the contract had been performed.[14] In the present context, the purpose of 'loss of bargain' damages is, in the words of McGregor, to give the injured party the market value of the benefit of which he has been deprived through the breach.[15]

10.05

As has been pointed out, the phrase 'loss of bargain' can be used in two different senses.[16] The first, and more general sense, is to denote the loss suffered by the claimant through being deprived of the benefit of the promise broken.[17] This is a general measure, not confined to cases of termination.[18] However, the term is also used more precisely to denote the loss of the benefits of future performance of obligations released following discharge or termination,[19] and in this sense it corresponds to Lord Diplock's concept of the 'anticipatory secondary obligation'.[20]

10.06

---

[8] See para 10.02.

[9] This phrase first appears during the course of argument in *Worthington v Warrington* (1849) 8 CB 134, 141, 137 ER 459, 462, and was adopted by Cleasby B in *Bain v Fothergill* (1870–71) LR 6 Ex 59, 64 in the context of the former rule that such damages could not be recovered in cases of failure to make good title to land. See now J W Carter, *Carter's Breach of Contract* (Hart, 2012) para 13-02; AS Burrows et al (eds), *Chitty on Contracts* (31st edn, Sweet & Maxwell, 2012) para 26-188; H McGregor, *McGregor on Damages* (18th edn, Sweet & Maxwell, 2009) para 2-002; A Tettenborn and D Wilby (eds), *The Law of Damages* (2nd edn, LexisNexis, 2010) para 19.54.

[10] See paras 10.39–10.41.

[11] (1880) 5 App Cas 25 (HL).

[12] *Livingstone v Rawyards Coal Co*, 39 (n 11); McGregor, *McGregor on Damages*, para 1-022 (n 9).

[13] (1848) 1 Ex 850, 154 ER 363.

[14] *Robinson v Harman*, 855, 365 (n 13); McGregor, *McGregor on Damages*, para 1-023 (n 9); D Winterton, 'Money Awards Substituting for Performance' [2012] LMCLQ 446.

[15] McGregor, *McGregor on Damages*, para 2-002 (n 9).

[16] M Hetherington, 'Contract Damages for Loss of Bargain following Termination: the Causation Problem' (1983) 6 UNSW LJ 211, 219, note 2.

[17] Hetherington, 'Contract Damages', p 219, fn 2 (n 16).

[18] Carter, *Carter's Breach of Contract*, para 13-02 (n 9).

[19] Hetherington, 'Contract Damages', p 219, fn 2 (n 16).

[20] See para 10.03.

In the pages which follow we shall consider *when* such damages are available following termination before going on to look at *how* loss of bargain damages are calculated in such cases.

(1) Availability

10.07   It has been argued by some that loss of bargain damages should be available as a matter of course in cases of termination.[21] However, whatever the position may be in other jurisdictions,[22] this is not the position taken by English law. Instead, we have to distinguish between a number of possibilities.

(a) Unliquidated damages: the 'bifurcated' principle

10.08   The first possibility is that the contract makes no provision for liquidated damages. Here the recovery of loss of bargain damages depends on the reason why the contract was terminated, the general rule being that such damages can be recovered in cases of termination at common law, but not where termination takes place under an express provision to that effect. Though this is sometimes referred to as the 'bifurcated' principle,[23] there are in fact not just two but three situations to consider.

10.09   **(i) Repudiation**   In cases of repudiation or fundamental breach, damages for loss of bargain can generally be recovered as a matter of course.[24] In *Yeoman Credit v Waragowski*[25] the defendant took a van on hire-purchase from the plaintiffs, paid the deposit, and took delivery, but subsequently failed to pay any of the instalments. The plaintiffs then repossessed the van, which they sold for £205, and then sued for arrears or rental up to the date of repossession plus damages. These were subsequently calculated by taking the full hire-purchase price less the sale price of the van, the deposit and the arrears already awarded.[26] It was held by the Court of Appeal that this was the correct measure; this was not a case of mere failure to pay instalments, but a total refusal to carry out the terms of the agreement, and the plaintiffs should therefore be awarded damages on that basis.[27] In *Overstone v Shipway*,[28] it was held by the county court judge on a similar set of facts that the loss had been caused not by the defendant's breach but by the

---

[21] B Opeskin, 'Damages for Breach of Contract Terminated Under Express Terms' (1990) 106 LQR 293; Tettenborn and Wilby, *The Law of Damages*, para 19.31 (n 9).

[22] See para 10.15.

[23] Opeskin, 'Damages for Breach of Contract' (n 21).

[24] One possible exception is in relation to leases: see *Reichman v Beveridge* [2006] EWCA Civ 1659. However, this has been criticized as unsound and contrary to principle: see M Pawlowski, 'Tenant Abandonment—Damages for Loss of Future Rent' (2010) 126 LQR 361.

[25] [1961] 1 WLR 1124 (CA).

[26] *Yeoman Credit v Waragowski*, 1128 (n 25).

[27] *Yeoman Credit v Waragowski* (Davies, Ormerod, and Upjohn LJJ) (n 25).

[28] [1962] 1 WLR 117 (CA).

plaintiff's election to terminate,[29] but this reasoning was rejected by the Court of Appeal.[30] In the words of Davies LJ:[31]

> It seems to me that if a hirer under a hire-purchase agreement is guilty of such a breach or non-observance of the terms of the agreement as would satisfy any court, not merely that the hire-purchase company had a right to terminate the contract but that, in all the circumstances, it would be reasonable to terminate the contract, it cannot thereafter be said on behalf of the hirer: 'You exercised your remedy for my breach of contract by terminating the contract, and having done that you cannot claim damages for my non-performance or breach of contract during such period as it had to run thereafter.'

Though the principle is couched here in terms of whether it was reasonable for the innocent party to terminate in the circumstances, these cases were later explained by the Court of Appeal in *Financings Ltd v Baldock*[32] on the ground that the defaulting party had repudiated the contract.[33] In this situation the innocent party had no choice but to terminate, and it was therefore entirely appropriate that damages should be awarded on the basis of total non-performance by the party in default. In the words of Diplock LJ:[34]   **10.10**

> Read in its context, I do not think that the phrase 'the reasonable solution' was intended to refer to anything other than the well-settled rule of law that a party to a contract has an option to treat as rescinded a contract which the other party has wrongfully repudiated by conduct which evinces his intention no longer to be bound by the contract. Such conduct is in itself a breach of contract, apart from any antecedent breaches there may have been, which entitles the party exercising his option to treat the contract as rescinded, also to recover from the party in default damages for non-performance of his future obligations under the contract.

(ii) **Termination under express provision**   It is different where the innocent party terminates under an express provision to that effect. In *Financings Ltd v Baldock*[35] a contract for the hire-purchase of a van provided for a total price of £762, payable by way of a deposit of £100 and twelve monthly instalments. The contract also gave the owners an express power of termination if any instalment was over ten days late. The hirer paid the deposit but defaulted on the first two instalments, following which the owners exercised their right of termination. They then sought to recover some £530 by way of loss of bargain damages, but   **10.11**

---

[29] This decision came one day before the report of the Court of Appeal decision in *Yeoman Credit v Waragowski*, so the county court judge had had no chance to read it: [1962] 1 WLR 117, 122.

[30] *Yeoman Credit v Waragowski*, 123 (Holroyd Pearce LJ), 125 (Willmer LJ), and 130 (Davies LJ) (n 28). Willmer LJ dissented from the decision of the court, but on a different issue.

[31] *Yeoman Credit v Waragowski*, 130 (n 25).

[32] [1963] 2 QB 104 (CA); see further para 10.11.

[33] *Financings Ltd v Baldock*, 113 (Lord Denning MR), 115 (Upjohn LJ), and 122–3 (Diplock LJ) (n 32).

[34] *Financings Ltd v Baldock*, 122–3 (n 32).

[35] *Financings Ltd v Baldock* (n 32); *Brady v St Margaret's Trust Ltd* [1963] 2 QB 494 (CA); *Capital Finance Co Ltd v Donati* (1977) 121 SJ 270 (CA); *United Dominions Trust (Commercial) v Ennis* [1968] 1 QB 54 (CA).

this was disallowed by the county court judge, following *Overstone v Shipway*,[36] on the ground that the owners' decision to terminate was not reasonable in the circumstances.[37] Though the Court of Appeal, as we have seen, was unanimous in rejecting this test,[38] it was held nevertheless that the owners were restricted to claiming damages on the basis of the arrears of instalments outstanding at the date of termination. Three reasons were given for this.

10.12 The first reason was that it was illogical to allow the owners to claim damages for breach of obligations from which the hirer had been discharged by termination. In the words of Lord Denning MR:[39]

> It seems to me that where an agreement of hiring is terminated by virtue of a power contained in it, and the owner retakes the vehicle, he can recover damages for any breach up to the date of termination but not for any breach thereafter, for the simple reason that there are no breaches thereafter.

10.13 The second reason was that in cases of this sort the loss was caused not by the breach but by the owners' decision to terminate. In this connection Lord Denning MR quoted with approval[40] a passage from the judgment of Salter J in *Elsey & Co Ltd v Hyde*,[41] which was to the following effect:[42]

> Then there is a...case I take, and that is this one, where the hire is determined by the owner, because the hirer is in arrear with his payments. It is proved that this is a breach of this contract, and it is proved that that breach, apart from any termination of the hirer, would give the owner a right to damages against the hirer. But what would those damages be? They would be interest on the amount unpaid and nothing more. The fact that the hirer is in arrear with his payments will not entitle the owner to any damages for depreciation of these things. The reason that they have suffered is that they have secondhand goods put on their hands before they have received very much money in respect of them. That is not the result of the hirer's breach of contract, in being late in his payments, it is the result of their own election to determine the hiring...

10.14 The third reason, given by Diplock LJ, was that a stipulation giving one or other party the right to terminate should not necessarily be construed as allowing for any more than that; in particular, just because the innocent party was entitled to terminate did not mean that he was entitled to any other remedy. Referring to his seminal judgment in *The Hongkong Fir*,[43] he pointed out that in the absence of

---

[36] See para 10.09.
[37] [1963] 2 QB 104 (CA) 105–6.
[38] See para 10.09.
[39] *Financings Ltd v Baldock* [1963] 2 QB 104 (CA) 110.
[40] *Financings Ltd v Baldock*, 111–12 (n 39).
[41] (1926), reported in CG Jones and R Proudfoot, *Notes on Hire-Purchase Law* (2nd edn, 1937) pp 107, 112, quoted by Jenkins LJ in *Cooden Engineering Co Ltd v Stanford* [1953] 1 QB 86 (CA) 102.
[42] *Cooden Engineering v Stanford*, 102 (n 41).
[43] *Hongkong Fir Shipping Co Ltd v Kawasaki Kisen Kaisha Ltd (The Hongkong Fir)* [1962] 2 QB 26 (CA); see Ch 6, paras 6.03–6.08.

express provision to the contrary the mere failure to pay two instalments would not give rise to a right of termination, and went on to say:[44]

> As I ventured to point out in *Hongkong Fir Shipping Co Ltd v Kawasaki Kisen Kaisha Ltd*, parties to a contract may incorporate in it provisions which expressly define the events, whether or not they amount to breaches of contract, which are to have this result. But such a provision may do no more than define an event which of itself, or at the option of one or other of the parties, brings the contract to an end and thus relieves both parties from their undertakings further to perform their obligations thereunder. Whether it does more than this and confers any other rights or remedies on either party on the termination of the contract, depends on the true construction of the relevant provision. If it does not, then each party is left with such causes of action, if any, as had already accrued to him at the date the contract came to an end, but acquires no fresh cause of action as a result of the termination.

All three of these reasons are open to criticism. The idea that the innocent party **10.15** cannot recover damages for breaches following termination as there are no such breaches goes against the principle seen earlier with regard to the anticipatory secondary obligation, namely that in the case of termination the outstanding obligations of the party in default, though indeed discharged, are replaced by a secondary obligation to pay damages for the loss caused thereby.[45] In the same way, the causation argument put forward by Salter J has been criticized as commercially naive by Carter,[46] who says that it is somewhat artificial to draw a contrast between what the common law permits by reference to commercial convenience and what the parties agree for reasons of commercial convenience.[47] Last but not least, whilst Diplock LJ may well be right in saying that termination under an express clause need not give rise to any fresh cause of action, a party who terminates for breach is at least entitled to be compensated for that breach, and if the result of that breach has been to cause a loss of bargain why should the innocent party not be compensated for it?[48] For these and other reasons the so-called 'bifurcated principle' has been rejected in Canada,[49] but it is followed in Australia and

---

[44] [1963] 2 QB 104, 120–1.

[45] See para 10.02.

[46] Carter, *Carter's Breach of Contract*, para 13-07 (n 9). It may, however, be defended on the basis of the general principle that the free and voluntary act of the victim breaks the chain of causation between the wrongdoer's conduct and any resulting loss: see further para 10.23, and see JE Stannard, 'Delay, Damages and the Doctrine of Constructive Repudiation' (2013) 29 JCL 178.

[47] Carter, *Carter's Breach of Contract*, para 13-07 (n 9). Carter nevertheless defends the bifurcated principle on different grounds, namely that a breach of condition, fundamental breach, or repudiation at common law, unlike an express right to terminate, discharges the promisor from liability even before the right of termination is exercised: 'Discharge as the Basis for Termination for Breach of Contract' (2012) 128 LQR 283, 290–2. Though his arguments are sound in principle, it is doubtful that they can stand in the light of *Geys v Société Générale, London Branch* [2012] UKSC 63, [2013] 1 AC 523 (see Ch 4, para 4.14).

[48] Tettenborn and Wilby, *The Law of Damages*, para 19.31 (n 9).

[49] *Keneric Tractor Sales v Langille* (1987) 43 DLR (4th) 171; JS Ziegel, 'Damages for Breach of Finance Leases in Canada' (1988) 104 LQR 513.

other jurisdictions,[50] and continues to be accepted as part of the English law of contract to this day.[51]

10.16   (iii) **Breach of condition**   Where do breaches of condition fit into the picture? The answer seems to be that loss of bargain damages can be recovered in these cases too. In *Lombard North Central plc v Butterworth*[52] a computer was hired[53] to the defendant for five years, with an initial down payment of £584.05 to be followed by nineteen quarterly rentals of the same amount. The contract also provided: (1) that prompt payment of each quarterly instalment of rental was to be 'of the essence'; (2) that in the event of the hirer defaulting in punctual payment of any of these instalments the owner might, after due notice, repossess the computer; and (3) that in the event of repossession the hirer was to pay to the owners all arrears of rentals, all further rentals which would have fallen due, and damages for breach of the agreement. The first two rentals were promptly paid, but the next three were late. The owners having repossessed the computer, and resold it for a small sum, then claimed damages based on the arrears of rental together with the twelve instalments still outstanding. It was subsequently argued by the owners that loss of bargain damages could be obtained either as liquidated damages or on the basis of repudiation.[54] The Court of Appeal held that the liquidated damages clause was unenforceable as a penalty,[55] and that on the facts there was no evidence of actual repudiation by the hirer,[56] but nevertheless allowed the claim for loss of bargain damages at common law.[57] This case was not one where the owner had merely exercised a common law right to terminate. Rather, the effect of the clause making time of the essence was to elevate timely performance into a condition, breach of which was equivalent to a repudiation of the entire contract. In the words of Nicholls LJ:[58]

> I must now consider a further submission advanced by the plaintiffs that, time of payment having been made of the essence by this provision, it was open to the

---

[50] *Shevill and anor v Builders' Licensing Board* (1982) 149 CLR 620, 42 ALR 305; *Progressive Mailing House Pty Ltd v Tabali Pty Ltd* (1985) 157 CLR 17, 57 ALR 609; *Wallace-Smith v Thiess Infraco* (2005) 218 ALR 1; *Morris v Robert Jones Investments Ltd* [1994] 2 NZLR 275; K Nicholson, 'Loss of Bargain Damages for Breach of non-Essential Term' (1988–89) 1 JCL 64.

[51] *ENE 1 Kos Ltd v Petroleo Brasileiro SA (The Kos)* [2009] EWHC 1843 (Comm), [2010] 1 Lloyd's Rep 87, para 38 (Andrew Smith J). The case went to appeal on a different issue, but the bifurcated principle itself was accepted both in the Court of Appeal and in the Supreme Court: [2010] EWCA Civ 772, [2010] 2 Lloyd's Rep 409, para 16 (Longmore LJ); [2012] UKSC 17, [2012] 2 Lloyd's Rep 292, para 7 (Lord Phillips PJSC and Lords Sumption and Walker JJSC).

[52] [1987] QB 527 (CA).

[53] Strictly speaking the contract was one of hire, not hire-purchase, but in effect the hirer had the option of purchasing the goods at the end of the hire period for 5% of their then value: [1987] QB 527, 543–4 (Nicholls LJ).

[54] *Lombard v Butterworth*, 530–1 (n 52).

[55] *Lombard v Butterworth*, 535 (Mustill LJ), 542–3 (Nicholls LJ), and 547 (Lawton LJ) (n 52).

[56] *Lombard v Butterworth*, 535 (Mustill LJ), 545 (Nicholls LJ), and 547 (Lawton LJ) (n 52).

[57] *Lombard v Butterworth*, 535 (Mustill LJ), 545 (Nicholls LJ), and 547 (Lawton LJ) (n 52).

[58] *Lombard v Butterworth*, 545 (n 52).

plaintiffs, once default in payment of any one instalment on the due date had occurred, to treat the agreement as having been repudiated by the defendant, and claim damages for loss of the whole transaction, even though in the absence of this provision such a default would not have had that consequence. On this, the question which arises is one of construction: on the true construction of the clause, did the 'time of the essence' provision have the effect submitted by the plaintiffs? In my view, the answer to this question is 'Yes'.

The same conclusion was set out by Mustill LJ in the fifth and sixth of a series of nine propositions, which were as follows:[59]   **10.17**

> 5. A stipulation that time is of the essence, in relation to a particular contractual term, denotes that timely performance is a condition of the contract. The consequence is that delay in performance is treated as going to the root of the contract, without regard to the magnitude of the breach.

> 6. It follows that where a promisor fails to give timely performance of an obligation in respect of which time is expressly stated to be of the essence, the injured party may elect to terminate and recover damages in respect of the promisor's outstanding obligations, without regard to the magnitude of the breach.

The court was not particularly happy with this result,[60] which can be criticized on a number of grounds.[61] In particular, though the Sale of Goods Act[62] and some of the cases[63] speak of breach of condition in terms of repudiation, the two concepts, as seen earlier, are very different in their theoretical basis[64] and in their scope.[65] As well as this, the result of *Lombard North Central plc v Butterworth* puts a premium on sharp contractual drafting[66] and places a great deal of weight in the present context on the distinction between conditions on the one hand and express rights of termination for breach on the other—a distinction which is difficult to draw at the best of times.[67] All in all, the effect of this case, coupled with the 'bifurcated' principle, is to leave the law in an unnecessarily complicated state in so far as it deals with the recovery of loss of bargain damages following termination.[68]   **10.18**

---

[59] *Lombard v Butterworth*, 535 (n 52).

[60] *Lombard v Butterworth*, 540 (Mustill LJ) and 547 (Nicholls LJ) (n 52).

[61] GH Treitel, 'Damages on Rescission for Breach of Contract' [1987] LMCLQ 143; W Bojczuk, 'When is a Condition not a Condition?' [1987] JBL 353; AP Dobson, 'Late Payment of Instalments by Hirers' [1987] JBL 147; F Oditah, 'Assets and the Treatment of Claims in Insolvency' (1992) 108 LQR 459; Stannard, 'Delay, Damages and the Doctrine of Constructive Repudiation' (n 46).

[62] Sale of Goods Act 1893, s 11(1)(b); Sale of Goods Act 1979, s 11(3).

[63] See especially the influential dissenting judgment of Fletcher Moulton LJ in *Wallis Son and Wells v Pratt & Haynes* [1910] 2 KB 1003 (CA) 1012; see Ch 5, para 5.03.

[64] See Ch 2.

[65] See Ch 5, paras 5.04 and 5.06.

[66] [1987] QB 527, 546 (Nicholls LJ); as Jacobs puts it, the case shows 'ways in which drafting can reach the parts a penalty clause cannot reach'; E Jacobs, 'Leasing' (1987) 8 Business Law Review 255.

[67] See Ch 8, paras 8.02–8.04.

[68] The position is particularly unclear with regard to leases, even assuming that they can be brought to an end by termination in the first place (see Ch 4, para 4.16). In particular, if a landlord makes prompt payment of rent a condition, can he bring the lease to an end and then sue for loss of bargain damages? The better answer would seem to be that this is now possible subject to

(b) Liquidated damages

10.19 What if the contract specifically provides for liquidated damages calculated on this basis? Given that this is, *ex hypothesi*, what the claimant has lost, one would assume that the law would have no problem in enforcing provisions of this sort, but this is not the case in English law, where such provisions fall foul of the rule against penalties. In *Lombard North Central plc v Butterworth*,[69] the facts of which have already been discussed, the contract contained a provision (clause 6(a)) by which following repossession of the goods the hirer was to pay: (1) all arrears of rentals; (2) all further rentals which would have fallen due less discount for accelerated payment; and (3) damages for breach, including expenses and costs incurred by the owners in taking possession.[70] It was argued by the hirer that this was penal, on the ground that it made no provision for a resale price allowance, that is to say, it gave the hirer no credit for the net amount of the price obtained by the owner on resale of the goods following repossession.[71] However, the Court of Appeal disallowed the clause on the broader ground that it allowed the owners to claim a sum equivalent to full loss of bargain damages even in cases of termination under an express right, contrary to the principle in *Financings Ltd v Baldock*.[72] In the words of Nicholls LJ:[73]

> In my view, applying the principle enunciated in *Financings Ltd v Baldock* to this case leads inescapably to the conclusion that in the absence of a repudiatory breach clause 6(a) is a penalty insofar as it purports to oblige the hirer, regardless of the seriousness or triviality of the breach which led to the owners terminating the agreement by retaking possession of the computer, to make a payment, albeit a discounted payment, in respect of rental instalments which had not accrued prior to... [the relevant date].

10.20 Given that in such cases this figure is precisely—leaving aside the issue of the resale price allowance—the loss sustained by the claimant, this is, as Carter observes, a rather odd application of the rule against penalties,[74] and it is not without

---

the availability of relief against forfeiture in appropriate cases: see M Pawlowski and J Brown, 'Repudiatory Breach in the Leasehold Context' [1999] Conveyancer 361, but see *Reichman v Beveridge* [2006] EWCA Civ 1659; see n 24.

[69] [1987] QB 527 (CA); see para 10.16.
[70] *Lombard v Butterworth*, 532–3 (n 69).
[71] *Lombard v Butterworth*, 530 (n 69).
[72] [1963] 2 QB 104 (CA); see paras 10.11–10.15.
[73] [1987] QB 527 (CA) 542–3.
[74] Carter, *Carter's Breach of Contract*, para 13-09; H Beale, 'Penalties in Termination Provisions' (1988) 104 LQR 355. According to the principles set out by Lord Dunedin in *Dunlop Pneumatic Tyre Co Ltd v New Garage and Motor Co Ltd* [1915] AC 79, 87, a provision will be held to be a penalty if the breach consists only in not paying a sum of money, and the sum stipulated is a sum greater than the sum which ought to have been paid: *Kemble v Farren* (1825) 6 Bing 141, 130 ER 1234. However, the status of this principle is increasingly open to doubt, it being argued that the true test is simply whether or not the clause in question was intended to be a genuine pre-estimate of loss, and that it should only be struck down as a penalty if out of all proportion to the loss suffered; see further *United International Pictures v Cine Bes Filmcilik (re Yapimcilik)* [2003] EWCA Civ 1669;

significance that the courts of Australia allow the recovery of liquidated damages on this basis.[75] However, as far as the law of England is concerned, this will only be allowed if the clause is drafted in such a way as to reflect the measure of damages that *will* be awarded at common law; the fact that they *may* be so awarded is not enough.[76]

(2) Basis of assessment

Loss of bargain damages can be classified, in Fuller and Perdue's famous taxonomy,[77] as a species of 'expectation' loss; the innocent party is compensated for his or her failure to obtain the expected benefit of the contract entered into.[78] As Friedmann argues, they might better be termed 'performance damages', as they are intended to put the claimant in as good a position as that in which he or she would have been had the contract been performed.[79] The principles used in calculating these damages are the same as those used for the assessment of damages generally, and there is no point in repeating them at length in the present context. However, there are one or two issues of particular relevance to an award of damages following termination, to which we may now turn.

10.21

(a) Causation

Generally speaking, issues of causation have little part to play in the contractual context as opposed to that of damages in tort.[80] However, as noted previously, causation plays a crucial role in relation to the so-called 'bifurcated' principle, which allows the recovery of loss of bargain damages in cases of repudiation but not where the innocent party invokes an express provision in the contract allowing termination for breach.[81] One reason given for this is that in the latter case the loss of bargain is caused not by the breach but by the election of the innocent party to

10.22

Ringrow Pty Ltd v BP Australia Pty Ltd [2005] HCA 71, (2005) 224 CLR 656; *Murray v Leisureplay plc* [2005] EWCA Civ 963, [2005] IRLR 946; K Dharmananda and D Vujcich, 'Reinventing the Wheel: Recent Interpretations of *Dunlop* on the Penalty Doctrine' [2006] LMCLQ 154; E Peden and JW Carter, 'Agreed Damages Clauses—Back to the Future?' (2006) 22 JCL 189; JW Carter and E Peden, 'A Good Faith Perspective on Liquidated Damages' (2007) 23 JCL 15.

[75] *Esanda Finance Corp Ltd v Plessnig* (1989) 166 CLR 131 (HCA); JW Carter, 'Liquidated Damages and Penalties: the Saga Continues' (1989–90) 2 JCL 78. But where the contract subjects the defaulting party to a liability to pay all sums which would have been payable under the contract without discount for early payment or without taking any account of the possibility of mitigation it will still be a penalty: *AMEV-UDC Finance Ltd v Austin* (1986) 162 CLR 170; RM Goode, 'Penalties in Finance Leases' (1988) 104 LQR 25; Carter, *Carter's Breach of Contract*, para 12-27 (n 9).

[76] Carter, *Carter's Breach of Contract*, para 12-27 (n 9).

[77] LL Fuller and WR Perdue, 'The Reliance Interest in Contract Damages' (1936) 46 Yale LJ 52, 373.

[78] D Friedmann, 'The Performance Interest in Contract Damages' (1995) 111 LQR 628, 630.

[79] Friedmann, 'The Performance Interest in Contract Damages' (n 78).

[80] McGregor, *McGregor on Damages*, para 6.126 (n 9).

[81] See para 10.08.

terminate.[82] This distinction has been criticized by some as a distinction without a difference,[83] the argument being that whilst on the face of it the loss appears to be more closely connected with the breach in the case of repudiation than in the case of termination under an express power, the loss is a matter of choice by the innocent party in the first case no less than in the second, given that unless he or she elects to terminate the innocent party has no right to damages for loss of future performance.[84]

10.23 Whilst there is certainly force in these criticisms, it is nevertheless submitted that there is still a significant distinction between the two cases, namely the fundamental principle that the free and voluntary act of the victim breaks the chain of causation between the wrongdoer's conduct and any resulting loss.[85] Though this principle is more likely to be encountered in the context of criminal law[86] or tort,[87] its influence can be seen in a number of contractual contexts, most notably the requirement of mitigation[88] and the rule that a party cannot rely on self-induced frustration,[89] and this is arguably yet another illustration of the same principle.[90]

(b) Remoteness

10.24 The concept of remoteness of damage in contract can best be explained in terms of two applications, three cases, and three rules. The two applications are the two connections in which the concept of remoteness is used, the first being causation and the second the range of consequences for which the defaulting party must take responsibility;[91] obviously it is the second aspect which is of crucial significance here. The three cases are the three leading decisions on remoteness from which all

---

[82] *Elsey & Co Ltd v Hyde* (1926) reported in Jones and Proudfoot, *Notes on Hire-Purchase Law*, pp 107, 112 (Salter J) (n 41), quoted by Jenkins LJ in *Cooden Engineering Co Ltd v Stanford* [1953] 1 QB 86 (CA) 102; *Financings Ltd v Baldock* [1963] 2 QB 104 (CA) 111–12 (Lord Denning MR); see para 10.13.

[83] Opeskin, 'Damages for Breach of Contract' (n 21).

[84] Opeskin, 'Damages for Breach of Contract', p 317 (n 21); cf *Borealis AB v Geogas Trading SA* [2010] EWHC 2789 (Comm), [2011] 1 Lloyd's Rep 482.

[85] HLA Hart and AM Honoré, *Causation in the Law* (2nd edn, OUP, 1985) pp 41–4 and 136–42. G Williams, 'Finis for Novus Actus?' (1989) 48 CLJ 391; Stannard, 'Delay, Damages and the Doctrine of Constructive Repudiation', p 184 (n 46). Carter describes this argument as 'commercially naive', but nevertheless upholds the bifurcated principle on different grounds; see n 47.

[86] *R v Pagett* (1983) 76 Cr App R 279 (CA), 289 (Robert Goff LJ); *R v Latif* [1996] 1 WLR 104 (HL) 115 (Lord Steyn); *R v Kennedy (No 2)* [2007] UKHL 38, [2008] 1 AC 269, para 14 (Lord Bingham).

[87] *Quinn v Burch Bros (Builders) Ltd* [1966] 2 QB 370 (CA).

[88] *Koch Marine Inc v D'Amica Societa di Navigazione ARL (The Elena D'Amico)* [1980] 1 Lloyd's Rep 75, 88 (Robert Goff J); *Sotiros Shipping Inc v Sameiet Solholt (The Solholt)* [1983] 1 Lloyd's Rep 605 (CA) 608 (Sir John Donaldson MR).

[89] *Mertens v Home Freeholds Co* [1921] 2 KB 526 (CA); *Maritime National Fish Ltd v Ocean Trawlers Ltd* [1935] AC 524 (JCPC–Canada); JP Swanton, 'The Concept of Self-Induced Frustration' (1989–90) 2 JCL 206, 212–13.

[90] Stannard, 'Delay, Damages and the Doctrine of Constructive Repudiation', p 184 (n 46).

[91] McGregor, *McGregor on Damages*, paras 4-023 and 4-024 (n 9).

other rules derive, namely *Hadley v Baxendale*,[92] *Victoria Laundry (Windsor) Ltd v Newman Industries Ltd*,[93] and *The Heron II*.[94] The three rules are the three rules derived from these cases. The first rule is that the extent of the consequences for which the defaulting party must accept liability depends on the contemplation of the parties,[95] or as some prefer to put it, on the principle that a contractor should be liable for consequences of breach only if he or she could reasonably have been regarded as accepting some kind of responsibility for them at the time the contract was made.[96] The second is the distinction outlined in *Hadley v Baxendale* between losses likely to happen in the ordinary course of things (general damage) and other heads of damage specifically within the contemplation of the parties (special damage);[97] though for some purposes it may be more accurate to see these two limbs of the rule as different aspects of the same principle,[98] the distinction has nevertheless been described as a convenient analytical device,[99] and is now probably too well engrained in the terminology of the courts to be abandoned.[100] The third rule is

---

[92] (1854) 9 Ex 341, 156 ER 145. Though generally regarded as a seminal case, the practical significance of *Hadley v Baxendale* and of the foreseeability test has in recent years been called into question, most notably by Sir Robin Cooke in the New Zealand Court of Appeal, who said that in many cases its application was no more than a 'ritual incantation': *McElroy Milne v Commercial Electronics Ltd* [1993] 1 NZLR 39. It has also been argued that the test is really one of contractual construction: A Kramer, 'An Agreement-Centred Approach to Remoteness and Contract Damages' in N Cohen and E McKendrick (eds), *Comparative Remedies for Breach of Contract* (Hart, 2005); A Tettenborn, 'Hadley v Baxendale Foreseeability: a Principle beyond its Sell-By Date?' (2007) 23 JCL 120; A Robertson, 'The Basis for the Remoteness Rule in Contract' (2008) 28 Legal Studies 172. This approach was subsequently adopted by certain members of the House of Lords in *Transfield Shipping Inc v Mercator Shipping Inc (The Achilleas)* [2008] UKHL 48, [2009] 1 AC 61; see especially Lord Hoffmann at para 11 and B Coote, 'Contract as Assumption and Remoteness of Damage' (2009–10) 26 JCL 211. However, this approach has not been universally welcomed: see especially the comments of Stiggelbout, who argues that an approach which 'invites judges to use evidence they do not possess to seek answers that may not exist is likely to produce explanations that do not convince or results that do not please': M Stiggelbout, 'Contractual Remoteness, "Scope of Duty" and Intention' [2012] LMCLQ 97, 121. Though the issue is beyond the scope of the present work, the argument may be no more than a storm in a tea-cup; in the end, the formula in *Hadley v Baxendale*, like other features in the law of contract, is too well engrained in the collective consciousness of the common law to be discarded; see R Ahdar, 'Remoteness, "Ritual Incantation" and the Future of Hadley v Baxendale: Reflections from New Zealand' (1994) 7 JCL 53.

[93] [1949] 2 KB 528 (CA).

[94] *Koufos v Czarnikow (The Heron II)* [1969] AC 350 (HL).

[95] *Victoria Laundry (Windsor) Ltd v Newman Industries Ltd* [1949] 2 KB 528, 537 (Asquith LJ).

[96] *Transfield Shipping Inc v Mercator Shipping Inc (The Achilleas)* [2008] UKHL 48, [2009] 1 AC 61, para 16 (Lord Hoffmann); Coote, 'Contract as Assumption' (n 92); N Andrews, M Clarke, A Tettenborn, and G Virgo, *Contractual Duties: Performance, Breach, Termination and Remedies* (Sweet & Maxwell, 2011) para 23-012.

[97] (1854) 9 Ex 341, 354, 156 ER 145, 151 (Alderson B).

[98] *Victoria Laundry (Windsor) Ltd v Newman Industries Ltd* [1949] 2 KB 528, 537 (Asquith LJ).

[99] Andrews et al, *Contractual Duties*, paras 23-008–23-009 (n 96).

[100] See for instance *Parsons (Livestock) Ltd v Uttley Ingham & Co Ltd* [1977] QB 791 (CA) 798 (Scarman LJ); *County Personnel (Employment Agency) Ltd v Alan R Pulver & Co (a Firm)* [1987] 1 WLR 916 (CA) 925 (Bingham LJ); *Kpohraor v Woolwich Building Society* [1996] CLC 510 (CA) 515 (Evans LJ); *Glencore Grain Ltd v Goldbeam Shipping Ltd (The Mass Glory)* [2002] EWHC 27 (Comm), [2002] CLC 586, para 62 (Moore-Bick J); *University of Keele v Price Waterhouse (a Firm)* [2004] EWCA Civ 583, [2004] PNLR 43, para 14 (Arden LJ); *Transfield Shipping Inc v Mercator*

that if the type of damage incurred was foreseeable, the fact that it was unforeseeably serious will be of no consequence.[101] Whilst in the past this was thought not to apply to loss of profits,[102] the crucial question now seems to relate not to the foreseeability of the losses themselves, but rather to the foreseeability of the events which brought those losses about.[103] All of these principles are thoroughly discussed in the specialist works on damages,[104] and there is no need to go over the same ground here.

10.25 How do these principles apply in the context of termination? Since the effect of termination is to discharge the defaulting party from his or her outstanding primary obligations,[105] the result will be to deprive the innocent party of the benefit of those obligations. In some cases, indeed, the innocent party will get no performance at all from the defaulting party, as where a buyer of goods terminates by rejecting the goods and returning them to the seller. What will normally be expected in these cases is that the innocent party will go out and obtain a substitute performance elsewhere, in which case he or she will end up getting the expected benefit after all, albeit perhaps at a higher price. This perhaps may be termed the ordinary damages obtainable in the normal course of events under the first limb of the rule in *Hadley v Baxendale*.[106] In some exceptional cases, however, this will not be possible, and here the innocent party will have to do without. This will be a case of special damages under the second limb of the rule.[107] The crucial issue in either case is whether there is an available market into which the innocent party can go to recoup his or her losses, and it is to this notion that we must now turn.

(c) Available market

10.26 Where there is an available market, the computation of damages following termination is best illustrated by reference to the rules set out in the Sale of Goods Act

---

Shipping Inc (The Achilleas) [2008] UKHL 48, [2009] 1 AC 61, paras 58 and 59 (Lord Hope); *Sylvia Shipping Co Ltd v Progress Bulk Carriers Ltd* [2010] EWHC 542 (Comm), [2010] 2 Lloyd's Rep 81, para 59 (Hamblen J).

[101] *Vacwell Ltd v BDH Chemicals Ltd* [1971] 1 QB 88 (QBD); *Parsons (Livestock) Ltd v Uttley Ingham & Co Ltd* [1977] QB 791 (CA); *Transworld Oil v Northbay Shipping Co Ltd (The Rio Claro)* [1987] 2 Lloyd's Rep 173 (QBD: Commercial Ct), 175 (Staughton J); *Banque Bruxelles Lambert SA v Eagle Star Insurance Ltd* [1995] 2 WLR 607 (CA) 620 (Bingham LJ); *Homsy v Murphy* (1997) 73 P & CR 26 (CA) 45 (Hobhouse LJ); Andrews et al, *Contractual Duties*, para 23-048 (n 96).

[102] *Cory v Thames Ironworks and Shipbuilding Co Ltd* (1868) LR 3 QB 181; *Victoria Laundry (Windsor) Ltd v Newman Industries Ltd* [1949] 2 KB 528 (CA); Andrews et al, *Contractual Duties*, para 23-051 (n 96).

[103] *Homsy v Murphy* (1997) 73 P & CR 26 (CA); *Jackson v Royal Bank of Scotland plc* [2005] UKHL 3, [2005] 1 WLR 377; Andrews et al, *Contractual Duties*, para 23-051 (n 96).

[104] Tettenborn and Wilby, *The Law of Damages*, ch 6 (n 9); McGregor, *McGregor on Damages*, ch 6 (n 9); Andrews et al, *Contractual Duties*, ch 23 (n 96).

[105] *Moschi v Lep Air Services Ltd* [1973] AC 331 (HL) 350 (Lord Diplock); see Ch 9, para 9.02.

[106] See para 10.24.

[107] See para 10.24.

with regard to non-delivery and non-acceptance of goods.[108] If a buyer of goods terminates, then the seller is discharged from the obligation to deliver. So if the buyer wants the goods, he or she will have to go out into the market[109] and get them at the best price possible. In most cases of termination, that price will be higher than the contract price,[110] and this is the measure of damages that will normally apply under section 51(3) of the Sale of Goods Act 1979.[111] If, on the other hand, the market price is lower than the contract price, the buyer will end up getting the goods cheaper than he or she would have done in the first place, so the damages will be purely nominal.[112]

In a case where a seller terminates, a mirror image of the same rule applies.[113] Since the buyer will no longer be bound or entitled to take the goods, the seller will have to go out into the market[114] and sell them to someone else. In most cases of termination, the price the seller will get will be lower than the contract price,[115] and this is the measure of damages that will apply under section 50(3) of the Sale of Goods Act 1979.[116] If, on the other hand, the market price is higher than the contract price, the seller will end up getting a better price than he or she would have got in the first place, so once again the damages will be purely nominal.[117] **10.27**

The same principle applies in other contexts too. For instance, where a buyer under a contract for the sale of shares in a company refuses to accept and pay for them, **10.28**

---

[108] McGregor, *McGregor on Damages*, ch 20 (n 9).

[109] For the meaning of an 'available market' in this context, see *Lesters Leather & Skin Co Ltd v Home and Overseas Brokers Ltd* (1948–49) 82 Ll L R 202 (CA); McGregor, *McGregor on Damages*, para 20-008 (n 9); Tettenborn and Wilby, *The Law of Damages*, para 22.06 (n 9).

[110] But not all by any means; the buyer may have terminated on strategic grounds to get out of a bad bargain, and if this is so no loss will have been suffered.

[111] McGregor, *McGregor on Damages*, para 20-003 (n 9); *Barrow v Arnaud* (1846) 8 QB 604, 610–11, 115 ER 1004, 1006 (Tindal CJ); *Borries v Hutchinson* (1865) 18 CB (NS) 445, 144 ER 518; *Williams v Agius* [1914] AC 510 (HL); *Kwei Tek Chao v British Traders & Shippers Ltd* [1954] 2 QB 459; *Hong Guan & Co v R Jumabhoy & Sons Ltd* [1960] AC 164 (JCPC–Singapore); *Tai Hing Cotton Mill Ltd v Kamsing Knitting Factory* [1979] AC 91 (JCPC–Hong Kong); Tettenborn and Wilby, *The Law of Damages*, para 22.05 (n 9).

[112] *Valpy v Oakeley* (1851) 16 QB 941, 117 ER 1142; *Griffiths v Perry* (1859) 1 E & E 680, 120 ER 1065; *Erie County Natural Gas Co v Carroll* [1911] AC 105 (JCPC–Canada); McGregor, *McGregor on Damages*, para 20-004 (n 9).

[113] McGregor, *McGregor on Damages*, para 20-112 (n 9).

[114] For the meaning of an 'available market' in this context see *Dunkirk Colliery Co v Lever* (1878) LR 9 Ch D 20 (CA) 25 (James LJ); *Thompson v Robinson (Gunmakers) Ltd* [1955] Ch 177 (Ch D), 187 (Upjohn J); *Charter v Sullivan* [1957] 2 QB 117 (CA) 128 (Jenkins LJ); *Shearson Lehman Hutton Inc v Maclaine Watson & Co Ltd (No 2)* [1990] 1 Lloyd's Rep 441, 447 (Webster J); McGregor, *McGregor on Damages*, paras 20-113–20-115 (n 9); Tettenborn and Wilby, *The Law of Damages*, paras 22.74–22.82 (n 9).

[115] Though once again the seller may be wanting to get out of a bad bargain: see n 110.

[116] McGregor, *McGregor on Damages*, para 20-107 (n 9); *Barrow v Arnaud* (1846) 8 QB 604, 610–11, 115 ER 1004, 1006 (Tindal CJ); *RV Ward v Bignall* [1967] 1 QB 534 (CA); *Shearson Lehman Hutton Inc v Maclaine Watson & Co Ltd (No 2)* [1990] 1 Lloyd's Rep 441 (QBD: Commercial Ct); Carter, *Carter's Breach of Contract*, para 13-04 (n 9); Tettenborn and Wilby, *The Law of Damages*, para 22.73 (n 9).

[117] See n 112.

the measure of damages for the seller is the difference between the contract price and the market price at the date of the breach, with an obligation on the part of the seller to mitigate the damages by getting the best price available upon that date.[118] Again, where a shipowner terminates a time charterparty, he or she may recover from the charterer the difference between the agreed hire and the market rate for an equivalent charterparty for the outstanding period.[119] And where a vendor of land refuses to complete, the purchaser may recover the difference between the contract price and the market value of the land at the date of the breach.[120] In all of these cases the basic assumption is the same; now that the innocent party will not be obtaining the benefit contracted for from the party in default, he or she will be expected to go out into the market and get it some other way.

10.29   However, in some cases there will be no available market. For instance, a seller may agree to deliver a specific item which is not generally available, as where the contract is one for specific goods,[121] or for goods to be manufactured to the buyer's order;[122] or the market may have collapsed;[123] or the contract may be of a kind where it will not be possible to get an identical benefit elsewhere, such as a contract of employment.[124] In these cases the effect of termination will be that the innocent party will have to do without. In some cases the court may be able to apply an approximation of the market rule,[125] but in others the computation of damages will be more difficult. In such cases, the innocent party will have to prove the relevant loss on the basis of the second limb of the rule in *Hadley v Baxendale*; indeed, it may not be possible to claim loss of bargain damages at all, and the innocent party may therefore have to rely on a totally different measure of compensation.[126]

---

[118] *Jamal v Moolla Dawood, Sons & Co* [1916] 1 AC 175 (JCPC–Burma); *Oxus Gold plc v Templeton Insurance Ltd* [2007] EWHC 770 (Comm).

[119] *Goldberg Ltd v Bjornstad & Broekhus* (1921) 8 Ll L Rep 7 (CA); *Snia Societa di Navigazione Industriale et Commercio v Suzuki & Co* (1924) 18 Ll L Rep 333 (CA); *Koch Marine Inc di Amica Societa di Navigazione arl (The Elena d'Amico)* [1980] 1 Lloyd's Rep 75 (QBD Commercial Ct); *Glory Wealth Shipping Pte Ltd v Korea Line Corp (The Wren)* [2011] EWHC 1819 (Comm), [2011] 2 Lloyd's Rep 360. The same approach has been used in relation to voyage charterparties: see *Zodiac Maritime Agencies Ltd v Fortescue Metals Group Ltd (The Kildare)* [2010] EWHC 903 (Comm), [2011] 2 Lloyd's Rep 370.

[120] *Engel v Fitch* (1868–69) LR 4 QB 659; *Diamond v Campbell-Jones* [1961] Ch 22; cf *Brading v F McNeill & Co Ltd* [1946] Ch 145 (sale of business).

[121] *Lyon & Co Ltd v Fuchs* (1920) 2 Ll L R 333 (KBD: Commercial Ct); *Mott & Co v Muller & Co (London) Ltd* (1922) 13 Ll L R 492 (KBD).

[122] *Hydraulic Engineering Co Ltd v McHaffie, Goslett & Co* (1878) 4 QBD 670 (CA).

[123] As in *Yukong Line Ltd of Korea v Rendsburg Investments Corp of Liberia (The Rialto) (No 2)* [1998] 1 WLR 294 (QBD: Commercial Ct) 304 (Toulson J); *Glory Wealth Shipping Pte Ltd v Korea Line Corp (The Wren)* [2011] EWHC 1819 (Comm), [2011] 2 Lloyd's Rep 370.

[124] *Shindler v Northern Raincoat Co Ltd* [1960] 1 WLR 1038 (Manchester Assizes) (Diplock J); Carter, *Carter's Breach of Contract*, para 13-04 (n 9).

[125] For instance, by looking at the cost of the nearest substitute: see *Hinde v Liddell* (1875) LR 10 QB 265 (sale of goods); *Shindler v Northern Raincoat Co Ltd* (Diplock J) (employment) (n 124); *SIB Intl SRL v Metalgesellschaft Corp (The Noel Bay)* [1989] 1 Lloyd's Rep 361 (CA) (charterparty); Carter, *Carter's Breach of Contract*, para 13-04 (n 9).

[126] See paras 10.39–10.40.

(d) Mitigation

There are two basic rules of mitigation in the contractual context. The first debars **10.30** the innocent party from recovering any loss which he or she could have avoided by taking reasonable steps.[127] The second debars the innocent party from recovering any loss which has in fact been avoided, whether or not it would have been reasonable to expect this to be done.[128] Both of these principles are fully discussed in the standard works on damages,[129] and there is no point in repeating that discussion here. There are, however, two points worth highlighting in relation to termination.

(i) **Mitigation and the market rule**   First of all, as has been pointed out, the **10.31** market rule discussed previously incorporates a mitigation requirement;[130] the rule that in the normal run of events the innocent party can only obtain the difference between the contract price and the market price, reflects the expectation that he or she will go into the market and obtain a substitute performance at the best price possible.[131] However, there are limits to what the innocent party can be expected to do. This is well illustrated by *Lesters Leather & Skin Co v Home and Overseas Brokers*,[132] where the buyers of a cargo of snakeskins rejected them as unmerchantable and then sued the sellers for loss of profit. It was argued by the sellers that there was a market for such skins in India, and that therefore the damages should be restricted to the difference between the contract price and the market price. However, it was held that in the circumstances the buyers could not have been expected to buy on that market, given the unstable political situation in India at the time and the fact that the goods would have taken nine months to arrive. In the words of Lord Goddard CJ, the buyers were not expected to go 'hunting the globe' to get their skins.[133]

(ii) **Mitigation and election**   The other key point to note is that the duty of the **10.32** innocent party to mitigate only relates to a claim for damages following termination; it does not apply to a claim for the contract price following affirmation.[134] In *White and Carter (Councils) Ltd v McGregor*[135] the defendants' manager signed a contract engaging the claimants to display advertisements for the defendants' business. The defendants repudiated the contract later that very day, but the claimants decided to ignore the repudiation, went ahead and displayed the advertisements, and then

---

[127] Burrows et al, *Chitty on Contracts*, para 26-079 (n 9).
[128] Burrows et al, *Chitty on Contracts*, para 26-093 (n 9).
[129] Burrows et al, *Chitty on Contracts*, paras 26-077–26-103 (n 9); McGregor, *McGregor on Damages*, ch 7 (n 9); Tettenborn and Wilby, *The Law of Damages*, ch 5 (n 9).
[130] *Copley v Lawn* [2009] EWCA Civ 580, [2010] Bus LR 83, para 6 (Longmore LJ); Carter, *Carter's Breach of Contract*, para 13-04 (n 9).
[131] *Dimond v Lovell* [2002] 1 AC 384 (HL).
[132] (1948–49) 82 Ll L R 202 (CA).
[133] *Lesters Leather v Home and Overseas Brokers*, 205 (n 132).
[134] McGregor, *McGregor on Damages*, para 7-023 (n 9).
[135] [1962] AC 413 (HL(Sc)).

claimed the contract price. The House of Lords held by a majority[136] that, though there might be cases where in such circumstances the innocent party would have no legitimate interest in carrying on performance in the face of a repudiation, this did not apply to the present case.[137] Though the question of mitigation was argued,[138] and indeed referred to by the minority,[139] the doctrine played no part in the reasoning of the majority. No doubt if the claimants had accepted the repudiation, they could not have then claimed the contract price, nor could they have claimed their full loss of profit without making some attempt to mitigate by getting another advertiser. But their decision to affirm left the contract in full force, and so no issue of mitigation arose.[140]

(e) The date of assessment

10.33 The final issue relating to loss of bargain damages relates to the date of assessment.[141] The basic rule here is said to be that damages are normally assessed as on the date of the breach.[142] However, the rule is not an invariable one. In particular, a distinction has to be drawn here between actual breach and anticipatory breach.

10.34 **(i) Actual breach** The normal practice of the courts in awarding damages for breach of contract is to assess them as on the date of the breach.[143] The rationale for this is said to be that this is the point at which the claimant could reasonably be expected to go into the market to mitigate his or her loss.[144] It follows that if there is no relevant market, or a good reason for the innocent party not to go into it, some other date will be chosen.[145] In *Johnson v Agnew*[146] the vendors of a plot of

---

[136] Lord Reid, Lord Tucker, and Lord Hodson, Lord Keith and Lord Morton dissenting.

[137] [1962] AC 413, 431 (Lord Reid): see further Ch 12, paras 12.12–12.34.

[138] *White and Carter v McGregor*, 419, 420, 424, and 425 (n 135).

[139] *White and Carter v McGregor*, 434 (Lord Morton) and 435–6 (Lord Keith) (n 135).

[140] *White and Carter v McGregor*, 419 (J G Wilmers *arguendo*) (n 135).

[141] Andrews et al, *Contractual Duties*, paras 21-085–21-096 (n 96); Carter, *Carter's Breach of Contract*, paras 13-03 and 13-010–13-014 (n 9); SM Waddams, 'The Date for the Assessment of Damages' (1981) 97 LQR 445.

[142] Andrews et al, *Contractual Duties*, para 21-086 (n 96); Tettenborn and Wilby, *The Law of Damages*, para 5.79 (n 9).

[143] According to Lord Wilberforce the 'breach date rule' has a long history, possibly going back to the Year Books: see *Miliangos v George Frank (Textiles) Ltd* [1976] AC 443 (HL) 459. It is codified in relation to the sale of goods by the Sale of Goods Act 1979, ss 50(3) and 51(3), and also merits frequent judicial mention, as in *Jamal v Moola Dawood, Sons & Co* [1916] 1 AC 175 (JCPC–Burma) 179 (Lord Wrenbury); *Diamond v Campbell-Jones* [1961] Ch 22, 36 (Buckley J); *Miliangos v George Frank (Textiles) Ltd* [1976] AC 443 (HL) 468 (Lord Wilberforce); *Standard Chartered Bank v Pakistan Shipping Corp* [1999] CLC 761 (QBD: Commercial Ct), 777 (Toulson J); *Total Spares & Supplies v Antares SRL* [2004] EWHC 2626 (Ch) para 218 (Richards J); *Seatbooker Sales Ltd v Southend United Football Club Ltd* [2008] EWHC 157 (QB) para 113 (Richard Seymour QC); *Grange v Quinn* [2013] EWCA Civ 24, [2013] 1 P & CR 18, para 31 (Arden LJ).

[144] *Radford v De Froberville* [1977] 1 WLR 1262 (Ch D), 1285 (Oliver J); Tettenborn and Wilby, *The Law of Damages*, para 5.97 (n 9).

[145] *Ogle v Vane (Earl)* (1867) LR 2 QB 275; *Hickman v Haynes* (1875) LR 10 CP 598; Tettenborn and Wilby, *The Law of Damages*, para 5.98 (n 9).

[146] [1980] AC 367 (HL).

land were seriously in arrears with their mortgage, and therefore agreed to sell the land to the purchasers, the aim being to pay off the sums owing. The purchasers having failed to complete, the vendors obtained a summary order of specific performance with which the purchasers failed to comply. The mortgagees then sold the land off themselves for a lower price, but this was insufficient to discharge the debts owed by the vendors. The vendors therefore sued for damages, and in allowing the claim the House of Lords refused to tie themselves to the date of the breach. In the words of Lord Wilberforce:[147]

> The general principle for the assessment of damages is compensatory, i.e., that the innocent party is to be placed, so far as money can do so, in the same position as if the contract had been performed. Where the contract is one of sale, this principle normally leads to assessment of damages as at the date of the breach... But this is not an absolute rule: if to follow it would give rise to injustice, the court has power to fix such other date as may be appropriate in the circumstances. In cases where a breach of a contract for sale has occurred, and the innocent party reasonably continues to try to have the contract completed, it would to me appear more logical and just rather than tie him to the date of the original breach, to assess damages as at the date when (otherwise than by his default) the contract is lost.

So even in cases of actual breach the so-called 'breach date rule'[148] is not really a rule at all, but only a starting point, the overriding principle being the need to put the innocent party into the position he or she would have been in if the contract had been performed.

(ii) Anticipatory breach   The position is more complicated in relation to antici-   **10.35** patory breach, the reasons being: (1) that such a breach is of no effect at all unless and until it is accepted by the innocent party; and (2) even when this has taken place, it is hard to see what loss the innocent party suffers, since the time for performance has not yet arrived. The general rule seems to be that though a right of action arises immediately the repudiation is accepted, the damages are assessed on the basis of the loss at the time of performance.[149] Thus where a seller contracts to deliver goods at a fixed date in the future, and then repudiates the contract, damages are fixed, subject to the requirements of mitigation, on the basis of the market price of the goods at the date of delivery.[150] In the words of Bailhache J:[151]

> In my opinion the true rule is that where there is an anticipatory breach by a seller to deliver goods for which there is a market at a fixed date the buyer without buying against the seller may bring his action at once, but that if he does so his damages

---

[147] *Johnson v Agnew*, 400–1 (n 146).

[148] The term first appears in the context of argument by Wilberforce QC (as he then was) in *Re United Railways of Havana and Regla Warehouses Ltd* [1961] AC 1007 (HL) 1030 and then by Lord Wilberforce in his judicial capacity in *Miliangos v George Frank (Textiles) Ltd* [1976] AC 443 (HL) 459.

[149] Andrews et al, *Contractual Duties*, para 21.087 (n 96).

[150] *Melachrino v Nickoll and Knight* [1920] 1 KB 693.

[151] *Melachrino v Nickoll and Knight*, 699 (n 150).

must be assessed with reference to the market price of the goods at the time when they ought to have been delivered under the contract. If the action comes to trial before the contractual date for delivery has arrived the Court must arrive at that price as best it can.

Subject to this, there are a number of particular issues that have to be addressed in the context of the assessment of damages for anticipatory breach.

10.36 The first relates to the problem of contingencies. It is all very well awarding damages on the basis of a future obligation, but can account be taken of the fact that it may never fall due for performance? In *Frost v Knight*[152] the defendant promised to marry the plaintiff once his father was dead, and then repudiated the contract while his father was still alive. The plaintiff then claimed damages for anticipatory breach on the basis of *Hochster v de la Tour*.[153] One of the reasons argued by the defendant for not allowing the plaintiff to recover was the difficulty in assessing damages, given the possibility that he might predecease his father. However, the court had no difficulty in brushing this objection aside. In the words of Cockburn CJ:[154]

> It has been urged that there must be great difficulty in thus assessing damages prospectively. But this must always be more or less the case whenever the principle of *Hochster v De la Tour* comes to be applied. It would equally exist where one of the parties, by marrying another person, gave rise…to an immediate right of action. It cannot be said that the difficulty is by any means insuperable, and the advantages resulting from the application of the principle of *Hochster v De la Tour* are quite sufficient to outweigh any inconvenience arising from the difficulty of assessing the damages.

However, it may be necessary when carrying out this task to factor in the contingency in question. In *Synge v Synge*,[155] as part of a pre-nuptial agreement, the defendant agreed to leave property to the claimant in his will, but then conveyed it to a third party. It was held by the Court of Appeal that the claimant was entitled to damages at once, but that these should be calculated on the basis of the value of the possible life estate to which the claimant would be entitled if she survived her husband.[156] Obviously this would depend on a number of factors, not least the comparative ages of the parties, and the court accordingly ordered an inquiry into damages on this basis.[157]

10.37 In computing damages the court may also take into account events that were certain to occur at the time the repudiation took place.[158] For instance, the innocent party may terminate prematurely in circumstances where he or she would inevitably have

---

[152] (1871-72) LR 7 Ex 111 (Exchequer Chamber).
[153] (1853) 2 E & B 678, 118 ER 922.
[154] (1871–72) LR 7 Ex 111, 117.
[155] [1894] 1 QB 466 (CA); Carter, *Carter's Breach of Contract*, para 13-11 (n 9).
[156] *Synge v Synge*, 472 (Kay LJ) (n 155).
[157] *Synge v Synge*, 472 (Kay LJ) (n 155).
[158] Carter, *Carter's Breach of Contract*, para 13-12 (n 9).

acquired the right to do so lawfully at a later stage.[159] In these circumstances only nominal damages can be recovered, as the innocent party would have suffered no loss at the end of the day.[160] In *The Mihalis Angelos*[161] a charterparty for the carriage of ore from Haiphong contained a clause specifying that the ship was expected ready to load at the beginning of July 1965, and giving the charterers a right of cancellation if the ship was not ready by 20 July. On 17 July the charterers purported to cancel the charter on the grounds of *force majeure*, saying that there was no ore available because of the Vietnam War. The owners treated this as an unlawful repudiation, and sued for damages. At the time the ship was still in harbour at Hong Kong, and it was found by the arbitrators that there would have been no prospect of her making it to Haiphong by the 20 July deadline. In the event it was held by the Court of Appeal that the charterers were entitled to terminate when they did,[162] but the court also dealt with the question of what damages would have been awarded if the termination had been wrongful. The charterers had argued that in this event the damages would be nominal, as they would inevitably have exercised their right of cancellation when the ship failed to arrive on time,[163] and it was held by the Court of Appeal that this was the correct approach.[164] In the words of Megaw LJ:[165]

> In my view, where there is an anticipatory breach of contract, the breach is the repudiation once it has been accepted, and the other party is entitled to recover by way of damages the true value of the contractual rights which he has thereby lost, subject to his duty to mitigate. If the contractual rights which he has lost were capable by the terms of the contract of being rendered either less valuable or valueless in certain events, and if it can be shown that those events were, at the date of acceptance of the repudiation, predestined to happen, then in my view the damages which he can recover are not more than the true value, if any, of the rights which he has lost, having regard to those predestined events.

The courts will also be allowed to take subsequent events into account where they have in fact happened, whether or not they were bound to occur at the time of **10.38**

---

[159] See MG Lloyd, 'Ready and Willing to Perform: the Problem of Prospective Inability in the Law of Contract' (1974) 37 MLR 121, 124–6.

[160] As Lord Porter pointed out, in such a case as this the same loss would have been suffered by the innocent party even if the repudiation had not taken place: *VOS of Moscow v Temple SS Co Ltd* (1945) 62 TLR 43 (HL) 46; Carter, *Carter's Breach of Contract*, para 13-12 (n 9).

[161] *Maredelanto Compania Naviera SA v Bergbau-Handel GmbH (The Mihalis Angelos)* [1971] 1 QB 164 (CA); *Engineering Construction Pte Ltd v A-G of Singapore* (1998) 14 Const LJ 120 (High Court of Singapore); *BS&N Ltd v Micado Shipping (Malta) (The Seaflower) (No 2)* [2000] 2 Lloyd's Rep 37 (QBD: Commercial Ct); *Tele2 Intl Card Co SA v Post Office Ltd* [2009] EWCA Civ 9.

[162] This was not on the grounds of *force majeure*, as this was rejected by the arbitrators, nor under the cancellation clause, as this could not be exercised in advance: see Ch 8, para 8.06. However, the charterers were entitled to terminate for breach of the 'expected ready to load' clause, which was held by the Court of Appeal to be a condition: [1971] 1 QB 164, 193–4 (Lord Denning MR), 200 (Edmund Davies LJ), and 205 (Megaw LJ).

[163] [1971] 1 QB 164, 185–6.

[164] *The Mihalis Angelos*, 196–7 (Lord Denning MR), 201–3 (Edmund Davies LJ), and 209–10 (Megaw LJ).

[165] *The Mihalis Angelos*, 209–10.

termination.[166] In *The Golden Victory*[167] a time charterparty included a war clause giving either party the right to cancel in certain eventualities. The charterers repudiated the contract in 2001, and the owners having accepted the repudiation, the case was then referred to arbitration. By the time the arbitration took place, war had broken out in the Persian Gulf. It was held by the arbitrators that though at the time of termination an outbreak of war could not have been said to have been certain or even probable, they could not close their minds to the fact that it had broken out, and that the owners would then inevitably have exercised their right of cancellation.[168] Once again this was held by the House of Lords, albeit by a bare majority,[169] to be the correct approach.[170] In this connection Lord Scott said that if a contract for the sale of goods over a period of time were frustrated between the acceptance of a repudiation and the assessment of damages, it would clearly be unrealistic to allow the innocent party compensation for a hypothetical loss sustained after the frustrating event had occurred.[171] The same was true in the context of termination. In the words of Lord Scott:[172]

> The same would, in my opinion, be true of any anticipatory breach the acceptance of which had terminated an executory contract. The contractual benefit for the loss of which the victim of the breach can seek compensation cannot escape the uncertainties of the future. If, at the time the assessment of damages takes place, there were nothing to suggest that the expected benefit of the executory contract would not, if the contract had remained on foot, have duly accrued, then the quantum of damages would be unaffected by uncertainties that would be no more than conceptual. If there were a real possibility that an event would happen terminating the contract, or in some way reducing the contractual benefit to which the damages claimant would, if the contract had remained on foot, have become entitled, then the quantum of damages might need, in order to reflect the extent of the chance

---

[166] Carter, *Carter's Breach of Contract*, para 13-13 (n 9).

[167] *Golden Strait Corp v Nippon Yusen Kubushika Kaisha (The Golden Victory)* [2007] UKHL 12, [2007] 2 AC 353; *Dalwood Marine Co v Nordana Line SA (The Elbrus)* [2009] EWHC 3394, [2010] 2 Lloyd's Rep 315; *Slocom Trading Ltd v Tatik Inc* [2013] EWHC 1201 (Ch); GH Treitel, 'Assessment of Damages for Wrongful Repudiation' (2007) 123 LQR 9; B Coote, 'Breach, Anticipatory Breach, or the Breach Revisited' (2007) 123 LQR 503; J Morgan, 'A Victory for "Justice" over Commercial Certainty' [2007] CLJ 263; Q Liu, 'The Date for Assessing Damages for Loss of Prospective Performance under a Contract' [2007] LMCLQ 273; JW Carter and E Peden, 'Damages following Termination for Repudiation' (2008) 24 JCL 145; D Capper, 'A "Golden Victory" for Freedom of Contract' (2008) 24 JCL 176.

[168] [2005] EWHC 161, [2005] 1 CLC 138, para 10 (Langley J).

[169] Lords Scott, Carswell, and Brown, Lords Bingham and Walker dissenting.

[170] *The Golden Victory*, para 38 (Lord Scott), para 68 (Lord Carswell), and para 85 (Lord Brown) (n 167). However, the principle may not be of universal application; in particular, it may not apply in the context of 'one-off' sale of goods contracts that do not involve performance over an extended period of time: *Bunge SA v Nidera BV* [2013] EWHC 84 (Comm), [2013] 1 Lloyd's Rep 621 (Hamblen J).

[171] *The Golden Victory*, para 35 (n 167). The same principle seems to apply even if the relevant event is due to the fault of the party seeking to rely on it, as where the contract is terminated at a later stage due to a subsequent breach by the defaulting party: see *Leofelis v Lonsdale* [2012] EWHC 485 (Ch D); D Winterton, 'Prospective Liability for Breach and Repudiation' [2012] LMCLQ 619.

[172] *The Golden Victory*, para 36 (n 167).

that that possibility might materialise, to be reduced proportionately. The lodestar is that the damages should represent the value of the contractual benefits of which the claimant had been deprived by the breach of contract, no less but also no more. But if a terminating event had happened, speculation would not be needed, an estimate of the extent of the chance of such a happening would no longer be necessary and, in relation to the period during which the contract would have remained executory had it not been for the terminating event, it would be apparent that the earlier anticipatory breach of contract had deprived the victim of the breach of nothing.

B. Other Cases

Though most cases of termination will lead to loss of bargain damages, there may be situations where this is not an appropriate measure. Two situations merit brief mention in the present context, one being the recovery of reliance loss[173] and the other recovery for non-pecuniary losses.

10.39

(1) Reliance loss

In some cases following termination the innocent party will not be able to sue for loss of bargain damages because no such damages can be proved.[174] In *Wallington v Townsend*[175] the defendant agreed to sell a bungalow to the claimant, but then repudiated the contract. The claimant sued for the return of her deposit and for damages, but could not show that the value of the property was higher than the purchase price. It was held that in this situation the claimant was entitled instead to sue for the recovery of wasted expenditure, including the loss of the use of the deposit, for the costs of approving and executing the contract, investigating the title and preparing the conveyance, and of searches.[176] Another situation where it is better to sue for reliance loss is where the contract is a speculative one in which it is impossible to estimate what if any loss of profit there will

10.40

---

[173] Other possibilities include restitutionary damages and even so-called 'vindicatory' damages: see D Pearce and R Halson, 'Damages for Breach of Contract: Compensation, Restitution and Vindication' (2008) 28 OJLS 73. For the award of restitutionary relief following termination, see Ch 11, paras 11.02–11.43.

[174] However, if it can be proved that the innocent party has suffered no loss at all on an expectation basis—for instance, where the contract was an unprofitable one—he or she cannot get round the problem by suing for reliance loss: see *Omak Maritime Ltd v Mamola Challenger Shipping Co (The Mamola Challenger)* [2010] EWHC 2026 (Comm), [2011] 1 Lloyd's Rep 47; DW McLauchlan, 'The Redundant Reliance Interest in Contract Damages' (2011) 127 LQR 23; A Tettenborn, 'Of Damages, Expenses and Unprofitable Charterparties' [2011] LMCLQ 1.

[175] [1939] Ch 588 (Ch D); *Lloyd v Stanbury* [1971] 1 WLR 535 (Ch D); *Commonwealth of Australia v Amann Aviation Pty Ltd* (1991) 66 ALJR 123; GH Treitel, 'Damages for Breach of Contract in the High Court of Australia' (1992) 108 LQR 226.

[176] [1939] Ch 588 (Ch D), 591.

be.[177] In *Anglia Television Ltd v Reed*[178] the claimants engaged the defendant to appear in a forthcoming TV series, but the defendant repudiated the contract soon afterwards. It was held that they could recover their wasted expenditure from the defendants; indeed, this could include expenditure incurred *before* the contract, provided that it was such as would reasonably be in the contemplation of the parties as likely to be wasted if the contract was broken.[179]

(2) Non-pecuniary losses

10.41   Claims for non-pecuniary loss in the contractual context are relatively rare,[180] and claims for such loss following termination rarer still. However, such claims are possible. For instance, in *Bailey v Bullock*[181] the claimant engaged the defendant solicitors to obtain possession of his house, which he had let to a tenant, saying that he needed the house for himself and his family. The defendants assured him on several occasions that the matter was being taken care of, but in fact did nothing. In the end the claimant terminated the contract, secured another solicitor, and obtained possession of the house. It was held by Barry J that the claimant was entitled to damages for the physical inconvenience of having had to live in cramped accommodation with his wife's parents during the interim.[182] In the same way, it was held by the Court of Appeal in *Marbé v George Edwardes (Daly's Theatre) Ltd*[183] that an actress who had been engaged and then forbidden to perform could recover compensation not only for loss of earnings but also for loss of reputation, that is to say for the opportunity to gain an audience.[184] However, no recovery is allowed for mental distress caused by wrongful termination. In *Addis v Gramophone Company*[185] the claimant was wrongfully dismissed by the defendants, and sought to recover not only for loss of earnings but for the harsh and humiliating way in which the dismissal had taken place. However, this was ruled out by the House of Lords, which held that in such a case damages could not be obtained for injured feelings, or even for the fact that the dismissal made it more difficult for the claimant to obtain

---

[177] cf *McRae v Commonwealth Disposals Commission* (1951) 84 CLR 377 (HCA).

[178] [1972] 1 QB 60 (CA); *CCC Films (London) Ltd v Impact Quadrant Films Ltd* [1985] QB 16 (QBD).

[179] [1972] 1 QB 60, 64 (Lord Denning MR).

[180] McGregor, *McGregor on Damages*, paras 3-013–3-032 (n 9).

[181] [1950] 2 All ER 1167 (KBD); *Burton v Pinkerton* (1867) LR 2 Ex 340; *Hobbs v London and South Western Rly* (1875) LR 10 QB 111 (QBD); *Stedman v Swan's Tours* (1951) 95 SJ 727 (CA).

[182] [1950] 2 All ER 1167, 1170.

[183] [1928] 1 QB 269 (CA); *Clayton v Oliver* [1930] AC 209 (HL); *Withers v General Theatre Corp* [1933] 2 KB 536 (CA). A similar principle applies to a wrongfully dismissed apprentice, who can recover for loss of training: *Maw v Jones* (1890) 25 QBD 107; *Dunk v George Waller & Son* [1970] 2 QB 163 (CA).

[184] *Withers v General Theatre Corp* [1933] 2 KB 536 (CA) 554 (Greer LJ).

[185] [1909] AC 488 (HL); *Bliss v South East Thames RHA* [1987] ICR 700 (CA); *Johnson v Unisys Ltd* [1999] ICR 809 (CA).

fresh employment.[186] The only situation in which such loss might be recovered is where the essence of the contract is, in the words of Bingham LJ, to provide 'pleasure, relaxation, peace of mind or freedom from molestation';[187] after all, the law allows damages here where the contract is badly performed,[188] so there is no reason why it should not do so just as well where it is not performed at all.[189]

---

[186] [1909] AC 488, 491 (Lord Loreburn LC).

[187] *Watts v Morrow* [1991] 1 WLR 1421 (CA) 1445.

[188] *Jarvis v Swan's Tours* [1973] 2 QB 233 (CA); *Jackson v Horizon Holidays* [1975] 1 WLR 1468 (CA); *Heywood v Wellers (a Firm)* [1976] QB 446 (CA).

[189] It has been argued that though the rule in *Addis v Gramophone Co* can be justified on pragmatic grounds it is too restrictive, that it conflicts with the basic principles on which contractual damages are awarded, and that it sits ill with the approach of the House of Lords in *Farley v Skinner* [2002] 2 AC 732 (HL): E Macdonald, 'Contractual Damages for Mental Distress' (1994) 7 JCL 134; J Hartshorne, 'Damages for Contractual Mental Distress after Farley v Skinner' (2006) 22 JCL 118. Such damages can, however, be recovered where the dismissal also involves a breach of the implied term of trust and confidence between employer and employee: *Malik v Bank of Credit and Commerce International SA (in liq)* [1998] AC 20 (HL).

11

RESTITUTIONARY RELIEF

This chapter is concerned with several inter-connected instances where the **11.01** non-breaching party in a contract terminated for the other's breach might seek restitutionary relief under the law of unjust enrichment as opposed to damages for breach of contract. It is also concerned with some situations where the claimant seeks relief which has been thought to be the province of the law of unjust enrichment but is not strictly speaking something falling within that branch of the law of obligations. What causes it to be placed in this chapter is that it is not necessarily a contract remedy. This chapter will also analyse some situations where the breaching party seeks, on the termination of a contract, to recover restitution of money and other benefits transferred to the other party. As the remedy here is not contractual, it is not particularly surprising that the breaching party should be entitled to relief in certain circumstances. As restitution (or unjust enrichment as some prefer to call it) has been recognized as a discrete branch of the law of obligations comparatively recently,[1] some of the discussion of older authorities will require re-interpretation of decisions in the light of the more modern vocabulary used today.

A. Claimant Recovery

For claims where the claimant seeks to recover benefits transferred under a contract **11.02** now terminated it is still conventional to distinguish between claims for restitution

---

[1] The first judicial recognition of the existence of restitution as an independent subject came in the decision of the House of Lords in *Lipkin Gorman v Karpnale Ltd* [1991] 2 AC 548 (HL).

of money benefits and claims for non-money benefits. But before examining these two claims in turn it is worth asking why the claimant might be seeking restitution? The claimant has a claim for breach of contract against the defendant which would in principle extend to loss of bargain damages and claims for consequential loss, and in most cases these losses would exceed the sum likely to be recovered in a claim for restitution. The answer is that sometimes, particularly when the contract is not a profitable one from the claimant's perspective, restitution provides the claimant with a higher recovery than contract. Whether and to what extent this should be allowed is a question that must be revisited.

11.03 The relationship between the potential claim for breach of contract and the claim in restitution requires some clarification. A claim in restitution cannot be brought so long as the contract is subsisting.[2] The law of restitution is subservient to the law of contract and should not be used to undermine the contractual allocation of risk. Hence, for a claim in restitution to succeed the contract must be terminated first although bringing a claim in restitution could be construed as an effective exercise of the right to terminate. However, as the following text will demonstrate, the contract's provisions can continue to have an effect upon the remedies available in the event of a breach. The High Court of Australia has said that a claimant cannot combine a claim in restitution with a claim for damages for breach.[3] In the relevant case the claimant was evacuated from a cruise ship which sank off the south-east coast of New Zealand. She claimed a refund of her fare plus contractual damages for, *inter alia*, distress and disappointment. The contractual damages claim ultimately succeeded but the claim for a refund of the fare failed because the claimant could not show a total failure of consideration. Had this claim succeeded there is no reason why it should not have been included as part of the damages award for breach. What the High Court's decision comes to is that the claimant could not obtain a double recovery of fare refund as part of her damages for breach and also a separate claim in restitution.[4]

(1) Money benefits—total failure of consideration

11.04 If the claimant has transferred money to the defendant before the contract was terminated there may be a right to restitution of that payment provided the consideration for that payment has totally failed. This requires two questions to be addressed—what is the meaning of consideration in this context and what does it mean to say that the consideration has failed totally?

---

[2] G Virgo, *The Principles of the Law of Restitution* (2nd edn, OUP, 2006) pp 305, 310–11.
[3] *Baltic Shipping Co v Dillon* (1993) 176 CLR 344 (HCA).
[4] See K Barker, 'Restitution of Passenger Fare' [1994] LMCLQ 291, where this is explained.

(a) Meaning of 'consideration'

For the meaning of 'consideration' the following two judicial statements are **11.05** helpful. First, in *Fibrosa Spolka Akcyjna v Fairbairn Lawson Combe Barbour Ltd* Viscount Simon LC said:[5]

> In English law, an enforceable contract may be formed by an exchange of a promise for a promise, or by the exchange of a promise for an act ... and thus, in the law relating to the formation of a contract, the promise to do a thing may often be the consideration, but when one is considering the law of failure of consideration and of the quasi-contractual right to recover money on that ground, it is, generally speaking, not the promise which is referred to as the consideration, but the performance of the promise. The money was paid to secure performance and, if performance fails the inducement which brought about the payment is not fulfilled.

Then in *Stocznia Gdanska SA v Latvian Shipping Co* Lord Goff said:[6]

> ...the test is not whether the promisee has received a specific benefit, but rather whether the promisor has performed any part of the contractual duties in respect of which the payment is due.

From these two statements the following important conclusions can be drawn. First, consideration does not mean in this context what it means when determining whether an agreement is enforceable as a contract. Secondly, and more importantly in this context, one does not ask what benefits the claimant has received but whether the defendant has performed any part of its contractual obligations. As *Treitel: The Law of Contract* has expressed it 'the test is whether performance has been *rendered*, not whether it has been *received*'.[7] The court's task is to determine whether the defendant has done anything to justify retention of the money benefit it has received. The only thing that is capable of justifying that retention is the performance of at least some of the contractual obligations promised in return for the promise to pay the money.

(b) Failure of consideration must be total

To succeed in recovering money paid pursuant to a contract that has now been **11.06** terminated the claimant must show that the failure of consideration was total. Officially, partial failure of consideration will not do. As will become apparent, the application of this total failure of consideration test has often proved to be a difficult exercise and it cannot be maintained dogmatically that all the decisions can be convincingly reconciled. A comparatively straightforward case is *Baltic Shipping Co v Dillon*.[8] The claimant's claim to a full refund of her fare was unsuccessful

---

[5] [1943] AC 32 (HL) 48.
[6] [1998] 1 WLR 574 (HL) 588.
[7] E Peel, *Treitel: The Law of Contract* (13th edn, Sweet & Maxwell, 2011) para 22-003, note 10.
[8] (1993) 176 CLR 344 (HCA) (n 3).

because she was evacuated from the ship after eight days of a fourteen-day cruise and thus the defendants could not be said to have rendered none of their agreed contractual performance. This was not, in the end, an inequitable outcome because the defendants had refunded that part of the claimant's fare which pertained to the six days' cruising she did not enjoy.

11.07   Application of the 'total failure' test has yielded some quite perplexing results. A leading authority is *Rowland v Divall.*[9] In this case the buyer of a motor vehicle innocently bought it from someone who was not the owner. The buyer was himself a dealer and after two months resold the vehicle to a third party. The police traced the vehicle and it was returned to its true owner. The buyer reimbursed the third party and sought to recover the price paid to the seller as money paid for a consideration that totally failed. The obvious problem with the buyer's claim was that he had two months' possession of the vehicle before he sold it to the third party. The Court of Appeal, however, held that under the contract of sale between the seller and the buyer the seller was obliged to transfer ownership of the vehicle to the buyer and this he had totally failed to do. As for the possession which the buyer enjoyed, that was also meant to be given to him under the contract, so this can be rationalized as total failure as well because the buyer contracted for a lawful right to possession which the seller was unable to confer. If the consideration that fails is to be seen in terms of consideration rendered as opposed to benefits received, this decision can be viewed as reasonably sound. It is also worth pointing out that in theory the true owner could have sued the buyer in conversion. And in unjust enrichment terms the buyer's possession of the vehicle was at the expense of the owner, not the seller, so should not be seen as a proper subject for counter restitution to the defendant.[10] The same approach was taken and same result reached in *Butterworth v Kingsway Motors Ltd*[11] and in *Barber v NWS Bank plc.*[12]

11.08   A somewhat contrasting case is *Yeoman Credit Ltd v Apps.*[13] The claimant hire-purchase company entered into a hire-purchase contract with the defendant. The car had numerous defects, about which the defendant protested to the claimant. However, he paid three hire-purchase instalments before he defaulted on the next two. The claimant sued to recover the arrears of instalments and damages and the defendant counterclaimed for the three instalments paid on the ground that the defective condition of the car reduced these payments to sums for which the consideration totally failed. The Court of Appeal held that there had been no total failure of consideration because the defendant contracted for lawful possession of the vehicle and that was what he got. If the contract had been one for work and

---

[9] [1923] KB 500 (CA).
[10] See A Burrows, *The Law of Restitution* (3rd edn, Hart, 2011) p 342.
[11] [1954] 1 WLR 1286 (Liverpool Assizes) (hire-purchaser had used a car for eleven months).
[12] [1996] 1 WLR 641 (CA) (conditional purchaser had used a car for twenty-two months).
[13] [1962] 2 QB 508 (CA).

materials or services and the quality of the work done by the recipient of payment had been completely useless, the outcome would have been different.[14]

Where the contract is entire it would seem that total failure of consideration is rela- **11.09** tively easy to establish. As the claimant paid the money for the defendant's entire performance any failure by the defendant to meet the strict requirements of the contract will be held to be a total failure of consideration. This seems to be the best explanation of the old case of *Giles v Edwards*.[15] The claimant paid the defendant in advance for cordwood which the defendant was to cord. The defendant corded only some of the wood and the claimant recovered the advance payment on the ground of total failure of consideration.

There will be a total failure of consideration if money is paid in advance for the **11.10** purchase of goods and the goods are not delivered. Thus in *Fibrosa Spolka Ackyjna v Fairbairn Lawson Combe Barbour Ltd* (a frustration case)[16] the claimant entered into a contract with the defendant to purchase machinery which the defendant manufactured. An advance payment was made but the outbreak of the Second World War frustrated the contract and no machinery was delivered. The claimant recovered the advance payment on the ground of total failure of consideration even though the defendant had begun to manufacture the machinery. The contract was construed as one of sale of goods only and as none of the machinery had been delivered to the claimant the consideration for the money paid had totally failed. A different outcome was reached in *Stocznia Gdanska SA v Latvian Shipping Co*,[17] where the claimants part manufactured a ship for the defendants and exercised a contractual right to terminate the contract for the defendants' repudiatory breach. The claimants sought summary judgment for an instalment due under the contract and were faced with the defendants' defence that as this would have been a payment for a consideration that totally failed they were not entitled to it. The House of Lords held that this was a contract to build and sell the ship so that the construction work done to date prevented total failure of consideration. Assuming the correctness of the decision that the contract was not just for the sale of the ship but for its construction and sale, it has to be correct to hold that there had been no total failure of consideration. Consideration in this context means not benefits transferred but performance rendered. Furthermore in the language of unjust enrichment scholarship the defendants would not be permitted to argue that they received no enrichment (the subjective devaluation argument) because the claimants had done precisely what the contract required of them and the contract was not entire. The difficulty with these cases, however, is that they show how the

---

[14] *Heywood v Wellers (a Firm)* [1976] QB 446 (CA), 458.
[15] (1797) 7 Term Rep 181; 101 ER 920 (KB).
[16] [1943] AC 32 (HL).
[17] [1998] 1 WLR 574 (HL).

distinction between a contract to sell goods and a contract to manufacture and sell goods is not always easy to draw.

11.11   An effect resembling partial failure of consideration may be produced where it is possible to apportion payments among separate parts of the contractual performance due from the defendant. Thus the buyer of 100 tons of a commodity could recover half the payment if only 50 tons were delivered.[18] In *Goss v Chilcott*[19] lenders of money on mortgage were able to recover the principal sum even though the borrowers had paid two instalments of interest. The obligations to pay interest and to repay capital were treated as separate and distinct and as no part of the capital sum had been repaid the consideration for lending it had totally failed once the contract of loan was terminated. Subtle as this distinction between interest and capital is, it makes nothing like the inroads into the total failure requirement that the following passage from the judgment of Lord Goff makes:[20]

> But even if part of the capital sum had been repaid, the law would not hesitate to hold that the balance of the loan outstanding would be recoverable on the ground of failure of consideration; for at least in those cases in which apportionment can be carried out without difficulty, the law will allow partial recovery on this ground.

Apportionment seems also to have been applied rather strangely in *DO Ferguson & Associates v M Sohl*.[21] The employer in a building contract had paid £26,738 for contract work that was actually worth only £22,065. The overpayment of £4,673 was recovered on the ground of total failure of consideration. It is difficult to contest the validity of Ralph Cunnington's comment that 'the Court of Appeal effectively broke up the consideration pound by pound to enable them to find a total failure of the severed part. Such analysis removes any real distinction between partial and total failure of consideration'.[22]

(c) Making sense of total failure of consideration

11.12   In order to make sense of the right to recover money paid before the termination of a contract, it is useful to begin by explaining why a claimant might prefer to bring such an action. The claimant does have, it must not be forgotten, a right to claim damages for breach of contract and in the great majority of cases this right, which compensates for disappointed expectations, will yield a higher return than the restitutionary action to recover money paid. To begin with there are those cases where the non-breaching party has made a bad bargain and thus has no expectation losses. Here a restitutionary action is better. It is sometimes protested that this subverts the contractual

---

[18] Peel, *Treitel*, para 22-004 (n 7). The Sale of Goods Act 1979, s 30(1) states that if the seller delivers short the buyer may reject the goods but if the goods are accepted the buyer must pay pro rata.

[19] [1997] 2 All ER 110 (JCPC–NZ).

[20] *Goss v Chilcott*, 117 (n 19).

[21] (1992) 62 BLR 95 (CA).

[22] R Cunnington, 'Failure of Basis' [2004] LMCLQ 234, 246.

allocation of risk and that it is wrong in principle to allow a claimant to do better in restitution than in contract. But the positing of an example given by Tettenborn[23] and Virgo comprehensively answers this argument. If A buys a car from B for £10,000 but which is worth only £8,000 A's damages for breach of contract would be nominal as there is no difference on these facts between what A got and what A should have got. By pursuing a restitutionary claim A gets the £10,000 back and returns the car to B. To limit A to £8,000 would leave B with a quite undeserved profit of £2,000.[24] It may also be advantageous for A to sue in restitution and avoid the sometimes difficult issues in breach cases concerning proof of loss, remoteness, and mitigation.[25] It will, of course, be rare for a defendant to breach a profitable contract.

The next question which needs to be addressed is why the failure of consideration **11.13** needs to be total. Why can it not be partial? In addressing this question it should be pointed out that the claimant does have a right to sue for breach of contract and that cases of partial failure of consideration closely resemble cases requiring measurement of loss. It should also be acknowledged that the official commitment to total failure of consideration does not often seem to have denied a remedy, either in restitution or breach, to a claimant who should have one. In the *Rowland v Divall*[26] type of case the buyer gets restitution because the seller cannot provide lawful ownership and possession. In *Yeoman Credit Ltd v Apps*[27] the hire-purchaser still had a contractual counterclaim for the wretched condition of the vehicle. And in the apportionment cases a way was found to grant restitution to claimants the courts believed deserved it. So it may well be that sticking with the total failure requirement will not produce any significant injustice.

So what are the reasons for the current commitment to total failure of consideration? **11.14** First, it has been argued that to recognize partial failure of consideration would subvert the contractual allocation of risk. This argument points out that the claimant does have a right to seek damages for breach and maintains that cases of partial failure would lead to claimants doing better in restitution than in contract.[28] The argument is unconvincing because it does not clearly explain why subverting the contractual allocation of risk is no problem in cases of total failure but a real difficulty in partial

---

[23] A Tettenborn, *The Law of Restitution in England and Ireland* (3rd edn, Routledge-Cavendish, 2002) para 6.20; Virgo, *Principles of the Law of Restitution*, p 307 (n 2).

[24] If authority need be cited that restitution may be granted in this scenario consider *Wilkinson v Lloyd* (1845) 7 QB 25, 115 ER 398 (QB). The claimant agreed to buy shares in a company conditional upon the defendant obtaining the directors' consent to the share transfer. The defendant failed to obtain the directors' consent and the claimant sued to recover the price paid. He succeeded even though the value of the shares had decreased in the meantime. Supporting dicta for this decision may be found in *Ebrahim Dawood Ltd v Heath Ltd* [1961] 2 Lloyd's Rep 512 (QBD).

[25] Burrows, *The Law of Restitution*, p 346 (n 10), where it is pointed out, for example, that the claimant's use of the motor vehicle in *Rowland v Divall* (see n 9) would reduce his damages for breach but would not be a matter of counter restitution as the seller was not the owner of the vehicle.

[26] See para 11.07.

[27] See para 11.08.

[28] Peel, *Treitel*, para 22-004 (n 7).

failure. In any event, restitution is only available in the rare event of the contract being discharged, so it is difficult to see what threat it poses to contract law.[29] Secondly, it has been argued that partial failure would involve difficult problems of counter restitution which would clearly not be present where the consideration totally failed. This argument is convincingly answered by Burrows, who states that 'simplicity is hardly justice' and points out the 'vast tracts' of the law of unjust enrichment where restitution is granted on the condition that counter restitution be provided.[30]

11.15 Against these unconvincing reasons the following more persuasive reasons are offered as to why partial failure should suffice. First, there remains an unjust enrichment even if the failure of consideration is not total. Secondly, open acknowledgement of partial failure would obviate the need to manipulate total failure as arguably occurred in some of the apportionment cases discussed previously. Thirdly, partial failure of consideration underlies the award of restitution under section 1(2) of the Law Reform (Frustrated Contracts) Act 1943 where a defendant obliged to make restitution of a payment made prior to a frustrating event is entitled to deduct from it expenses incurred in the performance of the contract. Arguably, the common law should develop in step with this statutory reform.[31]

11.16 There is precious little academic support for the total failure rule and, it is submitted, very convincing reasons why a partial failure rule should replace it. However, the current rule does not seem to be causing a great deal of injustice and judicial hints about its future present a rather nuanced picture. In *Westdeutsche Landesbank Girozentrale v Islington LBC* Lord Goff said:[32]

> There has long been a desire among restitution lawyers to escape from the unfortunate effects of the so-called rule that money is only recoverable at common law on the ground of failure of consideration where the failure is total, by reformulating the rule upon a more principled basis; and signs that this will in due course be done are appearing in judgments throughout the common law world.

In *Roxborough v Rothmans of Pall Mall Australia Ltd* Gummow J stated that the total failure requirement would not apply where the contract was no longer subsisting and there was no difficulty in apportioning the consideration.[33] However, Lord Goff was more cautious in *Stocznia Gdanska SA v Latvian Shipping Co* where he said:[34]

> This rule has been subject to considerable criticism in the past; but it has to be said that in a comparatively recent Report (Law Com. No. 121 (1983) concerned with

---

[29] See Barker, 'Restitution of Passenger Fare', pp 293–4 (n 4); Burrows, *The Law of Restitution*, p 330 (n 10).

[30] See Burrows, *The Law of Restitution*, p 331 (n 10); Barker, 'Restitution of Passenger Fare', pp 293–4 (n 4); Virgo, *Principles of the Law of Restitution*, p 324 (n 2).

[31] See Burrows, *The Law of Restitution*, pp 331–2 (n 10); Barker, 'Restitution of Passenger Fare', pp 293–4 (n 4); Virgo, *Principles of the Law of Restitution*, p 323 (n 2).

[32] [1996] AC 669 (HL) 682.

[33] (2002) 76 ALJR 203 (HCA).

[34] [1998] 1 WLR 574, 590.

Pecuniary Restitution on Breach of Contract) the Law Commission has declined to recommend a change in the rule, though it was there considering recovery by the innocent party rather than by the party in breach.

Recently in *Giedo van der Garde BV v Force India Formula One Team Ltd* Stadlen J dismissed a restitutionary action for failure of consideration because it was only for partial failure.[35] The judge said:[36]

> I am bound to say that I reach this conclusion with considerable regret, joining as I do the growing list of judges and academic writers who have expressed the view that the requirement of proof of total failure of consideration as a necessary condition for an award of restitution is unsatisfactory and liable in certain cases to work injustice.

His Lordship did award the claimants £1,865,000 damages in line with the principle in *Wrotham Park Estate Co Ltd v Parkside Homes Ltd*.[37]

(2) Non-money benefits

Where a contract is terminated before completion the non-breaching party has, in addition to its claim for damages for breach, a right to seek restitution of any benefits conferred upon the defendant. In unjust enrichment terminology there has to be an enrichment at the expense of the claimant and an unjust factor. Whether the enrichment takes the form of money benefits as in the previous section of this chapter or non-money benefits as in this section, the unjust factor is failure of consideration.[38] But so far as restitution for non-money benefits is concerned, there is no requirement that the failure of consideration be total, which is perhaps another reason why partial failure should suffice when restitution of a money payment is sought. The two principal issues that must be addressed are whether the defendant has been enriched by the claimant's contractual performance prior to termination and whether restitution is measured by the value received by the defendant or a pro rata portion of the contract price. It will be seen that these two issues overlap to some extent. **11.17**

(a) Enrichment

In relation to the first issue, whether the defendant has been enriched, cases cited in support of this proposition do not always exhibit clear evidence of enrichment. Thus in *Planché v Colburn*[39] the claimant was contracted to write a book for the defendant publisher for £100. After starting to write the book but before tendering **11.18**

---

[35] [2010] EWHC 2373 (Ch).
[36] *Giedo van der Garde v Force India Formula One Team*, para 367 (n 35).
[37] [1974] 1 WLR 798.
[38] Burrows, *The Law of Restitution*, p 341 (n 10).
[39] (1831) 8 Bing 14 (Court of Common Pleas).

any part of it the claimant validly terminated the contract for the defendant's repudiatory breach in abandoning publication of the series of which this book was part. The Court of Common Pleas awarded the claimant £50 damages on a *quantum meruit* basis. It is not clear precisely what benefit (enrichment) was conferred on the defendant but Virgo's suggestion that the defendant was estopped from denying enrichment has merit.[40] It simply does not lie in the mouth of someone who has contracted for something to repudiate the contract and then contend (s)he was not enriched. In *De Bernardy v Harding*[41] the defendant erected seats for the public to view the funeral of the Duke of Wellington. He contracted with the claimant for the latter to advertise the funeral abroad and sell tickets for it. The claimant was to be paid an allowance of 10 per cent of the money raised from ticket sales abroad. The claimant incurred expense advertising the funeral abroad but before he had sold any tickets the defendant repudiated the contract and decided to sell the tickets himself. The defendant met the expenses incurred by the claimant but refused to pay any remuneration to the claimant himself. The claimant brought an action upon a *quantum meruit* against the defendant which the judge dismissed on the ground that he should have sued for breach of contract. On appeal it was held that the claimant was entitled to bring a *quantum meruit* action and that the issue should have been left to the jury. Once again the enrichment is not clear but the estoppel argument suggested earlier in connection with *Planche v Colburn* seems a suitable rationale.

11.19   In *Chandler Bros Ltd v Boswell*[42] the defendant main contractors repudiated a sub-contract under which the claimants were excavating a tunnel. The claimants were held to be entitled to recover on a *quantum meruit* for the work they had done. In this case the enrichment of the defendant is somewhat easier to see and the real issue raised by the case is whether a restitutionary claim should be allowed whenever the claimant has an obvious case for breach of contract. Greer LJ said 'it has long been settled that the plaintiff whose contract is broken is entitled, if he so chooses, to claim damages or claim on a *quantum meruit* basis'.[43] While this choice is undoubtedly well settled, its rationale is not as clear as the choice between suing for restitution of money paid for a consideration that totally fails and the recovery of contract damages. There are clear advantages to claiming restitution of money payments, in the context of bad bargains especially and in terms of avoiding some of the difficult quantification issues that can arise when suing for breach. But as will be shown, there is a serious unresolved issue as to whether the claimant can recover the value of the benefit received by the defendant if it exceeds what would have been earned under the contract.

---

40 Virgo, *Principles of the Law of Restitution*, pp 90–3 (n 2).
41 (1853) 8 Exch. 822 (Court of Exchequer).
42 [1936] 3 All ER 179 (CA).
43 *Chandler Bros v Boswell*, 186 (n 42).

(b) Whether enrichment is measured by benefit to defendant or contract value

It has been argued that the claimant is not entitled to full restitution of the value **11.20** of the benefit to the defendant where this exceeds the rate that would have been payable under the contract. This, it is said, is to undermine the allocation of risk provided by the contract itself. If the claimant has made a bad bargain it should be required to live with that and not seek to improve its position by framing its claim in restitution. So the claimant should not be able to do better by partial performance than by full,[44] and where the claimant's performance is complete only the price should be recoverable.[45] This is the view taken in the only recent English authority on the subject, *Taylor v Motability Finance Ltd*,[46] although as will be argued later, this decision can be explained on a different basis.

Decisions from other common law jurisdictions support a different view. This is **11.21** that the contract has been terminated and does not provide the governing framework of analysis. The defendant therefore cannot set up a contract it has caused to be terminated as a defence to the claimant's unjust enrichment action. So in *Lodder v Slowey*[47] the Privy Council dismissed an appeal from a decision of the New Zealand Court of Appeal allowing the claimant remuneration on a *quantum meruit* basis for the partial completion of a tunnel constructed under a contract repudiated by the defendant. In *Boomer v Muir*[48] another building contractor was awarded $258,000 on a *quantum meruit* despite there being only another $20,000 due under the contract. Carter attempts to reduce the significance of these cases by arguing that they proceeded on a theory of rescission *ab initio*.[49] While restitution follows as a matter of principle in a case where the contract has been rescinded *ab initio*, it does not seem to follow that it would be inappropriate where the contract has been terminated prospectively.

The argument in favour of allowing recovery exceeding the sum due under the **11.22** contract is perhaps most clearly articulated in the judgment of Meagher JA in the New South Wales Court of Appeal decision of *Renard Constructions (ME) Pty Ltd v Minister for Public Works*. His Honour said:[50]

> There is nothing anomalous in the notion that two different remedies, proceeding on entirely different principles, might yield different results...Nor is there anything anomalous in the prospect that a figure arrived at on a *quantum meruit* might exceed, or even far exceed, the profit which would have been made if the contract had been fully performed...The most that one can say is that the amount

---

[44] Tettenborn, *The Law of Restitution*, paras 6.11 and 6.31 (n 23).
[45] Tettenborn, *The Law of Restitution*, para 6.24 (n 23).
[46] [2004] EWHC 2619 (Comm) (QBD).
[47] [1904] AC 442 (JCPC–NZ), affg [1900] 20 NZLR 321 (NZCA).
[48] 24 P 2d 570 (1933) (District Court of Appeal of California). A different view is, however, taken in the Restatement Third, Restitution and Unjust Enrichment § 38 and comment.
[49] JW Carter, *Carter's Breach of Contract* (Hart, 2012) para 13-55.
[50] (1992) 26 NSWLR 234 (NSWCA) 267–8.

contractually agreed is evidence of the reasonableness of the remuneration claimed on a *quantum meruit*; strong evidence perhaps, but certainly not conclusive evidence. On the other hand, it would be extremely anomalous if the defaulting party when sued on a *quantum meruit* could invoke the contract which he has repudiated in order to impose a ceiling on amounts otherwise recoverable.

It is submitted that this dictum accurately states the law, subject to two qualifications, one impliedly and the other expressly acknowledged in the statement itself.

11.23 The first qualification, impliedly acknowledged previously, is that if the contract expressly or as a matter of clear implication, states that the contractual measure of relief shall apply, then it shall apply.[51] Contractual provisions can exist beyond the grave, as is the case with liquidated damages clauses, choice of law clauses, and dispute resolution clauses to give just some examples. The speech of Lord Goff in the analogous context of *Pan Ocean Shipping Ltd v Creditcorp Ltd (The Trident Beauty)*,[52] provides further support for this view. Shipowners had assigned charter hire to assignees and then failed to undertake contractually required repairs to the chartered vessel. The charterers sued the assignees to recover advance payments of charter hire in respect of a period when the ship was off hire awaiting the repairs that had not been carried out. The owners were not worth suing, hence the restitutionary claim was brought against the assignees. The leading speech was given by Lord Woolf (with whom Lords Keith, Lowry, and Slynn agreed), who essentially held that the charterers had no restitutionary action against the assignees in any event. Lord Goff held that this kind of action had not yet been recognized but appeared to be developing. It would not be available in this case because the contract between the charterers and the owners had expressly provided for any overpaid hire to be refunded by the owners. The contract thus expressly provided for the situation that had arisen in that case and therefore there was no role for the law of restitution to play.

11.24 The second qualification, expressly acknowledged by Meagher JA, is that the contract price will sometimes, maybe often, provide the best evidence of the value of the defendant's enrichment. This is the view taken by Burrows and is used to re-interpret *Taylor v Motability Finance Ltd*,[53] and the other cases cited previously as supporting the view that the claimant is not restricted to a contract measure of relief.[54] In *Taylor* the claimant was wrongfully dismissed from his employment as a finance director. He sued for a bonus payment for negotiating a highly successful insurance settlement. He claimed that a negotiation consultant would have charged 0.5 per cent of the settlement figure, a sum amounting to £375,000. The defendants accepted that they were contractually obliged to pay the claimant £67,500 and

---

[51] This is the view of Virgo: *Principles of the Law of Restitution*, p 334 (n 2).
[52] [1994] 1 All ER 470 (HL).
[53] [2004] EWHC 2619 (Comm) (QBD).
[54] Burrows, *The Law of Restitution*, pp 348–50 (n 10).

this argument was accepted by Cooke J who, as stated earlier, held that the claimant was entitled only to the contractual measure of compensation. As Burrows has argued, rightly it is submitted, a sounder basis for this decision is that the claimant was entitled to the benefit actually gained by the defendant but that the contract sum of £67,500 was the most accurate measurement of that benefit. In principle the claimant should be entitled to restitution of the defendant's enrichment in both money and non-money cases. However, there is likely to be considerable scope for argument in non-money cases as to the value of the defendant's enrichment. Hence it will often be better to limit the claimant to the contract measure as the most certain and reliable method of calculating the restitution measure.

(3) Breach of fiduciary duty

Where the contractual duties of a party whose breach of contract has led to the termination of the contract are of a fiduciary nature, the claimant may have a remedy for breach of fiduciary duty. Fiduciary law is a large subject and this book is not the place to analyse it in detail.[55] Fiduciary relationships are based essentially on trust and confidence. The typical fiduciary relationship is well described in the following statement of Millett LJ in *Bristol and West Building Society v Mothew*:[56] **11.25**

> A fiduciary is someone who has undertaken to act for or on behalf of another in a particular matter in circumstances which give rise to a relationship of trust and confidence. The distinguishing obligation of a fiduciary is the obligation of loyalty.

The normal context with which this book is concerned does not import fiduciary duties. Arm's length transactions governed by bargained for contractual terms should not readily be re-characterized as fiduciary in order to bring about what might be considered a more just outcome. This can subvert the bargain the parties have actually made and re-allocate the risks among them differently from the contract's true intent.[57] One fact pattern exhibiting features of the commercial contract and fiduciary relationships is the joint venture, as illustrated by the facts of *Murad v Al-Saraj*.[58] The claimants and the defendant entered into a joint venture to purchase a hotel. After the hotel was purchased the claimants discovered that the defendant had deceived them by reaching a deal with the hotel's vendor whereby his contribution of £500,000 to the purchase price was rendered illusory because it consisted partly of a bribe to him and the discharge of various debts the vendor owed him. The breach of fiduciary duty which the defendant was guilty of was his non-disclosure to the claimants of the true nature of his contribution.

---

[55] See further M Conaglen, *Fiduciary Loyalty: Protecting the Due Performance of Non-Fiduciary Duties* (Hart, 2010).

[56] [1998] Ch 1 (CA) 18.

[57] See *Re Goldcorp Exchange plc* [1995] 1 AC 74 (JCPC–NZ); Sir Peter Millett, 'Equity's Place in the Law of Commerce' (1998) 114 LQR 214, 217–18; Virgo, *Principles of the Law of Restitution*, p 481 (n 2).

[58] [2005] EWCA Civ 959 (CA).

11.26 Where a breach of fiduciary duty has occurred and the claimant has suffered loss as a consequence, a remedy may be sought through equitable compensation.[59] This remedy is similar to damages but not identical as different approaches apply to causation and remoteness. Where the claimant has a claim for an injunction or specific performance, damages may be awarded in lieu of the equitable remedy under Lord Cairns' Act.[60] The latter is different from ordinary common law damages in so far as it is able to provide relief in respect of future loss that would usually be the subject of an injunction or specific performance, as well as past loss.[61] The remainder of this section will focus on restitutionary remedies for breach of fiduciary duty.

11.27 It is necessary to commence this discussion by issuing a health warning about the contents of the next few paragraphs. No comprehensive cataloguing and analysis of fiduciary duties and the remedies for breach of them can be attempted in a book of this nature. The area of law with which we are concerned is in a considerable state of flux and there is a striking difference in approach between the position currently taken in England and Wales and that in other common law jurisdictions such as Australia, New Zealand, Canada, and some of the American states, at least so far as the nature of the restitutionary remedy awarded to the claimant is concerned. It is possible that an important case decided by the Supreme Court of the United Kingdom in the next few years could effect radical change to the current understanding of the law in this area.

11.28 It has been customary to distinguish between two broad case categories in terms of the remedy awarded to the claimant, although the most recent pronouncement by the Court of Appeal in *FHR European Ventures LLP v Mankarious* calls that classification into question.[62] The distinction, for what it is worth, is between cases where the fiduciary makes a secret profit, and cases where he or she is in receipt of a bribe or secret commission paid by a third party. In the first of these case categories, the secret profit, the fiduciaries obtain a profit for themselves by virtue of their fiduciary position. Important illustrations include *Regal (Hastings) Ltd v Gulliver*[63] and *Boardman v Phipps*.[64] In both of these cases fiduciaries acquired shares in companies that their principals were unable, for different reasons, to

---

[59] IE Davidson, 'The Equitable Remedy of Compensation' (1982) 13 Melbourne University L Rev 349; WMC Gummow, 'Compensation for Breach of Fiduciary Loyalty' in TG Youdan (ed), *Equity, Fiduciaries and Trusts* (Carswell, 1989) pp 57–92; D Capper, 'Damages for Breach of the Equitable Duty of Confidence' (1994) 14 Legal Studies 313; C Rickett, 'Compensating for Loss in Equity—Choosing the Right Horse for Each Course' in P Birks and F Rose (eds), *Restitution and Equity* (Mansfield Press, 2000) pp 173–91; J Getzler, 'Equitable Compensation and the Regulation of Fiduciary Relationships' also in P Birks and F Rose (eds) pp 235–57; Conaglen, *Fiduciary Loyalty*, pp 85–96 (n 55).

[60] Now the Senior Courts Act 1981, s 50.

[61] See JA Jolowicz, 'Damages in Equity—A Study of Lord Cairns' Act' [1975] CLJ 224.

[62] [2013] EWCA Civ 17 (CA).

[63] [1967] 2 AC 134 (HL).

[64] [1967] 2 AC 46 (HL).

acquire for themselves.[65] Liability arose from the mere fact of profit being made, the courts taking a very strong prophylactic approach to these situations, reasoning that if fiduciaries cannot obtain profit for themselves without full consent from the beneficiaries they will not be tempted to try to do so at the principal's expense. Although never made crystal clear in either case, mainly because it did not actually matter on the facts, it seems that the remedy granted to the claimant was the imposition of a constructive trust.[66] The strict nature of the duty imposed on fiduciaries and the remedy enforcing it may be mitigated in an exceptional case by the award of an allowance to the fiduciary for the work done in earning profit also accruing to the beneficiaries.[67]

The remedial position with respect to bribes and secret commissions has proved **11.29** to be an extremely controversial issue. In *Lister v Stubbs*[68] the claimant's agent was charged with obtaining goods from a third party by whom he was paid secret commissions for placing orders. The Court of Appeal held that he was liable to account to the claimant for these payments but the remedy was personal and not proprietary. It was regarded as startling to contend that the claimant should have priority over the fiduciary's general creditors were he insolvent or that any profits made by the defendant through investing the ill-gotten gains should belong in equity to the claimant. An entirely different view was taken by the Privy Council in *Attorney General for Hong Kong v Reid*.[69] In this case the defendant had been a senior prosecutor in Hong Kong and received a considerable sum of money from criminal gangs for ensuring that they were not prosecuted. The defendant invested the money in property in New Zealand over which the Privy Council, relying on the maxim that equity regards as done that which ought to be done, imposed a constructive trust.

An enormous amount of academic ink (not to say angst) has been spilt over this **11.30** issue. The volume of literature is extensive and very strong positions have been taken by different commentators. Very broadly opinions fall into two camps. Those who support *Reid* tend to emphasize that as *Reid* should not have had this money in the first place neither should his creditors. It is also argued that imposing a constructive trust furthers the strong prophylactic policy of fiduciary law by ensuring that the fiduciary cannot benefit from breach of duty. Those who disagree

---

[65] In *Regal* this was due to a lack of finance and in *Boardman* it was because the trust required the sanction of the court to make what would have been an unauthorized investment.

[66] This seems to be confirmed by the court order issued by Wilberforce J, as he then was, in *Boardman v Phipps* [1964] 1 WLR 993 (Ch D). Wilberforce J had a strong claim to being the leading Chancery practitioner of his day and his order was confirmed by the House of Lords. Counsel for the appellants in *FHR European Ventures LLP v Mankarious* [2013] EWCA Civ 17 (CA) researched and confirmed this point—see para 91 (Etherton C).

[67] An allowance was given in *Boardman v Phipps* (see n 66), but refused in *Guinness plc v Saunders* [1990] 2 AC 663 (HL).

[68] (1890) LR 45 Ch D 1 (CA).

[69] [1994] 1 AC 324 (JCPC–Hong Kong).

with *Reid* argue that a constructive trust fails to explain why one particular creditor should obtain all of an asset or a fund in priority to others, and that personal liability to account ensures that the fiduciary does not enjoy the ill-gotten gains. If the issue is expressed in these general terms *Reid's* critics seem to the present authors to have the better of the argument, a proposition which receives strong support from the decision of the Court of Appeal in *Sinclair Investments (UK) Ltd v Versailles Trade Finance Ltd*.[70] The Court of Appeal decided that it would follow *Lister v Stubbs* in preference to *Reid* and administered some fairly sharp criticisms of the latter authority.

11.31   But as the recent decision of the Court of Appeal in *FHR European Ventures LLP v Mankarious*[71] shows, it is not just so easy to express the issue in the terms set out earlier. The facts of this case were that the defendant was employed by the claimants to negotiate the purchase of a hotel from the third party. The defendant arranged a sale of the hotel to the claimants for €211.5 million. What the claimants did not know, because the defendant had not told them, was that he had also been engaged by the third party to introduce it to would be purchasers including the claimants and he earned €10 million that was effectively paid to him from the money paid by the claimants. The Court of Appeal in *FHR* acknowledged that in *Sinclair v Versailles* three broad categories of situations where a fiduciary obtains a benefit in breach of fiduciary duty had been recognized:

(1)   where the benefit is or was an asset belonging beneficially to the principal (most obviously where the fiduciary misappropriates or misapplies the principal's property);

(2)   where the benefit is obtained by taking advantage of an opportunity which was properly that of the principal—included in this category are cases where, as in *Regal (Hastings) v Gulliver* and *Boardman v Phipps*, the principal is unable to pursue the opportunity;

(3)   all other cases.[72]

The issue in *FHR* was whether the secret commission fell into category (2) or (3). This was crucial because categories (1) and (2) give rise to constructive trust liability and category (3) personal liability to account only. Placing the secret profits cases in category (2) clearly also does damage to the distinction between secret profits, on the one hand, and bribes and secret commissions, on the other. The Court of Appeal, reversing Simon J, held that the facts of *FHR* fell into category (2), to some extent because the claimants had been deprived of an opportunity to purchase the hotel for a price minus the commission (or some lesser figure). But the Court of Appeal emphasized two particularly important weaknesses in the earlier Court of

---

[70]   [2011] EWCA Civ 347, [2012] Ch 453. See C Conte, 'The Death Knell Tolls for *A-G for Hong Kong v Reid*' [2012] 20 Restitution Law Rev 118.

[71]   [2013] EWCA Civ 17.

[72]   *FHR v Mankarious*, para 83 (Etherton C) (n 71).

Appeal judgment. One was the tendency to over-simplify the distinction between categories (2) and (3), and the other was the very large number of authorities not cited in the judgments of the earlier decision and the contribution this made to the over-simplifying tendency. In this context it is surely no surprise that the judgment of Etherton C draws attention to the different views taken by superior courts in other jurisdictions[73] and the possibility that the Supreme Court might re-draw the line on this question at some stage in the future.[74] In the light of this decision it may be a little premature to state that *Reid* is completely dead. The distinction between cases attracting proprietary relief and those where there is only a personal liability to account is more than a little fuzzy.

(4) Interference with property right

Where a breach of contract takes the form of an interference with the claimant's property rights, for example through trespassing on the claimant's property, damages may be assessed as a measure of the defendant's gain as opposed to the claimant's loss. So in *Penarth Dock Engineering Co Ltd v Pounds*[75] the claimant sold a floating pontoon to the defendant. The pontoon occupied part of dock premises which the claimant leased from the British Transport Commission. As the Commission wanted to close the dock and the claimant to shut down its ship repairing business, it was made an express term of the contract of sale between claimant and defendant that the defendant would remove the pontoon as soon as possible. The defendant was dilatory in removing the pontoon and the claimant sued for damages for breach of contract and trespass. Lord Denning MR, sitting at first instance, observed that the claimant had not suffered any loss, either through extra rent paid to the Commission or any benefit it missed out on because the dock was occupied by the pontoon. Damages were assessed by analogy with what the defendant would have had to pay if the pontoon had been moved elsewhere. Although this decision is technically about breach of contract, in truth it is one of a 'family' of tort (mainly trespass) cases where damages were assessed either on the basis of the defendant's gain or as an estimate of the rent the claimant might have charged for use of its land.[76] These cases all contribute to the debate referred to later as to whether damages on the *Wrotham Park* measure[77] are compensatory or restitutionary. For present purposes all that needs to be said is that damages for the invasion of the claimant's property rights are essentially tortious and only merit inclusion in a book on breach of contract in the relatively infrequent instance where the breach takes the form of a tort.

11.32

---

[73] *FHR v Mankarious*, para 80 (n 71).

[74] *FHR v Mankarious*, para 116 (n 71).

[75] [1963] 1 Lloyd's Rep 359 (QBD).

[76] *Phillips v Homfray* (1883) 24 Ch D 439 (CA); *Whitwham v Westminster Brymbo Coal & Coke Co* [1896] 2 Ch 538 (CA); *Stoke-on-Trent City Council v W & J Wass Ltd* [1988] 1 WLR 1406 (CA); *Ministry of Defence v Ashman* (1993) 66 P & CR 195 (CA).

[77] *Wrotham Park Estate Co Ltd v Parkside Homes Ltd* [1974] 1 WLR 798 (Ch D).

(5) Exceptional gain-based recovery

11.33 Aside from the 'interference with property rights' cases dealt with previously, there is also a growing body of jurisprudence in contract law where damages for breach have been measured by the defendant's gain. Usually this involves taking a part of that gain as damages for the claimant but exceptionally the defendant may be stripped of the entire gain. To the extent that any damages awarded here are restitutionary it is important to point out that this is restitution *for* breach of contract as opposed to restitution *following* breach of contract, as was the case in previous sections of this chapter.[78] To explain the current position the case law will be analysed chronologically.

(a) Wrotham Park Estate Co Ltd v Parkside Homes Ltd

11.34 The first case to discuss is *Wrotham Park Estate Co Ltd v Parkside Homes Ltd*.[79] The claimant was the successor in title to land subject to a restrictive covenant that limited owners' rights to develop it for building purposes. The claimant sold the land to the first defendant, who bought with notice of the covenant. In breach of covenant the first defendant built a housing estate and sold the houses to the second defendants. The claimant sought an injunction to compel demolition of the houses but did not seek any interim relief while the properties were being erected. Brightman J refused to grant an injunction to compel the demolition of the completed homes but awarded the claimant damages in lieu of an injunction under the Chancery Amendment Act 1858 (Lord Cairns' Act).[80] The judge's assessment of damages was 5 per cent of the reasonably anticipated profits of the first defendant, that being his not particularly scientific estimate of the likely sum the claimant would have charged for relaxing the covenant. The decision is technically more of an invasion of property rights case than breach of contract but it is close to breach of contract and has been used, as we shall see, as a means of remedying breaches of contract where conventional compensatory damages are not available.[81]

(b) Surrey County Council v Bredero Homes Ltd

11.35 Restitutionary damages for breach of a contractual covenant were sought in *Surrey County Council v Bredero Homes Ltd*.[82] The claimant council sold land to the defendants for the purpose of building houses. In breach of contract the defendants built eighty-two houses on the land sold, five more than the contractually agreed number. The claimant did not seek any injunctive relief, either interim or permanent, and because it had suffered no identifiable loss sought to strip the

---

[78] Virgo, *Principles of the Law of Restitution*, p 479 (n 2).

[79] [1974] 1 WLR 798 (Ch D).

[80] The current statutory provision preserving this jurisdiction is Senior Courts Act 1981, s 50.

[81] See also *Bracewell v Appelby* [1975] Ch 408 (Ch D) where 40% of the value of a house to which the only access was along a private road owned by the defendants was the sum awarded on the same principles.

[82] [1993] 1 WLR 1361 (CA).

defendants of the entire profit grossed from building an additional five houses. The Court of Appeal held that as the claimant had suffered no loss there could be only nominal damages. As far as *Wrotham Park* damages were concerned the easy way to explain why they were not awarded in that case would be that the claimant did not apply for an injunction or specific performance and hence there was no basis for awarding damages in lieu of the equitable relief. Virgo prefers the subtly different explanation that *Bredero* was a case about breach of contract whereas *Wrotham Park* involved invasion of a property right,[83] but it seems to the present authors that *Wrotham Park* damages can be suitable for breach of contract.[84]

(c) Attorney General v Blake

The principal decision in which a complete disgorgement of the defendant's profits **11.36** from a breach of contract was ordered is *Attorney General v Blake*.[85] George Blake, a notorious traitor and former MI5 officer, who defected to the Soviet Union in the early 1960s, published a book about his career and traitorous activities. This involved using a lot of information that his contract with the secret services did not permit him to use even after he had left that employment. By the time the book came to be published the information Blake was disclosing in breach of contract had ceased to be confidential so an action in breach of confidence would not have availed the Crown. Whether it would have been possible for the Crown to obtain an injunction to restrain publication of the book was the subject of some disagreement between Lord Nicholls for the majority of the House of Lords, who held that it was not, and Lord Hobhouse in dissent, who held that it was. Assuming that an injunction could not be obtained the question was whether the Crown could be awarded damages in the absence of any identifiable loss. The award of *Wrotham Park* damages, amounting to a portion of the defendant's profits, was not considered. This may have been because there was no jurisdiction to grant an injunction,[86] or because no property right was infringed,[87] or more likely than the foregoing because the breach of contract was so outrageous that only stripping the defendant of all gains derived from the breach of contract would suffice.

So when will an account of the defendant's profits be ordered? The following pas- **11.37** sage from the speech of Lord Nicholls is worth quoting in full:[88]

> An account of profits will be appropriate only in exceptional circumstances. Normally the remedies of damages, specific performance and injunction, coupled

---

[83] Virgo, *Principles of the Law of Restitution*, p 484 (n 2).
[84] Burrows, *The Law of Restitution*, pp 665–6 (n 10) treats *Wrotham Park* as involving both contract and invasion of property rights.
[85] [2001] 1 AC 268 (HL).
[86] It does not take much to establish jurisdiction to grant an injunction. See *Hooper v Rogers* [1975] Ch 43 (CA) 48 where Russell LJ said of a mandatory injunction that the critical question was whether the court 'could have (however unwisely...) made a mandatory order'.
[87] Virgo, *Principles of the Law of Restitution*, p 485 (n 2).
[88] [2001] 1 AC 268 (HL) 285.

with the characterisation of some contractual obligations as fiduciary, will provide an adequate response to a breach of contract. It will only be in exceptional cases, where those remedies are inadequate, that any question of accounting for profits will arise. No fixed rules can be prescribed. The court will have regard to all the circumstances, including the subject matter of the contract, the purpose of the contractual provision which has been breached, the circumstances in which the breach occurred, the consequences of the breach and the circumstances in which relief is being sought. A useful general guide, although not exhaustive, is whether the plaintiff had a legitimate interest in preventing the defendant's profit-making activity and, hence, in depriving him of his profit.

Later in his speech Lord Nicholls identified three circumstances which individually would not constitute a good reason for ordering an account of profits: 'the fact that the breach was cynical and deliberate; the fact that the breach enabled the defendant to enter into a more profitable contract elsewhere; and the fact that by entering into a new and more profitable contract the defendant put it out of his power to perform his contract with the plaintiff'.[89] 'Expense saved' or 'skimped performance' does not fall into the exceptional category either.[90] What made *Blake* such an exceptional case was that it came so close to breach of fiduciary duty.[91]

11.38   This is not the place in which to engage in an evaluation of *Blake*. It has received a mixed press.[92] At the time of writing it has been followed in only one English decision, *Esso Petroleum Co Ltd v Niad*.[93] The defendant owned a petrol station and was supplied by the claimant with petrol subject to a 'price support' provision. In breach of this the defendant overcharged its customers. This meant that the defendant paid the claimant less for its petrol than it would have had to pay if charging in line with the 'price support' agreement. Sir Andrew Morritt V-C awarded the claimant an account of profits based on the gains made by the defendant from breaching the contract. Compensatory damages were inadequate because there was no way to ascertain the sales lost because of the defendant's breach. The claimant had a legitimate interest in preventing the defendant profiting from the breach as it undermined the Pricewatch scheme in the area in which the defendant traded and the claimant had complained to it several times. An account of profits was rejected in *AB Corporation v CD Company (The Sine Nomine)*[94] where

---

[89] *Attorney General v Blake*, 286 (n 88).
[90] *Attorney General v Blake*, 286 (n 88).
[91] Burrows, *The Law of Restitution*, p 670 (n 10).
[92] For analysis see J Edelman, *Gain-Based Damages* (Hart, 2002) ch 5; PD Maddagh and JD McCamus, *The Law of Restitution* (looseleaf, Canada Law Book, 2004) ch 25. For hostile views see D Campbell and D Harris, 'In Defence of Breach: A Critique of Restitution and the Performance Interest' (2002) 22 Legal Studies 208; D Campbell and P Wylie, 'Ain't No Telling (Which Circumstances are Exceptional)' [2003] CLJ 605.
[93] 22 November 2001, unreported (Ch D).
[94] [2002] 1 Lloyd's Rep 805 (QBD).

shipowners withdrew a vessel from a charterparty because the market had risen and higher rates of hire were available elsewhere. This is an example of a case Lord Nicholls said was not suitable for an account of profits and one where compensatory damages were sufficient.

(d) Experience Hendrix LLC v PPX Enterprises Inc

In none of the cases decided after those mentioned previously was an account of **11.39** profits seriously considered. In all the issue was whether or not to award *Wrotham Park* damages. The most important appears to be *Experience Hendrix LLC v PPX Enterprises Inc.*[95] In this case a settlement was reached in 1973 of a dispute between the rock star Jimi Hendrix and the defendant record company. By that settlement it was agreed that certain master tapes could be retained by the defendant but that the remainder (non-Schedule A material) should be delivered up to Jimi Hendrix. In breach of contract the defendant continued to use master tapes that should have been delivered up to Jimi Hendrix. The estate of the late Jimi Hendrix obtained an injunction against any further breaches of the settlement agreement and in respect of past losses sought substantial damages. Compensatory damages were ruled out and damages awarded by reference to profits made by the defendant for reasons aptly summarized in this passage from the judgment of Peter Gibson LJ:[96]

> In my judgment, because (1) there has been a deliberate breach by PPX of its contractual obligations for its own reward, (2) the claimant would have difficulty in establishing financial loss therefrom, and (3) the claimant has a legitimate interest in preventing PPX's profit-making activity carried out in breach of PPX's contractual obligations, the present case is a suitable one (as envisaged by Lord Nicholls) in which damages for breach of contract may be measured by the benefits gained by the wrongdoer for the breach. To avoid injustice I would require PPX to make a reasonable payment in respect of the benefit it has gained.

The Court of Appeal was not required to assess the damages, just to decide whether these should only be nominal because losses could not be calculated or based on the defendant's profits; and, if the latter, whether this should be an account of all profits or a *Wrotham Park*-like notional fee which the claimant would have demanded as the price of relaxing the contractual condition. Significant points of distinction from *Esso v Niad* were that the defendant was not close to being a fiduciary, no issue analogous to national security was involved, and the contractual provision breached was not central to the claimant's whole mode of operation. Virgo draws attention to the fact that both *Wrotham Park* (restrictive covenant) and *Hendrix* (intellectual property rights) were concerned with the invasion of the claimant's property.[97] He

---

[95] [2003] EWCA Civ 323, [2003] 1 All ER (Comm) 830.
[96] *Experience Hendrix LLC v PPX Enterprises*, para 58 (n 95).
[97] Virgo, *Principles of the Law of Restitution*, p 491 (n 2).

also points out that in *Hendrix* the *Wrotham Park* damages were not, as was originally suggested in *Bredero*,[98] awarded in lieu of an injunction.[99]

(e) Three subsequent decisions

11.40   There have been three subsequent decisions awarding *Wrotham Park* damages. In *Amec Developments Ltd v Jury's Hotel Management (UK) Ltd*[100] the defendant breached a restrictive covenant by building a hotel several metres closer to the claimant's land than permitted. Anthony Mann QC, sitting as a Deputy High Court judge, assessed the fee that would be charged by the claimant for relaxing the covenant by looking to the benefit the defendant actually acquired from the breach and discounting the fee from that.[101] In *Lane v O'Brien Homes Ltd*[102] the defendant developer built four houses instead of the permitted three, in breach of a collateral contract with the claimant seller of the land. David Clarke J estimated that an additional £280,000 profit was earned from building the extra house and he calculated *Wrotham Park* damages at £150,000. The last of these cases is *Pell Frischmann Engineering Ltd v Bow Valley Iran Ltd*,[103] which is authority for the proposition that *Wrotham Park* damages can exceed the profit eventually made from the breach of contract. Confidentiality agreements in a failed joint venture for an offshore oilfield were broken by the defendants proceeding with a joint venture with a different partner to the claimants. Profits of $1.8 million were eventually made from the project but at the time prior to breach when it was assumed that the hypothetical release bargain would have taken place the parties were assuming greater profits. The Privy Council awarded $2.5 million because the release fee would have been based on the much higher profit margin anticipated at this earlier stage.

(f) WWF-World Wide Fund for Nature v World Wrestling Federation Entertainment Inc

11.41   The final authority to which reference should be made is *WWF-World Wide Fund for Nature v World Wrestling Federation Entertainment Inc*.[104] After a dispute between the parties about the use of the initials WWF, a settlement agreement was reached which the claimant alleged the defendant had broken. At first instance Jacob J held

---

[98] See nn 83–84.

[99] Virgo, *The Principles of the Law of Restitution*, pp 491–2 (n 2).

[100] (2000) 82 P & CR 286 (Ch D).

[101] cf *Lunn Poly Ltd v Liverpool and Lancashire Properties Ltd* [2006] EWCA Civ 430 in which a landlord breached its covenant of quiet enjoyment with its tenant by bricking up a fire door. Neuberger LJ said that in assessing *Wrotham Park* or 'negotiating damages', post-breach events were normally irrelevant. This approach was approved in *Pell Frischmann Engineering Ltd v Bow Valley Iran Ltd* [2009] UKPC 45 (JCPC–Jersey), discussed later.

[102] [2004] EWHC 303 (QB).

[103] [2009] UKPC 45 (JCPC–Jersey).

[104] [2007] EWCA Civ 286, [2008] 1 WLR 445.

that an account of profits for breach of this agreement was inappropriate.[105] The question then arose of whether the claimant could be entitled to *Wrotham Park* damages as a reasonable payment for the claimant releasing its rights under the settlement agreement and Peter Smith J held that in principle this was possible.[106] On appeal it was held that, for procedural reasons, this should not be allowed. The appeal is significant because of the following passage in the judgment of Chadwick LJ, with which Maurice Kay and Wilson LJJ agreed:[107]

> The circumstances in which an award of damages on the *Wrotham Park* basis may be an appropriate response, and those in which the appropriate response is an account of profits, may differ in degree. But the underlying feature, in both cases, is that the court recognises the need to compensate the claimant in circumstances where he cannot demonstrate identifiable financial loss. To label an award of damages on the *Wrotham Park* basis as a 'compensatory' remedy and an order for an account of profits as a 'gain-based' remedy does not assist an understanding of the principles on which the court acts. The two remedies should, I think, each be seen as a flexible response to the need to compensate the claimant for the wrong which has been done to him.

Burrows has described this passage as 'infamous' and criticized it as erroneous for regarding the account of profits as compensatory and not restitutionary.[108]

(g) Summary and discussion

The quotation in paragraph 11.41 prompts some summary of the main principles **11.42** in this area and some reflection on the essential nature of the exceptional remedies awarded here. The starting point is the recognition of a case where the claimant has suffered no loss that could be compensated by conventional compensatory damages. Where this is so the usual response is to award nominal damages to mark the technical infringement of the claimant's rights. But where the defendant has made some tangible gain from breaching the contract the question then arises of whether the defendant should be required by order of the court to hand over some or all of those gains to the claimant. Disgorgement of all of the defendant's gains is, in the light of *Attorney General v Blake*, clearly an exceptional remedy among these circumstances where the claimant has suffered no identifiable loss. Among those circumstances where an account of profits might be appropriate are cases where the claimant has a clear interest in preventing the defendant's profit-making activity and where the defendant occupies a position close to fiduciary. Burrows' position that it is wrong to describe these damages as compensatory is understandable but it is also important to bear two other things in mind as well. One is that others, notably Virgo,[109] do not regard the account of profits as restitutionary because

---

[105] [2002] FSR 32 (Ch D).
[106] [2006] EWHC 184 (Ch).
[107] [2007] EWCA Civ 286, para 59.
[108] Burrows, *The Law of Restitution*, pp 675–6 (n 10).
[109] Virgo, *Principles of the Law of Restitution*, pp 496–7 (n 2).

it does not reverse an enrichment at the claimant's expense. If not restitutionary damages then what are they? The other is that Chadwick LJ may have been going no further than to say that the overriding objective of monetary relief in this area is to find more subtle ways of responding to a breach of contract which has not caused obvious loss.

11.43 Turning now to *Wrotham Park* damages, it is clear that this will be a far more usual response to the 'no identifiable loss' scenario than an account of profits. This award will usually take the form of an assessment of what the claimant might conceivably charge as a fee for releasing the defendant from the obligation to observe the claimant's contractual rights. There has been a vigorous debate among academic commentators as to the nature of these damages.[110] What follows is only an attempt to sketch the main positions that have been taken and does not do justice to the depth or range of the scholarship in this area. One line of analysis, inspired largely by a seminal article by Waddams and Sharpe, sees *Wrotham Park* damages as compensating for the claimant's lost opportunity to bargain for a fee to release the defendant from the contractual obligation. Another, championed by Burrows, states that the lost opportunity to bargain is a fiction because in most cases the claimant would not be prepared to bargain for release at any price. According to this theory it is better to see *Wrotham Park* damages as restitutionary because they are based on a proportion of the defendant's gain from the breach and have nothing to do with compensation. A possible third theory, supported by Jaffey and by Virgo,[111] is that a remedy is being granted for the invasion of the claimant's property rights. It may be that the significance of this debate does not go far beyond the integrity of the Law of Restitution as an independent subject but that is not a major concern of this book.

B. Defendant Recovery

11.44 The essential question to be examined in the remainder of this chapter is the converse of the one examined in the first two subsections of Part A. There we examined situations where the contract had been discharged following the defendant's breach and the innocent party was seeking restitution of money and non-money benefits transferred under the contract. Here we are also dealing with situations where one party has committed breach and the contract has been discharged but this time the party that committed the breach is seeking restitution of money

---

[110] See S Waddams and R Sharpe, 'Damages for Lost Opportunity to Bargain' (1982) 2 OJLS 290; A Burrows, 'Are "Damages on the Wrotham Park Basis" Compensatory, Restitutionary or Neither?' in D Saidov and R Cunnington (eds), *Contract Damages* (Hart, 2008) p 165; P Jaffey, 'Licence Fee Damages' [2011] Restitution Law Rev 95; B Mason, 'Unravelling the Hypothetical Bargain' [2012] Restitution Law Rev 75.

[111] See n 97 and accompanying text.

and non-money benefits transferred under the contract. The first question to be addressed is why that breach does not of itself bar any restitutionary claim. As Virgo points out,[112] this is largely because the innocent party is sufficiently protected by its breach of contract claim, which is capable of placing it in the financial position it would have been in if the breach had not occurred. English law has never seen a need to remedy breach any further than that and where the innocent party seeks restitution following a breach it is always required to give counter restitution of any benefits it has received. In principle, where a contract has been discharged the law of restitution takes over and the contract should only continue to influence the remedial position where it clearly provides that it is to do so. Later, we shall see how fully this is all worked out in the case law. The same division between money and non-money benefits applies as in innocent party recovery.

(1) Money benefits

The position can be expressed fairly shortly and succinctly. Any pre-payment may **11.45** be recovered if there is a total failure of consideration. Any deposit or payment subject to forfeiture is irrecoverable. How, why, and whether that should continue to be the case will be examined now.

The conventional starting point seems to be *Dies v British and International Mining* **11.46** *and Finance Co.*[113] The claimant contracted to buy rifles and ammunition from the defendant for £270,000 and made a pre-payment of £100,000. The claimant breached the contract by refusing to take delivery and the defendant validly terminated it. The claimant recovered the £100,000 but not on the ground of total failure of consideration. The judge, Stable J, reasoned that this was because the contract impliedly provided for restitution in these circumstances.[114] Burrows points out that this reasoning was dictated by the earlier decision in *Chandler v Webster*,[115] where it was held that restitution for total failure of consideration was only possible where the contract was rescinded *ab initio*.[116] Now that the House of Lords has corrected this error in *Fibrosa Spolka Akcyjna v Fairbairn Lawson Combe Barbour Ltd*,[117] the decision can now be rationalized as one based on total failure as subsequent decisions clearly do.

In *Rover International Ltd v Cannon Film Sales Ltd*[118] Proper Films Ltd entered **11.47** into a contract with Thorn EMI for the exhibition of films on Italian television. Under the contract EMI granted a licence to Proper to exhibit nine films for a

---

[112] Virgo, *The Principles of the Law of Restitution*, pp 334–5 (n 2).
[113] [1939] 1 KB 724 (KBD).
[114] *Dies v British and International Mining and Finance Co*, 744 (n 113).
[115] [1904] 1 KB 493 (CA).
[116] Burrows, *The Law of Restitution*, p 355 (n 10).
[117] [1943] AC 32 (HL).
[118] [1989] 1 WLR 912 (CA).

total fee of $1.8 million. The fee was to be paid in three instalments with the last of $900,000 due on 30 September 1986. Cannon took over Thorn EMI in May 1986 and thereafter relations between the parties deteriorated. In the light of the disputes which developed, Proper refused to pay the last instalment directly to Cannon, insisting that it be paid into a joint account maintained by the parties' solicitors pending resolution of the disputes between them. Cannon elected to terminate the contract for this and then sued for recovery of the $900,000. The Court of Appeal dismissed this claim for the reason that if Proper were forced to pay the sum it would have an immediate right to recover it for a total failure of consideration. This was regardless of whether it was the guilty or innocent party in the termination of the contract. *Dies* was explained as a total failure of consideration case, a proposition supported by dicta of McHugh J in *Baltic Shipping Company v Dillon (The Mikhail Lermontov)*[119] and of John Martin QC (sitting as a Deputy High Court judge) in *Clowes Development (UK) Ltd v Mulchinook*.[120] The decision most important to settling this question is *Stocznia Gdanska SA v Latvian Shipping Co*,[121] where again the issue was whether money should not be paid by a party in breach of contract because it would be immediately recoverable on grounds of total failure of consideration.

11.48 There is no right to recover in restitution where the payment is a deposit or of the nature of something understood to be forfeited in the event that the payer breaches the contract. This is one of those situations where the law of restitution is subservient to the contract. If the parties have agreed what is to happen in the event of a breach, restitution has no role to play. Like other parts of the general law it only prescribes solutions where the parties have not worked one out for themselves. So there is nothing inherently implausible in Stable J's reliance on an implied contractual obligation to refund the pre-payment in *Dies*. The danger lies in reading the contract to mean what you want it to mean. If you think there should be restitution you find an implied obligation to make restitution. The better approach is not to go looking for contractual terms to solve the problem but to recognize that the solution lies outside the contract unless the contract clearly provides a solution within.

11.49 Where the contract expressly or by clear implication provides that money is paid as a deposit or is to be forfeited in the event of the paying party's breach, there is a clear solution within the contract. In *Howe v Smith*[122] a party in breach could not recover a payment because it was a deposit. Fry LJ defined a deposit as an 'earnest to bind the bargain so entered into [which] creates by the fear of its forfeiture a

---

[119] (1993) 176 CLR 344, 390–1.
[120] 24 May 2001, unreported (Ch D).
[121] Explained in n 17 and accompanying text.
[122] (1884) 27 Ch D 89 (CA).

motive in the payer to perform the rest of the contract'.[123] In *Mayson v Clouet*[124] a contract for the sale of land provided that if the purchasers defaulted they were to forfeit the deposit paid. The purchasers paid the deposit and two instalments and then defaulted. It was held that they could recover the instalments but not the deposit. Deposits and other similar payments are subject to those equitable principles governing penalties so that in the event that a deposit or forfeiture provision is struck down as a penalty the payer's right to restitution would be reinstated, subject to the innocent party's claim for damages for breach.[125] Birks explained deposits and similar payments not on grounds of contracting out of restitution but as cases where there would be no total failure of consideration or unjust enrichment.[126] It is not thought that this makes for any practical difference ultimately.

As the right to restitution depends largely on the removal of the contract from the   **11.50**
analytical terrain, save for those cases where express or clearly implied contractual provision governs post-discharge issues, the contract breaker should in principle be treated comparably to the innocent party seeking restitution. Just as the innocent party can only have restitution in preference to breach where it provides a better remedy or can have restitution as part of breach where breach is the better remedy,[127] the guilty party can have restitution because the innocent is entitled to damages for breach putting it into the financial position it would have been in had the contract not been breached. From this it should follow that the guilty party, no more than the innocent, should not be required to demonstrate a total failure of consideration. The contract has gone and no longer should there be any concern about a party doing better than the contract would allow. If there is concern about that, the parties should agree a contractual provision to prevent it.

(2) Non-money benefits

It may come as some surprise to the reader to discover that the law in respect of res-   **11.51**
titution for non-money benefits by a party in breach of contract is really quite different from restitution for money payments. If there were to be a right to restitution the restitutionary ground would probably be failure of consideration and one might expect to meet similar issues as to whether that failure had to be total and to what extent restitution was capped by the terms of the contract. But actually it would be more accurate to say that the party in breach has no right to restitution at all.

---

[123] *Howe v Smith*, 101 (n 122). cf *Chillingworth v Esche* [1924] 1 Ch 97 (CA) where a deposit 'subject to contract' was recovered by the payer. No contract was ever signed so the payer was not in breach. The payment was thus not a true deposit but 'an anticipatory payment intended only to fulfil the ordinary purpose of a deposit if and when the contemplated agreement should be arrived at' (Sargant LJ at 115).

[124] [1924] AC 980 (JCPC–Singapore).

[125] *Stockloser v Johnson* [1954] 1 QB 476 (CA); *Workers Trust and Merchant Bank Ltd v Dojap Investments Ltd* [1993] AC 573 (JCPC–Jamaica).

[126] P Birks, *An Introduction to the Law of Restitution* (Clarendon Press, 1989) pp 235–8.

[127] Double recovery is avoided in both instances.

(a) Sumpter v Hedges

11.52   Explaining the law logically begins with the decision of the Court of Appeal in
Sumpter v Hedges.[128] In this case the claimant builder did a little more than half
of the work of constructing certain buildings for the defendant when he ran out
of money and abandoned the contract. The defendant completed the buildings,
using materials left on site by the claimant. At first instance the claimant recovered
for the value of the materials left on site but he failed both there and in the Court
of Appeal to recover on a *quantum meruit* for the value of the work he had done
before abandoning the contract. It was pointed out by all the judges in the Court
of Appeal that the contract was entire so the claimant was not entitled to be paid
under the contract until the work was completed. As far as a restitutionary claim
was concerned, the claimant could not get that either in the absence of a fresh
contract to pay for the same.[129] No authority need be cited for the proposition that
the latter is a deeply flawed basis for the decision. Recovery in restitution depends
on unjust enrichment, a principle independent of the law of contract so that the
absence of any fresh contract, either express or implied, is not a reason to bar recovery. Whether the contract being entire is a reason to bar recovery in restitution
is another question to which further consideration will be given in due course.
It would appear to be the basis for the later Court of Appeal decision in *Bolton v
Mahadeva*.[130] The claimant agreed to install a combined heating and domestic hot
water system in the defendant's home for £560. The work was found to be defective
and meriting a deduction of £174 from the bill. The contract was entire and the
defects in the standard of the work too much to invoke the doctrine of substantial
performance.[131] In the absence of the latter, this meant that the claimant was not
entitled to recover anything for the work he had done, although the defendant had
paid £400 into court so that the outcome of the case primarily affected the claimant in liability for costs.

(b) Substantial performance

11.53   Mention was made in the last paragraph of substantial performance. The origins
of this doctrine lie in the famous New York case of *Jacob and Youngs Inc v Kent*.[132]
In the construction of a house a builder used a different kind of piping to the one
contractually stipulated. It was cheaper but it had no effect whatever on the building's structural integrity or its value. The contract was entire and the defendant
maintained that no payment was due as the contractor had not performed precisely
as the contract required. Cardozo J for the majority ruled that in cases where the

---

[128] [1898] 1 QB 673 (CA).

[129] All this was said in relation to the claim for compensation for work done beyond the supply
of materials.

[130] [1972] 1 WLR 1009 (CA).

[131] See *Hoenig v Isaacs* [1952] 2 All ER 176 (CA).

[132] 129 NE 889 (1921, NY CA).

contract was substantially performed the contractor should receive the contractual payment minus a small deduction to reflect the defective performance. In *Hoenig v Isaacs*,[133] discussed previously, the contractor was allowed the agreed price of £750 subject to a set-off of £56 to allow the owner to rectify some defective workmanship. It is important to recognize that in none of these substantial performance cases is the contract discharged. Indeed the contractor's right to payment minus a small deduction for defective performance is a contractual right and has nothing to do with the law of restitution. Restitution will only apply where the defective performance goes beyond the minor, so that in no sense imaginable can it be said that entire performance has been rendered.

(c) Support for restitutionary right

There is some support for a right to restitution for a party in breach on termination of the contract. In *Hain Steamship Co Ltd v Tate & Lyle Ltd*[134] the question of whether a shipowner who deviates from the agreed voyage route, thereby committing a repudiatory breach, but who delivers the goods on time to the cargo owner at the agreed port of discharge, should be entitled to payment on a *quantum meruit*. The question was obiter because the parties had intended that the charterers, not the cargo owners, would pay the freight. Lord Wright posed the following hypothetical situation:[135] **11.54**

> Let me put a quite possible case: a steamer carrying a cargo of frozen meat from Australia to England deviates by calling at a port outside the usual or permitted route: it is only the matter of a few hours extra steaming: no trouble ensues except the trifling delay. The cargo is duly delivered in England at the agreed port. The goods owner has had for all practical purposes the benefit of all that his contract required; he has had the advantages, of the use of a valuable ship, her crew, fuel, refrigeration and appliances, canal dues, port charges, stevedoring. The shipowner may be technically a wrongdoer in the sense that he has once deviated, but otherwise over a long period he has been performing the exacting and costly duties of a carrier at sea. I cannot help thinking that epithets like 'unlawful' and 'unauthorised' are not apt to describe such services; it may be that by the maritime law the relationship of carrier and goods owner still continues despite the deviation, though subject to the modifications consequent on the deviation. Nor can I help feeling that the court would not be slow to infer an obligation when the goods are received at destination to pay, not indeed the contract freight, but a reasonable remuneration...

To similar effect was the speech of Lord Maugham.[136] As well as being obiter the preceding quotation may also be reflective of a special maritime law rule.[137] In any

---

[133] [1952] 2 All ER 176 (CA).
[134] [1936] 2 All ER 597 (HL).
[135] *Hain Steamship Co v Tate & Lyle Ltd*, 612 (n 134).
[136] *Hain Steamship Co v Tate & Lyle Ltd*, 616 (n 134).
[137] See also B McFarlane and R Stevens, 'In Defence of *Sumpter v Hedges*' (2002) 118 LQR 569, 592–4.

event one wonders if a deviation as slight as that posed would not be better rationalized as a case of contractual substantial performance.

11.55 In *Miles v Wakefield MDC*[138] a council employed registrar of births, deaths and marriages engaged in industrial action, refusing to perform marriage ceremonies on Saturday mornings but performing all his other contractual duties on that day. The defendants refused to pay him anything for his work on Saturdays and the claimant sued to recover for that part of his work on a Saturday that was attributable to the work he actually did. His claim failed because the House of Lords held that in order to recover his salary under his contract of employment the claimant had to prove that he was ready and willing to perform all his duties under his contract. On the question of whether the employee was potentially entitled to claim in restitution for the value of the services he rendered Lords Brightman and Templeman were in favour, Lord Bridge was against, and Lords Brandon and Oliver reserved their opinion. As Burrows points out, the value of the views of Lord Brightman and Lord Templeman is somewhat diminished in the present context because the employer did not elect to terminate the contract of employment.[139] One also has to wonder if the views expressed here are not too context-specific to offer any real basis for a general restitutionary right to recover the value of work done prior to the termination of an entire contract.

(d) Specific exceptions

11.56 It is probable that there would be a right to restitution where there was a free acceptance of the contract breaker's performance after the termination of the contract. There is no specific authority for a free acceptance principle but there is academic support.[140] This principle holds that where the defendant chooses to accept a benefit provided by the claimant in the full knowledge that it was not intended to be gratuitous, there is an obligation to pay for it. It develops to some extent from section 30(1) of the Sale of Goods Act 1979, which provides that if the seller delivers to the buyer less than the agreed quantity of goods and the buyer accepts them the buyer must pay for them at the contract rate. Free acceptance would not have availed the non-breaching party in *Sumpter v Hedges* or *Bolton v Mahadeva* as neither had any real option but to take the partial performance rendered and make the best of it.

11.57 One other exception is where the Apportionment Act 1870 applies. Section 2 of the Act provides that all periodic payments in the nature of income, including rents, annuities, and dividends, are to be considered as accruing from day to day 'and shall be apportionable in respect of time accordingly'. The effect of this provision is that payment obligations and the consideration for them are not regarded as entire

---

[138] [1987] AC 539 (HL).
[139] Burrows, *The Law of Restitution*, p 360 (n 10).
[140] See Virgo, *The Principles of the Law of Restitution*, pp 340–1 (n 2).

contracts. Thus in *Item Software (UK) Ltd v Fassihi*[141] an employee's salary was payable one month in arrears. He was sacked on 26 June and the employer refused to pay him any of his June salary. His claim to be paid his salary up to 26 June was successful, his salary being deemed to be payable day by day instead of monthly. It must be stressed, however, that for the 1870 Act to apply the claimant must be entitled to payment *periodically*.

(e) Should there be a restitutionary claim?

The last issue to be addressed in this chapter is whether the law needs to be changed **11.58** to allow a party in breach to obtain restitution of the value of any benefit conferred on the other party? To do so would be to recognize that the contract is gone and to effect some symmetry with the position where the non-breaching party seeks restitution. The crucial question here is whether the parties have expressly or impliedly provided in their contract that there shall be no restitution following discharge by breach. In the absence of an express contractual term barring restitution this question often turns on whether the contract is entire. It is often assumed that if the contract is entire both contractual and restitutionary payment is barred. But is this necessarily so? Burrows puts the matter thus:[142]

> While it may be true that sometimes that is the best interpretation of what was meant by the contract, in many and probably most entire contracts the parties have not thought about the restitutionary consequences for the part performer. A contract may require payment after the completion of the work, and hence may be entire, not because the parties intend the payor to get something for nothing in the event of non-completion of the work, but because, for example, the payor fears that he will be unable to recover an advance payment in the event of bankruptcy or abandonment of the job by the other party or simply because his financial circumstances make it more convenient for him to pay at the end.

It should be a question of construction in each case whether the contract excludes a restitutionary claim in the event of an entire contract being terminated. A rebuttable presumption that it does may make sense but it should not be automatically assumed. All this would change the situation for the better without really changing the law. It would also be broadly consistent with the majority report of the Law Commission on *Pecuniary Restitution on Breach of Contract*.[143] The recommendation was that the contract breaker should be entitled to the value of the benefit conferred on the other party, subject to a pro rata contract price ceiling and the other's right to counterclaim damages for breach.

---

[141] [2004] EWCA Civ 1244, [2005] ICR 450.
[142] Burrows, *The Law of Restitution*, p 358 (n 10).
[143] Law Commission, *Law of Contract: Pecuniary Restitution on Breach of Contract* (Law Com No 121, 1983) paras 2.37–2.40. Brian Davenport QC dissented.

12

THE CONSEQUENCES OF AFFIRMATION

12.01 In this chapter the focus is upon the situation where the innocent party with an option to terminate the contract instead decides to affirm it. What are the obligations of the innocent party in that situation and what are its rights? In particular what remedies may the innocent party be entitled to in the event that it decides in effect to carry on with the contract? Broadly speaking the innocent party affirming the contract would be required to continue performing its own primary obligations under the contract and would be entitled to sue for damages for losses caused by the other party's breach. As regards the other party's continuing obligations, the innocent party might be able to seek to enforce them through an action for an agreed sum if they were money obligations or an order for specific performance if they involved non-monetary acts of performance.

A. Continuation of Innocent Party's Primary Obligations

12.02 If the innocent party is going to try to enforce the other party's continuing contractual obligations it is only fair and just that it be obliged to continue performing its own. This is the general rule to which there is one exception. If one party's obligation is dependent upon prior performance of the other's obligation there will

319

be no requirement for the innocent party to perform until the prior obligation is performed. Thus an employer is not obliged to pay wages to an employee who has not done the work earning those wages unless payment of wages was to be made in advance.[1] Why the innocent party might wish to affirm the contract as opposed to electing for termination is something better addressed in the context of the specific remedy the innocent party seeks, an action for an agreed sum or specific performance.

12.03 The manner in which the right of election between affirmation and termination may be exercised has been discussed previously and need not be repeated here.[2] Once the election is made it is irrevocable, so if the innocent party elects to affirm it cannot then seek a remedy for termination.[3] The contract will be kept alive and events subsequent to affirmation will have the same effect as they would have had if there had been no previous breach. The consequences of affirmation are well summarized in the following passage from *Frost v Knight*:[4]

> In that case [the innocent party] keeps the contract alive for the benefit of the other party as well as his own; he remains subject to all his own obligations and liabilities under it, and enables the other party not only to complete the contract, if so advised, notwithstanding his previous repudiation of it, but also to take advantage of any supervening circumstance which would justify him in declining to complete it.

So in *Avery v Bowden*[5] the defendant chartered the claimant's ship at a Russian port and agreed to load her with cargo within forty-five days. Before this period had elapsed the defendant issued several advices to the claimant that he should go away as it would be impossible to supply a cargo. The claimant remained at the port hoping the defendant would be able to perform his contractual obligations but this was to no avail. Before the forty-five day period elapsed the Crimean War broke out between the United Kingdom and Russia. The effect of this was to frustrate the contract between the claimant and the defendant and so the claimant's decision to affirm in the end cost him any chance of obtaining a remedy for what would undoubtedly have been a repudiatory breach by the defendant. Then in *The Simona*[6] a ship charterparty required a ship to sail to Durban and carry a cargo of steel coils to Bilbao. The charterparty contained a cancellation clause under which the charterer could cancel if the vessel were not ready to load on or before 9 July. On 2 July the shipowners asked if they might have an extension of the cancellation date because they wished to load another cargo first. In response

---

[1] E Peel, *Treitel: The Law of Contract* (13th edn, Sweet & Maxwell, 2011) para 18-019.
[2] See generally Ch 4.
[3] *Fercometal SARL v Mediterranean Shipping Co SA (The Simona)* [1989] AC 788 (HL); *Vitol SA v Norelf Ltd (The Santa Clara)* [1996] AC 800 (HL).
[4] (1871-72) LR 7 Ex 111 (Exchequer Chamber) 112 (Cockburn CJ).
[5] (1855) 5 E & B 714, 119 ER 647 (QB).
[6] *Fercometal SARL v Mediterranean Shipping Co SA (The Simona)* [1989] AC 788 (HL).

the charterers purported to cancel the charterparty. As clear authority established that a charterparty cannot be cancelled in advance no matter how clear it was that the ship would not be loaded in time, this put the charterers in repudiatory breach. However, the shipowners decided to carry on with the contract. The ship did not load on time or at all and the charterers loaded the cargo on to another ship. The shipowners' action for dead freight failed. By affirming the contract the shipowners kept it alive for all purposes, including the charterers' right to cancel if the ship was not ready to load in time.

So affirmation carries with it some dangers arising out of subsequent events. **12.04** However, if those subsequent events take the form of fresh or continued breaches of contract by the defendant, the innocent party will acquire a fresh right to elect between affirmation and termination.[7] The decision to affirm allows for no blowing hot and cold. A strategic choice must be made and has to be lived with.

B. Damages for Past Breach by the Other Party

If the innocent party elects to affirm the contract after the other party's breach, **12.05** this effectively treats the breach that would have entitled the innocent party to terminate the contract like a breach of a warranty that allows the innocent party to claim damages only. If the innocent party elects to terminate the contract it may claim damages for loss of bargain as well as for past loss. If the breach is treated like a breach of warranty, loss of bargain damages are not available for the innocent party but damages for past loss are. The principles for the calculation of past losses in this context are the same as those applicable to past losses in respect of a breach terminating the contract.[8]

C. Action for an Agreed Sum

Where the innocent party has affirmed the contract, the key objective is to obtain the **12.06** other party's contractual performance. If that performance takes the form of delivering goods or providing agreed contractual services, the claimant will most likely seek an order of specific performance or something similar. If it consists of the payment of money, then the claimant will most likely bring an action for an agreed sum.

(1) What is an action for an agreed sum?

In most actions for an agreed sum the claimant has sold goods or performed ser- **12.07** vices for the defendant and seeks payment of the agreed sum (price). Any defence

---

[7] *Johnson v Agnew* [1980] AC 367 (HL).
[8] See Ch 10.

which the defendant raises to this claim is likely to be along the lines of alleging that the goods were defective or the services were inadequate or the claimant's performance was in some way short or inadequate. Sometimes the defendant may bring a counterclaim against the claimant and the entire dispute may be resolved by assessing the merits of claim and counterclaim and arriving at an aggregate figure in favour of one party or the other. Usually this task is undertaken through a process of negotiation, producing an out of court settlement. In the majority of cases where an agreed sum is claimed the promisee has performed its side of the bargain and is claiming the agreed price earned by its performance. In the minority of cases with which this section is mainly concerned, the claimant has not completed the agreed work (or maybe has not even started it) but seeks to complete or do it and be paid the agreed sum. The defence will usually be that the claimant should not be allowed to do work which the defendant no longer wants done and should settle for damages for breach of contract. Those damages would usually include reliance expenses incurred in performing the contract or preparing to perform it[9] together with those profits which the claimant can show would probably have been earned if the work had been completed. The issue with which this section is mainly concerned is whether the claimant should be entitled to go on and deliver a contractual performance which the defendant has made clear is not wanted.

(2) Why bring an action for an agreed sum?

12.08 It seems that debt actions, of which the action for an agreed sum is a typical example, are the most common kind of actions in the civil courts.[10] By claiming the price as opposed to damages for breach of contract the claimant will be seeking a larger sum in cases where contractual performance is incomplete, but this is not the principal reason why the agreed sum is claimed because if the claimant were to cease performance at the defendant's request much expense would be avoided and provable profit could still be recovered. The principal advantage of the action for an agreed sum is that the amount of the claim is liquidated and no assessment of damages has to be undertaken. The court need not embark on a calculation of reliance expense or expectation loss. It does not have to take account of remoteness, mitigation, causation, or contributory negligence. In most cases a straightforward 'yes' or 'no' question is all that has to be answered. The claimant can invoke the summary judgment procedure of the civil courts and effectively force the defendant to show cause why judgment should not be entered for the claimant. If the

---

[9] *Anglia Television Ltd v Reed* [1972] 1 QB 60 (CA).

[10] See M Zander, 'The Woolf Reforms: What's the Verdict?' in D Dwyer (ed), *Civil Procedure Rules Ten Years On* (OUP, 2009) pp 417, 427 n 46, referenced in N Andrews, *Contract Law* (CUP, 2011) para 18-02. Zander sources the annual *Judicial and Court Statistics* to note that debt actions in the county courts numbered around 2 million in the years 2004 to 2007.

claimant has suffered loss over the agreed sum then these damages can be sought in addition to the price.[11]

As Chen-Wishart has pointed out, the quick and easy procedure for the claimant to seek judgment in respect of a debt does not come without protection for the defendant,[12] especially where the latter is a consumer. The obligation on the claimant to perform its contractual duties before being able to force the defendant to pay is strictly interpreted. At common law the claimant must at least substantially perform the contract[13] and paragraph 1(o) of Schedule 2 to the Unfair Terms in Consumer Contracts Regulations 1999 specifies as indicatively unfair (and thus invalid) any term 'obliging the consumer to fulfil his obligations (usually paying money) where the seller or supplier does not perform his'. Where the defendant has a right to set off what the claimant owes it against what is owed to the claimant, the Court of Appeal held that a contract clause barring this right was unreasonable under the Unfair Contract Terms Act 1977.[14] Such a clause is also indicatively unfair under paragraph 1(q) of Schedule 2 to the Unfair Terms in Consumer Contracts Regulations 1999 in contracts between sellers or suppliers and consumers. And as the later discussion will examine, there is always a defence for a contracting party who has not received its contractual performance at the time of breach to argue that it should not have been rendered afterwards. This context also presents some other reasons why the claimant may wish to put itself in a position where it can claim the agreed sum.

12.09

(3) When is an action for an agreed sum available?

The short answer to the question 'When is an action for an agreed sum available?' is whenever the claimant's case is a claim for a debt as opposed to damages. Usually this is not difficult to determine but there have been some problematic cases. It has been held that where an insurer is obliged by a contract of insurance to indemnify the insured against any damages the latter has to pay to a third party, the insurer's claim sounds in damages.[15] The better view, it is submitted, is that this is the insurer's primary obligation, a liquidated debt ascertained by calculation of the damages the insured is liable to pay the third party.[16] A more coherent view was taken by the Court of Appeal in the separate but analogous context of *Jervis v Harris*.[17] In this case a lease provided that on the tenant's breach of his covenant

12.10

---

[11] *Overstone Ltd v Shipway* [1962] 1 WLR 117 (CA).
[12] M Chen-Wishart, *Contract Law* (2nd edn, OUP, 2008) para 15.1.
[13] See *Hoenig v Isaacs* [1952] 2 All ER 176 (CA); *Bolton v Mahadeva* [1972] 1 WLR 1009 (CA).
[14] *Stewart Gill Ltd v Horatio Myer & Co Ltd* [1992] QB 600 (CA).
[15] See *Chandris v Argo Insurance Co Ltd* [1963] 2 Lloyd's Rep 65 (QBD); *Hong Kong Borneo Services Ltd v Pilcher* [1992] 2 Lloyd's Rep 593 (QBD); *The Kyriaki* [1993] 1 Lloyd's Rep 137 (QBD); *Phoenix General Insurance Co of Greece SA v Halvanon Insurance Co Ltd* [1988] QB 216 (CA).
[16] Peel, *Treitel*, para 21-003 (n 1).
[17] [1996] Ch 195 (CA).

to repair the landlord could execute the repairs and recover the cost from the tenant. It was held that this claim was for debt, not damages. Like the insurance cases the agreed sum was not ascertained when the contract was made but it was still ascertained when the tenant's payment obligation arose. This should be the time for determining the status of the obligation. In contractual indemnity cases, where A agrees to indemnify B against any loss or liability incurred in certain events, one of which may be a breach of the A-B contract by A, it seems to be largely a question of construction whether B's right against A sounds in debt or damages.[18]

12.11 As these authorities also indirectly demonstrate, the obligation to pay must sound in debt and also have arisen. In *Mount v Oldham Corporation*[19] a local education authority wrongfully withdrew boys from a school without giving the customary one term's notice. It was held that the headmaster could bring an action for unpaid school fees as there was an implied term in the contract that these should be paid in advance. The claim had therefore arisen. To say that the claim has arisen is in effect to say that the price has been earned. In a contract for the sale of goods the seller's action for the price arises in accordance with section 49(1) and (2) of the Sale of Goods Act 1979. Section 49(1) is the general rule and states that the price is payable when the property in the goods has passed to the buyer,[20] the rationale for the rule being that at this stage the seller has done everything it is required to do to earn the price. However section 49(2) provides that the parties may agree instead that the price is payable on a 'day certain irrespective of delivery'. The remainder of this section will examine the question of whether a promisee who is faced with a promisor's clear intimation that it wants to terminate the contract may go ahead and earn the price notwithstanding.

(4) The *White and Carter* principle

12.12 Where a contract is executed, ie. where at least one party has performed all or substantially all of its obligations under the contract and all that remains to be done is for the other to pay the price, then the price is the remedy which the innocent party should have if the other party defaults and refuses to pay. One way of demonstrating this is to take an example which shows that damages for breach would, in most instances anyway, be the same as the price. Suppose a builder (A) agrees to build a house for B for a price of £200,000. It will cost A £180,000 to complete the contract work in terms of labour, materials, and other costs, so A's profit is £20,000. If it is supposed that A has built the house in accordance with the contract and that B has refused to pay, A would be entitled to the contract price of £200,000. If A were to sue for damages for breach A would be entitled to that sum by way of compensation that would put A into the position it would have been in if the contract had

---

[18] Peel, *Treitel*, para 21-004 (n 1).
[19] [1973] QB 309 (CA).
[20] This generally depends on the Sale of Goods Act 1979, ss 16–20B.

been performed. This would involve paying A all reliance expenses in carrying out the contract work (£180,000) plus the profit A could show would have been earned from performing the contract (£20,000), a sum of £200,000 in total.

In the previous example, if B's default is anticipatory, ie if it happens before the contract work is substantially completed, then the question arises of whether A should be allowed to continue with the contract work and earn the price or whether A should be required to settle for damages. Suppose that at a time when A has spent only £10,000 in preparatory work B indicates to him that B does not want the house. Damages for breach would require B to pay to A his reliance expenses (£10,000) plus the £20,000 profit, making £30,000 in total. Should A be required to settle for this or should he be entitled to complete the contractual work and be paid the price of £200,000? It may be recalled from Chapter 7 that an anticipatory breach does not automatically terminate a contract,[21] so in theory A could decide to affirm the contract and claim the price. As the following narrative will demonstrate, sometimes A will not be entitled to the price and will have to settle for damages. This is usually explained not in terms that A is barred from affirmation because that would mean that the contract was terminated automatically by B's breach; rather the explanation is that the price is not a remedy A is entitled to in those circumstances, only damages.[22] In deciding this very complex question two competing policy considerations come into play. On the one hand, there is sanctity of contract which requires that the innocent party should be allowed to do what the contract entitles it to do and get what the contract gives it in return. On the other hand, there is the need to avoid extravagant waste, which would certainly occur in the earlier example if A were entitled to claim a £200,000 price when £30,000 damages would adequately compensate. It should be stressed, however, that few cases are quite as simple as this one.[23] **12.13**

The starting point of this analysis has to be the decision of the House of Lords in *White and Carter (Councils) Ltd v McGregor*,[24] a Scottish appeal from the Second Division of the Court of Session, although it has never been suggested that the decision was not reflective of English law. The appellants (pursuers in the trial court) were in the business of supplying litter bins to town councils in urban areas. They were paid, not by councils, but by advertisers who paid the appellants for the use of advertising space on litter bins. There was an annual charge of 5 shillings towards each advertising plate and a weekly charge of 2 shillings for the advertising. The appellants had contracted with the respondents (defenders in the trial court) for the **12.14**

---

[21] See Ch 7, para 7.37; a rule to which employment contracts do not serve as an exception; see *Geys v Société Générale, London Branch* [2012] UKSC 63, [2013] 2 WLR 50.

[22] See *Decro-Wall Intl SA v Practitioners in Marketing Ltd* [1971] 1 WLR 361 (CA) and *Geys v Société Générale, London Branch* (see n 21).

[23] See Q Liu, 'The *White & Carter* Principle: A Restatement' (2011) 74 MLR 171, to which this part of the chapter is much indebted.

[24] [1962] AC 413 (HL).

use of advertising space for a period of three years from 1954 to 1957. In 1957 the contract was renewed for a further three years by the respondents' sales manager but cancelled later that day by Mr McGregor himself. Condition 8 of the renewed contract stated that in the event that one instalment of the contractual payments should be outstanding for four weeks then the entire three years of payments would become due. The appellants refused to accept the respondents' repudiation of the contract, then proceeding to go ahead with the preparation of the plates for the ensuing three years. On the respondents' default the entire three years' of payments were claimed as an agreed sum.

12.15   The lower courts all held for the respondents but the House of Lords by a bare three to two majority held for the appellants. The majority did not all concur on the same reasons so there is some difficulty in stating precisely what the *ratio decidendi* of *White and Carter* actually is. Lord Hodson for the majority, with whose speech Lord Tucker concurred, essentially took the line that the innocent party has a completely free choice as to whether to affirm and seek the agreed sum or to terminate the contract. He founded himself upon a dictum of Asquith LJ in *Howard v Pickford Tool Co Ltd*: 'an unaccepted repudiation is a thing writ in water and of no value to anybody: it confers no legal rights of any sort or kind'.[25] To the argument that this would be wasteful and potentially hard on the respondents, Lord Hodson answered thus:[26]

> It may be unfortunate that the appellants have saddled themselves with an unwanted contract causing an apparent waste of time and money. No doubt this aspect impressed the Court of Session but there is no equity that can assist the respondent. It is trite that equity will not rewrite an improvident contract where there is no disability on either side. There is no duty laid upon a party to a subsisting contract to vary it at the behest of the other party so as to deprive himself of the benefit given to him by the contract. To hold otherwise would be to introduce a novel equitable doctrine that a party was not to be held to his contract unless the court in a given instance thought it reasonable so to do. In this case it would make an action for a debt a claim for a discretionary remedy. This would introduce an uncertainty into the field of contract which appears to be unsupported by authority either in English or Scottish law save for the one case[27] upon which the Court of Session founded its opinion and which must, in my judgment, be taken to have been wrongly decided.

Lord Reid's speech for the majority will be discussed separately later. For the minority Lords Morton and Keith emphasized that the effect of holding for the appellants was to give specific implement (the Scottish equivalent of specific performance) of a money obligation when damages would be an adequate remedy, and to excuse the appellants from all and every obligation to mitigate their loss. Both found the

---

[25] [1951] 1 KB 417 (CA) 421, quoted at [1962] AC 413, 444.
[26] [1962] AC 413, 445.
[27] *Langford & Co Ltd v Dutch* 1952 SC 15 (CS).

implications of holding for the appellants startling, Lord Keith giving the example of a consultant hired to go to Hong Kong and prepare a report for a client. If the other party were to inform him before the time for performance that his services were no longer required it would seem that the consultant would be entitled to go to Hong Kong, prepare the report and afterwards receive the agreed fee.[28]

This dead heat between four of their Lordships made Lord Reid's speech the all-important one in this case. Lord Reid accepted the general principle of Lord Hodson in the following words:[29]   **12.16**

> It might be, but it never has been, the law that a person is only entitled to enforce his contractual rights in a reasonable way, and that a court will not support an attempt to enforce them in an unreasonable way. One reason why that is not the law is, no doubt, because it was thought that it would create too much uncertainty to require the court to decide whether it is reasonable or equitable to allow a party to enforce his full rights under a contract.

To this general principle Lord Reid added two caveats. The first was that where the innocent party needs the cooperation of the other party to perform its side of the contract there is no right to sue for the agreed sum.[30] This is not, in truth, any exception to the right to recover an agreed sum. It is a condition precedent to the recovery of an agreed sum that the party claiming it has done everything it has to do[31] to earn the agreed sum. It will not matter whether the failure of the condition precedent is the fault of the claimant or the defendant; in each case the contractual remuneration has not been earned. That this is a fundamental principle and not an exception to the general rule is confirmed by Lord Morton's acknowledgement of it in the same case.[32]

The one true caveat in Lord Reid's speech came in the following passage:[33]   **12.17**

> It may well be that, if it can be shown that a person has no legitimate interest, financial or otherwise, in performing the contract rather than claiming damages, he ought not to be allowed to saddle the other party with an additional burden with no benefit to himself. If a party has no interest to enforce a stipulation, he cannot in general enforce it: so it might be said that, if a party has no interest to insist on a particular remedy, he ought not to be allowed to insist on it. And, just as a party is not allowed to enforce a penalty, so he ought not to be allowed to penalise the other party by taking one course when another is equally advantageous to him. If I may revert to the example which I gave of a company engaging an expert to

---

[28] *White and Carter v McGregor*, 442 (n 24).
[29] *White and Carter v McGregor*, 430 (n 24).
[30] *White and Carter v McGregor*, 429 (n 24).
[31] Subject to the doctrine of substantial performance.
[32] [1962] AC 413, 432: 'If the appellants are right, strange consequences follow in any case in which, under a repudiated contract, services are to be performed by the party who has not repudiated it, *so long as he is able to perform these services without the co-operation of the repudiating party*' (emphasis added).
[33] *White and Carter v McGregor*, 431 (n 24).

prepare an elaborate report and then repudiating before anything is done, it might be that the company could show that the expert had no substantial or legitimate interest in carrying out the work rather than accepting damages: I would think that the de minimis principle would apply in determining whether his interest was substantial, and that he might have a legitimate interest other than an immediate financial interest. But if the expert had no such interest then that might be regarded as a proper case for the exercise of the general equitable jurisdiction of the court.

Several comments on this passage may be offered. First, it is the only acknowledgement in this case of the need to balance the competing policy considerations of sanctity of contract and the avoidance of waste referred to earlier.[34] Secondly, Lord Reid does not clearly distinguish between barring the right to affirm and barring the remedy of agreed sum, although in the light of the recent Supreme Court decision in *Geys v Société Générale, London Branch*,[35] it is better to understand this as a bar on the remedy. Thirdly, the analogy with penalty is out of place because this is a doctrine regulating sums payable on breach of contract rather than the exercise of contractual entitlement.[36] Fourthly, Lord Reid's thinking is clearly influenced by an intuitive sense that the innocent party should mitigate its loss, yet mitigation analysis is not applied to a claim for damages for breach of contract where it could be relevant, but to the prior question of whether the claimant should sue for the price or for damages. Fifthly, Lord Reid brings in equitable, discretionary factors to an issue to which they seem to have no principled application. An action for an agreed sum is something to which a contracting party is either entitled or not entitled; it is not a matter of the court's discretion.

12.18 This confused conceptual thinking makes it difficult to understand what Lord Reid's 'legitimate interest' test really means. Two things are clear and these are that the onus rests on the party in breach to demonstrate that the innocent party has no legitimate interest in claiming the price, rather than the innocent party demonstrating that it has a legitimate interest; and secondly, that the concept of 'legitimate interest' is a broad one, encompassing things other than direct financial benefits. The absence of a clear connection with principle also shows that Lord Reid's test is policy driven, reflecting a judicial concern to place some limits on the innocent party's right to render contractual performance which is not wanted. Lastly, in relation to the *White and Carter* case itself it has to be understood that Lord Reid's speech with the caveats added is the true *ratio decidendi* of the decision. In *Hounslow LBC v Twickenham Gardens Developments Ltd*[37] Megarry J pointed out that without Lord Reid there would have been no majority in that case, and, in any event subsequent decisions have treated the general right to affirm and claim the agreed price as limited by the two caveats expressly recognized by Lord Reid.

---

[34] See para 12.13.
[35] [2012] UKSC 63, [2013] 2 WLR 50.
[36] See D Winterton, 'Reconsidering White & Carter v McGregor' [2013] LMCLQ 5, 8.
[37] [1971] 1 Ch 233 (Ch D) 254.

(a) The defendant's cooperation

The practical need for some measure of cooperation from the defendant promisor **12.19** explains why there are comparatively few successful cases where an agreed sum has been successfully recovered in the face of a defendant's anticipatory breach. As Liu has pointed out: 'In most cases the contract-breaker can prevent a claim for the contract price by simply withholding its co-operation. Co-operation does not necessarily require active steps to be taken. A buyer, by refusing to take delivery, thus withholds its co-operation necessary for the delivery to take place.'[38] It matters not that withholding cooperation is a further breach of contract. However caused it simply prevents the innocent party from doing what it has to do to earn the contract price.

Another illustration of the passive way in which non cooperation can prevent a **12.20** successful claim for the price is provided by *Hounslow LBC v Twickenham Gardens Developments Ltd*.[39] Megarry J held that a building contractor in physical possession of council land on which it was carrying out contract works still needed the permission of the council to be able to carry out those works validly. So even were the council in breach of contract in seeking to expel the contractors from the land the contractors could not just affirm the contract, carry on with the work, and claim the contract price afterwards. His Lordship gave another example of where cooperation by the defendant would be required. A, the owner of a large and valuable painting, contracts with B, a picture restorer, to restore it over three months. Before the work begins A receives a lucrative offer from C to purchase the painting in an unrestored condition because C doubts B's competence. So long as the painting remains in A's house he can obviously prevent B from carrying out the contract work. If the painting is placed in A's locked barn but B has been given a key to the barn the answer is the same because B needs A's cooperation in not barring the way to the barn and not changing the lock.[40]

In *Ministry of Sound v World Online Ltd*[41] Nicholas Strauss QC, sitting as a deputy **12.21** High Court judge, allowed an appeal against the dismissal of an action for an agreed sum claiming the last instalment payment under a two-year contract to produce a branded internet service. It was agreed between the parties that the claimant had suffered no loss so would not be entitled to substantial damages. The defendant argued that the action for the last instalment was barred because the claimant still had a number of outstanding obligations to perform under the contract and needed the defendant's cooperation in order to perform them, which cooperation was not going to be forthcoming. Although the deputy judge refused the claimant summary judgment he allowed the action for the agreed sum (the last instalment)

---

[38] Liu, 'The *White & Carter* Principle', p 184 (n 23).
[39] [1971] 1 Ch 233 (Ch D).
[40] *Hounslow v Twickenham Gardens Developments*, 253 (n 39).
[41] [2003] EWHC 2178 (Ch), [2003] 2 All ER (Comm) 823.

to proceed to trial because the right to payment of this sum was in no way dependent upon any of the claimant's outstanding obligations for which it needed the defendant's cooperation to perform.

12.22   In *Isabella Shipowner SA v Shagang Shipping Co Ltd (The Aquafaith)*[42] time charterers of a vessel chartered for fifty-nine to sixty-one months stated their wish to re-deliver the vessel several months early. This was in admitted breach of contract and the owners commenced an arbitration seeking an award of outstanding hire. Cooke J allowed the owners' appeal against the arbitrator's decision that the *White and Carter* principle did not apply both because the charterers' cooperation was needed to earn the hire and because of the absence of any legitimate interest in claiming hire. The legitimate interest point will be revisited later, but in relation to the cooperation argument the judge held that in a time charter the charterers' cooperation was not needed. The owners supplied the vessel and the crew who were at the charterers' disposal. No cooperation, active or passive, was needed from the charterers for hire to be earned. Although the charterers were obliged to provide and pay for fuel for the vessel, the owners could charge this to the charterers' account so this did not affect the earning of hire either. The judge recognized that the position would be different under a demise charterparty because there possession of the vessel was given to the charterers. This would mean that if the owners took re-delivery of the vessel they would not be entitled to hire any longer.

(b) Legitimate interest

12.23   In this section the aims are twofold—to paint as accurate a picture as possible of the meaning of 'legitimate interest' from the decided cases; and to assess how effectively the court balanced the conflicting policy considerations of sanctity of contract and avoidance of waste as recommended by Liu.[43] A chronological approach will be taken, beginning with *White and Carter v McGregor* itself. It is reasonably clear that the appellant pursuers in that case did not need any cooperation from the respondents to carry out the contract work so nothing was said about that earlier. On the legitimate interest question it is more difficult to make a judgment because the respondents could not reasonably have been expected to lead evidence and argument on this issue as there had been no indication in any of the precedents that this issue was even relevant. The appellants relied much on an unreported decision of the Court of Appeal in *White and Carter (Councils) Ltd v Harding*[44] and the respondents on an earlier Court of Session decision, *Langford & Co Ltd v Dutch*,[45] which the House of Lords overruled.[46] Reliance on these authorities would have led

---

[42] [2012] EWHC 1077 (Comm), [2012] 1 CLC 899.
[43] Liu, 'The *White & Carter* Principle' (n 23).
[44] (1958) May 21 (CA).
[45] 1952 SC 15.
[46] The respondents might well have cited a substantial amount of American authority which is hostile to the notion that an agreed sum may be claimed for an executory contract. See LJ Priestley,

most advocates to the conclusion that either the price was recoverable in the event of an anticipatory breach always or never, not that it would be unless the party in breach could show that the innocent party had no legitimate interest in claiming it. Of interest is a note by the late Lord Rodger of Earlsferry in the Law Quarterly Review, where he notes that a study of the record in *White and Carter v McGregor* indicates that the appellants made no effort to procure another advertiser to take up the advertising space not needed by the respondents, and that no finding was made as to whether any such effort would have been likely to meet with success.[47]

A short time after *White and Carter* was decided there was the case of *Anglo African*   **12.24** *Shipping Co of New York Inc v J Mortner Ltd*.[48] The claimants acted as confirming house and shipping agents for the defendant importers. Their contractual duty was to obtain delivery of plastic sheeting from the United States within two to three weeks. The defendants alleged that the delivery date had passed so that the claimants had breached the contract but this stance was not vindicated in the courts. On the contrary it was held that the defendants had repudiated the contract so that the issue arose as to whether the claimants were entitled to affirm the contract and claim payment of the contract price. Megaw J held that they were and that *White and Carter* applied. The judge held that it would have been commercially unjust if the claimants had had to receive the goods in New York, selling them there with all sorts of arguments about whether they obtained the best price or could have resold them for a higher price in another market. The judge also took into account that the claimants had made various subcontracts for the purpose of performing the contract, for example booking shipping space, and that the cancellation of these contracts would have been very damaging commercially.[49] The legitimate interest point was not directly addressed but it seems clear from these considerations that the claimants did have a legitimate interest in claiming the price instead of mitigating and seeking damages for breach of contract. The facts when analysed in terms of sanctity of contract and the need to avoid waste fully justify preferring the sanctity of contract.

If *Anglo African Shipping Co v Mortner* changed nothing the same cannot be said   **12.25** for sure of *The Puerto Buitrago*.[50] This case concerned a demise charterparty of a ship for seventeen months between January 1974 and May 1975. After six months the vessel developed engine trouble and had to be towed from Rio de Janeiro in Brazil to Gdynia in Poland. A cargo of soya bean meal was unloaded there and

---

'Conduct after Breach: the Position of the Party not in Breach' (1991) 3 JCL 218; J W Carter, *Carter's Breach of Contract* (Hart, 2012) paras 11-53–11-56.

[47] (1977) 93 LQR 168.

[48] [1962] 1 Lloyd's Rep 81 (QBD: Commercial Ct). An appeal on issues different to those of relevance here was dismissed at [1962] 1 Lloyd's Rep 610 (CA).

[49] [1962] 1 Lloyd's Rep 81, 94–5.

[50] *Attica Sea Carriers Corp v Ferrostaal Poseidon Bulk Reederei GmbH (The Puerto Buitrago)* [1976] 1 Lloyd's Rep 250 (CA).

afterwards the vessel was towed to Kiel in northern Germany for repairs estimated to cost $2 million. This compared with an estimated value of $1 million for the vessel if the repairs were carried out. A clause in the charterparty provided that the vessel should be re-delivered to the owner in the same good order and condition as on delivery. The charterers admitted liability for $400,000 of repairs but otherwise re-delivered the vessel and terminated the charterparty. The owners refused to accept re-delivery, contending that the charterers were bound to repair the vessel whatever the cost and pay charter hire until it was repaired. These proceedings occurred some three months after the charterparty expired, by which time the vessel was still in Kiel. The owners claimed that the vessel should be repaired and hire paid until then. The Court of Appeal held that the obligation to repair the vessel was not a condition precedent to the right to redeliver but an obligation sounding in damages only; and further that on the true construction of the charterparty re-delivery was effective notwithstanding that the vessel was not in proper repair. These holdings made the issues of the charterers' repudiatory breach and the proper response of the owners strictly obiter but the highly nuanced views of the Court of Appeal on this issue are important to the subsequent development of the law.

12.26 Lord Denning MR, in characteristically robust fashion, described the owners' claim to have the ship repaired at a cost of $2 million when its value once repaired was $1 million and it would probably be sold for scrap for around $500,000, as economic nonsense.[51] *White and Carter* should only be followed in a case precisely on all fours with it. In the words of Lord Denning: 'It has no application whatever in a case where the plaintiff ought, in all reason, to accept the repudiation and sue for damages—provided that the damages would provide an adequate remedy for any loss suffered by him.'[52] Upholding the owners' claim for hire while the ship remained unrepaired would mean that either the charterers paid hire forever if the ship remained unrepaired, or it would be repaired at twice its value and then sold for scrap. This amounted to specific performance of the contract when damages would be an adequate remedy.[53] Orr LJ agreed with the judgment of Lord Denning MR but added some words of his own on the *White and Carter* question. He quoted two passages from the speech of Lord Reid in *White and Carter* dealing with the issues of the defendants' cooperation and 'legitimate interest' and said that neither led him to a different conclusion on the very different circumstances of this case.[54] Browne LJ agreed with Orr LJ on the *White and Carter* question.[55] In these judgments only Lord Denning MR is attempting to explain what 'legitimate interest' really means but the allusions to specific performance and the adequacy of damages are not particularly helpful because they refer to a discretionary remedy to be

---

[51] *The Puerto Buitrago*, 254 (n 50).
[52] *The Puerto Buitrago*, 255 (n 50).
[53] *The Puerto Buitrago*, 255 (n 50).
[54] *The Puerto Buitrago*, 256 (n 50).
[55] *The Puerto Buitrago*, 256 (n 50).

awarded exceptionally, whereas affirming the contract and claiming the agreed sum is the rule and denying this for want of legitimate interest is the exception. By eschewing elaboration the judgments of Orr and Browne LJJ essentially amount to the conclusion that whatever legitimate interest means the owners had no legitimate interest here.

The next case to consider whether the price or damages should be the remedy where there is a repudiatory breach of an executory contract was *The Odenfeld*.[56] This case concerned the time charter of a ship for a ten-year period from May 1973. The claimants were the assignees of the charter hire on which repayment of the loan they provided the owners was secured. The loan contract required the owners to 'take all necessary steps to procure due performance' by the charterers of the charter. In January 1976 the charterers wrongfully repudiated the charterparty and in September 1976 the vessel was transferred to the claimants who then accepted that the charterparty was at an end. From January to September 1976 the claimants had held the owners to their contractual obligation to hold the charterers (defendants) to the charterparty and the issue before the court essentially became whether the claimants were entitled to hire for that period. The defendants' argument was that the owners should have accepted the defendants' repudiation of the contract in January 1976 and sued for loss of bargain damages. **12.27**

Kerr J reviewed *White and Carter* and *The Puerto Buitrago* and concluded that the innocent party's right to affirm the contract and seek payment of the price was the general rule which would only be fettered in extreme cases:[57] **12.28**

> It follows that any fetter on the innocent party's right of election whether or not to accept a repudiation will only be applied in extreme cases, *viz.* where damages would be an adequate remedy and where an election to keep the contract alive would be *wholly unreasonable*.

It was not wholly unreasonable for the owners to seek payment of charter hire in this case. The loan agreement entitled the lender to call in the loan if the charter were terminated and the owner failed to find alternative employment for the vessel in sixty days. In the then state of the market no alternative employment was likely so the lenders wisely required the owners to hold the defendants to the charter. It was true that any damages claim of the owners had been assigned to the lenders but assessing damages for a lost charterparty with six and a half years left to run would be a very difficult exercise involving many possible variables concerning market rates and the performance of the vessel.[58] Kerr J acknowledged that in time the legal position of the parties might be altered. Deadlocked situations were usually resolved by practicalities. All that had to be decided was the position as of September

---

[56] *Gator Shipping Corp v Trans-Asiatic Oil SA (The Odenfeld)* [1978] 2 Lloyd's Rep 357 (QBD: Commercial Ct).
[57] *The Odenfeld*, 374 (emphasis added) (n 56).
[58] *The Odenfeld*, 374 (n 56).

1976.[59] The formula applied in this case was superior to that of *The Puerto Buitrago* as it avoided unhelpful allusions to specific performance, although whether all three judgments in that case do truly come to this position is not entirely clear. Through his reference to the adequacy of damages and the other considerations in play in this dictum Kerr J can be understood as balancing respect for sanctity of contract against the need to avoid extravagant waste, as recommended earlier.

12.29 Four years on, another ship's charter case, *The Alaskan Trader*,[60] contained a further review of the authorities on the question. After nearly a year's service under a twenty-four month time charter the vessel suffered a serious engine breakdown requiring several months' repairs. In this time the market rate for hire declined from $13 to $14 per ton to $8 to $9 per ton and the charterers indicated that they had no further use for the vessel. The owners went ahead with repairs at a cost of $800,000 which were completed and the ship made ready for further service with a little over six months of the charter period left to run. The charterers treated the charterparty as having come to an end but the owners maintained the vessel at anchor with a full crew ready to sail until the charter period expired. Hire was paid throughout this period but the charterers referred to arbitration the question of whether they were entitled to a refund on the basis that the owners should have accepted that the charterparty had ended earlier. The arbitrator decided that the owners had no legitimate interest in keeping the charterparty alive and were thus only entitled to damages. On appeal Lloyd J upheld the arbitrator's decision. His review of the authorities is worth examining in some depth.

12.30 Lloyd J began with an analysis of *White and Carter*. He accepted that what Lord Reid said in that case about legitimate interest was strictly speaking obiter and also tentative. He observed that Lord Reid had not gone very far in explaining what he meant by legitimate interest except that the *de minimis* principle would apply and that it would be insufficient to establish that the innocent party was acting unreasonably. Neither did Lord Reid explain the juristic basis for confining the claimant's remedy to damages.[61] However, without expressly stating it, Lloyd J clearly regarded Lord Reid's speech as laying down the law on this question. Next Lloyd J considered *The Puerto Buitrago*. He seemed a little unsure what to make of the judgment of Lord Denning MR on legitimate interest but at the very least there was the strong persuasive authority of the majority of the Court of Appeal (Orr and Browne LJJ) in support of Lord Reid in *White and Carter*.[62] Lloyd J lastly discussed *The Odenfeld*, which he regarded as entirely consistent with Lord Reid's speech and the views of the majority of the Court of Appeal in *The Puerto Buitrago*.[63] The

---

[59] *The Odenfeld*, 375 (n 56).
[60] *Clea Shipping Corp v Bulk Oil Intl Ltd (The Alaskan Trader)* [1984] 1 All ER 129 (QBD: Commercial Ct).
[61] *The Alaskan Trader*, 133 (n 60).
[62] *The Alaskan Trader*, 135 (n 60).
[63] *The Alaskan Trader*, 136 (n 60).

conclusion which Lloyd J ultimately came to was that the innocent party had in general an unfettered right to elect between claiming the price or claiming damages for breach of contract, but that the court would in exceptional cases, in the exercise of its general equitable jurisdiction, refuse to allow the innocent party to receive its full contractual remedies where it had no legitimate interest in asserting them.[64] The burden of proof lies on the contract breaker to show that the innocent party should have accepted damages and it must be shown that the latter is acting wholly unreasonably. On the facts of this case it had not been shown that the arbitrator had erred in law in making his decision. Judging this decision in terms of the balance between sanctity of contract and the avoidance of extravagant waste it seems quite a marginal one, much dependent on the need to respect arbitrators' decisions where there is a rational basis for doing so.

The next decision of significance, *The Dynamic*,[65] is also a charterparty case but this time the arbitrator's decision was quashed. In this case the charterers arrested the vessel one day before it was due to complete discharge. The vessel remained under arrest for fifteen days and the issue before the arbitrator was whether it remained on hire for this time and the owners were thus entitled to claim hire. The arbitrator held that the charterers were in repudiatory breach but that the owners were entitled only to damages. This decision was quashed by Simon J because on the remedies question the award did not make clear how the relevant principles were applied. The judgment is valuable for this statement of the principles applying to legitimate interest:[66]   **12.31**

(1) The burden is on the *contract breaker* to show that the innocent party has no legitimate interest in performing the contract rather than claiming damages.
(2) This burden is not discharged merely by showing that the benefit to the other party is small in comparison to the loss to the contract breaker.
(3) The exception to the general rule applies only in extreme cases where damages would be an adequate remedy and where an election to keep the contract alive would be unreasonable.

The arbitrator's failure to ask the right questions makes it impossible to express a clear view as to how the test proposed by Liu should be applied in this case.

An important case breaking the string of charterparty cases is the Court of Appeal's decision in *Reichman v Beveridge*.[67] Two solicitors practising in partnership took a five-year lease of office premises from January 2000 at a rent of £23,101 per annum. In February 2003 they quit the premises and in January 2004 the   **12.32**

---

[64] *The Alaskan Trader*, 136–7 (n 60).
[65] *Ocean Marine Navigation Ltd v Koch Carbon Inc (The Dynamic)* [2003] EWHC 1936 (Comm), [2003] 2 Lloyd's Rep 693.
[66] *The Dynamic*, para 23 (n 65). In the previous paragraph Simon J had said that the word qualifying 'unreasonable'—'wholly'—added nothing to the test.
[67] [2006] EWCA Civ 1659, [2007] Bus LR 412.

landlords commenced proceedings claiming a full year's rent arrears. The defence was that the landlords had failed to take steps to mitigate their loss, such as by forfeiting the lease and attempting to re-let the premises to another tenant. This defence failed at every stage of the case's history. In the Court of Appeal the court reviewed the cases dealt with in the preceding paragraphs and came to the following conclusion on the law:

> There is, therefore, a very limited category of cases in which, although the inno-
> cent party to a contract has not accepted a repudiation by the other party, and
> although the innocent party is able to continue to perform all his obligations under
> the contract despite the absence of co-operation from the other party, nevertheless
> the court will not allow the innocent party to enforce his full contractual right to
> maintain the contract in force and sue for the contract price. The characteristics of
> such cases are that an election to keep the contract alive would be wholly unreason-
> able and that damages would be an adequate remedy, or that the landlord would
> have no legitimate interest in making such an election.[68]

If the word 'or' in the last sentence of this passage were replaced by 'and', this passage would be a completely accurate statement of the law. As applied to the facts
the Court of Appeal held that the tenants had not satisfied the burden on them of
showing that the landlords were acting wholly unreasonably in seeking rent arrears
and not seeking new tenants.[69] This was mainly because it appeared that English
law did not allow a landlord forfeiting a lease to claim damages for loss of future
rent so if the premises had stood vacant for any substantial period of time before
a new tenant were found, this loss would have been irrecoverable. Neither did the
Court of Appeal think that the responsibility of finding a new tenant should fall on
the landlords; on the contrary it should have been the tenant who shouldered this
burden on the facts here. This decision is not completely satisfactory because the
tenants were represented by one of the solicitors who practised from the demised
premises and the landlords did not instruct anyone to appear for them to resist
the appeal, the case contrary to that presented by the tenants being entrusted to
an advocate to the court. Certainly the conclusion reached about the unavail-
ability of damages for future rent loss has been vigorously challenged in academic
literature,[70] but nothing in the Court of Appeal's discussion of the affirmation and
agreed sum issues seems otherwise questionable.

12.33 The last case on this question of legitimate interest is another charterparty case,
The Aquafaith, the facts of which were outlined previously.[71] Cooke J held that the
arbitrator had applied the wrong test in deciding that the owners had no legitimate
interest in claiming hire for ninety-four days as opposed to accepting that the

---

[68] *Reichman v Beveridge*, para 17 (Lloyd LJ, Auld and Rix LJJ concurring) (n 67).

[69] *Reichman v Beveridge*, paras 40–41 (n 67).

[70] See M Pawlowski, 'Tenant abandonment—damages for loss of future rent' (2010) 126 LQR
361; J Morgan [2008] Conveyancer 165.

[71] *Isabella Shipowner SA v Shagang Shipping Co Ltd (The Aquafaith)* [2012] EWHC 1077
(Comm), [2012] 1 CLC 899; see n 42.

charterparty was over and trading on the spot market while claiming damages for the difference. He had never asked whether it was 'wholly unreasonable' to keep the contract alive; and whether the charterers had discharged the burden of showing that this was an extreme case where damages would be an adequate remedy and that an election to keep the contract alive was so unreasonable that no contracting party should be allowed to do it. He failed to explore whether there was any benefit to the owners and whether or not this was small in comparison to the loss to the charterers. It appeared that the charterers were in financial difficulties and that absolving them from the obligation to pay hire timeously would give rise to the risk that funds would be diverted to meet other liabilities with only an uncertain spot market to rely on in the meantime and a precarious damages award to compensate the owners in the future.[72]

In the light of the foregoing it would seem that some theoretical confusion remains **12.34** about the meaning of Lord Reid's legitimate interest test. However, the only decision about which real doubt persists as to the correctness of the result seems to be *White and Carter* itself and this is purely because neither party knew to advance any evidence or argument on the question. Liu has persuasively argued that the policy considerations at play in these cases are sanctity of contract and the need to avoid extravagant waste and it may well be that courts have been intuitively balancing these considerations in the reported cases. This section can be concluded by commending, subject to some later qualification, Liu's reformulated legitimate interest test, the principal part of which is stated thus:

> The principal test for a legitimate interest is whether, in the particular circumstances of the case, the wastefulness of the victim's continuing performance outweighs its performance interest in earning the contract price. By its nature this test is equitable and confers on the court a discretionary power, which is exercised only in exceptional cases, to hold that the victim has no legitimate interest in continuing to perform and is thus not entitled to the contract price. There must be some very cogent reason for doing so, as the victim would otherwise suffer inconvenience and injustice.[73]

The qualification added to this statement is that the restriction on the victim's right to continue performance should not be seen as some kind of equitable discretionary power of the court to compel the victim to settle for damages. Only Lord Reid in *White and Carter* has ever seriously suggested that equitable considerations might apply in this area. The truth is that if the victim is prevented from claiming the price the court is making an adjudication that it is not entitled to claim the price in

---

[72] *The Aquafaith*, [42–48] (n 71). In this connection it is worth noting the comment by Carter that: 'Given the ever-present risk of insolvency in the commercial world, it is difficult to envisage any situation in which it could seriously be argued that a plaintiff has no legitimate interest to prefer a claim in debt over a claim in damages': JW Carter, 'White and Carter v McGregor—How Unreasonable?' (2012) 128 LQR 490.

[73] Liu, 'The *White & Carter* Principle', p 192 (n 23).

these circumstances. This is more like a common law reasonableness test or a good faith principle than an equitable discretionary power of the court.[74] Ultimately it may not make much practical difference whether these cases are analysed in terms of discretion or entitlement but framing the question in terms of the latter is more consistent with the general approach of the law to contractual remedies.

D. Specific Performance

12.35 It was stated previously[75] that where the breaching party's unperformed contractual obligation is the payment of money, the affirming party's principal remedy is likely to be an action for an agreed sum. Where the breaching party's unperformed obligations are otherwise, the affirming party is likely to need an order for specific performance. Put simply, specific performance is an order of the court which requires a party in breach of contract actually to perform the contract instead of opting to pay damages for its breach. It constitutes something of a refutation of the observation made over a century ago by the United States Supreme Court Justice Oliver Wendell Holmes Jr that 'the duty to keep a contract at common law means a prediction that you must pay damages if you do not keep it—and nothing else'.[76] Since specific performance is an equitable remedy, a strict reading of this statement would be that it fully and accurately summarizes the position at common law but it was probably intended to go further than that and emphasize that the law very rarely ever makes someone perform their contractual obligations. This is because failure to obey an order of the court is a contempt of court and as such potentially punishable by an order for committal to prison.[77] Specific performance is also available in cases where the defendant is presently just threatening to breach the contract so long as this threat is real.[78]

12.36 Specific performance is an equitable remedy guided by the maxim that equity regards as done that which ought to be done. If specific performance is awarded to a litigant, this represents the judgment of the court that the litigant has an equity to have their contract actually performed. But specific performance does not provide proprietary relief so a party granted specific performance has no priority over other creditors in the event of the defendant's insolvency. It operates *in personam*,

---

[74] Professor John Carter, in correspondence with the authors, is acknowledged as the originator of this point.

[75] See para 12.01.

[76] OW Holmes, 'The Path of the Law' (1897) 10 Harvard L Rev 457, 462. At this time, Holmes was a member of the Supreme Judicial Court of Massachusetts, afterwards being raised to the United States Supreme Court in 1902.

[77] Other forms of punishment are fines and sequestration orders, where assets of a company or an unincorporated association may be taken from it. See Contempt of Court Act 1981.

[78] See A Burrows, *Remedies for Torts and Breach of Contract* (3rd edn, OUP, 2004) p 456, citing *Hasham v Zenab* [1960] AC 316 (JCPC–Eastern Africa) and *Zucker v Tindall Holdings plc* [1992] 1 WLR 1127 (CA).

against the person of the defendant only, and hence is enforceable by those personal contempt orders referred to previously.

Specific performance is very much an exceptional remedy and will only be awarded where damages are clearly an inadequate remedy. Factors suggesting the inadequacy of damages include situations where successive breaches of contract seem likely so that the claimant would have to bring successive actions for damages, where loss is difficult to quantify, and where damages are otherwise insufficient to meet the justice of the case. But what must be emphasized is that the inadequacy of damages is simply a necessary but by no means sufficient condition for the award of specific performance. The remedy is rarely granted outside its traditional territory of contracts for the sale of an interest in land. It has generally been assumed that for the purchaser each parcel of land is unique and therefore monetary compensation will not do where the land is not conveyed. Some challenges to that theory will be discussed later but it remains the starting position for a purchaser who has not received what the contract promised. Although the obligation of the purchaser in a contract for the sale of an interest in land is to pay money, specific performance, as opposed to an action for an agreed sum, is usually granted to the vendor. This is because of the mutuality principle and the equitable maxim that equality is equity. As the purchaser is normally entitled to specific performance so also should the vendor be entitled to it. There has also been some challenge to this viewpoint as will become clear. Beyond these cases, however, the most that inadequacy of damages can do for a litigant is to allow the court to consider whether this might be the kind of exceptional case requiring a different approach to the usual one of leaving the claimant to the remedy at law. **12.37**

The framework for the remainder of this section will first discuss those cases where damages are not an adequate remedy and then move on to the typical grounds on which specific performance is refused in the exercise of the court's discretion. As specific performance is an equitable remedy, there are no hard and fast rules. There are settled principles but the individual circumstances of a case may justify a departure from the usual approach. Before that there shall be a discussion of a particular contract type, contracts involving personal services, where some special principles apply. **12.38**

(1) Contracts for personal services

These contracts are essentially employment or employment-like contracts where mutual trust and mutual confidence between the parties is essential to making the contract work. The importance of mutual trust and confidence means that it is virtually impossible to obtain specific performance of a contract like this. A court order requiring two parties to work together or get along together will almost certainly 'beat upon the air' and should not even be contemplated. There is a statutory rule for contracts of employment, section 236 of the Trade Union and **12.39**

Labour Relations (Consolidation) Act 1992, which provides that no decree of specific performance requiring an employee to perform a contract of employment and no injunction restraining an employee from breaching it may be granted. There is no equivalent rule barring an employee from obtaining such orders against the employer but the availability of statutory unfair dismissal remedies of reinstatement, re-engagement, and compensation[79] effectively means that no permanent relief of this kind would ever be granted. A temporary injunction restraining an employer from dismissing an employee until an applicable contractual appeal procedure could be exhausted, was granted by Warner J in *Irani v Southampton and South West Hampshire Health Authority*,[80] but this fell a long way short of specific performance for even a limited period as it was made a term of the order that the employer was not required to give the employee any work in the meantime. The judge also emphasized that trust and confidence had not broken down between the employer and the employee, as the only relationship problem the employee had was her relationship with a senior consultant with whom she did not get along.[81]

12.40   Moving away from employment contracts as such, prohibitory injunctions have been granted against parties to contracts for personal services restraining the defendant from working for someone else. The first time this happened seems to have been in the celebrated case of *Lumley v Wagner*.[82] The claimant engaged the services of the operatic diva, Miss Johanna Wagner, to sing at his theatre in London for the summer season. When Miss Wagner got to London she was offered more money to sing for Mr Gye's theatre. The claimant obtained an injunction to restrain Miss Wagner from singing for Mr Gye. This would have been a breach of her contract with the claimant but the order did not in terms require her to sing for the claimant. She had a choice between singing for the claimant or singing for nobody. In subsequent cases where the principle of *Lumley v Wagner* has been followed the courts have emphasized that the defendant must not be put in a position where (s)he has no effective choice but to perform the contract with the claimant.[83] In these scenarios equity, it seems, looks to substance rather than form.

(2) Inadequacy of damages

12.41   Contracts for the sale of an interest in land are the most typical example of cases where damages are considered to be an inadequate remedy. This is so much so that

---

[79] Employment Rights Act 1996, ss 113–117.
[80] [1985] ICR 590 (Ch D).
[81] A temporary injunction restraining dismissal without going through the disciplinary procedures was granted by Morland J in *Robb v Hammersmith and Fulham LBC* [1991] ICR 514 (QBD) even though the claimant had lost the trust and confidence of the defendants. The judge considered that the order was perfectly workable and was anxious not to allow the defendants to snap their fingers at the claimant's rights.
[82] (1852) 1 De G M & G 604, 42 ER 687 (Lord Chancellor's Court).
[83] *Warner Bros Pictures Inc v Nelson* [1937] 1 KB 209 (KBD); *Page One Records Ltd v Britton* [1968] 1 WLR 157 (Ch D).

the question of 'adequacy of damages' is not addressed in the typical sale of land case. Where it is addressed it will be on the defendant's initiative and not a prior question which needs to be answered in the affirmative before the equitable remedy is considered. The theory on which this is based is that every parcel of land is unique so that damages for losing out on buying it would never do. Recently this view has been challenged in Canada particularly in respect of investment property, large suburban housing estates, and multi-unit developments.[84] In Canada the position is now that the purchaser must demonstrate some level of uniqueness about the property to justify a decree of specific performance. This controversial view has not been adopted in England and Wales but could have some contribution to make to the 'can't pay' cases discussed in the following paragraphs.

Contracts for the sale of personal property are nearly the opposite of sale of land **12.42** cases because a substitute purchase is usually available. One exceptional case was *Falcke v Gray*[85] where the court refused on other grounds specific performance of a contract for the purchase of two china jars of unusual beauty, rarity, and distinction but clearly indicated that these were reasons otherwise justifying the making of an order. Uniqueness was the reason for ordering specific performance of a contract to sell the arch-stone, the spandrill stone, and the Bramley Fall stone of old Westminster Bridge in *Thorn v Public Works Commissioners*.[86] Wright J ordered specific performance of a contract to sell a ship in *Behnke v Bede Shipping Co Ltd*[87] because the vessel was of unique practical value to the purchaser. An even more exceptional case was the award of an interim injunction restraining the defendant from refusing to supply a commodity (petrol) to the claimant in *Sky Petroleum Ltd v VIP Petroleum Ltd*.[88] The exceptional circumstances justifying this were that it was the oil crisis of the early 1970s, the petroleum market was in turmoil, and supplies from the defendant were the only viable way of keeping the claimant's business afloat. This was not a specific performance order as a matter of form but it was in substance, an injunction being sought because specific performance is a final order only and no interim relief can be obtained. Specific performance would not generally be ordered of a contract to sell shares whose price was quoted on a stock exchange because suitable substitute shares would be available but where substitute shares are not available the position may be different.[89]

Another exceptional case where specific performance was granted because of the **12.43** utter inadequacy of damages was *Verrall v Great Yarmouth BC*.[90] The defendant

---

[84] *Semelhago v Paramadevan* [1996] 2 SCR 415 (SCC); *Southcott Estates Inc v Toronto Catholic District School Board* (2012) SCC 51 (SCC).
[85] (1859) 4 Drew 651, 62 ER 250 (Court of Chancery).
[86] (1863) 32 Beav 490.
[87] [1927] 1 KB 649 (KBD).
[88] [1974] 1 WLR 576 (Ch D).
[89] *Harvela Investments Ltd v Royal Trust Co of Canada* [1986] AC 207 (HL).
[90] [1981] QB 202 (CA).

council granted the claimant a contractual licence to use a public hall for the two-day annual conference of the National Front. After a council election the new council attempted to terminate the contract but the claimant obtained a specific performance order because a new venue could not be obtained at the last minute and damages would be an inadequate remedy. This case was not treated as one concerning any interest in land because contractual licences were not treated then as conferring any interest in land.

12.44　An example of a most exceptional case is provided by *Beswick v Beswick*.[91] Peter Beswick transferred his coal merchant business to his nephew subject to two conditions—one that he would retain Peter Beswick as a consultant for life and the other that after his death to pay his widow an annuity of £5 per week for the rest of her life. After the uncle's death the nephew made one payment to the widow and then stopped. The widow brought an action for specific performance of this promise but faced two principal difficulties in securing success. First, in her personal capacity the widow had undoubtedly suffered loss but she had not been a party to the contract between Peter Beswick and the nephew so had no personal standing to bring the case.[92] Secondly, as administratrix of her late husband's estate she had personal standing to sue but only for such loss as the estate had suffered, which was nothing. The House of Lords held that the widow should succeed because the case was exceptional and significant injustice would be caused if the nephew were able to avoid keeping his promise. Two considerations seem to have influenced the House—one being a desire to ensure that procedural technicalities did not serve as an impediment to justice; the other being a desire to avoid the unjust enrichment of the nephew who would not have obtained the coal merchant business without promising his uncle that he would look after the widow after her husband's death.[93] It is the most vivid example of how the principles of specific performance cannot be treated as fixed and immutable.

(3) Constant supervision

12.45　A very important equitable maxim in relation both to injunctions and specific performance is that equity does not act in vain, ie that equitable relief will not be granted where inadequate practicable means are available for ensuring that the court's order will be carried out. One such ground where those practicable means are absent is where the award of a decree of specific performance would require the court to engage in an excessive amount of supervision of the defendant in carrying out the order. Constant supervision does not mean court officials going down to a work site to give orders to the defendant's staff as to what they should do; it

---

[91] [1968] AC 58 (HL).

[92] The Contracts (Rights of Third Parties) Act 1999 had not then come into force.

[93] This aspect of the case is stressed by SM Waddams in *Dimensions of Private Law* (CUP, 2003) 49–51.

means that it is not possible to set the terms of a decree of specific performance so that it can be clearly seen whether the defendant is or is not carrying out the order. That this is the issue with constant supervision can be seen by comparing two cases, one late nineteenth century and the other late twentieth, on the lease of a building with a resident porter obligation. The first case is *Ryan v Mutual Tontine Westminster Chambers Association*,[94] where the lease simply stated that the tenants were entitled to the constant attendance of a resident porter 'to be and act as the servant of the tenants'. The second is *Posner v Scott-Lewis*,[95] where the resident porter's obligations were spelled out in greater detail—cleaning of the common parts of the building, refuse disposal, and the maintenance of heating services. Specific performance was awarded in the latter but not the former because in the latter it had been made much clearer exactly what the resident porter was to do.

In *Wolverhampton Corporation v Emmons*[96] specific performance was granted of an **12.46** obligation to build houses in accordance with a local authority scheme of improvement on land sold to the defendant by the local authority. The constant supervision problem was overcome because the building work had been very clearly defined in the contract. Other important considerations in decreeing specific performance were that the claimant had a very substantial interest in having the work done (development of the area) and the fact that the land had been specifically sold to the defendant for this purpose. A landlord's repairing covenant was specifically enforced in *Jeune v Queen's Cross Properties Ltd*,[97] again largely because the obligation was clearly defined. In *Rainbow Estates Ltd v Tohenheld Ltd*[98] Lawrence Collins QC, sitting as a deputy High Court judge, granted specific performance of a tenant's repairing covenant. This owed much to the absence of any other means of getting the repairing work done, such as terms in the lease allowing the landlord to forfeit the lease or to enter and do the work itself. But the court's order had to be clear and precise in its terms so that it could be seen whether the tenant had actually done the work.

The nature of the constant supervision ground for refusing specific performance **12.47** was the subject of detailed consideration by the House of Lords in *Co-operative Insurance Society Ltd v Argyll Stores Ltd*.[99] The claimant landlords leased a large unit in a shopping centre to a supermarket. The lease was for thirty-five years and the tenant was the 'anchor' tenant of the entire development. As such, it was intended that it should draw customers into the shopping centre and thus attract custom

---

[94] [1893] 1 Ch 116 (CA).
[95] [1987] Ch 25 (Ch D).
[96] [1901] 1 KB 515 (CA).
[97] [1974] Ch 97 (Ch D).
[98] [1999] Ch 64 (Ch D).
[99] [1998] AC 1 (HL). This decision has spawned a considerable amount of literature: see A Tettenborn, 'Absolving the Undeserving: Shopping Centres, Specific Performance and the Law of Contract' [1998] Conveyancer 23; comments by Jones [1997] CLJ 488, Phang (1998) 61 MLR 421, and Luxton [1998] Conveyancer 396.

to the other units in the centre. As the closure of the anchor tenant would have potentially serious and detrimental consequences for the viability of the centre as a whole the defendant's lease contained a 'keep open' covenant which provided that the tenant had to keep the supermarket shop open for the entire duration of the lease and could not surrender it before the thirty-five years had expired. As the supermarket was losing money, the defendant closed it and purported to surrender the lease. The landlords treated this as a repudiatory breach of contract and sought an order of specific performance requiring the tenant to keep the premises open for the outstanding period of the lease. Although the Court of Appeal granted specific performance, the House of Lords unanimously refused it. Lord Hoffmann's speech, with which the other members of the House agreed, gave several reasons for this decision but they can largely be summarized as follows:

(1) It could not be stated with sufficient certainty what keeping open the supermarket would actually mean. As the tenant was losing money in these premises it was likely to adopt a minimalist approach to compliance with the obligation to stay open and this was likely to result in the case coming back to court over and over for rulings on whether the shop was sufficiently open to comply with the keep open covenant.

(2) The means of enforcing any court order, which ultimately could result in the imprisonment of executive officers of the defendant, were not considered suitable.

(3) It would be contrary to public policy to keep the parties together in a hostile relationship.

(4) It was unfair to force the tenant to trade at a loss. Those losses were likely to exceed the benefits to the landlords and could ultimately result in the landlords extracting a very large ransom fee for releasing the tenant from the covenant.

(5) The general legal advice that had been given to contracting parties about these covenants was that they were not specifically enforceable and this made it unfair to upset assumptions which tenants were entitled to make about the effect of the agreement they were signing when entering into it.

The Inner House of the Court of Session in Scotland came to the opposite conclusion on the same issue in *Highland and Universal Properties Ltd v Safeway Properties Ltd*.[100] While it is true that Scots law favours specific performance (specific implement is the Scottish term) more than English law, the judgments turn more on a different evaluation of the policy considerations involved.

12.48 All of the cases on this issue discussed so far have related to contracts for the sale of an interest in land. However, the issue before the courts in all of those cases

---

[100] [2000] Scot CS 28. See H McQueen, 'Specific Implement, Interdict and Contractual Performance' [1999] Edinburgh L Rev 239.

concerned the specific enforceability of covenants within those contracts rather than the contracts themselves. Hence these cases should not be understood primarily as cases where there would have been a decree of specific performance unless some discretionary factor resulted in refusal, as is the approach taken in contracts for the sale of land, although they are authoritative on the significance of constant supervision as a discretionary factor militating against specific performance. In these cases the adequacy of damages and the discretionary grounds militating against specific performance all went into the mix together.

(4) Impossibility and futility

Another application of the maxim that equity does not act in vain comes in those **12.49** cases where it is simply impossible for the defendant to comply with a specific performance order or it would otherwise be futile to grant it. Specific performance will not be granted of a vendor's obligation to convey land he does not own.[101] In *Warmington v Miller*[102] specific performance of an under-lease was refused because the defendant had granted it in breach of his covenant against sub-letting in the head lease. An example of futility is provided by the old case of *Hercy v Birch*[103] in which specific performance of a partnership agreement terminable at will was refused because it could be validly terminated any time.

Impossibility is illustrated by cases that have arisen out of the collapse of the prop- **12.50** erty market in both parts of Ireland in recent years. The specific context in which this problem has arisen is important to understanding the way in which the 'impossibility' defence has been applied. A developer obtains planning permission to erect an apartment building. Units in the building are then offered to purchasers 'off the plans', ie the purchaser buys not an apartment as such but a right to an apartment once the building is complete. The building process can take up to two years and a lot can change in that time. An important feature of a typical 'off the plans' apartment sale was that the contract of sale did not usually contain any 'subject to finance' clause. This meant that if the purchaser needed a mortgage to purchase the property (s)he was still contractually bound to purchase even if a mortgage could not be obtained. When the property market crashed a lot of purchasers who had entered into contracts at the top of the market found themselves unable to pay when the completion stage was reached. Sometimes this was because they had lost their jobs or livelihoods in the economic recession which accompanied the collapse or because they could not get a mortgage sufficient to enable them to complete, as lenders would only lend against the current market value of the property, now much lower than the contract price.

---

[101] *Castle v Wilkinson* (1870) 5 Ch App 534; *Ferguson v Wilson* (1866) 2 Ch App 77.
[102] [1973] QB 877 (CA).
[103] (1804) 9 Ves 357 (Lord Chancellor's Ct).

12.51   The High Court in both Irish jurisdictions has recognized that if the purchaser simply cannot pay then specific performance should not be granted to the vendor. First it was the High Court in the Republic of Ireland that made this move with the decision of Clarke J in *Aranbel Ltd v Darcy*.[104] Then Deeny J in the High Court in Northern Ireland came to a similar conclusion in *Titanic Quarter Ltd v Rowe*.[105] Strictly speaking this was a summary judgment specific performance application and the judge went no further than ruling that the defendant's inability to pay because he was unemployed and had no other property he could sell to meet the contract price could be a defence at trial. Deeny J said that if the defendant had a job come trial, then specific performance might become an option again but this takes nothing away from the fact that the principle is established that inability to pay can be a defence to a claim for specific performance. In Northern Ireland the practice has now developed of filing a 'Rowe affidavit' of means to substantiate a defendant's claim that he or she is unable to pay.

12.52   Notwithstanding the highly significant nature of this development it is important not to make too much of it. The defence that has been recognized is 'impossibility', that the purchaser simply cannot pay. In *Rowe* Deeny J heard argument on the separate issue of 'hardship' and, while not expressly ruling it out, he was careful not to base his decision on it. Hence as the law currently stands it would appear that if the 'Rowe affidavit' revealed that the defendant was buying an apartment as an investment rather than a home and had a substantial equity in a family home the defendant would be expected to sell the family home to raise the finance to purchase the apartment. This would be a hardship but it would not be impossible for the defendant to pay.[106] Even the impossibility defence may not necessarily apply outside the specific context of 'off the plans' apartment sales. In most other land sales the time between contract and completion is usually much shorter and 'subject to finance' clauses are not deliberately omitted. Dowling has challenged the assumption that a specific performance order would necessarily be futile in the sense that nothing would be accomplished by granting the order.[107] There is no sign yet that courts in England or Ireland are likely soon to travel down the road taken by the courts in Canada and refuse specific performance to purchasers unless the property can be shown to be unique in some sense.[108] If this lead were followed, the basis for awarding the vendor specific performance would be compromised where

---

[104]   [2010] IEHC 272.

[105]   [2010] NICh 14.

[106]   Financial difficulties were not regarded as a reason to refuse specific performance in *Francis v Cowcliffe Ltd* (1976) 33 P & CR 368 (Ch D); neither was it relevant that in a rising market the defendant vendor was finding it difficult to obtain suitable alternative accommodation: *Mountford v Scott* [1975] Ch 258 (CA).

[107]   A Dowling, 'Vendors' Applications for Specific Performance' [2011] Conveyancer 208. The vendor might be able to take advantage of the vendor's lien and force a sale at a time when the market had partially recovered, thus losing less when damages eventually replaced specific relief.

[108]   See *Southcott Estates Inc v Toronto Catholic District School Board* [2012] SCC 51.

the vendor was a developer because the purchaser's obligation is to pay money and specific performance is afforded to the vendor on the mutuality principle. Where the vendor is a private person who may have to sell their house before being able to move to another one, different considerations may apply. Lastly, the bottom line remains that a purchaser who escapes a specific performance order on the grounds of inability to pay, does not escape a judgment for damages measured by the difference between the contract and the market price of the property. This is likely to be a financially crippling sum and in many cases unenforceable.

(5) Hardship

Specific performance may be refused if the decree would involve excessive hardship **12.53** for the defendant. In *Denne v Light*[109] specific performance was refused against the purchaser of farming land to which there seemed to be no access. In *Wroth v Tyler*[110] specific performance was refused against a vendor because it would have required him to commence uncertain litigation against his wife to obtain vacant possession of the property and thus bring about a likely break-up of the family. In *Patel v Ali*[111] there had been a long delay in the completion of the sale of a house by married vendors. This was nobody's fault so did not affect the disposition of the case. After the contract was executed the husband vendor became bankrupt and was later imprisoned. The wife developed bone cancer and had a leg amputated while heavily pregnant. The vendors were members of the Muslim community and the wife spoke very little English. She became heavily dependent on the support of family and friends in the area where she lived and it would have involved great hardship to her if she had been forced to move. For these exceptional reasons specific performance was refused and the purchasers were left to their remedy in damages.[112]

(6) Mutuality

One side to the mutuality principle has already been mentioned. This is that the **12.54** vendor in a sale of land case can get specific performance of the purchaser's obligation to pay the price because the purchaser can get specific performance against it. The other more complex side was originally understood as Fry expressed it in 1858:[113]

> A contract to be specifically enforced by the court must, as a general rule, be mutual, that is to say, such that it might at the time it was entered into have been enforced by either of the parties against the other of them.

---

[109] (1857) 8 De GM & G 774.
[110] [1974] Ch 30 (Ch D).
[111] [1984] Ch 283 (CA).
[112] Sympathetic members of the Muslim community paid the damages.
[113] GD Northcote, *Fry on Specific Performance* (6th edn, Sweet & Maxwell, 1921) p 219.

This rule was not supported by authority and was challenged by Ames, who maintained that the defendant will not be ordered to perform unless there was sufficient assurance that the claimant will in turn perform. As Ames wrote:[114]

> Equity will not compel specific performance by a defendant if after performance the common law remedy of damages will be his sole security for the performance of the plaintiff's side of the contract.

The leading case is now *Price v Strange*.[115] The defendant was the head lessee of some flats in a house. She orally agreed to grant the claimant a new under-lease of his flat in return for the claimant's promise to effect certain repairs to the house. The claimant did about half the repairs but the defendant did not allow him to complete, instead completing the repairs at her own expense and refusing the defendant the new under-lease. The claimant was granted specific performance subject to compensating the defendant for the expenses she had incurred. The defendant relied upon Fry's rule to argue that as the claimant's obligation was not specifically enforceable from the time the contract was made specific performance could not be ordered against her. Fry's rule was held to be wrong and specific performance granted because there was no risk of the claimant not performing obligations that had already been performed. As to the precise rule of law that should be applied in similar cases, there seems to have been a slight difference between Goff LJ and Buckley LJ. Goff LJ would seem to have preferred Ames' formulation but Buckley LJ was tentatively of the view that where the defendant could not be assured of actual performance by the claimant, specific performance could still be granted if damages were an adequate remedy for the defendant in respect of any default by the claimant.[116] Burrows' preference for Buckley LJ's formulation, on the ground that the defendant contractually undertook the risk of the claimant's non-performance, should be supported.[117]

(7) Conduct of claimant

12.55 There are various grounds on which a claimant may be refused specific performance because it would be unconscionable for the claimant to have equitable relief. Two well established equitable maxims are: 'He who seeks equity must do equity' and 'He who comes to equity must come with clean hands'. The former means that the claimant must have complied with all of his or her obligations of conscience under the contract and be ready and willing to perform those that have not matured. Burrows cites the example of *Chappell v Times Newspapers Ltd*,[118] where employees were refused an injunction amounting to specific performance of their

---

[114] JB Ames, 'Mutuality in Specific Performance' (1903) 3 Columbia L Rev 1, 2–3.
[115] [1978] Ch 337 (CA).
[116] *Price v Strange*, 367–8 (n 115).
[117] Burrows, *Remedies for Torts and Breach of Contract*, p 493 (n 78).
[118] [1975] 1 WLR 482 (CA); Burrows, *Remedies for Torts and Breach of Contract*, p 500 (n 78).

contracts of employment because they would not give undertakings to perform their contracts by not engaging in industrial action. An exceptional case would have to have been shown in any event as this was a contract of employment but the claimants' unwillingness to do equity themselves made this task impossible. The latter means that the claimant must not have engaged in any tricky or unfair behaviour in the context of the contract. So, in *Quadrant Visual Communications Ltd v Hutchison Telephone (UK) Ltd*[119] the claimant contracted to sell its car and portable telephone business to the defendant. The price depended on the number of the claimant's customers prior to the completion date. The claimant made two marketing deals prior to completion, informing the defendant of one but not the other. On the defendant's breach specific performance was refused because the claimant had tricked the defendant and not come to equity with clean hands.

By section 36(1) of the Limitation Act 1980 contractual limitation periods do not apply to specific performance actions. They are usually too long for relief of this nature. A claimant may be refused equitable relief if (s)he has been guilty of laches, ie such inexcusable delay in seeking relief that it would be unfair to the defendant to grant it. In *Frawley v Neill*[120] the Court of Appeal said that the claimant did not have to show itself eager and zealous to obtain relief but specific performance would be refused if the claimant's actions made it unconscionable to assist it. How long delay must last before relief is refused cannot be measured. Regard is had to the length of the delay, the degree of prejudice to the defendant and the degree to which this can be attributed to the claimant's actions.   **12.56**

A degree of procedural unconscionability, such as misrepresentation, mistake known to the claimant, duress, undue influence, or unconscionable bargaining can lead to the refusal of specific performance. This is so even though these are reasons that are capable of resulting in the contract being rescinded. So, if A has been guilty of misrepresentation but B's right to rescind the contract is barred, A may still be refused specific performance. Mistake can be a reason to refuse specific performance if hardship amounting to injustice would otherwise be caused. In *Tamplin v James*[121] the defendant purchaser of land made a unilateral mistake about the extent of the land. The vendor had accurately described the property in the plans but the purchaser failed to consult them because he had first hand knowledge of the property. Specific performance was granted because any mistake here was down to the defendant's carelessness. Any contribution made by the claimant to the defendant's mistake will help the defendant. In *Denny v Hancock*[122] specific performance was refused because the vendor claimant's plans were carelessly misleading. Burrows has queried whether this power to refuse specific performance   **12.57**

---

[119] [1993] BCLC 442 (CA).
[120] [2000] CP Rep 20 (CA).
[121] (1880) 15 Ch D 215 (CA).
[122] (1870) 6 Ch App 1.

is much more than a historical relic of pre-Judicature Act days that is not needed today after the expansion of the grounds for rescinding a contract entirely.[123] The view taken in this book is that where unconscionable conduct falling short of a basis for rescission is shown, it is fair and just for the claimant to be left to a remedy in damages which post-Judicature Act is more easily obtained in the same court.

(8) Damages and specific performance

12.58 Section 49 of the Senior Courts Act 1981 allows for the award of common law damages in addition to specific performance. This would be useful as a means of compensating the claimant for loss suffered between the completion date and the date when specific performance is ordered. Section 50 of the 1981 Act, the successor to the Chancery Amendment Act 1858 (Lord Cairns' Act), allows for equitable damages to be awarded in lieu of or in addition to specific performance. This power is of considerable importance to injunctions restraining a nuisance or a trespass because in that context there is often an important distinction to be drawn between cases where a tort is complete and where it is ongoing. If it is complete, common law damages would be an adequate remedy and there would be no case for an injunction at all. If it is ongoing, there would be a case for awarding damages for losses suffered up until the grant of an injunction in addition to the injunction, or in lieu of an injunction if the injunction were considered inappropriate.[124] This distinction is not meaningful in the context of specific performance as all breaches of contract are ongoing and the House of Lords held in *Johnson v Agnew*[125] that the same measure of damages applies under Lord Cairns' Act as at common law.

12.59 Prior to Lord Cairns' Act the Court of Chancery had the power to award specific performance with some abatement of the purchase price or compensation where the land sold was not entirely as promised. The power to do this has not been abolished but in view of the power to award damages in addition to specific performance one may question whether it might not be better if it were.[126]

12.60 For the protection of the defendant specific performance may be granted subject to certain conditions. In *Baskcomb v Beckwith*[127] the defendant contracted to buy land without realizing, owing to the plans being unclear, that the vendor was retaining a small plot of land nearby not covered by restrictive covenants preventing the building of a public house. The vendor was given a choice—either specific performance with the restrictive covenant extended to the retained plot of land or

---

[123] Burrows, *Remedies for Torts and Breach of Contract*, p 497 (n 78).

[124] JA Jolowicz, 'Damages in Equity—A Study of Lord Cairns' Act' [1975] CLJ 224; *Shelfer v City of London Electric Lighting Co Ltd* [1895] 1 Ch 287 (CA); *Jaggard v Sawyer* [1995] 1 WLR 269 (CA).

[125] [1980] AC 367 (HL).

[126] This is the view of Burrows in *Remedies for Torts and Breach of Contract*, p 507 (n 78).

[127] (1869) LR 8 Eq 100.

no specific performance. In *Langen and Wind Ltd v Bell*[128] specific performance of a sale of shares for a price to be fixed in the future was made subject to an order that the shares be transferred to the claimant's solicitors until payment. In *Price v Strange*[129] specific performance was granted subject to the claimant compensating the defendant for the repairs she had carried out at her own expense. Finally, in *Harvela Investments Ltd v Royal Trust Co of Canada Ltd*[130] specific performance was granted subject to the condition of paying the seller interest from the completion date to payment.[131]

If the specific performance order breaks down and it becomes impossible to imple- **12.61** ment it the claimant will become entitled to seek damages. In *Johnson v Agnew*[132] this happened because mortgagees of the land subject to specific performance enforced their security and sold off the land. Much of the speech of Lord Wilberforce (with which the other Lords agreed) was given over to why the claimant could still be awarded damages and need not concern us. What matters is the following passage in Lord Wilberforce's speech which establishes that the claimant does not have an automatic right to damages:[133]

> Once the matter has been placed in the hands of a court of equity...the subsequent control of the matter will be examined according to equitable principles. The court would not make an order dissolving the decree of specific performance and terminating the contract (with recovery of damages) if to so do would be unjust, in the circumstances then existing to the other party, in this case to the purchaser.

Burrows' qualification to this statement, that it is only where the claimant's default has brought about this situation that the court may refuse the award of damages, seems correct.[134]

E. Revival of the Right to Terminate

This chapter concludes by considering in a little more detail the question of whether **12.62** a promisee who affirms a contract after a breach by the promisor entitling the promisee to terminate, would be entitled to terminate in the event of a subsequent or continuing breach by the promisor. In principle the answer is 'yes' as was stated earlier,[135] but three qualifications must be entered to that basic proposition.

---

[128] [1972] Ch 685 (Ch D).
[129] [1978] Ch 337 (CA).
[130] [1986] AC 207 (HL).
[131] See further on this Burrows, *Remedies for Torts and Breach of Contract*, pp 507–8 (n 78).
[132] [1980] AC 367 (HL).
[133] *Johnson v Agnew*, 399 (n 132).
[134] Burrows, *Remedies for Torts and Breach of Contract*, p 509 (n 78).
[135] See para 12.04.

12.63 The first qualification is that if a breach is 'once and for all' there can be no revival of the right to terminate. The distinction between a continuing breach and a 'once and for all' breach was explained by Dixon J in the Australian case of *Larking v Geat Western (Nepean) Gravel Ltd* as follows:[136]

> If a covenantor undertakes that he will do a definite act and omits to do it within the time allowed for the purpose, he has broken his covenant finally and his continued failure to do the act is nothing but a failure to remedy his past breach and not the commission of any further breach of his covenant. His duty is not considered as persisting and, so to speak, being for ever renewed until he actually does that which he promised. On the other hand, if his covenant is to maintain a state or condition of affairs, as, for instance, maintaining a building in repair, keeping the insurance of a life on foot, or affording a particular kind of lateral or vertical support to a tenement, then a further breach arises in every successive moment of time during which the state or condition is not as promised, during which, to pursue the examples, the building is out of repair, the life uninsured, or the particular support unprovided.

In the *Larking* case itself the defendant granted an exclusive fifty-year licence to the claimants to remove sand gravel from a river. In return the claimants promised to fence a particular area and to construct and maintain a gate as an extension of one of the fences erected. The claimants commenced the removal of gravel in 1937, paid royalties, but did not erect the fencing and gate. On 26 October 1939 the defendant gave notice requiring the claimants to remedy their breach within 14 days. The claimants failed to comply with the notice but continued paying royalties which the defendant accepted. Further notice was given on 1 December and then on 12 December the defendant purported to terminate the contract by revoking the licence. The High Court of Australia held that by continuing to accept royalty payments after the expiry of the notice the defendant had elected to continue with the performance of the contract and no longer had the right to terminate for past breaches. The notice converted the obligation to erect the fence from a continuing obligation in the second part of Dixon J's dictum (quoted earlier in this paragraph) into a 'once and for all' obligation in the first part. The claimants were granted an injunction restraining the defendant from acting contrary to the terms of the licence.

12.64 In a case of continuing breach, just as with initial breach, the promisee will not be permitted to terminate the contract where it has estopped itself from exercising that right. An example is provided by *Bull v Gaul*,[137] where a contract for the sale of land provided for the payment of a £100 deposit and weekly instalments of £3 towards the remainder of the purchase price of £1,200. Time was of the essence of the contract and various payments were made late but accepted by the vendor. Subsequently the vendor purported to terminate on the ground of the purchaser's

---

[136] (1940) 64 CLR 221, 236 (HCA); Carter, *Carter's Breach of Contract*, para 11-15 (n 46).
[137] [1950] VLR 377.

failure to pay on time and sought a declaration that her election was effective. This declaration was refused because by leading the purchaser to believe that she would not insist on timely payment the vendor had made it unconscionable to treat this as a ground for termination without first giving notice to the purchaser that timely payment would be insisted on in future.

That notice can revive the right to terminate a contract for breach is illustrated by the Court of Appeal's decision in *Charles Rickards Ltd v Oppenhaim*.[138] In 1947 the defendant ordered a Rolls Royce chassis from the claimants. After delivery the defendant decided to have a body built on the chassis and the claimants found a firm of coachbuilders who said they would have this done in six to seven months. A contract was then entered into between the claimants and the defendant on the footing that the claimants would enter into a sub-contract with the coachbuilders. The latest time for delivery was 20 March 1948 but the work was not completed by then. The defendant then pressed for delivery by Ascot June 1948 but that time passed too. On 29 June 1948 the defendant wrote to the coachbuilders that they would be unable to accept delivery after 25 July. That letter was passed to the claimants but nothing of significance happened. The vehicle was completed on 18 October 1948 but the defendant refused to take delivery as it had acquired another vehicle elsewhere. The claimants sued to recover the balance of the price and the defendant counterclaimed for the chassis or its value. The court held for the defendant. **12.65**

The Court of Appeal held that time was originally of the essence of this contract but that the defendant was effectively estopped from relying on this as it led the claimants to believe this would not be insisted on. However the defendant could overcome this estoppel bar by serving notice requiring the work to be done within a reasonable time. Reasonable notice was given by the notice of 29 June 1948 so the defendant was entitled to terminate the contract because this notice had not been complied with. As Carter has pointed out, a rationale for this view lies in the need to ensure that the promisee is not bound to the contract forever.[139] **12.66**

---

[138] [1950] 1 KB 616 (CA).
[139] Carter, *Carter's Breach of Contract*, para 11-70 (n 46). For further discussion of revival of the right to terminate see Carter at paras 11-57–11-70.

INDEX